DR. SUSAN LOVE'S
BREAST BOOK

SECOND EDITION
FULLY REVISED

DR. SUSAN LOVE'S BREAST BOOK

SECOND EDITION
FULLY REVISED

Susan M. Love, M.D.

with Karen Lindsey

Illustrations by Marcia Williams

A MERLOYD LAWRENCE BOOK

PERSEUS BOOKS

Reading, Massachusetts

Table 14-1, page 178, is used with the kind permission of Elsevier Science Publishing Company, Inc.

Table 14-2, page 179, is used with the kind permission of the American Cancer Society.

Table 14-3, page 179, is used with the kind permission of J.B. Lippincott/ Harper and Row.

Table 14-6, page 188, is used with the kind permission of the American Medical Association.

Table 21-1, page 292, is used with the kind permission of McGraw-Hill Publishing Company.

Physician/Patient Statement in Appendix F is used with the kind permission of the Wellness Community.

Many of the designations used by manufacturers and sellers to distinguish their products are claimed as trademarks. Where those designations appear in this book and Perseus Books was aware of a trademark claim, the designations have been printed in initial capital letters (e.g., Lactaid, Motrin).

Library of Congress Cataloging-in-Publication Data

Love, Susan M.
    [Breast book]
    Dr. Susan Love's breast book / Susan M. Love, with Karen Lindsey, illustrations by Marcia Williams. — 2nd ed.
       p. cm.
    "A Merloyd Lawrence book."
    Includes bibliographical references and index.
    ISBN 0-201-40835-X
    1. Breast—Diseases—Popular works.   2. Breast—Cancer—Popular works. I. Title.
RG491.L68   1995   94-48593
618.1'9—dc20   CIP

Perseus Books is a member of the Perseus Books Group

Cover design by Hannus Design Associates
Text design by Anna George
Set in 10-point Palatino by Weimer Graphics, Indianapolis, IN

15 16 17 18 19 20–MA–02010099

*This book is dedicated
to the memory of Verna and Watson Lindsey,
to Helen and Katie with all my love,
and to all of the women over the years
who have given me the honor of caring for them,
learning from them.*

Contents

PART FOUR: THE CAUSES OF BREAST CANCER

APPENDICES

Acknowledgments

The authors have many people to thank. Without them this book would never have been completed. We would like to thank all the patients who took the time to fill out questionnaires regarding their feelings about their breasts. Particularly we would like to mention Rebecca Cooper, Carolyn Cummings-Saxton, Mary Carmody, Thalia Dulchinos, Ann Marotto, Elizabeth MacDougal, Karen Paine-Gernee, Cathi Ragovin, Susan Shapiro, Rose Thibault, and Joyce Toth.

In addition, we would like to thank those medical professionals who freely gave of their time in interviews on specific subjects: Ted Chapman, M.D., Estelle Disch, Ph.D., Hester Hill, LIC.S.W., Robert Goldwyn, M.D., Jean Hubbuch, M.D., Susan McKenney, R.N., M.S.N., and Leo Stolbach, M.D. Other professionals graciously critiqued chapters: Jay Harris, M.D., I. Craig Henderson, M.D., Stuart Schnitt, M.D., Paul Stomper, M.D., and Walt Willet, M.D. We appreciate all their help.

Many other people contributed in a significant way, including: Jennifer Abod, Enid Y. Burrows, Ann Caspar, Micki Dickoff, Joan F., Dede Herlihy, Carolyn Muller, and Lori Lowenthal Stern. Our thanks to Amy Schiffman from NABCO for her help with the resource list.

We owe a special debt of gratitude to the staff of the Faulkner Breast Centre for putting up with "the book" for the past three years.

Special thanks to Julie Shea as well as Ann Walsh, Rita Lawler, Cynthia Lemack, Diane Connelly, and Barbara Kalinowski, R.N. Thanks also to Beth Siegel, M.D., and Susan Troyan, M.D., for those last-minute reference checks. My partner Kathy Mayzel, M.D., not only put up with my working on the book but read it for me. She gets my appreciation. And gratitude to Cyndi Saint who not only kept the home fires burning but did numerous errands, and read the book cover to cover as a test reader.

Mark Kramer assisted mightily in getting this project off the ground. Sydney Kramer was very helpful in getting it going. And Merloyd Lawrence was invaluable in getting it completed. To all of these literary professionals I give my thanks.

Finally, those who suffer most in the writing of a book are those from whom our time is stolen. Special thanks to Helen Cooksey and Katie Love-Cooksey who have lived with this book from its conception through a long and arduous labor and finally to this birth.

Susan Love, M.D.
Karen Lindsey
April 1990

The second edition has had much assistance from my new colleagues on the West Coast as well as from some of my Boston friends. I especially want to thank those who read chapters or submitted to interviews: Leslie Bernstein, Bill Shaw, Patricia Ganz, John Glaspy, I. Craig Henderson, Jay Harris, David Wellisch, Anne Coscarelli, Ronnie Kaye, Wendy Schain, Sanford Barsky, PJ Viviansayles, Barbara Kalinowski, Stephanie Chang, Lisa Winslow, Fran Visco, Bertha Adams, Jane Reese Coulbourne, Corey Anderson, Kathy Albain, Larry Bassett, Carol Fred, Lois Martin, Marie Cargill, and Roberta Apfel. Connie Long spent many hours working on the appendices and the notes. And my staff at the UCLA Breast Center has been a continuous support during the past year, especially: Lisa Gotori-Koga, Christi Dearborn, Shannon Tucker, Sherry Goldman, Tamara Sutton-Kasum, Leslie Laudeman, and Claudine Breant.

Susan Love, M.D.
Karen Lindsey
May 1995

Introduction
to the Second Edition

When we set out to write the second edition of this book, we thought it would be a simple matter of updating the first edition, adding a few things here, subtracting a few things there. But as we began to work, we realized that almost every chapter needed some updating and that several new chapters were necessary. The only chapter that remains untouched is Chapter 1 on anatomy. (The breast, I'm glad to report, is still located on the chest!)

There are many new issues and old issues which we discuss now in light of new findings. For example, because of the uproar over silicone implants, they are covered at far greater length than they were in the first edition; and new methods of biopsy for breast tissue have changed our approach to fibroadenomas and pseudolumps.

But the area of greatest concern to most readers is breast cancer, and it is here where most of the changes in our knowledge of the breast have occurred. Thus, much of what's new in this edition concerns issues around that disease. I have lessened my focus on breast self-examination. The evidence continues to mount that breast self-examination does not lead to a decrease in mortality from breast cancer. We have added a lengthy discussion on the controversy over mammography screening in young women, and the pros and cons of hormone therapy are discussed in light of its possible effect on breast cancer risk.

There are a few new treatments for breast cancer, such as bone marrow transplant and neoadjuvant chemotherapy; these are explored in all their complexity. There have also been many discoveries made in the studies on risk and prevention. In 1990 there was no need for a chapter on the cause of breast cancer; we just didn't know enough. Now we have all kinds of leads to help us find the cause of this killer and to assist us in finding newer, more subtle therapies. Prevention is a major issue, as the first breast cancer gene was discovered while we were finishing the writing of this edition. It now merits a whole chapter.

After the publication of the first book I traveled around the United States speaking. Women who had metastatic disease would invariably come up to me and ask why there was so little information on what was happening to them. It made me realize that the public knows little about metastatic disease. In this second edition I have added considerably more information on metastatic disease and recurrence. Women who find thinking about it too scary can skip those parts; those who are curious and feel more brave will want to read them. Each woman who has to contend with this phase of breast cancer will find we are there with her holding her hand.

The psychosocial and mind/body connections are given fuller discussion as scientific evidence, showing they can affect how long a woman with breast cancer will live, continues to mount. We have also devoted a chapter to explaining how clinical trials help researchers find the causes and cure of breast cancer as well as a host of other problems. We hope that the inclusion of this information will encourage both healthy women and breast cancer patients to consider becoming involved in such trials.

Finally, we look at the importance of political action in the fight against breast cancer. In some ways the first edition helped to launch the breast cancer movement, and I hope we can continue the battle with this new edition.

With all these changes the book has gotten a little fatter. My hope is that one of these days we will make a discovery so earthshaking that most of the conjecture, hypotheses, and wishful thinking you find here will be unnecessary.

As in the first edition, there may be some chapters that some women don't want to read. Some people don't mind the "gory details" of surgery; others would just as soon not know what happens while they are asleep. There are some who want to know what happens with metastatic disease, and others prefer to ignore it if they're not facing it themselves. Some readers will be concerned about the possibility of plastic surgery, either because of mastectomy or because they're unhappy with the way their breasts have developed. Others will find the subject irrelevant to them. All that is fine; we have designed the book with the understanding that some readers will want to read it cover to cover while others will want to choose only the sections of particular interest to them. Take what you want from our book. We wrote it for all of you.

Introduction

"I've always felt unattractive because I'm so flat-chested. Would plastic surgery help?"

"My breasts are lumpy—what does that mean?"

"My mother and grandmother had breast cancer. Will I get it too?"

"My doctor says I have breast cancer. Does this mean I have to choose between dying and losing my breast?"

In my years as a breast surgeon, I have constantly been asked questions like these. Women worry about their breasts in a different way than they worry about the rest of their bodies—and for good reason. For women in many cultures, breasts have had a deep, often mythical significance. They are the external badge of our womanhood. While the uterus is the center of reproduction, it is invisible; it does not identify us to the world outside as female. When we see an androgynous-looking person, we instinctively glance at the chest to determine the person's gender. If there are no obvious breasts we assume the person is male; the presence of breasts assures us we are looking at a woman.

Perhaps because of this, or because of the breast's associations with nurturance and hence survival, most cultures have eroticized breasts. In America in our century, this eroticization is highly pronounced, yet inconsistent, and a source of confusion and anxiety for most women. On the one hand, we are constantly asked to compete with select and unrealistic images of breasts: Playboy bunnies, billboard bikinis, newsstand sex symbols with their seductive cleavages. But these images themselves change from era to era. In the 1930s, we had to compete with the small, firm, but clearly outlined breasts of a Jean Harlow; in the '50s it was the large, very cleavaged breasts of a Marilyn Monroe. In the '20s, breasts were de-emphasized; in the '60s small breasts were highlighted by the braless look. Now, fashion magazines alert us, in all seriousness, that breasts are "coming back." Whatever the prevailing social aesthetic, we have never been able simply to accept our breasts. We are always made conscious of their centrality to our "womanhood."

At the same time, we're taught to be ashamed of them. Only the sex symbols are permitted, and only in clearly defined contexts, to display their breasts. Just as Muslim women hide their faces behind the veil, we must hide our breasts in public. Women who violate these rules can suffer legal penalties, or at least social ridicule. A woman may not breast-feed in public—despite the fact that feeding babies is precisely what breasts are for. Women posing barebreasted for the cover of *Playboy* are accepted. A woman basking barebreasted in the sun for her own pleasure is violating a social taboo, and, as in a celebrated 1985 case, may find herself in jail.[1]

The result of this taboo is that, even in our supposedly liberated, sophisticated era, most women know little about their breasts. They seldom see other women's breasts, except in the "idealized" versions in magazines. In reality, women's breasts come in a rich variety of sizes and shapes. But many of us go through life consciously or unconsciously assuming our breasts are unusual and unattractive, and we are embarrassed by them. We also tend to be ignorant about the workings of our breasts. What are they made of? What happens during breast feeding? How do they change with the menstrual cycle, and how does menopause affect them?

Familiarity with our breasts is also clouded by the twin fears of cancer and mastectomy. Many women avoid regular breast examinations because, consciously or unconsciously, they don't want to know if they have cancer; they don't want to face the possibility of a treatment they see as mutilating. Ignorance about our breasts thus leads to emotional pain, confusion, and sometimes serious health problems. Many of these fears—so common for women today—are not necessary. Most women who are afraid they have cancer don't—they have a variety of other, benign conditions that are usually fairly harmless.

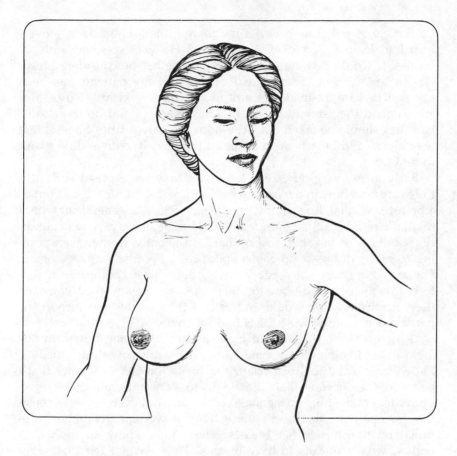

But, of course, some women do get breast cancer—one out of every 8 women in our country, in fact. And these women find themselves dealing with a largely male dominated medical establishment that is often astoundingly insensitive to the double terror women feel: the terror of death and the terror of mutilation. Ironically, the male culture that emphasizes the importance of beautiful breasts often becomes extremely cavalier about removing those breasts. Despite years of research showing that many mastectomies are unecessary, a frightening number of male surgeons still recommend them when a less severe operation would be equally helpful—and some even recommend "preventive" mastectomies for women they feel *might* get cancer. (I find it interesting that the ovaries, the uterus, and the breasts are practically the only organs taken out to prevent cancer.) This attitude finds its way into both the privacy of the doctor's office and the medical literature. One prominent Boston surgeon wrote in the *Journal of*

Clinical Surgery that he believed in "tossing the excess baggage over-board to keep the ship of life afloat."[2] He was speaking only of breasts; it would be interesting to learn whether he considered testicles to be "excess baggage." A doctor one of my patients had been to—and fled from—made his attitude even more clear: "No ovaries are so good they should be left in," he told her, "and no testicles so bad they should be taken out." (Perhaps it's only ovaries he feels that way about, and breasts are a different matter. My patient didn't wait to find out.)

Early in my surgical career, I realized how widespread such attitudes are, and how much harm they do to women. I didn't start out as a breast specialist; I began my practice in 1980 as a general surgeon. I treated a number of patients, female and male, for a variety of conditions, but I soon began to realize that, consistently, women were coming to me with breast problems specifically because I am a woman. For any other form of surgery, they might have chosen, even preferred, a male doctor—but for their breasts, they wanted someone they instinctively felt would understand their bodies and respect the particular meaning their breasts had for them.

I soon realized that I could make a particular contribution in this area: I could combine my experience as a woman with my medical knowledge. I decided to specialize in breast problems. It's not that I believed, then or now, that all male doctors are uniformly insensitive. I have had many fine, caring male colleagues. But even the most sensitive, sympathetic men can't understand a woman's complex emotional relationship to her breasts. They don't know, in their own bodies, what it means to have breasts. They haven't felt that slight adolescent itching as the small bump on the chest grows into a real breast; they haven't set out self-consciously with their mothers to buy a "training bra"; they haven't fretted over whether a party dress shows too much or too little cleavage. And they haven't faced the nightmare of mastectomy that haunts almost every woman in our culture, and surfaces with even the most harmless breast problem.

And so I chose my specialty with the hope of combining my medical knowledge with the understanding of breasts built into my own body. In the years since, I have worked with thousands of patients. I have learned much from them, both about the physiology of the breast and about the varied emotional responses women have to their breasts.

I have also geared my research to learning more about the breast and its workings. I've been studying breast pain, duct anatomy, and the various symptoms that doctors have called "fibrocystic disease." In a paper on fibrocystic disease, challenging the accuracy and the implications of the term, I was able to clarify our understanding of the concept and its relationship to cancer.

Because I want to share this knowledge with as many women as possible, I spend part of my time teaching and lecturing about breasts to medical students, health care professionals, and women's groups, as well as appearing on radio and television. This book is an extension of that work. I have written it because as a woman and a mother I have experienced the same excitement, joy, fear, and confusion that most women have experienced about their breasts, and as a breast surgeon, I have both the technical knowledge most women are denied and the human knowledge gained from working with thousands of patients.

Unfortunately, much that is published about medical issues is difficult for readers to comprehend. Medical jargon is confusing and intimidating; medical fact is less so. Yet even when the lay reader can understand the jargon, she often finds herself bewildered. Without a statistical and medical context, the significance of research findings can be difficult to judge.

My co-author and I have tried to make this book easily accessible for any woman who wants to know more about her breasts, for whatever reason; and we have broken down the topics in such a way that a reader concerned with only one particular question can find the section of the book relating to it and, if she chooses, read only that section. Most medical terms are explained in the glossary at the back of the book. I have combined my own medical information with the knowledge my patients have shared with me about their subjective experiences of various breast problems and treatments. As a doctor, my expertise is purely objective: I can diagnose a condition with reasonable accuracy, and I can administer a treatment with reasonable competence. But I do not live the experience as the patient does; I do not know, except when she tells me, what it *feels* like to her. And so I have included, in their own words, information given me by my patients.

The women I see in my practice generally fall into one of four categories, and I have so divided the book to include sections dealing with each of those categories.

The first group of women come because they are concerned with some aspect of their breasts' development: they are unsure about whether their breasts are normal, or indeed about what "normal" breasts really are. They are "flat-chested" and want to know if this will affect breast-feeding; their breasts are huge and they worry that it might mean something is wrong with them. Often mothers come in with concerns about their pubescent daughters: one breast is growing more quickly than the other; the girl has hairs around her nipple; she's 14 and her breasts haven't yet begun to develop.

Second, I see women with benign breast problems—lumpy breasts, discharge, infections, and so forth. Often they fear these conditions are indicators of cancer, but in any event they are concerned and uncertain about what the symptoms mean.

The third category is composed of women I call the "worried well." These are usually women with a family history of breast cancer—sometimes their mothers or grandmothers, sometimes a favorite aunt—and they are worried that they will inherit the illness. Occasionally it isn't a family member but a friend who has breast cancer. The patient is worried about whether there are behavioral or nutritional causes for cancer. Such patients want to know how likely it is that they'll get cancer themselves, and whether there are preventive measures that will lessen their vulnerability. Sometimes a woman with breast cancer comes to me because she's worried that her daughter will inherit the disease.

Finally, there is the woman who has been diagnosed as having breast cancer. What she needs is information about the various treatments available, and which would be most likely to save her life—as well as which would be the least disfiguring.

There is an understandable, but unfortunate tendency on the part of many patients to want the doctors to offer infallible solutions—and on the part of many doctors to pretend they can offer them. The doctor-patient relationship is all too often that of a paternalistic authority and a blindly obedient child. But doctors are neither infallible nor omniscient: at our best, we are skilled consultants with useful, specialized knowledge. We can tell people what options are open to them in a given situation, and we can give them statistical information about how these options have worked. We cannot tell a particular patient which option she *should* follow: it is her body and her life, and what is right for one patient may be wholly wrong for another.

In this book I have described a variety of alternatives for each situation I've presented. I have not endorsed or dismissed any of them. I've tried to include different women's experiences—and decisions—with each situation I've presented. Many of the decisions are different from each other, and this is important. In dealing with our own lives, there is no objective right or wrong; each of us must decide for herself, based on the most complete information possible.

The most frightening thing about breast problems isn't the possibility of cancer. The most frightening thing is not knowing, not understanding what's happening to one's own body. Even the most life threatening situations are less terrifying when people understand what they're facing. Knowledge is power, and most women have been denied real knowledge about their own breasts. With this book, I hope to give readers some of that power.

PART ONE

THE HEALTHY BREAST

1

The Breast and Its
Development

Most women don't know what "normal" breasts look like. Most of us
haven't seen many other women's breasts, and have been constantly
exposed since childhood to the "ideal" image of breasts that permeates our society. But few of us fit that image, and there's no reason
why we should. The range of size and shape of breasts is so wide that
it's hard to say what's "normal." Not only are there very large and
very small breasts, but in most women one breast is slightly larger
than the other. Breast size is genetically determined—it depends
chiefly on the percentage of fat to other tissue in the breasts. Usually
about a third of the breast is composed of fat tissue. The rest is breast
tissue. The fat can vary as you gain or lose weight; the breast tissue
remains constant. A "flat-chested" woman's breasts will grow as she
gains weight, just as her stomach and thighs do; if she loses that
weight, she'll also lose her larger breasts.

Breast size has nothing to do with capacity to make milk, or with
vulnerability to cancer or other breast disease. Very large breasts, however, can be physically uncomfortable, and, like very small or very
uneven breasts, they can be emotionally uncomfortable as well (we
discuss this in Chapter 4). Usually the breast is tear-shaped. There's
breast tissue from the collarbone all the way down to the last few ribs,
and from the breastbone in the middle of the chest to the back of the

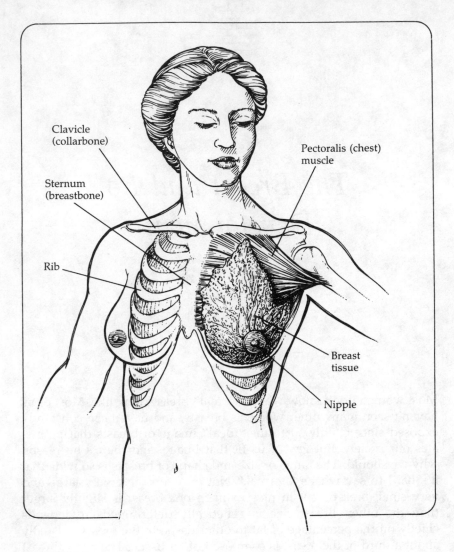

Clavicle (collarbone)

Sternum (breastbone)

Rib

Pectoralis (chest) muscle

Breast tissue

Nipple

FIGURE 1-1

armpit (Fig. 1-1). Most of the breast tissue is toward the armpit and upper breast; fat tissue is mainly in the middle and lower part of the breast. Your ribs, which lie behind the breast, sometimes feel hard and lumpy. When I was in medical school I embarrassed myself horribly one day when I found a "lump" in my breast. Frantically I ran to one of the older doctors to find out if I had cancer. I found out I had a rib.

Often there's a ridge of fat at the bottom of the breast. This "infra-mammary ridge" is normal, the result of our breasts folding over

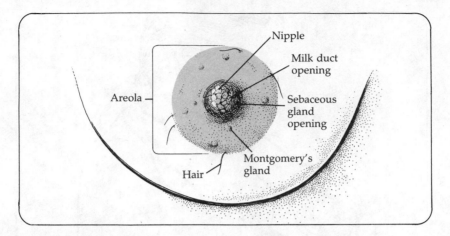

FIGURE 1-2

themselves because we walk upright. The areola is the darker area of the breast surrounding the nipple (Fig. 1-2). Its size and shape vary from woman to woman, and its color varies according to complexion. In blondes it tends to be pink; in brunettes it's browner, and in black-skinned people, it's black. In most women, it gets darker after the first pregnancy. Its color also changes during the various stages of sexual arousal and orgasm. Many women find that their nipples don't face front; they stick out slightly toward the armpits. There's a reason for this. Picture yourself holding a baby you're about to nurse. The baby's head is held in the crook of your arm—a nipple pointing to the side is comfortably close to the baby's mouth (Fig. 1-3).

There are hair follicles around the nipple, so most women have at least some nipple hair. It's perfectly natural, but if you don't like it you can shave it off, pluck it out, use electrolysis, or get rid of it any sensible way you want—it's just like leg or armpit hair. And, like leg or armpit hair, if it doesn't bother you, just ignore it. You may also notice little bumps around the areola that look like goose pimples. They're little glands known as *Montgomery's glands*. The nipple also has sebaceous glands that secrete tiny amounts of a lubricating material. Sometimes nipples are "shy." When they're stimulated, they retreat into themselves and become temporarily inverted. This is nothing to worry about; it has no effect on milk supply, breast feeding, sexual pleasure, or anything else. (Permanently inverted nipples are discussed in Chapters 4 and 5.)

Inside, the breast is made up primarily of fat and breast tissue (Fig. 1-4). The breast tissue is sandwiched between layers of fat, and behind the tissue and fat is the chest muscle. The fat has some give to it,

5

FIGURE 1-3

which is why we bounce. The breast tissue is firm and rubbery. One of my patients told me while I was operating on her that she thought the breast was constructed like a woman—soft and pliant on the outside, and tough underneath.

Like the rest of the body, the breast has arteries, veins, and nerves. Included in the breast tissue are the all-important ducts and lobules. The lobules make the milk, and the ducts are the pipes that bring the milk to the nipple. There are between five and nine separate ductal systems. They don't connect with each other but intertwine, like the roots of a tree. Each has a separate opening at the nipple, so milk comes from more than one opening. There haven't been many studies done on the patterns of the ductal system; it's one of the areas of research I'm involved in now. (Some readers will be interested to know that the breast is actually a modified sweat gland, and the milk it produces is a modification of sweat.) The breast also has its share of the connective tissue that holds the entire body together. This tissue creates a solid structure—like gelatin—in which the rest of the body parts are loosely set.

There's very little muscle in the breast. There's a bit of muscle in the areola, which is why it contracts and stands out with cold, sexual stimulation, and, of course, breast feeding. This too makes sense: if the nipple stands out, it's easier for the baby's mouth to get a good grip

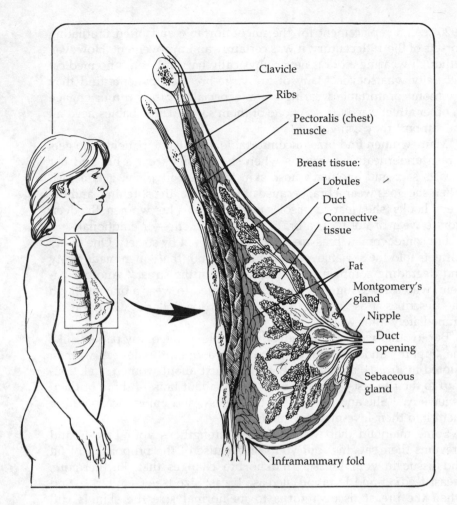

Clavicle

Ribs

Pectoralis (chest) muscle

Breast tissue:

Lobules

Duct

Connective tissue

Fat

Montgomery's gland

Nipple

Duct opening

Sebaceous gland

Inframammary fold

FIGURE 1-4

on it. There are also tiny muscles around the lobules that help deliver milk, as we will discuss in Chapter 3. But the major muscle in the area—the pectoralis—is *behind* the breasts. Because of this, the idea that you can grow larger breasts through exercise is false. You can grow stronger pectorals—like body-builders do—but all that means is that your breasts will rest on an expanded chest.

Bras

In our society breasts and their coverings have become almost a fetish. The bra is a relatively recent invention—it became popular in the

1920s. As a replacement for the uncomfortable and often mutilating corsets of the 19th century, it was certainly an improvement. However, although wearing a bra is never physically harmful, it has no medical necessity whatsoever. Many of my large-breasted patients find they are more comfortable wearing a bra, especially if they run or engage in other athletic activities. As one of them said, "These babies need all the support they can get!"

Many women find bras uncomfortable. I have one patient who gets a rash underneath her breasts when she doesn't wear a bra and her breasts sag; and another whose skin is so sensitive she gets a rash when she does wear a bra, because of the elastic, the stitching, and the metal hooks (she wears camisoles instead). For other women, the decision to wear or not wear a bra is purely aesthetic—or emotional.

For some women, bras are a necessity created by society. One of my patients told me she enjoyed going braless, but that "men made nasty and degrading comments as I walked down the street." Another patient, who teaches high school, feels obligated to wear a bra, although she describes it as "a ritual object, like a dog collar . . . I take it off immediately after work."

But to other women bras can be enjoyable. Some of my patients like the "uplift" and the different contours a bra provides. A woman quoted in *Breasts*, a book of photos and text about women's relationship to their breasts, said she was "crazy about bras—I think of them as jewelry."[1] She and others find them sexy, and enjoy incorporating them into their love-making rituals.

Some maintain that wearing a bra strengthens your breasts and prevents their sagging. But you sag because of the proportion of fat and tissue in your breasts, and no bra changes that. Furthermore, breast feeding and lactation increase breast size (see Chapter 3), and when the breast tissue returns to its normal size the skin is still stretched out and saggy. (This, and lack of nutrition, account for the extremely saggy breasts one sees in photos of many aged African women.) As I noted earlier, except for the small muscles of the areola and lobules, the only breast muscles are behind your breast—muscles that will not be affected by whether or not you wear a bra. If you've been wearing a bra regularly and decide to give it up, you may find that your breasts hurt for a while. Don't be alarmed. The connective tissue in which the ducts and lobules are suspended is suddenly being strained. It's the same tissue that hurts when you jog or run. Once your body adjusts to not wearing a bra, the pain will go away.

No one type of bra is better or worse for you in terms of health. Some of my patients wear underwire bras and are told they can get cancer from them. This is nonsense. It makes no difference medically whether your bra opens in the front or back, is padded or not padded, is made of nylon, cotton, or anything else, or gives much support or little support. The only time I would recommend a bra for medical reasons is after any kind of surgery on the breasts. Then the pull from a hanging breast can cause more pain, slow the healing of the wound, and create larger scars. For this purpose, I recommend a firmer rather than a lighter bra. Otherwise, if you like bras for aesthetic, sexual, or comfort reasons, by all means wear one. If not, and job or social pressures don't force you into it, don't bother. Medically, it's all the same.

Breast Sensitivity

Breasts are usually very sensitive—as you'll notice if you get hit in the breasts. It's painful, but if you're told that injury in the breast leads to cancer, ignore it. A bruised breast causes only temporary pain. Similarly, scar tissue that results from an injury to the breast won't cause cancer. The sensitivity of women's breasts has been used as an excuse to keep girls from playing contact sports. (It is interesting that the extreme sensitivity of testicles has rarely been used to keep men from such sports.) Your own pain threshold, and your enthusiasm for the game, should determine whether or not you want to risk pain by playing. A bruised breast will hurt, but so will a bruised shin.

The sensitivity of the breast changes within the menstrual cycle. During the first two weeks of the cycle it's less sensitive; it's more sensitive around ovulation, and it's less sensitive again during menstruation.[2] There are also changes during the larger process of development—little sensitivity before puberty, much sensitivity after puberty, and extreme sensitivity during pregnancy. After menopause, sensitivity decreases slightly, but never fully vanishes. As in most aspects of the normal breast, sensitivity varies greatly among women. There's no "right" or "healthy" degree of responsiveness.

Breasts also vary greatly in their sensitivity to sexual stimuli. Physiologic changes, or phases of response, are an integral part of the female sexual experience. In the excitement phase the nipples harden and become more erect, the breasts plump up, and the areola swells. In the plateau just before orgasm breasts, nipples, and areola get larger still, peaking with orgasm and then gradually subsiding. For most women, breast stimulation contributes to sexual pleasure. Many women enjoy having their breasts stroked or sucked by their lovers, but they too have been told that this, like breast injury, can also lead to cancer. It can't. Breasts, after all, are made to be suckled, and your body won't punish you because it's a lover and not a baby doing it. Some women's breasts are so erogenous that breast stimulation alone can bring them to orgasm; others find breast stimulation uninteresting or even unpleasant. Neither extreme is more "normal"; as we all know, different people have different sexual needs and respond to different sexual stimuli. Patients ask me whether their lack of sexual excitement around their breasts means that something is wrong with them. It doesn't. There is an unfortunate and destructive stereotype in our society—that women whose sexual needs don't correspond to those of their (usually) male partners are "frigid." Ironically, the opposite stereotype persists: a woman who is easily sexually stimulated is still too often seen as a "tramp." If your breasts contribute to your sexual pleasure, enjoy them. If not, enjoy what you do like, and don't worry about it.

Lumpiness

Lumpy breasts have inspired yet another unfortunate misconception about our bodies. Women are told that their lumpy breasts are a symptom of "fibrocystic disease" (see Chapter 6). These women suffer from needless fear, even to the point of undergoing disfiguring surgery. Lumpy breasts are caused by the way the breast tissue forms itself. In some women, the breast tissue is fairly fine; in others it is very clearly lumpy, somewhat like a bumpy cobblestone road. Still others are somewhere between the two extremes—just a bit nodular. There's nothing at all unusual about this—breasts vary as much as any other part of the body. Some women are tall and some short; some women are fair-skinned and some dark; some women have lumpier breasts and some have smoother breasts. There are also differences within the same woman's breasts. Your breasts might be a little more nodular near your armpit, or at the top, for example; or the pattern may be the same in both breasts or occur only in one. You'll find, if you explore your own breasts, that there's a general pattern that stays fairly consistent. As I discuss in Chapter 2, it's important to become acquainted with your breasts and get a sense of what your pattern is.

How the Breast Develops

To understand how the breast typically develops, we need to know what it's for. The breast is an integral part of the woman's reproductive system. It actually defines our biological class: mammals derive their name from the fact that they have mammary glands, and feed their young at their breasts. Different mammals have different numbers and sizes of breasts, but the most interesting, and probably the most significant difference between human females and the other

mammals is that we're the only ones to develop full breasts long before they're needed to feed our young. Humans are also the only
animals that are actively sexual when not fertile, suggesting that our
breasts have an important secondary function as contributors to our
sensual pleasure.

It is also worth noting that although women traditionally are often
thought of as "the other sex" (to quote Simone de Beauvoir) in our
male-dominated culture, biologically we're the norm. The genitalia of
all embryos are female. When testosterone is produced at the direction
of the Y chromosome, the fetus starts to develop male genitalia. If the
testes are destroyed early in fetal development, the male fetus will
develop breasts and retain female genitalia. It makes sense to ask
whether the basis of "mankind" is, in fact, woman.

EARLY DEVELOPMENT

Human breast tissue begins to develop remarkably early—in the sixth
week of fetal life. It develops along lines from the armpits all the way
down to the groin, and is known as the *milk ridge* (Fig. 1-5). In most
cases, the milk ridge soon regresses, and by the ninth week it's just in
the chest area. (Other mammals retain the milk ridge, which is why
they have multiple nipples.) When you're born you already have
breast tissue, and it's sensitive to hormones even then (your mother's
sex hormones have been circulating through her placenta). Infants
actually have little breasts, and may even have nipple discharge. This
"witch's milk," as it's called, goes away in a couple of weeks because
the infant is no longer getting the mother's hormones. Between 80 and
90 percent of all infants of both genders have this discharge on the
second or third day after birth.

PUBERTY

After early infancy, not much happens to the breast until puberty.
Soon after the pubic hair begins to grow, the breasts start responding
to the hormonal changes in the girl's body. (Typically, her period
won't start until a year or two after her breasts have begun growing.)
They begin with a little bud of breast tissue under the nipple—it can
be itchy, and sometimes a bit painful. The rudimentary ducts begin to
grow, and the breasts expand more and more until they've reached
their full growth—usually by the time menstruation begins (Fig. 1-6).
One little girl quoted in *Breasts* described it beautifully: "At first they
were flat, then all of a sudden the nipples came out like mosquito

Milk ridge at 6 weeks

Milk ridge in adult—
common locations
of extra nipples

FIGURE 1-5

bites. And three or four days ago I noticed that my breasts were coming out from the sides. When I first started they were just little lumps by the nipple."[3]

The first tiny breasts can be confusing to children, and to their parents as well. One of my patients was an 11-year-old girl whose mother had breast cancer, and they found what they were sure was a lump under the girl's nipple. I was certain it was just the beginning of her breast development, but everyone, including the child, was so upset I did a needle aspiration just to reassure them. It's never advisable in a situation like that to remove this newly forming breast tissue, since it will never grow back, and the child will never have that breast.

The rate at which breasts grow varies greatly from girl to girl; some start off very "flat-chested" and end up with large breasts; others have large breasts at an early age. Often one breast grows more quickly than the other. (We'll discuss this more in Chapter 4.)

The emotional confusion of puberty can be intensified for girls growing up in a society that both mystifies and obsesses about

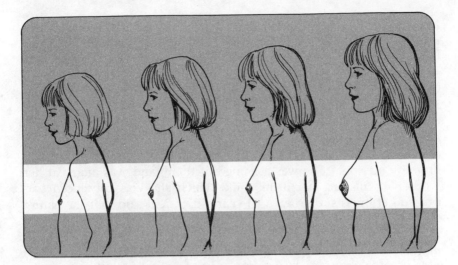

FIGURE 1-6

breasts. For the adolescent girl, the growth of her breasts can be a source of extreme pleasure or extreme dismay—and often both at once. In a 1980 British survey, researchers learned that 56 percent of the women they questioned had been pleased with their breast development, while 33 percent were shy and 24 percent embarrassed. Ten percent had been "worried" or "unhappy."[4] I did an informal survey among my own patients, with similar results. Of about 200 who filled out questionnaires in my office, 70 recalled having been happy or proud of their budding breasts; 61 had been embarrassed and angry; 20 confused; and 9 ambivalent. One had been "amazed." Not surprisingly, only four were "indifferent."

I've also talked with a number of my patients about their memories of how they felt when their breasts began to develop. Again, I found a range of feelings. Two of my youngest patients had opposite reactions to their breasts' growth. One, 13, said that when her breasts began to grow, "I felt older and I felt mature, that I was becoming a woman." She's proud of her new breasts: "I think that for my age, my boobs are just right," she says. But a 16-year-old patient tells me she was embarrassed when her breasts began to grow, because she "always felt as if people were staring at me and talking about me." She doesn't like her breasts, which she sees as "too hard and lumpy, and triangular, not round."

Similar differences in attitude appear in the recollections of my older patients. One 48-year-old recalls the first day she wore her bra to school: "I was so proud—I was the second girl in the sixth grade to have one. All the other girls gathered around me and I showed them my bra." A 44-year-old remembers "anticipating with joy and awe that my body was changing, and the blossoming of my breasts was such a delightful, exciting period for me. I was becoming a woman!" Others were less delighted. A patient who is now 39 remembers thinking, "Oh, shit, now I'm supposed to be a girl!" To her, developing breasts represented confusion and "the world getting much worse." Another, 45, hated her new breasts so much that she would fantasize about ways "to cut them off with my grandmother's long, thin embroidery scissors." She was ashamed of them, and was angry at her mother for making her drink milk, which she was convinced had caused her breasts to grow. A 65-year-old patient said that she hadn't been "ready for this sign of growing up. It was like going down a roller coaster and not being able to stop it." And a middle-aged mother recalls that for many years she wore overlarge sweaters to hide the breasts that embarrassed her. "My teenage daughter does the same thing now," she says, "and it makes me a bit sad to remember that stage of my life." For many women, breasts represented enforced femininity. They could no longer play ball with the boys, and felt they had lost forever a kind of freedom little boys still had.

On the other hand, the absence of breasts can be equally upsetting. One of my friends, whose breasts didn't begin developing until her mid-teens, recalls her feelings of inadequacy. "I was so upset," she says. "My grandmother had told me that I'd get breasts if I rubbed cocoa butter on my chest. So for months, every night, before I went to sleep, I rubbed cocoa butter on my flat little chest, hoping I'd wake up with breasts."

Sometimes, adolescent boys' hormonal development results in a condition called *gynecomastia*—which translates into "breasts like a woman." The boys' reactions don't parallel that of the girls—for the boys, breast development is uniformly embarrassing. I remember my seventh-grade boyfriend being so humiliated he paid another boy to push him into the swimming pool. That way, he didn't have to take off his shirt to swim, and didn't have to explain to the other kids why he was swimming with his shirt on. I occasionally have patients suffering from gynecomastia, and their mental anguish, as well as their acute embarrassment at having to show me their chests, is painful to see. Fortunately, the condition usually regresses on its own in about 18 months; if it doesn't, it can easily be helped through surgery.

THE MENSTRUATING YEARS

Initial breast development is soon followed by the establishment of the menstrual cycle, as a young girl's body begins to prepare for reproduction. Hormones play a crucial part in this development, as they do in all aspects of reproductive growth. On the ovary are follicles (eggs encased in their developmental sacs) (Fig. 1-7). These, stimulated by follicle-stimulating hormone (FSH) in the pituitary gland, produce estrogen. The resulting high levels of estrogen in the blood tell the pituitary to turn off the FSH and start secreting LH (luteinizing hormone). When the estrogen and LH are both at their peak, you ovulate—the follicle bursts and releases its egg into the fallopian tube, where it starts its journey down toward potential fertilization.

The ovarian follicle is now an empty sac, but it still has a job to do: it becomes what is known as the *corpus luteum,* and starts producing *progesterone,* which prepares the lining of the uterus for pregnancy (progesterone means "pro-pregnancy"). If the egg gets fertilized, it starts to produce HCG (human chorionic gonadotropin), which maintains the progesterone level until the placenta takes over the production, and you're well on your way to a baby. If it doesn't get fertilized, the progesterone level falls off, the lining of the uterus is shed, and you start all over again.

In addition to maintaining fertility, these cyclical hormones are preparing the breast for a potential pregnancy each month. In a very general sense, estrogen causes the increase of ductal tissue in the breast, and progesterone causes the increase in lobular tissue. This obviously has something to do with the cyclical changes women's breasts go through—swelling, pain, tenderness—but exactly how it does it is still unclear.

BREAST FEEDING

Breast feeding, as I've mentioned before, is what the breast is designed for. In a purely technical sense, your breast isn't fully mature until—or unless—you've given birth and your body has begun to produce milk. The breasts of women who do not give birth remain in the earlier stage of development until menopause. Because breast feeding is so complex, and so central, I've given it a chapter of its own (Chapter 3).

MENOPAUSE

By the time you're in your late 40s or 50s, most of your ovarian follicles have been used up and you're ready for menopause (Fig. 1-8). At this point, the remaining follicles are unable to produce perfect levels of estrogen and progesterone, and you start having some unusual hormonal symptoms. The cycles start getting shorter because insuffi-

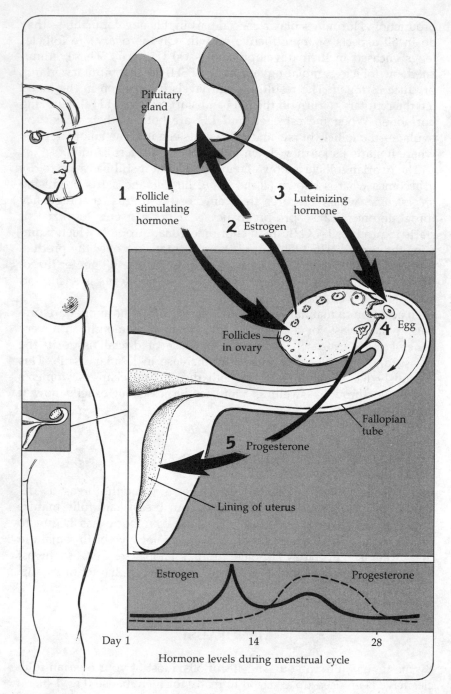

Pituitary gland

1 Follicle stimulating hormone

2 Estrogen

3 Luteinizing hormone

Follicles in ovary

4 Egg

Fallopian tube

5 Progesterone

Lining of uterus

Estrogen

Progesterone

Day 1   14   28

Hormone levels during menstrual cycle

FIGURE 1-7

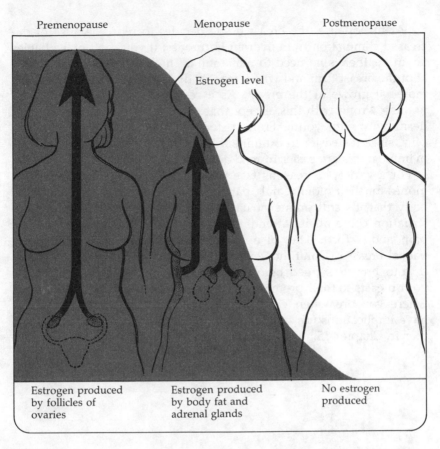

Premenopause   Menopause   Postmenopause

Estrogen level

Estrogen produced   Estrogen produced   No estrogen
by follicles of   by body fat and   produced
ovaries   adrenal glands

FIGURE 1-8

cient estrogen is being produced. Because the stimulation is abnormal, your bleeding can start getting heavier. Your breasts may get sore and lumpy, and sometimes form cysts (see Chapter 9). Finally, you reach a point where there's not enough estrogen, so you miss a cycle. As the estrogen levels in the bloodstream decrease, you may start having symptoms of estrogen withdrawal, such as hot flashes. Once the ovary stops producing, then the adrenal gland produces androgen, which is converted to estrogen—so there's still some estrogen produced, but it's no longer cyclical. (With all the bad press fatness gets, and with all the health problems it causes, this is an area where weight is an advantage: heavy women have fewer menopausal symptoms than thinner women, probably because fat makes estrogen and gives them a boost.) After a while, at about age 70, there are no more androgens produced and you have total estrogen withdrawal.

At menopause, the breast tissue decides to retire because of decreased stimulation from ovarian hormones. If you can't make babies anymore, there's no need to make milk. The breast tissue, which has kept the breast firm and which was ready to make milk, shrinks, and more fat grows in the breast. As a result, the breasts sag. There's nothing wrong with this, except that our society equates beauty and desirability with youth. From a doctor's standpoint, it's actually a plus, since it's easier to examine a breast with less breast tissue, and mammograms are easier to read accurately.

For a variety of reasons (see Chapter 15) doctors prescribe hormones for their older female patients. These hormones persuade the body that it's still premenstrual, and so, along with renewed menstruation come all its attendant breast symptoms: swelling, breast pain, and so forth. They also may halt the sagging of the postmenopausal breasts. (Don't, however, look for a fountain-of-youth effect. If your breasts sagged before menopause, hormones won't restore your breasts to their premenopausal firmness. They simply keep you where you are when you start taking them.) Hormone therapies have implications for cancer and its risks, and I'll discuss them further in Chapter 15.

2

*Getting Acquainted
with Your Breasts*

One of the most useful concepts to come out of the women's health movement in the 1970s was the idea that women should become fully acquainted with their own bodies. This had a twofold purpose: the first was a medical one, if we know what our bodies normally feel like, we are better able to know when something is wrong with them. The other, more profound purpose was to help us know, accept, and cherish our bodies. In our culture, people, and particularly women, are too often taught to feel shame and alienation around their bodies. And we're taught this early in childhood.

Babies, unconditioned as yet by social constrictions, are wiser than their elders. Watch babies gleefully playing with their toes. We smile at this, without learning its real lesson. We stop smiling when the baby's joyful self-discovery begins to include genitals. Early on, children learn that body parts associated with sexuality are taboo. We need to reverse this process, to teach little children to respect and cherish their bodies. And as adults, we need to reclaim that lesson for ourselves.

This is as true for breasts as it is for any other part of the body. Little girls should be encouraged to know their breasts, so that when the changes of puberty come about, they can experience their growing breasts with comfort and pride, and continue to do so for the rest of their lives. Most of us were not raised that way, however, and it's often hard for an adult woman to begin feeling comfortable with her breasts. Yet it's important to do so—to know what they feel like, and what to expect from them, so that you can truly live an integrated life. No part of your body should be foreign to you.

This chapter helps you get acquainted with your breasts, how to explore them and learn about them. It isn't as easy as it seems because of all the taboos against "erogenous zones." Our culture overemphasizes and at the same time negates sexual arousal, and that makes it difficult to allow yourself to touch your breasts unself-consciously.

There are two things to remember as you read this chapter. One is that breasts are a body part, just as elbows and ribs are, and there's nothing shameful about exploring them. The other is that for many women breasts are centers of erotic feelings, and in the process of exploring them you might experience some sexual arousal. So what? That's a perfectly reasonable response. We've finally come to realize, in childrearing, that it's a bad idea to teach kids to be ashamed of their sexual feelings, that we should help them understand and cherish them. Similarly, we need to give ourselves permission to feel the entire range of reactions to our own bodies—sexual as well as nonsexual.

To begin getting acquainted with your breasts, simply look at them. Stand in front of a mirror and look at yourself. See how your breasts hang, and get a sense of how they project. If you're young, they'll stick out more; if you're older they'll be more droopy. There's a fold where the breast actually folds over itself, called the *inframammary ridge*. The breast tissue is suspended over the underlying pectoralis major and minor muscles (see Chapter 1). Look at your nipple—what color is it? Does it have hairs or little bumps on it? If so, that's perfectly normal. You might want to swing your arms around and watch how your breasts move, or don't move, with the motion. Put your hands on your hips; flex your muscles, stretch your arms up. How do your breasts look with each change of position?

It's important to do this nonjudgmentally. You're not evaluating the possibility of becoming a *Playboy* centerfold; you're learning about your body. Forget everything you've heard about what breasts are supposed to look like. These are your breasts, and they look fine.

Then the next step is to feel the breasts. It's best to do this soaped up in the shower or bath; your hands slip very easily over your skin. You can put the hand on the side you want to explore behind your head. This shifts the breast tissue beneath your armpit so that it lies over your chest wall. Since the tissue is sandwiched between your skin and your chest bones, this gives you good access to it. If you're very large-breasted, you might want to do this lying down, in the bathtub or even in bed. You can then roll on one side and the other to shift the breast closer to your chest wall so that you can feel what is there more easily.

Breast tissue generally has a particular texture: it's finely nodular, or granular, like pebbles, or cobblestones. A lot of this more or less bumpy feeling of the breast is simply the normal fat intermingled with the breast tissue.

In the middle part of your chest you can feel your ribs. They jut out from your breastbone. If your ribs are prominent, you may feel them under the breast tissue. Many women have congenital deformities in their ribs, which affect the flatness of the rib cage. This can show in different ways. One is the condition called "chicken-breasted," in which the ribs arch outward. Then there's a sunken chest, in which the breastbone is depressed. Women can have either of these conditions and not realize it because their breasts camouflage their chest structure. Sometimes when I do a mastectomy, the patient will discover this unusual rib cage formation, and think I created it in surgery.

Another common variation in the rib cage occurs with scoliosis. Many women have minor scoliosis and never realize it. As you feel your breast tissue you may notice that your ribs are more prominent on one side or the other. This occurs because your back is not entirely straight. It has no real significance except that it can cause this asymmetry. Like the breasts themselves, everybody's rib cage is a little different, which affects the feel of the breast area differently in different women.

Usually you'll feel more tissue up toward your armpit and less in the middle of the breast. The tissue toward the armpit is the tissue that is apt to get lumpier premenstrually and less lumpy after your period. There are lymph nodes in the armpits, as there are in many other parts of the body, and if you've had any sort of infection you might feel those nodes. The inframammary ridge, where the breast folds over itself, is an area of thickening, and the older you get, the thicker that area gets. It usually has some large fat globules, larger than in other areas. There's a hollow spot under the nipple where all the ducts come together to exit the nipple. Around this area is a ridge of tissue—shaped rather like the crater edge of a volcano.

All of this you can easily get to know just by using the pads of your fingers and running your hand over your breast area, getting a sense of how it feels (Fig. 2-1). There's no point in grabbing at the breast. You won't get a good idea of the texture of the breast tissue, because you're pulling it forward into a big wad.

You can squeeze your nipple if you're curious about how that feels. Don't be surprised if there's some discharge—squeezing the nipple produces discharge in many women. (If you're concerned about it, see Chapter 8.)

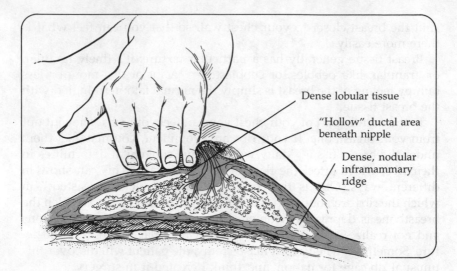

Dense lobular tissue

"Hollow" ductal area beneath nipple

Dense, nodular inframammary ridge

FIGURE 2-1

To be thoroughly acquainted with your breasts, explore them during different times of the month. Hormones affect your breasts, and they'll feel different at different points in your menstrual cycle. (Monitoring your breasts may even help you know where you are in your menstrual cycle.) Be aware of changes. Are your breasts lumpier, or more tender, before your period? If you've had a hysterectomy but you still have your ovaries, the hormone patterns continue. If you're postmenopausal, or if you've had your ovaries out and aren't taking hormone replacement, the changes no longer occur. Your breast tissue in general will be less sore, less full, less lumpy. If you take hormones—estrogen, or estrogen and progesterone—postmenopausally, that too will affect your breasts. They will often become more sore and bigger although not necessarily firmer. Similarly, if you take birth control pills, your breasts may respond to hormonal changes by becoming more sore or less lumpy.

There's a good practical, as well as psychological reason for knowing your breasts. Such knowledge can help prevent needless biopsies. In our mobile era, we rarely have the same doctor all our lives. If you've got a lump from, say, silicone injections or scar tissue from a previous biopsy, and you go to a new doctor who doesn't know your medical history, the doctor may think a biopsy is necessary. If you can say with conviction, "Yes, I know about that lump. It formed right after my operation 10 years ago, and it's been there ever since," the doctor will know the lump is okay. I've often been through this with patients. Even if a doctor thinks a lump is okay, but the patient doesn't know whether or not it's been there a long while, the doctor has to assume it might be dangerous, and will want to do a biopsy. If you know it's an old lump, your doctor won't have to worry.

If the doctor argues with you, argue back. Remember that you are a perfectly valid observer of your own body. You don't need to be a medical expert to know that you've had the same lump in the same place and it hasn't grown at all in 10 years. I had one 80-year-old patient who came to me after her doctors insisted that she'd been wrong about a lump in her breast that looked troublesome on her mammogram. Sexism and ageism can unite into a potent force, and obviously the doctors had decided that the "little old lady" didn't know what she was talking about when she told them her breast had been that way since her last child was born, 50 years earlier. They intimidated her enough so that she decided they must be right and had me do a biopsy. What I found was a congenital condition, perfectly harmless, that she'd probably had all her life and noticed after breast feeding. She knew her body, as her doctors couldn't.

IS THIS BREAST SELF-EXAMINATION?

This may all sound a bit like "breast self-examination." However, there's a very crucial difference. In breast self-examination, or BSE, you're hunting for something. What I'm talking about is very different—knowing your body, apart from anything ominous that may or may not occur there. For example, whereas advocates of BSE tell you to examine your breasts once a month, at the same time each month, to see if there's a lump, I'm suggesting that you check out your breasts at different times of the month to know how they feel at all times. Once you do know, you don't have to keep checking on a rigid schedule every month, unless that pleases you. (Do keep in mind that breasts, like the rest of your body, change over time, so that it's worth exploring your breasts regularly, every couple of months, even after you feel fully acquainted with them. But again, there's no timetable.)

As you can see, I am deliberately not presenting the idea of getting to know your breasts in terms of breast self-examination. The idea is to become familiar with your breasts as one significant part of your body, and to experience all their variations. Breast self-exam, on the other hand, is designed to monitor your breasts for cancer. Why am I making such a big point of this? I have very strong feelings about the concept of breast self-exam and its overuse. I think it alienates women from their breasts instead of making them more comfortable with them. It puts you in a position of examining yourself once a month to see if your breast has betrayed you. It becomes you against your breast: can you find the tiniest lump that may be cancer?

Admittedly, breast cancer is scary, and, as I discuss later, it has become almost an epidemic. At the same time, the majority of women will never get breast cancer. To set up this alienation is a mistake. I get particularly alarmed when I hear people talk about teaching breast self-exam in the high schools. Instead of teaching young girls who are just developing breasts to revel in their changing bodies, this means teaching them to see the breast as an enemy, something alien that has the ability to hurt them. It's a destructive way to define breasts.

Ironically, for all the fuss about breast self-exam, most women don't do it—even women who are at high risk because they have a mother or sister with breast cancer.[1] Only about 30 percent of women do BSE with any regularity. If you talk to women about BSE, most of them say they don't do it because they're scared of what they'll find. Sometimes they have lumpy breasts (see Chapter 9), and they can't tell whether one of the little bumps is actually a lump. But even when women are not doing BSE, it often dominates their thinking about their breasts. I keep coming across women in their 30s and 40s who are very fearful of breast cancer—out of proportion to the real risk they face. Some of this comes from having been saturated with the idea of breast self-exam and the "need" to search their bodies constantly for signs of betrayal.

Where does the idea of breast self-exam come from? It originated with Cushman Haagensen, who was a breast surgeon at Columbia University in New York in the 1950s, before the existence of mammography. Haagensen and his colleagues had women coming in who had huge lumps in their breasts, far too big to be removed surgically. This was also an era when women were taught that it was bad to touch themselves "down there"—and "down there" was any place below the chin. Haagensen hoped that BSE would encourage women to touch their breasts and find cancerous lumps earlier, when they were still operable.

There are a couple of problems with his thinking, well intentioned though it was. He assumed that most of these women didn't touch their breasts because they were ashamed to. But that may not have been the case. They may have touched their breasts and found the lumps long before they came to the doctor: shame and fear may have prevented them not from touching their breasts, but from admitting it to the doctor, or from going to a doctor about a problem in that "shameful" area.

In its early days BSE might have been useful to some women who did indeed feel ashamed to touch themselves without a medical directive. But the idea soon grew into something more than a permissible way for women to touch their breasts. It became standardized into a technique to find a cancer early, with the implication that this would save lives. That assumption is really not true, as we'll discuss in Chapter 23.

This rigid, standardized technique has become ubiquitous and serves mostly to make women very anxious. They'll read a book or go to a lecture about breast self-examination, and come home and stand in front of a mirror and do the exam. Then they feel these little bumps, and if they've never felt their breasts before, they begin to get scared. There are these lumps here, and then they feel the other breast and the bumps are there too, and they think the "cancer" has spread. This gets them so upset they avoid touching their breasts at all. They feel guilty if they don't keep doing their BSE every month, and scared if they do.

Many women will stop me at this point and tell me that they or their friend found their cancer themselves. This is undoubtably true: 80 percent of cancers not found on mammography are found by the woman herself. But when I question these women, it turns out very few cancers are actually found during a formal breast self-exam—as seen on those shower cards you get from the American Cancer Society. More typically, the woman just rolled over in bed, or felt a lump while soaping up in the shower, or had it pointed out by a lover. This touching and knowing your body is what we are after, not the rigid routine of looking for cancer.

As currently presented, breast self-exam is not a good model. It's important to learn how your breasts feel, but not so that you can go on a search-and-destroy mission once a month, cataloguing every grain-sized nodule you feel because it might kill you. Getting well acquainted with your breasts is important because it helps give you a good, integrated sense of your body.

This process should start with adolescence. Its side benefits are marvelous—it can teach the girl to be comfortable with her own body, and it can be a pleasing rite of passage, a confirmation and exploration of her womanhood. And all women should continue to explore their breasts periodically for the rest of their lives, noting and embracing each change that all the stages of life entail in her breasts, as in the rest of her body. There is a powerful feeling that comes from knowing and becoming comfortable with your body—a feeling and a power that is yours alone, and that no one can take from you.

3

Breast Feeding

The purpose of the breast is to make milk, and your breast doesn't reach its full potential development until you've been through a full-term pregnancy. This stage of the breast's development begins to be evident quite soon after conception. Even before you've missed your period, you may notice that your breasts are unusually tender or your nipples unusually sore. I've had a few patients coming to me complaining of unusual breast pain and I've asked when their last periods were. "Oh, about four weeks ago," they say—and I say, "Well, you could be pregnant." And they either groan or grin, depending on how interested they are in motherhood at that time—and a couple of weeks later they call back to say, "Guess what? I'm pregnant."

Your breasts enlarge very rapidly when you're pregnant, and they become very firm. The Montgomery's glands—those little glands around your areola (see Chapter 1)—become darker and more prominent, and the areola itself darkens. The nipples become larger and more erect, preparing themselves for future milk production (Fig. 3-1).

Two hormones are mainly responsible for milk production—prolactin and oxytocin. Both come from the pituitary gland, stimulated by an area of the brain known as the *hypothalamus*. The first, *prolactin*, is sometimes known a bit sentimentally as the "mothering hormone" because it causes you to make milk and, some theorists believe, has a

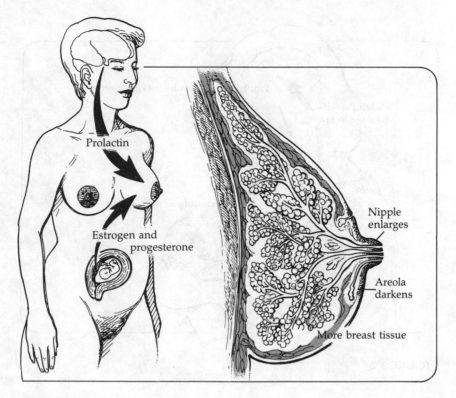

Prolactin

Estrogen and progesterone

Nipple enlarges

Areola darkens

More breast tissue

FIGURE 3-1

tranquilizing effect which presumably makes you feel more maternal. This latter theory, while pretty, is so far unproven.

Prolactin is absolutely crucial to your potential to breast-feed— without it, you'll never have any milk. It begins its work about the eighth week of pregnancy and slowly gets higher for the next seven months, peaking at your baby's birth (Fig. 3-2). With this high level of prolactin coursing through you, you would begin to spout milk right away except that your body is also producing high levels of estrogen and progesterone, which block some of the prolactin receptors and inhibit milk production.

Once your baby is born and the placenta has been delivered, your levels of estrogen and progesterone plummet, while the prolactin levels begin a much slower decline, and this is the sign for your breasts to begin producing milk. The milk, however, doesn't come right away. It takes between three and five days, during which time your breasts are making another liquid, a sort of pre-milk called *colostrum*, which the baby can drink instead of the milk it will soon get. Colostrum is filled with antibodies, which help the infant fight off

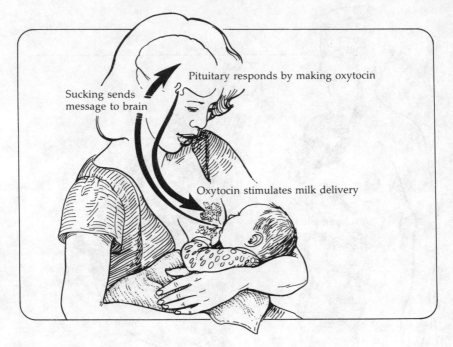

Sucking sends message to brain

Pituitary responds by making oxytocin

Oxytocin stimulates milk delivery

FIGURE 3-2

infections. It's also believed that colostrum decreases the baby's chances of later developing allergies and asthma. Soon the baby's own immune system has begun to develop, and it no longer needs the antibodies supplied by colostrum.

The other major hormone, *oxytocin*, delivers the milk that prolactin has produced. The baby's suckling at your breast does two things—it brings some of the milk out with its suction, and it sends an important message to the pituitary, via the nipple's nerve endings, the thoracic nerves, and the hypothalamus: send more milk out! The pituitary responds by manufacturing oxytocin, which makes the tiny muscles lining the lobules contract and squirt milk out from the breast. So while some of the milk is actually sucked out by the baby, some simply gushes into the baby's mouth. The mother experiences this as "letdown"—her milk is literally being let down into her nipples. The milk now exists in two places inside her breasts: the fore milk is at her nipples, the hind milk up in the lobules. When the hind milk is called forward by the oxytocin, new hind milk is created, ready to be called forward. Unlike prolactin, oxytocin doesn't exist in the body until the suckling process calls it forth (Fig. 3-2).

So suckling does two things: it stimulates prolactin to make milk,

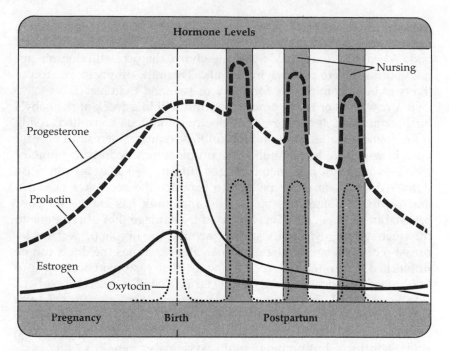

Hormone Levels

Progesterone

Prolactin

Estrogen

Oxytocin

Nursing

Pregnancy   Birth   Postpartum

FIGURE 3-3

and it stimulates oxytocin to deliver milk. It's very much a demand-and-supply process. Your prolactin level, high during pregnancy, slowly drifts down toward its normal level after the baby is born (Fig. 3-3). By the end of the first week after birth, prolactin is down to 50 percent of its normal level, and after three or four months, it's the same as it was before pregnancy. But every time your baby suckles, there's a new burst of prolactin telling your body to make milk and a burst of oxytocin telling it to release the milk into the baby's mouth. The more you nurse the baby, the more milk your body will produce. The baby can't ever use up the milk in your breasts; suckling is the message to your body to make more of it.

Meanwhile, other hormones are at work in the background—insulin, thyroid, cortisol, and background nutritional hormones. These take part of the food you eat and remanufacture it in a new way so that it can become part of the baby's milk.

In the 1950s, when breast feeding was unpopular, doctors typically gave new mothers milk-inhibiting drugs. Often this was done by blocking prolactin with the drug bromocriptine. This is rarely used today, partly because social mores have changed: women are much more inclined to breast feed at least for a while, even if they then perhaps switch over to bottle feeding. Often you hear that having unused milk in your breasts is extremely painful, but it's rarely all that bad. When you don't suckle your newborn, the prolactin doesn't signal your breasts to produce more milk. The milk simply stops. You're likely to be uncomfortable for a day or two and then feel fine.

If a new mother is not producing milk within a week of the baby's birth, something is wrong and a doctor should be consulted. Aside from deliberate attempts to inhibit milk, several problems can prevent your breasts from having milk. One problem may be in your pituitary gland—you might have hemorrhaged into it, or it may be otherwise damaged, and you won't be able to produce the necessary prolactin and oxytocin. Sometimes you'll find that milk has come into your breast, but can't get out. This is caused by damage that's been done to the duct system, usually by surgery around the nipple or perhaps by breast reduction surgery (see Chapter 5). Sometimes the ducts can be unblocked, but often they can't, and in that case, you will have to bottle feed instead of breast feed. (The milk will be reabsorbed back into your body.) This happened to a patient of mine in the ob/gyn section of the hospital where I work. I was called in to look at her because her milk had come in, but nothing was coming out. I tried to probe her ducts, but nothing would pass. I discovered that an operation she'd had done on a nipple abscess many years before had scarred over, sealing off her milk ducts.

If you've been breast feeding and you suddenly stop, your body will stop creating prolactin and oxytocin, so milk isn't being let down. Milk production will taper off and stop. For this reason, if you need to stop breast feeding temporarily—for instance, if you have to travel or are about to be on medication that you don't want the child to consume—you should keep expressing milk manually or with a pump, so that the production continues. Otherwise it may be difficult to resume breast feeding—the body has to start the whole business over again, and it takes time.

On the other hand, once you've had a baby you can always breast feed in the future. If, for example, you adopt a child some time after you've breast fed your biological baby, you can have the new baby suck your breast, and, with time, that can eventually start the whole process up again.

Breast milk looks different at each stage of its production. According to standard teaching, colostrum is yellow and clear; early breast milk is bluish-white, mature milk is white and creamy—what we think of as "milky"—and late milk, as you begin to breast feed less and less, is thin and white. But it may vary. I found my own early milk to be white and the later milk to be blue. It was also interesting to me to find that milk left to stand in the refrigerator layered out with the cream at the top. If I skipped a meal there would be less cream, "skim milk." When I ate regular meals, there was more cream. The milk of a premature baby's mother is different from that of a mother whose baby was delivered at full term: the preemy's nutritional needs are different, and the mother's body knows this and adjusts the milk to her child's needs. Similarly, if you have twins your body will adjust to that, and provide you with twice as much milk. You can even nurse two consecutive children at the same time, tandem nursing. I discovered something else from my own experience: if you freeze early milk and give it to the baby weeks later, it will put the baby to sleep; it has a natural sedative effect.

Another important fact worth noting: you should alternate breasts and not just feed from one. One of my patients found it comfortable to feed on one breast, and ignored the other—which in turn ignored her and stopped making milk. The result is she now has an asymmetry she never had before. Though having your first baby late in life can have other effects on your body, it won't affect your breast milk at all. You can produce good milk for your child at 40 just as you did at 20.

After you've stopped breast feeding, you'll still have some secretions for two or three months, sometimes as long as a year, afterward. Usually you can breast feed for two or three years, though you'll probably want to combine breast feeding with bottle feeding of breast milk or formula or juice after a while, both for your own convenience and to move your baby on to other foods. The length of time is up to you. Your child probably won't be traumatized by the change. My sister decided to stop breast feeding her daughter after three years. She was sure the child would be shattered, and spent a lot of time working out her explanation. When she broached the subject, my niece's response was a cheerful, "It's okay, Mom, I understand."

Breast feeding has some contraceptive effect, but only in the first three or four months—and even then, it isn't 100 percent effective. Don't assume that because you're breast feeding you can engage in intercourse without other contraceptives—unless you want to be breast feeding again in nine months.

If you plan to go back to work while you're still breast feeding, you can pump your breasts every three or four hours, freeze the milk or just refrigerate it, and use it to feed your baby later. Pumping can be done by manually expressing milk into a clean container or by using a breast pump (Figs. 3-4 and 3-5). They come in a number of forms—there are hand pumps, electric pumps, and battery-operated pumps. Depending on the type of pump, it takes 10 to 15 minutes on each side—there is even an extra attachment for the electric pump that allows you to empty both breasts simultaneously. As one of my busy doctor colleagues says, "Why waste a letdown?" Many workplaces

FIGURE 3-4

(especially hospitals) have pumps available, and many others will rent one for you. It's certainly worth asking your employer, since it is to their advantage to keep you at work. After my daughter was born, I was explaining to a patient how the breast was a milk factory, and in the middle of my session with her I had to interrupt and go pump my breasts—nicely illustrating my metaphor.

Sometimes breast feeding is interfered with by problems in the mother's body. One is sore nipples, created by the infant's suckling. You can often alleviate this by alternating the position in which the child is nursing. Avoid soaps, which irritate the delicate nipple skin. You can buy a rubber nipple shield to help relieve some of the pain during breast feeding. Some experts have actually suggested toughening up the breast ahead of time by rubbing in various creams or by sunbathing topless! (Obviously, if you're going to try this latter method, be aware that the law might not agree with your decision; either find a private place to sunbathe, or be prepared for a court case!)

Women with inverted nipples usually have trouble breast feeding (I discuss this in Chapter 4). There's a shell you can buy and put over the nipple, squeezing down and making it more available to the child (Fig. 3-6.)

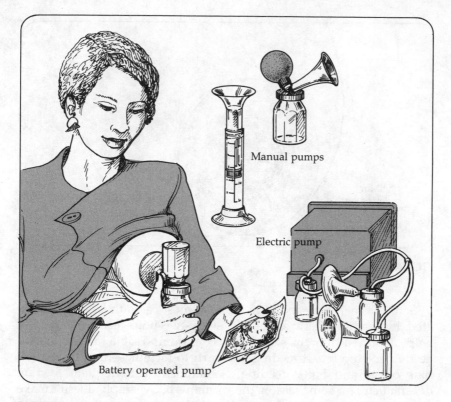

Manual pumps

Electric pump

Battery operated pump

FIGURE 3-5

Some women suffer from engorgement of the breasts: they fill up too fast and don't empty enough, and then the nipple is so stretched out the child can't get his or her mouth around it, and the problem gets worse. This is especially true when the milk first comes in, before the body has figured out the right amount of milk to produce—the first three or four days. It can be very uncomfortable, as I learned when my own baby was born. The best thing to do then is to express the milk manually between feedings, or to pump, and to feed the baby as often as possible. Frequent massage, hot tubs, and hot showers will help to express the milk; ice packs and aspirin or Tylenol can help relieve the pain.

Sometimes a duct can become blocked (Fig. 3-7). You'll know this has happened if you find a lumpy area in one segment of the breast that doesn't go away after breast feeding. It's important to treat it right away, because it can lead to infection and, in rare cases, the infection can turn into an abscess. Again, you can treat it with hot soaks, hot showers, and massage; if those don't work, call your doctor. There's a detailed description of these problems in Chapter 8.

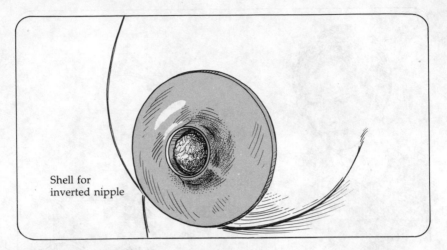

Shell for
inverted nipple

FIGURE 3-6

Some women have too little milk. In most cases this can be allevi-ated by feeding more often—an every-two-hour-feeding generally helps. If such a rigorous schedule becomes impossible for you, it may be time to stop breast feeding and turn to formula—or at least com-bine breast and bottle feeding. Sometimes even frequent feeding doesn't help; for some reason, the woman's body simply doesn't make enough milk, no matter what she does. Many women feel guilty when this happens, as though they've failed in their "motherly duties." They haven't—it's a biological idiosyncrasy, not a cosmic flaw.

At the other extreme is the woman whose body produces too much milk, and she finds herself leaking between feedings, or having her milk squirt out into the baby's face when she starts to nurse. This can be dealt with by expressing the milk between feedings, or pumping it and storing it in the refrigerator.

In any case, if you find yourself under physical or emotional distress over aspects of breast feeding, or just want moral support, contact the La Leche League, or one of the other breast feeding organi-zations which offer counseling, peer support groups, and practical advice (see Appendix C).

Breast Feeding and Lumps in the Breast

Pregnancy and lactation don't prevent lumps from occurring: you can get any of the usual fibroadenomas, cysts, or pseudolumps (see Chap-ter 9). In addition, a nursing mother can get a galactocele, a milk cyst

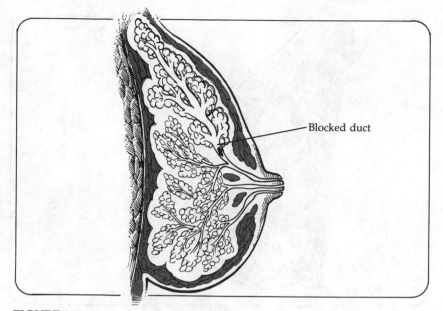

Blocked duct

FIGURE 3-7

that forms when some of the milk closes off in a sac and ultimately gets thick and cheesy. A needle aspiration can determine if the lump is a galactocele (Fig. 3-8). It's harmless, as is any cyst, but you want to be sure that's what it is. I recently had a patient who had two milk cysts, which had been there for at least two years.

And, of course, you can get a cancerous lump, just as you can when you're not breast feeding. Any dominant lump that doesn't go away with massage should be checked out. It appears that prognosis may be worse for a woman who gets breast cancer during pregnancy or breast feeding than at another time.[1] In addition, it usually gets diagnosed at a later stage, because a pregnant woman and her doctor are focused on the pregnancy and not thinking about cancer.[2] It's important to be as aware of the possibility of cancer during pregnancy and lactation as at any other time. Continue to explore your breasts (see Chapter 2), and be aware of the normal changes that pregnancy and breast feeding have created in them. Again, this is not about hunting for cancer. You're having a new and probably wonderful relationship to the breasts that are now feeding your baby, and it's nice to know how your breasts feel during this time. A pregnant breast will feel like a premenstrual breast; it is usually sore and lumpy in the first trimester and less so in the second and third; a lactating breast feels both full and lumpy, as if it had cottage cheese inside, because it's filled with fluid.

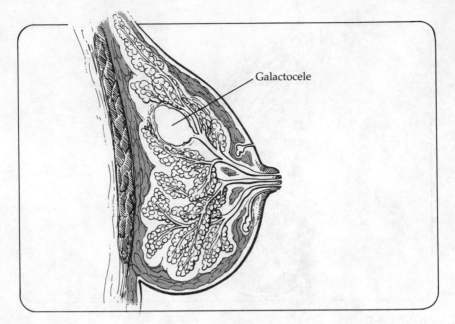

Galactocele

FIGURE 3-8

If you do find a suspicious lump, get it checked out. If a biopsy is called for, neither pregnancy nor breast feeding need prevent it. When you're pregnant, it's best to do a biopsy under local anesthetic, since the general anesthetic may harm the fetus.

A nursing mother can have either a general or a local anesthetic. I prefer to operate right after a woman has fed her baby, or expressed the milk. I use the lowest percentage of local anesthetic possible, since the child may suck some of it later. It's not terrible for the child to swallow a bit of anesthetic, but I want it to be as little as possible. I also advise the mother not to feed the baby from that breast for 12 hours after the surgery, since a large gulp of the lidocaine might be harmful, and you want to give it time to disperse through the breast.

It's messier to perform surgery on a lactating woman than on a nonlactating woman, and it's always possible that the operation will create a milk cyst or leakage. It's really no great tragedy, though, if it does. It can temporarily make the milk messy, too, since blood from the operation can mix with the milk. Blood won't hurt your baby, so it's mostly a matter of aesthetics.

Some surgeons will tell a lactating woman she has to stop breast feeding if she needs a biopsy. She doesn't. If your surgeon tells you this at a time when you're thinking of stopping breast feeding anyway, it's probably a good time to stop. Otherwise, find another surgeon who will operate while you're lactating.

There are some myths about cancer and breast feeding that need to be addressed. The first is that if you have breast cancer and your child drinks from the cancerous breast, the child will get your cancer. This theory is based on a study of one species of mouse, which does transmit a cancerous virus to its female offspring through breast feeding. At this time, it hasn't been found in any other species of mouse, or any other animal, or in humans.

Another myth is that a baby won't drink milk from a cancerous breast. Normally this isn't so. If a breast has a lot of cancer, it probably won't produce as much milk, so the baby will, quite sensibly, favor the milkier breast. There's nothing wrong with this; in fact, many babies prefer one breast to another, even with a very healthy mother.

A third notion is that breast feeding helps prevent breast cancer. This statement often sounds slightly moralistic. If the breast is doing what it's supposed to do, it won't get cancer. Overall research hasn't shown a consistent effect. Your odds of getting breast cancer appear to be nearly the same whether or not you've ever breast fed a baby.[3] A study of Chinese women indicated that women who breast feed their children for at least nine consecutive years have less breast cancer.[4] Another study showed that women who first lactated before the age of 20 and breast fed their infants for six months had half the risk of breast cancer than did women who had been pregnant and did not breast feed. Unfortunately, after age 20, breast feeding demonstrated only a slight reduction of risk for most women.[5] (The age at which you first have a baby does affect your vulnerability to breast cancer—see Chapter 14.) These are interesting findings, but not very useful for most women in our culture.

Sex and Breast Feeding

There's no reason for breast feeding to interfere with an active sex life. Breast stimulation may cause some milk to flow out. Sometimes lovers enjoy sucking at breasts and getting some milk. If this is pleasing to you, it's fine—your lover won't be using up your child's milk, only stimulating the breast to produce more. If either of you finds stimulation of the breast unappealing at this time, you can adjust your sexual practices accordingly. On the other hand, you may find that your general libido is markedly reduced while you are breast feeding, and you're not as interested in sex as you usually are. You and your partner should be aware of this possibility, so your partner doesn't feel rejected and you don't feel like you've suddenly become "frigid."

Many women feel sexual stimulation during breast feeding, and it's perfectly natural—oxytocin causes the uterus to contract. Don't worry about it. It doesn't mean you're a potential child molester. It's usually a fairly mild form of sexual feeling, and there's no reason not to just enjoy it. (If you don't feel it, don't worry about that either; just enjoy the sensations you do feel.)

Breast Feeding When You Haven't Given Birth

If you've never breast fed or been pregnant before, you can still do a form of breast feeding. This must be done in conjunction with bottle formula (or milk from another woman's breast, as in the case of lesbians raising the biological child of one partner together). Stimulated by suckling which increases prolactin, the breast will produce a kind of pre-milk fluid, which can provide a small amount of nutrition to the child. Since many women find breast feeding pleasurable, and since breast feeding intensifies the bonding of mother and infant, this can be a good idea, as long as the baby is given other forms of nutrition. (Men, by the way, don't have this fluid, since their breasts haven't developed through puberty the way women's have.) This kind of breast feeding can be enhanced by using an invention called a Lactaid kit (Fig. 3-9). It has a bag into which formula (or pumped breast milk) is placed, and a long plastic tube that winds around the breast and ends up at the nipple. The child sucks the milk from a catheter next to the nipple, thus creating the bonding effect of breast feeding.

The kit might also help a woman who has had a baby (or been pregnant for several months) in the past to revive her own milk-producing abilities. In this case she will eventually produce full milk. The virtue of the kit is that it helps you bond with the child and experience breast feeding, even if your own milk isn't available. Hormones have also been used to stimulate breast feeding, with varying results.

Breast Feeding versus Bottle Feeding

When I was born, breast feeding was very out of fashion. Bottle feeding was considered less messy, and it gave mothers more mobility than they had with breast feeding. In the past decade or so, the tendency has reversed itself, and breast feeding is definitely "in." I think it's unfortunate that there are fashions in baby feeding. They tend to include pressures and guilt trips, or the idea that there's a universally

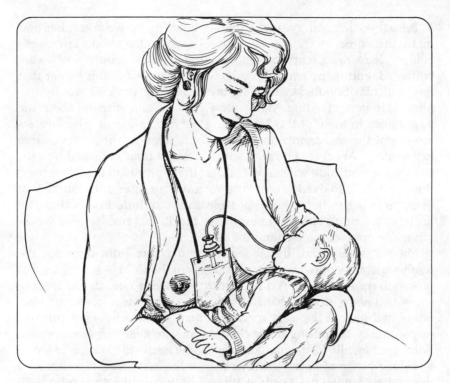

FIGURE 3-9

correct way to feed your baby, and that there's something odd and probably immoral about doing it any other way. In reality, there are advantages and disadvantages to both methods of baby feeding, and you need to weigh them all before you decide what you want to do.

What are the advantages of breast feeding? Probably the most important advantage is the nutritional composition of breast milk. It's tailor-made for the human baby's needs—it's got the perfect combination of water, protein, carbohydrates (mainly lactose), immunoglobin (which helps create immunity against disease), lots of cholesterol (which, though unhealthy for adults, is great for babies), and vitamins and minerals. Cow's milk, on the other hand, is tailor-made for the needs of baby cows, which are obviously somewhat different from those of the human baby.

Formula is our attempt to modify cow's milk to make it as close as possible to human milk. We've done a pretty impressive job, but it's not perfect. For one thing, cow's milk isn't as digestible as human milk. It takes a baby four hours to digest formula, and only two to digest human milk. And no formula has been able to duplicate the immunity-providing properties of colostrum.

Breast feeding also creates a unique bonding between mother and infant that some psychologists feel is essential to the child's later well-being. There are plenty of emotionally healthy people who were bottle-fed, and many neurotics who were breast-fed, but it's clear that the particular bonding created by breast feeding can't be wholly duplicated in bottle feeding. Many of my patients talk with me about the importance to them of this bonding. "The realization of what breasts are meant for was tremendous," says one, who calls it a "generative experience." Another, who was self-conscious about her small breasts, changed her attitude when she realized that "my small breasts nursed three sons." I enjoyed breast feeding my daughter and found that even pumping milk for her was a pleasant interlude in an otherwise hectic day. I think being able to fill her nutritional needs while working made me feel more connected to her.

On the other hand, breast feeding can create difficulties for the mother that may outweigh the advantages to the child—difficulties that proselytizers for breast feeding sometimes under-rate. Breast feeding every two hours may be hard for a woman who has a job outside her home, and it's not that easy for the woman at home who has primary responsibility for raising other children and maintaining a household. Bottle feeding allows the mother to get some rest, and to do other work, while her husband or another member of the household does some of the feeding. Sometimes a combination of breast feeding and bottle feeding (using either formula or breast milk expressed by the mother at an earlier time) can be a useful compromise, but some women still find breast feeding too demanding of time and energy. Also, lactation can cause problems even for the mother combining breast and bottle feeding. Oxytocin can be produced by an emotional as well as a direct physical response to the baby. Many mothers find to their embarrassment that, while they're thinking about their baby, milk suddenly begins to flow. A surgeon colleague of mine stopped breast feeding when the thought of her baby came to her during an operation, and suddenly milk started dripping onto her patient.

Still other women find the idea of breast feeding unpleasant, even repugnant. This isn't an indication that the woman will be a bad mother; reactions to physical experiences vary greatly among human beings. Forcing oneself to go through with it would be counterproductive to the bonding experience between mother and child. Some women feel more comfortable with bottle feeding because they know how much nutrition the child is getting, since it's premeasured, and the exact amount of breast milk is not something she can know for certain.

There are also women whose own food habits can interfere with breast feeding. Babies consume, through breast milk, everything the mother consumes, and many women cherish their cups of coffee and their evening martinis. Although small amounts of liquor and caffeine are probably all right, limit them if you want to breast feed. A study from the University of Michigan[6] demonstrated a slight decrease in motor development, but not in mental development, in the year-old offspring of mothers who drank one alcoholic drink per day. Thus, although some data suggest that a glass of beer a day improves milk production, it probably isn't worth the slight but potentially harmful consequences. And, of course, there are other recreational drugs that are just as dangerous. It's probably safest to remain drug- and alcohol-free while breast feeding. Some women can do this easily, and for them it's worth the sacrifice; for others, it's not, and they may prefer to bottle feed. Similarly, some mothers are on medication for chronic illnesses and some (though certainly not all) medication will harm a breast feeding baby. Sacrificing your own health or comfort may not be the best thing either for you or for your child. As we discuss in Chapter 5, it is possible that silicone from a breast implant can leak into breast milk and harm the baby, so if you have implants it may be wisest to bottle feed.

Many women today feel pressured to breast feed, regardless of their own needs, and often others play unconsciously into those pressures. A patient recently came to see me in her eighth month of pregnancy. She reminded me that, four months earlier, I'd said to her, "I'll see you again toward the end of your pregnancy, and then again when you've finished breast feeding." She was concerned because she didn't want to breast feed, and felt I'd been implying that she should.

At the same time, there are still parts of our culture that have retained the old prejudices against breast feeding, and they can be very damaging to a mother. There's still some feeling that, because the breast is a sexual organ, it shouldn't be exposed in public (men don't cover their chests, even though some people view men's breasts as erotic). Thus, a woman who's breast feeding may find herself pressured to give it up, or to confine it to her own home. I remember going to a wedding and seeing my cousin's wife sitting off in a corner, very discreetly breast feeding her baby. Some of the other guests were horrified. Feeding your baby is a perfectly natural and sensible thing to do, and you shouldn't be made to feel like some kind of slut for doing it. Obviously, given social mores, it's usually unwise to bare your whole breast in public, but sensibly chosen clothing can allow for discreet feeding anywhere, and you shouldn't feel guilt-tripped by other people's puritanism.

There's another prejudice that gets in the way of breast feeding. The breast-fed baby doesn't gain weight as rapidly as the bottle-fed baby does. That's perfectly fine, except that we've been raised with the image of the chubby, healthy baby. But chubby isn't necessarily healthy, and breast feeding may in fact produce a healthier child.

Opposition to breast feeding originated in the early days of formula feeding, and it was very much in the interests of the manufacturers of baby formula. This had a tragic effect in Third World countries, where poor mothers were told that formula was better for their babies than breast milk, then given formula until their own milk dried up, and were then forced to buy more formula at a cost they couldn't afford. Many babies died as a result.

Most women in the United States are well enough off to be able to choose between breast and bottle feeding. Make your own choice realistically, taking into consideration your own needs and priorities. If the various social criticisms make sense to you, consider them. If they don't, ignore them. You want to do what's best for you and your baby, and for the relationship that develops between you. Only you can best determine what that is.

4

*Variations in
Development*

Breasts are found in many different shapes and sizes. Medically speaking, a "normal" breast is one that is capable of producing milk, so there's nothing "abnormal" about large, small, or asymmetrical breasts, or about extra nipples.

There are a number of common variations in breast development. They fall into one of two categories: those that are obvious from birth, and those that don't show themselves until puberty. The latter are far more common. (There are also variations due to accident or illness, the surgical remedies for which are essentially the same as those used for genetic variations.)

Variations Apparent at Birth

The most common variation to appear at birth is *polymastia*—an extra nipple, or nipples. These can appear anywhere along the milk ridge (Fig. 1-5). Usually the milk ridge—a throwback to the days when we were animals with many nipples —regresses before birth, but in some people it remains throughout their lives. Between 1 and 5 percent of extra nipples are on women whose mothers also had extra nipples. Usually they're below the breast, and often women don't even know

43

they're there, since they look very much like moles. I've frequently pointed out an extra nipple to a patient, and it's the first time she's known about it.

They cause no problems, and because of their size and resemblance to moles usually don't appear cosmetically unattractive. One of my patients is actually very fond of her extra nipple. She told me that her husband has one too, and that's how they knew they were meant for each other! Men do sometimes have extra nipples, though as far as we know, less frequently than women. This may be due to some biological factor we don't yet know about, or it may simply be that men and their doctors don't notice the nipples because they're covered by chest hair.

Extra nipples may lactate if you breast feed. There's nothing wrong with this, unless it causes you discomfort. Sometimes a woman will have an entire extra breast, which causes no medical problems.

A variation of the extra nipple is extra breast tissue, without a nipple, most often under the armpit. It may feel like hard, cystlike lumps that swell and hurt the way your breasts do when you menstruate. Like extra nipples, this extra breast tissue is often unnoticed by doctor and patient. One of my patients found that, during her second pregnancy, she had swelling under both armpits. It was probably caused by extra breast tissue and it went down again after she finished lactating. The extra tissue is subject to all the problems of

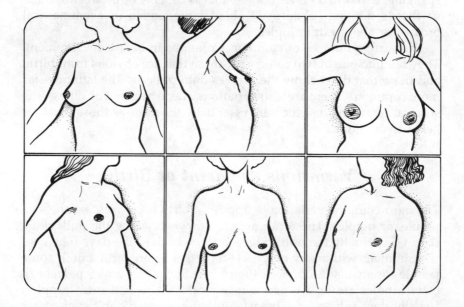

normally situated tissue. I have had patients with cysts, fibroadenomas, or even cancers in this aberrant breast.

Unless the extra nipple or breast tissue causes you extreme physical discomfort or psychological distress, there's no need to worry about it. If it does bother you, it's easy to get rid of surgically. The nipple can be removed under local anesthetic in your doctor's office, much the way a mole can, and the breast tissue can be removed under either local or general anesthetic.

A much rarer condition is *amastia*—being born with breast tissue but no nipple. Amastia is usually associated with scoliosis and rib deformities. Aside from whatever medical procedures you may need, you might want to have a fake nipple created by a plastic surgeon, in the same way a nipple is created during reconstruction after a mastectomy. A skin graft is taken from tissue on the inner thigh; the skin becomes darker after it's grafted, and, if it still doesn't match the color of your other nipple, it can be tattooed to a darker shade. This artificial nipple looks real but it won't feel completely like a real nipple. There is no erectile tissue, so it won't vary like your other nipple does; it's usually constructed midway between erect and flat. It will have no sensation because it has no nerves. And, of course, it won't have ducts and so it can't produce milk. Its advantages are wholly cosmetic.

Some women have practically no breasts at all. This condition is sometimes called Poland's syndrome, and it involves not just the breast but also the pectoralis muscle and the ribs, as well as, in some cases, abnormalities of the arm and one side of the body. At times, a woman with Poland's syndrome does have a small but very deformed breast. A recent patient of mine in Los Angeles was doubly unlucky. She had been born with Poland's syndrome and had a very undeveloped breast on one side. When she developed breast cancer in the good breast, she was anxious to have a lumpectomy rather than a mastectomy, because she very much wanted to preserve her only functional breast. Some women have permanently inverted nipples (they grow inside instead of out)—a congenital condition that usually won't manifest until puberty.

Various kinds of injuries can affect breast development. This may happen surgically or with trauma. If the nipple and breast bud are injured before puberty, the potential adult breast is destroyed as well. Sometimes injuring the skin can limit future breast development. Most commonly this occurs as a result of a severe burn: scars are so tight they don't allow the breast tissue to develop. In the past, some congenital conditions such as *hemangiomas* ("birthmarks") were treated with radiation, which damaged the nipple and breast bud and prevented later growth. Any serious injury to the breast bud can cause this arrested development.

Variations Appearing at Puberty

Three basic variations appear when the breasts begin to develop: extremely large breasts, extremely small breasts, and asymmetrical breasts.

VERY LARGE BREASTS

Very large breasts can occur early in puberty—a condition known as "virginal hypertrophy." After the breasts begin to grow, the shutoff mechanism, whatever it is, forgets to do its job and the breasts keep on growing. The breasts become huge and greatly out of proportion to the rest of the body. Sometimes the condition runs in families. In rare instances virginal hypertrophy occurs in one breast and not the other. It's worth noting here that "large" is both a subjective and a variable term. A five-foot-tall woman with a C cup is very large-breasted; a five-foot-eight woman with a C cup may not feel especially uncomfortable with her size. A five-foot-eight woman with a DD cup is likely to be very uncomfortable.

Large breasts are a source of distress for a number of my patients. "I almost never wear a bathing suit," one patient told me, "because people stare at my breasts." Another, at 71, still "hunches over" when she walks to avoid having her breasts stared at. Teenage girls with huge breasts face ridicule from schoolmates and—unlike small-breasted girls—extreme physical discomfort as well. A large-breasted young girl may be unable to participate in sports, and may have severe backache all the time. She usually needs a bra to hold the breasts in, but the bra, pulled down by the weight of the breasts, can dig painful ridges into her shoulders.

If the breasts cause this much discomfort, the girl might want to have reduction surgery done while she's still in her teens. There are a number of procedures. Though they're all major surgery, because they're done on the body's surface they're less dangerous than other equally complex operations, and the recovery period is speedier. (We discuss plastic surgery in the next chapter.) The procedures vary according to the size of the breasts. If they're really huge, the nipple will have to be moved further up on the newly reduced breast. In this case, the ducts are cut and so breast feeding will never be possible.

For this reason, some mothers refuse to let their daughters have reduction surgery, urging them to wait until they've had their children. This concern must be weighed against the physical and emotional damage the girl will go through first. If she decides to have children, pregnancy may make things worsen. When breasts become engorged with milk they become even larger and thus, in a woman with huge breasts, more uncomfortable. It's too bad that someone so young is faced with a decision that will affect her whole life, but it's important to realize that not having surgery will also affect her life. Many girls of 15 or 16 are mature enough to make their own decisions if all the facts are carefully explained to them, including the possibility of bottle feeding. In any case, the losses and gains of either choice are the girl's, and she should be given the right to decide for herself what to do. She should be encouraged to talk to doctors, mothers of young children, and very large-breasted women; to read all the material she can find about the pros and cons of the procedure and of breast feeding; and to make her decision only when she feels she is fully informed.

Not all problems with huge breasts appear right after puberty; some comfortably large-breasted women find their breasts have expanded considerably after pregnancy. Many women become uncomfortable when their breast size increases with an overall weight gain. Surgeons are often reluctant to operate on these women, preferring to wait until they lose weight. Sometimes, however, this can backfire psychologically. I've known women so depressed by huge breasts that they compensate by overeating, thus compounding their distress. In such cases, the pleasing appearance of their breasts created by reduction surgery can be a spur to continue the process of self-improvement.

In all cases, the decisions must be made by the women themselves. Each one lives with the problem and can best judge its impact on her life. Some women with very large breasts don't mind them. One patient, who admits they cause her discomfort, says she nonetheless enjoys their size. "They feel feminine and sexy," she says.

VERY SMALL BREASTS

The opposite is extreme flat-chestedness. Like "large-breasted," the notion of "small-breasted" is subjective and relative, and to some extent culturally determined. Some women, however, have breasts so small that their chests look like men's. This causes no physical or medical problems. Yet it can cause psychological ones, making a woman feel unattractive and sexless. Plastic surgeons often inaccurately call very small breasts a "disease," contributing even further to the woman's lack of comfort with her anatomy.

For many women, the solution often lies in the padded bra or "falsies." Others want to have the breasts themselves altered. For years there was nothing that could be done for women who wanted larger breasts. Some surgeons experimented with paraffin injections, with fairly awful results. In the 1960s, the silicone implant and silicone injections were introduced. These implants, their safety and the surgery involved, are discussed in Chapter 5.

Drs. Andrew and Penny Stanway in their book *The Breast*[1] suggest a somewhat surprising alternative to augmentation surgery—hypnosis and visualization. Visualization is a form of self-hypnosis in which you put yourself in a state of deep relaxation and then see yourself, as vividly as possible, achieving the state you want to be in. (We discuss this in Chapter 29, where we talk about nonmedical components of cancer treatment.)

The Stanways describe a study in which volunteers, put into a trance, were asked to visualize a wet warm towel over their breasts. They were told to concentrate on the warmth of the towel and on the breasts' pulsation. They did this exercise every day for 12 weeks. At the end of that time half the patients reported having to buy bigger bras! The authors suggest that the deep relaxation and visualizing might effect a hormonal change that influences breast size. Although the study is hardly conclusive, it is certainly interesting, and you might want to give visualization a try before considering surgery. It's painless, it has no harmful side effects, and it might just produce the results you want in a less expensive and physically invasive way than through surgery. (See Appendix B for books on visualization techniques.)

ASYMMETRICAL BREASTS

There is a third situation that often occurs in puberty: the breasts grow unevenly. In some cases, this is simply a question of the rate of the breasts' growth, and in a year or two the breasts are fairly symmetrical—for example, one breast will be an A cup size, the other is a B cup size. (Keep in mind that most people's breasts are slightly uneven, as are their feet and hands.) But sometimes the breasts remain extremely asymmetrical. Again, asymmetrical breasts are perfectly "normal" from a medical viewpoint: they can both produce milk. But they can also create extreme psychological distress, causing some adolescent girls—and later the grown woman—to feel like a sexual freak. Some girls refuse to date in their teens because their condition may be discovered and ridiculed. (My co-author had her first date at the age of 20—two weeks after her last silicone injection.) A falsie—or a pile of several falsies—can be worn on one side, of course, but that can still leave a feeling of something ugly and somehow shameful that must be hidden from the world.

For a woman who is bothered by extreme asymmetry, cosmetic

surgery can help achieve a reasonable match. Either the larger breast can be reduced or the smaller one augmented—or a combination of both can be done. It's important for the surgeon to discuss these options—often we assume a woman will want a small breast made larger, and neglect to suggest the possibility of reducing the larger breast. What a woman decides will depend on the size of both breasts, the degree of asymmetry, and, above all, her own aesthetic judgment.

It's fortunate that plastic surgery techniques exist for women who want them. But don't assume that because you have atypical-looking breasts you have to get them altered. Many women are quite pleased with how their breasts look. Some women with large breasts, like the patient I mentioned earlier, think their breasts are "feminine and sexy." Small breasts, too, have their advantages. One of my patients likes her small breasts because "they're unobtrusive, and they worked well during nursing. Occasionally some male person will intimate that they're less than optimal. That's his problem, not mine." Another likes her tiny breasts ("they're really just enlarged nipples") because they don't get in her way when she engages in sports. A patient with very asymmetrical breasts says she used to feel self-conscious, but has "come to terms with them" after nursing her child.

And another patient tells a wonderful story about a friend of hers who had inverted nipples. "When I was 12 and my cousin was 14, we stood before the bathroom mirror and compared breasts. I noticed how different her nipples were; they didn't protrude, the way mine did. We had this big discussion about whose were 'normal.' I was convinced mine were, but she insisted hers were, and since she was older and, I thought, more knowledgeable, I decided she must be right.

"After she graduated from college and was studying in Paris, she became ill and had to be hospitalized. The doctor who was examining her asked if her nipples 'had always been like that.' That's how she learned that she had inverted nipples—and that mine were the normal ones!"

Obviously, the woman's inverted nipples hadn't caused her any distress. If you don't object to the way your breasts look, don't think about plastic surgery. You're fine as you are.

5

Plastic Surgery

Many women with atypical breasts are perfectly comfortable with them, and never consider having them altered. On the other hand, some women are very unhappy with the way their breasts look. For them, cosmetic surgery is worth thinking about. In our society women are often made to feel that having cosmetic surgery is frivolous and "vain"; at the same time they are expected to meet an impossible, Hollywood-style standard of beauty. It's no more vain to alter your breasts than it is to wear contact lenses instead of glasses, or to get discolored teeth capped; it's certainly no more vain than it is for a man to wear a toupee or get a hair transplant.

Plastic surgery on breasts has been around for a long time. The first recorded breast surgery was done on a man with gynecomastia, in A.D. 625.[1] It was not until over a thousand years later (1897) that mammoplasty was performed on a woman—but we needn't feel too deprived. With the primitive state of surgery in the past, that poor man in the seventh century can't have had too comfortable a time with it. Good breast reduction techniques have now been with us for decades. Augmentation, as I mentioned earlier, is a much more recent procedure.

From a surgical standpoint the procedures themselves are quite safe. They are often labeled "unnecessary surgery," and, of course, they are unnecessary, in the sense that you won't die without them. But for many women the risk is worth the chance of an improved self-image, and, in the case of large breasts, increased physical comfort.

Plastic surgery has always been an issue of ethical concern, especially for feminists. Women have always been told when their looks weren't "right"; that they needed to change their looks to please men, or a particular man. Cosmetic surgery can be seen as a high-tech version of all the painful assaults on the body that women have experienced for centuries—footbinding, corsets, genital mutilation. Activists in the women's health movement argue that rather than subjecting our bodies to procedures that carry the risk of surgery and that may cause other health problems as well, we should change society's approach so we don't feel the need to have "perfect" or "ideal" bodies.

But that doesn't seem reasonable to me. First of all, it takes a very paternalistic—or maternalistic—view of what's best for other people. Second, some women have a practical need for bodies that society defines as "ideal"—like many of the young women I meet in my Los Angeles practice who are trying to succeed as actresses and models. Third, some women have needs that are emotional, their feelings are deeply ingrained—they can't just decide not to feel a certain way. Years spent in an uphill battle against internalized social expectations can be as devastating as physical illness. A nose job, a face lift, or enlarged breasts can make a major difference in a woman's life—and whether that would or would not be the case in an "ideal" world is beside the point.

Not everyone who wants to alter her body is a bimbo. I've had a range of patients who've wanted their breasts augmented. Among them is a gynecologist, married to a surgeon. A well-educated, professional, not terribly young, she had silicone implants and said they had made a tremendous difference in her life, and that she'd do it again if she had to make the choice today. Another had gotten her implants in 1980 at the age of 40. "For the first time in my life I was proud of my figure," she says. "I felt like a new woman." Perhaps it's a pity that society has made these women feel this way, and perhaps we should work to change the way we're taught to view our bodies. But meanwhile, we all have irrational feelings that deeply affect our lives, and none of us needs to be a martyr.

Before we get into the various kinds of plastic surgery, there's a practical consideration you need to address: insurance. You'll need to check with your insurance company about what forms of plastic surgery they will or won't pay for. You'll also want to find out if the insurance company has a disclaimer or exclusion for coverage of future implant-related health problems (medical/surgical). You may have to shoulder the financial responsibility for the procedure yourself.

Silicone Implant Controversy

The plastic surgery debate has been ignited further by the recent silicone implant controversy. When silicone was introduced in the United States in the 1960s as a tool for breast augmentation, it seemed like a godsend. Early experiments with substances like paraffin, polyurethane foam, and even steel had proven disastrous. But silicone—a synthetic plastic composed of the natural material silicon, blended with carbon, hydrogen, and oxygen—was considered an inert substance, perceived at the time as harmless. It had been (and continues to be) used in a variety of medical devices: artificial limbs, pacemakers, and implants for replacing surgically removed testicles and penises.

In its early use for breast augmentation, it was given to women in two forms—injections of silicone gel into the breast over a period of weeks, and pockets of silicone gel in a harder, breast-shaped silicone shell implanted into the breast.

Some women have had excellent, long-term results from the injections, but many others have developed problems. The silicone often traveled through the body, causing unsightly and alarming lumps to form in unexpected spots. The injections were eventually banned, and women wanting their breasts enlarged got the, presumably safer, implants.

Saline implants were actually used before silicone, but they leaked, and were less firm-appearing than a young woman's breast. The silicone implant seemed more appealing at the time, and doctors began developing it. Saline implants are similar to silicone, except that saline (salt water)—not silicone gel—is in the silicone shell. Saline is no more likely to leak than silicone, but when it does it becomes absorbed by the body fairly quickly so that you realize suddenly your breast has shrunk. Gel implants, on the other hand, may rupture or leak but the bulk of the material stays together inside the fibrous scar capsule, so the outside appearance may not change for some time. The saline implant feels somewhat less realistic than silicone. Dr. William Shaw, a plastic surgeon and a colleague of mine at UCLA, describes it as feeling "less fleshy than silicone; it's more like a bag of water, particularly when the covering tissue is thin." Leakage of saline won't cause any medical problems, and to date, there have been no complaints about saline.

In 1990, women began to complain about health problems they were certain were related to silicone implants.[2] There were congressional hearings in which patients and doctors testified about their negative effects. Many problems were thought to be caused by the casing rather than the silicone itself. Some implants were encased in a covering of polyurethane foam which was supposed to lessen the likelihood of *capsular contracture* (the formation of a thick, spherical scar tissue that causes the breast to harden). The foam, however, was suspected of causing worse problems—it could increase the risk of infection and release into the body a substance called 2-*tolunediamine* (TDA) that might be carcinogenic. Tests on animals and women did not show such effects,[3,4] but the foam-encased implants were withdrawn from the market. (Women with foam coverings can get their urine tested for TDA, although we don't know what good that will do them.)

Most of the women's complaints, however, were about the silicone itself. The questions raised about silicone implants continued, as more and more women testified about health problems from their implants. In 1992, the Food and Drug Administration (FDA) banned silicone implants. According to FDA head David Kessler, they did this not because silicone implants were known to pose a risk, but because manufacturers had not fulfilled their legal responsibilities to collect data on the question.

Despite the lack of data, the media reportage of the FDA decision led the public and most judges and juries to believe that there was indeed a connection between the implants and a variety of health problems. Over 18,000 lawsuits were filed against manufacturers of breast implants. Three finally decided, on April 1, 1994, that a global settlement would be the easiest way out, and they set up a fund of $4.2 billion to compensate women with implants who had developed one of eight different diseases.

Under the 1992 FDA ruling, women wishing to have silicone implants can now have them only in conjunction with a long-range study, and only certain categories of women are eligible for these studies. Women with mastectomies, serious injury to the breast, or severe breast asymmetry or abnormality, or those who need new implants due to a rupture in the old one, will be accepted for the study. Women who simply want their breasts enlarged will not be. We'll discuss the implications of all this in the section on breast augmentation later in this chapter.

With the current controversy over silicone many plastic surgeons have shifted back to saline as a the implant of choice. Saline leakage, which can be repaired by simple surgery, seems less frightening to most women. But saline implants may not eradicate the danger of silicone because one could have a reaction to the harder silicone shell as well as to silicone gel.

There's a variant on the implant called the *expander* (see section on reconstruction in Chapter 26). It's still in a silicone envelope, and it can leak, so it may have some of the same problems as the silicone implant.

The FDA hearings on saline implants resulted in a requirement that manufacturers undertake further studies. However, the implants were not taken off the market. Activists are angry that the implants have been used for so long without being studied by manufacturers, scientists, or the FDA. That anger is justified. Women were led to believe by their doctors that the absence of data meant they were safe (much as with fertility drugs and postmenopausal hormones today).

As it now exists, I have trouble accepting the FDA ban. We may not have had data showing that implants were safe, but neither do we have data showing they are dangerous. Despite the testimony of hundreds of women who attributed their health problems to implants, we can't be certain there is any connection between the two.

The American Society of Plastic and Reconstructive Surgeons put a lot of money into fighting the move to ban silicone implants. They got a group of women who were happy with their implants and trained them how to testify to the lobbyists and talk to the media. We can be cynical about the society's motives, but the fact remains that these women were neither forced nor bribed to testify—they were happy with their implants, just as the women who testified against them were unhappy with theirs. Even complaints to the FDA suggest that not all women are unhappy with the implants themselves. The FDA reviewed 112 letters received in January 1992.[5] When analyzed, they revealed four main themes: the women didn't get enough information prior to surgery; they weren't taken seriously by their doctors when they complained of pain; some of them had difficulty with normal activities, and they had concerns about the future. Most of those complaints are about doctor/patient communication, not medical problems with the implants.

There are other indications that the majority of women who have had silicone implants are not unhappy with them. A group of researchers from Duke University did telephone interviews with 174 women who had had silicone implants after mastectomies. Even after the reports of problems with silicone were publicized, most said they were pleased with their implants.[6] Studies on women who have had implants for breast augmentation showed similar results.[7] Whereas over half of the women in the Duke study were worried about their implants, only slightly more than one fifth had even considered having them out.

These stories never reached the general population, because the media weren't interested in reporting them. Presumably, contented consumers make less exciting copy. When the FDA hearings were going on, a number of people from the press called my office asking to interview some of my patients with silicone implants who were having health problems. I agreed to put them in touch with patients who were willing to be interviewed, as long as they also included patients who were happy with their implants. They weren't interested. This is shabby, unbalanced journalism, and it is harmful to women with implants who have had no problems but who were now seeing only the horror stories on television. I got calls from some of my scared patients, and I had to reassure them they weren't necessarily going to have trouble—that lots of women didn't.

I don't mean to dismiss women's concerns about silicone implants. Larger studies may turn out to validate the suspected links to some diseases. And there are less dramatic but still significant problems for which we do have data.

Implants interfere with how well mammograms can detect tumors in the breast. A study by Mel Silverstein and his colleagues[8] showed that implants create shadows on mammograms, blocking areas from the picture and leading to a decrease in accuracy of a mammogram. While small breasts themselves are hard to visualize on a mammogram and mammography is not always a surefire way to detect breast cancer, it is still the best tool we have for finding breast cancer. Any process that interferes with its effectiveness should be entered into only with great forethought.

Furthermore, Dr. William Shaw, Chief of Plastic Surgery at UCLA, says silicone isn't the wholly inert substance it was once thought to be, and it always creates some reaction around it. Minuscule amounts of silicone will always leak. The reaction may be something that you'd never notice or be bothered by—the sort of thing that only shows up if the breast is biopsied. But it can cause some kind of inflammatory reaction or irritation in other parts of the body. Furthermore, he says, "every patient who has an implant develops a capsule around the implant, and the capsule itself is a form of inflammation—like the callus that can develop around a sore spot on your foot after you've stepped on a thorn. And the fact that you have a chronic inflammation can create biological mediators that can, in turn, create some uncomfortable symptoms—soreness around the breast, for example."

Contracture—the formation of a thick, spherical scar tissue that causes the breast to be overly firm (Fig. 5-1)—is a real possibility with most implants. It occurs in 1 to 18 percent of cases in which the implant is under the muscle, and between 18 and 50 percent of cases in which it's between the muscle and breast. This firmness can be so

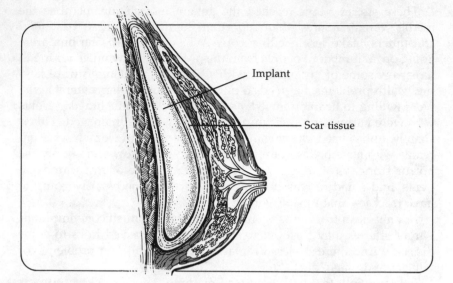

Implant

Scar tissue

FIGURE 5-1

minimal that it's unnoticeable, or it can feel like solid wood—or anything in between. Contracture can be painful, and it can change the appearance of the breast. Contracture, warns Dr. Shaw, may happen to one implant and not the other, or may happen differently in the two implants. "One side is higher, the other lower."

There is also the possibility that the implant can rupture, causing the gel to leak into the breast and sometimes beyond the breast. There have been cases in which the leaked silicone has migrated to the vicinity of the brachial plexus nerves to the arm, causing chronic irritation and pain. We don't know if that leakage is dangerous or not. There has never been a study done on the long-term health of women who had silicone injections before they were banned. Such a study might tell us if silicone in the breast and other parts of the body causes harm. Dr. Shaw has had a number of patients who had silicone injections years ago, and has seen cases in which hard lumps have formed in the breast, making cancer detection impossible, and other cases in which there was infection and dead tissue in the breast itself. This does suggest that similar problems can occur with leakage from implants.

But the biggest concern of the activists is one that remains unproven. They believe that the gel might cause autoimmune disorders and connective tissue diseases such as rheumatoid arthritis and lupus. Many of the women testifying at the FDA hearings had such disorders. However, we have no way of knowing what, if any, relationship there is between the disorder and the implants. It's possible that there is no relation—that the percentage of women with silicone implants who have these conditions is the same as that of women with no implants who have these conditions. A 1994 Mayo Clinic[9] study suggests that this is the case. Here, 749 women with implants were studied, using a control group of 1,498 other women. All were from Olmsted County, Minnesota, and all their medical records were in the nearby Mayo Clinic. The study found that there was no difference in the incidence of connective tissue and autoimmune diseases between the two groups. It's an early and a small study, and more work needs to be done, but it certainly tells us that we can't assume that all the women with implants who had these kinds of health problems had them as a result of the implants. At least one clearly didn't—her own doctors testified that her condition had existed before she got the implants. (She won her case against Dow Corning Wright, the implants' manufacturer, anyway, getting $7.3 million.)

One hypothesis is that some women are allergic to silicone, and that for them a leak causes autoimmune disorders or other health problems. Women who aren't allergic to silicone have no negative reactions to it. In any case, we certainly can't rule out the possibility that the implants cause health problems until proper studies are done.

One positive finding is that no increase in breast cancer has been discovered among women with silicone implants. In fact, the studies that have looked at it have shown a decrease.[10] This is probably because plastic surgeons may be more reluctant to put silicone into women who are very high risk and are thus selecting people who are low risk. I find it hard to imagine that silicone prevents breast cancer—though it would be ironic if it did!

Another concern has been whether small amounts of silicone that leak from the breasts can show up in breast milk. To date, there is no information about whether this occurs, or whether, if it does occur, it could harm a breast-feeding baby. One small study from Long Island showed that infants breast-fed by women with silicone implants had trouble swallowing, which can be an early sign of one autoimmune disease, *scleroderma*.[11] This information is provocative at best. We need more information to know whether there is a difference. In the absence of information, however, it might be wise, if you have implants, to consider bottle-feeding rather than nursing your child.

If you've had a silicone implant and problems with the implant occur later, it may have to be removed and a new one put in. Also, the silicone ruptures, it may leave you with an unattractive breast and the danger that the silicone, now loose in your breast, will spread to other parts of your body. That can happen relatively soon, six months or a year after the implants are put in, or years later. You will need to have the implants removed and replaced—with the possibility that the same thing will happen again.

Because of this, Dr. Shaw advises looking for changes in size, shape, or consistency, or the appearance of a new lump, which may suggest either a possible rupture or a tumor growth. If you've read Chapter 2, you know I have reservations about formal breast self-exam, but am certainly in favor of women becoming acquainted with their breasts, and here's another case where that makes sense. Certainly you should be very aware of your breasts and how they feel with the implant, so you'll know if the implant has indeed ruptured. I'd also recommend that you know the size of your implant to be sure the replacement is the right size.

So there are some proven problems with silicone implants. But they do not seem to me severe enough to justify the FDA's ban—and even if the worst suspicions about their connections with other diseases turn out to be accurate, I'm still not sure I'd support a ban. I suspect a bit of paternalism in permitting implants for certain categories of women while keeping it from others. I distrust the whole concept that an operation the FDA perceives as too dangerous for "normal" women is somehow all right for women it sees as suffering so much they're permitted to take the risk. It's insulting from both perspectives. It assumes that someone outside can judge subjective suffering. There are women with asymmetry, injured breasts, or even mastectomies, who aren't traumatized by their condition and prefer not to use surgical procedures to change it. And there are women who are terribly traumatized by small breasts. It's not up to the government, the plastic surgeons, or even the feminist movement to judge an individual woman's pain.

I'm not convinced women should be deprived of an option that's very important to them. It might be a lot better to make certain that plastic surgeons give patients full information and then let them decide for themselves. Implants may cause problems, but that's no reason to deprive a woman who, fully informed, chooses to take the risk. People take risks every day. My co-author, Karen Lindsey, had silicone injections in the mid-1960s. In the feminist newspaper *Sojourner*, she wrote, "I can, if I choose, drink a quart of whiskey a day and smoke a pack of cigarettes a day. I can eat fats and sugar by the pound. I can fly in airplanes and ride motorcycles and walk alone down dangerous dark streets. I can do all kinds of dangerous things if I choose to do them—and I should be able to." Implants, adds Dr. Shaw, aren't all bad or all good, and he, too, believes the ban goes too far. "The ban implies it's all bad. It limits what we can do, and it creates tremendous fear. It's too simplistic."

I agree—the answer lies not in banning silicone but in studying it, using a number of tests. If, for example, it turns out that some women are allergic to silicone, we might be able to devise a test to find out who is and who isn't allergic, and to discover if the allergy extends to the solid capsule of silicone that contains the silicone gel or the saline implant. In fact, the whole silicone controversy should demonstrate to the government and the scientific community how crucial clinical trials are. With any health care reform, we should require that new procedures, drugs, and treatments that are introduced should be paid for by insurance only if they are part of a trial that will answer questions about their safety. The time to withhold a questionable medical process isn't after it's been available for 20 years, but at its inception.

Luckily for women who want implants, complete with accurate information on known and suspected risks, there are studies looking at the possibility of using peanut oil or soy oil rather than silicone and saline. These oils are lighter than saline solution and would show up better on a mammogram; if there were a rupture, both oils, as organic material, would be digested by the body, as silicone is not. Other substances are also being studied. But, warns Dr. Shaw, we should not expect future implants to be completely trouble free. We don't know if they would cause infection. Furthermore, they would still be in a silicone pouch. In addition to the pouch itself, there might be reactions caused by the silicone rubber interacting with the oil on the one side and the patient's body on the other. "In the best possibility, it's still a foreign implant," he warns. "Not every patient will have a good result." Unfortunately, there are no studies on possible substitutes for the silicone pouch, because there is no solid substance more inert than silicone.

Breast Augmentation

It's been my experience that, when considering surgery, some patients want to know all the details of the operation; others just want to know what the operation will do for them. The details are left to the doctor. For this reason, I've begun each discussion of cosmetic surgery by mentioning briefly what the procedure sets out to accomplish. Readers content with that can skip the rest. But for those of you who want the "gory details," read on!

Before considering augmentation surgery, women over 35 should have a mammogram to make sure there's no cancer in their breasts. In addition, the surgeon should check for cysts that will require needle aspirations (see Chapter 9). As Robert Goldwyn, a plastic surgeon and colleague from my Boston days, puts it, "You don't want to be sticking needles into the patient's breast when there's a silicone gel bag inside it." The plastic surgeon should take a careful history.

The surgeon should show you pictures of breasts that have been augmented, including pictures of operations that have left visible scars, so you know both the best and the worst of what to expect. You and the surgeons should also discuss what size you want your new breasts to be, and you need to be realistic about that—you won't have enough breast tissue to turn tiny breasts into huge ones. Dr. Goldwyn tells of a petite woman who wanted to go from a size 34-A to a size 34-D. "Not only did she lack sufficient soft tissue to harbor such implants," he says, "but the results would have been poor, even bizarre." Dr. Shaw emphasizes that the augmentation should be appropriate for the size and build of the patient.

If you're married, some surgeons will want to make sure your husband feels okay about your having augmentation, since an angry husband might later try to sue the doctor. Dr. Shaw points out that it is not so important for medical or legal reasons, but may be for the marital relationship. If you feel that it is your decision alone, let the surgeon know, and try to work it out. If you can't, find a surgeon willing to do what you want.

The operation can be done under either local or general anesthetic. Some patients, says Dr. Shaw, prefer to use general anesthetic because they fear pain, and some surgeons also prefer it.

The incision is made through the armpit, underneath the breast, or around the areola (Fig. 5-2). All of these have their proponents. The

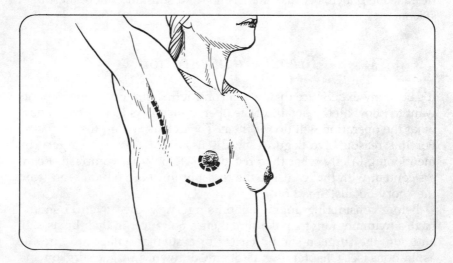

FIGURE 5-2

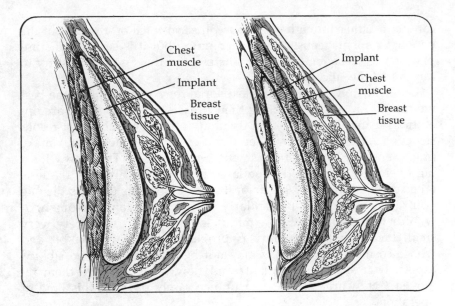

FIGURE 5-3

implant can be placed under the breast tissue between the breast and the chest muscle or under the muscle itself (Fig. 5-3). Putting the implant under the muscles has two disadvantages, according to Dr. Shaw: a tendency for a flatter breast and the possibility of movement of the breast with the muscle. But it has two advantages: it seems to carry less risk of contracture and, even more important, it's less likely to hide a cancer if one develops in the future.

The operation is usually done on an outpatient basis; it takes about two hours or more, depending on whether or not the surgeon puts the implant under the muscle, which takes more time. You go home after the operation. The stitches are removed about 10 days later. You'll be out of work for about a week or 10 days, and shouldn't drive a car for a week. In three weeks you'll be able to jog or play tennis.

Side effects include infection, which occurs in less than 1 percent of cases, and bleeding, which is equally rare. There may be a permanent altering of sensation in the nipple or areola, which occurs in less than 2 percent of cases, and there is also a slight possibility of reduced sensation in the breast itself. There's also the possibility of visible scarring and of contracture, both of which we mentioned earlier. And there is some possibility that lactation will be interfered with if the surgeon makes the incision around the areola and the ducts are severed.

Implant rupture, also discussed earlier, is another complication. It can occur either through strenuous physical force on the part of the patient or spontaneously. It's not common but it is serious. The implant needs to be removed immediately and the surgeon must try to remove all the silicone.

Unfortunately, for now at least, some form of implant is the best we can do for women wanting their breasts enlarged. There are operations using the body's own tissue that are done for breast reconstruction after mastectomy (see Chapter 26), but these don't make much sense for less drastic cosmetic purposes, says Dr. Shaw. "It's a big operation, and you'd have large scars on the area the tissue is taken from, so you'd create an aesthetic problem as great as the one you're trying to fix. Particularly for a very young woman, it wouldn't be worth it. For a middle-aged woman with very, very small breasts, whose tummy is probably pushing out a bit and whose cosmetic expectations may not be as great, it's a possibility, especially if she's had implants and now needs to have them removed." He warns also that insurance rarely pays for this kind of operation.

Surgery for Asymmetry

To correct asymmetry, doctors can use one of three procedures. It's important for you as the patient to be sure about which one of the three you want. You can have an implant put in the smaller breast, or you can have the larger breast made smaller, or a combination of both. Your doctor might assume you want the smaller breast augmented; if you don't, make that clear. (Silicone, as I noted earlier, is still legal for this kind of surgery, provided you're followed up in the study set up after the 1992 FDA ruling.)

The procedures used to reconstruct a breast with tissue from elsewhere in the body are also possible, but far more complicated. Particularly if you're young and healthy, and the asymmetry is severe, it might be worth putting your body through the discomfort only one time, knowing that with an implant you're likely to have to have it removed and replaced at a later date. If your asymmetry results from Poland's syndrome or from an injury such as discussed in Chapter 4, an entire artificial breast can be constructed from your own tissues. Unlike the situation of women with small but symmetrical breasts, the scars created in the area the tissue is taken from will likely disturb you less than the cosmetic problems you have with your breasts.

If you're thinking of implants for asymmetry, keep in mind that exact matching is unlikely. If there's a difference in nipple and areola size, the implant operation will stretch the nipple and areola on the smaller breast, but it may be a little less elastic as a result. And, since silicone has now been added to the distribution of fat and tissue in the breast, the breasts will probably sag at different rates as you grow older. If these differences are minor compared to the original asymmetry, it's likely that you yourself will be the only one to notice. Remember, you may need to have your implant replaced at some point, so be sure you know what size it is.

Breast Reduction

Most women come in for breast reduction because they're embarrassed by their large breasts or because they have discomfort from neck and back pain. If a woman is over 35, she should have a mammogram first to make sure there's no cancer.

On the patient's first visit, says my Boston colleague Dr. Goldwyn, "I show them photos of breasts that have had reduction surgery to make sure they know there will be scars." The doctor will explain what sizes are possible; most of Dr. Goldwyn's patients want to be a B, and some want to be a C. Dr. Shaw points out that the patient and the surgeon must agree on what a "B" or "C" cup is. He often has patients bring in pictures from magazines, to be sure what their expectations are. It's not always possible to get the exact size you want, but a good surgeon can approximate it well. Then the operation is scheduled. There are a number of variations, but all begin with the same basic procedure.

The operation is usually done under general anesthesia, in the hospital, and takes place the day you're admitted. It can last up to four hours. Your nipples can be either removed and grafted back or left on breast tissue and transposed. Doctors today usually prefer not to graft the nipples except in extremely large reductions, since they lose sensitivity when all the nerves are severed.

Most procedures involve some variation of the "keyhole" technique. The amount of tissue to be removed is determined and a pattern drawn on the breast (Fig. 5-4). The nipple is preserved on a small flap of tissue, while the tissue to be removed is taken from below and from the sides. The surgeon can then elevate the nipple and bring the flaps of tissue together, allowing for both uplift and reduction. The scars are below the breast in the inframammary fold and come right up the center to the nipple. Dr. Shaw says that in recent years there is a preference for shorter incisions under the breast. In some cases only

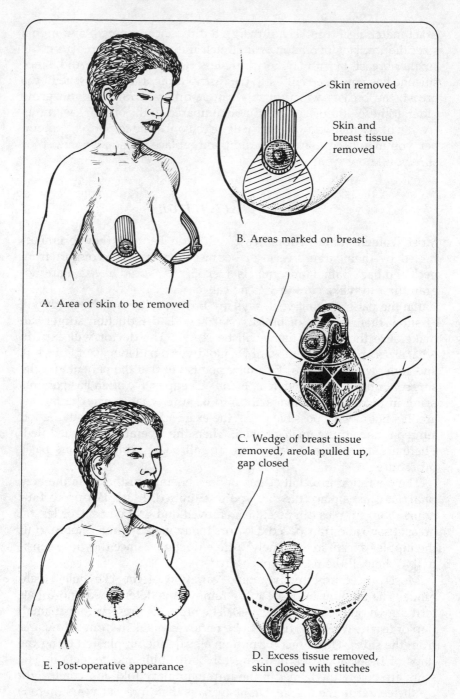

Skin removed

Skin and
breast tissue
removed

B. Areas marked on breast

A. Area of skin to be removed

C. Wedge of breast tissue
removed, areola pulled up,
gap closed

E. Post-operative appearance

D. Excess tissue removed,
skin closed with stitches

FIGURE 5-4

a circular incision around the nipple is made—the so-called doughnut or concentric reduction pattern.

Patients experience pain the first day after the operation, but there's not much pain after that. You can go home two or three days later, wearing a bra or some form of support. The stitches are out in one to two weeks, and you can go back to work. In three to four weeks you can even jog and play tennis.

Side effects include infection, which can occur with any operation. There's a slight risk that you'll need one or more blood transfusions, but it's very rare. Dr. Shaw and Dr. Goldwyn have been doing this operation for years and have never had to give transfusions. If you're worried, however, you can give your own blood to the hospital two or three weeks in advance, and it will be there in case you need it. There's some danger of the operation interfering with the blood supply of the nipple and areola; if this happens the nipple and areola die and need to be artificially reconstructed. It's not a very great danger— it happens in less than 4 percent of operations. The larger your breasts are, the greater the danger. Reduction does not affect a woman's risk of cancer. Your ability to breast-feed will be decreased; studies show that about half of women who have had reductions can still nurse their babies.

Some of the erotic sensation in your nipples and in your breasts themselves may be reduced, though for many women the increased relaxation actually makes sex more pleasurable after reduction surgery. Also, because the nerves in the nipple of the overlarge breast are so stretched out the nipple is unlikely to have much sensitivity to begin with, and the loss of sensation—both in sexual activity and breast feeding—will probably go unnoticed. There's also a possibility of some slight reduction of sensitivity in the breast itself. There's no way to know whether or not you will experience reduced sensation, so you have to decide for yourself between full sensation and whatever physical or emotional discomfort your large breasts create for you. In any case, you'll retain most of your breast sensation.

If you do decide to get reduction surgery, be aware that if you later gain weight, your breasts will probably also gain weight, just as they would without the surgery. This has happened to a number of my patients. One woman had her size 36EE breasts reduced to a 36B, but they are now 36D. According to Dr. Goldwyn as well as Dr. Shaw, "The more the patient regards the operation as reconstructive, the happier she'll be; the more she sees it as cosmetic, the fussier she'll be about the result. If it's only cosmetic, she's more likely to focus on the scars; if it relieves pain and discomfort, she'll be happier."

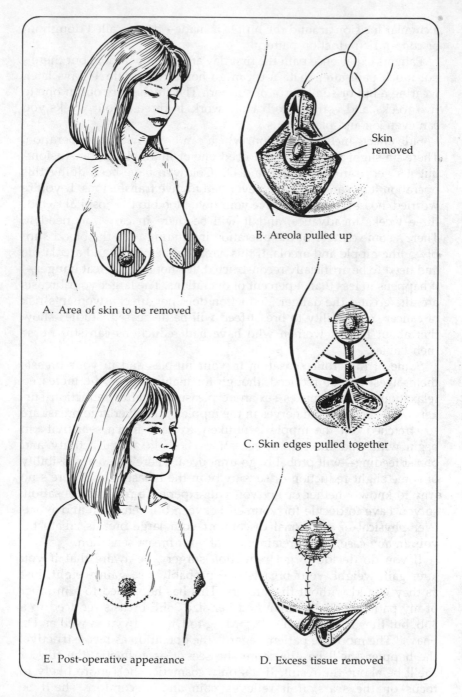

A. Area of skin to be removed

B. Areola pulled up

Skin removed

C. Skin edges pulled together

D. Excess tissue removed

E. Post-operative appearance

FIGURE 5-5

The Breast Lift

Sagging breasts (known medically as "ptosis") can be made firmer through an operation called a *mastopexy*, which Dr. Goldwyn describes as "a face lift of the breasts."

A mastopexy can give your breasts uplift, Dr. Goldwyn warns, but it will not make your breasts look like a 20-year-old's. And the operation will leave scars—sometimes bad ones, depending on how your body usually scars. Like a face lift, it won't last forever. Remember, you've got gravity and time working against you.

Your first step is to set up a meeting with your plastic surgeon, who will take a very thorough medical history. You should get a mammogram before proceeding, if you haven't had one recently. Be sure to get a full description of both the best and the worst possible results of a mastopexy.

This operation usually involves removing excess skin and fat and elevating the nipple (see Fig. 5-5). If you're very large breasted, you may want reduction surgery as well, especially since a mastopexy is less effective on very large breasts: gravity pulls them down. If you're very small breasted, you may want an augmentation. (Both of these procedures were described earlier in this chapter.)

If your operation doesn't involve reduction or augmentation, it's a simpler procedure, and can be done either in the hospital under general anesthetic or in the doctor's office under a local anesthetic. Insurance won't pay for it, so most women prefer the latter. The operation lasts about two and a half hours; the stitches are removed in two weeks. By three weeks, you'll be able to participate in sports. You should wear a bra constantly for many weeks after surgery. Follow-up is minimal—three or four visits during the year after surgery. You may experience some very slight loss of sensation in the nipple or areola. Other than that, there are no particular side effects to mastopexy.

Inverted Nipples

There is an operation that can reverse inversion of nipples, but it doesn't always work, and the inversion may recur. It's a very simple procedure, usually done under local anesthetic with no intravenous medication, and you can go back to work two or three days later. The stitches will come out in about two weeks.

The nipples are usually inverted because they are tethered down by scar tissue or other tissue from birth. To reverse it, the surgeon will reach down, pull the nipple, stretch it, and make an incision, releasing the constricting tissue (Fig. 5-6). There are a number of procedures, and each one has its advocates. If the inversion recurs, the operation can be redone.

This operation can make a psychological difference for teenagers, who often feel extremely self-conscious about their inverted nipples. It definitely interferes with breast feeding, but women with inverted nipples usually have difficulty breast feeding in the first place.

Thinking About Plastic Surgery

None of these operations are medically necessary. Still, we're lucky to live in an age when they're available. For a woman deeply unhappy with the way her breasts look, plastic surgery can make a major psychological difference in her life. No operation will make you look "perfect" (whatever that is), but all of these procedures can help you look more normal and feel more comfortable in your body.

If you're thinking about any of these forms of surgery, you should ask yourself a few questions. The first and probably most important is, Who wants the surgery? If you're contented with your breasts, but your mother or boyfriend or someone else is pressuring you into it, you probably shouldn't do it. It's your body, not theirs.

The second question is, How realistic are your expectations, and

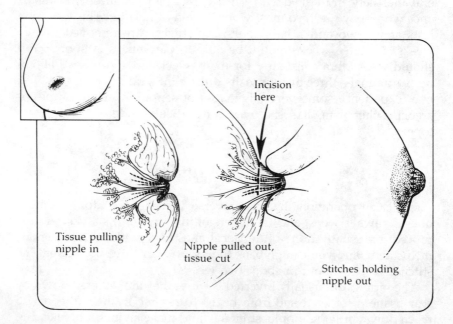

Incision here

Tissue pulling nipple in

Nipple pulled out, tissue cut

Stitches holding nipple out

FIGURE 5-6

how clear are you about the kind of breasts you want? Dr. John T. Heuston,[12] a noted plastic surgeon, has written some wise words about reduction surgery that can apply equally well to all forms of cosmetic surgery for the breasts. "The concept of an ideal operation," he writes, "carries with it the concept of an ideal breast. The surgeon seeks the best means to construct the breast form—but for whom? For him or her, or for the patient, or both?" As Heuston notes, there is no objectively ideal breast; each of us has her or his own ideal. So you should have a clear sense of what size and shape breast you want, and what your own goals are. The surgeon can't make your breasts absolutely "perfect," but if your goals are fairly reasonable, they can come pretty close to being met. If you do decide on plastic surgery make sure you know the range of possible results. Some plastic surgeons like to "sell" their operation—a practice Dr. Goldwyn abhors. "Too often doctors use pictures to seduce patients into surgery," he says. "I think it's a form of hucksterism." If you're shown pictures of a surgeon's best results, insist upon seeing pictures of the average and worst results as well." Dr. Shaw concurs. "Communication between plastic surgeon and patient can be very tricky," he says. "It requires a tremendous amount of honesty and self-restraint. Both the patient and the surgeon constantly need to separate 'wishes for perfection' from the reality of what can be reasonably expected."

Once you know what you want, don't hesitate to shop around for the right plastic surgeon. Choose someone you feel absolutely comfortable with and confident in; above all, someone who respects your ideal and doesn't seek to impose her or his ideal on you. The surgeon's "beautiful breast" and yours may be very dissimilar. Make sure you find someone who will construct *your* breast. And make sure you find someone who respects who you are, and why you're making your decision. One woman I know went to a plastic surgeon when she was 20, hoping to have her painfully large breasts reduced. The surgeon wanted her to wait until she had children and had breast-fed them. She told him that she was a lesbian and didn't plan to have children. "In that case," he told her, "you won't need your breasts— why don't we just cut them both off?" The experience so embittered and intimidated the woman that, more than 20 years later, she still hasn't had her breasts reduced. Remember that you don't have to submit yourself to the surgeon's prejudices: if the surgeon you've approached acts insulting or condescending, get out and find someone with a more professional and more humane approach.

Of course, there's no guarantee that you'll be happy with your operation after it's done, even if you have taken every precaution possible. But the odds are on your side. I've had very few patients who have regretted having their breasts cosmetically altered, but I've had several who've regretted not having it done. One of my Boston patients was an 80-year-old woman with huge, uncomfortable breasts. When she was younger, she went to a surgeon to try and get her breasts reduced. He told her she shouldn't have the operation. She took his advice—those were the days when doctors were gods, and you didn't question them—and has been uncomfortable and unhappy with her breasts ever since. After we talked about this, she decided to have her surgery done, and she is now very happy with her small breasts—and very sad for all the years she could have been this comfortable.

Another of my patients was a sophisticated career woman in her early 30s. During our first visit, I noticed that her breasts were extremely asymmetrical, and after a few visits, I asked her if she'd ever thought about plastic surgery. Her face lit up. "Can I really do that?" she asked. I assured her she could, and gave her a list of plastic surgeons. She didn't even wait till she got out of the building to call; she found a phone booth downstairs, made an appointment, and had her implant within the month. She's absolutely delighted with it—but she needed me to suggest it, and to "give her permission" to seek help for her asymmetry. My co-author, who had silicone injections for her asymmetry, has found that her breasts are no longer perfectly matched, and, as she grows older, the augmented breast sags much more than the natural one. But she is very happy about her decision and says she would make the same choice today. She keeps in her closet an old V-neck sweater her mother gave her after she finished her injections—a symbol of a freedom she hadn't known before.

We have seen so much news in the past couple of years about women who are unhappy with their silicone implants that it's easy to forget that most patients—those who don't get in the news—are happy with their decision to alter their breasts. Psychologist Sanford Gifford writes about a patient feeling she had "gained something lost in early puberty."[13] He observes that the degree of satisfaction is much greater among women who have had plastic surgery for their breasts than among those who have had face lifts or nose jobs—they don't have the same unrealistic expectations. Often they're happier with their still-imperfect breasts than the surgeon thinks they should be. For some reason, people don't go into this kind of plastic surgery with the same dreams of impossible perfection they bring to facial surgery.

If you want plastic surgery for your breasts, make sure you have all the information you need about risks, dangers, and reasonable expectations—and then do what you want. And don't let age deter you from the cosmetic surgery you want. My 80-year-old patient was delighted with her belated operation, and I've had many women in their 50s, 60s, and 70s who have had their breasts reduced or augmented. If your health is good enough to sustain surgery, it doesn't matter how old you are.

PART TWO

COMMON PROBLEMS
OF THE BREAST

6

The Myth of Fibrocystic Disease

You're concerned about your breasts: they get swollen and hard just before your period. Or they're painful, so painful you can't get any work done. Or there's discharge when you squeeze your nipple.

So you go to the doctor, who examines you carefully and gravely announces, "Well, I've got good news for you. It isn't cancer. It's only fibrocystic disease." The doctor seems to think this will cheer you up, and in away, it does—you *are* relieved to know you don't have cancer.

But you're also a bit disturbed—you do have another disease, and that's scary, even if it won't kill you. So you decide you'd better find out a little more about this illness you've got, and you check around. You find an article in one of the women's magazines, and you learn about fibrocystic disease. And now, you're really scared. Fibrocystic disease, you read, can increase your risk of cancer.

So, very sensibly, you go back to your doctor and demand treatment. The doctor prescribes vitamin E, or tells you to eliminate caffeine from your diet (see Chapter 15).

By now, whatever your physical discomfort is, your mental anguish is far worse. Every little breast pain seems like cancer. You stare at your breasts in the mirror: surely they look different than they used to? You start seeing signs of malignancy everywhere. And it's all unnecessary. Because, in reality, there's no such thing as fibrocystic

73

disease. Your symptoms, however—and I can't stress this enough—
are very real. It is the diagnosis that is unreal.

"Fibrocystic disease" is a meaningless term—a wastebasket into
which doctors throw every breast problem that isn't cancerous. The
symptoms it encompasses are varied and unrelated to each other.
More and more doctors recognize this and have stopped using the
term; others, unfortunately, have not. When they do, what are they
talking about? To begin with, it depends on the doctor.

First, there's the doctor who examines you. This doctor can be addressing one or more symptoms. His (or her) "fibrocystic disease" can
be swelling, pain, tenderness, lumpy breasts (a condition not to be
confused with breast lumps—see Chapter 9), nipple discharge—any
noncancerous thing that can happen in or on the breast. That's the
clinical version of our mythical disease.

If the doctor is concerned that your problem might be a symptom of
cancer, your breast will be biopsied, and the tissue examined under a
microscope by another doctor called a pathologist. And what does the
pathologist find? You've got "fibrocystic disease." But it's not the same
fibrocystic disease the examining doctor discovered. The pathologist's
report has to do not with your original symptom, but with any one of
about 15 microscopic findings that exist in virtually every woman's
breasts, and which never reveal themselves except through a microscope. They cause no trouble, and they have no relation to cancer—or
to anything else, except the body's natural aging process. They are the

result of natural wear and tear, no more a disease than gray hair or age lines. And the only reason for such a finding in a particular breast tissue that was biopsied is that it *was* biopsied: if you'd had another area of your breast biopsied, they'd find it there, too. These harmless little changes take place throughout your breasts. (Only one—a fairly rare one—is a danger sign. It's called *atypical hyperplasia*, and, combined with a family history of breast cancer, it can suggest an increased breast cancer risk. I'll discuss atypical hyperplasia in Chapter 16.) But your doctor may not make this distinction. He or she may only tell you what you already know: you've got "fibrocystic disease." Again, you're grateful not to have cancer, but upset that you're diseased.

If this isn't confusing enough, there's a third kind of "fibrocystic disease," discovered by the radiologists who read your mammogram. Mammography has only been around 30 or 40 years. When the radiologists began reading mammograms, they wanted to get in on the game. They discovered that younger women tend to have very dense breast tissue and older women tend to have less dense breast tissue. "Why?" they asked the surgeons. And the surgeons answered—what else?—"fibrocystic disease." So the radiologists have their very own fibrocystic disease to diagnose—completely different from the clinical or pathological version.

What causes the radiologists' "fibrocystic disease" is exactly the opposite of what causes the pathologists' version: it's simply youth. You know those firm, unsagging breasts that women in their teens and early 20s so often have—the breasts the rest of us are supposed to envy? Well, they're firm because they've got comparatively little fat and comparatively more breast tissue, and the more breast tissue you've got, the denser the tissue is. If you've read Chapter 1 you'll know that dense breast tissue is, in fact, normal, especially in young women. There's nothing diseased about it, except in the imaginations of some doctors.

If you're beginning to feel a little like Alice after she fell through the looking glass, you should. "Fibrocystic disease" is as fanciful as anything Lewis Carroll ever invented. It's not only fanciful, it's dangerous. It causes problems for women who, as we say in the medical world, "carry the diagnosis." The dangers fall into three categories.

The first danger isn't a medical one; it's economic. Many insurance companies won't insure a woman who's been diagnosed as having fibrocystic disease—as they won't insure people diagnosed as having any chronic disease. If they'll insure you at all, they may exclude breast problems—with the result that you won't have insurance coverage should you ever get a real breast disease.

At the same time, if you're already insured when you're diagnosed, your company might pay for your mammograms. Because of this, a well-meaning doctor might be tempted to diagnose fibrocystic disease so your mammogram will be paid for. But your advantage then lasts only as long as you remain with the same insurance company. Should you ever want to sign up with another company, your "disease" will work against you, and you'll be stuck with the label for the rest of your life.

Medically, the dangers range from minor to very serious, indeed. First of all, your mental health isn't going to be improved by your conviction that you're especially prone to breast cancer. Second, the medical "treatments" can be anything from ineffective (like eliminating caffeine from your diet) to devastating. Some doctors even recommend a form of mastectomy to prevent the cancer you're supposedly likely to get. Finally, the existence of the diagnosis "fibrocystic disease" has negatively affected the research done on the specific clinical symptoms women experience—symptoms which, as I said earlier, are as real as the disease is unreal. The research done in the United States on nonmalignant breast symptoms isn't very good—and you can see why. A large number of completely different symptoms have been thrown together. They're not studied individually, as they need to be if we're going to learn anything useful about them. We aren't sure, for example, why some women have extreme breast pain before or during their periods, or why some women have especially lumpy breasts—and we're certainly not sure that there's any relationship among the various symptoms so conveniently thrown together in the same useless term. If we're to help alleviate these symptoms, we need to research each one on its own terms.

Origins of the Term

If fibrocystic disease is a useless and inaccurate diagnosis, how did it gain such widespread acceptance? It's not only the popular press that's responsible for the misinformation—the medical literature also talks about fibrocystic disease and its supposed associations with breast cancer.

The problem is that medical literature tends to be a bit incestuous—doctors read a study, are impressed with it, and use its information in their own articles. Their work, in turn, is rewritten, often without attribution, by other doctors. Hence it can appear that impressive numbers of medical authorities have independently come to the same conclusion.

With the help of some associates, I investigated the literature on fibrocystic disease and found that almost all of the articles were based on the same data. I researched this data and learned that the evidence linking so-called fibrocystic disease with breast cancer was, at best, extremely shaky.[1]

To do our research, my colleagues and I first had to separate the papers referring to clinical symptoms from those talking about people who'd had biopsies. Most of the early work—done in the 1930s and 1940s—was done on people who'd had biopsies, not on people who'd simply had symptoms. This in itself made its universal application highly suspect, because most people with symptoms don't ever have biopsies.

We found the studies broke down into three types. In the first, breasts that had been removed because of cancer were studied to see what else was there. "Fibrocystic disease" was found in most of these breasts, and so the researchers brightly concluded that fibrocystic disease was linked to cancer. Their findings were ludicrous: a kind of medical guilt-by-association. They might as well have decided that, since all the cancerous breasts had nipples, nipples cause cancer. When these studies were compared with other studies done from autopsies on women who had died from a variety of noncancerous causes, it was discovered that the women without cancer actually had a higher incidence of "fibrocystic disease." (This makes sense when you remember that what the pathologists call fibrocystic disease is simply the wear and tear that happens over the course of time, and that many of the women autopsied had died in old age whereas many of the cancer victims biopsied were still comparatively young.) So the first category of studies could be dismissed.

Another, different type of study also suggested that women with fibrocystic disease were more likely than others to get cancer. These studies looked at women who had cancer and asked them if they had had previous biopsies. The researchers compared these women with others who didn't have cancer, but who went to the breast clinic for one reason or another. They were also asked if they had had biopsies. The studies were fairly specious, since they equate having a biopsy with having fibrocystic disease. All they showed is that a woman who has had one biopsy is likely to have others, probably because she is now aware of her breast problems and more likely to keep checking to make sure her breasts are all right. This is interesting, but it says nothing at all about the relation of the entities that have been dubbed "fibrocystic disease" to cancer.

There was, however, one category of study that seemed to have some validity. These were studies done on women who'd had biopsies that showed fibrocystic disease and who were followed over a period of years to see if they developed cancer. They were compared to a group of women who had never been diagnosed as having fibrocystic disease. This kind of study might show that women with microscopic fibrocystic disease got cancer more often than those without it.

Indeed, as we examined some of these studies, we discovered that they appeared to show that the women diagnosed as having fibrocystic disease after being biopsied appeared to have twice the incidence of breast cancer that women in the general population had. But it didn't seem to matter what the biopsy showed. Even more perplexing, it didn't seem to matter which breast the biopsy was done on: a woman who'd had a biopsy done on something found in her left breast might later develop cancer in her right breast.

The studies, we realized, hadn't taken into account the subjective nature of the decision to do a biopsy. A surgeon doesn't do a biopsy on every woman with a breast problem. It depends on how worrisome the particular situation seems to be. If, for example, a 20-year-old woman comes into my office with a questionable area in her breast and has no risk factors that would make cancer likely, I probably won't do a biopsy. If, however, I've got a 40-year-old patient with the same kind of area, and her mother and two sisters both had breast cancer, then I'll probably do a biopsy. So the decision is influenced somewhat by the patient's cancer risk.

One study did take cancer risk into consideration. Dr. Page of Vanderbilt University[2] had corrected for risk factors, making sure that both the women who'd been biopsied and the control group of women who hadn't been biopsied had the same number of risk factors. What he found was that the increase in the rise in breast cancer risk among the biopsied women was smaller—1.3 instead of 2.

Since then, Page has done another study, looking at 10,542 biopsies to see if any of the microscopic entities led to breast cancer. He distinguished the various forms of "fibrocystic disease" from one another, and it was in this study that the relationship between breast cancer and the rare entity *atypical hyperplasia* was discovered (see Chapter 16). None of the other, far more common entities were found to have any connection at all to cancer. This explains most of the increased risk of breast cancer associated with biopsies that have revealed "fibrocystic disease."[3]

I wrote about my findings in the *New England Journal of Medicine* in 1982. It is interesting that no doctors wrote to the journal to argue against my findings. But it took four years for the American College of Pathologists to come out with a statement that fibrocystic disease doesn't increase the risk of cancer.[4]

Caffeine, Vitamin E, and "Fibrocystic Disease"

Just as doctors have foisted on women the concept of "fibrocystic disease," they've also come up with a number of fairly useless "treatments"—which, like the idea itself, have gained a lot of publicity and generated a lot of anxiety. For some of the specific symptoms that do exist, there are more-or-less effective treatments, and I'll go into them in the next three chapters. Meanwhile, here I'll discuss some of the popularly accepted "fibrocystic disease" treatments.

Probably the most popular treatment is the removal from the woman's diet of caffeine, which supposedly causes fibrocystic disease in all its alleged manifestations. The idea originated with an Ohio surgeon named Dr. Minton,[5] who in 1980 decided to test his theory on 40 women with "clinical symptoms"—pain, lumpiness, swelling, etc.—and told them to stop all caffeine intake. Twenty of them ignored his advice; of the remaining 20, 13 said their breasts felt better as a result. He accepted their reports on face value and did no objective testing—mammograms, for example. While it's true that we need to respect women's definitions of their own sensations, it's also true that a study without objective components is never valid: for one thing, there's always the placebo effect, which I'll discuss a bit later in this chapter.

For this type of study to be valid it needs to be randomized, controlled and double-blinded—that is to say, a given number of randomly chosen subjects must be taking the substance under study while an equal number of subjects, also randomly chosen, must not be taking it. Neither researcher nor subject must know which subjects are getting the treatment and which are being given a placebo—an ineffective, "sugar pill" substitute. The latter is very important; it prevents the unconscious expectations of both subject and researcher from clouding the perceived results.

In spite of its glaring inadequacy, Minton's research got a lot of press, and it wasn't long before it was extended in the popular imagination to include cancer prevention. Since fibrocystic disease led to cancer and caffeine consumption led to fibrocystic disease, people reasoned, then obviously cutting caffeine from the diet reduced the risk of breast cancer. So we now have a double fallacy to contend with: the symptoms associated with "fibrocystic disease" don't lead to cancer, and caffeine doesn't cause the symptoms in the first place. So giving up caffeine, however beneficial this may be in other health areas, won't keep you from getting breast cancer.

Other studies, slightly better designed than Minton's but still far from conclusive, followed in the wake of the newly popular caffeine theory. One San Francisco study,[6] reported in 1984–1985, limiting itself to the effects of caffeine on lumpy breasts, did have a randomly chosen control group. Both groups were studied by a nurse practitioner who examined the women's breasts every month for several months. She divided each breast into quadrants, and graded each quadrant on a scale of 1 to 4, repeating the procedure with each examination. A score of 16 indicated that a breast was very lumpy; a score of 2 indicated that it had little lumpiness. One problem was that, since the nurse checked each quadrant, even a small change—say, half a point—in each quadrant could create a 4-point difference in a woman's breasts, giving the impression of greater overall change than really existed.

But there were problems worse than this. The nurse was not blinded: she knew whether she was examining a woman in the caffeine-consuming group or one in the noncaffeine group. So her own prejudices may have been a factor in the significant improvement she found among the women who had given up caffeine. Two circumstances strongly suggest that this was the case. The first is that there were other components to the study: they also did mammograms on all the subjects, as well as needle biopsies (see Chapter 12), to determine if there was caffeine in the breast tissue. Neither test showed a difference between consumers and nonconsumers of caffeine.

The other circumstance clearly illustrates the extent to which even a trained medical professional can be misled by preconceptions. Unknown to the nurse or the researchers, several of the women in the caffeine-consuming group (who had not been told what it was they were testing) had heard that caffeine was linked to breast problems and had independently given it up. The nurse, who, of course, believed they were still taking caffeine, found that their lumpiness had gotten worse.

Another, more recent, study shows both the lack of substantiation for the anti-caffeine theories and the power that the belief that caffeine decreases breast symptoms can have on people. Dr. Sharon Allen in Minnesota[7] conducted a randomized and blinded study of caffeine and its possible connection to breast pain and lumpiness. She divided 56 women into three groups. One, the control group, was given no dietary advice, and the second, the experimental group, was put on a caffeine-free diet. A third group was asked to eliminate cholesterol from their diet. This group was added to see if a major change in the diet could, in and of itself, improve breast symptoms. At the beginning of the study patients were examined and their breasts were graded for lumpiness by one of three "blinded" examiners. In addition, they were asked to describe the amount and severity of their breast pain in a five-item questionnaire, which was then scored. The women in all three groups were followed two months later and again four months later.

The study showed that decreasing caffeine had no effect on either the pain experienced by the patients or the lumpiness found by the examiners. The patients on the cholesterol-free diet likewise experienced no change in their breast symptoms.

Aside from suggesting that diet has no effect on breast pain or lumpiness, this study has another intriguing component. In the months following the study, the participants were telephoned and interviewed. They were asked if they had previously heard of a connection between caffeine and fibrocystic disease and whether they had decreased their caffeine intake on their own before the study. In addition, they were asked whether or not their pain had worsened after the study when they had resumed caffeine. Finally, the women in the study group were questioned about their recollection of the effect that decreasing caffeine had had on their symptoms. Seventy percent of the participants were reached, and of these 82 percent said they'd heard about the supposed link between caffeine and breast disease before the study. Fifty-three percent of those who had previously (average one and a half years before) decreased caffeine on their own reported a decrease in pain, tenderness, or lumpiness as a result. Of the 10 patients who had increased their caffeine intake after the study, three reported an increase in pain and tenderness. What is interesting is that of the 36 percent who did decrease their caffeine as part of the study, 25 percent reported they had experienced less pain and 27 percent reported less lumpiness. This is in contrast to the objective data, which showed no change in patients' accounts of pain or examiners' accounts of lumpiness. In other words, retrospective self-reporting appears different in many respects from actual data. This may explain some of the discrepancies in other studies: those using patient recall may be less accurate and more prone to selective memory than those with objective measurements.

Other studies of the effect of caffeine have been done on women who had been biopsied and diagnosed as having fibrocystic disease. Their caffeine consumption was determined and compared to that of women in a control group with no breast complaints. If women who consumed caffeine were more likely to have biopsies, presumably this would mean they had more lumpiness. The study found that caffeine consumers were no more likely to need biopsies than those who did not consume caffeine.

A study[8] done with rats pretreated with caffeine and then injected with a carcinogen that usually gives rats cancer showed that the rats actually got less breast cancer than those not given caffeine! The caffeine seemed to stabilize the cells, and kept them from responding to the carcinogens. (See Chapter 13 for a description of how carcinogens work.) Rats, of course, aren't people, and we can't conclude from this that drinking coffee will keep you from getting breast cancer—but it doesn't help the caffeine-leads-to-fibrocystic-disease-leads-to-breast-cancer theories.

Neither does an epidemiological—number-based—study done in Israel.[9] There they looked at 854 women who had been diagnosed with histological (as seen under microscope) fibrocystic disease, and compared them to 755 women who had had surgery for some other reason and to 723 women who were living in the same neighborhood. Their intake of caffeine and all methylxanthines (a substance found in tea, chocolate, and other foods) was examined. No association between coffee or methylxanthine intake and benign breast disease was found. In a second study[10] of 818 newly diagnosed breast cancer patients, their intake of methylxanthines was compared to that of others in the same neighborhood and with the same surgical controls. They found, interestingly, that the coffee drinkers had a slightly lower incidence of breast cancer.

This study, too, has major limitations, since they didn't look into other aspects of the women's lives that might or might not affect cancer risk. But again, it offers no support to the idea that caffeine causes breast problems.

Vitamin E has also been put forth as a preventive for "fibrocystic disease" and thus, by extension, of breast cancer. Unfortunately, studies have shown this effect also to be chimerical. Dr. Abrams[11] in Boston first articulated the theory back in 1965. It was later popularized in 1978 by Dr. London[12] of Baltimore, but he abandoned it when his own tests—a double-blinded, randomized, controlled study[13]—showed vitamin E had no effect on breast symptoms. Though some studies have suggested that a low-fat diet may prevent breast cancer (see Chapter 15), no evidence has in any way linked such a diet to the easing of benign breast symptoms.

Having said all this, let me add that individual women report that specific dietary changes have indeed lessened some of their breast symptoms—lumpy breasts, painful breasts, swelling, or all of these. I see no reason to doubt these women; they know what they're feeling. One of three possibilities—or a combination of them—is likely to cause the changes.

It may be that the diet actually did cause the change. While our bodies are essentially similar, there is also large variation from person to person—and medicine doesn't always know what the variations are, or what causes them. Thus, it is quite possible that, for example, giving up coffee, or taking vitamin E, or drinking herb tea, or any of an infinite number of dietary additions or subtractions will ease your breast pain or lessen your lumpiness, while the same thing will have no effect, or even a reverse effect, on your sister or your next-door neighbor.

Second, 54 percent of all benign breast conditions go away on their own after a while. If the condition vanishes after the woman has changed her diet, she may very reasonably attribute this to cause and effect.

Finally there is the "placebo effect," which researchers have noted and named but rarely given the study it deserves. The placebo effect is what occurs when a person's belief that something will work actually makes it work. In other words, your belief that a particular substance (or withdrawal from a particular substance) will relieve your lumpiness or pain or swelling may, in itself, cause it to do so. (This is probably what happened in the follow-up in Dr. Allen's study.) This doesn't mean you're gullible or stupid or imagining things; it means that the mind affects the body in ways we don't yet fully understand, and that fortunately the body-mind interaction is working in your favor.

Fair-minded doctors will acknowledge the individual variations in patients' bodies and the placebo effect. It's very important that we all do take these things into consideration. Unfortunately, however, the placebo effect can also be used in a manipulative manner. Some doctors present patients with unproven data and tell them, or imply, that it is proven, in order to trigger a placebo effect. An honest statement about the effects of caffeine might be as follows: "Some women have found that reducing caffeine in their diets has helped alleviate their breast symptoms. We have no medical evidence to back it up, but it works for them and you might want to try it for a while and see if it helps you." Unfortunately, too often that's not what doctors say; instead they tell you that you have fibrocystic disease and that it's caused by caffeine, so you have to give it up.

When they're challenged on this, many doctors will admit there's no evidence, but still defend their actions. Coffee, they reason, isn't good for you anyway, and it's easy to give up, and it makes you feel better to be given a diagnosis and a "cure." This is extremely insulting to an adult woman, who is entitled to honesty from her doctor, and it ignores the social importance of caffeine in our culture. For many people, giving up caffeine is a hardship. They give up not only coffee but tea, cola, and chocolate. These may or may not be socially or emotionally important to them. Giving them up because you've thought about it and decided, based on accurate information, that it's worth it to you is fine. But you shouldn't give them up because of your doctor's prejudices, presented as medical fact. Giving a patient a nonexistent cure for a nonexistent disease is hardly in her best interest.

When the American College of Pathologists issued their statement admitting that "fibrocystic disease" didn't cause cancer, they suggested altering their terminology by substituting "fibrocystic condition" or "fibrocystic change." Neither term helps much: a "condition" still sounds like a disease, and a "change" suggests it was something else before. And we still end up with a catch-all term. I have similar objections to other terms that have been used over the years: chronic mastitis, chronic cystic mastitis, cystic disease. They're all useless at best, misleading and frightening at worst.

If we throw away these terms, how can we classify the various symptoms? It might be useful, for a start, to look to European medicine. In Europe they've kept the term "fibrocystic disease,"but only to define one specific symptom—lumpy breasts. They call breast pain "mastalgia," a sensible enough term, since "mast" is Latin for breast and "algia" for pain. By separating out the different symptoms, they allow each symptom to be studied on its own—a vast improvement.

We can also look to our own history. In the late 19th and early 20th centuries there was no fibrocystic disease; there were only symptoms: you had breast pain, or lumpiness, or nipple discharge. It was only later that the silly term came into existence and became the wastebasket into which everything that wasn't cancer got thrown. I suggest dropping the term "fibrocystic disease" altogether and replacing it with the following six categories:

1. Normal physiological changes, such as the minor tenderness and swelling and lumpiness most women experience during or before their periods
2. Mastalgia, which is severe breast pain, cyclical or noncyclical, that interferes with the patient's normal life
3. Infections and inflammations
4. Discharge and other nipple problems
5. Lumpiness or nodularity, which is a general lumpiness beyond the amount most women have
6. Dominant lumps, such as cysts and fibroadenomas

The next few chapters will discuss these symptoms, and their treatments, in detail.

7

Breast Pain

If you don't have fibrocystic disease, what do you have? This and the following two chapters discuss the various kinds of benign breast conditions.

One common breast symptom is pain—frequently called *mastalgia*, or *mastodynia* (one's Latin, the other is Greek; both translate to "breast pain"). The medical approach to breast pain has been somewhat contradictory. On the one hand, its reality is acknowledged as part of the conglomeration of "fibrocystic disease" symptoms. On the other hand, its reality is denied, as menstrual pain was denied 10 years ago. It's "psychosomatic"; all in our heads.

So prevalent has this belief been that in 1978, Dr. Preece,[1] as part of a larger study of breast pain done in Cardiff, Wales, did a study measuring the degree of neurosis in female patients in three of the hospital's clinics: the breast pain clinic, the psychiatric clinic, and the varicose vein clinic. To the surprise of the doctors, who expected to find the breast pain sufferers highly neurotic, the breast pain and varicose vein patients showed the same degree of neurosis, which was significantly lower than that of the psychiatric patients. It seems like an awful lot of time, energy, and expense to find out what any woman could readily have told them, but the study did give validation to what we've known all along—many women experience breast pain that's as real as a bellyache or a broken arm. And it runs the gamut of discomfort—from a minor irritation a couple of days a month through permanent, nearly disabling agony, and everything in between.

Unfortunately, studies of breast pain are few and far between—chiefly because of the dual misconceptions about it. Those who call it fibrocystic disease think it's already been covered, so what need is there to do more research? And those who think it doesn't exist aren't about to explore its causes, except in psychiatric terms—which won't say much about a physical reality. So we know very little about what creates breast pain and thus how to treat it.

Failure to acknowledge breast pain is relatively recent. Literature from the 1850s[2] describes "pain syndrome" as something distinct from "cystic disease," their term for lumpiness (see Chapter 9). But by the 1940s[3] the literature that mentions breast pain treats it as interconnected with lumpiness. In the United States it has been believed that lumpiness causes breast pain,[4] whereas in Europe it's believed that breast pain eventually leads to lumpiness.[5]

Actually, there is no evidence of relationship at all. Some women have breast pain and never have lumpiness, some have lumpiness and never have breast pain, and some experience both. Dr. J.W. Ayres of Chicago took 15 fertile women who complained of mastalgia and 15 fertile women with no breast pain complaints and studied their breasts and their hormonal levels.[6] First he did ultrasound examinations to try and quantify the degree of lumpiness. To his surprise, he found that the degree of lumpiness had no connection to the amount of pain the woman was experiencing. About half of the women with mastalgia showed lumpiness on ultrasound and half did not; and half of the asymptomatic women had lumpiness on ultrasound and half did not. He concluded that lumpiness and pain were two distinct problems.

The Welsh clinic in Cardiff that conducted the study mentioned earlier has documented three main categories of breast pain: cyclical (pain related to the menstrual cycle), noncyclical ("trigger-zone" pain), and pain that is nonbreast in origin. Of these, the most common by far is cyclical.[7]

Cyclical Pain

We know that cyclical mastalgia is related to hormonal variations. The breasts are sensitive right before menstruation, then less sensitive once the period begins. For some women tenderness begins at the time of ovulation and continues until their period, leaving only a couple of pain-free weeks during their cycles. Sometimes it's barely noticeable, but some women are in such pain they can't wear a t-shirt, lie on their stomachs, or tolerate hugs. Sometimes it's only in one breast, and other times it radiates into the armpit, and even down to the elbows, causing its poor victim to think she's got cancer spreading to her lymph nodes.

Our understanding of the part hormones play in cyclical mastalgia is clouded by the fact that women's hormonal cycles haven't been that well researched. Although we know roughly how the levels of estrogen and progesterone go up and down during each cycle, and that follicle stimulating hormone and luteinizing hormone are the main pituitary hormones, we don't yet understand the "fine tuning" of these hormones, and how they regulate and affect the different parts of the body. Just as we don't understand menstrual cramps and bloating and premenstrual syndrome (PMS), we don't understand breast pain.

Studies in Europe have given us some preliminary clues to the role hormones play in breast pain. Dr. Mauvais-Jarvis[8] in France has shown that the amount of progesterone put out by the ovary in the second half of the menstrual cycle seems to vary in patients with breast pain. He found a decreased ratio of progesterone to estrogen in patients with mastalgia. Other investigators[9,10] have found that an abnormality in the regulation of prolactin seems to affect breast pain. Although prolactin blood levels in the subjects of these studies appear to be normal, these women are much more sensitive to stimulation with thyroid-stimulating hormone: they are "hyper-reactive." Dr. Ayres's study, mentioned earlier, confirmed both of these hormonal abnormalities. He found that the patients with mastalgia had a lower progesterone to estrogen ratio, as well as a hyper-reactiveness in the regulation of prolactin; the women in the control group did not. Predictably, the lumpiness demonstrated on ultrasound did not relate to the hormonal aberrations—only pain did.

Hormones can also affect cyclical breast pain in a more subtle way; for example, as a result of stress. We know that stress affects the menstrual cycle: you can miss your period, or have a particularly heavy period, or an early or late period, when you're under a great deal of stress, positive or negative. Similarly, your breast pain can increase or change in its pattern with the hormone changes of stress. We also know that hormones vary at different points in your life and that the incidence of breast pain often follows these shifts. It's usually most intense in the teens and then again in the forties—at both ends of the fertile years. It almost always ends with menopause, although in some rare cases, it lasts beyond menopause—perhaps because of the continuing estrogen production of the adrenal glands (see Chapter 1). And, of course, if a postmenopausal woman is taking hormones, her body thinks she's still premenopausal and she's just as likely to get breast pain as she was before. We also know it's common in pregnant women; indeed, unusual breast pain can be an early sign of pregnancy.

The relation to hormones doesn't appear to be absolute—there must be other factors, since most often the pain is more severe in one breast than in the other, and a purely hormonal symptom would have to affect both equally. It appears to be caused by a combination of the hormonal activity and something in the breast tissue that responds to that activity. More research clearly needs to be done; I hope my own current work will contribute to our understanding of cyclical mastalgia. Breast pain is annoying, but it usually isn't unbearable—what can be unbearable is the fear that it's cancer. The best "treatment," therefore, is reassurance. The study in Cardiff suggests that 85 percent of women with breast pain are worried much more about the possibility of cancer than about the pain itself. Most of them, when reassured that their problem has no relation to cancer, are relieved, and feel they can live with their pain. Only 15 percent of the women have pain that's incapacitating and needs treatment.

Treatments for cyclical breast pain are many and varied; unfortunately, none of them works very well. In the last chapter I discussed some of the specious remedies for so-called fibrocystic disease such as stopping caffeine or taking vitamin E. Some physicians believe pain comes from water retention, and recommend diuretics ("water pills"). These give little relief. Others have tried everything from ginseng tea, vitamin A, vitamin B complex, and iodine to a firm support bra. A group of doctors in Wales[11] has recommended Evening Primrose Oil (a naturally occurring triglyceride), which, taken on a regular schedule, will relieve cyclical mastalgia in 20 percent of women.

All of these therapies are interesting, but cyclical mastalgia is a hormonal problem, so it makes more sense that the treatment be hormonal. Various hormones and hormone blockers have been tried and several have had good results. All have side effects, however, and, as always, weigh carefully the risks and benefits of any treatment you are about to undergo. (Figure 7-1 illustrates where some treatments—described below—have their effects.)

One hormonal treatment is birth control pills, which stabilize the amount of hormone each month, unlike the ovaries which vary the hormone amount. I recommend it for patients in their early 20s who are planning to use a contraceptive measure anyway, since the pill is actually the safest form of contraception for that age group, especially among nonsmokers. This holds true in spite of reports that it may slightly increase your risk of cancer.[12] (See Chapter 15 for a discussion of this risk.)

Other hormones have been tried. In England, bromocriptine,[13] which blocks prolactin in the hypothalamus, has been used. This helps

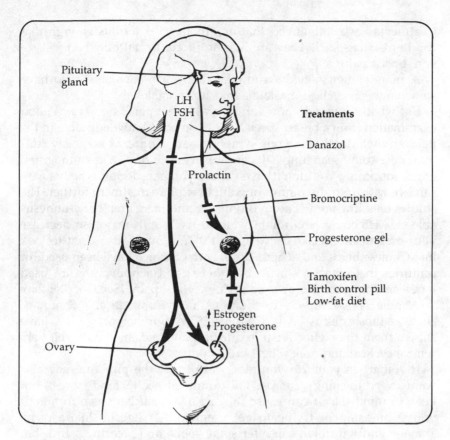

Pituitary gland

LH FSH

Treatments

Danazol

Prolactin

Bromocriptine

Progesterone gel

Tamoxifen
Birth control pill
Low-fat diet

↑ **Estrogen**
↓ **Progesterone**

Ovary

FIGURE 7-1

around 30 to 40 percent of women who've tried it, but it has some bad side effects, and shouldn't be used for any length of time. Right now it's more useful in research, helping us understand the causes of breast pain. Danazol[14] has the greatest effect on breast pain, but it's a male hormone; you might get hair on your chin, your voice might get lower, and you will probably stop getting your period. It also costs $200 a month. So, unless you're seriously incapacitated by pain (and well-insured or rich), danazol is not appropriate.

Some investigators believe thyroid hormones[15] can help, since they're related to prolactin. But there are no good controlled studies at this time. Tamoxifen is an estrogen blocker (see Chapter 17). According to an English study,[16] it's very good at relieving mastalgia. We don't know its long-term effects on premenopausal women. We do know that it increases estrogen and progesterone levels generally while blocking estrogen in the breast tissue. All of these hormonal treatments have side effects that are, or may be serious enough that caution is suggested. They are inappropriate for all but the most severe breast pain.

A more benign remedy, a low-fat diet,[17] has been shown to have some effect on cyclical mastalgia and hormone levels.

But what can you do now for cyclical breast pain? First, get a good examination from a breast specialist, or someone knowledgeable in the field and who will take your symptoms and concerns seriously (this may take some searching). If you are over 35, have a mammogram. Once you know you don't have cancer you can decide whether you can live with your discomfort or want to explore treatment further. The studies on a low-fat diet seem promising and there aren't any undesirable side effects, so you might want to try that; it may also decrease your breast cancer risk (see Chapter 15). You might also want to look into Chinese herbs and acupuncture, both of which have been used for centuries in China; in some cases, herbs and acupuncture are used together. They can also be used for noncylical pain. (See Chapter 28.)

Another possibility is meditation and visualization techniques, such as those discussed in Chapter 28. A number of studies have shown them to be effective in reducing pain, and they may well help relieve cyclical and noncyclical breast pain.

If you are in your 20s you may want to try the pill. You may also want to try Evening Primrose Oil (found in health food stores), but keep in mind that it can cause miscarriage, so it isn't safe to take if you're pregnant or trying to get pregnant. Analgesics like aspirin, Tylenol, and ibuprofen can offer some relief, and wearing a firm bra will at least prevent bouncing breasts from increasing your discomfort. If none of these helps you might ask to try danazol.

Eventually, we will be able to invent something specifically for breast pain like the prostaglandin inhibitors (ibuprofen) that work so well with menstrual cramps, and women will no longer have to suffer from it.

Noncyclical Pain

Noncyclical pain is far less common than cyclical pain. It also feels a lot different. To begin with, it doesn't vary with your menstrual cycle—it's there, and it stays there. It's also known as "trigger-zone breast pain," because it's almost always in one specific area: you can point exactly to where it hurts. It's anatomical rather than hormonal—something in the breast tissue is causing it (although we usually don't know what). Very rarely, it can be a sign of cancer, so it's always worth checking out with your doctor.

One cause of noncyclical breast pain is trauma—a blow to the breast will obviously cause it to hurt. A breast biopsy is likely to leave some pain (see Chapter 12). Many women get slight shooting or stabbing pains up to two years or more after a biopsy. You're never quite perfect after any surgery—just as after breaking a leg you can always tell when it will rain. This kind of pain is usually pretty obvious: it's on the spot where your scar is. It's unpleasant, but it's nothing to worry about.

Often, we simply don't know what causes noncyclical breast pain. We'll operate and remove the area, have the tissue studied, and find nothing abnormal.

The treatment for this kind of breast pain is more difficult than that for cyclical breast pain. Again, you must start with a good exam, and, if you're over 35, a mammogram. If there's any obvious abnormality, it can then be taken care of. For example, sometimes a gross cyst (see Chapter 9) will cause localized breast pain or tenderness and can be cured with aspiration.

Hormonal treatments are less likely to work in these patients because noncyclical pain is rarely caused by hormones. Some women, however, will find relief with the other kinds of treatments mentioned earlier under cyclical breast pain,[18] and you may want to try them. Sometimes (not invariably) having a biopsy of the area will relieve the pain—although, of course, the biopsy itself will cause pain. As a test your doctor can inject local anesthesia into the spot. If it gives relief, then surgery may well work; if not, then it probably isn't worth it.

The best treatment is a good exam and a negative mammogram with the reassurance that goes with it. This does nothing to relieve your pain, but it does relieve what's usually much worse than the pain—the fear that you have cancer.

Non-Breast-Origin Pain

The third category isn't really a form of breast pain, although it feels like it to the patient. It's usually in the middle of the chest, and doesn't change with your period. Most frequently, it's arthritic pain in the place where the ribs and breastbone connect—an arthritis called *costochondritis*[19] (Fig. 7-2). When men get costochondritis, they think it's a heart attack; when women get it, they think it's breast cancer. You can tell it's arthritis by pushing down on your breastbone where your ribs are—if it hurts a lot more, that's probably what you've got. Similarly, if you take a deep breath and the middle part of your breast hurts, it's probably arthritis. If you take aspirin

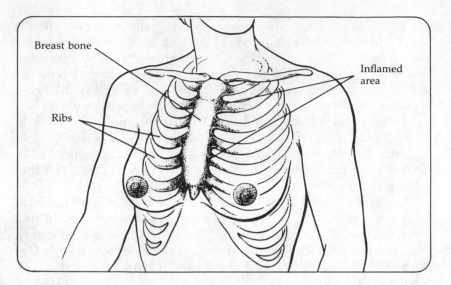

Breast bone

Inflamed area

Ribs

FIGURE 7-2

or Motrin and it relieves the pain, it's probably arthritis. Both are anti-inflammatory agents and thus work especially effectively on conditions like arthritis.

You can also get non-breast-origin pain from arthritis in the neck (a pinched nerve),[20] which can radiate down into the breast the way lower back arthritis goes into the legs. There's also a special kind of phlebitis (inflamed vein) that can occur in the breast, called Mondor's syndrome. It gives you a drawing sensation around the outer edge of your breast that extends down into your abdomen. Sometimes you can even feel a cord where it is most tender. These problems aren't serious. When a nonbreast condition appears in the breast area, it's treated as it would be on any other part of the body. That usually means, for the conditions mentioned, aspirin or another anti-inflammatory agent. These pains are usually self-limited and will go away in time.

Cancer Concerns

How likely are these forms of breast pain to be cancer? Cyclical pain never has any relation to cancer at all, so don't worry. Noncyclical pain is rarely a sign of cancer, but it can be, so it's worth checking out. One of my patients discovered while she was traveling in Europe that her breast hurt when she lay on her stomach. Although she couldn't feel any lump she had it checked when she came home and discovered she did indeed have a very tiny cancer on the spot. About 10 percent of all target-zone breast pain is cancer. Non-breast-origin pain is probably arthritis, and you can confirm this by the methods suggested in the last section. If you're still in doubt, have it checked by your doctor.

8

Breast Infections and Nipple Problems

Like pain, breast infections and nipple discharge are symptoms that are often misdiagnosed as either fibrocystic disease or its equally invalid synonym, cystic mastitis (see Chapter 6). They're fairly uncommon, and usually not much more than a nuisance, but they can cause much anxiety to the woman who experiences them.

Breast Infections: Intrinsic

There are two major categories of breast infection: intrinsic and extrinsic. Intrinsic breast infections—those occurring only to the breast itself—break down into three categories: lactational mastitis, nonlactational mastitis, and chronic subareolar abscess.

LACTATIONAL MASTITIS

Lactational mastitis is the most common of these infections.[1] It occurs, as its name suggests, when the woman is breast feeding. The breast is filled with milk, a medium that encourages the growth of bacteria. A baby is regularly biting and sucking on your breast, causing cracks in the skin and introducing bacteria—it's amazing that more nursing mothers don't get infections.

Probably it happens as seldom as it does because the milk is always flowing through and flushing the bacteria out. However, sometimes when you're breast feeding, a duct will get blocked up with thick milk that doesn't flow well. Then it's a setup for infection: the bacteria is trapped in the breast, the milk helps it grow, and suddenly you've got a reddened, hot, and very painful breast (Fig. 8-1).

Your doctor will probably suggest initially that you try to unblock the duct with massage and warm soaks; sometimes heat will be suggested (which liquifies the milk for better flow, but unfortunately increases metabolic rate of breast tissue and thus accelerates the bacteria's growth), or ice packs (which slows the bacteria's growth rate but unfortunately hardens the milk). If the infection persists, antibiotics are the next step. Usually that will take care of it. Don't worry about the antibiotics affecting your nursing child. Your obstetrician will know which antibiotics are safe for children to ingest, and will be careful about which are given to you. Nor will the bacteria hurt the child. Since it's going into the gastrointestinal system, the bacteria will be killed by the baby's stomach acid. It's actually good for you if the child goes on nursing: the sucking helps keep the duct unblocked.

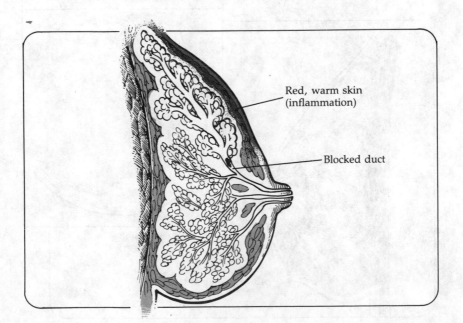

Red, warm skin
(inflammation)

Blocked duct

FIGURE 8-1

Antibiotics will almost always get rid of the infection, but in about 10 percent of cases an abscess forms, and antibiotics are useless in eliminating abscesses. An abscess, like a boil, is basically a collection of pus, and the doctor has to drain the pus. If it's an extremely small abscess, the pus can be aspirated with a needle. If it's bigger, the doctor will have to make an incision large enough to allow the pus to drain (Fig. 8-2). This can be done under local anesthetic, but it's difficult because the inflamed tissue is highly sensitive and it's hard to inject an anesthetic that will really numb the area well. If it's an extremely small infected area, I'll tell my patient to bite the bullet, the pain will soon be over—and go with the local. But if it's a large area, I find it far more effective to give the patient some anesthetic drugs. (See Chapter 25 for a discussion of monitored anesthetic.)

Once the cut is made, the pus drains out and the pain abates quickly. The surgeon will never sew up a drained abscess; that would lock the bacteria into the abscess, and almost ensure the infection's return. I tell my patients to go home and rest, then, after 24 hours, begin taking daily showers; let the water run over the breast and wash away the bacteria, and then put a dressing over it to absorb oozing fluids from the incision. Some surgeons will put a wick, or a drain, in

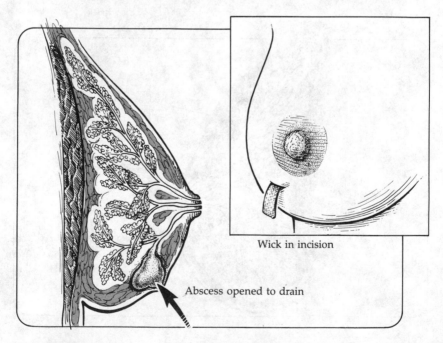

Wick in incision

Abscess opened to drain

FIGURE 8-2

the corner of the incision to keep it open; that way it heals from the inside out, and closes within a week or two (Fig. 8-2).

Some surgeons will tell you that if you need an operation, you have to stop breast feeding. Many women really want to breast feed, and there's no reason they should give it up. It is messy, since not only are you oozing fluids, you're also oozing milk. But if you're willing to put up with the mess, there's no reason not to breast feed. It's usually just one breast, and just a segment of the breast at that; there's plenty of room for your baby to suckle.

NONLACTATIONAL MASTITIS

Although the kind of mastitis described above is usually found only in lactating women, it can sometimes occur in nonlactating women, especially in particular circumstances. For example, it may occur in women who've had lumpectomies followed by radiation (see Chapter 26), in diabetics, or in women whose immune system is otherwise depressed. Such women are prone to infections, either because some of the lymph nodes, which help fight infection, have been removed, or because their immune systems are generally less strong than those of most people. This type of infection will usually be a *cellulitis*—an infection of the skin—red, hot, and swollen all over rather than just in one spot. It's generally accompanied by high fever and headache, both characteristics of a strep infection (staph infections, by contrast, are usually local). It will be treated by your doctor with antibiotics, usually penicillin, and you may be briefly hospitalized.

Skin boils (or staph infections) can form on the breast just as they do on other parts of the body. If you're a carrier of staph and prone to infection as well—as in the case of diabetics—this is more likely to occur than it would in noncarriers or people less infection prone. It's also possible to get an abscess in the breast when you're not lactating and don't have any of the other risk factors, although this is unusual. Both cellulitis and these abscesses can mask cancer (as we'll discuss below), so, although such cancer is rare, if you've got one of these conditions, it's important to have it checked out by a doctor.

I have recently seen several women who have what has been called *chronic mastitis*. In each case the patient had an infection, which her doctor drained. Unlike the lactational infections discussed earlier, these infections are abscesses, and so the first treatment should indeed be to drain them. When the condition recurred or failed to heal completely the women were sent to an infectious disease specialist who started them on antibiotics. Some of the women I saw had been on these antibiotics for years, often given intravenously at home through a Hickman catheter (see Chapter 28). Most of the time I found that the problem was one that was easily treated with a minor operation, which the infectious disease specialist, who has no experience in breast surgery, has overlooked. If you have a "chronic" infection make sure you see a breast surgeon early on. You may save yourself a lot of suffering and expense. As we do for the next condition, the chronic subareolar abscess, we have to remove the diseased tissue to eradicate the disease.

CHRONIC SUBAREOLAR ABSCESS

The second most common breast infection—and it's pretty infrequent—is the chronic subareolar abscess. We really don't understand it well, but we're getting some insights from Dr. Bruce Derrick[2] at Temple University and the late Dr. Otto Sartorius[3] in Santa Barbara, California.

Until recently, this infection was believed to be a blocked duct. The nipple has about 15 to 20 little holes around it, and we've always believed these holes were all ducts. But Dr. Sartorius has shown that they're not all ducts; only about half of them are. The others are little glands that make a sebaceous material; it's a white, oily, cheesy substance, like the stuff you find in a whitehead pimple. These glands are found all over the body. We don't know what they're for, or why there are so many around the nipple. My own theory is that the body produces them to provide a coating and protection for the skin—sort of your own little skin-care system. The nipple, designed to be sucked on, is especially vulnerable to getting chapped and sore, so it makes sense that it would have a lot of these glands.

Whatever their function, these small, dead-ended glands can get infections, whether you're nursing or not. Bacteria from the skin or mouth of your child or lover gets into the gland; thickened secretions block it so it can't drain well, and it gets infected. This kind of infection is most common in women with inverted nipples, because their glands have narrower openings.

When this infection occurs, an abscess can form. The abscess can't drain through the usual exit, and therefore tries to drain through the weakest part of the skin in the area—the border of the areola and the regular skin (Fig. 8-3). The abscess is a red, hot, sore area on part of the border of the nipple—like a boil. It looks and feels fairly awful, and the frightened woman often thinks she's got breast cancer. She doesn't, and the infection doesn't affect her vulnerability to breast cancer.

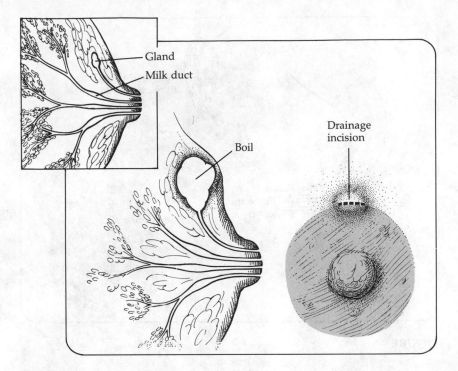

Gland

Milk duct

Boil

Drainage incision

FIGURE 8-3

If the infection is caught very early, before an abscess forms, it can be helped by antibiotics, but often it can't be; it needs an incision and draining. I prefer to do the incision on the border of the areola, so that it doesn't show later. Once the pus is drained, it's okay—for the time being. The trouble is that this type of infection tends to recur. The gland is a little blind tract, with no internal opening, so it tends to reinfect itself and drain again at the same point. Eventually this leaves a permanent open tract.

We've had some luck reducing these recurrences by removing the entire gland or tract. To get the whole tract, we have to excise a wedge of nipple. It isn't perfect, but the success rate is a lot better than that of the other methods.

Since the gland is small and the surgery is relatively minor, I used to do it under local anesthetic. But it's hard to get a chronically infected area thoroughly numb, especially as sensitive an area as the nipple—the same problem we faced above in lactational mastitis, only more severe. So I found that in my anxiousness to end my patient's discomfort, I sometimes didn't get the whole gland out, and the

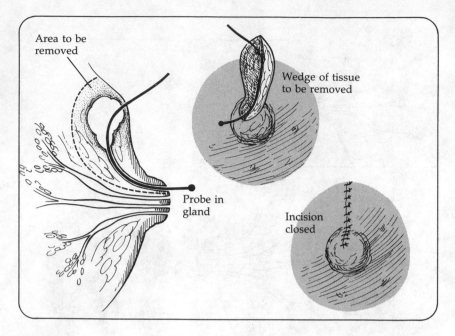

Area to be removed

Wedge of tissue to be removed

Probe in gland

Incision closed

FIGURE 8-4

infection would often recur. Now I tend to give women short-acting drugs to complement the local anesthetic. I pass a probe through the tract and then take out the wedge of nipple that contains the tract, including both openings (Fig. 8-4). The nipple is then closed and sewn up.

There's some controversy about whether or not to close the incision. Some doctors are afraid that if there are lots of bacteria to begin with there's a greater chance that the gland will reinfect itself if it's closed off; others are more concerned with the cosmetic loss if the nipple is left with a hole in it. I prefer to close it, but I always tell my patient the pros and cons of both, and then do what she wants.

Unfortunately, even in the best-done operations, the problem often recurs.[4] Perhaps the infection spreads from one gland to another, or perhaps there's still lining left from the old gland that the surgeon isn't aware of.

So if you have a chronic subareolar abscess, it's well worth trying to have it taken care of. But you have to understand that you might have to keep dealing with it. About 40 percent of these infections do recur, sometimes as often as every few months.

As so often happens with women's bodies, many doctors think disfiguring surgery is called for. One patient came to me after her doctor said he was fed up with these recurrences and wanted to remove both breasts. Fortunately, she had the sense not to listen to him. A well-planned, nonmutilating operation solved her problem—but even if it hadn't, the most drastic procedure that would have made any sense at all would have been to remove the nipple and leave the breast—then at least a plastic surgeon could reconstruct a new nipple, leaving the breast intact (see Chapter 5).

But if you have this condition, it's unlikely you'd want even that done. The condition is unpleasant and a nuisance, but it's not life-threatening. It doesn't interfere with breast-feeding, nor should it restrict your sexual life, except insofar as you're obviously not likely to want your nipple touched while it's hurting from the infection.

Extrinsic Infections

Extrinsic breast infections are those that involve the whole body and show first on the breast. These are extremely rare, especially in this country, so I'll mention them only briefly. TB and syphilis have both been known to emerge first on the breast; such an infection would be treated the same way the disease would be treated if it showed anywhere else.

Infection and Cancer

Breast infections never lead to breast cancer; however, some breast cancers lead to infections, or can look like infections (see Chapter 24). As the cancer cells grow, some cancer cells die off for lack of blood supply, and the necrotic (dead) tissue can get infected. So it's possible for a breast cancer to show up first as a breast abscess, but it's extremely unusual.

There is a form of breast cancer, called inflammatory breast cancer, that can be mistaken for infection (see Chapter 24). This starts with redness of the skin, warmth, and swelling. There usually is no lump. What distinguishes it from infection is that it doesn't get better with antibiotics. Anyone with a breast infection that persists after 10 days to two weeks of antibiotics should see a breast surgeon, who will probably want to do a biopsy.

If you get an infection, don't worry about it—but do see your doctor right away. The infection won't give you cancer, but it should be treated and gotten rid of, and you do want to make sure it is an infection.

Discharge and Other Nipple Problems

DISCHARGE

The nipple is an especially sensitive area, and it is subject to a number of problems, such as the subareolar abscess discussed earlier. The most common nipple problem—or rather, concern, since it's not always a problem—is discharge. Its significance has been exaggerated by the public and the medical profession as well. The American Cancer Society, for example, says that if you have any nipple discharge you should go to your doctor immediately. Those movies that show you how to do breast self-exam always show the woman squeezing her nipple to find out if there's any discharge. And a lot of internists and gynecologists will squeeze your nipple to see if there's discharge.

It's a pointless and self-defeating exercise. Most women do have some amount of discharge when their breasts are squeezed, and it's perfectly normal. A study at the Boston Lying-in Hospital breast clinic was conducted,[5] in which women had little suction cups, like breast pumps, put on their nipples and gentle suction applied. Eighty-three percent of these women—old, young, mothers, nonmothers, previously pregnant, and never pregnant—had some amount of discharge. Yet women are continually being encouraged to be frightened by breast discharge.

The typical scenario is this: a woman is bathing and washing her breasts, or her lover is squeezing her breast, and she discovers a little bit of discharge, produced by the pressure on her breasts. Alarmed, she squeezes the nipple to see if there's something in there—and more discharge comes out. What she doesn't realize is that the very act of squeezing the nipples creates more discharge, because it increases prolactin. Prolactin, as we discussed at the beginning of Chapter 3, is the hormone in the brain that stimulates the breast of a lactating woman to produce milk; the sucking of the infant is what usually announces to the brain that it's time to send in the prolactin; we need more milk here. So when you squeeze your breasts you're telling your brain to please produce some liquid for the breasts, and the brain obliges (Fig. 8-5). So the discharge increases, and the poor woman is convinced she's not only got cancer, but a terrible, advanced cancer at that. She runs to her doctor in a state of terror. I've had women come in with breasts they've bruised and battered, after wringing them out in a desperate attempt to find out how bad their "cancer" really is. Often by this point the discharge is bloody, and no wonder—they've beaten their poor nipples to a pulp.

It's a pity, because most discharge is nothing to be alarmed about. The kinds that are have very specific characteristics which I'll discuss

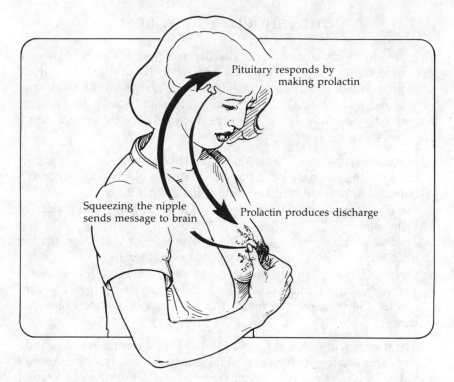

Pituitary responds by making prolactin

Squeezing the nipple sends message to brain

Prolactin produces discharge

FIGURE 8-5

below. The ducts of the nipple are pipelines; they're made to carry milk to the nipple. The fact that there's a little fluid in the pipes shouldn't be surprising. (This fluid may come in a number of colors— gray, green, and brown, as well as white.)

Sometimes people confuse nipple discharge with other problems— weepy sores, infections, abscesses (see above). Inverted nipples (see Chapter 5) sometimes get dirt and dried-up sweat trapped in them, and this can be confused with discharge.

Some women are more prone to lots of discharge than others. Women on birth control pills, on antihypertensives such as Aldomet, or major tranquilizers such as thorazine, tend to notice more discharge because these medications increase prolactin levels. It may seem aesthetically displeasing, but beyond that there's nothing to worry about.

There are also different life periods when you're more likely to get discharge than others. There's more discharge at puberty and just before menopause than in between. Newborn babies often have a little discharge, called "witches' milk." This makes sense, since the discharge is a result of hormonal processes.

WHEN SHOULD YOU WORRY?

The time to worry about nipple discharge is when it's spontaneous, persistent, and unilateral (only on one side). It comes out by itself without squeezing; it keeps on happening; and it's only from one nipple and usually one duct. It's either clear and sticky, like an egg white, or bloody. You should go to the doctor. There are several possible causes:

1. *Intraductal papilloma*. This is a little wartlike growth on the lining of the duct. It gets eroded and bleeds, creating a bloody discharge. It's benign; we remove it to make sure that's what it is.
2. *Intraductal papillomatosis*. Instead of one wart, you've got a lot of little warts.
3. *Intraductal carcinoma in situ*. This is a precancer that clogs up the duct like rust: it's discussed in detail in Chapter 16.
4. *Cancer*. Cancers are rarely the cause of discharge. Only about 4 percent of all spontaneous unilateral bloody discharges are cancerous. (See Chapter 16 for further discussion of discharge with cancer.)

The doctor will first test for blood by taking a sample, putting it on a card, and adding a chemical called guaiac. If it turns blue, there's blood (which may not be visible to the eye alone, because of the color of the discharge itself). He or she may do a Pap smear, very like the Pap smear you get to test for cervical cancer. Discharge is put on a glass slide, and sent to the lab for the cells to be examined. This is not as accurate as testing for blood in the discharge, but occasionally it can demonstrate if there are abnormal cells.

Next the doctor will try and figure out the "trigger zone," by going around the breast to find out which duct the discharge is coming from, although often the woman herself can give the doctor this information. If you're over 30 you'll be sent for a mammogram to see if there's a tumor underneath the duct.

You can then be given a ductogram—a test I find vital. The radiologist takes a very fine plastic catheter and, with a magnifying glass, threads it into the duct, squirts dye into it, and takes a picture (Fig. 8-6). The procedure sounds uncomfortable, but it really isn't that bad—the duct is an open tube already, and the discharge has dilated it. The ductogram provides a "map" for the surgeon who will do the biopsy and may also show the source of the discharge. Not all surgeons order a ductogram, but I find it extremely worthwhile.

The biopsy itself is fairly simple; it's a specialized form of the regular breast biopsy (see Chapter 12). It can be done under local anesthetic and on an outpatient basis. A tiny incision is made at the edge

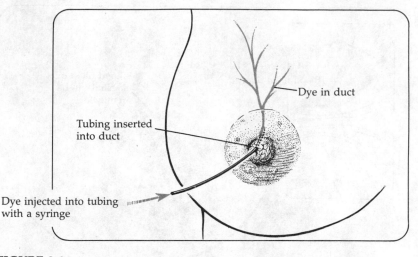

Dye in duct

Tubing inserted
into duct

Dye injected into tubing
with a syringe

FIGURE 8-6

of the areola; the areola is flipped up, and the blood-filled duct located and removed (Fig. 8-7). Sometimes during the ductogram we will have the radiologist cut a fine suture and pass it into the duct to the point to be removed, or blue dye can be injected into the duct to help identify it. Both techniques will help pinpoint the right area. Sometimes if the ductogram has shown the lesion to be far from the nipple, we will localize the area with a wire, as described in Chapter 12. In that way, we can avoid cutting the ducts, which interferes with breast feeding, or numbing the nipple, which interferes with sexual pleasure.

Because the lesion can be far from the nipple itself, we've largely abandoned the old standard surgical practice of removing all of the ductal system to make sure that the discharge has stopped. Although this procedure stops the discharge (by disconnecting the ducts from the nipple), it may or may not remove the pathology causing the discharge.

In Japan, they're using duct endoscopy to figure out what's causing the discharge. A little thin endoscope is put directly into the nipple duct, and the surgeon can see the inside of the ducts on a video screen. I'm working on this technique so that we can make the diagnosis without surgery.

Another form of problematic discharge is one that is spontaneous, bilateral (on both sides), and milky. If you're not breast feeding, and haven't been in the past year, this is probably a condition called *galactorrhea*. It occurs because something is increasing the prolactin levels— sometimes a small tumor in the brain. This may not be as alarming as it sounds. Often it's a tiny tumor which may not require surgery. A

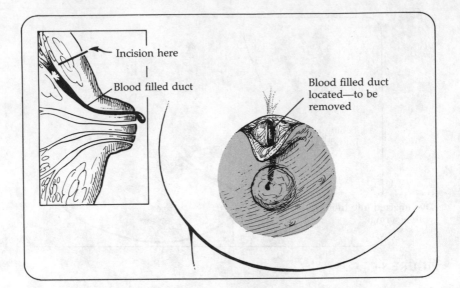

Incision here

Blood filled duct

Blood filled duct located—to be removed

FIGURE 8-7

neurosurgeon and an endocrinologist together need to check this out. Sometimes bromocriptine is given to block the prolactin. Galactorrhea is often associated with amenorrhea—failure to get your period. It can also be caused by major tranquilizers, marijuana consumption, or high estrogen doses.

Galactorrhea is diagnosed only when the discharge is bilateral. Many doctors don't understand this, and send patients with any discharge for prolactin-level tests. They shouldn't; unilateral discharges are not associated with hormonal problems. Unilateral spontaneous discharge is anatomical, not hormonal, and the money spent on prolactin tests is wasted.

OTHER NIPPLE PROBLEMS

Discharge is the most common nipple problem women experience, but there are a few others, as well. Some patients complain of itchy nipples. Usually itchy nipples don't indicate severe problems, especially if both nipples itch. You can get dry skin on your nipples, as elsewhere. You may be allergic to your bra, or to the detergent it's washed in. And, of course, pubescent girls with growing breasts often experience itching as the skin stretches itself. Otherwise, we don't know what causes itchy nipples—but they're not usually a problem.

If they bother you, you can use calamine lotion or other anti-itch medication.

There is a form of cancer known as Paget's disease that doctors and patients often confuse with excema of the nipple. It looks like an open sore area, and it itches. If it's only on one nipple, and it doesn't go away with standard excema treatments, check it out. A biopsy can be performed on a small section of the nipple. (Paget's disease is discussed at length in Chapter 24.) If the rash is on both nipples and you tend to get excema anyway, don't worry. Anything that can happen to other parts of the skin can happen to the nipple.

Most of these various infections and irritations are benign—they're more of a nuisance than anything else. If they appear, get them checked out just to make sure they're what they appear to be, and to get the relief available.

9

Lumps and
Lumpiness

To begin with, you need to remember that lumpiness, as I discussed in Chapter 2, isn't the same as having one dominant lump. It's a general pattern of many little lumps, in both breasts, and it's perfectly normal. The distinction between "lumps" and "lumpiness" is an important one; the confusion of the two can cause a woman days and weeks of needless mental anguish. Lumpiness is not a disease—"fibrocystic" or otherwise. It's simply normal breast tissue.

Patients aren't the only ones who get lumpiness and lumps confused. Doctors who don't usually work with breast cancer—family practitioners and gynecologists—often get nervous about lumpy breasts and are afraid they're malignant. So your doctor may send you to a specialist—a surgeon or a breast specialist—to make sure you don't have a cancerous lump. If you or your doctor are uncertain about whether you've got a lump or just lumpy breasts, it's probably not a bad idea to check it out further. But understanding more about what a lump really is might make the trip to the specialist unnecessary.

The most important thing to know about dominant lumps—benign or malignant—is that they're almost never subtle. They're not like little beebee gun pellets; they're usually at least a centimeter or two, almost an inch, or the size of a grape. The lump will stick out prominently in the midst of the smaller lumps that constitute normal lumpiness. You'll know it's something different. In fact, that's why most breast cancers are found by the woman herself—the lumps are so clearly distinct from the rest of her breast tissue.

The obvious question here is, how do I know the beebee-sized thing isn't an early cancer? The answer is that you usually don't feel a malignant lump when it's small. The cancer has to grow to a large enough size for the body to begin to create a reaction to it—a fibrous, scarlike tissue forms around the cancer, and this, combined with the cancer itself, makes up the palpable lump. The body won't create that reaction when the cancer is tiny, and you won't feel the cancerous lump until the reaction is formed.

At the same time, if it's much bigger than a walnut—if it feels like a quarter of the breast itself—you're probably still okay. You'll know when you check it through a couple of menstrual cycles, and see that it changes through different parts of your cycle. A cancer lump that large would probably have been noticed earlier, by even the most absentminded person. But if it doesn't go away or change significantly after two menstrual cycles, have it checked out; it's not likely that it's a cancer, but it could be, and you don't want to take the chance. It will be easier for you to notice changes if you've become acquainted with your breasts, as we discussed in Chapter 2.

There are four types of dominant lumps, three of which are virtually harmless. It's the fourth type, of course—the malignant lump—that you're worrying about when you have your lump examined by a doctor. I'll discuss cancerous lumps at length in Chapter 20. It's worth noting here, however, that in premenopausal women only one in 12 dominant lumps is malignant, and in postmenopausal women, 1 of 2. We don't know the cause of any of the noncancerous lumps, though we do know they're somehow related to hormonal variations (see Chapter 1). Two kinds of lump—cysts and fibroadenomas—are formed only during a woman's menstruating years, but can show up years later, when breast tissue has shifted. Pseudolumps can occur in women of any age. It's interesting that two of the three kinds occur most often at opposite ends of a woman's fertile years: fibroadenomas occur when the woman is just starting to menstruate, and cysts when she's heading toward menopause.

Cysts

Usually when you think of nonmalignant lumps, you think of cysts, because doctors have a tendency to describe all nonmalignant lumps as cysts. They're not. A cyst is a particular, distinct kind of lump. Typically it occurs in women in their 30s, 40s, and early 50s, and is most common in women approaching menopause. It will rarely occur in a younger woman, or in a woman who's past menopause. However, I've had patients with cysts in both categories—including a teenager and a woman who had finished with her menopause long ago and wasn't on artificial hormones. (If a woman is taking estrogen to combat menopausal symptoms, she'll have fooled her body into thinking it's still premenopausal.)

A gross cyst—gross meaning "large," not, as in popular usage, "disgusting"—is a fluid-filled sac, very much like a large blister, that grows in the midst of the breast tissue. It's smooth on the outside and "ballottable"—squishy—on the inside, so that if you push on it, you can feel that it's got fluid inside. This, however, can be deceptive. Cysts feel like cysts only when they're close to the surface (Fig. 9-1). Cysts that are deeply imbedded in breast tissue distend the tissue and push it forward, so that what you're feeling is the hard breast tissue, not the soft cyst. In these cases, the cyst feels like a hard lump.

The classical cyst story goes something like this. A woman in her 40s will come to me and say, "I went to the gynecologist six weeks ago and everything was fine. I had a mammogram, and that was fine, too. Then all of a sudden, in the shower last night, I found this lump in my breast, and I know it wasn't there before." So I examine her and, sure enough, there's a hard lump in her breast.

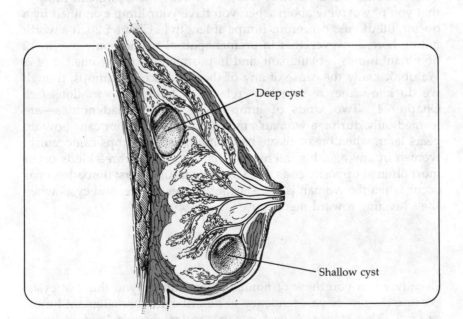

Deep cyst

Shallow cyst

FIGURE 9-1

Because of its overnight appearance, I'm pretty sure it's a harmless cyst; but, of course, it's something the doctor—not to mention the patient—wants to be absolutely certain about: cancers sometimes do seem to appear overnight. So I try to aspirate it.

To aspirate a cyst, the doctor takes a tiny needle, like the needle used for insulin injections, and anesthetizes the sensitive skin over the breast lump. Then a larger needle—like the kind used to draw blood—is attached to a syringe and stuck through the breast into the cyst, where it draws out the fluid (Fig. 9-2). The cyst collapses like a punctured blister, and that's that.

Aspirating cysts is one of the medical procedures I most enjoy doing. It's very easy, and as soon as it's done my patient and I both know she's okay. We're both delighted that she doesn't have cancer, and she thinks I'm the greatest doctor in the world, having simultaneously diagnosed and cured her condition. It does wonders for my ego.

An added pleasure is that it's usually almost painless for the patient. It sounds scary and grim—a little like descriptions of acupuncture—but most of the nerves in the breast are in the skin, and that's been anesthetized. Some women with greater sensitivity to pain or who have especially sensitive breasts do find it painful, but most don't. The only complications from aspirating a cyst are bruising and bleeding into the cyst, which are only slightly uncomfortable.

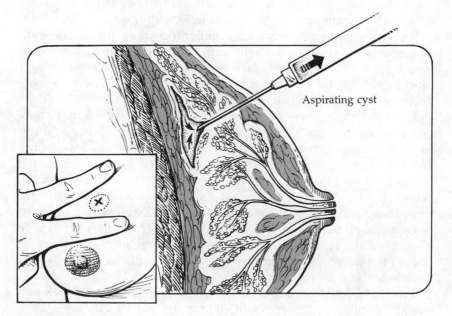

Aspirating cyst

FIGURE 9-2

The fluid itself is pretty disgusting looking, but it's harmless. It can be almost any color—usually it's green or brown or yellow. Sometimes the fluid can even be milk—a breast-feeding woman can form a milk-filled cyst called a *galactocele*, which is treated the way any other cyst is. There can be any amount in it—from a few drops to as much as a cup. One patient came to me with asymmetrical breasts; after I aspirated her cyst, her breasts were the same size.

Some doctors have the fluid analyzed in the lab, but frankly, I think it's a waste of the patient's money. The chances of getting a correct diagnosis from cyst fluid are very low, and false positives are common. The fluid has usually been around a while; it's old, and its cells, though harmless, often look weird when they're checked. The tests are useless and costly. Most specialists just throw the stuff down the sink.

In Sweden, they think injecting air into the cyst after it's been aspirated prevents the cyst from recurring.[1] It's an interesting theory, but it hasn't been proven. Still, it's worth a try if the cyst has recurred many times.

Usually a woman will get only one or two cysts in her entire life. But some get many, and they get them often. If a patient has recurring multiple cysts, I like to see her every three to six months, and aspirate as many as I can to keep the multiplication of cysts under control. If a malignant lump is forming, the cysts, harmless in themselves, can obscure it, and that, of course, is dangerous. If a woman has multiple cysts, the chances are she'll go on getting them until menopause—only rarely are multiple cysts a one-time occurrence.

If cysts are harmless, why do we bother to aspirate them? There are a number of reasons, but the most important one is that we need to be sure it really *is* a cyst. You can't be sure a lump in the breast isn't cancer until you find out what it really is. Once we know it's a cyst, doctor and patient can both rest easy.

There are other ways of finding out you have a cyst—it may show up as an area of density on a routine mammogram, and then you can have an ultrasound test done to see whether it's a cyst or a solid lump. The ultrasound test works like radar. If you have a solid lump, the waves from the ultrasound will bounce back and there'll be a shadow behind it. If, however, it's a cyst, the sound waves will go right through it and there won't be a shadow. (See Chapters 10 and 11 for discussions of mammograms and ultrasound techniques.) If you've discovered a cyst through a mammogram and ultrasound and it doesn't bother you, you don't need to have it aspirated as well—you already know it isn't cancer.

Sometimes cysts are painful, especially if they've developed quickly. Aspirating the cyst will relieve the pain. Cysts are almost never malignant. There's a 1 percent incidence of cancer in cysts, and it's a seldom-dangerous cancer called *intracystic papillary carcinoma* (Fig. 9-3). It usually doesn't spread beyond the lining of the cyst, and unless there are specific signs that it might be present, it's not worth the risk of a biopsy. A biopsy is surgery, though minor surgery, and it's better to avoid it when you can.

If there are signs that cancer might be present in the cyst, I do operate on it—never otherwise, and only after I've aspirated it. I may operate if the cyst has recurred after I've aspirated it three times. I'll also operate if the fluid comes out bloody—that usually means something else is going on, and I want to find out what it is. Finally, I'll do a biopsy if the lump doesn't go away after I've aspirated the cyst.

Sometimes a doctor will aspirate a cyst and won't get any fluid. This isn't a cause for panic. It can happen for a number of reasons. The lump may not be a cyst after all, but a nonmalignant solid lump like those discussed below. Or the doctor may have missed the middle of the cyst. The doctor tries to get the cyst between her or his fingers and then puncture it, but it's easy to miss the middle, especially in a fairly small cyst. When this happens to me, I'll decide how sure I am it's a cyst and, if I have doubts, I'll send the patient for an ultrasound test rather than operate. Operating on a cyst should only be a last resort—it simply isn't necessary in any but the most unusual situation.

It used to be believed that aspirating a cyst was dangerous if someone unknowingly had breast cancer—that the process of aspiration would spread the cancer over the needle's track. We now know that's not true.[2] Any dominant lump should be aspirated before it's biopsied. It might be a cyst, and surgery can be avoided.

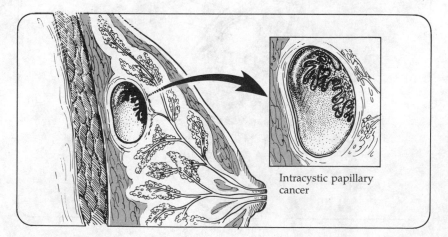

Intracystic papillary cancer

FIGURE 9-3

Cysts don't increase the risk of cancer. Only one study—that of Cushman Haagensen[3] of Columbia University—suggests it does, and his evidence is sketchy. David Page's[4] research is a little better; he's found that there is a slightly increased risk in women who have gross cysts and who have a first-degree relative with breast cancer—a mother or sister. Most other research shows no relation between cysts and cancer.

The real risk is mental rather than physical. A woman with frequent cysts is likely to feel a lump and shrug it off as just another cyst—only to learn later that it was a malignant growth. Every lump should be checked out to be sure it isn't dangerous.

Fibroadenomas

Another common nonmalignant lump is the *fibroadenoma*. This is a smooth, round lump that feels the way most people think a cyst should feel—it's smooth and hard, like a marble dropped into the breast tissue (Fig. 9-4). It moves around easily within the breast tissue, and is often found near the nipple, but can grow anywhere in the breast. And it's very distinct from the rest of the breast tissue. It can vary from a tiny 5 millimeters to a lemon-sized 5 centimeters.

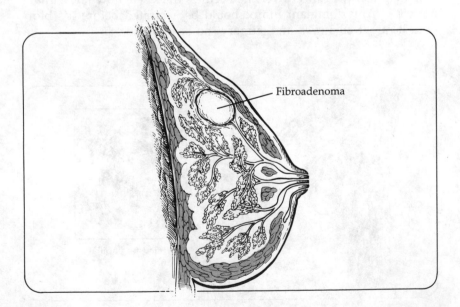

Fibroadenoma

FIGURE 9-4

The largest are called "giant fibroadenomas." A doctor can usually tell simply by feeling the lump that it's a fibroadenoma; if a needle aspiration is done and no fluid comes out, the doctor knows it isn't a cyst and is even more convinced it's a fibroadenoma. We can get a few cells by doing a fine needle aspiration (see Chapter 12) and sending the tissue off to the lab just to make doubly sure. Fibroadenomas will usually be clear on a mammogram (Chapter 10) or ultrasound test (Chapter 11). Core biopsy can also prove that they are fibroadenomas (see Chapter 12). Fibroadenomas are harmless in themselves, and they don't have to be removed, as long as we're sure they're fibroadenomas. Teenagers are both more prone to fibroadenomas and less likely to get breast cancer than are older women, so we do not remove fibroadenomas in them. In women middle-aged or older, we tend to remove all fibroadenomas to be sure they're not cancer.

In the spring of 1993, a new study by Dr. Page[5] showed that women with a certain kind of fibroadenoma might have an increased risk of subsequent cancer. The special kind of fibroadenoma was called a "complex fibroadenoma" because not only were there glands and surrounding tissue as is usual in this lesion, but the women had other microscopic entities such as *sclerosing adenosis* and *apocrine metaplasia* (see Chapter 6). It is important to note that the complex fibroadenomas studied had not turned into cancer. Rather, they were a marker for a future risk, like having a strong family history. About one third of all fibroadenomas are complex. Page found that, when associated with a family history in a first-degree relative, these fibroadenomas increased the subsequent risk of cancer three times. This might make us more likely to remove a fibroadenoma in a woman with a first-degree family history to see if it is a complex one.

Fibroadenomas are easy to remove—it can be done under a local anesthetic; the surgeon simply makes a small incision, finds the lump, and takes it right out (Fig. 9-5). (Some surgeons prefer to make a small incision around the nipple and then tunnel their way to the lump, since an incision at the nipple scars less noticeably. I don't think this is a great idea, however; it's harder to find the lesion that way. If you cut over the fibroadenoma, you're bound to get it, and the scarring doesn't usually remain all that noticeable in most patients.) If you feel nervous about your fibroadenomas, it's probably a good idea to get it removed for your own peace of mind; if there's no reason to get it removed and you don't want to, don't worry about it.

In most cases a woman has only one fibroadenoma; it's removed, and she never gets any more. But some women do get several over their lives—and a few women get many of them. One of my patients had a fibroadenoma in her left breast, and I removed it; she returned a

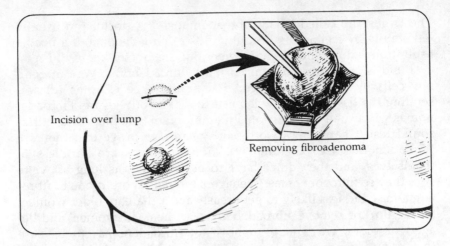

Incision over lump

Removing fibroadenoma

FIGURE 9-5

couple of years later with another one on the exact same spot in her other breast—a kind of mirror image.

Patients often call their fibroadenomas "fibroids"—and, while it's inaccurate, it makes sense in a way. Fibroids by definition exist only in the uterus, but there are similarities between the two conditions. In both cases, one section of glandular tissue becomes autonomous, growing as a ball in the midst of the rest of the tissue. But there's no correlation except for that—having one doesn't mean you're likely to get the other. In fact, they usually occur at different times in a woman's life: fibroids when you're heading toward menopause, fibroadenomas in your teens or early 20s.

They can, however, occur at any age, up until menopause. Like cysts, you can get them after menopuase if you're taking hormones that trick your body into thinking it's premenopausal. It's true that, as we do more mammograms on "normal" women, we find more and more fibroadenomas in women in their 60s and 70s. Probably they've had them since their teens and simply, in those premammography days, didn't know about them. There are some very rare cancers that can look like fibroadenomas on a mammogram, so, in women this age, we usually do either a fine needle aspiration or core biopsy or, if that doesn't give us the information, an excisional biopsy (removal of the whole lump), just to make sure it is a fibroadenoma.

There's also a rare cancer called *cystosarcoma phylloides* which can occur in a fibroadenoma. (See Chapter 24 for a discussion of this cancer.) It only occurs in about 1 percent of fibroadenomas, and those are usually giant fibroadenomas—lemon-sized or larger. It's generally a relatively harmless cancer, in that it doesn't tend to spread to other parts of the body. Some doctors will insist on removing all fibroadenomas on the theory that this cancer might be present. It's not a very sensible attitude, both because of the rarity and because of the lack of danger. Unless the lump is large, it's almost never going to contain this cancer—and even if the cancer is present for a long time, it probably isn't going to kill you. When it's discovered, the surgeon simply has to remove the lump and it's gone.

Finally, fibroadenomas in no way predispose you to cancer. They're a nuisance, and they can scare you into thinking you might have cancer—but that's the only bad thing about them.

Pseudolumps

Studies show that pseudolumps are the lumps that most confuse surgeons. If you line up patients with fibroadenomas, with cysts, and with breast cancers, and have surgeons examine them, surgeons who haven't been told which patient has which kind of lump, usually the surgeons will agree in their diagnoses. Give them patients with pseudolumps, however, and you'll get all kinds of different diagnoses. These innocent lumps of breast tissue cause no physical problems, but all kinds of confusion.

"Pseudolump" is a descriptive term for an area of breast tissue that feels more prominent and persistent than usual. The surgeon checks it out and just can't be sure that it isn't a dominant lump.

If I think a patient has a pseudolump, I'll usually see her at least twice, several months apart and at different parts of her cycle, just to make sure it isn't normal lumpiness. Deciding what is or isn't a lump in these cases can be very subjective. If I've recently done a lot of biopsies and they've all turned out to be pseudolumps, I'll tend not to operate; but if I've missed a cancer, I'll operate on a lot of them. Unfortunately, diagnosis is not an exact science. That's the other reason I like to see the patient a few months after my first diagnosis—to balance out whatever effect my mood has had on my decision.

A pseudolump, then, is usually just exaggerated lumpiness. It's distinct and persistent enough, however, that we have to check to be certain that's all it is. It's usually what's meant when doctors say you have fibrocystic disease (see Chapter 6). Or a pseudolump can be caused by a rib pushing against breast tissue and causing it to feel hard and lumpy (Fig. 9-6). Sometimes women who had silicone injections years ago to enlarge one or both breasts (see Chapter 5) will get lumps that turn out to be hardened chunks of silicone. If you've had injections and get a lump, check with either a breast surgeon or a

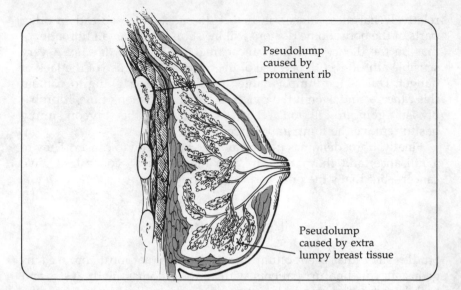

Pseudolump caused by prominent rib

Pseudolump caused by extra lumpy breast tissue

FIGURE 9-6

plastic surgeon (preferably one who's old enough to have worked with silicone injections when they were legal). Surgery on the breast can cause pseudolumps through hardened scar tissue. A pseudolump can also be caused by "fat necrosis"—dead fat—resulting from trauma due to a lumpectomy and radiation in the removal of an earlier, cancerous lump (see Chapter 27), or to breast reconstruction surgery (see Chapter 26). But in all these cases, the best judge will be a breast surgeon who's done all the procedures.

Cancer

The fear of cancer is, of course, the main reason we worry about these lumps. You get a cyst aspirated, or a fibroadenoma or pseudolump biopsied, chiefly to make sure they aren't cancer.

It's reasonable to be afraid of getting breast cancer, and to check out any suspicious lump. But remember that a dominant lump doesn't mean you have cancer. In premenopausal women, as we said earlier, there are 12 benign lumps for every malignant one. The statistics change to 50/50 in postmenopausal women who aren't taking hormones, not because they get that much more cancer but because they no longer get the lumps that come with hormonal changes, cysts and fibroadenomas. We'll discuss malignant lumps in Chapter 20. The main thing to remember is to be cautious, but not paranoid. If you've got a lump, it may be cancer, but it probably isn't. Get it checked out right away. Then if it's cancer, you can start working on it; if it isn't, you can stop worrying.

What to Do If You Think You Have a Lump

If you have something that feels like it might be a lump, the first thing to do, obviously, is go to your doctor. The chances are that the doctor will check it out, tell you it's not a lump, and send you home. A doctor who's a general practitioner or a gynecologist and hasn't spent years working on breasts might not be sure, and may send you to a breast surgeon for further examination. Often when you hear the word "surgeon" you get scared—sure the doctor knows you've got something awful and will have to undergo major surgery.

Probably you won't. The doctor is simply, and sensibly, taking no chances, and sending the patient on to someone who has more experience with breast lumps and is thus more able to determine whether or not it's a true dominant lump. But sometimes even the surgeon can't be sure. In this case, depending on your age, the surgeon will probably send you for a mammogram for additional information (Fig. 9-7). The mammogram might show evidence of a real lump, or a pseudolump. If it doesn't—if even the combination of an examination and a mammogram doesn't give the surgeon the necessary clarification—it's wise to do a biopsy to find out what it is. In the past, we were afraid of unnecessary surgery, and didn't want to biopsy these "gray-area" lumps. The problem is, you don't know until you have done the biopsy that it is a pseudolump, so the operation isn't unnecessary at all. It's far wiser to risk a fairly safe operation than to take the chance on letting a cancer go.

One thing is important to stress, and I'm becoming more and more aware just how important it is. If you're sure something is wrong with your breast, get it biopsied, whatever the doctor's diagnosis. Often a woman is sure she has a lump, the doctor is sure she doesn't, and a year or two later a lump shows up on her mammogram. She's sure the doctor was careless. She's not usually right: a cancer that is difficult to feel but shows on a mammogram probably wasn't a lump two years earlier, or it would be a huge lump at that point. But I think it's very likely that the patient—who, after all, experiences her breast from both inside and outside; the doctor only from outside—has sensed something wrong, and interpreted that in terms of the concept most

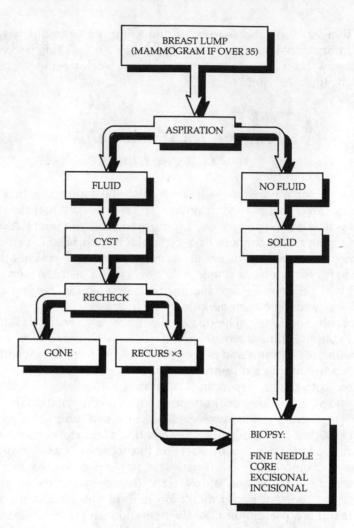

FIGURE 9-7

familiar to her, a lump. I'm convinced that this is the basis of many of the malpractice suits that arise when a doctor has "failed" to detect what later proves to be cancer. If you really feel something is wrong in your breast, insist on a biopsy. If you're wrong, you'll put your mind at rest—and if you're right, you may just save your own life. It's a minor procedure with low risks and potentially high gains.

PART THREE

DIAGNOSIS OF BREAST PROBLEMS

10

Diagnostic Mammography

Although mammography is most commonly thought of in relation to cancer, it's actually a diagnostic tool for a variety of breast problems. It shares this capacity with a number of other imaging techniques. (Imaging means ways of seeing body tissue; see Chapter 11.) For example, a woman with localized breast pain might have a mammogram to see if she has a cyst. A woman with an abscess might need an ultrasound to delineate its extent. A woman with nipple discharge might have a ductogram (type of mammogram; see Chapter 8) to find the lesion and plan surgery. Both magnetic resonance imaging (MRI) and ultrasound are being used to determine whether silicone implants have leaked.

In this chapter we look at diagnostic mammography, and in the next we discuss other commonly used diagnostic tools. Later, in Chapter 19, we discuss the use of mammography as a method of screening for breast cancer. (The same equipment is used for screening and diagnostic mammography, but different types of pictures are taken.)

A mammogram is an X ray of the breast—"mammo" means breast and "gram" means picture. It isn't the same as a chest X ray, which looks through the breast and photographs the lungs. Mammograms look at the breast itself, and take pictures of the soft tissue within it, allowing the radiologist to see anything unusual or suspicious.

Mammography can pick up very small lesions—about 1/2 centimeter (or 1/5 inch), whereas you usually can't feel a lump till it's at least a centimeter (2/5 inch). These lesions can be benign or malignant. In addition, mammograms can pick up precancers (see Chapter 16), which are even earlier.

Mammography has its limits, though. The mammogram can take a picture only of the part of the breast that sticks out—the plates are put underneath the breast, or on the sides of the breast—so it's easier to get an accurate picture of a large breast than of a small one. The periphery of the breast will not get into the picture at all (Fig. 10-1). In addition, if your breasts are dense, the lump may not be visible through the tissue. So a mammogram isn't perfect. Physical exams and mammograms are complementary, not substitutions for each other. You can see some lumps on a mammogram that you can't feel, and you can feel some lumps through palpation that you can't see on a mammogram.

You get a diagnostic mammogram when you find a lump or have another breast complaint and your doctor wants to get a better sense of what the problem is. If, for example, you have lumpy breasts and there's one area that may be a dominant lump, your doctor may send you for a mammogram. If a lump looks jagged, not smooth, on the mammogram, it's a sign that further investigation may be called for. If you've got a lump your doctor thinks may be cancerous, a mammo-

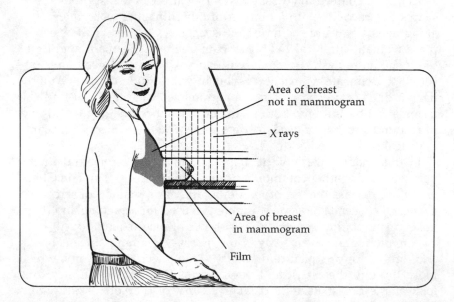

Area of breast
not in mammogram

X rays

Area of breast
in mammogram

Film

FIGURE 10-1

gram can help determine if there are other lumps that should be biopsied at the same time; it can also document the location of the lump.

Radiation Risks

When mammography first started, it was seen as the Great New Hope; in typical American fashion, it was hyped as the answer to all breast problems. All a woman had to do was get a mammogram every six months and she had nothing to worry about. Then, in 1976, Dr. John C. Bailar III[1] calculated that if young women in their 20s started having mammograms every six months, we'd cause more cancer than we'd cure. There were scary news stories, and mammograms were viewed as a major health hazard.

Predictably, the truth is somewhere in between. These days, mammography offers very little radiation risk. In recent years we've reduced the amount of radiation significantly. As we note in Chapter 15, the risk of getting cancer from exposure to radiation is greater when you're young, and decreases as you grow older. In terms of mammography, this works very well, since mammography is less useful in most young women, who tend to have much more dense breast tissue than fat, and it's increasingly useful as women age and breast tissue gives way to fat. Most specialists now feel that the radiation risk of mammography after age 35 is negligible or nonexistent.

What Mammograms Show

A mammogram, like any other X ray, is a two-dimensional picture of a three-dimensional structure in which dense areas appear as shadows. Breast tissue, for example, is very dense, and shows up white on the mammogram. Fat, which is not very dense at all, shows up gray. (See photographs on page 126).

As you'll recall from our discussion in Chapter 1, the breasts of young women in their teens and early 20s are usually made up mostly of breast tissue, and are very dense. As you grow older, the breast ages, much as your skin does, and as it ages, there's less breast tissue and more fat. When you're in your 30s and 40s, it's about half and half. (This varies with weight; if you're very heavy there'll be a lot more fat; if you're thinner, there'll be more breast tissue.) Once you're in menopause, the breast tissue goes away, and there are usually only a few strands of it left. However, women vary in the proportion of breast tissue remaining after menopause. If they take hormone replacement therapy (see Chapter 15) their tissue may remain as dense as it was, or may even become more dense.

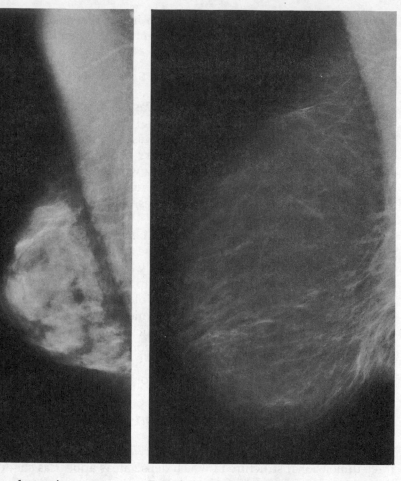

Dense breast in young woman   **Fatty breast in older woman**

How does this affect the reading of a mammogram? Cancer and benign lumps are the same density as breast tissue and both show up white. A lump in the middle of an area of dense tissue won't show up on the mammogram—the tissue will hide it. But if the same lump is sitting in the middle of fat, it'll be very obvious—a white spot in the midst of gray. So mammography is more useful in older women, who have more fat, than in younger women, who have more breast tissue. Sometimes I'll get a patient who's been for a mammogram and has been told that her breasts are so dense that mammography isn't useful to her. That's ridiculous—what it means is that mammography isn't as useful to her as it would be if she had fatty breasts. Often the woman

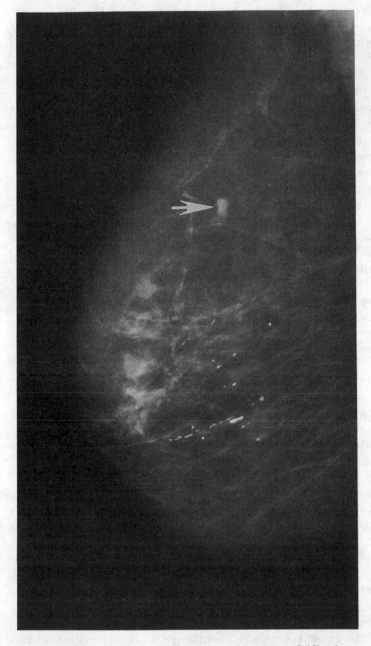

Small cancer in fatty breast (arrow) and benign calcifications

is around 30, when her breasts should be dense. What it really means is that there's a higher chance that something could be missed (9–20%), which still means an 80–90 percent chance of picking up something. I'm not recommending screening mammograms for women at 30; diagnostic mammograms may have some value if there is a breast problem that needs to be explored.

When mammograms show something round and smooth, it's likely to be a cyst or a fibroadenoma (see Chapter 9). Then, since the mammogram can't distinguish between cysts and fibroadenomas, you'd follow up with an ultrasound (see next chapter) to see if it's a cyst. If there are jagged, distinct, radiating strands, pulling inward, it's more likely to be cancer. But until it is biopsied, we can't tell for sure. Several benign conditions can mimic cancer on a mammogram. Scarring or fat necrosis will look very suspicious; as will a noncancerous entity called a radial scar. This lesion can be confusing even under the microscope and often requires a breast pathologist to be sure it is not cancer.

A mammogram may also show intramammary (in the breast) lymph nodes. In fact, until the invention of the mammogram, we didn't know there *were* lymph nodes in the breast. We now know that about 5.4 percent of women will have them.

Sometimes you'll hear about a "normal" mammogram. But there's really no one pattern you can call normal, since there's no real "normal" breast.

In mammography reports, some radiologists use words loosely—as if they can see what the pathology is when they're looking at the shadows on the mammogram. So they'll tell you you've got "cystic changes," which is a variation of our old nemesis, fibrocystic disease. All that means is that you've got dense breast tissue. Or they'll tell you you've got "mammary dysplasia," which sounds very serious and means you've got abnormal cells—cells en route to cancer. But you can't see the cells on the mammogram—only a biopsy can show cells. What they really mean is, once again, you've got dense tissue in your breasts. All a radiologist can tell you is how much breast tissue there is and how much fat tissue, and whether there are abnormal areas of density.

Twenty percent of women have some degree of variation in the size of their breasts, and that variation is reflected on the inside as well. It will appear on the report as "asymmetry," and it probably doesn't mean anything at all—though sometimes, rarely, an asymmetry can be caused by cancer, so you might want to get a second mammogram several months later, just to make sure. If it's cancer, it's likely to have changed somewhat during that time. One of the most absurd cases I've come across is one in which a patient who'd had a mastectomy on one side came to me and had a reconstruction done. The report on the mammogram said it showed "marked asymmetry." Of course it did!

The breasts were completely different in their composition; they were meant to look the same on the outside, not the inside.

Types of Mammograms

Mammography has changed over the years. In the beginning, in the 1950s, they used big X-ray machines—the same ones they used for chest or bone X rays. These produced only a fair amount of radiation, and the pictures weren't very clear. So they began refining the process, and designed an X-ray machine specifically geared to do mammograms, one that could be aimed more precisely at the breast, and could rotate to get most of the breast tissue. Over the years they've also refined the X-ray techniques, so that now very little radiation is actually used. It's commonly said that a mammogram exposes you to the same amount of radiation you'd get in a plane flying over Denver. One radiologist I used to work with in Boston explained it in more colorful terms: the amount of radiation of one mammogram is equal to the amount of radiation you would get by walking on the beach nude for 10 minutes or until you got caught.[2]

Several years ago, they developed a mammographic technique called the xerogram. It was a form of X-ray very different from the earlier mammogram, whose X-ray pictures came out looking like a negative of a photo. The xerogram's picture came out on blue and white paper, giving a very clear picture that was easier for the radiologist to read. It also used less radiation.

Now there's an even better technique—film-screen mammography. It goes back to negative-type pictures, but gives a much more precise definition of what the tissue looks like, and it uses even less radiation. Although there have been advances in the xerography technique, most radiologists agree that film screen is the best technique we have, with xerography a distant second.

Film-screen mammography is a bit more uncomfortable than xerography; the breasts have to be squeezed more between the plates to get an accurate picture. Sometimes patients will complain that the technologist isn't as good as the one who did their last mammogram, because this one is more uncomfortable. It may not be the technologist's fault—it's just a different method. And the slight discomfort is well worth the gain in accuracy and in lower radiation. A recent study tried letting women control the compression themselves. Not surprisingly, they ended up with the same amount of compression, equally good quality films, and fewer complaints.[3]

Newer techniques, called digital mammography, are being developed, which will show the tissue with even better resolution. What we try to do, with each of these types of mammogram, is get better and better resolution—a sharper picture. Digital mammography is a way of computerizing the image and then recreating it. Because it's a computer rather than a photograph technique, the radiologist can move things around to see what she or he wants to see. All the fat can be blocked out so only breast tissue shows up, or the breast tissue can be erased so that only fat shows up. People have great hopes that digital mammography will solve some of the limitations of mammograms. It may be more accurate in women with dense breasts, for example, since it could erase some of the breast tissue and make a lump more evident. (It still involves radiation, so will continue to have limited application in very young women.)

I think we've gotten almost as far as we can with mammography. Each advance is a small, incremental advance. The problem is that it's limited by the breast tissue. No matter how great the technique becomes, the body it's photographing is still the same.

Calcifications

One of the more important discoveries from the study of mammograms is that often cancer is associated with very fine specks of calcium that appear on the picture—they look a bit like tiny pieces of dust on a film.

We discovered that these microcalcifications, as we called them, were sometimes an indication of cancer, or of precancer (see Chapter 16). So the radiologist will always mention in a report any microcalcifications that show up. But it's nothing to panic about—80 percent of microcalcifications have nothing to do with cancer; they're probably just the result of normal wear and tear on your breast.[4] Ironically, when you age, calcium leaves your bones, where it's needed, and shows up in other places, where it's not. It can show up in arteries, causing them to harden, and in joints, causing arthritis. The microcalcifications in your breast won't cause problems if they're not indications of cancer or precancer. (The appearance of this calcium in your body has no relation to how much calcium you eat or drink, by the way.)

How can we tell which are the bad and which the harmless kinds of calcifications? We look at the shape, the size, and how many there are. If they're very tiny and tightly clustered, and there aren't a whole lot of them, they're more likely to be precancer. If they are all over the place they're more likely to be benign (see page 127).

Precancer occurs in the duct, which is very small. For the calcifications to fit in a duct, they have to be very tightly clustered and very small. The big chunks of calcium we see on the mammogram couldn't possibly fit in the ductal system, so we know they're benign. They're usually old fibroadenomas that you had as a teenager, which have faded and become soft and less dense and now are calcifying. Or they can be calcifications in a blood vessel as it gets older and harder.

There's a middle group of calcifications which are less easy to characterize. They may be new, but there are just one or two of them. In that situation, we'll usually repeat the mammogram in six months.[5] If it's precancer, we might see more calcifications, or a change in the shape or size, whereas if there's no change, it's more likely to be benign. Patients get nervous about that. If it's cancer and we wait six months, won't it grow and kill you? In fact, if we wait six months it's probably because we don't think it's cancer. And even in the worst-case scenario, it's precancer, not cancer, and precancer takes 10 years to develop into cancer. So six months won't make any difference, and you don't want to have needless biopsies.

It's true that some precancerous calcifications don't grow or change, so we don't pick them up on the second mammogram. But that's because they aren't growing and thus aren't becoming cancer.

Any time we're worried about calcifications we can, of course, proceed to a biopsy. This can be a core biopsy or an open biopsy, depending on the available facilities. (See Chapter 12).

Mammographic Workup

One thing that's very important in diagnostic mammography, as opposed to screening, is that something that appears abnormal to the radiologist needs to be evaluated. A good radiologist will do other X rays and maybe an ultrasound to try and figure out what is going on. A biopsy should be done only as a last step.

One of these extra X rays is a *compression spot view* — the technician presses on the breast tissue and takes a picture of a particular area. We do this when there is a density on the original mammogram that we're unsure of. A mammogram is a two-dimensional picture of a three-dimensional structure, so we are often looking at overlapping shadows. (It's like a transparent balloon with two different pictures on front and back. If you take a photo from the front, the two pictures look like one complex image. If you push down on the balloon squashing it somewhat or look at it from a different direction you will see them both.) Thus the technician either compresses the spot or takes a picture from a different angle so that things aren't perfectly superimposed.

If there is an abnormal density on a mammogram, or a lump that you can feel but isn't visible on a mammogram, you may be sent to get an ultrasound (see Chapter 11).

If you have a palpable lump, the mammographer should put a marker on your breast to be sure the lump is located on the film. If the lesion is at the periphery of the breast it may be necessary to take special mammographic views to get it in the picture—like changing the angle of your camera to make sure that Aunt Mabel's head doesn't get cut off in the photograph. This is especially important for lumps that are near the armpit or in the lower fold of the breast.

If you have calcifications, we very often do a *magnification view*, which is a mammogram that magnifies the area of the breast with the calcifications, so that we can see them and characterize them better. So, for the most part, if you're told that the calcifications on your mammogram are worrisome, make sure they do a magnified view to see if the calcifications still look bad and how many there are. Sometimes mammographers will want to skip this step and send you for a biopsy. Don't let them. Why subject yourself to surgery if it may not be necessary?

Some problems arise because many radiologists don't have much experience reading mammograms. (See Where to Get a Mammogram, below.) How familiar your radiologist is with the procedure may well be reflected in how well the X ray is read. A more experienced mammographer may be willing to state his or her opinion that something is almost certainly benign. A radiologist anxious about missing something will be more likely to say, "I don't think it's cancer, but it could be, and a biopsy is recommended to be absolutely sure." As a result of these kinds of readings, we're doing more operating than ever on benign lumps. In the next decade or so, as mammograms become more common and routine, we may be able to avoid some of this unnecessary surgery.

So it's very important if you're told you need a biopsy for an abnormal mammogram that you get a second opinion. Take your mammogram to another center—preferably a place that specializes in mammography—and have them review it. Studies show that 60 to 70 percent of biopsies done for abnormal mammograms could be avoided if the mammogram were reviewed by an expert.

A mammogram can't tell for certain what you have. To do that we need to have tissue we can look at under a microscope. But there are some situations in which the view from the mammogram shows signs that clearly suggest a diagnosis. It's a bit like seeing someone from the back—you don't know for sure that it's your friend Mary until she turns around and faces you, but if it's Mary's shade of red hair, in the kind of ponytail Mary always wears, and she walks like Mary does and carries the kind of large briefcase Mary likes to carry, you can make a pretty good guess that it's Mary. How often you are right will, of course, depend on how well you know Mary. An experienced mammographer is better able to diagnose breast problems than an inexperienced one.

A typical story these days is a patient in her early 60s who comes to the center after her first mammogram and tells me they found something strange. I look at the X rays and I see a little asymmetry, and send her back for a compression spot mammogram and the asymmetry completely disappears. Because the radiologist didn't take it the next step, the patient was scared needlessly.

In another frequent scenario, a woman tells me they found something strange on her mammogram. I look at the X rays and see a small and smooth lump, like a fibroadenoma, but it is new. The radiologist has written, "possible fibroadenoma; cancer can't be ruled out." I can do one of two things. I can have her wait six months and check it out again. If it's cancer, it probably will have grown. If she's really anxious, I can do a new form of minor surgery. This is much less invasive than an open biopsy. It's a kind of needle biopsy, called a stereotactic biopsy, done under X-ray control. There are two kinds: one is done with a fine needle, the other with a larger "core" needle. If it's not cancer, that's fine; if it is, we can plan for the cancer surgery. If the diagnosis can't be made this way, we can do a wire localization biopsy. (We'll discuss these forms of biopsy further in Chapter 12.)

Where to Get a Mammogram

While standards of quality in mammography have improved greatly, it is still worth your while to investigate and find the best place in your area to get a mammogram. Start by calling the American Cancer Society and asking for their recommendations (see Appendix E). Once you have a few names, you can begin calling the places on your list and asking them some questions. Since the newest equipment uses the least radiation, you want to be sure the place you go to uses dedicated (used only for mammography) modern equipment purchased within the last few years. Also, since taking and interpreting mammograms requires skill, you want to find the place that has a designated and certified mammography technologist. The technologist who does an occasional mammogram, along with foot and lung and kidney X rays, is less likely to do an excellent mammogram than the technician who does mammograms all day. The same applies to the radiologist reading the mammogram. You should ask if there is a radiologist who has had special training and experience and has been singled out as the local expert. Some parts of the country have breast centers, which are specialized and do no X rays but mammograms. There are even mobile vans now that go to workplaces to do mammograms. They're usually very good; generally they send the mammograms they've taken to a mammographer who does nothing but read mammograms.

Actually, since I wrote the earlier edition of this book, the quality of mammograms available has improved greatly. The mammographer I work with, Dr. Larry Bassett, director of the Iris Cantor Center for Breast Imaging, has been working to get national standards for mammography and mammogram reports. The technology of mammography grew up pretty quickly, so, until recently, a lot of people never got the training they needed. Now mammography technologists can get special courses in how to take mammograms. Radiologists too have special training. The equipment and film are checked. It's become probably the best monitored medical diagnostic tool we have, and it should be a model for the rest of medicine. Now you have the assurance that when you get a mammogram, it will be a good one.

Two bills have been passed by the U.S. Congress, due to the work of the activists in the women's cancer movement. One is the Medicare coverage of screening mammography in 1990 and the other is the Mammography Quality Standards Act of 1992. Both include mammography quality assurance provisions. As a result of the Medicare bill, on-site inspections of Medicare screening sites began in the fall of 1992, and the Mammography Quality Standards Act went into effect on October 14, 1994. All mammography units must be accredited. So there now are national standards not only for how the mammograms are taken, but for who takes them. Mammography now is one place where we really do have quality control—something we have little of in the rest of breast care, and indeed in much of medicine.

Procedure

How do you actually proceed to get a mammogram? To begin with, don't wear talcum powder or deodorant the day you're scheduled for a mammogram—flecks of talcum can show up as calcifications. Also, avoid lotions that can make the breast slippery. Some places tell you not to consume caffeine for two weeks before the X ray; unless you have a problem with caffeine, ignore them (see Chapter 6).

The atmosphere you face when you get there will vary from hospital to hospital—some are cold and clinical, others provide a warm ambience and reassuring, friendly personnel. But the actual procedure is pretty standard. You have to undress from the waist up, and you're usually given some kind of hospital gown. You'll probably be X rayed standing up. The technologist—usually, but not always, a woman—will have you lean over a metal plate, and help you place your breast on the plate. It can be cold and a bit uncomfortable, and when the plates press your breast together, it can be somewhat unpleasant. Two pictures of each breast are usually taken, one in a lateral position, the other vertical. But 20 percent of the time it will be necessary to take additional views, or do special magnification or spot pictures. This isn't a sign that you have cancer—it just means that the mammography technologists and radiologists are being painstakingly careful to get an accurate picture. In addition, the way the technologist takes the X rays is important. The tighter they can squeeze your breasts, the more accurate a picture they can get.

The process really isn't all that painful. Paul Stomper[6] did a multicenter study interviewing people right after their mammograms, asking how painful the process was, and what point they were at in their menstrual cycle. He was pleased that 88 percent of the women reported no pain or discomfort at all, and was surprised to learn that their cycle didn't seem to have any effect on their comfort level.

Sometimes women are surprised that a mammogram doesn't hurt. A patient of mine, an older woman, asked her gynecologist if she should have a mammogram—he told her not to because it would be too painful. Recently she decided to do it anyway. "It didn't hurt at all," she told me indignantly. "I shouldn't have listened to my doctor in the first place."

There's a small percentage of women whose breasts are unusually sensitive, and for them a mammogram can be painful. In Stomper's study none of the women who reported that the procedure was painful felt that it would stop them from having another mammogram exam. It's unfortunate that it's not painless, but I think it's well worth the slight—and brief—pain. At UCLA we timed the technologists and found that compression lasted at most 10 seconds. It's only uncomfortable for a few seconds. It doesn't leave bruises or tender spots when it's over.

The whole process lasts only a few minutes; when it's done, you have to wait for a while till the pictures are developed, so you might want to bring a good book or a Walkman along. The radiologist (an M.D., not the technologist) who looks at the pictures will sometimes see something on the periphery that isn't completely clear, and will want to take another picture, focusing on that area. Or they'll want a magnification view, which can magnify the breast in a certain area to show it more clearly. This latter is usually done when there are microcalcifications.

In some places, the radiologist will come out and tell you what the mammogram shows. This is nice because, even if you're there for just a screening mammography, it's still a reminder of the possibility of cancer and you are apt to be nervous. But some radiologists are uncomfortable talking to the patients, and some doctors feel a bit territorial about other doctors giving their patients information. So often you're just told to go home and wait for your doctor to call you in a couple of days. I find this unfortunate. If there are no problems, you're stuck with a few days of needless worry, and if there are problems, you're stuck with frustrating uncertainty. If you have your X ray at a high-volume low-cost center, the X rays aren't read right away, and you have to wait several days to a week to find out the results.

Don't ask your technologist to interpret the mammogram for you. Technologists aren't M.D.s: their job is taking the pictures, not reading them.

Although I am often quoted as having said that diagnostic mammography must have been invented by a man (and that there should be an equally fun test for them), it is the best tool we have. We have to be careful when we discuss the risks and benefits of screening (see Chapter 19) not to throw the baby out with the bath water. It's an imperfect tool but, particularly for women with complex breast problems, it's an important one.

11

Other Imaging Techniques

Frustration with some of the limitations of mammography has led to the exploration of other ways of looking at the breast. The reasons we're looking for other tests are that mammography uses radiation, which is potentially dangerous, and that it is limited in its ability to see through dense breast tissue and to determine clearly whether a lump is benign or malignant. Some of the techniques we've looked at are old techniques, and some are new. The amount of promise varies significantly with each technique.

Ultrasound

In the ultrasound method, high-frequency sound waves are sent off in little pulses, like radar, toward the breast.

A gel is put on the breast to make it slippery, and a small transducer is slid along the skin, sending waves through it. If something gets in the way of the waves, they bounce back again, and if nothing gets in the way, they pass through the breast. Ultrasound never picks out the small details, as an X ray can, but it can show other characteristics of a lump. Ultrasound is appealing because it doesn't use radiation. While there has been little study of the long-term effects of high-frequency sound waves, no problems have yet been shown.

This technique is used mostly for looking at a specific area; if we know a lump is there, we can use ultrasound to get more information about it. It can help us determine whether a lump is fluid-filled or solid—if it's fluid-filled, like a cyst, the sound waves go through it, and if it's solid, like a fibroadenoma, pseudolump, or cancerous lump, the sound waves will bounce back. So if a lump shows up on a mammogram that we can't feel in a physical examination, and we want to determine whether it's a cyst or a solid lump, ultrasound can give us the answer.

Ultrasound can also be quite useful in helping us interpret a mammogram. If the doctor feels a lump and the mammogram shows just dense breast tissue, the ultrasound can sometimes see if there's a lump within the dense breast tissue. Mammography will show only overlapping shadows, but ultrasound can sometimes distinguish differences in the density of the tissues causing the shadows. Remember the image of the transparent balloon in Chapter 10? Now imagine that the balloon has a few colored balls inside it. An ultrasound can distinguish the balls inside, which are different from the balloon itself. Ultrasound isn't perfect, but it adds another dimension to the imaging possible with mammography. Many cancer centers, therefore, if they see a lesion on mammogram, will also do an ultrasound.

Ultrasound, because there is no radiation involved, and, as far as we know, sound waves are harmless, is also often the best tool for studying benign problems at length, particularly in women under 35 who have denser breast tissues. So, if a doctor has a younger patient who has a lump and wants to determine if it's likely to be a fibroadenoma or just dense breast tissue, ultrasound in that area is often the technique of choice because it can show distinct lesions with edges or mixed areas with no definite lumps.

One of the down sides of ultrasound is its dependence not only on the technologist's skill in manipulating the transducer but also his or her ability to interpret the image. Ultrasound pictures, unlike mammography, are difficult to interpret later on because images are the result of the angle at which the transducer is held over the lesion, and this is clear only to the technologist doing the procedure.

Ultrasound might appear like the ideal test, with no radiation and the capacity to tell a cyst from solid tissue. Why then don't we just use ultrasound and forget about mammography? The problem is that we cannot ultrasound the whole breast accurately. The breast shows so many changes in contour and density that it becomes very difficult to differentiate normal breast tissue from a lesion. Its best use is in investigating one lump or area which has already been identified by physical exam or mammography.

We can also use ultrasound to guide needle biopsies and core biopsies (see Chapter 12) in much the same way we use mammograms.[1] Sometimes ultrasound is a more effective tool for guiding us into the lesion than mammography. We have the leeway to get around corners, since the technologist is holding the transducer and can move it around to the side and hard-to-reach areas of the breast. In mammography we are constrained by the breast having to remain compressed on the machine. Of course, we have to be able to see the lesion on ultrasound to use this technique. Microcalcifications or other lesions visible on a mammogram may not be identifiable on an ultrasound.

Ultrasound has also been used to look at women with silicone implants to decide whether or not the implant has ruptured or leaked. With a highly skilled technologist and radiologist, it's very accurate for that purpose.[2]

Just as digital mammography is attempting to make mammography clearer, there are many scientists working on improving the resolution of ultrasound. Three-dimensional ultrasound with even better resolution will be more useful in the diagnosis of breast problems, especially in young women with dense breasts.

MRI

Magnetic resonance imaging (MRI) takes advantage of the electromagnetic properties of the hydrogen nucleus. Hydrogen is part of water, and water is part of our bodies. MRI is a huge magnet. You get put in the middle of the magnet; the magnetic field is turned on and then turned off again. The way the magnetized cells return to normal gives an image. This test was initially used in the brain, and has been very accurate in diagnosing brain tumors. It's now been applied to the breast. It is definitely useful, but its most effective role in the diagnosis of breast lesions has not yet been determined. A recent study done in Texas[3] looked at 41 women who were about to have mastectomies for breast cancer. They did MRI's on them first. The MRI detected 85 lesions which were later evaluated by pathological examination. Of these, 64 lesions proved to be malignant. This shows that MRI is very good at finding lesions, but so far less useful in determining what they are. The study was announced at a press conference before it was announced to the medical community. The press touted MRI as the Great New Hope that would immediately replace mammography.

But it isn't quite as wonderful as that. A quarter of the lesions the MRI detected weren't cancer, and were completely irrelevant. This means that a lesion indicated by a positive MRI might be cancer or might be benign. We need further studies to define the best use of this technique before it is widely used.[4]

The MRI exam is done with the patient lying face down on a table with her breasts hanging down into the machine. To get good results the woman should have an injection of contrast material that is picked up by lesions and not by normal tissue. We do this by injecting a dye, gadolinium, intravenously before the study. The dye is absorbed better and faster by cancers than by benign lesions. Though this improves the accuracy of the MRI, it is not foolproof: it often lights up with a fibroadenoma, and it still misses some cancers.

Another problem with the current use of MRI is that as yet we have no way to localize the lesion that we do find. If there is an abnormality on mammogram which cannot be felt, it can be biopsied by a needle or by using a wire localization (see Chapter 12). With MRI we haven't yet figured out how to do this. We can't use the same techniques we use for mammography because this is a three-dimensional image instead of a two-dimensional one. Furthermore, the needles and wires, being made of metal, are attracted away from the breast by the huge magnet used in MRI. Researchers are working on ways to solve this problem. One patient came to me with a normal mammogram, normal ultrasound, and lesion on MRI. There was no way to biopsy it to see if it was a cancer or a fibroadenoma. She was left fearing she might have cancer, and we had no way to reassure her. This is the trouble with using a technique clinically before all of the research is done. If you want to have an MRI of your breast, make sure it's in a research setting and that there's a plan for dealing with any lesion that is found.

There are two uses of MRI that are more helpful. MRI can sometimes delineate with more accuracy than mammography, the extent of a cancer that has already been found.[5] And, as we said, it's also a good tool for discovering if a silicone implant has leaked.[6]

MRI is not going to replace mammography, at least at this stage. It's not as good a screening test—it's too expensive; it's too hard to do; and it's not yet accurate enough. Nonetheless, much research is going on to determine MRI's role in the detection and diagnosis of breast cancer. I predict we will see more of it in the future.

PET Scanning

Positron emission tomography (PET) is another technique that's gotten a lot of press. PET is a completely different way of imaging breast tissue. The others all create pictures; in PET scanning we look not at the structure itself, but at the activity going on in it. All tissues need glucose as fuel to survive. Cancers are rapidly growing and turning over, so they use more glucose than normal tissue. PET scanning looks at how much and how fast glucose is being used by a tissue. To do this scan we give the patient a radioactively labeled glucose molecule, which is taken up and metabolized by the tissue. The scanner can demonstrate how much and how fast. Like MRI, the tracer is injected intravenously prior to the scan.

The PET scanner was first developed to study the brain, and has been very useful. We can have the patient do a number of things that use different parts of the brain. If the patient talks, the scan lights up in the area of the brain that connects for talking; if he or she reads, it lights up another area. So it's very useful in mapping the brain and seeing where different problems lie.

PET scanning could be the answer to detecting virtually any cancer, since it can examine the whole body. Cancers are faster growing and use more glucose than normal tissues, so they should light up better than normal tissues. PET scans have been able to demonstrate areas of metastatic disease that cannot be seen by other imaging techniques. The major question is how small a lesion it can pick up—how sensitive it really is. If it can demonstrate only the lesions we already know about through other techniques, it is not particularly useful. But if it can pick up micrometastatic disease it could be very helpful.

In the breast, it does not show the exact area involved very clearly and therefore is not good for finding a cancer and helping us know where to biopsy. Like MRI, we are still in the process of determining its usefulness. It may have a role in distinguishing benign lesions from malignant ones based on how much glucose they use. It may also be useful in detecting cancerous lymph nodes in the armpits prior to surgery.[7] This would be particularly helpful; women with normal scans could avoid lymph node surgery.

Another thing we're looking at is whether PET scanning can be used to monitor how well a tumor is responding to chemotherapy. If we give a person chemotherapy and then follow up with a scan to see if there's less glucose utilization than there was before the treatment, we might be able to tell if the chemotherapy is slowing the tumor growth.

MIBI Scan

An MIBI scan (Sesta MIBI scan) is another nuclear medicine imaging technique. MIBI stands for 2-Methoxy IsoButyl Isonitral. It can be useful in determining the difference between benign lumps and cancer.

Gallium, a radioactive particle, is injected intravenously, and a scanner, much like a bone scan machine, takes a picture and shows whether the gallium is taken up by the breast lump more than the rest of the tissue. Since cancer is likely to pick up more gallium it will often light up. Sesta MIBI scans may prove useful in determining the difference between benign lumps and cancer. It's only been tested in very limited studies, and it's too soon to know how well it will work.[8]

It's not particularly good for screening, because you need an injection of radioactive material, and also because it doesn't localize things very well. It's very fuzzy and far less distinct than a mammogram.

CT Scanning

Another type of test, CT (computed tomography) scanning, also uses radiation—far more than mammography does. It works by visually cutting a part of the body into cross-sectional slices. It's very good for detecting brain tumors and cancer in the belly and the lungs, because of the composition of those organs. But the amount of radiation needed to make slices close enough to pick up a 5-millimeter lump in the breast is simply too high for safety, and you're wiser to stick with mammograms.

Thermography

Thermography is based on the concept that cancer gives off more heat than normal tissue. It was originally a much-heralded technique, since it doesn't involve putting radiation, or anything else into the body. A sensor is put on the breast and heat coming from different parts of the breast is measured. From this a map is constructed, making beautiful colored pictures in which blue shows cold areas and red shows hot areas. The hot areas are supposed to be the cancerous ones. Unfortunately, this technique hasn't proved accurate—there are too many false positives and false negatives. Not all cancers give off heat, and of those that do, some are too deep, or are located under wedges of fat, and the heat doesn't register on the device.

Thermography doesn't detect cancer; still, some doctors in Europe believe it can define the aggressiveness of a cancer they know exists: the more aggressive a cancer is, the more heat it gives off. This hasn't been substantiated, and thermography hasn't been used in the United States for this purpose.

Transillumination and Diaphanography

Transillumination is a very old technique used long before mammography appeared on the scene. Its purpose was to help determine whether a lump was a cyst or solid. It functioned like a flashlight; if the light shone through the lump, the lump was assumed to be a cyst, and if it didn't, the lump was solid and potentially dangerous. The technique became more sophisticated, and equipment was developed to monitor the exact amount of light in transmission. It's called diaphanography. Since it doesn't use radiation, there was great hope that diaphanography would replace mammography, but it hasn't proven to be a great screening test. I know some practitioners who have found it useful in conjunction with mammography.

All of these techniques are attempts to find ways to diagnose breast lesions other than mammography, because what we really need is a diagnostic test that does not involve radiation and that can determine the difference between dense breast tissue and benign lumps and cancer. We don't have that yet, which is why there's this long list of potential candidates. At the moment there are a lot of nominees, but no winner—none of them will revolutionize the diagnosis of breast diseases. So far, they can't replace mammography, but may have a role in diagnosis.

Researchers are also exploring whether or not there are diagnostic tests that are different from imaging, like a blood test that could determine whether or not a lesion is malignant. Possibly we can come up with a way to analyze nipple duct fluid and find a factor in it that would predict a problem. All that is being explored vigorously, but the answer isn't here yet.

12

Biopsy

When the doctor tells you you'll need a biopsy, you'll want to find out what kind. There are four different kinds of biopsies—two done with needles, and two "open" biopsies that require surgical cutting (Fig. 12-1). A fine needle (like the kind used to draw blood) biopsy takes only a few cells out of the lump; a larger needle biopsy, called a "tru-cut," or core, cuts a small piece out of the lump. An incisional biopsy takes a much larger piece of the lump out, while in an excisional biopsy the entire lump is removed (Fig. 12-2).

If you aren't clear about what kind of biopsy the surgeon is planning, ask. Otherwise you may discover that whereas you assumed only a little piece would be removed, the surgeon really meant to remove the whole thing. Then you'll end up angry (and the surgeon will end up defensive) because you were told you were getting a "biopsy" but what you got was an "operation." The term *biopsy* refers to the operation itself, not the process of studying the lump in the laboratory, which the pathologist does later. Anything cut out of the body is always sent to the pathologist for analysis. The connection between the two procedures is confusing to some people. If you're having a biopsy, you need to know the precise meaning of the term.

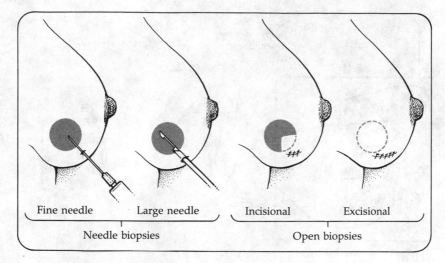

FIGURE 12-1

Fine needle Large needle Incisional Excisional

Needle biopsies Open biopsies

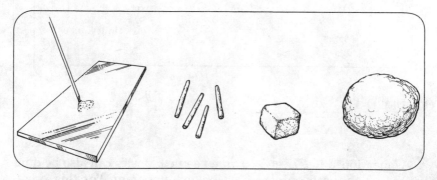

FIGURE 12-2

Fine Needle and Stereotactic Biopsy

In a fine needle biopsy of a *palpable* lump (a lump that can be felt), the surgeon anesthetizes the breast with a small amount of lidocaine and then uses a needle and syringe to try to get a few cells (Fig. 12-3). The material can be squirted onto a slide, which is examined under a microscope. This often shows whether something is benign or cancerous.[1] However, since there's no tissue to look at, just the individual cells, the procedure requires a good cytologist—a specialist in the field of looking at cells rather than tissue—who can look at cells out of context.

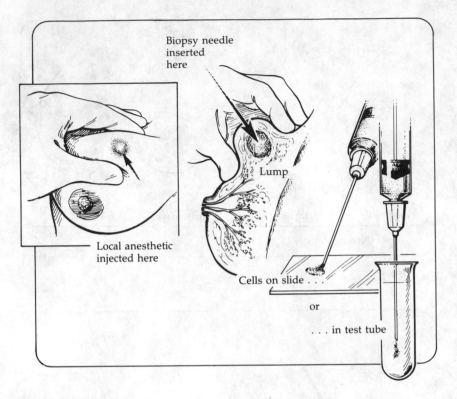

FIGURE 12-3

As mentioned in Chapter 10, fine needle biopsies can also be done on lesions that can only be seen on mammogram. For this procedure, we use a machine called the stereotactic biopsy machine. The patient usually lies face down on a table with her breasts hanging down (Fig. 12-4). Mammograms are taken, and a computer calculates exactly where the lesion is. Then a device holding a needle (similar to the puncher that's used to pierce ears) quickly shoots in and removes a few cells from the lesion. Often several passes are taken to make sure the lesion is well sampled. Here too a cytologist is needed.

Three elements should be consistent to determine if a lesion is benign.[2] If on examination I think that it's a fibroadenoma, and it looks like one on the mammogram, and it also looks like one under the microscope after a needle aspiration, then I feel certain that's what it is. But if one of those elements is different—if it seems like it's not a fibroadenoma to me, even though the mammogram and needle aspiration suggest it is; or if I think it is but either the mammogram or the needle aspiration biopsy suggest something different, then we go on to a larger biopsy.

Tru-cut or Core Biopsy

A tru-cut, or core, biopsy is done in much the same way as a fine needle biopsy. The major difference is that we use a larger needle. We give the woman some lidocaine to numb the area, then make a small nick in the skin with a scalpel so that the biopsy needle can enter. We put the biopsy needle into the lump and remove a core of tissue. Then we close the nick in the skin with a single stitch. The patient feels mild pressure when the core is taken, but otherwise no real pain. The advantage of a tru-cut over a fine needle biopsy is that a piece of tissue is removed, rather than just cells. This is easier for a pathologist to read. On the other hand, the lesion is not as well sampled. When a fine needle biopsy is done, several passes are made through the lesion in different directions to ensure that all of it is sampled. The core biopsy removes a core from the center of the lesion, in the hope that it is representative. There are pros and cons with both procedures, but most surgeons have a bias toward one or the other. The best policy is

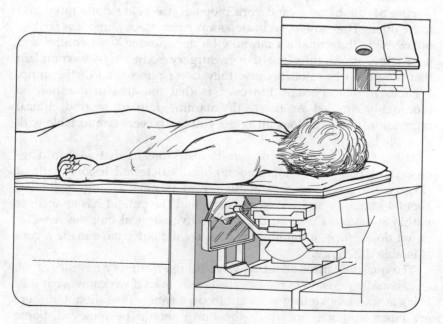

FIGURE 12-4

to follow your surgeon's advice in this and use the technique with which he or she has the most experience.

In mammographic lesions we can also do a core biopsy. This is often useful if there are calcifications (see Chapter 10). The cores that have been removed can be X-rayed so we can be sure that some calcifications have actually been sampled.

Core biopsies are particularly good in areas of the country where good cytology is unavailable. Because it drills out a core of tissue rather than just cells, we no longer need a cytologist to look at it. A general pathologist can do that, and see the cells in the context of the surrounding tissue.

For this procedure, the patient lies down on the table with her breast suspended below her between two X-ray plates, just as she does with the stereotactic fine needle biopsy (Fig. 12-4). A nick is made in the skin for the biopsy needle. After exactly localizing the area, the biopsy device enters the breast at 72 mph and drills a core of tissue. Usually we take out four to five cores. After the biopsy we can actually take an X ray of the breast and see the line of air in the middle of the lump and know that we've taken out what we were going after. (The inventor of these things was clearly a man: they were first called "biopsy guns." Only a man would think of aiming a gun at women's breasts! In my UCLA breast center, I've gotten them to use the less militaristic term "biopsy device.")

Fine needle biopsies and core biopsies are being done more and more often. They are as accurate as an open biopsy, and are far less invasive.[3] Both techniques can now be done under X-ray control and have largely taken the place of open surgery. Some surgeons complain that they can't be good because they don't remove all of the lump. What is most important, however, is that the area in question be thoroughly sampled. As long as the mammogram, ultrasound, clinical impression, and pathology all agree, you can be very comfortable with a needle biopsy.[4]

Using these fine needle or core biopsies means that we can diagnose most palpable or mammographically detected lesions without surgery. The procedure costs about a third as much as surgery; it takes about 45 minutes and leaves no scars, and the patient has an answer within 36 hours. I used to do four or five surgical biopsies a week; now I do a couple a month. The new technologies have made a considerable difference.

The question arises about why we do open-surgery biopsies at all. Occasionally we want to remove the lesion, even if we know what it is. If it's a cancer, obviously we want to do a cancer operation, but there are other situations in which the lump should be removed. Some women want fibroadenomas removed, even though they know they're harmless: a lump in your breast can be very unnerving. Sometimes the fine needle or core biopsy doesn't give completely clear information, and we need to do an open biopsy to see what's going on.

Surgical Biopsy

What is the process of an incisional or excisional biopsy like? Well, to begin with, there's the setting. You may have your biopsy performed in your doctor's office or, more frequently, in the hospital's "minor" operating room. If you had a biopsy several years ago, you might find this confusing—especially the minor operating room. In the past, most surgery was performed in what we now call the main operating room, and the surgical rituals may be very different from those you recall.

Most hospitals have two or three kinds of operating rooms. I like to think of them as types of restaurants in which the food is basically the same, but different varieties are served in different places and the rituals accompanying them are different.

In the hospital where I work there are three kinds of rooms. The minor operating room is like the snack bar—you can go in barefoot and wearing your bathing suit, and order your hamburger, and it's cheap and it tastes good. The ambulatory surgery room is more like the coffee shop; you have to wear shoes and be fully dressed, but it's okay to wear jeans, and you sit at a table and are waited on. There's a larger menu, which still includes your hamburger. And finally there's the main operating room, which is like the formal dining room—you've got to be a bit dressed up, and there's a fancier menu, and the waiter grinds pepper onto your salad. Again, you can still get your hamburger, though it will cost you more. In each place, the hamburger's the same, but the rituals around it are different.

Similarly, you can have your biopsy in any of the three operating rooms, though the ambulatory and main rooms are equipped with a larger "menu" that includes more complex operations as well. The difference is in the ritual. And the rituals are always defined by the room they're performed in, not by the particular operation.

There's nothing wrong with the rituals—every profession has its rituals, and they're very useful to us. But if you don't know what the rituals are, or even that they *are* rituals, they can be intimidating.

Most of the surgical rituals are holdovers from the turn of the century, when they served a very practical purpose. Earlier, little was known about germs and the danger of spreading them through unsanitary practices. So doctors would go straight from the morgues, where they were doing autopsies, into the operating rooms where, without washing their hands or changing their clothing, they performed

surgery—and then wondered why so many of their patients were dying on them. Then I. P. Semmelweis, a Hungarian obstetrician, figured out in the late 1840s that washing hands between autopsies and operations would save patients' lives—it was quite a revolutionary discovery.

So the majority of the rituals began then—the frequent handwashing, the surgical gowns and masks, etc.—but nowadays, when people shower every day and wash their hands a lot and we have antibiotics to combat infections, the extreme degree of attention to completely sterile cleanliness is less necessary, and, as I said, partially ritualistic. Predictably, the fancier the operating room, the fancier its attendant ritual.

Much of the breast surgery today is done in either outpatient, freestanding ambulatory clinics or in the minor operating room. It's much cheaper than the same surgery performed in the main operating room. In the latter, you're paying for all that specialized equipment used for complicated procedures like open-heart surgery. Neither patients nor their insurance companies want that, so more and more, the "snack bar" facilities are being used. (The ambulatory room is a bit more sophisticated than the minor operating room, but far less so than the main.) Often the ambulatory and minor operating rooms are used interchangeably. Keep in mind, however, that all this varies from hospital to hospital, and region to region.

So, if you had a biopsy 10 years ago in the "formal dining room," you may be expecting all the formal ritual, and be disturbed at its

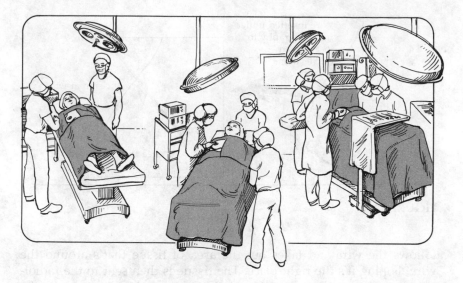

absence. Don't be. The operation and the care you're receiving are the same, and they are what matter.

If a patient has other medical problems—a heart or a respiratory condition, for example—then it's probably wiser to perform the operation in the main operating room, in case complications arise that need more sophisticated equipment. If you're concerned about complications and how they'll be handled, talk with your doctor beforehand about which room will be used and what you're likely to need.

So much for the setting—now let's get to the procedure itself.

WIRE LOCALIZATION BIOPSIES

One form of surgery we might use, if your lesion isn't a palpable lump and a needle biopsy is not possible, is a wire localization biopsy. As you might imagine, it's difficult to biopsy something you can only see on an X ray. In this procedure we use a thin wire to show the surgeon where the lesion is. It's usually done in the X-ray department. The radiologist will give you a local anesthetic, put a small needle into the breast under X-ray guidance, pointing toward the lesion. He or she will then pass a wire with a hook on the end through the needle, and then position the hook so the end of the wire is where the calcifications or density is. The wire is left in the breast and you're taken to the operating room. The biopsy procedure is similar to the procedure used to take a lump out, except we use the wire to direct where we'll remove the tissue (Fig. 12-5). You may be given a sedative as well as more local anesthetic before the surgeon makes an incision. He or she

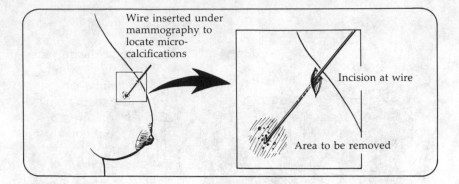

FIGURE 12-5

follows the wire and takes out the area of tissue that's around the wire, hoping it's the right place. The tissue is then sent to the radiology department. There they X-ray it to make sure it's the area with the calcifications or lesion, and then it's sent to the pathology department for further study. There they make slides and look at it under the microscope. Meanwhile the surgeon sews you up.

This last X ray will tell you if the surgeon got the calcifications or area that was seen on the mammogram. It won't, however, tell you if the surgeon got all the calcifications in your entire breast. If the area is benign this won't matter, but you will want to know that there are still some benign calcifications inside. So it's important that you get another mammogram three to six months later to show how you look after the surgery. The surgeon can't see or feel calcifications, so it's possible to miss them with the surgery. In this case the specimen mammogram will not show calcifications and you may need to have another biopsy.

Whether it's a wire localization or a regular biopsy, the procedure can be done under either local or general anesthetic. Most doctors and patients prefer the former. Some doctors like to give their patients a tranquilizer, but I prefer to help them stay calm through reassuring conversation. Whereas tranquilizers require the patient's pulse, oxygenation, and blood pressure be monitored during the operation, I want to be able to focus my attention on the operation itself. In every case it is important to use a device called a pulse oximeter—this fits over your finger (like the pulse monitors used by fitness enthusiasts) and monitors your pulse and how much oxygen there is in your blood—as a safeguard whenever sedation is used. In some cases "local/standby" is used, that is, the operation is done under local anesthesia but an anesthesiologist or nurse-anesthetist is standing by, ready to give some mild drugs, if necessary, which will make the patient indifferent to the procedure. The anesthesiologist can put the patient to sleep if general anesthesia becomes necessary.

Recently drugs have been developed that are very fast acting and don't last long. They put you into a kind of twilight sleep, in which you don't care about what happens and won't remember it, even though you're not completely unconscious. These are often used in conjunction with local anesthetic. This is known as monitored anesthesia, or MAC. If MAC is used, we need to do all the preoperative preparation just as we do for general anesthesia. When local anesthesia alone is used, you arrive, have your procedure, and go home. So it's a trade-off between being relatively more comfortable with a longer procedure and having more discomfort but getting in and out more quickly. MAC is definitely a cafeteria, not a snack-bar procedure. Which people choose depends very much on their own personalities. Some people just don't want to know what's going on, and they're willing to put up with the extra inconvenience. Others who hate being out of control would rather know. Discuss with your doctor which way makes more sense for you. Some drugs allow the patient to be awake and talking but to have no memory of the experience afterward. If a woman wants to have the full experience of surgery she needs to tell the anesthesiologist or anesthetist so that drugs, such as Versed, for example, are not given to her. Dr. Corey Anderson, an anesthesiologist I work with at UCLA, recommends the patient make a list of questions to discuss with the anesthesiologist so that the stress of the moment doesn't distract her.

If the biopsy takes place in the minor operating room or the doctor's office, the patient usually just has to change from the waist up; in the main operating room, where the dress code is more formal, the patient has to change into a hospital johnny and the surgeon wears a scrub suit.

Often in a biopsy, the surgeon uses a machine called an electrocautery to seal off the small blood vessels and prevent bleeding. Since there's a small risk of a short circuit, which would give the patient an electric shock, a grounding pad is put on the leg, back, or abdomen to ground the current and prevent electric shock. It's a plastic pad with a cool gel inside that will initially feel freezing cold.

Next, the surgeon will wash her or his hands and put on surgical gloves, and then paint you with an antiseptic solution. Usually this is done two or three times—no particular reason, but three is a nice ritualistic number, so why not? Then sterilized towels (paper or cloth, depending on which operating room you're in) are framed around the area that's going to be operated on (Fig. 12-6).

Then, with a sterile felt-tipped pen, the surgeon marks the spot over the lump, and injects, through a small needle, the local anesthetic. (We

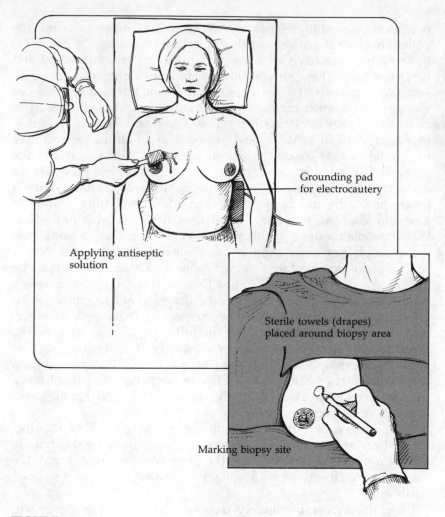

Grounding pad
for electrocautery

Applying antiseptic
solution

Sterile towels (drapes)
placed around biopsy area

Marking biopsy site

FIGURE 12-6

usually use lidocaine, not novocaine, these days, but "novocaine" is still the popular term—like calling any facial tissue "Kleenex.") When the needle first goes in, there's a little pain and a little burning. The slower the anesthetic goes in, the less pain there is, so it's worth taking the time to do it slowly.

But don't be misled by the "novocaine"—it's not the anesthetic you get at the dentist's. For one thing, it hurts a lot less. The dentist has to poke around your mouth looking for a nerve, and then deaden it, and you have to wait till the novocaine takes effect, and then your whole mouth goes out and you end up chewing the inside of your cheek. It's not the dentist's fault; dental work requires a nerve block, since drilling into a tooth is felt all through the jaw.

But the process in the biopsy is different. We're cutting only into soft tissue, so we can use "local infiltration," which numbs only the area where it's put, not the whole breast. And it works immediately. (This confuses some patients, who get scared when the surgeon starts to work right after injecting the anesthetic.) It's possible that you will feel some pain, even with the local anesthetic we give you for the biopsy. Some people are especially sensitive to pain. This is not a bad thing; you are not being weak. Everyone's pain sensitivity is different. It can change, depending on a number of factors that include medications you may be taking, stress, and your experience with pain.

I usually test the anesthetic right after I inject it, by pinching the skin with small tweezers. This assures both the patient and me that the area is really numb. Then I point out to her that it's only the area we're operating on that's numb, and she'll feel me touching her in other parts of the breast.

I also point out that *I* won't feel any pain, so she has to tell me if something hurts. Occasionally the surgeon unknowingly wanders outside the anesthetized area. Never feel embarrassed to yell if it hurts—there's plenty of anesthetic, and we can always give you more, at any time during the operation. Don't try to be "polite," or be a "good girl." There's no reason for you to suffer.

Now the surgeon makes the incision, going through skin, fat, and tissue to get to the lump. Most of the process isn't actually cutting; it's just spreading tissue apart till the lump is reached. There's little bleeding, because there aren't many blood vessels here, and the cautery takes care of the few there are. The lump or sample (in an incisional biopsy) is cut away from the surrounding tissue and removed (Fig. 12-7).

The incision is then sewn up, usually in layers—tissue, then fat, then skin. This prevents a dent from forming in the breast when it heals. Most surgeons use dissolvable stitches that tend to leave less scarring.

Sometimes you'll feel some pressure when the surgeon is pulling the lump out and clamping it before cutting it out. This is painless, but unpleasant-feeling. Occasionally patients feel a sharp, stinging pain when the surgeon is tying off the blood vessels—there are nerves in the lining of the blood vessels, and sometimes the surgeon can't avoid them. If this happens, tell the surgeon, who can immediately anesthetize the spot.

By the way, you don't have to keep perfectly still—it's not that kind of an operation. Obviously you can't be jiggling around all over the place, but you can wiggle your toe or bend your knees or your fingers,

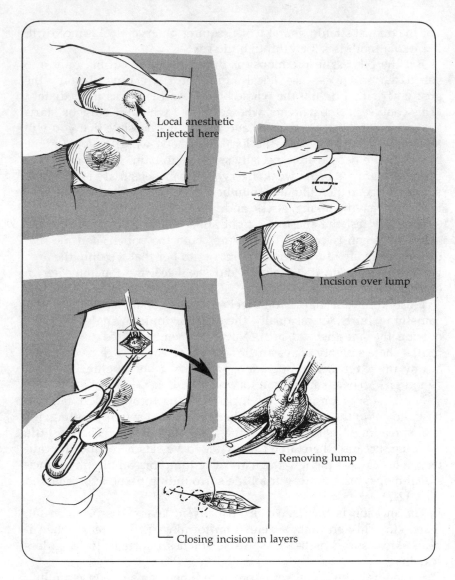

Local anesthetic
injected here

Incision over lump

Removing lump

Closing incision in layers

FIGURE 12-7

and it's a good idea to let your body move a bit. Sometimes a patient is so nervous she lies there perfectly rigid throughout the whole operation; afterward her breast feels fine but her muscles are killing her.

I like to play music while I operate, to entertain both the patient and myself. If we like different kinds of music I give the patient my Walkman so I can play what I like and give her what she likes. It's a good idea to pick something soft and soothing that you like, but that isn't your favorite music—you don't want to ruin your future enjoyment by associating your favorite songs with surgery. One of my patients chose Vivaldi, and now says that every time she hears Vivaldi her breast hurts!

Some surgeons get distracted if their patients talk to them while they're operating, but I don't mind it at all—a pleasant chat can make it a more comfortable experience for both of us.

Many surgeons drape their patients in such a way that the patient can't see the surgeon; I find that alienating and impractical. Often when patients are in pain they don't consider intense enough to bother the doctor with, they won't complain, but will wince or grimace, and if I see that I can ask if they'd like more anesthetic.

After the surgery, what happens? Well, the surgeon, who has bandaged the incision, will probably tell you when you can take the bandage off and when you can shower. I usually have the patient remove the bandage the next day and shower as soon as she wants to. We used to think you shouldn't shower until the stitches came out, but we've found that water doesn't hurt stitches at all. The more you bounce, the sorer you'll be, so whether or not you usually wear a bra it's a good idea to wear one for a couple of days after the surgery—a good, firm, sensible bra, not a pretty, lacy, flimsy one. You'll probably want to keep it on all night as well. On the other hand, some women find the bra so uncomfortable in bed that they prefer the soreness. If the incision is near the bra line, the bra may cause more discomfort than it's worth. Use your own judgment; the point is that you be as comfortable as possible.

The anesthetic wears off much more quickly than the dentist's does. Just as it goes to work right away, it wears off right away, generally within an hour after the biopsy is finished. You're usually not in much pain after the operation—many patients find that Tylenol is all they need. Do not, however, take aspirin or any non-steroidal pain medication such as Motrin, Nuprin, or Aleve; they increase the chance of bleeding or bruising after the operation. By the next day, you can usually go back to work and resume your normal activities. (Be sensible, of course; if your normal activities include weight lifting, give it another couple of days.)

Usually there won't be a lot of scarring, but there will be some so you should talk with your surgeon about it before you have the procedure done. You and your surgeon may have different ideas about what makes an acceptable scar. For example, surgeons often learn in training that the most cosmetic scar results if they make the incision right around the areola, and then tunnel up to the lesion, so that the scar is camouflaged by the color change between the areola and the rest of the breast. If that's done well, it can indeed give you a very cosmetic scar. Sometimes, however, depending on the length of the scar or the amount of tissue that's removed, it can decrease the sexual sensation in your nipple, or create other changes in your nipple and areola such as numbness or puckering. And the scarring might cause difficulties in breast feeding. Further, the tunneling increases the chance that you'll have bleeding complications and a hematoma (see later in this chapter). You need to discuss clearly with your surgeon whether having a pretty scar is worth those consequences. An alternative, and one that I personally favor, is to make the incision directly over the lesion. It's usually a smaller incision that way, and there's less chance of damaging the nipple.

Most surgeons are sensitive to their patients' concerns and will try to give them the incision that most suits their needs. If you feel your surgeon is being flippant or not taking your concerns seriously, find another. At the same time, be aware that some people have bodies that make big keloid (thick) scars, and the best surgeon in the world can't prevent that. If you're one of these people, you probably know it, although there's always the chance that, if you've never had a major cut before, you won't know till after the surgery.

With wire localization biopsies, it's important to know how much tissue the surgeon plans to remove. Some surgeons make their incision where the wire enters the skin, and will take out the tissue surrounding the whole length of the wire. This procedure usually creates more deformity than if the surgeon were to make the incision over where the end of the wire is—going in directly and taking out the lesion. With the increasing use of the core biopsy and the stereotactic needle aspiration, we're able to obtain more information before the surgery, so we don't have to remove as much tissue. Find out exactly how much tissue the surgeon plans to remove, and ask questions if it seems to you that it is too much.

While you're resting up from the operation and getting on with your life, the lump, having been immediately sent to the pathologist by the surgeon, is analyzed by the pathologist. Sometimes he or she does a "frozen section," which is a quick but crude method of testing the lump. The lump is cut in half; a piece is quickly frozen to make it solid, then thinly sliced, placed on a slide, and stained right away. Sometimes this will give you the answer, but it's not 100 percent accurate. In the old days, when we were doing immediate mastectomies if the lump was found to be malignant, this was the method always used—to allow the surgeon to proceed with the operation immediately. Nowadays, however, we usually do it in two steps—the biopsy is performed and the results are discussed with the patient, then, if further surgery is called for, it's done later. So we don't often do a frozen section anymore.

Far more reliable is the regular procedure, the "permanent section."

Here the tissue is removed and cut into small pieces. It goes through several stages: first it's dehydrated by being put in different strengths of alcohol, then fixed in paraffin wax, so the piece of tissue is imbedded in a block of paraffin. This is then put on a microtome, a knife that cuts it into very thin slices. Each slice is then put on a slide, the wax melted away, and the tissue stained with different colors. The whole process takes about 24 to 36 hours.

When the slides are ready, the pathologist looks at them and makes a diagnosis; this will probably take another day. The pathologist then dictates a report, which is sent to the doctor, probably within a week. Some doctors wait till the report comes in, but others prefer to call the pathologist the day after the operation. This is what I do, because I like to let my patient know what's happening as soon as possible, and because for all patients the waiting and uncertainty can be terrifying. But whatever your doctor's practice, you'll know in a week or so what the biopsy has shown.

Like any surgical procedure there are sometimes complications in a breast biopsy. The two most common are *hematoma* (a blood blister) and infection. If a hematoma occurs, it will be within a day or two of the procedure. It's caused by bleeding inside the area where the surgery was done (see Fig. 12-8). There will be a lump and some bruising under the skin. The body usually absorbs the blood and recycles it, as it does with any bruise, but sometimes, before the body can do that, you'll bump into something, or someone will bump into you, and it bursts open, causing black blood to come out. It looks gross and you think you're dying but don't worry—you're not. It's old blood; you're not bleeding now. What you need to do is

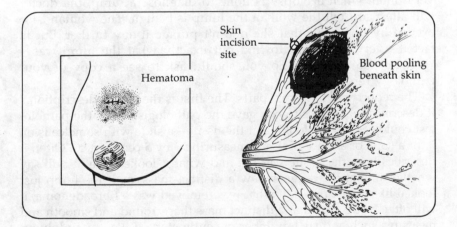

Skin incision site

Blood pooling beneath skin

Hematoma

FIGURE 12-8

go home, clean up the mess, and take a shower. If you're worried about it, call your doctor.

If an infection occurs, it will show up a week or two after surgery—there'll be redness and swelling and fever, and the doctor will treat it as infections are usually treated, with antibiotics. Again, it's more of a nuisance than anything else. Sometimes, you'll get a combination of infection and hematoma—the blood mixes with pus, like an abscess or a boil, and needs to be drained by the doctor.

Sometimes, when stitches are removed after breast surgery—either a biopsy or a cosmetic procedure—a small, non-dissolvable stitch is overlooked and remains in the breast, which then gets infected, as was the case with one of my patients (no, I wasn't the surgeon who removed the stitches!). It's easy to treat with antibiotics and removal of the stitch.

And, yes, the worst patient nightmares do occasionally occur—I had one patient who had a persistent infection following a biopsy, and when they finally operated on her they discovered that her surgeon had left a sponge inside her. I'm not quite sure how a surgeon could manage to do that, but this one did. Fortunately, it's very, very rare—and my patient is fine now.

These complications are pretty infrequent—all together they occur only in about 10 percent of breast biopsies. Even though they're unpleasant and inconvenient they're not life-threatening and they don't have any long-term effects.

How to Read Your Biopsy Report

Very often, when a biopsy is done to diagnose a lump, the doctor will afterward tell the woman the lump is benign. The woman is so excited by this news that she doesn't pursue it any further. But in fact it's very important to find out exactly what the lump was—"benign" isn't enough. So you should ask to see a copy of your pathology report.

The report will have two parts. The first is the "gross description." It describes what the surgeon gave the pathologist, what the pathologist could see just by looking at the tissue—a slide with some cells on it, or a core, or a piece of tissue measuring 3 by 5 centimeters. Often it describes how the tissue was cut and what it looked like. It will say whether or not the surgeon saw a distinct mass, or if the lump just looked like breast tissue. If what was removed was a fibroadenoma, it will often be described as a distinct mass that's round and smooth and measures such and such number of centimeters. If it's a pseudolump and it's just breast tissue, it may be described as a piece of fibro-fatty tissue that contains no obvious lesions. If it's microcalcifications, the pathologist won't see them, so they won't be described.

The second part of the pathologist's report describes what the lump looks like under the microscope. Some give a detailed description—what the cells look like, what the surrounding tissue is like, and so forth. Others just cut to the chase and give the final diagnosis. So it might read, "1. fibroadenoma." It almost always adds, "2. fibrocystic disease" or "fibrocystic change." That's because, as we said in Chapter 6, the "fibrocystic change" is the background that we see normally in breast tissue, so it's always there. The report may say "fibrocystic change" alone if it's just breast tissue. That's not an adequate diagnosis. If your report says that, ask for more specifics, even if it means making the pathologist go back and look at the slides again and describe exactly what's there. Under the rubric of "fibrocystic disease" there is one entity that does increase your risk of subsequent breast cancer: atypical hyperplasia. You will want to know if that's what you have. (Atypical hyperplasia, mentioned at the beginning of Chapter 6 on fibrocystic disease, will be discussed in Chapter 16.) Usually if it says fibrocystic disease (or change) alone, you don't have atypical hyperplasia, because today most pathologists are aware of its importance and are likely to mention it if it's there. But they might not. I wouldn't risk assuming they have and doing nothing.

Often you'll have hyperplasia that isn't atypical—extra cells in the lining of the duct that are normal. So if it says "hyperplasia of the usual kind," that's fine.

In addition, if you had a biopsy done for calcifications you want to be sure the pathologist saw them under the microscope so you know they're looking at the right tissue. Sometimes, if you have a very small area of calcifications and a big piece of tissue is taken out, when they make the slides they don't get the area where the calcifications are. They then look at the tissue and say "totally benign." That's happened to me: I took out calcifications and the report came back benign. I asked if they'd seen the calcifications and they said no, but they'd put all the tissue through. I said, "You need to see the calcifications." So they took the blocks of paraffin, X-rayed them, found which ones had the calcifications, and made additional slides. Then they found the calcifications, and indeed there was precancer, which they would have missed. It's important to make sure the pathologists look at what they are supposed to look at. You might think it's your doctor's job to take care of all that, and you're right. But you can't assume that this has been done, and you need to double check.

Get a copy of the report and save it. It may be relevant at some later time, and it's important for you to have it in your records. One of the things we're starting to realize is that some of the changes in the basic molecular biology of the breast tissue (see Chapter 13) can be identified in earlier biopsy tissue. For example, suppose you have a family history of breast cancer and you have a biopsy for what turns out to be a fibroadenoma. In the past we thought that was all you needed to know. But, as we discussed in Chapter 9, we've recently discovered that one kind of fibroadenoma can, when you have a family history of breast cancer, markedly increase your risk. It is important for you to be able to have the pathologist go back and look at the slides and determine what kind of fibroadenoma you actually had. Probably they won't keep the tissue, but if you at least keep a record of your biopsy, with the date and the name of the hospital, you can go back and find the slides. That can be very important.

In fact, however, you may be able to have them keep some of the tissue itself. You can ask your doctor if there's a possibility of saving extra tissue from the biopsy in a tissue bank. As we do more and more research on benign and malignant breast problems there's an enormous need to have tissue to test. Some of that needs to be saved fresh, and some can be saved in paraffin blocks. It's to your advantage to have the tissue saved because, as new discoveries come along, we can go back and test them out on this tissue. One of the things we're trying to do on a political level is create a regional network of tissue banks so that everybody will be able to have some tissue saved when they have surgery (see Chapter 14).

If you had a biopsy because of a lesion seen on a mammogram, it is important to have a new baseline mammogram done a month or two after the procedure. If the doctor doesn't suggest it, you should. Sometimes, even when we take out calcifications, we don't get all of them. If it's benign, that doesn't matter; but it's good to have it documented so that a year from now if you have a mammogram it won't seem like there are new calcifications.

Similarly, if you have something taken out, your breast is going to look different: there will be scarring. A year later that might look like something new and alarming, unless there's a baseline mammogram fairly soon after the surgery to compare it to.

PART FOUR

THE CAUSES OF BREAST CANCER

13

Genes and
Environment

Until about 1940, it was widely believed that cancer was an inevitable consequence of aging. Somehow the process of living included the inevitable creation of cancer cells at some significant frequency, and they were bound to get you eventually in one form or another, unless something else got you first, like an infectious disease (this was before the discovery of antibiotics). The idea was that, since cells constantly divide, DNA (*deoxyribonuclease*, the acid in the nucleus of cells that transfers genetic characteristics) has to replicate, and this replication will inevitably include some mutations. Eventually one of these mutations would be a cancer. ("Mutation" is one of those words that science fiction has made sound very sinister, but many mutations are in reality perfectly harmless.)

The theory wasn't completely crazy—cells do mutate and cancer is created by lots of different kinds of cell mutations. But there are diverse causes for cell mutations, some external and some internal and many not inevitable.

For example, rates of cancer are different in different geographical areas, in different societies, and in different occupations. This suggests that there are external, or environmental, factors that contribute to cancer, such as chemicals called carcinogens and radiation. At the same time there are differences in cancer rates in different ethnic groups. Therefore there must also be internal factors explaining why not everyone who is exposed to the same environment gets cancer. So cancer is caused by a combination of something in a person's physical makeup and something in the environment.

It's becoming more and more clear that all cancers have a strong genetic basis. That doesn't mean they're necessarily hereditary; it means they're caused by something going on in the genes. The genes regulate cell growth. But just as cancer rates vary in different external environments, genetic changes in the cells vary in different internal environments (organs, tissues, etc). The whole process is interactive both in a cellular and in a societal sense.

Basically a tumor is caused by normal cell division and growth that run amok, so you have cells that are dividing constantly, without the normal controls. Normal cell division is a good, necessary process. It causes hair to grow, skin to recreate itself, and a dozen other important, healthy things. It happens in a nice, orderly fashion—just as much as is needed. Sometimes something occurs that forces cells to reproduce more—like an injury or an operation, in which the healing process requires more cell division than usual. A message goes out via certain "messengers"—for example, growth factors and *cytokines*—that there's an emergency and they've got to mobilize the forces and get the cell division speeded up until the injury is healed. When the message is received by the cells, certain growth factor receptors signal internal enzymes that tell the cells to divide more, multiply more, and clean up the mess. Then when it's cleaned up, the message gets sent that the job is done. The growth factors can turn off, and stay turned off till the next time they're called on. Sometimes they do their job a little too enthusiastically, and don't turn off quite as quickly as they should, causing small problems. For example, a keloid scar—those thick, raised scars some people are prone to—is caused by growth factors that haven't stopped in time; benign fatty tumors under the skin are an overgrowth of fat; and some age spots in the skin are an overgrowth of a spot of skin. But even in these situations, growth eventually stops.

And that's the key. Healthy or reparative cell growth, whether it goes at its normal pace or escalates for an emergency, is controlled. In addition, every cell has planned obsolescence: it is programmed to die at a certain point. This planned cell death is called *apoptosis*. In cancer, this growth is generally unregulated and cell death is delayed or reduced. As a result a cancer grows and grows. In addition to growing uncontrollably, cancer cells develop the ability to spread from their site of origin to distant sites in the body. This process is called *metastasis* and is the main reason cancers cause illness and ultimately death.

As colonies of cancer cells grow throughout the body they become parasites, using up all the nutrition, the glucose, and oxygen the body needs to keep going. That's among the reasons why people with end-stage cancer start to lose weight and look so drained—all their nutrition is going to the cancer cells. Depending on what organs the cells are in, they soon interfere with some vital structure or function, and end up killing the person.

The key to understanding cancer, then, is figuring out the genetic controls to cell growth, invasion, and metastasis. What makes cells grow? What makes them stop growing? What blocks their programmed death? What makes them invade and metastasize? How does the environment in which the cell finds itself affect its growth? All that is programmed in the genes.

Most cellular genes are found in the nucleus of the cell in structures called *chromosomes*. Normal cells have a total of 46 chromosomes but cancer cells usually have many more and occasionally fewer. The 46 chromosomes consist of 23 pairs, and you inherit half of the pair from each parent. Those chromosomes contain your genetic code.

From either of your parents, you can inherit a flawed gene that makes you susceptible to cancer. If that happens, the flawed gene will show up in every cell in your body. Even if you inherit flawless genes from your parents a gene can subsequently mutate if you become exposed to an environmental carcinogen (Fig. 13-1). For example, smoking can injure some of the cells in the lining of the lung and damage the DNA, leading eventually to lung cancer.

But it's still more complicated than that. Not everyone with an

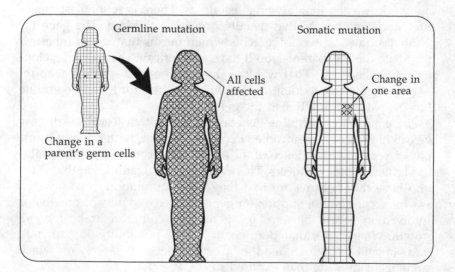

FIGURE 13-1

167

inherited damaged gene will get the cancer that the gene predisposes them to, and not everyone who acquires a damaged gene will get the cancer that gene can cause. The reason for this is that for human cancers the cooperation of multiple genes is required so that mutations in only a few genes alone will not cause cancer. For example, we all know people with a strong family history of cancer who escape the cancer themselves, just as we all know people who smoke a pack of cigarettes every day for years and live to be 90.

Different kinds of gene damage expose you to different levels of risk. Partly this has to do with whether or not the gene affected is a dominant gene or a recessive one. We have two copies of every gene in our cells, each coming from one of our parents. If a dominant gene is affected, only one copy of the pair has to be mutated; if a recessive gene is affected both copies have to be mutated in order for cancer to be set in motion. Genes that cause cancer when mutated, called *oncogenes. Tumor suppressor genes* are brakes which when mutated, can also cause cancer. Most human cancers are caused by mutations in dominant and recessive genes that are present in the *somatic cells* of our body, the cells that make up all of our tissues. Only a handful of human cancers are the result of genes that are inherited: genes that are present in our *germ cells*, either sperm in our testes or eggs in our ovaries. Therefore, the tendency to develop most human cancers is not passed on from generation to generation. But there are a few situations where an inherited mutation or set of mutations predisposing to cancer is passed on from parents to sons and daughters.

To understand how a dominant germline mutation and a somatic one work, we can look at some examples. There is retinoblastoma, a rare cancer of the eye that usually occurs in children. The gene for retinoblastoma is a recessive gene, which means that if you inherit it from both of your parents you'll have a significant chance of developing retinoblastoma.[1] That was the first cancer-predisposing gene researchers were able to identify, enabling us to test for it and determine that the patient actually had the gene.

There are other germline genetic mutations that lead to a disease we call Li-Fraumeni syndrome.[2] People in families with this syndrome have a very high incidence of all kinds of cancers—sarcomas, childhood cancers, breast cancers. There are about 100 families in the world who have this. It turns out that they have a mutation in p53, which was the second tumor suppressor gene isolated and may be one that is involved in breast cancer. This gene is a common brake for cell growth. When it is mutated a person has the possibility of getting all kinds of cancers. Which one they develop depends largely on which carcinogens they are then exposed to.

Another germline defect that contributes to cancer risk is the *ataxia-*

telangiectasia (AT) gene.[3] Ataxia-telangiectasia is a rare, recessive disease in which there is progressive brain deterioration and spots on the eyes and skin. Since it is recessive, both copies of the gene have to be affected to get the disease. The people who have one copy but not the other don't get the disease, but they do have an increased risk of getting cancers, including breast cancers. This increased risk is poorly understood. One possible explanation is that women with only one copy of the gene are very sensitive to the effects of radiation, including the exposure in routine X rays such as mammograms. This means that there's a danger that a lot of mammography in women who have a single copy of the AT gene may actually increase their vulnerability to breast cancer. (Unfortunately, we have no way to identify them.)

In most cancers, and undoubtably in breast cancer, many more mutations are involved in developing the disease. Every cancer has its own unique set of mutations, but some mutations, such as p53, are seen in common in many different cancers. Still, no one given mutation in one given gene is common to all human cancers.

In addition to mutations, some cancer-causing genes can increase in number above the normal two copies per cell. This phenomenon is called *gene amplification*. Oncogene amplification is best illustrated by the *Her 2 neu gene*.[4] This gene is a member of the *epidermal growth factor receptor* family of cell receptors, that is to say, receptors that make cells grow. It's been found that in about one third of breast cancers there are more than two copies of the Her 2 neu gene. It's as if you put something into the Xerox machine to make two copies, but the machine goes crazy and spits out 40 copies. The oncogene is thus amplified. It produces much more growth factor receptor than you normally produce. As a result, the cancer cells may grow in a more uncontrolled manner from the greater growth stimulus of the increased growth factor receptors. Her 2 neu is amplified in only one third of breast cancers; in two thirds it is not, and the controls for cell growth in these women await discovery.

There is a lot of work still necessary, but we're much closer than we used to be. In the first edition of this book I didn't include a chapter on the causes of breast cancer since we didn't have enough knowledge even to begin making good guesses. Now at least we have some idea about how all this fits together. That's because in the past few years there has been an enormous amount of research in molecular biology and molecular genetics, and we've come a lot closer than we ever were. One recent advance that illustrates the accomplishments of basic molecular research in breast cancer is the discovery and mapping and cloning of the BRCA1 gene, a possible tumor suppressor gene that is inherited and that predisposes women to early-onset breast and ovarian cancer.[5]

The history of its discovery is interesting. Researchers looked at large families with a high incidence of breast or ovarian cancer and studied three generations of each family. Thus they knew which family members had ovarian cancer, breast cancer, or no cancer. They constructed family trees and then obtained blood from everybody. They obtained the DNA from the lymphocytes (a type of white blood cells) and, using a battery of genetic markers, were able to map the disease gene by doing so-called *linkage analysis* (Fig. 13-2). Genes located next to one another on a given chromosome are usually inherited together. So that by intensive screening and some luck they were able to find a marker located close to the disease gene. By using modern molecular techniques, the researchers could locate and sequence the actual gene and determine the mutation it contained.

Using a molecular probe of the gene, we will soon be able to create a blood test that allows us to tell a woman with a strong family history of breast cancer whether she has or doesn't have this gene. This will be a big step forward, but it will cover only the 4 or 5 percent of women with strong family histories of breast or ovarian cancer. There are probably other germline mutations, leading to breast cancer in other families, that await identification. Even though most breast cancers arise sporadically and are not inherited, similar mutations may exist. Unfortunately, since the BRCA1 gene isn't the only one that contributes to breast cancer, the blood test will be of only limited use. We can tell women with the gene that they're at high risk for breast

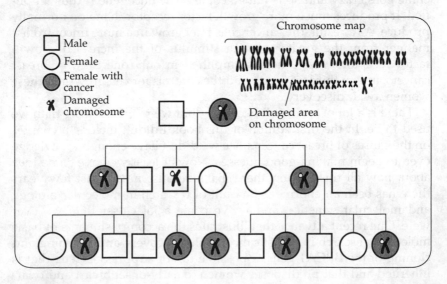

FIGURE 13-2

cancer, but we can't tell the women without it that they're at low risk. Even with these limitations, we're left with a lot of hope for the future. It's not likely that there will be thousands of dangerous genes—it's more likely that it will be a handful. So we've made a promising start.

We're still not wholly certain about what makes the genes that cause cancer mutate in the first place. What is it in the woman's environment or in her life that does the damage? Is it hormones? If so, is it her own or the ones she takes? Or is it pesticides or a virus or radiation or who knows what which makes the genes mutate? If we could figure that out, and block the key factor, it wouldn't matter quite as much which genes are mutating. A good example is lung cancer. We know that smoking triggers the disease, so it must cause the mutations. Thus, it's less crucial to find out what the mutations are, because we don't have to try and alter the genes; we can just tell people to stay away from cigarette smoke and that will dramatically reduce the incidence of lung cancer. So, in terms of breast cancer, we're studying things like diet, alcohol consumption, hormone medications, pesticides in the environment, and electromagnetic waves to find the carcinogens (see Chapter 15).

There is another question we need to examine in our study of gene mutation: whether these mutations have to happen in a certain sequence or whether they can happen randomly. A lot of the risk factors, as we'll discuss in the next chapter, seem to be most important around puberty or earlier—having radiation in puberty causes breast cancer 20 years later. This delayed problem may happen because, even though that radiation sets up one mutation that isn't enough by itself to give you cancer, it will do so in combination with others. Over the years, further mutations occur.

So both the environmentalists and the basic scientists are right, at least to an extent. You can't simply say, "Pesticides are the cause of cancer." Alone, they aren't. Many people are exposed to pesticides and never get cancer. But on the other hand, you can't simply say, "All cancers are genetic, so pesticides are irrelevant." It is the interaction between genes and the environment that explains cancer in the end (Fig. 13-3).

I have been working on yet a third scenario—or rather, a third line of inquiry to follow. That is the cell environment interaction. We know that there is "cross talk" between the cells and the *stroma* (the surrounding supporting tissue in which cells are suspended) (Fig. 13-4). As the cells grow they make certain proteins—growth factors, cytokines, enzymes—that are messengers telling the surrounding cells what to do. The surrounding cells then respond to these messages with messages of their own. This cross talk is called *epigenetic interaction*. It results in change in gene expression rather than mutations in

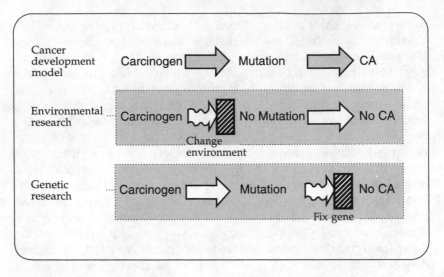

FIGURE 13-3

the genes themselves. Epigenetic interaction is probably an important determinant of cancer cell growth and metastases, and hence potentially amenable to therapeutic intervention. For an analogy, let us say there is a certain plant that can be pollinated only if there is a particular kind of bee in the environment that will take some of the pollen on its body to another plant. The original flower secretes a message, in the form of a smell, which attracts the bee. The bee then responds by cross-pollinating the plant. If you could block the scent of the flower, that species might well die out. Or you could change the environment so that it is inhospitable for the bee but not the flower. This also would eliminate the species. We don't want to eliminate any species of flower, of course; but we would love to be able to eliminate species of cancer cells by blocking this type of interaction.

In summary, we now believe that cancer is probably caused by a combination of genes that are mutated by carcinogens and then find themselves in an environment conducive to growth and spread.

How does this play out in breast cancer? On the practical level, it seems that you first have uncontrolled growth in cells strictly confined to the ductal or lobular units of the breast (so-called precancerous lesion of the breast, see Chapter 16). Then, possibly with additional mutations or epigenetic changes, these cells develop the ability to break out of the duct or lobule into the fat and the tissue around it. It may be only one cell that breaks out, but once it does it starts dividing and multiplying, and soon you've got an invasive tumor.

While it's growing, it needs nourishment. So it sends out protein

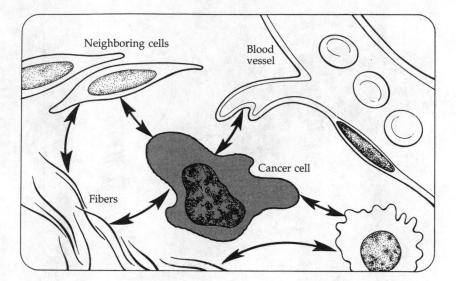

FIGURE 13-4

messengers called *tumor angiogenesis factors.* These proteins cause new blood vessels to form and bring nourishment to the growing tumor. It's survival of the fittest: the cells that develop the capability to send these messages are the ones that make it, and all the other ones die.

If all these steps take place, you've got a tumor sitting in the breast tissue. It has made a new blood supply and is doing fine. And then come further changes that give the cell the ability to break through its wall and into a blood vessel. It does that, and then maybe just dies out. Or maybe it survives in the bloodstream and is killed by the immune system. Eventually it may acquire other changes that allow it to elude the immune system. The cells circulate throughout the body and attach and grow in different organs. They don't go into just any organ, however. There may be factors in the lining of the blood vessel in certain organs that attract the cells, like the scent of the flower. (Breast cancer, as we discuss in Chapter 31, is typically attracted to the lungs, liver, and bones.) Once the cancer cell attaches to the blood vessel in an organ (say, the lung) and passes through the vessel into the organ, it has to be able to again set up a new blood supply and make the lung more conducive to its growth. It has to send out new messages to the surrounding lung tissue and get the growth factors it needs. Finally, the breast cancer is triumphant: it has successfully metastasized to the lung (Fig. 13-5). In time it will take up all of the space needed by the person to breathe. Eventually the burden of cancer becomes too much and the person dies.

173

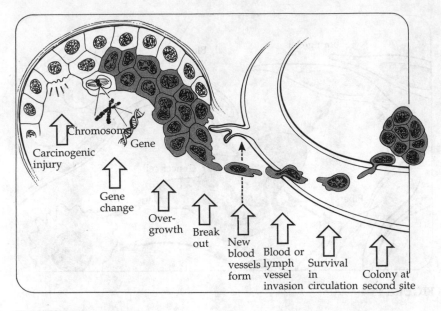

FIGURE 13-5

So it actually isn't that easy for cancer to spread and kill someone. There are a whole lot of steps it must take, and the steps may take a relatively long time. What that means is, if you're lucky, and although your cancer is growing in your breast, it may take a long time for it successfully to establish a growing metastatic colony.

Even when early metastasis has occurred it doesn't necessarily spell doom. Some of these steps may well be reversible. If the cancer cells are sitting in the lung but the lung tissue cannot supply the needed growth factors, they may become dormant for a while (maybe years), waiting for just the right circumstances to arise in order to resume their growth (Fig. 13-6). This would explain why some women have a recurrence of breast cancer many years after the first diagnosis. Those cells were there from the beginning but were dormant until the right conditions induced them to grow again.

Although we can examine and diagnose breast cancer and determine some of the biomarkers that correlate well with its behavior in the patient, we still cannot determine many of its biological properties. As a surgeon, I can't look at your lump and say, this is a lump that has mutated three times and it's gotten as far as the bloodstream but it hasn't hit another organ yet. We don't know what the precise mutations or messages are.

What's exciting about breast cancer research now is that we're on the verge of figuring this out. We've got the tools of molecular biology

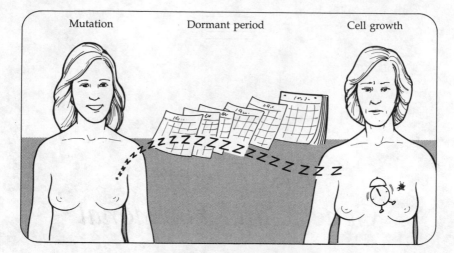

FIGURE 13-6

to help us find some of these mutations and to identify some of the messengers. Once we've done that, our current means of treating this disease—radiation and chemotherapy and surgery—will be obsolete. Those kinds of treatments aren't subtle—they blast you, because the cancer is advanced or advancing, and it needs the blast. As we come to understand the subtleties of cancer and its molecular mechanisms, we won't need all that any more. We will be able to treat the cancer by directly correcting the gene mutation or blocking its effect.

We currently treat breast cancer as if it were a hardened criminal leading a relentless life of crime. The only way to stop the villain is with the death penalty (slash, burn, or poison). However, as we've said, the cancer cell, like many criminals, is in constant contact with its environment. If we can change the environment, we may be able to rehabilitate the evil cell and make it less dangerous. At the moment this sounds like a fantasy, but we have the potential to make it a reality in the not too distant future.

14

===

Risk Factors:
Genetic and Hormonal

Every woman wants to know what her risk of getting breast cancer is and what she can do about it. Before discussing the figures, however, we need to be clear about their derivation, since they're often used in confusing and misleading ways. For example, an advertisement calling milk "99 percent fat-free" might suggest that it has 1 percent as much fat as whole milk. What is meant, however, is that 1 percent of the milk is made up of fat. Since only 3.6 percent of whole milk is fat, whole milk could be called "96.4 percent fat-free." Whereas this is still a substantial difference, what it means is that whole milk has three and one half times as much fat as 1 percent fat milk—not 99 times as much. Likewise, when the media headlines say that three drinks a week increase breast cancer risk by 50 percent they don't mean you have an additional 50-percent chance of getting breast cancer. A 50-percent increase in a lifetime risk of 3.3 percent is about 5 percent. Thus, it is important that we examine the common statistics used in breast cancer and review exactly what they mean.

Understanding Risk

There are three kinds of risk commonly referred to in discussing breast cancer: absolute risk, relative risk, and attributable risk (Fig. 14-1).

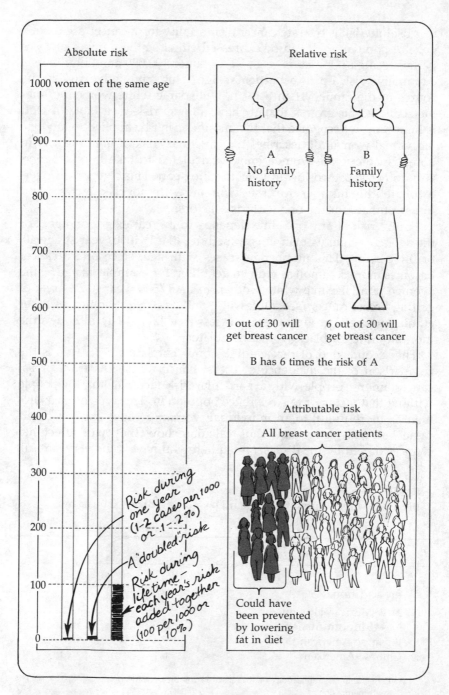

FIGURE 14-1

Absolute risk is the rate cancer or mortality from cancer occurs in a general population. It can be expressed either as the number of cases per a specified population (e.g., 50 cases per 100,000 annually) or as a cumulative risk up to a particular age. This cumulative risk is the source of the familiar 1 in 8 for non-Hispanic white women. (Other racial and ethnic groups actually have a lower risk—see Table 14-1). It is important to recognize that this number can't be applied to any one individual woman. It describes the "average" risk of breast cancer in non-Hispanic white women and is calculated to take into consideration other causes of death over the life span. This figure will over-estimate the number for the woman with no risk factors and underestimate for the one with risk factors.

Future risk at any one time depends to a great extent on age. For the average white woman, it is something like 1/1000/year at age 40, or 0.1 percent. This number increases with age, since breast cancer becomes more common as women get older: for example, at age 50 the average non-Hispanic white woman has a 1/500/year (0.2%) risk of getting breast cancer (see Tables 14-2 and 14-3). For women of other ethnic and racial groups, the risk is less (see Table 14-1), although the mortality rate for black women is greater.

The second kind of risk we talk about is relative risk. This is the comparison of the incidence of breast cancer or deaths from breast cancer among people with a particular risk factor to that of people without that factor, or to a reference population. This type of measure-ment is more useful to an individual woman because she can deter-mine her risk factors and thus calculate how they will affect her chances of getting the disease. Even here you have to be very careful.

Table 14-1. Probability of a Woman Developing Breast Cancer by Age 75[a]

Ethnic/Racial Group	%	No.
White	8.2	1 in 12
Black	7.0	1 in 14
New-Mexican Hispanic	4.8	1 in 21
New-Mexican American Indian	2.5	1 in 40
Japanese-American	5.4	1 in 19
Chinese-American	6.1	1 in 16

[a]J.W. Berg, "Clinical Implications of Risk Factors for Breast Cancer," *Cancer* 53 (1984): 589. Reprinted with permission.

Note table calculates risk to age 75 (1 in 12) rather than the familiar 1 in 8 calculated to age 85.

Table 14-2. The Average Risk of Developing Breast Cancer in a Given
Year in White Women[a]

Age	Risk Per Year
30	1 in 5,900
35	1 in 2,300
40	1 in 1,200
50	1 in 590
60	1 in 420
70	1 in 330
80	1 in 290

[a]Adapted from P.C. Stomper, R.S. Gelman, J.E. Meyer, and G.S. Gross, "New England
Mammography Survey 1988: Public Misconceptions of Breast Cancer Incidence," *Breast Disease*,
May 1990.

Table 14-3. Probability of Developing Breast Cancer for the Population
of White Women[a]

Age Interval	Risk of Developing Breast Cancer	Risk of Dying of Breast Cancer
Birth to 110	10.2%	3.60%
20–30	0.04	0.00
35–45	0.88	0.14
50–60	1.95	0.33
65–75	3.17	0.43

[a]H. Seidman et al., *CA: A Cancer Journal for Clinicians* 35 (1985): 36–56. Reprinted with permission.

For comparison, you can't use the 1 in 8, or 12 percent, generated in
the absolute risk equation (see above) because that is based on all
women regardless of their risk. Rather, you need a number that will
reflect the risk of a woman without the factor being considered. For a
woman with no clear risk factors at all (no previous cancers, no family
history, menarche after 11, menopause before 52, first pregnancy before 30), this is 1/30, or 3.3 percent, significantly lower than the average of 12 percent.[1]

If you call the risk of the woman without a particular risk factor 1.0,
you can report the risk of those with a particular risk factor in relation
to this. This is how relative risk is derived. A woman whose mother

had breast cancer in both breasts before the age of 40, for example, has a relative risk of 2.7 over her lifetime—that is, 2.7 times that of the woman with no family history— not, as it might appear, 2.7 times the 12 percent we mentioned above.

How any increase in relative risk will affect your absolute risk is also dependent on your age at the time. For example, a threefold relative risk (compared to the general population) at a young age will increase your absolute lifetime risk to about 20 percent, while by age 50, the woman with the threefold increased relative risk has a lifetime risk of about 14 percent. (She has used up some of her risk by making it through to 50 unscathed.) One third of the breast cancers occur before age 50 and so her risk is only 2/3. She has about a 4.5-percent chance of developing breast cancer over the next 10 years and about 10.5 percent in the next 20 years, compared with the average risks of 1.5 percent and 3.5 percent, respectively.[2]

When you read about a study or hear one reported on the media, it is important to check the basis for the relative risk numbers. Most authors compare women with a specific risk factor to women without it. They assume that all the other risk factors are equal in both groups, so that only their risk in terms of the risk factor of interest is being compared. It's like the fat in the milk: the numbers can be very misleading if you don't take the time to put them in context.

Finally, we must consider the attributable risk. This concept relates more to public policy. It looks at the amount of disease in the population that could be prevented by alteration of risk factors. For example, a risk factor could convey a very large relative risk but be restricted to a few individuals, so changing it would only benefit a few individuals. Dr. Anthony B. Miller[3] has hypothesized that if every woman in the world were to have a baby before 25, 17 percent of the world's breast cancer would be eliminated. If you were looking at this from a public health policy perspective, you'd have to weigh the possible advantages of pushing early pregnancy against the problems of young and possibly immature parents, and increased population growth. Miller also estimated other possible attributable risk formulas. He thought postmenopausal estrogen caused 8 percent of breast cancer, and total fat in diet 26–27 percent (see Chapter 15). This is interesting, because the largest factor here is fat intake, and that's changeable. Nevertheless, 75 percent of breast cancers would not be affected by decreasing dietary fat.

Defining Risk Factors

But what do we mean by risk factors and how are they determined? "Risk factors" is a term referring to identifiable factors that make

Table 14-4. Family History and Risk of Breast Cancer[a]

	Relative Risk
First-degree relative with breast cancer (mother, sister, daughter)	2.3
premenopausal	2.7
postmenopausal	2.5
mother	2.1
sister	2.1
mother and sister	13.6
Second-degree relative (aunt, grandmother)	1.5
First- and second-degree relative	2.2

[a]Adapted from R.W. Sattin, G.L. Rubin, L.A. Webster, et al., "Family History and the Risk of Breast Cancer," *Journal of the American Medical Association* 253 (1985): 1908.

Table 14-5. Reproductive Factors and the Risk of Breast Cancer

	Relative Risk
Menstrual History	
Age at first period < 12	1.3
Age at menopause > 55 with > 40 menstruating years	2.0
Pregnancy[a]	
First child before age 20	0.8
First child between ages 21 and 29	1.3
First child after age 30	1.4
Nulliparous (no pregnancies)	1.6

[a]Adapted from W.D. Dupont and D.L. Page, "Breast Cancer Risk Associated with Proliferative Disease, Age at First Birth, and a Family History of Breast Cancer," *American Journal of Epidemiology* 125 (1987): 769.

some people more susceptible than others to a particular disease: for example, smoking is a risk factor in lung cancer, and high cholesterol is a risk factor in heart disease. Medical researchers attempt to define risk factors in order to discover who is most likely to get a particular disease, and also to get clues as to the disease's cause and thus to the possible prevention and/or cure. (See Tables 14-4 and 14-5.)

A risk factor is usually determined by taking a large population of people—say, 20,000–30,000 or more—and identifying a variety of features about them, determining who gets the disease under study, and then seeing what the relationship is between the disease and the features that commonly occur within the group.

You have to be careful how you use your findings. If you determine that out of your 20,000 people under study, 5,000 got the disease and all 5,000 drank milk as infants, you can't decide from this that milk-drinking causes cancer. If none of the other 15,000 drank milk as infants, you might be on the right track; if, as is more likely, all 15,000 did drink milk, you've learned nothing except that most people drink milk as children. (This is the kind of flaw that led researchers to decide that "fibrocystic disease" causes cancer. See Chapter 6.)

Sometimes, as in the case of lung cancer and smoking, risk factors are dramatic, and can make a clear difference in the individual's likelihood of getting the disease. Unfortunately, it usually doesn't work that way. In breast cancer, we have come up with some risk factors—such as family history—which we'll look at in this chapter. But so far, there is nothing comparable to the connections found between cholesterol and heart disease or between smoking and lung cancer. With breast cancer, the sad reality is that we can't say, as with lung cancer, "You're fairly safe because you're not in this particular population." In fact, 70 percent of breast cancer patients have none of the classical risk factors in their background.[4] It's important to understand this for two reasons. Overestimating the importance of risk factors can cause needless mental anguish if you have one of the risk factors in your background. On the other hand, you may create a false sense of security if you don't have them. I can't count the number of times patients have come to me with a suspicious lump that turns out to be malignant and, stunned, say, "I don't know how this happened! No one in my family ever had breast cancer!" I tell them they're in good company—most breast cancer patients don't have a family history of breast cancer. By virtue of being women, we are at risk for breast cancer.

Another thing to note is that risk factors don't necessarily increase in a simple, arithmetical fashion: if one risk factor gives you a 20-percent risk of getting breast cancer, and another gives you a 10-percent chance, it doesn't always mean that now you're up to 30 percent. The interaction of risk factors is a tricky and complicated process. One interesting example are the recent studies on alcohol and breast cancer (see Chapter 15), which show that women with other risk factors who also drink liquor don't increase their risk at all, while women with no other risk factors who drink tend to increase toward the risk level of women who already had risk factors.

It would be much more convenient if we could say, "This causes breast cancer so don't do it." But breast cancer, as we noted in Chapter 13, is what is known as a "multifactorial disease"—that is, it has many causes which interact with each other in ways we don't understand yet.

As I noted earlier, the older you are, the higher are your chances of getting breast cancer. The publicity about breast cancer, which has

FIGURE 14-2

increased rapidly in recent years, gives the impression that the disease is hitting younger and younger women. That's not entirely true. The *percentage* of young women getting breast cancer is the same as it's always been. The number of younger women in the country has risen in recent years, because the baby boomers are reaching their 40s and 50s. If you take 10 percent of 40, you get 4; if you take 10 percent of 400, you get 40. There are more 40-something women with breast cancer because there are more 40-something women around. (There's no breast-cancer rise in the generation after boomers, by the way. There are fewer of them than boomers, and breast cancer in really young women—teens and 20s, has always been rare.)

Most breast cancer still occurs in women over 50—about 80 percent of cases. Your risk at age 30 (see Table 14-2) is one in 5900 per year. By age 40, it's 1 in 1200. So the risk of getting breast cancer before you're 50 is very small. The median age for breast cancer diagnosis is 64, which means that half of women who get breast cancer will get it before age 64 and half will get it after.

But the media show you constant images of women with breast cancer who look 25 or 30. Articles, TV news features, public service announcements—they all give the impression that it's a disease of young women (Fig. 14-2). It's true that breast cancer is the leading cause of death in women between 40 and 44. However, that isn't quite as grim as it sounds: most women don't die between 40 and 44, so the "leading cause" doesn't necessarily imply huge numbers. But we've now got hundreds of young women who are scared to death they've got breast cancer. At the same time, older women aren't scared enough, because they're not getting the message that this disease becomes more common the older you are. Thus we're finding that only 30 percent of women over 50 are getting screening mammograms, while something like 50 or 60 percent of women under 50 are getting them.

So whenever you look at risk factors you need to think about age. Whatever other factors exist—family history, hormonal factors, etc.—will be most likely to cause breast cancer in combination with rising age.

Another factor we need to look at is the variation among ethnic groups. Almost all the data you read are based on non-Hispanic Caucasian women. If you look at Table 14-1, you see that the risk for black, Asian, and other non-white women is less than for white women. This is a disease found predominantly in non-Hispanic Caucasian women. That isn't necessarily comforting news to African American women, however; although breast cancer is less common in that group, it's often more deadly. Five-year survival for African American women diagnosed in 1983–1988 was 62 percent compared to 70 percent in white women diagnosed in the same time period.[5] That has to do in part with screening and being diagnosed early. But this doesn't appear to be the whole answer. It may also have to do with different estrogen metabolism, or exposure to carcinogens, the degree of dietary fat, or some other factor we don't now understand. I don't believe that it's exclusively early detection, because the statistics for white and black women with ovarian, colon, and lung cancers are the same.

There's also a class variation. White women of higher socioeconomic status get more breast cancer than poorer white women.[6] Black women of higher socioeconomic status also have a higher risk than poorer black women. Breast cancer seems to "discriminate" in an opposite way to the way society discriminates.

There are a number of possible factors in this intriguing situation. It may be that one of the elements in the cancers affecting the women in these different ethnic and social groupings is environmental. I'm not certain that's the case, and, if it is, I don't know what the environmental factor is—I doubt that it's any of the obvious things that would come to mind: I don't think African American women are less exposed to, say, pesticides, than white women are. Another possibility, especially in terms of racial difference, is the genetic factor. There may be a gene that makes a non-Hispanic Caucasian more susceptible to a cancerous mutation. The difference in vulnerability to breast cancer works on an international level as well. Third World countries have less breast cancer than highly industrialized countries.

The only likely possibility we've come up with so far is one I'll discuss later in this chapter. These days many white middle- and upper-class women tend to have their first child later in life, and a small subset of these women choose to have no children at all. This trend doesn't follow in other racial and ethnic groups and lower socio-economic groups in the United States, nor in women of Third World countries. But that's not enough to explain the whole difference.

In 1993 there was a lot of publicity about the possibility that lesbians are at a higher risk of breast cancer—1 in 3 instead of 1 in 8. This was based on some research done by Suzanne Haynes from the National Cancer Institute.[7] She had looked at several studies that had been conducted on lesbians who had been asked to fill out questionnaires about their lifestyles in the 1980s. She took special care to choose studies that had representative samples of lesbians. Then she took the characteristics that those studies had reported and matched them with known breast cancer risk factors. She hypothesized that there should be a larger amount of breast cancer than in heterosexual women. The factors she was looking at were not directly related to their sexual preference, but to the lifestyle common to many lesbians. Several different national and city samples indicated that 1 out of 4 lesbians over 50 were heavy drinkers. Seventy to eighty percent had never been pregnant. These are risk factors for breast cancer and may put lesbians at a two- to three-fold greater risk of breast cancer than heterosexual women. But there hadn't been any actual studies on lesbians and breast cancer, and she was trying to show the research establishment that it was a population that needed to be studied. As a result of her work studies are now being done. The Women's Health Initiative, (see Chapter 32) which is researching estrogen diet and other aspects of women's health, includes a question about sexual behavior so that we can begin to get information that will tell us whether lesbians are indeed at higher risk, or have particular risks.

The one problem area we do know exists is the one that is true of any minority women. Bigotry against lesbians causes many of them not to seek medical care until there's an emergency, because they know from their own and their friends' experiences that they risk censure from medical professionals who disapprove of them. Thus it may turn out that there is a higher mortality risk from breast cancer because they're not detected early enough. But all this is only speculative at this point: we don't know that lesbians have greater risk than any other women.

So much for overall populations and their risks. Now let's look at the two major categories of risk itself—genetic and hormonal.

Genetic Risk Factors

Genetic factors are often exaggerated. Women come to me convinced that, because their mother and aunt had breast cancer, they have a 50 percent chance of getting it. It's true that breast cancer in the family increases a woman's chance of getting it, but the additional risk for most women may not be that great.

Genetically, we divide breast cancer occurrences into three group-ings. The first, and most common, is *sporadic*—that's the 70 percent of breast cancer patients who have no known family history of the dis-ease. The second is *genetic*—there's one dominant cancer gene, and it's passed on to every generation. Most people assume that these are the only two kinds of breast cancer: the kind that is inherited and the kind that isn't. In fact, there is a third group that is much more common than the genetic group. It's what we call *polygenic*, and it occurs when there is a family history of breast cancer that isn't directly passed on through each generation in one dominant gene—some members of the family will get it and others won't.

Dr. Henry Lynch[8] of Creighton Medical School's oncology clinic did a study looking for percentages of these genetic groupings of breast cancer within a particular population. He looked at 225 patients with breast cancer and found that 82 percent had sporadic breast cancer (or no family history), while 13 percent had polygenic, and only 5 percent had true genetic breast cancer.

Most estimates are that pure hereditary breast cancer is rare, but it does occur—between 5 and 10 percent of all breast cancers fall into this category. In this case, the mother (or father) has a breast cancer gene, as mentioned in Chapter 13, and there's a 50–50 chance it will be passed on to the daughters (Fig. 13-2). If a daughter, or son, has inher-ited the gene, that gene again has a 50–50 chance of passing on to the next generation. I've had one family with a dramatic instance of ge-netic cancer. The grandmother had it, and the mother had it. She's fine now, but two of her five daughters died of breast cancer, and two others have had the disease. (This is a very different situation from the more common one, when the family members with breast cancer are aunts or cousins rather than mother and sisters.) We have found some evidence that people with breast cancers transmitted through a domi-nant gene have a better overall survival rate than other breast cancer patients. This interesting finding may have to do with ways in which that particular form of cancer works, or it may simply reflect the ten-dency of women with breast cancer in their immediate family to have frequent exams.

As noted in Chapter 13, several mutations in sequence are probably needed to get breast cancer (Fig. 14-3). For example, initially you'd be

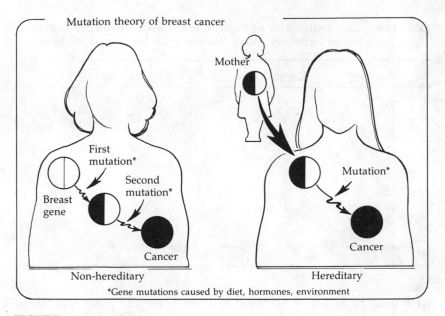

Mutation theory of breast cancer

Mother

First mutation*

Second mutation*

Breast gene

Cancer

Mutation*

Cancer

Non-hereditary

Hereditary

*Gene mutations caused by diet, hormones, environment

FIGURE 14-3

susceptible to a mutation caused by hormones, in the second to a mutation caused by diet. The person with genetic breast cancer has passed the gene on to her daughter, so the girl is born with her first mutation and needs only the second to get breast cancer. If the second mutation were something that could be altered (e.g., diet, which we'll discuss in the next chapter), it is possible that changing the situation (e.g., switching to a low fat diet) could prevent the daughter from getting breast cancer. Unfortunately, at this stage we have no way of determining what the sequence is likely to be, or who is vulnerable to which risk factors, or if a low fat diet even works. But it's interesting to think about, and if it turns out to be true it would tell us a lot about the link between environment and genetics.

There are some rare syndromes in which people tend to have a run of combinations of cancers in their family, and several of these include breast cancer. One mentioned in Chapter 13 is Li-Fraumeni syndrome, where families tend to have clusters of sarcomas, breast cancers, lung cancers, leukemias, and adrenal cancers.

As we discussed in the preceding chapter, we've now identified the BRCA1 gene, the tumor-suppressor gene thought to be linked to genetic breast and ovarian cancer. The families who have a mutation of this gene tend to have a high incidence of breast cancer and ovarian cancer, often at a young age. The risk estimates are as high as 80 percent by age 80 (Table 14-6).[9] Now that this gene has been identified

Table 14-6.   Cumulative Risk of Breast Cancer to Women in the United
              States Generally and to Women With Inherited BRCA1

Age	General Population	Inherited BRCA1
40	0.5%	16%
45	1 %	42%
50	2 %	59%
55	3 %	72%
60	4 %	77%
65	6 %	80%
70	7 %	82%
75	9 %	84%
80	10 %	86%

(Used with permission, Copyright 1993, American Medical Association.)

we'll soon be able to do a blood test for women in these families to determine whether or not they have that mutated gene. Although this is an important breakthrough, it will also bring up a lot of difficulties for these women.

Should every woman in these families be tested? We are aware that in the case of other hereditary illness, people often don't want to know. Then there's the question of when to test. Should you know at age 8, or 25, or 30? Or should we do it as part of amniocentesis? And once you have the information, what should you do with it? As we discuss in Chapter 17, we don't have any foolproof methods for preventing breast cancer, so the information may or may not be useful. And if you test negative it won't necessarily mean that you don't have hereditary breast cancer—only that you don't have that particular genetic mutation. If you test positive it means you have a very high chance of getting breast cancer. Having that in your medical record could affect insurance and employment. So it won't be a simple issue.

There's a lot of research going on right now about how best to counsel women about their genetic risk, and about the pros and cons of getting tested.

Other genes will soon follow. There has been mapping of BRCA2 which should soon be identified. And BRCA3 is not far behind. Will any of these genes be mutated in *nonhereditary* breast cancer as well? These issues will be answered within the lifetime of this book. I hope we can move ahead as fast on prevention, or these newly identified "carriers" will be in a difficult position.

In any case, tests would not be useful in the more common, polygenic breast cancer. Here there is a familial tendency but not a dominant gene. There are a number of explanations for polygenic breast cancer. It's possible that there's one gene that, while not a cancer gene itself, makes a woman particularly vulnerable to environmental causes of cancer. If, for example, you are particularly vulnerable to the carcinogenic effects of a high fat diet, and you've always eaten a high fat diet, and so have your sisters and cousins, you may find that some family members have breast cancer. Or you may be genetically inclined to begin menstruating early and/or going into menopause late, and that increases your risk and that of other family members. Or you may come from a family of women whose lifestyle and values tend to cause them to postpone childbearing until their 30s.

Support for the possibility that external factors increase some women's genetic vulnerability to breast cancer comes from immigrant studies. Some families may not be at high risk in their native country (like the women in Japan), but on moving to a different country they have more breast cancer, and their daughters have even more. Thus genetic and nongenetic factors mix to increase breast cancer risks slightly in the same family. Most family history cases of breast cancer fall into this category.

The critical question for any particular woman is whether her family has the genetic or the polygenic type of breast cancer and what her risk is. Once all of the genes have been identified and the blood tests have been developed that question will be easily answered.

Until we have those tests, we use circumstantial evidence to guess who has genetic cancer. We look at large groups of women and try to guess who seems likely to have inherited a breast cancer gene and who doesn't. Epidemiological studies have looked at large groups of women and tried to see what the consistent factors were. Two major studies have laid the groundwork for this.

Dr. David Anderson[10] of M.D. Anderson Hospital looked at all the patients at the hospital from 1944 to 1969, and found 6,550 who had had breast cancer. Of those, he picked out the ones who had relatives with breast cancer—there were 500, or 7.6 percent of the total. He studied these to try and determine whose cancer was caused by dominant genes and whose was polygenic. He concluded from his study that it was important to know whether the relative had breast cancer in only one breast, or in both, and whether the relative was first or second degree—that is, a mother or sister versus a cousin. Though his earlier studies suggested that the risk was affected by whether the affected first-degree relative was pre- or postmenopausal, his later work found this to be insignificant. On the basis of his findings, he described what he felt were criteria for the dominant gene (hereditary) type of breast cancer: a 30-year-old woman who had two first-degree relatives (mother and sister, or two sisters) with breast cancer, one of whom had cancer in both breasts, had a 25–28-percent risk of getting breast cancer by age 70, since she had a higher chance of having hereditary breast cancer; but if she had a sister and a second-degree relative with breast cancer, her risk was actually only slightly different from that of the general population.

These characterizations were studied by Dr. H. O. Adami,[11] in Sweden, who looked at a general population. Since Sweden is a small country and has socialized medicine, he was able to get records of all the women in the country who'd been treated for breast cancer over a period of 14 months (1,423 women altogether), and to examine how many of them had a family history of breast cancer and what its pattern was. He looked at all the factors in that family history—was the cancer pre- or postmenopausal? Uni- or bilateral? Unlike Anderson, he found no relationship to age or to whether the cancer was in one breast or both. This might have been because he had only 149 patients who had an additional relative with breast cancer. This small number would make it harder to demonstrate an association with clinical findings. In addition he found that, overall, when a mother or sister had breast cancer, an individual's chances of getting the disease were only 1.7—a small increase in risk (instead of 1/1000/year at age 40, 1.7/1000/year). Since Adami studied all the women with breast cancer rather than just those with risk factors, his work is probably more representative of most women with the disease than Anderson's.[12]

Other factors may well enter into this, and it's important when you give a history to look not just at the breast cancers that have been in your family, but at other kinds of cancers as well. For example, one study suggests that daughters of men who have prostate cancer are at higher risk for breast cancer.[13] It may be a simliar gene—the same genetic marker that makes women susceptible to breast cancer makes men susceptible to prostate cancer. Endometrial and uterine cancer in the family can also affect whether you get breast and ovarian cancer. We don't know yet whether other cancers in your family affect your chance of breast cancer, although it appears that lung cancer and melanoma don't predispose offspring to breast cancer. It's likely, though uncertain, that hormonal cancers are related to each other.

The other area that's so crucial is the gene environment interaction. Is it just having a gene for a kind of cancer, or is it having a gene that makes you susceptible to a carcinogen like the ones in pesticides? So when we look at the studies that show Japanese women in Japan not getting breast cancer, but then getting it when they move to the United States, we need to look at the possibility that something in our environment affects a gene they have. There's a lot of research going on in this area, as we discuss in Chapter 15.

What's critical in this kind of research for figuring out genes is having tissue or blood or some other way of investigating all of the different family members. We're starting to develop high-risk tissue banks. Women with a strong family history of breast cancer might want to participate in one of these banks. It may mean giving a blood sample, having a breast biopsy, or collecting nipple duct fluid. If you've had a breast biopsy it may involve getting the block of tissue for the researchers to analyze. This is vital for pushing this kind of research forward.

Currently there are several groups working on these genetic issues, and, as we said before, there's a push to get a national tissue depository. This will save researchers identifying a new gene from having to put massive amounts of time and energy into seeking appropriate subjects—they can go to the bank, pull out a thousand cases, run the tests, and see what percentage has or doesn't have the gene. There also will be many studies involved in the initial testing for these genes. If you're interested in participating in these studies you should enroll in the nearest high-risk program or approach the nearest medical school and see if they're involved in any research. If they're not, they can tell you where some of it is being done.

If you're going to have any kind of breast biopsy, or breast surgery, we recommend that you ask your surgeon to ask the pathologist to save some of the tissue. If possible, the tissue should be frozen rather than saved in paraffin, because some of the tests can only be done on frozen tissue. You can have them save it and find out later who needs it and get it to them then (Fig. 14-4).

This kind of patient involvement in research procedures is very important. We've seen how effective it can be in the case of the estrogen receptor test. Few doctors were doing this test until author Rose Kushner, in her book *Alternatives* and in her speeches around the country, told women to demand their surgeons make sure that the estrogen receptor test is done. Now estrogen receptor tests have become routine (they no longer have to be done on fresh tissue so are easier to do). The way to make such things happen is not to wait for your doctor to suggest it. It's extra work for doctors and they're not going to volunteer. But if you push them, they may do it.

All the studies done to date make it clear that family history does affect your risk of getting breast cancer. But so far we don't really know for certain how great the effect is and, more importantly, how it relates to other risk factors. As more of the molecular markers become available—not just the BRCA1 gene, but, for example, a gene we might discover that makes you more susceptible to pesticides or fatty diet or estrogen effects—then all these epidemiological studies of risk will become less important. So it won't matter whether your mother had bilateral, early-onset breast cancer: the test will determine whether you do or don't have it.

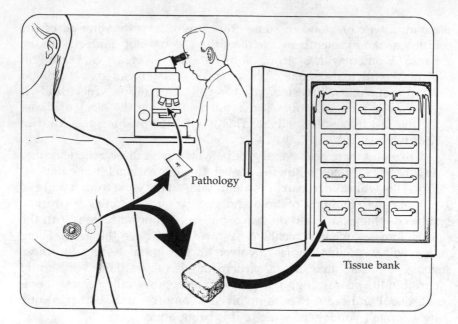

Pathology

Tissue bank

FIGURE 14-4

Hormonal Risk Factors

Aside from the genetic risk factor, the other most obvious risk factor is hormonal. We know that hormones play a large part in breast cancer because it's a form of cancer common in women and rare in men and, as we discussed in Chapter 1, women's breasts undergo a complex hormonal evolution that men's don't. We don't yet understand what the hormonal risk factors are, but we have some interesting clues. We know it has something to do with age and menstrual cycle: the younger a woman is at her first period, and the older she is when she goes into menopause, the more likely she is to get breast cancer. It seems that the more periods a woman has over her lifetime, the more prone she is to breast cancer. If she menstruates for more than 40 years, she seems to have a particularly high risk. If the ovaries are removed early, and no hormone therapy is given, the risk of breast cancer is greatly reduced.[14] It's not exactly a cure-all, however, since removing a woman's ovaries greatly increases the danger of osteoporosis and coronary heart disease. If a woman has had a hysterectomy, it may or may not influence her vulnerability to breast cancer, depending upon whether the ovaries, as well as the uterus, were removed. If the ovaries are not removed, hormonal cycles continue, even though the woman doesn't have periods.

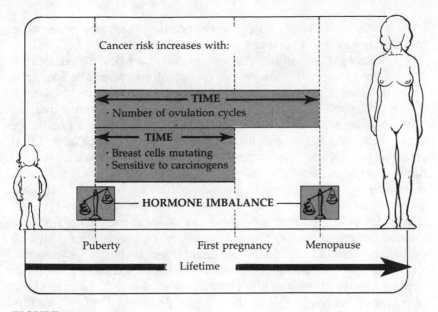

Cancer risk increases with:

TIME
· Number of ovulation cycles

TIME
· Breast cells mutating
· Sensitive to carcinogens

HORMONE IMBALANCE

Puberty   First pregnancy   Menopause

Lifetime

FIGURE 14-5

Pregnancy also appears to affect breast cancer risk. Women who have never been pregnant seem to be more at risk than women who have had a child before 30. And women who have their first pregnancies after 30 have a greater risk than women who have never been pregnant at all. The hormones of a pregnancy carried to term will mature the breast tissue in a young woman. The same hormones after 30 may actually stimulate breast tissue that has already mutated by earlier carcinogenic exposure. Although unconfirmed through further research, some studies indicate that a pregnancy that ends in a miscarriage or abortion slightly increases the risk.[15,16]

The key seems to be the amount of time between the first period and the first pregnancy (Fig. 14-5). There are theories about why this is so. One explanation is that between menarche and first pregnancy the breast tissue is especially sensitive to carcinogens. This seems to be true. As we discuss a little later, diet, alcohol consumption, and radiation exposure all seem to have a greater effect on a woman's breasts between her first period and her first pregnancy than they do later. So it may indeed be that the "developing breast" is more susceptible to carcinogens than the breast that has gone through its complete hormonal development. This increased sensitivity may relate to the breast cells' capability of mutating up until the first pregnancy. There may be something about first pregnancies that stops young women from being able to sustain a mutation; thus, the more time cells have to sustain a mutation, the greater the chance they'll mutate in response to a carcinogen and in a way that develops into cancer.

Dr. Malcolm Pike[17] thinks that one factor in a woman's vulnerability to breast cancer is the number of ovulatory cycles she has gone through, since it's the length of time between menarche and menopause that seems to count. In fact, a Swedish study[18] found that the number of regular menstrual cycles prior to the first full pregnancy was a better predictor of risk than age at first period or age at first pregnancy. This may be because early menarche is associated with rapid onset of ovulatory menstrual cycles.[19] Within two years of early menarche (ages 8–11) all cycles become ovulatory; however, late menarche is associated with delayed onset of regular ovulatory cycles— that is, for young women who are 13 or older at menarche, no more than 50 percent of their cycles are ovulatory four years after their first period. In anovulatory cycles estrogen doesn't always become elevated. Also, it is usually accompanied by a shortened *luteal phase* (after ovulation)—which means less cumulative exposure to high levels of hormones. This has been shown by Leslie Bernstein, Professor of Preventive Medicine at the University of Southern California. She suggests it's another explanation for the difference in breast cancer rates in white and Japanese women in the United States. Asian women in the United States have a later age at menarche and menstrual cycles that are, on average, two days longer than those of white women (30 vs. 28 days). This increase in days is almost completely in the *follicular phase* (before ovulation), where estrogen levels are lower.[20]

Another factor relating to the number of menstrual cycles is breast feeding. Studies have shown that women who breast feed for a long time (more than six consecutive years) have a decreased risk of breast cancer.[21] In addition, women who have had early pregnancies and have breast-fed have a decreased risk of subsequent breast cancer.[22] This is probably not a question of using the breast as it was meant to be used but rather one of preventing ovulatory cycles at a crucial time in reproductive life.

As you can see, we're still very much in the theorizing stage. As yet, we don't know why there is this vulnerable time in a woman's life or why or how internal hormones affect breast cancer. Theories are interesting, but more useful to scientists than to individual women, who can't control heredity, ethnicity, or menarche. In the next chapter we look at some external factors, which we *can* control.

15

Risk Factors:
External

The things we discussed before—genetic factors and the body's own hormones—are things over which you have no control. But equally important are external, environmental factors, which can create a breast cancer causing mutation or accelerate the growth of breast cancer—or, for that matter, prevent the growth of breast cancer. Diet, alcohol, and certain medications carry risks over which we have some control. The amount of fat and liquor you consume can increase your susceptibility to breast cancer. Hormones taken by postmenopausal women, as well as birth control pills, are also a matter of choice and are being studied in relation to breast cancer. Radiation has always been known to increase cancer risk, and may or may not be something you can control.

Diet

Although different theories have connected breast cancer to all kinds of foods, the most compelling studies are those involving fat in the diet. So far, these studies are by no means definitive, and frequently are at odds with each other. They are also unclear as to whether the danger that seems to exist comes from all fats, animal fats alone, some combination of animal and vegetable fats, or even just calories. Finally, it's important to remember that even the most convincing studies suggest that only about 27 percent of breast cancers are attributable to dietary fat.[1] This is a significant percentage, but it also suggests that 73 percent of breast cancers aren't connected to fat intake at all.

These studies are of great interest to researchers, yet only hint at the kind of diet that might help lessen the odds of breast cancer or the disease's severity once it occurs (see Chapter 28). Each is well worth looking at, and worth considering as a basis for a different diet, but is no amulet against breast cancer.

ANIMAL STUDIES

In the 1940s, Albert Tannenbaum discovered that giving rats a high-fat diet increased their rate of breast cancer. Rat studies done since then have confirmed that the percentage of fat in their diet affects their vulnerability to breast cancer—as does the total intake of calories. Ernst Wydner[2] has established an apparent threshold level: rats with 20 percent or less fat in their diet have a lower breast cancer rate, and once above 20 percent, it doesn't seem to matter what percentage of fat they consume; the rats with 30 percent fat in their diet do as badly as those with 40 percent or more.

Most of this animal research indicates that the fat consumption doesn't cause breast cancer, it simply promotes it. Something else probably initiates the process, or causes the first mutation—possibly a virus, or a gene.

DESCRIPTIVE EPIDEMIOLOGY

Epidemiological studies are the most useful, but obviously can't be done on human subjects. For a study on dietary fat to have value, we would have to put subjects on a high-fat diet at about the age of five and follow them through a lifetime, making sure their diets were unchanged—clearly an impossible task. So we have to rely on less direct means of studying the effects of diet on breast cancer in humans. One technique is called "descriptive epidemiology." In this, we take a particular group of people—possibly a specific geographical population—and compare it to another group. Diet varies from culture to culture, so the rate of breast cancer and the dietary habits of one culture can be compared with those of another culture. But if women in country X get more breast cancer than women in country Y, and they also eat more fat, it doesn't prove that fat is the cause of the increased cancer. These women might also be chewing more bubble-gum, marrying younger, exercising more, wearing different fabrics, and doing a hundred other things differently than women in country Y, any of which may or may not relate to their cancer rate.

Nevertheless, this type of epidemiological study has produced interesting data. A chart of breast cancer incidence plotted against dietary fat intake shows a correlation.[3] For instance, women in Japan have had a lower rate of breast cancer than women in the United States, and their fat intake has also been much lower—12 to 15 percent of their calories is fat, as opposed to 40 percent of American women's calories (Fig. 15-1). But as Japanese women have become more westernized, their average fat intake has increased to about 25 percent, and their breast cancer rate has increased somewhat.[4]

In Iceland, the typical diet was low in fat, and the breast cancer rate was also low. Again, as fat in the diet increased, so did the incidence of breast cancer.[5] But there's an important difference: Icelandic women's breast cancer is rising at a much faster rate than that of the Japanese women. This suggests that fat alone isn't the issue. Perhaps the Icelandic women have more genetic or hormonal susceptibility to breast cancer—or perhaps there are other changes involved in the westernization process: different stress levels, for example.

For Japanese women who have migrated to California, gradually switching to a more westernized diet, studies have found that breast cancer rates increased—not only for the women themselves but even more for their daughters.[6] This might indicate that dietary factors make more of a difference when the body is young and still growing and less of a difference in older people. Often within the same culture there are subgroups whose diets are significantly different from those of the general population. One revealing study was done with a group of Seventh-Day Adventists in California.[7] Some are strict vegetarians

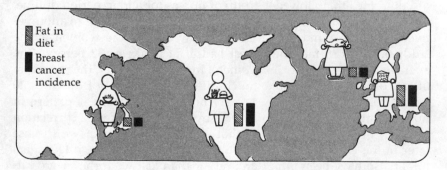

FIGURE 15-1

but others are not, and so the latter proved useful as the control group. The study showed there wasn't much difference in the rate of breast cancer between the vegetarian and nonvegetarian members. A similar study[8] of an order of vegetarian nuns in England had similar results: their breast cancer rates didn't vary significantly from the rates of other never-pregnant women who ate meat. A study of cancer rates in 65 rural counties in China where fat intake ranged from 5 to 47 percent of energy showed no correlation with breast cancer rates which were one tenth of those of the United States.[9]

These studies don't negate the fat-and-breast-cancer findings, however; both the vegetarian Adventists and the nuns ate a lot of dairy products, which may have kept the total amount of animal fat constant. A study of women on a strict macrobiotic diet, who eat no meat or dairy, might shed some light on this question.

The timing of the fat consumption might also be important. Both the nuns and the Adventists had adopted their lifestyles in adulthood, by which time the damage may well have been done. The time between the first period and the first pregnancy may be when women are most vulnerable to carcinogens.

Other kinds of research have been designed to look more accurately at this problem. Case control studies look at women with breast cancer along with a similar number of women picked at random. The diets of the women are then studied to see if there are any differences. Most of these studies show a weak association or no association between dietary fat and breast cancer. It is exceedingly difficult, however, to get an accurate evaluation of diet, and small differences might well be missed.

Cohort studies, on the other hand, identify a defined population exposed to a particular factor and another population not exposed, following both groups over time. A 1987 cohort study,[10] which received a lot of publicity when it was released, did not demonstrate a breast cancer dietary fat link. This study, done by the Harvard School of Public Health, followed a group of nurses for a long period of time, looking for a number of different things. They found no relation between fat intake and breast cancer. However, all the women in the study ate a lot of fat. The lowest had a fat intake of 32 percent (the average intake for most U.S. women). In rats, remember, the reduction of fats didn't seem to make much difference until it got down to 20 percent or below. That may or may not suggest a similar pattern in human females. (The Harvard study, by the way, did find a correlation between breast cancer and alcohol consumption, which we discuss later in the chapter.) What the nurses ate when they were teenagers might also have been important, rather than just what they were eating as adults.

Another factor may be that fats are not all the same. Fats from milk-producing animals (butter fat), other land animals, fish and shellfish, vegetables, and hydrogenated vegetable oils all differ substantially in their chemical properties. Two studies were reported in early 1995[11,12] demonstrating that women who consumed olive oil twice a day or more had less breast cancer than those who did not. Both of these studies were done in Mediterranean countries (Greece and Spain) where breast cancer overall is rarer than it is in northern Europe. The question remains whether it is olive oil which is protective or the fact that it replaces more dangerous fats in these women's diets.

FACTORS OTHER THAN FAT

Some studies suggest that the amount of fat we eat may be more of an indirect than direct cause of breast cancer. Being high in calories, fat creates greater weight. Some data show that the taller and fatter a postmenopausal woman is, the more susceptible she is to breast cancer. It's worth noting that one of the countries with the highest breast cancer rate is the Netherlands, whose people have high-fat diets and are typically much taller and heavier than the Japanese, who eat less fat and have less breast cancer. Other studies indicate that it may not be either height or weight, but the interaction of both—the lean body mass. This holds true in studies of rats as well: if you give rats a lower-calorie diet that stunts their growth, they have a lower rate of breast cancer.

The risks related to diet may also differ in pre- and postmenopausal breast cancer. F. de Waard suggested that premenopausal breast cancer has no relation to food but is purely hormonal. But postmenopausal breast cancer, he says, may result from a hormone imbalance caused by "overnutrition." He studied 7,259 postmenopausal women and found an increased risk of breast cancer among those who were taller and heavier.[13] Women who were over 154 pounds and over five-foot-five had 3.6 times the risk that women under 132 pounds and below five-foot-three had. Women whose height and weight fell in between those measurements had a risk that was also between that of the larger and smaller women. (Remember those second-generation Japanese American women we talked about earlier? As a result of their changed diet, they were taller and heavier than their mothers.) If height really is partly responsible for the increased risk, this fact would also support the theory of an early period of vulnerability: you can adjust your weight as an adult, but height is determined early in life, and though part of it is genetic, part is also nutritional.

So it's quite possible that the problem isn't fat itself, but overall nutrition: people who eat more may be more vulnerable to breast cancer. Overnutrition might have some connection with some of the other risk factors: girls with lower food consumption stay thinner and often begin menstruating later than more heavily nourished girls. People who eat more also tend to be those who can afford to—those with an overall higher standard of living appear to be at greater risk for breast cancer.

There is the possibility that fiber, rather than fat, is the important element. Usually diets very high in fiber are very low in fat. It may be that with a low fat-diet it's the fiber or the high-complex carbohydrates or the vegetables you're replacing the fat with that are helping you. Some new evidence suggests that soy protein may be a protective element as well.[14] Maybe the problem is not that the Japanese start eating fat, but that they stop eating tofu. There's growing evidence that certain vegetables, particularly those containing antioxidants such as vitamins A, C, and E, may be protective against breast cancer.[15]

Vitamin A, particularly the vegetable form, beta carotene, seems to decrease the incidence of several cancers. People with lower beta carotene levels have been shown to get more lung cancer, for example. It's not clear that massive doses of vitamin A or beta carotene supplements will change anyone's risk of breast cancer. But there are studies going on using 4HPR, which is a form of vitamin A, to see if it can prevent breast cancer. Vegetables with vitamin A include broccoli, kale, carrots, and lettuce. Vitamin C and folic acid also appear to offer some protection against all cancers.

The National Cancer Institute has come out with a major plan, the "five a day" plan, encouraging people to eat five servings of fruits and vegetables a day. That can sound pretty daunting, but when you find out what they call a serving, it's not all that bad—one carrot is a "serving."

Zinc may also have an effect on the growth of breast cancer, but the studies so far are extremely contradictory. Some even suggest that large amounts of zinc may actually increase the risk of breast cancer.

For a while there was a theory that a high consumption of foods that contained the element selenium decreased breast cancer risk. I worked on a study at the Harvard School of Public Health, with Dr. Walter Willett, looking at the relation between fat and breast cancer. Part of the study involved looking at selenium, vitamins, and fatty acids. We asked a group of women who developed breast cancer after menopause to fill out extensive dietary questionnaires. We then took samples of their body fat to analyze different fatty acids, analyzed their toenail clippings for selenium, and did blood tests for vitamins. We compared them to a control group of women without breast cancer. Unfortunately, we found no relationship between selenium, fat, and breast cancer susceptibility.[16]

If fat intake does indeed increase the risk of breast cancer, what makes it happen? There are a number of theories. Some researchers think it changes the metabolism of estrogen. According to one study[17] people with a high-fat diet tend to have more estrogen in their blood and low urinary excretion of estrogen; vegetarians who eat dairy foods excrete more estrogen, leaving less in the blood, and people on macrobiotic diets, which include a very low amount of fat, have even lower levels of estrogen in their blood and secrete less in their urine. As we noted in Chapter 1, your fat cells can make estrogen, so it is also possible that if you're obese, you have an oversupply of estrogen, which could increase your vulnerability to cancer. Studies attempting to confirm this hypothesis have been inconsistent.

It's also possible that cancer cells grow better in an environment with a lot of overnourished cells, and the fatter you are the more such cells there are for the cancer cells to grow with. (There's also some evidence that among victims of breast cancer, those with a low-fat diet have a better prognosis than those with a high-fat diet. The studies, however, are not extensive, and we can't be at all certain of them.)

The other possibility is that it isn't the food at all that contributes to breast cancer, but the carcinogens and hormones that are in the food. Beef in this country, for example, still has artificial hormones. Unfortunately meat isn't the only problem. Fish are very much contaminated, since most of our fresh and coastal waters are polluted. There is, among other things, a lot of mercury in the fish we eat. (Fish, by the way, isn't always as low fat as we've been led to believe. Lobster, shark, swordfish, and several others all have a lot of fat.) Even vegetables aren't that safe, since they're sprayed with pesticides.

THE RESEARCH CHALLENGE

Until recently, the medical profession hadn't embraced the theory of a high-fat diet contributing to breast cancer, for a number of reasons, good and bad. As we've seen, the evidence is far from conclusive, and many doctors are rightly unwilling to present unproven theories as fact. Many argue that they don't want to push women into trying to change eating habits that are difficult and uncomfortable to change; and many of them mean what they say. But given the alacrity with which doctors accepted the evils of caffeine and its effects on the nonexistent "fibrocystic disease," I'm puzzled and suspicious. The evidence linking fat to breast cancer is much better than the evidence against caffeine, and surely it's as hard to give up coffee as it is to reduce fat in one's diet.

Part of the doctors' hesitancy may stem from the fact that the dairy and meat lobbies are very strong: medicine is usually reluctant to go up against powerful lobbies, unless (as is the case with tobacco and lung cancer) the evidence against the lobbyists' product is unusually powerful. It's unfortunate that big business has such an effect on the medical profession, but it does, all too often. No doubt there are other nonscientific reasons for the resistance of the medical profession to this particular theory.

It's extremely difficult to do a good prospective intervention study (in which healthy women are asked to change their diets and are then followed to see how many get cancer) because it's hard for large numbers of women to change their diets permanently, and accurate results would mean studying huge numbers of women for a long period of time. A large prospective study was planned by the National Institutes of Health (NIH) and later canceled because of scientific and monetary difficulties. However, when Bernadine Healy, a woman in her early 40s, became head of the NIH, she wanted to see these questions answered, and developed the Women's Health Initiative. Part of this massive study will look at a low-fat diet in postmenopausal women to see whether it can reduce the incidence of breast cancer, heart disease, osteoporosis, and stroke (see Chapter 33). We're finally going to research this issue.

It won't, however, be the definitive study by any means. Postmenopausal women are more likely than younger women to get breast cancer, but the factors that give them the cancer may, as we discussed earlier, begin far sooner, during adolescence. So if it turns out that changing her diet at age 55 doesn't affect a woman's chance of getting breast cancer, that won't necessarily mean fat has no role in the disease. We need another study, one that starts in adolescence and monitors the young woman's diet throughout her life.

Designing such a study seems difficult at this point. I can barely get my six-year-old to eat vegetables, much less keep her on a low-fat diet; I can't imagine what it will be like to try when she's 13. Still, we need to figure out a way to create such a study. We desperately need research to tell us not only exactly what the culprits are in our westernized high-fat diet, but also when they do their dirty work. If it is during adolescence, then it is pointless for us to encourage 50-year-old women to change their diets as a method of lessening breast cancer risk.

Overall, it seems likely, from the material in the various studies, that fat consumption and calorie intake do have some effect on your vulnerability to breast cancer. Although the proof is nowhere near as solid as it is with smoking and lung cancer, the data are strong enough to make it worthwhile to consider seriously cutting back your animal fat consumption—especially when you consider that animal fat has been proven to be a factor in many other illnesses, and that nothing good has ever been shown about high animal fat consumption, except perhaps that it tastes good. If you're the parent of a teen

or preteen daughter, it may be particularly wise to consider encouraging her to eat a low-fat diet, since the evidence suggests that much of the fat-related damage may be done early in life. Without expecting miracles, you may do well to encourage your kids to spend a little less time at MacDonald's, and to eat a bit more low-fat, nutritious food.

Don't, however, expect miracles. Even if lowering the amount of fat in the diet does have an effect, it is likely to be a small one. Women on low-fat diets should not neglect screening (see Chapter 18).

Alcohol Consumption

Related to the question of diet is that of alcohol consumption. A number of studies suggest that drinking alcoholic beverages, even in moderate amounts, may increase your risk of breast cancer. Walter Willett of the Harvard School of Public Health conducted a study of the dietary habits of a group of nurses (cited earlier in this chapter).[18] He followed a group of 89,538 nurses between 34 and 59 years of age for four years after studying their nutritional habits. He found that consuming hard liquor, beer, and wine appeared to increase women's risk of breast cancer. Women who usually had between three and nine drinks a week had a 1.3 increase in relative risk of breast cancer (1 being the norm: see Chapter 14 for a description of relative risk). Those who had more than nine drinks a week had a 1.6 increase. It was interesting to note in this study that drinking had little effect on those women already at high risk—the effect was mainly on the women with no risk factors.

Also, women under 55 with no other risk factors who had more than nine drinks a week had a more dramatic increase than those over 55: they had a 2.5 increase—two and a half times the susceptibility to breast cancer of nondrinkers with no risk factors. (In all these cases, Dr. Willett looked to see if there were dietary differences as well: there weren't.) Studies in France and Italy, where wine is consumed regularly by virtually everyone, have supported this connection. Women in these countries do have a higher incidence of breast cancer than do women in the United States, though it's a fairly slight increase—only 1.2 to 1.9 times.

The same issue of the *New England Journal of Medicine* in which Dr. Willett's study appeared ran an article on a similar study from the National Cancer Institute (NCI). The study looked at 7,188 women between 25 and 77 over a 10-year period[19] and found that among the group of regular drinkers a woman's risk of breast cancer was increased by 1.5. The NCI published another study in 1987 comparing 1,524 women with breast cancer against a control group of 1,896 women without the disease.[20] They found that alcohol consumption increased the risk of breast cancer—but only in those who had drunk liquor at an early age, before 30. Consumption of alcohol after 30 didn't seem to matter at all. The authors looked for other possible compounding factors—differences in diet, socioeconomic position, age of first childbirth—and didn't find them.

Like fat consumption, it may well be that the main effect of alcohol in increasing breast cancer risk is during the vulnerable period of youth. More precise information as to when and how the effect manifests itself is needed before we can make concrete recommendations. Whether to stop drinking or not is one of the many decisions we all must make, unfortunately on inadequate information. The risk increase isn't great, but it definitely exists. You alone know how much pleasure you get from your glass of wine or beer, and how alarmed you are at the thought of breast cancer. If it's not all that important to you to drink, you might want to reduce your alcohol consumption to a glass of champagne on New Year's Eve and major celebrations. Although it's probably wise for a number of reasons to discourage your daughters from drinking, this is an area, like many in parenting, where you may not have a lot of control.

Radiation

One of the known risk factors for breast cancer, as well as a variety of other cancers, is radiation. At least three major studies have confirmed that there is indeed a link between radiation and increased risk of breast cancer.

The first study came out of one of the major tragedies of the 20th century—the bombings of Hiroshima and Nagasaki at the end of World War II. The people in the immediate area of the bombings died instantly, or shortly after the bombs were dropped. But it has become evident that those within a 10-kilometer radius of the bomb sites developed far more cancer than others in comparable populations, and scientists began studying these survivors to learn more about the dangers of radiation. They measured the amount of radiation these people had been exposed to, and then followed them over the years to see what cancers they developed.[21]

Among their other discoveries, the researchers found that, while breast cancer rates rose among the general female population exposed to the radiation, the increase was far more dramatic among women who were younger at the time of the bombing than among those who were older—thus strengthening other findings about the particular vulnerability of the developing breast to carcinogenic agents. The effects were greatest among women in their teens and early 20s, and nearly nonexistent in women in their 50s and 60s. More recent reports have indicated an increased risk in the women who were less than 10 years old at the time of the exposure. This effect took longer to be revealed because it didn't appear until the women had reached the age at which breast cancer normally occurs.

Other studies back up the atom bomb data. The first is a Canadian study that looked at women who had been checked for tuberculosis with fluoroscopy.[22] This was a common practice in the 1930s and 1940s, before we knew of the dangers of radiation and saw it as something of a magic cure-all. The typical treatment for TB was to collapse the infected lung to rest it, and then check it with X rays every day to see how it was doing. When the women were studied in the 1970s, they were found to have an increased incidence of breast cancer. I've come across a similar case in my own practice. A patient I just diagnosed with breast cancer, now 58, had had TB in her early 20s. She lived in France and received intensive radiation in a sanatorium. Her two best friends at the sanatorium, who received the same radiation therapy, have also developed breast cancer.

Another study examined a group of 606 women in Rochester, New York,[23] who had suffered postpartum mastitis—painfully inflamed breasts (see Chapter 7)—and had been given radiation (averaging between 50 and 450 rads for both breasts) to alleviate their pain. They too had a rate of breast cancer higher than that of the general population. The risk was also dose related. This study is interesting for a second reason: the radiation was given after the first pregnancy. Nonetheless it was during lactation, a time of high activity in the breast.

There are other studies that confirm the existence of radiation-induced breast cancer. One showed an increase in the disease among women who had scoliosis,[24] and who during the crucial time of puberty had a lot of X rays to monitor their backs. Another showed an increase among a group of women who had radiation therapy on their chests for acne—also during puberty.[25] Another study looked at women who had their thymus radiated in infancy or early childhood to shrink it. (The thymus, a normally large gland in the middle of the chest in childhood, shrinks with age. At one time, before we realized that it shrank normally, radiation therapy was used to shrink it.)[26]

All these studies show that the danger is from exposure to moderate doses of radiation (10–500 rads); the last two show that the danger is only to the area of the body at which the radiation has been aimed. Thus people exposed to radiation for cancer of the cervix did not show an increased rate of breast cancer.[27] The survivors of Nagasaki and Hiroshima had their whole bodies exposed to radiation and have suffered increased vulnerability to virtually all kinds of cancer. Another interesting finding in all these studies is the long latency period. The excess risk of cancer does not appear until the age at which breast cancer commonly occurs. This suggests that radiation is only part of the early picture and that there are other moderating influences which come later and affect the development of breast cancer. The duration of the increased risk from radiation is also not known, but in the atomic bomb survivors, fluoroscopy patients, and mastitis patients it appears to have lasted at least 35 years from the time of exposure.

This kind of exposure is very different from the kind of exposure you get with occasional diagnostic X rays such as chest X rays and mammograms. Many people are legitimately concerned about getting such X rays, but it's a mistake to throw out a highly useful diagnostic tool. Remember that the danger comes with a total cumulative dose of radiation. If you had a chest X ray every week for two years, you probably would risk increasing your risk of getting breast cancer. But the danger of leaving pneumonia undetected, if you have reason to believe it may exist, is far greater than any danger from infrequent chest X rays. Similarly, the level of radiation in up-to-date mammograms (1/4 of a rad) won't increase your risk of breast cancer, except in very rare instances (see Chapter 19). As we mention in Chapter 13 there may also be a gene (ataxia telangeltasia) which makes carriers more sensitive to radiation.

Radiation to treat cancer puts us at the other end of the spectrum: very high levels of radiation are used, on the order of 8,000 rads. In these cases, however, the risk of radiation is far outweighed by the risk of cancer. For example, radiation is used in the case of Hodgkin's disease, a cancer of the lymph nodes. By itself and in conjunction with chemotherapy it has been responsible for many cures. However, some women who had this treatment many years ago are now showing up with breast cancer. We suspect that the radiation to their chests, which saved their lives, is responsible now for their second cancers.[28] It won't be surprising if some of the children treated today for cancer with radiation in the chest region will also eventually have an increase in breast cancers.[29] This is unfortunate, but since radiation was responsible for their being around long enough to get a second cancer, few of those patients are likely to wish they had chosen otherwise.

Hormone Medications

BIRTH CONTROL PILLS

We discussed earlier the effects of your body's hormonal system on breast cancer. Since your own hormones can affect breast cancer, it stands to reason that hormones taken externally as drugs will also have an effect—and studies have shown this to be the case.

The birth control pill, originally seen as the magic solution to unwanted pregnancy, quickly became vilified as its negative side effects became apparent. As is often the case, the reality of the pill falls somewhere between its panacea/demon images. The pill did indeed, especially in its early forms, seem to contribute to a number of illnesses, including stroke (especially in combination with cigarette smoking in women over 30). Some studies, however, have suggested that it might also be useful in protecting against certain diseases such as ovarian cancer, because the more you ovulate, the more chance you have of getting the disease. So if you take the birth control pill and decrease the number of ovulations, you can decrease the risk of ovarian cancer. The pill has also consistently been shown to reduce *endometrial* cancer (cancer of the lining of the uterus) as well.[30,31]

In discussing the pill as though it were a single entity, part of the problem is that, like other inventions, the pill has gone through many permutations. Earlier pills used much more estrogen and progesterone than today's pills do. We've changed both the amounts and the proportions of those hormones. So early findings aren't necessarily applicable to the pill used today. A study looking at women who have been on the pill for 10 or 20 years is likely to be looking at women who have been on a number of different pills at different times— which explains in part why we seem to get so many contradictory results with studies on the relationship between breast cancer and the pill. Dr. Leslie Bernstein, at the University of Southern California, along with Dr. Malcolm Pike, did a careful meta-analysis of birth control pill use and breast cancer risk and found that the total months of use is the most important factor.[32] But even with that, the increased risk is about 3.3 percent per year of use, or 38 percent (relative risk of 1.38) for 10 years of use. This risk may be worth it for the benefit of a convenient, sure method of birth control, but it's a decision only you can make, weighing evidence of increased breast cancer against the risks of other contraceptives, unwanted births, and abortion.

There's a new type of progesterone that has just come out; at least in a test tube, it seems as if it might prevent breast cancer.[33] It hasn't been tested sufficiently in humans yet to know if these impressive test tube effects translate into practical usefulness.

DES

Another external hormone women have taken is the estrogen DES. It was used in the 1940s through the 1960s to increase fertility and to prevent miscarriage. A study in 1984 showed a slight increase—1.4—in breast cancer among women who took DES while pregnant.[34] Since there's a lot of estrogen going through your body anyway when you're pregnant, it's not clear why an increased external dosage would be harmful, but it appears to have been, at least for some women. One theory is that exposure to estrogen during the period of rapid growth of breast tissue during pregnancy may increase risk.[35] We don't know yet what effects DES had on the breast cancer rate among daughters of women who had taken it, since the daughters are only now approaching the age when breast cancer is most common. There has been an increase in vaginal cancer among this population, but it's not as aggressive as we once thought it was.

POSTMENOPAUSAL HORMONE THERAPY

The question I'm asked more often than any other in my practice is, What effects will taking postmenopausal hormones have on my risk of breast cancer? It's a question I hate getting, because I simply don't know the answer.

During the 1940s and 1950s, it was popular to give a woman going through menopause estrogen—gynecologists routinely prescribed it whether the woman had any complaints or not. And since in those days most women did whatever their doctors told them to do, they took it. Then studies appeared linking long use of estrogen with uterine cancer. There was a big scare, and everyone stopped taking it.

Like birth control pills, estrogen therapy pills have been changed over the years. Progesterone has been added to balance the estrogen, and it seems to help protect against uterine cancer. Some studies, however, show that taking estrogen for a long time (over 10–15 years) or at high doses may increase breast cancer (though other studies with shorter duration of use show no effect at all on breast cancer).[36] Also, there is no evidence that progesterone acts the same way on the breast as it does on the endometrium. The only study showing that progesterone (Provera), in addition to estrogen (Premarin, the brand name for conjugated equine estrogen, made from pregnant mare's urine), decreases breast cancer risk was a prospective survey done at Wilford Air Force Base in Georgia.[37] In this study, postmenopausal women, when they went for their routine visit, were registered according to epidemiological information as well as use of postmenopausal hormones. These women were then followed and their subsequent incidence of cancer was noted. Although the women on estrogen and progesterone had a decreased incidence of breast cancer, the study hardly proves the safety of adding progesterone. For one thing, it was not randomized or controlled. This means that there were probably biases as to which women were given which therapy. It may well be that the women who were at high risk for breast cancer were not given the hormones. Subsequent studies have counteracted this data.

There is concern that progesterone will block estrogen's good effects on the heart.[38] A randomized controlled study[39] published in early 1995 of 875 women looked at this issue. In this study there were four groups. In one, women were given a placebo; in one they received just Premarin; in one they received Premarin with the Provera given cyclically; in one they received Premarin and Provera with the Provera given consecutively; and finally in the last group they were given Premarin and micronized progesterone. The study monitored high-density lipoproteins, blood pressure, insulin and fibrinogen for three years. They found that estrogen alone is best for increasing the good cholesterol but can result in an increase in the lining cells of the uterus (hyperplasia, which could lead to uterine cancer). In women with a uterus, Premarin and micronized progesterone has the most favorable effect on cholesterol, with Premarin and Provera coming in a poor third. Unfortunately, this study (PEPI) has a very short follow-up and therefore will not be able to address the effect on breast cancer risk.

We have very little data on the long-term safety of Provera. In the only study looking at it thus far, the women taking Provera had more breast cancer than women taking Premarin alone.[40] The study is limited, however, because the women in the study used a different kind of estrogen than that which is used in this country (estradiol), and very few of them took Provera in addition. The side effects of Provera can be worse than those of Premarin, and include depression. It has also been suggested that natural progesterone may be safer than Provera. While this may well turn out to be true, it has yet to be put to the test of a well-designed study.

Some gynecologists have argued that hormone replacement therapy (HRT) is similar to the pill and the pill hasn't been shown to increase breast cancer risk. Not only has this fact been questioned, but also the logic is flawed. The pill is being given to women at a different age, and that may make a large difference. We need more studies to make even a reasonable guess about postmenopausal hormones and breast cancer.

I do have a problem with the idea that we're supposed to keep taking these hormones indefinitely—there must be some reason that menopause exists in the first place, and maybe our bodies really need to stop having these hormones at some point. I'm concerned because once again gynecologists are casually giving out hormones without sufficient research, and we may well end up with another DES-type situation on our hands.

Certainly the pharmaceutical companies have done a wonderful marketing job. Women now expect to crumble and dry up the minute they turn 50. This marketing is very subtle. Sandra Coney's book, *The Menopause Industry*[41] shows graphically the types of advertisements that gynecologists are barraged with in an attempt to convince them that all women need to be on hormones. Menopause has been redefined as a disease of "estrogen deficiency," rather than a normal passage of life. Therefore, being a disease, it should be treated. In fact, if "estrogen deficiency" is a disease, then all men have it. Imagine how we could decrease their risk of heart disease, prostate cancer, and osteoporosis if they took this "miracle drug." Notice we even call it "hormone replacement therapy" which implies we are missing something that needs to be replaced. We should use the term "hormone therapy" which would imply rightly that these are drugs being given to treat or prevent disease. A NOVA public television show on menopause in the fall of 1994 was very telling. All of the male experts thought all women should be on hormones until death. All of the women experts thought that a study should be done to see if these drugs were safe and actually prevented disease. The male experts reported that this was preventive medicine and everyone should be in favor of it. I disagree. These are powerful drugs which will inevitably have side effects, and we as women need to be well informed of the risks and benefits. There may well be a place for hormone therapy, but we all need to realize that there is no free lunch.

Those who favor hormone therapy argue, with some validity, that we're not "supposed" to live long enough to go into menopause in the first place: in the old days people died in their 30s and 40s. We live as long as we do because human intelligence has created artificial environments that prolong life. They are convinced that hormone replacement is needed to prevent osteoporosis and heart disease.

Estrogen will help prevent osteoporosis, but how much of a problem is it? These data are not as strong as we have been led to believe. In the early 1990s the bone density test was devised. In an attempt to see what the range of bone densities were in women, many women in their 40s and 50s were tested. The results were then looked at and a normal range defined. Anyone below that range was diagnosed as having osteoporosis. This is not entirely fair. Osteoporosis used to mean soft bones, fractures and much pain. It occurred in 25 percent of elderly women. We know estrogen can help in this situation.[42] What we don't yet know is if the bone density test done at 40 or 50 can predict accurately who will end up with fractures later on. Many women are being labeled as having osteoporosis when all there is is a bone density test that shows they are outside of an arbitrarily defined norm. It is as if we said that all kids who are under two and a half feet at three years old will be short when they grow up. In reality, some will and some won't—and what is the definition of "short" anyway?

In addition, we know that all women will show some bone loss with menopause. If our goal is to prevent that at all costs, then we all need to be on estrogen until we die. That is unrealistic, however. Men also show bone loss with time. It's part of aging. More important is that you build up as much bone as you can in your youth and 20s, with adequate calcium, vitamin D, and, in particular, weight-bearing exercise. Continuing that habit of exercise will help keep your bones, as well as your muscles, strong. If you didn't exercise when you were younger, starting now can still reduce your risk of fracture.

What we do know is that a 50-year-old white woman has a 15 percent lifetime probability of a subsequent hip fracture. The median age at first hip fracture is 79. If she takes estrogen (no good evidence about progesterone) therapy she can reduce this by 25 percent.[43]

Heart disease may be a more cogent problem. A 50-year-old white woman has a 46 percent lifetime probablity of developing, and a 31 percent chance of dying, of heart disease. Death from coronary heart disease occurs at a median age of 74 years. Epidemiologic studies have shown a lower risk of coronary heart disease among estrogen users compared to nonusers. Most of this evidence is limited. The studies looking at this are all observational and therefore flawed. Women who take hormones tend to be white, educated, and in the upper middle class. They are also usually thinner than women in lower socioeconomic groups. Thus they have a lower risk of heart disease than the women who don't take hormones. It is also true that women who continue to take hormones share the as yet unidentified advantage of compliant individuals. In the double-blind Coronary Drug Project trial, participants who were highly compliant with their prescribed placebo had a significantly lower risk of heart disease than those who did not take their placebo regularly. The only way to answer this dilemma is to do a randomized controlled clinical trial such as the Women's Health Initiative (see Chapter 32). It may well be that healthy, compliant women take hormones, not that hormones make you healthy.

It may also be that the protective effect of estrogen is higher in women who already have coronary heart disease. Nonetheless it appears that estrogen has to be taken for a prolonged period. The data on estrogen and progesterone together are limited.[44]

I think we need to look at this from an individual standpoint. All women do not need to be on hormones for prevention. Each woman has to weigh the risks and benefits for herself. I think it's important to look at the other possible causes of osteoporosis, stroke, and heart disease before jumping into using artificial hormones as a preventive for them. Is there a history of these diseases in an individual's family? And what other factors are involved in the diseases? Hormones are only one factor. Osteoporosis also seems to be connected with the amount of calcium in your diet, and with the amount and kind of exercise you do. Similarly, there are many nonhormonal factors that contribute to heart disease, and it might be worth your while to change diet, exercise, and smoking habits instead of taking hormones.

Many women need to take hormones not to prevent future illness, but to alleviate current discomfort, which makes a lot more sense. But their numbers are not as great as we are often led to believe. The media would have us assume that all women suffer from the symptoms of menopause. But the studies they cite are done on women in doctors' offices and so are skewed toward those women with complaints. Studies of the population as a whole are just being conducted. It appears that about one in five women will experience incapacitating hot flashes, or extreme vaginal dryness that ruins their enjoyment of sex. If you are one of these women, you may well decide it's worth the risk of taking hormones. At any rate you probably need to take them for only five or six years to get over the initial adjustment. If your symptoms are mild and don't disrupt your life particularly, you may not want to bother. You may well want to look into some of the nonhormonal ways to alleviate your symptoms, described in many up-to-date books on menopause (see Appendix B). There is some evidence that bioflavinoids (found in cabbage, broccoli, brussels sprouts, and cauliflower) and other plant estrogens (found in soy products) may both help relieve menopausal symptoms and prevent breast cancer.[45]

What we need in order to answer the prevention question is a randomized, controlled study with the same number of healthy women in each group. Once we control for all of the other factors the true influence of hormone replacement therapy will be apparent. We are finally going to have this study. The Women's Health Initiative (described in Chapter 33) will do a study on HRT. They will compare two groups of women—one taking estrogen and progesterone, and one taking a placebo. Unfortunately we won't have the results for 10 years. I encourage all women who live near a center for the Women's Health Initiative to participate (see Appendix B for the number to call and find the center nearest you). Meanwhile, every woman has to weigh the risks and benefits in her own case. If you decide you want to be on hormones, bear in mind that you have two options: you can take estrogen and progesterone, or estrogen alone. The latter option is often not given but it is one I am comfortable with, because we have more data on estrogen than on progesterone. You then are at increased risk for uterine cancer, so you'll want to have your uterus monitored with an endometrial biopsy once a year. If you are one of the unlucky 20 percent of women who are sensitive to estrogen and develop precancerous changes in your uterus you can decide whether to take progesterone, which protects you from uterine cancer, or have a hysterectomy.

What if you've had breast cancer, or a strong family history, and you have horrible menopausal symptoms or a high risk of osteoporosis—should you take hormones? I wish I had an answer, but I don't. We'll discuss the issue of hormones and breast cancer in Chapter 28.

FERTILITY DRUGS

Fertility drugs are being used a lot these days as the baby boomers who postponed childbearing are now trying to get pregnant. These drugs make you "hyperovulate," kicking your ovaries and making them work harder. We don't know how safe fertility drugs are or how they interact with breast cancer. There are data now that suggest that use of Clomid will increase the risk of ovarian cancer,[46] since the more you ovulate the stronger your chance of getting it. Another fertility drug is Perganol, which comes from the urine of pregnant mares, and also causes you to hyperovulate. There's also HCG, human chorionic gonadotropin, the hormone that actually goes up in pregnancy. By the time you're taking fertility drugs you're probably over 30 and you probably haven't had a child yet—a combination that already increases your risk of breast cancer. The drugs and hormones might also add a promoter effect. It's very important for women to realize that we don't know the relationship of these drugs to breast cancer, but it's likely that they have some effect, since DES and the other hormones do.

I have mixed feelings about all this. There's a tendency to look at hormones as prevention rather than treatment. You have your first period, and a few years later you get on the pill. You stay on the pill, with a few interruptions to have your kids. Or maybe you're already in your 30s when you get off the pill, and you don't get pregnant for a while. So you use fertility drugs. Otherwise you have your kids and go back to the pill, and stay on it till you hit menopause. Then you take postmenopausal hormones till you die. So you're always on some kind of hormonal medication. And that somehow says our bodies are wrong. It bothers me. It provides a great market for the pharmaceutical companies, but it may not do us any good in the long run. Rather than fixing our bodies we should be fixing the world we live in and fostering a healthy lifestyle from girlhood on. But that is harder and less lucrative.

Pesticides and Other Environmental Hazards

There are a number of other things that now contribute to your vulnerability to breast cancer. The most telling study has been one done by Dr. Mary Wolfe. Wolfe and her group looked at the levels of DDE, which is a breakdown product of the pesticide DDT (an organochloride), in the breast fat of women with breast cancer, comparing them to the levels of breast fat of women without breast cancer.[47] The levels were significantly higher in the women with breast cancer. This doesn't mean that DDE is the cause of the breast cancer, but it certainly suggests that there is a possibility. Another, larger study by Krieger and associates,[48] however, showed no relationship between blood levels of organochlorides and subsequent breast cancer risk.

Does it make sense that organochlorides used as pesticides might also be related to breast cancer? One theory is based on the fact that a lot of them are broken down in the body to forms of estrogen (xenoestrogens) which act in the body as estrogen.

Breast cancer activists on Long Island have been instrumental in developing this line of study. There is a very high risk of breast cancer on Long Island, and certain counties—Nassau and Suffolk—have a higher risk than others. *Newsday* did an intensive investigative report

and, although they found that breast cancer risk on Long Island wasn't the highest in the nation (Marin County north of San Francisco is the highest), they did find that most of the high-risk areas were inhabited by well-to-do white women. They also implied that the risk of breast cancer in these areas appeared to be related to the environment. This, like all risk factors, may be difficult to prove since it may well depend on when exposures to carcinogens in the environment occurred. Exposures at puberty may be more important than adult exposures.

In the 1950s, they used to spray DDT from trucks in the suburbs to kill the mosquitoes, and kids used to run after the trucks and play in the spray. Kids were sprayed in swimming pools; these were the years of the polio epidemic, and health experts thought this would protect the kids. Pesticides were used on the golf courses and lawns. Those chemicals do not go away. They sit in the ground contaminating groundwater and eventually drinking water. Most of these chemicals have subsequently been banned, but their residue persists in our lives and in our environment.

In addition, there are many contaminants in food. Some are now banned in this country but permitted to be sold to countries in Latin America. We import foods from those same countries, and so get our old contaminants back again. Interestingly, the rates of breast cancer are actually lower in these countries. Are they really not so dangerous, or are some ethnic groups more susceptible to the carcinogens than others?

Breast cancer activists on Long Island did a really historic thing. First they asked the Centers for Disease Control to investigate the high incidence of breast cancer on Long Island. The Centers held some hearings and concluded that the women had high rates of breast cancer because they were Jewish and of a high socioeconomic class and therefore at a higher risk in general. Needless to say, that answer wasn't acceptable to these women, so they decided to hold their own conference, in the fall of 1993, to investigate the link between environmental pollutants and breast cancer. I was asked to co-chair the conference, which included environmental scientists and people involved in breast cancer research as well as activists. It was a fascinating conference, and it raised a lot of important questions. We looked not only into the organochlorides and pesticides, but also at other issues. For example, it appears that much of the water contamination you're exposed to comes not from drinking water, but from showers and baths, because it's vaporized in the hot water and you inhale the gases. So if you go out and buy your nice bottled water and then take a long, hot shower after your exercise, you're still exposed to carcinogens. There's no avoiding it.

Now, in the wake of this conference on Long Island, the National Cancer Institute has launched, under a congressional mandate, the Long Island study, which is going to examine the risk of breast cancer on Long Island. They're also doing some cooperative studies with the National Institute of Environmental Health and Safety to start to explore pesticides and other risks. The Massachusetts Breast Cancer Coalition has gotten the state to fund a study on Cape Cod looking at many of the same environmental factors.

Another issue that was brought up, that hasn't yet been well studied, is that of electromagnetic fields, coming from telephone and other high-tension lines. There have been some reports of higher levels of leukemias and brain cancers in children who live under these lines. The electric appliances we use in our houses also subject us to electromagnetic fields. Women who work on the telephone lines have a higher incidence of breast cancer.[49] Artificial light is another source. There's a very interesting study that was done in Seattle on men with breast cancer. It showed that men who spent many hours under artificial light had a higher rate of breast cancer than men who didn't.[50] (They chose men because, since breast cancer is so rare in men, it's easier to find something in common in that group than in the much larger female population.) A similar study on women is now under way. There are several theories to explain this. One is that vitamin D in sunlight works as a form of breast cancer prevention, and artificial light, obviously, doesn't contain vitamin D.

The other argument, which the researchers in Seattle favor, is that the pineal gland, a small gland under the brain which helps you distinguish day and night, produces a hormone, melatonin. It appears that melatonin can be protective of the breast, and it's excreted mostly when it's dark. It doesn't get secreted if it's light, so if you stay up most of the night with the lights on, you may never get enough melatonin to do you any good.[51]

Studies are also being done with farm workers, who are exposed to high levels of pesticides, hormones, and other additives, to see if they are at higher risk of cancer than others. It may well be that people who live in smoggy L.A. are safer than people who live in farms in the San Joaquin Valley.

So there are a variety of external factors which haven't been very well explored that we're just now starting to look at. This is an area where having banks of tissue, both normal tissue and breast cancer tissue, is extremely important, because then you can test the tissues to see if they have traces of some of these carcinogens. (See Chapter 33 for how to become involved in tissue donation.)

Carcinogens come not only from where we live but also from what we do. As we mentioned, women who work on the telephone lines have a higher incidence of breast cancer—they're exposed to electromagnetic fields. I've taken to asking all my patients now if they have any environmental or occupational exposures to carcinogens. Almost every woman says no. Then I ask what they do for a living. Very often it turns out that in fact they do have exposures. One of my patients has been a manicurist for 15 years. She's been inhaling all those fumes from the nail polish remover and nail polishes in a fairly close area for a long period of time. Could that be a carcinogen? Another woman was a painter who used oil paints. She was exposed to all the solvents used to clean the oil paint, as well as to the cadmium in the red paint, which is a very strong carcinogen in some studies. I've had a number of women patients recently who are flight attendants. It may well be that they have a higher risk of breast cancer because of their exposure to radiation. At higher altitudes you get much higher radiation than you do on earth.

There are probably a lot of environmental exposures that haven't yet occurred to us because we're not used to thinking about life that way. In 1993 the National Cancer Institute held the first conference on occupational risks of cancer in women. (Until now, I think they assumed women didn't have occupations.) Even "housewives" are ex-

posed to cleaning solvents and insecticides. These may well be among the factors that lead to breast cancer.

As we mentioned in Chapter 13, the cause of breast cancer will probably turn out to be not just one thing but a combination of environment and genetic components. Research needs to be done on both fronts if we are to find an answer.

16

Precancerous Conditions

As we discussed in Chapter 6, virtually none of the symptoms mis-named "fibrocystic disease" is related to breast cancer. There are, however, certain microscopic findings in breast tissue that may well lead to cancer.

You'll recall that I've described the breast as a milk factory, with two parts—lobules that make the milk and ducts, like hollow tubes, that carry it to the nipples (Fig. 16-1). Over the years, you can get a few extra cells lining the tube—sort of like rust in a metal pipe. This is called *intraductal hyperplasia*, which simply translates to "too many cells in the duct." In itself, this "rust" is no problem. Sometimes the cells can begin to get a bit strange looking, and this condition is called *intraductal hyperplasia with atypia*. If they keep on getting odd-looking, and multiply within the duct, clogging it up, they're known as *ductal carcinoma in situ* (meaning "in place") or *intraductal carcinoma* (Fig. 16-2). These three steps are all reversible. We don't yet know how, but we suspect it has something to do with hormones. Finally, if cells break out of the ducts and into the surrounding fat, they are called *invasive ductal cancer*.

The first two conditions do not cause lumps (the third rarely does)—they take place inside the duct, so you can't feel them by exam-ining your breast. Though they're found during a biopsy, they aren't in

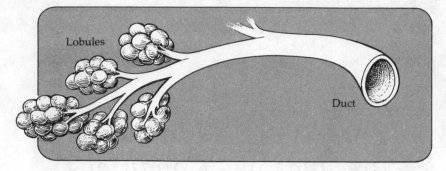

FIGURE 16-1

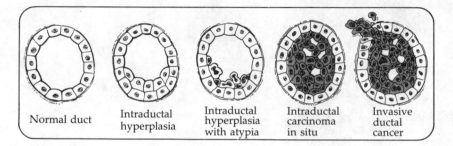

| Normal duct | Intraductal hyperplasia | Intraductal hyperplasia with atypia | Intraductal carcinoma in situ | Invasive ductal cancer |

FIGURE 16-2

the lump itself—they're next to the lump in the rim of "normal" tissue and the pathologist comes across them by accident. If you look at autopsy studies of women who've died of causes other than breast cancer, you'll see that 30 percent or so had some degree of either hyperplasia or atypical hyperplasia.[1] So probably a lot of us are walking around with these conditions, and we don't know it because we have no reason to have biopsies, and they don't show on mammograms.

David Page,[2] of Vanderbilt University, studied 10,000 biopsies and found, not surprisingly, that there is a progression of increased risk with each of these entities. The women with hyperplasia and no atypia had a slightly increased relative risk (barely significant), which was worse when compounded with family history (1.5 and 2.1, respectively). Interestingly, and not easily explained, he also found that women with gross cysts and family history had an increased relative risk of about 3. Finally, and most significant, the women with atypical hyperplasia had an increased relative risk of 3.5, and if they had a family history in a first-degree relative this rose to 8.9 over 15 years. Although this certainly sounds high, it must be pointed out that there were only 39 women who fulfilled these criteria. In fact, of the 10,000 benign biopsies Page reviewed, only 3 percent had atypical hyperplasia (see Table 16-1).

We're not quite sure whether atypical intraductal hyperplasia increases the risk of cancer because it's dangerous in itself, or because it's a response to something else that's dangerous and that we don't yet know about—the way, for example, a bruise that doesn't heal isn't harmful itself but may be failing to heal because it's over a cancer site. It is interesting to note that the risk of invasive cancer in these patients was equal in either breast, and some of the patients even had bilateral cancers. This makes it more likely that we are picking up women at high risk in this specific group rather than a condition which is dangerous in itself. It might be termed an intermediate marker.

There are obviously still many questions. The most vital, however, to the woman diagnosed with atypical hyperplasia is the question of what to do. At this time most surgeons would agree that the best program is close follow-up. This will not detect more atypical hyperplasia, but may detect an intraductal carcinoma (by mammogram) or invasive cancer in its early stages. A close follow-up means a physical exam by a doctor every six months and yearly mammograms. Some women may even consider a more drastic approach and have preventive mastectomies (see Chapter 17). Although I don't usually recommend it, because we can never be certain that it will get out all the breast tissue and therefore prevent the cancer from returning, there are some women who feel it is worth investigating if they have a first-degree family history and atypical hyperplasia.

Table 16-1. Benign Breast Disease and Risk of Breast Cancer[a]

	Relative Risk
Previous biopsy[b]	1.8
Gross cysts	1.3
with first-degree family history	2.7
Atypical hyperplasia	4.4
with first-degree family history	8.9
with calcifications on mammogram	6.5
with first birth after 20	4.5
Lobular carcinoma in situ	7.2
Ductal carcinoma in situ	11.0

[a]Adapted from W.D. Dupont and D.L. Page, "Breast Cancer Risk with Proliferative Disease, Age at First Birth, and a Family History of Breast Cancer," *American Journal of Epidemiology* 125 (1987): 769.

[b]S.M. Love, R.S. Gelman, and W.S. Silen, "Fibrocystic Disease': A Non-disease?," *New England Journal of Medicine* 307 (1982): 1010.

If we consider atypical hyperplasia as "pre-precancer," then in situ cancer, the next step along the path, can be considered precancer. Some doctors prefer to call it "noninvasive cancer"—a term I find misleading since in most people's minds cancer is by definition an invasive disease. I prefer the term "precancer" because the lack of invasion means that these lesions don't metastasize; therefore they can't kill you. I have had many battles over this nomenclature with some colleagues, doctors who say cancer is cancer whether it is invasive or not. I have finally figured out what the problem is. It's like arguing whether life begins at conception or once the fetus becomes viable. Those who call ductal carcinoma in situ cancer are like those who believe that life begins at conception. Cancer is cancer even if it can't spread or kill you. The other school is like those who say that life begins at viability: it isn't cancer until it has the ability to spread and kill you. Like the fetal viability debate, there is no "right" answer, but there are strong feelings on both sides.

Precancers in the breast, like atypical hyperplasia, rarely cause lumps, pain, or any other symptoms. They are also usually found incidentally. As opposed to atypical hyperplasia, however, they can sometimes show up on mammograms, and the increased use of mammography for screening has shown us that they're actually far more common than we had thought. The process of learning about and treating breast precancers is similar to that for cervical precancers, which were rarely seen until the routine use of Pap smears showed them to be fairly frequent.

There are two kinds of precancer of the breast: *ductal carcinoma in situ*, which we have mentioned and will discuss more below, and *lobular carcinoma in situ*. As its name suggests, lobular carcinoma in situ occurs in the lobules. The difference is not only in the lesions' locale: the two behave very differently.

Lobular Cancer in Situ

Under the microscope, lobular carcinoma in situ (LCIS) is seen as very small, round cells stuffing the lobules, which normally don't have any cells inside them (Fig. 16-3). If there are only a few cells and they're not too odd looking, you have lobular hyperplasia; whereas if they fill the whole lobule and do look very atypical (odd), you have LCIS. Such collections of cells are usually what we call "multicentric"—you can find them scattered throughout both breasts.

The natural history of LCIS became better known when Cushman Haagensen,[3] a leading breast specialist, did a study in which he carefully monitored his patients who had LCIS rather than perform mastectomies on them in his breast clinic. He saw them periodically for

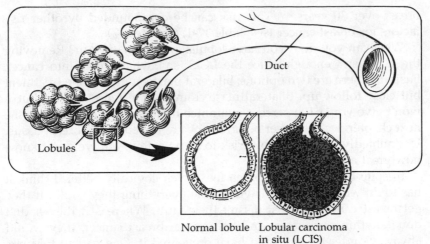

Normal lobule   Lobular carcinoma
in situ (LCIS)

FIGURE 16-3

about 30 years, examining them every four months (this was in the early days of mammography, and Haagensen, who didn't much trust mammography, used only physical examination). Out of 211 patients, only 36 (about 17%) developed invasive cancer over 30 years. This made their risk 7.2 times the normal risk: that is, if one patient per thousand per year, age 40–50, normally got breast cancer, then among patients with LCIS about seven per thousand per year, age 40–50, got breast cancer. These cancers occurred in either breast, and any place within the breast. They weren't confined to the spot where the original LCIS was found, or even to the lobular system itself. This strongly suggests that LCIS doesn't grow into cancer, but is simply a sign that cancer is a possible danger—the way, for example, an overcast day warns you it might rain. Because of this, some experts believe that lobular carcinoma in situ isn't, in fact, a true precancer. Having LCIS indicates a degree of risk similar to that faced by a woman whose mother and sister have or had breast cancer. It is cumulative risk, spread out over your entire life (see Chapter 14).

It's also important to note that of the women in Haagensen's study who did develop breast cancer, only six died of it. And none of the six had come back for regular examinations. In Haagensen's opinion, they died because they ignored the warning sign of LCIS, and didn't monitor the condition of their breasts after the LCIS diagnosis.

Haagensen's was the benchmark study, but others that have followed have had similar results, showing that people with LCIS have a range of between 16 and 27 percent risk of breast cancer in either breast over 30 years.[4,5,6] This risk can be compounded by other risk factors for breast cancer (see Table 17-1, Chapter 17).

What can you do if you have lobular carcinoma in situ? Removing the LCIS isn't enough, since the LCIS isn't what grows into cancer. Basically there are two options: bilateral mastectomy and no treatment but close follow-up. Bilateral mastectomy is the more drastic, but it won't give you a 100 percent guarantee because, as we discuss in the next chapter, we can never be sure we've removed all the breast tissue. Undoubtedly it reduces your risk to some extent, but we don't know how great an extent that is.

In spite of this, some women feel psychologically better. I think it has to do with a sense of having done everything they could. If they get breast cancer, at least it isn't their fault. Whereas if they hadn't done anything surgically and had gotten breast cancer, they would always wonder if they could have prevented it. One patient told me, "I knew instantly what my decision should be. I was astounded to see how greedy for life I was." This patient was already in a high-risk group because of her family history; she had seen members of her family go through breast cancer, and was determined to do all she could to avoid suffering with it herself. She was uncomfortable with the studies about monitoring, which she felt were too recent: mastectomy, she reasoned, had been around a long time.

This particular patient had reconstruction through one of the flap procedures discussed in Chapter 26, while others have had silicone implants. Since, as we discussed earlier (see Chapter 5), silicone has been seriously called into question, this will be one more factor in the decision for a woman with LCIS contemplating double mastectomies.

There's a variant of the bilateral mastectomy that's very popular with some doctors—the subcutaneous mastectomy, which leaves the nipple and outer breast skin intact and then fills in the gap with an implant of either silicone or saline. It's a little better cosmetically, but leaves more breast tissue than mastectomy. You can make the argument that since we're not likely to get all the breast tissue anyway, we may as well do the more cosmetically appealing surgery, and hope that it will reduce your risk as well. In the absence of data, however, I would lean toward the more aggressive approach if I were to do surgery at all.

Another possibility is to have a one-sided mastectomy with a quadrantectomy on the other breast—that is, the removal of the breast that contains the LCIS and the upper outer quadrant, where most of the breast tissue is, of the other.[7] I can't see much justification for this procedure. Cancers that follow the appearance of LCIS can appear in either breast and in any section of the breast, so all this procedure does is subject you to major surgery and disfigurement, without affecting the likelihood that you will or won't get breast cancer. There is no evidence that reducing the amount of breast tissue by a certain percentage reduces the risk of breast cancer proportionately. If you're going to subject yourself to the disfigurement of surgery, you may as well get whatever amount of protection goes with it—there is at least the possibility that total mastectomy will remove all the breast tissue

The alternative to surgery is to take the appearance of LCIS as a warning that you need to be closely watched. This means follow-up exams every six months, with a yearly mammogram. That way, if a cancer does develop, you're likely to catch it at an early stage and can decide then if you want to have a mastectomy, or a lumpectomy and radiation (see Chapter 23). If a cancer doesn't develop, you've been spared the ordeal of major and disfiguring surgery. This was Haagensen's recommendation, and for the most part I agree with him. Most of my patients have opted for this course.

There is a possible third option. The National Surgical Adjuvant Breast and Bowel Project (NSABP) is conducting a study (which we'll discuss at length in the next chapter) to see whether tamoxifen, an estrogen blocker, prevents breast cancer. Women with LCIS are eligible for this study. When its data are available, we will know whether tamoxifen is a good choice for women with LCIS. Until there is definitve proof that tamoxifen does prevent breast cancer, I don't recommend that anyone use it outside of a study—I think it's unethical for doctors to offer it for LCIS on their own.

What's important is that you give yourself time to figure out what you want to do. LCIS doesn't call for an immediate decision. When a patient of mine is undecided, I usually suggest she take the follow-up route, and see how she feels about it after six months or a year. If she's comfortable living with it, then she can continue this course for the rest of her life, or until a cancer occurs. If she finds herself in a constant state of anxiety, waking up every morning thinking, "This is it—this is the day I'll find the lump," then maybe a bilateral mastectomy is best for her. You can always decide on mastectomy later, but you can't undo a double mastectomy.

Radiation and chemotherapy are not necessary treatments for LCIS, because it's not really cancer. Nor is there any reason to obtain surgically clean margins. LCIS is usually scattered throughout both breasts. LCIS is only a marker for risk; it does not become cancer itself, so it does not need to be excised. Some clinicians don't understand this. If your surgeon or oncologist starts talking about wide excision, radiation, or chemotherapy for LCIS, make sure you get a second opinion from a doctor who is more familar with this process. I recently saw a woman from Southern California who had had a wide excision and radiation for LCIS. She was now being told to have chemotherapy "just in case." I reviewed her slides and indeed it was just LCIS. When I explained that she had been overtreated she said she had thought this was the case at the time. She had read the first edition of this book and had understood what she had. But she hadn't been able to convince her doctors, and had trusted their expertise. The moral is, when in doubt, get a second opinion.

Sometimes, when a patient has a lump that turns out to be cancer, the pathologist finds LCIS in the adjacent tissue. What does this mean? Well, it may mean that the patient was at a higher risk for breast cancer and sure enough she got it. But it may also mean that the other breast is also at a higher risk for breast cancer than that usually expected, so some surgeons like to do what we call a "blind biopsy" on that breast. It's called a blind biopsy because the surgeons have no way of knowing what they're looking for. Sometimes they take out the upper outer quadrant because that's where most of the breast tissue is, or they may take out the mirror image of the section they've removed from the breast with LCIS. It's pretty chancy since there's no evidence that cancer will occur in the mirror image, and they might find something that looks worrisome pathologically yet is biologically insignificant. In addition, they might be clear in one part and miss a cancer millimeters away. Most doctors prefer simply to follow the woman closely, with breast examinations every three to four months and yearly mammograms.

Ductal Carcinoma in Situ

Ductal carcinoma in situ (DCIS) is more complex than LCIS—and unlike LCIS, it's more than a marker that cancer may appear in the breast: it's a lesion that can in itself grow into a cancer. It rarely forms lumps, but may sometimes form a soft thickening (caused by the pliable ducts becoming less pliable because they're filled with cells. See Fig. 16-4).

DCIS is now found far more frequently because of mammograms, where it appears with microcalcifications. In fact, it's probably very common. Autopsies done on women who died from all kinds of causes show that between 6 and 16 percent had DCIS.[8,9] This suggests that many of us have it and never know it—it is probably not, as we used to believe, a rare condition.

In the past, standard treatment was a mastectomy on the breast with the lesion. That worked most of the time. But it might not have been necessary—and since the breasts had all been removed, we had no way of studying what happened when a breast that had DCIS wasn't removed. There have been a few small studies, however, that

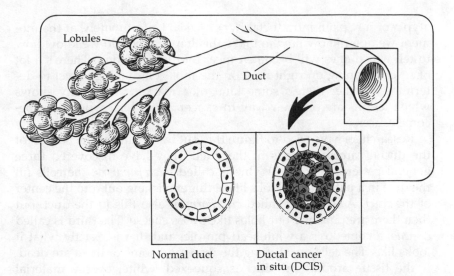

Normal duct   Ductal cancer
                     in situ (DCIS)

FIGURE 16-4

have given us a clue. Three studies followed people who were biopsied and thought to have something benign. W. L. Betsill[10] at Sloan Kettering reviewed all the pathology the hospital had done on 10,000 breasts between 1940 and 1950 and, on reexamining the pathology reports, found 25 cases of people who had been misdiagnosed. The biopsied tissue had been described as benign but actually had had early intraductal lesions. (These lesions are often small, and very easy to miss.) Obviously, no further treatment had been done. Of these 25, only 10 had been regularly followed for 22 years. They contacted these women and found out what their breast history had been since the biopsies had been performed. They found that seven had developed invasive cancer in the 22 years after the original diagnosis.

Other similar studies have led us to believe that about 20 to 25 percent of women with untreated DCIS will go on to get invasive cancer within about 10 years.[11]

All together the studies add up to only 78 patients, not enough to be sure they're representative. Furthermore, their lesions were on the border between atypical hyperplasia and DCIS, or they would have been diagnosed initially: the studies don't address the situation of women with obvious DCIS. What is clear from these studies, however, is twofold: untreated DCIS can go on to become invasive breast cancer and in the majority of women it does not seem to do so.

A further complexity is that some of the lesions don't stay in the precancerous stage but revert to either intraductal hyperplasia with atypia or just plain intraductal hyperplasia. Unfortunately, at the moment we don't know how to make this happen, nor do we know how to tell which ones will become cancer and which won't. There's a lot of research going on right now on the molecular biology level to determine whether there's some kind of a marker that clearly shows which lesions are on their way to cancer and which won't ever become cancer.

Researchers have tried to figure this out by looking at the pattern of the ductal carcinoma cells in the duct. They have discovered three general patterns (Fig. 16-5). One is called *micropapillary*: the cells fill the duct in a pattern that looks like a finger sticking out into the center of the duct. A second is called *cribriform*: it also fills in the duct, but then there are punched-out holes like Swiss cheese. The third is called *comedo*; a comedo is a whitehead pimple, and that is exactly what it looks like. The cells are stuffing the duct, and some of them are dead. If the tissue around the duct is squeezed, white, cheesy material comes out, just like squeezing a pimple.

Trying to predict the behavior of DCIS by examining the pattern it makes is crude at best. It is a little like trying to predict someone's behavior from a photograph—it may or may not be representative. Nonetheless, in the absence of data it is all we have.

Some researchers believe that the comedo pattern is the one most likely to progress on to invasive cancer, although their hypothesis hasn't been proved yet. Comedo DCIS has larger cells, and more atypical-looking nuclei than the other two types. Other measures of cell division and growth such as those we call *S phase* and *ploidy* (see Chapter 20) are also more prominent in comedo DCIS.[12]

In a study of wide excision alone,[13] all the recurrences that appeared after wide excision were of the comedo type. But that has only

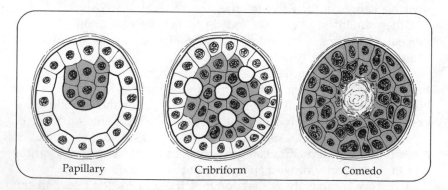

| Papillary | Cribriform | Comedo |

FIGURE 16-5

been after a short period of follow-up. We don't know if more recurrences will show up later in the other two forms.

Another study, by Mel Silverstein,[14] at the Van Nuys Breast Center, looked at wide excision and radiation. It showed that most of the initial recurrences showed up in the comedo type, but that later there were recurrences in the non-comedos as well.

In the smaller studies mentioned earlier in this chapter, with Betsill and Page, the women who went on to get cancer were all non-comedos, because, in order to be misdiagnosed in the first place, the lesions had to be borderline, less aggressive lesions. So there's no doubt that non-comedo DCIS can go on to become cancer. It seems either that the comedos are more likely to become cancers or that they do so more quickly.

In any case, it's too early to make treatment decisions, outside of the context of studies, based on the type of DCIS a patient has. Many cases of DCIS are mixed, with both comedo and non-comedo elements. The NSABP study (see page 232), with its 818 randomized patients, will be better able to tell whether one form of DCIS is more dangerous than the others.

Without a thorough understanding of the natural history of DCIS, it's hard to devise a logical treatment. However, there is increasing interest in treatments for DCIS that are less drastic than mastectomy—chiefly, wide excision. These are based on the same principle as the lumpectomy in breast cancer (see Chapter 23), except that there's usually no lump involved, so the surgeon tries to remove the entire area that has the DCIS, along with a rim of normal breast tissue.

Some experts[15] argue against this, claiming that DCIS, like LCIS, is multicentric. Their idea is that all the breast tissue is marching along toward cancer, and is precancerous to a greater or lesser degree, and this tissue just got a little further on. So, says this theory, we have to take off the whole breast, or even both breasts, because taking off just part of one isn't going to solve the problem.

This unfortunate theory evolved from a number of studies in which breasts that had been removed for DCIS were analyzed. The breasts were cut into four quadrants, and then examined under the microscope. If they found DCIS in more than one quadrant, the researchers designated it as multicentric.[16]

The problem is that this presupposes that the breast tissue is arranged in quadrants. It isn't. It's not an orange with nicely defined sections. The ductal system isn't structured in quadrants at all. It's more like an arbor: it comes from the nipple, branches out, and fills up a certain amount of space. There are between five and nine separate ductal systems in each breast, and they intertwine but they don't connect. So one system might take up the whole upper part of the breast.

If the breast is cut into quadrants, we would find DCIS in both quadrants even though it's all in part of one ductal system.

This was proven in a study done by Rolland Holland in Nijmegan in the Netherlands.[17] He took breasts that had been removed and cut them into four quadrants, and he too found that there was disease in several of the quadrants. But he went a step further. He very carefully mapped out the DCIS and found that in 80 of the 81 cases it was all contiguous. In other words, even though it was in more than one quadrant, it was in the same duct, which branched into several parts of the breast.

So this notion of multicentricity is wrong. Yet it persists in the medical literature. Like "fibrocystic disease," once something gets into the literature people keep quoting the earlier work without questioning it, and it becomes part of the canon.

Unfortunately, when pathologists look at DCIS on a slide, and see several duct profiles filled with cells, they too describe it as "multicentric" or "multifocal." The clinician interprets that as meaning there's DCIS all over the breast. But the pathologist just means that there are several different ducts seen in cross-section that have DCIS in them (Fig. 16-6). What this means is that if a doctor tells you that you have muliticentric DCIS and need a mastectomy, most of the time that's wrong.

The problem is that no one has ever mapped out the anatomy of the ductal system—something I'm working on in my own research now. If we had such a map, the surgeon could remove the ductal system that's affected and leave the rest of the breast alone. Then we would be sure of getting out the entire dangerous area. Now we just remove the area around the lesion, with no way of knowing whether or not we've gotten out the whole ductal system—which may account for the recurrences that happen.

What we do now is a wide excision based on a best guess of the extent of disease. We arrive at this guess by looking at the preoperative mammogram and then studying the tissue we remove from the breast. The pathologist coats the outer surface of this tissue with India ink, and the tissue is then fixed and made into slides and the slides are examined. If there is DCIS near ink it is said to be a "dirty margin"; if there is only normal breast tissue next to ink it is a "clean margin." But the pathologists can't look at every margin—it would mean more than 2,000 slides. They are only sampling the margins, so it's possible that even if all the margins they look at are negative there will be a DCIS-filled duct crossing into the breast that they have missed. This is a different situation than when we remove a single lump, in which case we know precisely where the lesion is and thus we know that we have gotten out the right surrounding tissue. So when there's a "re-

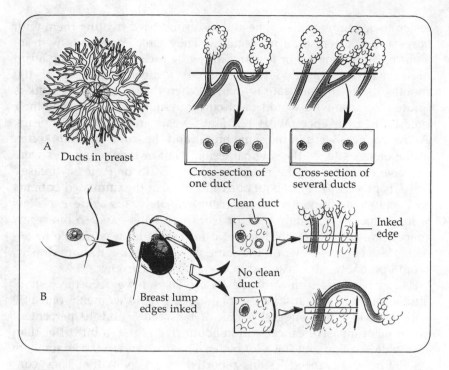

A Ducts in breast

Cross-section of one duct

Cross-section of several ducts

Clean duct

Inked edge

No clean duct

B Breast lump edges inked

FIGURE 16-6

currence" of DCIS, it's probably not a recurrence at all; it's DCIS that we left behind in the first place, in spite of what we thought were clean margins. This doesn't happen frequently, but it happens often enough (about 10–20 percent of the time) to make it significant. That's why mastectomy, though imperfect, tends to give a lower recurrence rate—it's the widest excision possible.

It is also important to look at a post-biopsy mammogram. DCIS usually shows up on the mammogram as calcifications. Even if calcifications have been removed, there are often some left, and this picture can add information regarding residual disease.

The best data we have on the results of limited surgery for DCIS come from Michael Lagios—a pathologist in San Francisco who's done some fine and careful work. He first looked at mastectomies done on women with DCIS to see if he could correlate the sizes of the lesions with the chance of having a tiny spot of invasion that could be seen only under a microscope. He found that if the lesion was less than 25 millimeters (one inch), there was almost no chance of hidden invasion, and if it was more than 50 millimeters (two inches), microinvasion was highly probable.[18] Once he believed invasion in the smaller lesion to be highly unlikely, he and his group tried treating them with surgery less severe than mastectomy. They took 79 patients with lesions of 25 millimeters or less and did wide excisions, including a rim of normal tissue around the lesion. At a mean follow-up of 100 months the recurrence rate is 16.6%. When this group of patients is limited to those who would meet current criteria and still have their breast, the recurrence rate is 12.7% at 5 years and 15.9% at 10 years. All recurrences were in the same breast and the same quadrant, often at the biopsy site, as the original lesion. Half of the recurrences were invasive cancers and the remainder were DCIS or Paget's disease[19] (see Chapter 24). That's about one third of what the untreated patients had shown in previous studies. Unfortunately, his wide excisions were "blind"—he couldn't see or feel the lesions—and so his recurrences probably represent leftover cancer cells he was unable to detect. Mastectomies done on the same women, although more drastic, would probably have resulted in even fewer recurrences.

Is radiation useful for treating DCIS? There have been three small studies on radiation and DCIS—one looking at 40 women,[20] one 14,[21] and one 34.[22] They suggest a risk of between 5 and 10 percent of subsequent invasive cancer within about five years—a bit better than just wide excision, but not a lot better. The first randomized data were on the more advanced lesions reported by the NSABP.[23] They conducted a nationwide study, called B 6, which looked at invasive cancer. It compared mastectomy, lumpectomy alone, and lumpectomy plus radiation. The pathologist Edwin Fisher reviewed all the slides. He reclassified 78 of the patients who he believed had DCIS rather than invasive cancer. The confusion was caused by the fact that the DCIS was right on the border of being invasive—lesions that had been perceived as invasive by the earlier pathologists. This study showed that patients who had had wide excisions plus radiation for their DCIS had 7 percent recurrence rate within four or five years, as opposed to 23 percent recurrence among those who had had only wide excisions. It's worth noting that most of these women had lumps or DCIS of 2.5 centimeters or larger. This suggests that lumpectomy and radiation is more effective in treating advanced DCIS than lumpectomy alone, probably because the radiation kills the cells that were inadvertently left behind. It may also be that radiation is more important the closer the lesion is to invasion.

But this study is still too small and too limited to draw generalizations from, so the NSABP has done a bigger study looking at this question. Called B 17,[24] it's the best to date. They took 818 women with DCIS throughout the country, randomly dividing them into one group that got wide excision alone and one that got wide excisions plus radiation. At three years, the data are very interesting. They show what we had seen before, a 16.4 percent recurrence in the wide excision alone group and 7 percent in the radiation group. What's very interesting about this study is that in the wide excision alone group, as had been seen before in Lagios's study and others, half the recurrences were precancer and half were invasive—so it was 10.4 percent precancer, 10.5 percent invasive. In the radiation group, 7.5 percent were precancer and 2.9 percent were invasive. So the radiation made a significant difference in the recurrence of invasive cancer, but not in the recurrence of precancer. The invasive cancer, of course, is what you're afraid of. And these lesions were all small and mostly mammographically detected, not the lumps studied in B 6.

There are a number of possible reasons for this. Maybe some of the precancers were already on the road to being invasive and we just couldn't tell that under the microscope. Maybe radiation is doing what we haven't been able to do: picking out the DCIS that is destined to go on to invasion from the DCIS that is stable. It will be very interesting to see if histological patterns such as comedo and noncomedo DCIS are a factor in these results.

This study, which came out in February 1993, has changed my treatment approach. I used to think I would only do radiation in cases of an invasive cancer that needed it. (As we discuss in Chapter 23, we can't radiate the same spot more than once.) Now I'm convinced it can really help prevent that cancer from occurring in the first place.

TREATMENT OPTIONS FOR DCIS

What does all this mean for you if your routine mammogram has shown a cluster of microcalcifications? How should you proceed from there? First, you'll need to have a core biopsy or a wire localization biopsy (see Chapter 12) to make certain that it is DCIS. The next step should always be to do another mammogram—to see if the biopsy has gotten rid of all the microcalcifications. However thorough your surgeon has been, there still may be a few remaining. Then you've got the three choices I described above: wide excision alone, wide excision and radiation, or mastectomy. Currently there is a lot of difference among doctors about the best ways to treat DCIS. Until more studies come out with definitive answers the controversies will rage. At UCLA, we approach the options in the following way.

You can have the breast removed, which is the ultimate wide excision. Most of the time this is more than adequate, but still there have been reports of recurrence of DCIS in the remaining breast tissue.[25,26] We do a mastectomy only if the DCIS is so extensive that it's the only choice, or if the patient strongly wants it.

The next option is a wide excision. This means taking out the area with a rim of normal tissue around it. Sometimes this has been done on the first operation and other times it is necessary to go back and remove more tissue (a re-excision).

The next question is whether or not it is necessary to add radiation therapy. This is still controversial. At the UCLA Breast Center we have devised practice guidelines to help direct our treatments. If it's a very small area of non-comedo DCIS and the margins are clean, or if there is no residual DCIS on the re-excision, then you don't need further treatment beyond close follow-up, since, as we discussed earlier, you have only between 10 and 20 percent chance of recurrence and only half of these will be invasive.

If there's residual disease on your re-excision, or if it was a comedo DCIS, then we generally add radiation therapy. As discussed above, there is still a 5–10% percent chance of local recurrence, but it is usually only DCIS, not cancer.

There is no reason to remove lymph nodes for small areas of DCIS since precancer can't spread at this stage. But if the lesions are big (greater than 5 centimeters—2 inches), some experts think they may hide microinvasion, and recommend removing the lymph nodes as well. On the other hand, as we mention in Chapter 23, many surgeons will forego lymph node dissection in this group as well, since even with microinvasion the chance of having positive nodes is so low.[27]

Since DCIS is not capable of spreading there is no reason to use tamoxifen or chemotherapy to treat systemic disease. The newest NSABP study has every woman with DCIS getting radiation and then randomizes them between placebo and tamoxifen. This will be interesting to follow. In England another study is looking at tamoxifen alone or in conjunction with radiation for DCIS. Both of these studies will give us more imformation. As of now, however, there is no evidence to support using tamoxifen for DCIS.

For the reasons discussed in Chapter 33, I try to encourage every woman to participate in a study, unless she has a definite preference or unless there are reasons to pick a particular treatment.

As new studies and information come in, we will be able to refine our understanding of DCIS and have a better basis for determining treatment. Every patient should have the final say in what treatment she gets: some women don't want a mastectomy no matter how big the lesions are; at the other extreme, some patients don't want to gamble even on the smallest lesion. When Nancy Reagan had precancer in the fall of 1987 she chose to have a mastectomy even though the lesion was tiny—7 millimeters. Remember, there's not one single treatment for precancer; there are a number of possible treatments. You don't have to rush into any one treatment because your doctor or your friend or anyone else says you should. It's your breast, and your life. Take the time to decide what is best for you.

17

Prevention

When we did the first edition of this book, we didn't have a separate chapter called "Prevention." That's because, at the time, there wasn't enough information for such a chapter. Now there is. So we're making some progress. We still, however, have more questions than answers. But the questions themselves are significant—and we're closer to the answers than we've ever been.

The issues of prevention are growing more important as we're becoming more able to identify the people with hereditary breast cancer. With these women we won't be talking about a theoretical risk, but real risk. We'll be able to say, for example, "You have a 50 percent risk by age 40 and an 80 percent risk by age 80." Once someone knows that, she's really going to want to find some form of prevention.

Taking into consideration all the risk factors we have reviewed, the question is, How far can we now go in preventing breast cancer? According to Canadian epidemiologist Anthony Miller, the major factors that seem amenable to change and therefore have potential for prevention are diet, reduction in obesity, reduction in the use of estrogens at menopause, and possibly a shift back to women having their first babies at an earlier age.

In Table 17-1 I list the attributable risks for some of these environ-

Table 17-1.   Attributable Risks for Breast Cancer[a]
(percent of breast cancer cases that can be attributed to each factor)

	Attributable Risk
Age 25 or greater with first birth	17%
Estrogen replacement therapy	8
High-fat diet	26
Obesity	12

[a]A.B. Miller, "Epidemiology and Prevention," in J.R. Harris, S. Hellman, I.C. Henderson, and D.W. Kinne, eds., *Breast Diseases* (Philadelphia: J.B. Lippincott, 1987).

mental and lifestyle risk factors. Remember, attributable risk is the amount of breast cancer that can be attributed to a certain risk factor (or eliminated if that factor is changed). The degree of certainty varies for each risk factor. These factors are all very interesting from a public health standpoint, but may or may not be applicable to any one individual woman, and I don't advise using them as the sole influence in decision making. For example, I had my first child at 40 and do not regret it. The advantages to me far outweighed the slight potential increased risk for breast cancer that this may entail. Would I have been wiser to have had a child in my 20s, when I wasn't ready for it? Or, since having no children is actually less of a risk than having a first child later in life, should I have deprived myself of the joy Katie has brought me? For me, there was no question. On the other hand, I do eat a low-fat diet. The occasional twinge I feel at the sight of a juicy hamburger or wedge of brie cheese is a reasonable price to pay for the fact that I may be decreasing my breast cancer risk and improving my overall health. These are very individual decisions.

Finally, it is important to realize that all of these factors have a long latency (time before an effect is seen). A proposal for reducing breast cancer by 25 percent in the United States by the year 2000 includes reducing the amount of fat in the diet to at most 100 grams per day and the amount of obesity to 5 percent of the population. While this is a laudable effort, the effect would not appear so soon. Miller has pointed out that the changes in diet would probably have to start at age five, and would have a 20-year lag until an effect would even be seen, and 80 years until the maximum effect would be realized.[1]

Intermediate Markers

If we're going to do prevention research we desperately need what we call "intermediate markers." That means we need to be able to find a sign that occurs before breast cancer—something in the blood or the nipple duct fluid, from which we could determine that a woman is on her way to cancer. The Pap smear has been able to do this for us in cervical cancer. It identifies cells that are just starting to become abnormal and allows us to try a variety of techniques to reverse them. We can then repeat it at a later date and recheck it. As of yet there is no easy way to check on breast tissue. Precancer sometimes gives us this information, but not every woman with breast cancer has precancer, and in any case we need to find something at an even earlier point. Then the woman could do something like go on a low-fat diet, or we could start with one of the noninvasive preventive measures, and then check back a year later and see if the early signs of cancer were reversed. At this point we don't have that, but we need to find a way to discover markers through something less drastic than surgery.

Some researchers are now working on this. They are doing blind breast biopsies every year to follow the breast tissue in high-risk women. Although this sounds great at first, it can be done only for so long before you run out of breast tissue. In addition, it presumes that the tissue you remove will be representative of the whole breast. Another center is doing multiple needle biopsies throughout the breast. Researchers there are hoping that this will get enough cells to analyze without resorting to surgery.[2] Another group is studying nipple duct fluid.[3] They've found that women who are at high risk are more likely to have nipple discharge than women who aren't at high risk. My own research involves trying to see if I can put a very small endoscope (like the scopes used in knee surgery these days but even smaller) into nipple ducts. If this turns out to be possible we will be able to biopsy the lining of the duct and monitor the cells much as is being done in the colon with colonoscopy. How we find an intermediate step in breast cancer development doesn't really matter—all that matters is that we do find it.

Meanwhile, here you are, reading this book and hoping to figure out a way to reduce your own chances of getting breast cancer, now. What can you do?

Diet

First we'll talk briefly about diet. (We looked at diet in Chapter 15, and discussed how it may have an effect on breast cancer risk.) It might make sense to eat a low-fat diet to try to help reduce your chance of breast cancer. This is currently being studied by the Women's Health Initiative. (See Appendix C.)

I highly advise any woman who has the opportunity to be a participant in this study to do so. There are many centers around the country that will be involved in this study. If you see an ad in the newspaper or on television, you should check it out, or call the 800 number listed in the appendix. (For more information about studies and their importance, see Chapter 33.)

Whether you do it through a study or not, you can get onto a low-fat diet, and I think it's wise for any woman to do so. There is no certainty that it prevents breast cancer, but it's healthier in terms of preventing heart disease and stroke. Further, we do know that obesity at later ages is a risk factor for breast cancer, and a low-fat diet makes you less likely to be obese.

Your diet should also be high in fiber, in antioxidants (food containing vitamins C, E, and beta carotene), and in green leafy vegetables. I concur with the National Cancer Institute's recommendation of five servings of vegetables and/or fruits a day. Some interesting research is also suggesting benefits to soy protein, perhaps a factor in the low incidence of breast cancer in East Asia.

It also makes sense to drink alcohol only in moderation, since, as we discussed in Chapter 15, regular consumption of liquor may affect your vulnerability to breast cancer, in addition to all its other effects.

Exercise

Exercise is important for cardiovascular health and for preventing osteoporosis and heart disease—and, probably, breast cancer.

A study by Leslie Bernstein at USC came out in the fall of 1994[4] demonstrating that women who participated in four or more hours of exercise a week during their reproductive years have a marked decrease in breast cancer risk. This is very exciting because it is one of the first lifestyle changes which has actually been shown to decrease risk. The key effect is hormonal. The study showed no association at all between body mass index, weight, or height and breast cancer risk. In fact, studies of body mass and breast cancer risk among premenopausal women are consistent in showing that at young ages obesity is not a risk factor for breast cancer—a few studies even show that being lean is a risk factor. There is a correlation, in young girls, however, with exercise and delayed menstruation patterns and changes in ovulatory frequency.[5] Since, as we discuss below, late onset of menstruation prevents against breast cancer, this is significant (Fig. 17-1).

A good long-term prevention approach would be to increase adolescent athletics and thus get girls into the habit of exercising. Rose Frisch[6] of Harvard Medical School and Harvard School of Public Health has also shown that women who were involved in athletics during high school and college have a decreased risk of breast cancer.

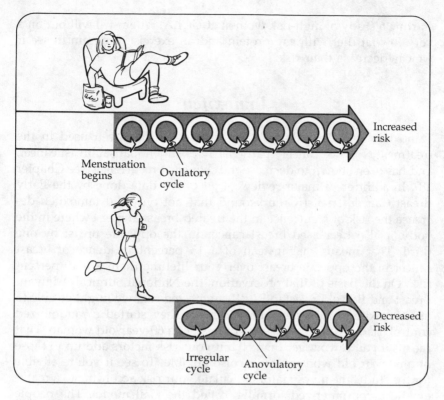

FIGURE 17-1

As a result, a theory has been very seriously put forth that I find delightful: put public health funding into high-school athletics for girls—not a bad use of our resources. This would likely decrease breast cancer; also, it strengthens bones and prevents future osteoporosis and helps to prevent heart disease. The next generation of women could probably dispense with the need for postmenopausal hormones if we could increase the exercise levels in girls and adolescents. (One caution in all this. There has been a near-epidemic of eating disorders among teenage girls desperate to conform to our culture's "thin is beautiful" image. "Low fat" doesn't translate to "no food," and to be beneficial, exercise requires a well-nourished body. Breast cancer will not be a big issue if a girl has so badly damaged her body with starvation that she doesn't live long enough to worry about it.)

Exercise in adult women is undoubtably of value as well, although with the exception of a few studies such as Bernstein's, just mentioned, its effectiveness in terms of breast cancer is less clear. We are starting a study of high-risk women at UCLA, whom we will put on a very low-fat diet with soy protein and an exercise program to see if we can decrease their risk.

Tamoxifen

Tamoxifen is a drug that blocks estrogen. It has been used in the treatment of breast cancer,[7] particularly postmenopausal breast cancer, and has been shown to decrease the chance of recurrence (see Chapter 28). In addition, a major review of all of the data done by the Early Breast Cancer Trialist Group found that not only did tamoxifen decrease the risk of recurrence in the treated breast and elsewhere in the body, it also decreased breast cancer in the opposite breast by one third. That means that instead of a 15 percent incidence of breast cancer in the opposite breast over your lifetime there is a 10 percent risk. On the basis of that observation, the National Surgical Adjuvant Breast and Bowel Project (NSABP) suggested that we might be able to use tamoxifen to prevent breast cancer. They started a randomized control trial, taking as a baseline the risk of a 60-year-old woman. That means if you're younger than 60 but your risk factors add up to those of a 60-year-old woman, you're also eligible. To see if you're eligible for the study, the investigators calculate your risk according to a mathematical, computerized formula, called the Gail model. The people who are eligible are then randomized to get either tamoxifen (in the form of a twice-daily pill) or a placebo for five years. (As in any such study, none of the participants know if they're getting the medication or the placebo until the study is finished.)

There are 16,000 women in the study, and the NSABP hopes to prevent 65 breast cancers, so it's not the answer to all prevention, but it's the first prevention study the National Cancer Institute has funded, and it will answer some questions.

There's been a lot of controversy about this study. Tamoxifen is a complicated drug. It blocks estrogen in the breast, but it acts like estrogen in the uterus, bones, and liver. That means it could cause endometrial (uterine) cancer much the way estrogen replacement therapy does. At the same time it tends to stabilize bone loss and, potentially, to decrease heart disease by reducing the "bad" cholesterol. One area of contention has been its use in premenopausal women. Most of the data on the safety of tamoxifen have been on postmenopausal women.

There are other less serious side effects of tamoxifen. These can include eye problems, depression, hot flashes, and bloating. Most of these symptoms haven't been considered very significant, because the drug was used only in women with cancer. If you have breast cancer and you're trying to keep it from recurring, you'll put up with a lot of unpleasant symptoms. Also, compared to chemotherapy, tamoxifen seems pretty gentle. But when we talk about using it on healthy women who don't have cancer and may never have it, then even those milder side effects become much more significant.

In 1994 there was a reevaluation of the study because information was revealed by the NSABP from another study that tamoxifen caused deaths from uterine cancer. We always knew that it could cause uterine cancer, but we thought that it would be a highly treatable kind, similar to the kind that is seen in women on estrogen replacement therapy. The reports of deaths, perhaps from a less treatable form of uterine cancer, shook everyone up, even though incidence of uterine cancer was not high—about 1/1000. However, after careful evaluation the National Cancer Institute decided to continue the trial with careful monitoring and informed consent.

I am pleased about this outcome since I feel very strongly that we need to learn whether tamoxifen can prevent breast cancer, and at what cost. There are risks, and potential subjects must be told of all the known and suspected dangers. They are taking a gamble in either direction since they're already at fairly high risk for breast cancer. That is what it means to be in a study.

It is important that we do prevention studies, and this is a useful one. I suggest that women who are eligible and interested should consider participating. It's taking place all over the country, and any woman who fits in the risk criteria should find out if she can participate, and give it serious thought (see Appendix C).

As always, it's worth a warning here. The fact that something is being studied doesn't mean it will turn out to be a means of prevention or a cure, only that we have some reason to think it might. And since something like tamoxifen, unlike exercise or low-fat diet, does have risks and side effects, I think it's extremely unwise for any woman to use it as a possible cancer preventive measure if she's not part of a study.

I also have mixed feelings about the notion that we should use drugs to prevent disease—the medical model of treatment as prevention. I'd rather see us eliminate the causes, such as improving diet, or cleaning up the environment.

4HPR

Another study being done on a possible breast cancer preventive is the 4HPR study.[8] 4HPR is a relative of vitamin A, a type of retinoid. In many cancers, particularly lung cancer, it has been shown to be preventive. It's being studied in Italy right now—the National Cancer Institute is funding a study in Milan looking at women who have had stage 1 breast cancer (see Chapter 21), to see if 4HPR will reduce the incidence of cancer in the opposite breast. There's also some evidence that combining tamoxifen and 4HPR creates a stronger effect than either alone. This is an agent that will probably be studied soon in this country as well.

Hormones

Another approach to preventing breast cancer has been through studying hormones. The earlier you have your first period and the later your menopause—the more menstruating years—the higher your risk of breast cancer. And the younger you are when you have your first child, the lower your risk. So there has been some thought that we might have an effect on breast cancer risk by coming up with a way to induce a hormonal "pregnancy," in which a teenager would be given the hormones of pregnancy for nine months to mature the breast tissue. To my knowledge, this hasn't yet been tried, but it's an interesting possibility.

A related idea, which is actually being tried at USC by Drs. Malcolm Pike and Darcy Spicer, is devising a type of contraceptive that might protect against breast cancer, based on the fact that too many ovulatory cycles lead to an increased risk.[9] So the women in the study who are at risk are given GnRH inhibitors, which are drugs that inhibit the pituitary gland from stimulating the ovary (see Chapter 1), which, in turn, puts the woman into a reversible menopause (Fig. 17-2). Staying indefinitely in this state would put young women at risk for osteoporosis and heart disease, so they are put on a low dose of estrogen, just enough to help prevent hot flashes and heart disease, but less than they'd have if they were menstruating regularly. Since if they received estrogen alone they would be at risk for endometrial cancer, every two or three months they receive a small amount of progesterone. The women have been carefully monitored (which included regular mammograms), and it was found after the first six to nine months of the study that they had an increase in bone loss, so a bit of androgen has been added as well.

This particular "cocktail" will, in theory, reduce breast, ovarian, and uterine cancer, while acting as a contraceptive. An interesting effect in the first 20 women to be studied on this new contraceptive was a change in their mammograms.[10] After a year on the study they were found to have reduced density of tissue. We don't as yet know whether this means that they are successfully preventing breast cancer

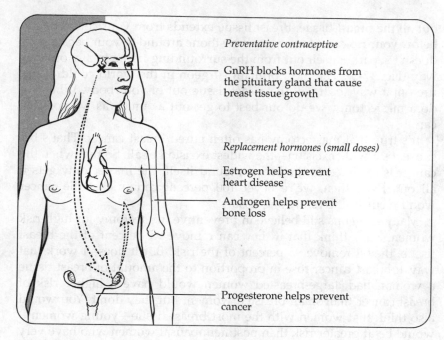

Preventative contraceptive

GnRH blocks hormones from
the pituitary gland that cause
breast tissue growth

Replacement hormones (small doses)

Estrogen helps prevent
heart disease

Androgen helps prevent
bone loss

Progesterone helps prevent
cancer

FIGURE 17-2

or whether it will just make a cancer easier to detect. It is provocative, however, and lends credence to Pike and Spicer's approach. It's a fairly complicated contraceptive, and it shouldn't be used by everyone. But it might be good for a woman whose family has hereditary breast cancer and who has a gene that makes it 80 percent likely that she'll get the disease. Again, I'm not too crazy about using medicine to prevent disease, but this could be right for a certain population of young women.

Preventive Mastectomy

Most people assume that the foolproof way to prevent breast cancer is to remove the breasts. If you don't have breasts, the reasoning goes, you won't get breast cancer. It's a pretty drastic solution. Most women like their breasts for aesthetic and erotic reasons, even if they're not planning to use them for breast feeding. Yet there are some women who are so terrified of the possibility of breast cancer that preventive mastectomy still seems to be a good idea.

Contrary to popular belief, however, it doesn't completely eliminate the risk of breast cancer. No mastectomy can be guaranteed to get out all the breast tissue. Breast tissue extends from your collarbone to below your rib cage, from your breastbone around to your back, and it doesn't separate itself out from the surrounding tissue in any obvious way (Fig. 17-3). The most brilliant surgeon in the world couldn't figure out a way to dig all the breast tissue out of your body. When we do a mastectomy, we do our best to get out as much as we possibly can.[11]

It's true that mastectomy has often cured breast cancer. That's because it's a wide excision—the widest excision of all. So that when the cancer is confined to the breast mound itself, the mastectomy gets it all out. Even then, we're never 100 percent certain that the cancer won't recur in the remaining tissue.

Many surgeons still believe in preventive mastectomy for high-risk women. They think that if they can remove 95 percent of the breast tissue, they'll remove 95 percent of the risk. But it doesn't work that way. If breast cancer rose in proportion to the amount of breast tissue a woman had, large-breasted women would have a higher risk of breast cancer than small-breasted women. But they don't. You would also think that women with the most breast tissue—young women—would be at greater risk than postmenopausal women who have very

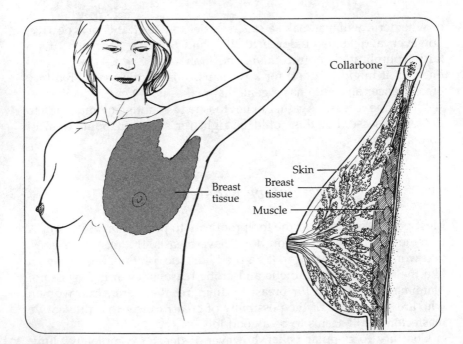

FIGURE 17-3

little breast tissue left. But as we know, younger women rarely get breast cancer and postmenopausal women often do. The question isn't how much breast tissue you have, it's how much whatever tissue you have is acted on by the carcinogens and the other factors that cause breast cancer.

No good studies have been done on women to find out. Preventive mastectomies probably do remove some of the risk, but we have no idea how much. There have been some studies done on rats, who have twelve breasts.[12] The researchers removed 3, 6, 9, or 12 breasts, and gave them a carcinogen (Fig. 17-4). The rats got the same number of cancers, regardless of how many breasts had been removed. A second experiment was done on mice that carry a gene for hereditary breast cancer.[13] They did the mastectomies on the mice, leaving out the carcinogens this time, and the mice still got the same amount of breast cancer. So, in rats and mice, removing a portion of the breast tissue doesn't remove the risk proportionately.

In humans, however, it probably depends on the stage your breast tissue is in, in regard to the development of cancer. If you look back at

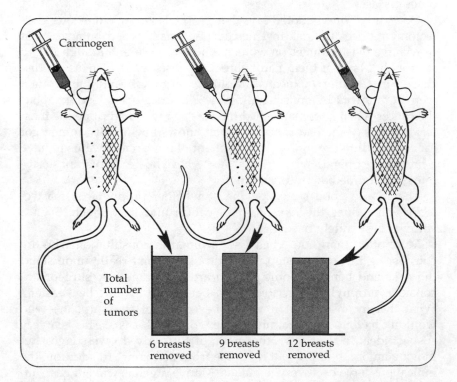

FIGURE 17-4

Chapter 13 on the causes of cancer, you'll see how a cancer goes through a series of mutations, then the growth of the cancer cells, then the invasion of the rest of the body by the cancer cells. If a mastectomy removes tissue that has already been triggered by a carcinogen, it probably does remove some of the risk of breast cancer. If carcinogens haven't acted yet on the tissue you've left in, then probably the mastectomy makes no difference.

There is a form of mastectomy that plastic surgeons around the country are offering called a *subcutaneous mastectomy* which I have to warn against.[14] They make a small incision and remove most (80–90%) of the breast tissue, keeping the nipple and areola intact. They then put a silicone implant either behind or in front of the pectoralis muscle (see Chapter 5) to reconstruct the breast mound. They say you will be good as new with greatly reduced cancer risk. But women have developed breast cancer after prophylactic subcutaneous mastectomies, so the operation may not alter your vulnerability to breast cancer. In addition, this particular operation has a high level of complications. And should the claims about silicone implants that we discussed in Chapter 5 prove true, you've also put yourself at risk for a number of other diseases.

One study[15] often quoted says that prophylactic subcutaneous mastectomy reduces the risk to 1 percent. But that's based on a series of preventive mastectomies on women who really weren't at high risk to start with. Many of them had "fibrocystic disease," which, as we discussed in Chapter 6, means absolutely nothing. And the women weren't followed in any scientific way. The researchers learned about the cancer when a woman called the surgeon who had done the mastectomy to say she had cancer. No one knows how many women got cancer and didn't report back. If a patient of mine really wants to have a preventive operation I suggest that she have bilateral total mastectomies with immediate reconstruction.

There is no good study looking at whether prophylactic mastectomy will reduce the risk of breast cancer and how much. Such a study is desperately needed.

More often than not, when I see women in consultation who are considering this drastic step, I find that they don't really understand the risks and benefits. Some women are encouraged by surgeons to consider prophylactic mastectomies because it would be "easier." What this means is that it would be easier for the surgeon—who wouldn't have to keep examining the woman's breasts. This is a very suspect idea: in very few other parts of the body do we suggest removing an organ to prevent a disease from occurring. In addition, the indications have been very nebulous. Many surgeons will suggest "increased risk" or "cancer phobia" as valid reasons to do the operation.

But their definition of increased risk is very broad. They often include women who have a second-degree relative with breast cancer, or women who have never had children.

In addition, cancer phobia is often induced by the surgeon. If a surgeon tells you that you are at very high risk for getting breast cancer and your breasts are so lumpy that they'll conceal a cancerous tumor until it's too late, you will very sensibly react with fear. Whether this fear is warranted and whether it justifies removing a normal breast is another matter. To put these recommendations into perspective, I suggested (on ABC's "Nightline") that we take out men's testicles and replace them with Ping-Pong balls to prevent testicular cancer. Somehow the men in the audience didn't take to the idea.

When consulting with anyone who is considering preventive mastectomy I suggest that she get several opinions as to what her risk of breast cancer really is and see several surgeons before she decides on such a drastic step. If your problem really is "cancer phobia," it might be wise to address it as you would any debilitating phobia, through psychotherapy rather than through mutilating surgery.

I have, with reluctance, occasionally done preventive mastectomies—four in my entire career. They were all in settings where, after spending almost a year discussing all the pros and cons, the patients still felt from a psychological standpoint that they needed to do it. If they did get breast cancer, they wanted to know they had done all they could to prevent it, so they didn't end up angry at themselves for contributing to their own disease. That's a highly individual decision. But any woman considering such a step must be absolutely clear that it is not a guarantee.

Will this approach change as we become close to having a blood test to identify the women with the BRCA1 gene and a very high risk? I don't know. For one thing, these women have a risk for both ovarian and breast cancer. Mary Claire King of Berkeley, an early researcher of the gene, tells of one woman, who was suspected to have the gene and had a very strong family history of breast cancer, who had preventive mastectomies when her twin sister got breast cancer; three months after her mastectomy, she was diagnosed with ovarian cancer.[16] It shows you that you can't count on anything as a panacea. Since, with the same gene, her sister got breast cancer and she got ovarian cancer, it's not just the gene, but something about external carcinogens that are also involved.

The true answer to prevention isn't surgical, it's systemic. We need to find ways either to block the carcinogens or do something that could reverse the damage to genes. We need a new way to solve this disease, and we need it soon.

So once again—what can you do? Not a whole lot—as I said in Chapter 15, there isn't one overriding factor in breast cancer, like cigarettes and lung cancer. But as we said above, there are some things you can do to affect your own and your daughters' risk. To summarize, you should follow what your mother told you when you were a kid: eat a low-fat diet, exercise, and drink alcohol in moderation. You can get breast exams and mammograms when it becomes appropriate. In addition, if you are at high risk you can participate in a clinical trial. At UCLA, where I've set up a breast program, we now have a high-risk program to follow women with a strong family history. We have an integrated program including physical therapy, stress reduction, and nutritional counseling, as well as exams, mammograms, and participation in the latest research, such as the tamoxifen prevention trial. There are other high-risk programs around the country—in New York, at the Strang Clinic, and many NCI designated cancer centers (see Appendix C). It's a good option for someone at high risk who doesn't want a medical procedure but wants to be followed in the most thorough, up-to-date manner.

Finally, you can get involved in political action. It's vital that we continue to press for prevention research. We can't just do one study and then wait for it to be over, and then another and wait for that to be over. That would take too long. What we need to do is have several studies going at once. And we have to demand that prevention becomes a priority.

18

≡

Screening

Screening is the process of looking at healthy people with no symptoms, in order to pick up early signs of disease. The Pap smear is the most successful screening technique to date—it has lowered the incidence of cervical cancer by picking up precancers and allowing them to be treated before they grow into cancer, and it has affected the cure rate of that cancer. Cervical cancer is now diagnosed and treated at an early stage, and significant numbers of lives are saved. We're still looking for a Pap smear equivalent for breast cancer.

We need a test that's easy to do, widely acceptable to patients (i.e., cheap and painless), sensitive enough to pick up the disease (avoid false negatives), and specific enough not to give false positives. To date we haven't such a test. What we do have are three screening tests which vary in their effectiveness—breast self-exam, breast exam by a doctor, and mammography.

Evaluating Screening Tests

There have been several studies examining the value of screening for breast cancer. Accepting that not all cancers will be found early, what evidence is there that our current tools are making a difference? Before

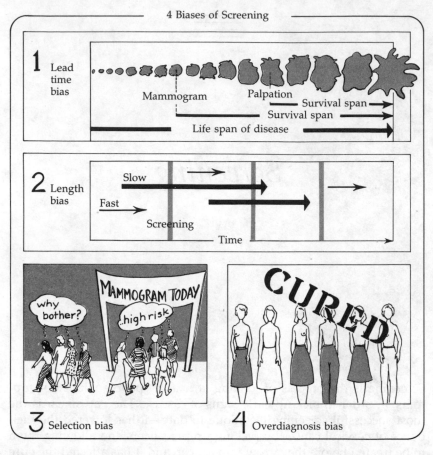

FIGURE 18-1

we go into the studies, it's useful to look at a few common biases that complicate the issue of early detection (Fig. 18-1).

The first is lead-time bias—the assumption that catching a disease early in its existence will necessarily affect its rate of progress. This is sometimes true and sometimes not. Let's assume you have a disease that usually kills you eight years after it starts. If we diagnose the disease in the fifth year, you'll live three years after the diagnosis. If we diagnose it in the third year, you'll live five years—and we gleefully proclaim that our early diagnosis has given you a longer survival span. Actually, it hasn't—it's just given you a longer time to know you've got the disease, which may or may not be a benefit. So just looking at years of survival after diagnosis isn't enough—we need to know how many people actually die of the disease with and without early detection. Most breast cancers have been around six to eight years by the time they appear on mammogram, and most women with breast cancer survive many years, so this bias can be very misleading.

The second bias is length bias. For instance, take a test done every two years on a large number of people. Fast-growing tumors aren't around as long, so there's less time in which they can be detected. Slow-growing tumors are around longer, so you have time to find them. If, for example, one tumor takes six years to become two centimeters, and you do a test every two years, you're likely to find it before the six years are up. Another, very aggressive tumor grows to two centimeters in nine months. You won't find it in your first test, and before you do your second, it's become a palpable lump and has been found. So screening tests select against fast-growing tumors, and catch the slow-growing ones—which have a better prognosis. It's like a nighttime security guard going around the bank every hour. The guard will catch a slow robber who takes three hours to get the job done, but the fast robber, who can do the job in 20 minutes, can be in and out before the guard shows up. The chances are that the fast robber is also the most efficient one; the guard will only get the slower, less competent criminal.

Then there's the selection bias. If you make mammograms available to all women over 50, and you don't offer any extra incentives to take the test, who's likely to take you up on your offer? For the most part, it'll be the people who perceive themselves as high-risk: they've already had breast cancer, or their mother has had breast cancer. The women who don't worry as much about getting the disease are less likely to bother getting the test. So usually the women who go for screening have a higher risk than those who don't.

Finally there's the overdiagnosis bias. You detect suspicious areas on a mammogram—they may or may not indicate cancer. Precancer (see Chapter 16) falls into this category: if it were never diagnosed, in many cases nothing would happen and you'd never know you had it. But if it's overtreated—that is, preventive mastectomies are performed wherever it's found—the cure statistics can get very inflated. If, as it currently appears, only 30 percent of precancers will ever become cancers, and mastectomies are performed on all women found to have precancer, large numbers of women will appear to have been cured, whereas the majority of these—70 percent—would never have gotten cancer in the first place.

What's needed for a truly accurate study is a randomized controlled study with mortality as its endpoint, to take care of the lead-time bias. If you take a group of women and pick randomly who'll get the test and who won't—that takes care of self-selection and overtreatment. If you have the same numbers of fast- and slow-growing tumors, this counters the length bias, and ensures that both the study group and the control group have the same risks of, and the same kinds of, cancer. But studies like this are few and far between. It behooves us to examine the data supporting each type of screening against this standard, however, if we are truly to understand its worth.

The final bias we need to contend with is the concept of early detection. As we discuss in Chapter 19, the notion of "early detection" is somewhat misleading. But is it a myth? Not really: there are some cancers that we truly can detect early. The myth is the notion that *every* cancer has the potential to be found early by our current techniques. We are unfortunately limited both by our techniques and by our understanding of breast cancer. Screening is still our current best tool for changing the mortality rate of breast cancer, We need to take full advantage of it while working very hard to find something better.

Breast Self-Exam

Until recently, breast self-exam (BSE)—much touted as the obvious first step in screening for breast cancer—had not been scientifically tested to see if it can change the mortality rate of breast cancer. The Russians, British, and Canadians are all now studying it, and the results will be forthcoming in the next decade. As of now there has never been a randomized controlled study showing that breast self exam makes any difference in the mortality from breast cancer.[1] The studies that have been done are inconsistent. Some women have never actually been instructed in how to do BSE, but even in those women who have been well taught there has been no effect.[2] Some studies show that cancers are found at an earlier stage (lead-time bias?) while others show no difference at all.[3,4] To date, all the evidence we have indicates that it is an ineffective tool in detecting breast cancer. By the time you can feel a lump it's been there so long that whether you find it this month, next month, or four months from now won't make a critical difference. Most lumps are, as we said in Chapter 2, found by the woman herself, not while she's doing formal breast self-exam but rather while she's bathing or scratching an itch or making love.

Why then does the health establishment keep pushing BSE? Partly because it's free and easy to do. Partly, perhaps, because it puts the blame back on the woman. If you die from breast cancer it isn't because the medical profession hasn't figured out how to cure or prevent the disease; it's because you didn't do your self-examination.

The other reason is that we haven't anything else, particularly for young women for whom mammography doesn't work well. Doctors and nurse practitioners have said to me, "I know breast self-exam doesn't work well, but what am I going to tell my 35-year-old patient to do?" My answer is: political action. It doesn't solve anything to tell women to do breast self-exam as though it's going to find all cancers early, when we know it doesn't work. Be honest about what we know and what we don't know. Tell her that breast self-exam hasn't been shown to change the mortality of breast cancer, and she should be lobbying for something that will make a difference in young women.

Some doctors say that doing breast self-exam makes a woman feel more in control of her body and empowers her. That hasn't been true in my experience. I think it is the *provider* who feels better, because she or he feels less impotent and more in control. I find that women themselves get scared to death and alienated from their bodies, feeling they need to go on this monthly search-and-destroy mission. I also think the ones who do feel empowered are often getting a false sense of security. But if doing breast self-exam every month, and not finding a lump, makes you feel more comfortable, then you should do it, as long as you understand that its benefits are psychological and that it probably won't make a difference in your physical health.

I get really frustrated about the amount of money and time that have gone into researching how to teach breast self-examination, and whether you should do it in a circle or radially. Those resources are needed to find a blood test or some other form of early detection that might really work.

Does BSE have any value at all? Possibly. Though it doesn't save lives, there may be other benefits. For example, as we mention in Chapter 2, it can be a way to become acquainted with your body—a pleasant and worthwhile activity.

In addition, it may help find the cancer a little bit earlier, when the lump isn't too large, and therefore help create a better cosmetic result from a lumpectomy.

I am not opposed to breast self-exam as a concept. I am opposed to the notion that women should look on their breasts as though they were enemy soldiers being searched for weapons. I am opposed to investing money in a technique which has not been shown to change mortality. And I am opposed to using breast self-exam as an excuse for not finding better methods of early detection.

Breast Physical Exam

Breast physical exam—examination by a doctor or other medical professional—has never been studied by itself in terms of its usefulness in detecting breast cancer.

There is, however, at least one good randomized controlled study in which both physical exam and mammography were combined, and it forms the basis for much of our understanding of the advantages of screening. In New York in 1962 the Health Insurance Plan (HIP)[5], a health maintenance organization, chose 62,000 of its female members between the ages of 40 and 64 and divided them into two matched groups of 31,000 each. They then offered the women in one group breast cancer screening, including mammography and physical examinations, with follow-up exams and mammograms once a year for three years. The women in the control group received their usual care. (This was before the days of routine mammography, so it is unlikely that many women in the control group received any mammograms.) The 31,000 women in the study group were invited to get mammograms, and two thirds of them accepted and had at least one mammogram. (To avoid selection bias here—since the women who were most likely to attend were those at higher risk—all the women who were invited were included in the statistics rather than just those who actually came. If anything, this would underestimate the benefit of mammography.) One third of the cancers detected were on mammogram only, while two fifths were on physical exam only and one fifth on both. After seven years of follow-up, there was a one-third reduction in mortality in the members of the screened group who were over 50. After 14 years of follow-up[6] this difference was maintained, and there is now also a significant difference in the mortality of the women under 50 as well. In fact, at 18 years follow-up the decrease in deaths from breast cancer was equal in the older and younger group.[7] This was the first study to show the advantage of screening for breast cancer, and it was done with the rather crude mammography being employed in the early 1960s. It's important to remember, however, that the HIP study included a physician's exam in the screening, and it is interesting to note that physical examination seemed to be more effective in the younger women (40–50) while mammography was more effective in the older group.

There was also a study done in Canada[8] that looked at whether in older women, mammograms added anything to a well-performed medical physical exam. After a seven-year follow-up, they found that in women between 50 and 59, mammography didn't decrease mortality any better than the physical exam alone.

One problem is that most doctors haven't been trained to do physical breast exams. The breast has always been thought to be the property of the general surgeon. So gynecologists and primary care doctors have almost never received formal training in the breast. Yet most women who have breast problems go to their gynecologists or primary care doctors. This is the source of a lot of problems, because gynecologists and primary care doctors, untrained in breast problems or breast cancer, often don't know what to do. Surgeons have always had the advantage of educating their fingers. They examine the breast and then do a biopsy. That way they can learn what different breast problems feel like. Primary care doctors do not have this advantage. We need to be sure that every woman has access to a good clinical breast exam as part of her yearly checkup.

Mammography

The third technique that's been used for screening is mammography. We discussed mammography in Chapter 10 as a diagnostic technique. Here we discuss it not as a tool for women who have breast complaints, but for all healthy women to find early disease. Because of the limitations of screening studies already discussed, the only ones we can really count on to get answers are randomized control studies, where women are randomly assigned to get mammography or not.

There have been eight randomized controlled trials of mammography over the past 30 years, which is an impressive number. The findings are striking. All the studies consistently show a reduction in mortality from breast cancer in women between 50 and 69. It's around 30 percent—nearly a third. This means that out of every 100 women over 50 with undetected breast cancer who underwent screening mammography, there were 30 who would have died of breast cancer had they not been screened, but who lived. This is the largest reduction in mortality we have seen in breast cancer and far overshadows any improvement in mortality we've been able to obtain from treatments with chemotherapy and surgery. In women over 50 there is no question that mammography screening can be lifesaving. We don't yet know how it affects women over 70, because there haven't been enough studies to give us that information, but there is no reason to believe that the result won't be the same. These benefits overall far outweigh any of the risks that having mammography may entail, and which we discuss below. We still need to stress, however, that mammography is not perfect and that a mammogram that shows nothing unusual does not guarantee that a woman does not have cancer.

What is so magic about the age of 50? It isn't actually 50 that matters, but rather menopause. Before menopause the breast tissue tends to be denser, because your breasts have to be ready to make milk at a moment's notice. After menopause, the breasts go into retirement and the breast tissue is replaced by fat. Cancer shows up against fat tissue, but not against dense breast tissue (see pages 126 and 127). Further, breast cancer is more common the older you are. The combination of these two facts makes mammography postmenopausally more accurate. There is no argument about the recommendation that every woman over 50 should be having yearly mammography.

The controversy is about the women under 50. There have been quite a number of randomized controlled studies looking at women between 40 and 74. The data are very clear: for women between 40 and 49, the trials have shown no effect on mortality after seven years of follow-up.[9] After 10 to 12 years, none of the four studies that had followed women out that long have found a statistically significant difference. The only trial with any data beyond 10 years is the HIP trial mentioned earlier, which shows a slight improvement in mortality between 10 and 18 years. This may, however, not be as positive as it sounds. One of the problems in definition is that if you study mammography screening in women over 40, and you're following them from 12 to 18 years, they're no longer 40 to 50 anymore—they're now in their 50s and 60s. So we have to ask if these women are being defined as between 40 and 50 at the time they entered the study, or 40 to 50 when their cancer was detected. If a woman was 40 when she entered the study but her cancer was detected when she was 52, it's no longer measuring mammography screening in a woman between 40 and 50 but in a woman over 50.

One pro–early mammography camp argues cancers that occur between 40 and 50 seem to be the faster-growing cancers. They feel the reason many studies are not showing the value of mammography in this group is because the mammograms are not being done frequently enough. They think we should close up the intervals in those years— especially since those are the years when you've still got a lot of dense breast tissue that can mask a cancer. So they suggest you have a mammogram every year between 40 and 50, and every two years after 50.

The other argument from those who favor mammography between 40 and 50 is that none of the randomized studies was designed specifically to address the younger woman. Because breast cancer is less frequent in this age group, many more women have to be in the study to be able to show the same difference in mortality. They also suggest that at least one third of women under 50 have fatty breasts, which are conducive to mammography. These proponents[10] contend that until there is a study that proves mammography is not helpful in this age group, we should continue to offer it.

It should be pointed out that these arguments refer to the value of recommending frequent mammography as a public policy: the benefit to the individual woman may be very different. If you have a strong family history of breast cancer, your chance of getting cancer is higher and therefore the chance of mammography finding it is better. Perhaps a good analogy would be a loaf of raisin bread. The more raisins you put in the bread, the better chance that you will see a raisin in an individual slice. For you, therefore, mammography screening may be worthwhile.

And some young women do have fatty breasts, which are good for mammography. There are always exceptions to any rule, and there are occasionally women under 50 for whom mammography screening will make a difference. One of my patients is a woman in her mid-40s whose cancer was detected by mammogram. She had a mastectomy, and seemed fine. But she was very concerned by the studies. "I keep hearing that mammography in women under 50 doesn't affect mortality," she said to me. "Does that mean I'm going to die?"

It doesn't mean that at all. In her case, the cancer was discovered very early, and will probably be cured. She may be one of the lucky ones where mammography was useful or she may have been cured whether or not she had the mammogram. Not all women who develop breast cancer between 40 and 50 die from it; even women in their 20s and 30s survive breast cancer, whether it is detected as a lump or on mammogram.

There can be goals other than reduced mortality, as we mentioned earlier with breast self-exam. It may be that if you get mammography screening you'll find a cancer when it's slightly smaller and you'll be able to have breast conservation that will leave you with less cosmetic damage.

Risk of Screening Mammograms

Is there any harm in doing screening mammograms? The risk:benefit ratio in women over 50 has been shown consistently, and few would argue against encouraging it in this group. In the 40–50-year-old group, however, the data aren't so clear. These days, mammography offers very little cancer risk, since we've reduced the amount of radiation significantly. However, David Eddy of Duke University has pointed out that certain "side effects" of mammography have not always been taken into consideration.[11] First of all, there is the anxiety provoked by having a screening test for cancer. Then there are the unnecessary biopsies that are performed because of false positive readings. The biopsies cause mental anguish, as do the risks of surgery, and the potential for scarring, which decreases the future ability to detect cancer. A false negative mammogram (one that is read as normal when the patient actually has cancer) could give a woman a false sense of security and might even delay the diagnosis of her lesion. Finally there is the cost of mammography, which is often not covered by insurance. In his analysis, the additional benefit of mammography over and above physical exam was not worth it in women under 50. He recommended that each woman decide for herself whether to have a screening mammogram and that no blanket recommendations be made for women in the 40–50 age group.

This was confirmed by a recent study in San Francisco showing that women under 50 who have mammograms are 12 times more likely to have unnecessary biopsies than are women over 50, because mammograms often show "false positives"—things that look ominous but are really harmless. That happens in part because in our entrepreneurial health system all the rewards are in doing procedures. So if there's the slightest question on a mammogram, some radiologists are likely to recommend a biopsy. The surgeon, the pathologist, the radiologist, and the hospital all profit financially when you have a biopsy—and they risk lawsuits if they don't operate and breast cancer is found. You yourself are likely to want the biopsy because the possibility of cancer, however remote, terrifies you. Yet 80 percent of biopsies done on the basis of lesions found on mammogram reveal wholly benign tissue. In Europe, it's 50 percent, because they're not as influenced either by financial gain or fear of lawsuits and they do many more needle biopsies for diagnosis.

While a biopsy is a fairly minor operation (see Chapter 12), it's still surgery. It causes scars, and there is always some risk in any surgical procedure. It also costs you, or your health care plan, money.

It's important as well to consider the question of the radiation you get from the mammogram itself. Generally, radiation risk is higher in young women, and goes down as you get older. Though mammogram radiation is low, it's not something to be taken lightly.

Further, some women who have a gene called the *ataxia-telangiectasia* gene are particularly sensitive to radiation (see Chapter 14). For them, the radiation from several screening mammograms could cause cancer—even breast cancer. Unfortunately we haven't a way to test for this relatively rare gene as yet.

So we need to be careful about how we present the idea of mammograms. We've tended to approach it with an attitude of "Oh, well, why not get one?" But we always need to realize that there is no free lunch.

Guideline Controversy

The mammography guidelines were originally formulated in 1977 by the American Cancer Society based on the HIP study and the Breast Cancer and Cervical Detection Project (BCCDP) suggesting mammograms for women over 50. Then, as more data came out from the BCCDP demonstrating the advantage in mammography for younger women (note that the BCCDP was not randomized and was subject to a large amount of selection bias), they decided to include younger women. It was at this time that a baseline mammogram at 35 was first suggested, as well as a regular mammogram every couple of years after 40. Now, with recent data, the guidelines have been reexamined and there is some question as to how they should be shifted to reflect the controversy regarding screening in younger women. The American Cancer Society has refused to change them because they think women will get confused. The National Cancer Institute initially agreed, but they re-studied the issue. The Institute's new policy is that women over 50 should have mammograms, and women under 50 should discuss the pros and cons of screening mammography with their doctors and decide for themselves.

I think this makes sense. Each woman under 50 needs to weigh the risks and benefits for herself and decide if it's worth it for her. It means making decisions based on inadequate information, but many major life decisions have to be made with inadequate information. In any case, inadequate information is better than false information. What we really need are some studies that will give the answers.

Screening Recommendations

So, if you want to do everything possible to protect yourself from dying of breast cancer, and from facing disfiguring surgery, what should you do? At the present time I recommend the following: If you're very young you should begin getting acquainted with your breasts. Have your doctor examine your breasts during your regular checkups. After 40, make sure to get this done at least once a year.

Many doctors stress the importance of a "baseline mammogram." Actually any time you have your first mammogram could be called your baseline. What's more important is that you have serial mammograms: several a year or two apart so that comparisons can be made. This is what makes mammography the most accurate.

What I recommend is doing a "baseline" mammogram in your early 40s to find out what your breast tissue looks like. Some women discover with their first mammogram that they have very dense breasts, in which case it makes sense to hold off and not do regular mammograms till 50. But some women have very fatty breasts in their 40s, and for them, it might make sense to have screening mammograms in their 40s.

Once you're in your 50s (or whenever your breast density makes it feasible), you should have regular mammograms, every year or two, so that we can compare one mammogram against the last one. Often that's how we catch a cancer: this year's mammogram has something that wasn't there last year and the year before. There are people who believe they can get one mammogram and that's it. Much as I oppose overdoing mammography, underdoing it is just as bad.

There are two different setups used for screening. One is the hospital or free-standing clinic that has a radiologist present who will check the quality of the films as they are taken and order extra films as necessary. The other is what is called low-cost, high-volume clinics. These have been set up in an effort to reduce the cost of mammography. They do a large number of X rays in a day. At the end of the day the radiologist will review all the films at once. If there is any question the woman will be sent a call-back card and told to return for more views. Again this doesn't mean there is cancer, only that a conscientious effort is being made to do the best studies possible. Both types of centers have their advantages and disadvantages.

It is important to point out that this discussion is about screening mammograms which are done on women who have no symptoms but just want to get checked out. If you have a lump you should have a mammogram regardless of your age. Mammography is still the best tool we have for detecting breast cancer or determining the nature of a lump. We need to make full use of it while we try to find something even better.

PART FIVE

THE DIAGNOSIS
OF
BREAST CANCER

Understanding Breast Cancer

One of the reasons there's been a major shift in the treatment of breast cancer is that there's been a shift in the whole way we think about breast cancer. In the mid-19th century, when breast cancer first began to be seen as a treatable disease, it was thought that the cancer started in the breast and then grew out from it in a continuous way—it would go directly into the lymph nodes, directly into the lungs, or directly through the liver (Fig. 19-1). Nobody realized that it spread through the lymphatics (the vessels that carry lymph through the body) or the bloodstream. In those days, by the time a woman with breast cancer came to a doctor, she probably had a large tumor that took up most of the breast: it had already metastasized to the liver and other organs, and the doctors didn't think to question how it had gotten there. Women didn't report lumps until they were large, since respectable women weren't supposed to touch their breasts any more than was essential for washing and dressing.

The theory of the continuous spread of cancer held sway until the late 19th century when doctors first began to realize the importance of the lymphatic system. At that point, the German surgeon Von Volkman demonstrated that extension wasn't the only way breast cancer spread—it also spread through the lymphatics. Cancer was then thought to start in the breast, get slowly bigger, and then go cell by

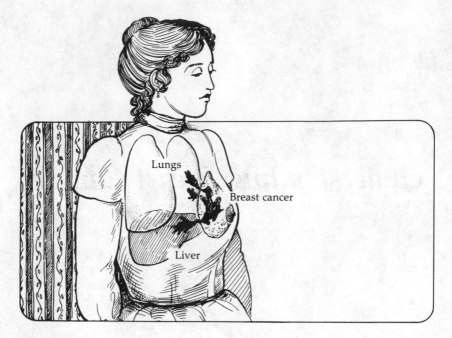

FIGURE 19-1

cell into the lymph nodes. When it got to the last lymph node, it went quickly into the rest of the body. Thus, the reasoning went, it was necessary to remove the lymph nodes as well as the breast and chest wall muscles—to get out the tumor and all the lymph nodes in the vicinity of the breast. Based on this reasoning, William Stuart Halsted developed the operation known as a radical mastectomy (it was first done in England in 1857 by Charles Moore) during the 1890s at Johns Hopkins. When this radical surgery didn't always work it was thought not to be extensive enough. Halsted tried removing the supraclavicular nodes (above the collarbone), and Sampson Handley, a London surgeon, included removing part of the breastbone and ribs to get the internal mammary nodes. Neither of these radical operations was shown to add to survival, but both became popular, and both are sometimes still done today.

The fact that extending the surgery didn't improve survival led to the thought that timing was the key element. If you don't operate immediately, they reasoned, the cancer might jump from the lymph nodes into the rest of the body, and the patient would be lost. This is the basis of the belief that held sway for many years—that as soon as the biopsy was performed a frozen section should be performed (see Chapter 12) and, if cancer were found, an immediate radical mastectomy should follow.

264

As early as the 1930s, critics started complaining that the radical mastectomy was of no use in patients whose cancer had spread and was too extensive for early lesions. Geoffrey Keynes in England and R. McWhirter in Scotland were both exploring combining radiation therapy and lesser forms of surgery. In the 1940s, D. H. Patey and W. H. Dyson, also in England, responding to an anatomical study of breast lymphatics by J. H. Gray, argued for a less extensive operation that removed the breast and axillary lymph nodes while leaving the chest muscles intact. This was termed a *modified radical mastectomy*.

In spite of the good reports from England, American surgeons were slow to try this lesser operation. But when educated women got wind of these new developments, they demanded that their doctors try the less mutilating form of surgery. Over time, studies comparing patients who had radical and modified mastectomies found no difference in survival rate or local recurrence. By the mid-1970s the modified radical mastectomy had replaced the radical mastectomy in most hospitals. While it was an improvement in terms of less disfigurement and impaired mobility, it still didn't increase the survival rate.[1]

By this time, pioneers such as Oliver Cope in Boston and George Crile, Jr. in Cleveland were pushing for even less disfiguring surgery and trying partial mastectomies, with and without radiation. However, the real shift came about when Bernard Fisher of Pittsburgh began to develop an alternative theory.[2] He looked at current research, including a study by J. Gershon-Cohen,[3] that followed breast cancer metastasis—areas where the cancer had spread—over time to see how fast they grew. He was able to calculate that the average doubling time for a cancer cell was about 100 days. It took 100 days for the first cell to become two cells, those two to become four, those four to become eight, and so on. It takes 100 billion cells to have a centimeter's worth of cancer. That means that most cancers have been around eight years before they can be seen on a mammogram and 10 years before they can be felt as a lump (Fig. 19-2). This isn't a hard-and-fast rule: some

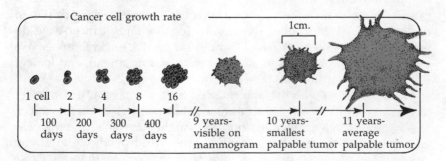

FIGURE 19-2

cancers grow faster, and some slower, and it's also possible that cancers grow in spurts, growing and then resting and then growing some more. But no matter how a cancer grows, it has had the opportunity to spread microscopically many years before we can detect it. In this case, Fisher reasoned, taking out the lymph nodes at the time of diagnosis shouldn't have much to do with survival. Rather, survival would be determined by how well the immune system handled whatever cancer cells had already spread from the breast. In 1971 Fisher set up a research protocol to study this, randomizing women into three treatment groups.[4] In one, women had a radical mastectomy, in one a simple mastectomy and radiation, and in the third only a simple mastectomy, leaving the lymph nodes intact. After 15 years the survival rates for the three groups were exactly the same.

There has been some concern that Fisher's study was not large enough to detect a small difference in survival with lymph node removal, but even the critics can only hypothesize that at most 7 percent of women would be likely to benefit if there is indeed an advantage to lymph node removal at the time of surgery.[5]

While this notion of very early cancer spread is a depressing thought, it's helpful in that it shows the folly of assuming that a mastectomy must be performed the instant a cancer is discovered. You won't stop the cancer from spreading because it probably already has, and if somehow it hasn't spread in 10 years there's no reason to assume it's going to suddenly begin in the next half hour. This research opened up the way to exploring treatment for breast cancer that involved less surgery than mastectomy, as well as pointing out the importance of some type of systemic treatment in addition to the local one.

When we first diagnose breast cancer, the question we have to ask is not whether the cancer cells have gotten out, but how well we think the patient's body has taken care of whatever cells might have gotten out. We determine this in a number of ways. One of these is to look at the places where the cancer is likely to have gone. Different cancers seem to have an affinity for different parts of the body, and breast cancer cells, although they can go anywhere, seem especially drawn to the lungs, liver, and bones (Fig. 19-3). In very large cancers, we do tests called staging tests (see Chapter 21) on these three areas. We examine the lymph nodes for signs of microscopic spread, and look at the tumor for any sign of aggressiveness.

What do we do with that information once we have it? The answer to this is what has really revolutionized the approach to breast cancer. If we think, for whatever reason, you might have microscopic cells elsewhere that the body hasn't successfully destroyed, we give you systemic treatments—either chemotherapy or hormone therapy. These

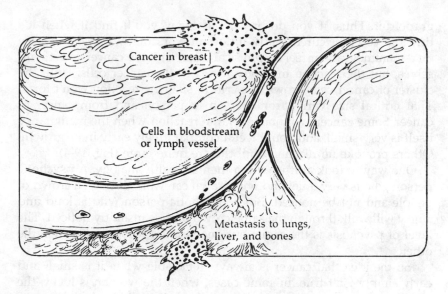

Cancer in breast

Cells in bloodstream
or lymph vessel

Metastasis to lungs,
liver, and bones

FIGURE 19-3

involve the use of drugs, given either intravenously or orally, that go into your bloodstream and circulate through it, getting to all the places the cells might be and trying to destroy them. Surgery can take care only of the large cancer in the breast itself—if one cell has left the breast and is sitting, alone, somewhere else in your body, untouched by the immune system, the most extensive mastectomy in the world won't keep the cancer from returning. That cell will multiply and the cancer will grow. Radiation is also a local treatment; it will clean up the cells around the area that's been operated on, but it doesn't get any cells that have left that area. If a systemic treatment is needed, we choose one that works well on breast cancer cells. Having decided on that, we then decide on a local treatment and determine what combination of surgery and radiation will be most effective. Both are important.

The Concept of Early Detection

Are there some women in whom we can find the cancers at an early stage, before there's been any metastasis at all? There's still some debate about this.

There's a common misconception that every cancer grows in a clear progression: it starts with a lump the size of a grain of sand, then grows to a beebee, to a pea, to a grape, to a walnut, to a lemon, to a grapefruit. Thus, if you do breast self-exam, you'll find it when it's tiny and you'll be cured. Sadly, it doesn't work that way. What we see on a mammogram or feel on physical exam isn't the cancer cells themselves, but the reaction the body forms to the cancer cells. Until the cluster of cancer cells grows to a critical size, the reaction won't form. That critical size varies from person to person and from cancer to cancer. Some cancers will incite a large reaction when the malignancy itself is very small, and you'll feel it comparatively early in its growth. Others provoke no reaction until they're quite large (Fig. 19-4).

One way to look at it is with a mental health analogy. A psychotic person who is very quiet and withdrawn can walk through a crowd of people and not be noticed. But a psychotic person who is loud and angry will walk through the same crowd and be instantly noticed. The level of psychosis is the same, but one is more recognizable than the other.

So the idea that cancer is always detectable when it is small and early simply isn't true. In some cases, when the woman is lucky, the cancer creates a reaction when it's still small, and she finds it early. When the woman is less lucky, the cancer doesn't create a reaction until it's larger. Because of the misconceptions about early detection, such a woman is likely to blame herself: she was foolish and didn't examine her breasts regularly.

By the same token, she can't assume that her mammogram was done badly, or that her doctor wasn't careful. Mammography (and most of

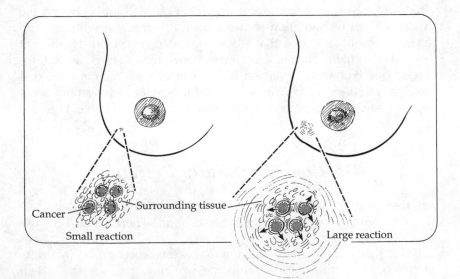

Cancer — Surrounding tissue

Small reaction

Large reaction

FIGURE 19-4

the other imaging techniques, for that matter) depends on the same reaction for detection. Some tumors will appear on a mammogram at an early point. Others will not. Often a woman comes into my office with a diagnosis made only on a mammogram. I do an operation and find a medium-sized tumor with positive nodes. The woman asks me why the tumor wasn't found earlier. It is the earliest we could detect your tumor, I answer. Is it early enough to save her life? I don't know.

At this point we come up against another misconception. Most people believe that the size of a tumor alone determines its severity. Generally speaking, they're right. Smaller lumps are less likely to have spread. But there are other factors that affect a woman's prognosis. The aggressiveness of the cancer is important. It's possible to have a very small cancer that has already spread. Thirty percent of cancers that are detected on mammogram but can't be felt as lumps have positive lymph nodes. On the other hand, a cancer that first appears as a large lump may not have spread.

Another important consideration is how well the woman's immune system is able to control the cancer. Unfortunately, we don't yet have a way to measure this.

So early detection won't always work. But there does appear to be a subgroup of women for whom it is effective. Mammography has been shown to increase the cure rate of breast cancer by 30 percent in women over 50.[6] For these women finding the cancer earlier did make a difference. This could mean that a cancer must reach a certain threshold before starting to metastasize, or that once there are a certain number of cells in the bloodstream the immune system can no longer handle them effectively. We don't have any scientific evidence about this, but I personally favor the latter theory. I think that any breast cancer large enough to be detected has already spread. But a smaller cancer may have sent fewer cancer cells into the bloodstream than a bigger one, and an aggressive cancer has sent off more cells than a slower-growing cancer (Fig. 19-5). So I think that in the early stages, if a cancer is small or nonaggressive, the body has probably been able to kill off whatever cells the cancer has thrown into it. And the cancer is curable with local treatment alone.

Some breast cancer that has spread microscopically is also curable. This will again depend upon the aggressiveness of the tumor, the strength of the immune system of the body the tumor finds itself in, and the sensitivity of the tumor cells to the chemotherapy drugs. In many cases we can cure the patient. The problem is that we can never know for certain whether we've succeeded. It's only when a breast cancer patient lives for 50 years and dies of a stroke that we can say she licked breast cancer.

The danger of cancer depends on the balance between the cancer and the ability of your body's immune system to fight it. Our

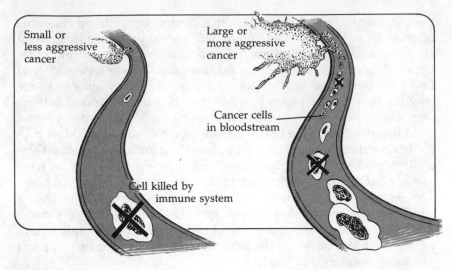

Small or
less aggressive
cancer

Large or
more aggressive
cancer

Cancer cells
in bloodstream

Cell killed by
immune system

FIGURE 19-5

treatments are based on shifting the balance. It's similar to infection and bacteria. In the old days, before antibiotics, pneumonia was often, but not always, fatal. Many of its victims died, but many others went through the crisis, their fever broke, and they survived. The survivors were those whose bodies were able to fight off the bacteria. Even after the invention of antibiotics, the body's immune system played a part: antibiotics don't kill every last bacteria, but they reduce the bacteria to a level the body can fight off.

Surgery and radiation reduce the bulk of cancer cells but not all of the microscopic ones. Chemotherapy helps to wipe out the microscopic cells, but it probably doesn't kill them all. We hope that it kills off enough so the body's immune system can take over and get the rest.

The next logical step would be to find some way to try and stimulate the immune system. Much research is being done on this matter, but so far we don't have a reliable method that can be used in all patients. Most of the complementary treatments (see Chapter 29)—whether meditation, diet, herbs, prayers, "positive thinking" techniques, or visualization—are methods that practitioners hope will strengthen the immune system to help it fight off the cancer. Theoretically they can work well in conjunction with chemotherapy—the chemicals kill the cancer while the complementary method bolsters the body's own fighting resources. Although we have no scientific proof, I feel from my experience that, if nothing else, their ability to empower the woman and give her a role in her own care can't help but be strengthening. The related possibility that stress may damage the immune system, lessening the body's ability to fight off cancer cells, also needs further research.

With breast cancer, unlike some other cancers, five years without recurrence doesn't mean you're cured. Because it's usually a slow-growing cancer, it can spread to another part of your body and go undetected for 10 or even 20 years. The longer you go without a recurrence, however, the less likely a recurrence is, and the more treatable it will be if it does happen. Many women will live out their normal life spans, though you will only know if this is true for you in retrospect when you reach a ripe old age. Therefore, you're wise to think of breast cancer as similar in some ways to a chronic disease, like high blood pressure or diabetes or asthma, that you'll always have in your life. You're also wise to remember that, like other chronic diseases, it's very likely something you can live with.

We have made some progress: if you look at all women under 65, the death rate from breast cancer has fallen by six percent. That's because those women respond best to chemotherapy. For premenopausal women with breast cancer under 50, the decrease in mortality is even more significant: it's decreased by 11 percent. The greatest decrease is in younger white women—13 percent. Our successes however, are not uniform. For premenopausal African American women, the mortality has risen by 2.5 percent. Even worse, for postmenopausal African American women, there has been a 22 percent increase in mortality in the last 17 years. Much of this is due to lack of access to care, but there may be other biological factors we don't understand as well.

Screening helps some, as do our new systemic therapies, but the real answers to breast cancer therapy must await an as yet undescribed paradigm which will give us the understanding we need to prevent this disease.

It might be useful here to clarify some cancer terminology that often confuses people (these and other words will be found in the Glossary). First of all, there's *metastasis*, which means the spread of the cancer to another organ. Sometimes we also call spread to the lymph nodes metastasis, acknowledging that the cells had to come through the bloodstream. But a cancer that has "metastasized" to the lymph nodes, as we have said, is considered differently than one that has spread to other organs. When we suspect these cells have spread to other organs but are too small to detect by modern techniques we call them *micrometastasis*. If breast cancer is found either locally or in another organ after treatment is finished it is termed a *recurrence*. A cancer that's recurred elsewhere in the body can rarely be cured—but it can be put into *remission*. A remission is essentially a slowing down of the cancer's progress for a period of time, so that you live longer—and, depending on a number of factors, that "longer" can be a few months or 20 years.

Finally, treatments for a primary cancer given in addition to the local therapy are called *"adjuvant treatments,"* which are different from metastatic treatments.

20

Diagnosis and Types of Breast Cancer

What are the symptoms that should alert you to the possibility of breast cancer? The most common finding is a painless lump, although occasionally painful lumps are cancerous. A thickening of the breast or a change in density should also be checked out. As we've mentioned in previous chapters, occasionally breast cancer can show up as a lump under the arm, redness of the skin over the breast, eczema of the nipple, or dimpling of the skin. Finally, the most common finding these days is an abnormality seen on mammogram with no physical findings at all.

Once you've discovered a symptom that alerts you to the possibility of breast cancer, you should see a doctor. Start with your own primary care physician or gynecologist. If you're over 35, your doctor should send you for a mammogram. Even if the mammogram shows no abnormalities, if the symptom persists, ask to be referred to a surgeon or a breast specialist. In some areas of the country there are surgeons like myself who specialize in breast disease; in other areas you may be referred to a general surgeon. Don't be scared by the word "surgeon"—the fact that you're going to see a surgeon doesn't automatically mean an operation. Surgeons are the doctors best trained to diagnose breast problems. And if you're unsatisfied with the answers you're getting from one surgeon, find another one.

Types of Biopsy

What might the surgeon suggest? Very possibly, some form of biopsy. As we discussed in Chapter 12, this covers four distinct procedures, so it's important that you understand which kind your doctor is talking about. Often the patient thinks it means taking out a small piece of tissue, while the surgeon really means removing the whole lump. The type of biopsy done depends in part on whether the lesion is palpable or not. If it is seen only on the mammogram it can be approached by a *stereotactic fine-needle biopsy*, *tru-cut (core) biopsy*, or *wire localization biopsy*. These all use the mammogram to find the location of the lesion before sampling it. (See Chapter 12.) If the lesion is palpable then it can also be tested with a *fine-needle aspiration* or a core biopsy, and mammography is not necessary. Finally, it can be removed entirely with an *excisional biopsy*, or a piece of it can be removed with an *incisional biopsy*. You should discuss with your surgeon which approach is best for you and why. Sometimes fine-needle aspirations or core biopsies are not offered because the hospital does not have the equipment or the surgeon doesn't know how to use it, rather than because they are not the best choice. You need to know what your surgeon is using as his or her criteria.

If a woman comes to me with a palpable lump or a lesion seen on a mammogram, I try to make the diagnosis with the least invasive procedure. That way I can often avoid leaving her with a scar or dent if it turns out to be a benign lesion. If the lesion is cancer, we can then discuss the options for treatment and proceed with the definitive operation. If the fine-needle or core biopsy do not give the information needed, I'll do an open biopsy.

As you see, biopsies and treatment can be done in one or two stages. The one-stage procedure was popular 10–20 years ago. You'd sign a form in advance, agreeing to an immediate mastectomy if cancer was found. This is still sometimes done today: it's what Nancy Reagan did in 1988. The one-stage approach is based on the old theory that when we operate on an area with cancer, we spread the cancer cells. Removing the breast quickly was thought to prevent any actual spread. However, there's absolutely no evidence that a one-stage procedure has any effect on survival or cure rates.[1]

A two-stage procedure is one in which the biopsy is performed, usually under local anesthetic, and then, later, you're given the diagnosis, after which you can take time to discuss the possible treatments and make your decision.

The advantage of a two-stage procedure is that it gives you time to think. Being told you have breast cancer is a shock, even if you've suspected it. You need time to adjust to the idea, to decide, with full information, perhaps including a second opinion, what you want to do. I don't think you can really make that decision before you know if you've got cancer. The hypothetical is very different from the real: what you think you'd decide *if* you have cancer may be very different from what you will decide *when* you have cancer.

For many women the thought of having cancer is so appalling that often, their first thought is, "I don't want to deal with this—just get it out of me and let me go on with my life." But with a day or two to reflect on this new reality, your panic may subside and you may decide on a less drastic treatment than your original horror dictated. Whatever treatment you decide on, you'll have to live with it for the rest of your life—and that life won't be shortened by giving yourself a little time to think it over.

Obviously, if you've got cancer you want it taken care of as soon as possible, and you don't want to wait several months before your treatment. But the week or so you give yourself to decide won't kill you, and it will help you to make the clearest decision possible. No one should be put to sleep without knowing whether she'll have her breast when she wakes up.

How to Interpret a Biopsy Report

A good pathologist looking at the tissue removed in an excisional biopsy can tell whether or not breast cancer is present, and if it is, what kind of breast cancer you have. Your surgeon should select a pathologist who has had a lot of experience in diagnosing breast cancer. The language of a pathologist's report can be puzzling and intimidating, and for this reason a patient should always discuss the pathology report with her surgeon.

Most breast cancers (86%) start in the ducts, while some (12%) start in lobules and the rest start in the surrounding tissues. Thus, your cancer will probably be described as either ductal carcinoma or lobular carcinoma. Next, the report will state whether or not the cancer is invasive. Invasive cancers are also known as infiltrating cancers—a sinister-sounding description which simply means the cancer has grown outside the duct or lobule where it started into the surrounding tissue (Fig. 20-1). In this case the report will read either invasive ductal (or lobular) carcinoma or "infiltrating ductal (or lobular) carcinoma."

Since lobules and ducts are kinds of glands, and the medical term meaning "related to a gland" is *adeno*, sometimes these cancers are called *adeno-carcinomas*. Some people get confused with this term, thinking it is a different kind of cancer. It is just a broader category—like calling me a Californian since I live in Los Angeles.

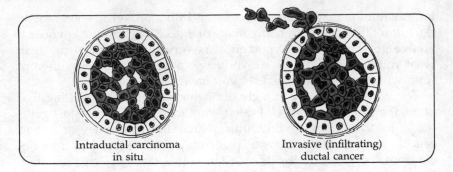

Intraductal carcinoma   Invasive (infiltrating)
in situ   ductal cancer

FIGURE 20-1

An infiltrating ductal cancer forms a hard, firm lump because it creates a lot of reaction caused by tough tissue (fibrosis) around the cells. Infiltrating lobular cancer tends to be a little more sneaky, and will send out individual cells in little fingerlike projections into the tissues without inciting a lot of reaction around them. You may feel it as a little thickening, rather than as a hard lump (Fig. 20-2). For this reason, it's harder for surgeons to tell if they've got the lobular cancer all out, because the little projections can't be felt as easily as a hard lump. Aside from that, however, one form is no worse than the other: neither has a better or worse prognosis. There's a slightly higher tendency for lobular cancer to occur in both breasts. An infiltrating ductal cancer has about a 15 percent chance of occurring in the other breast; a lobular cancer has about a 20 percent chance—an increase in risk, but not a very large one.[2]

If the cancer is not invasive, it will be called *intraductal carcinoma* or *ductal carcinoma in situ* or *lobular carcinoma in situ* or even *noninvasive carcinoma*. These are all names for what I call precancer, which was discussed in Chapter 16. Sometimes both cancer and precancer are present in one lump, and the report might read "infiltrating ductal carcinoma with an intraductal component." This finding will be discussed further in Chapter 23.

There are other names for cancers that may appear on the pathologist's report. For the most part they're variations on invasive ductal cancer, named by the pathologist according to the visual appearance of the cells under the microscope. *Tubular* cancer, in which the cancer cells look like little tubes, is very unusual—1–2 percent of breast cancers—and usually less aggressive. *Medullary carcinoma* has the color of brain tissue (the medulla) and can be aggressive or less aggressive. *Mucinous carcinoma* is a kind of infiltrating ductal cancer that makes mucous. *Papillary carcinoma* has cells that stick out in little papules, or fingerlike projections. (See Table 20-1.)

Table 20-1. Types of Breast Cancer and Frequency[a,b]

Infiltrating ductal	70.0%
Invasive lobular	10.0
Medullary	6.0
Mucinous or colloid	3.0
Tubular	1.2
Adenocystic	0.4
Papillary	1.0
Carcinosarcoma	0.1
Paget's disease	3.0
Inflammatory	1.0
In situ breast cancer	5.0
ductal	2.5
lobular	2.5

[a]There can be combinations of any of these types.

[b]Henderson, C., J.R. Harris, D.W. Kinne, S. Helman, "Cancer of the Breast," in V.T. DeVita, Jr., Helman, S., Rosenberg, S.A. eds. *Cancer: Principles and Practice of Oncology*, Vol. I, 3rd edition. Philadelphia: J.B. Lippincott, 1989, pp. 1204–1206.

Once the pathologists have decided what kind of cancer you have, they try to determine by studying the cells further whether or not they're likely to be aggressive. This isn't 100 percent accurate, however; it's a little like looking at a lineup to pick out who the criminal is. If one of the people is seedy and scruffy-looking and one is wearing a three-piece suit, you'll guess that the first one is the bad guy. But you could be wrong.

Similarly, the pathologist who sees wild-looking ("poorly differentiated") cells will know that such cells are usually more aggressive,

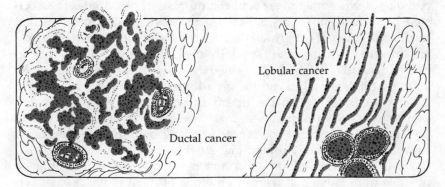

Lobular cancer

Ductal cancer

FIGURE 20-2

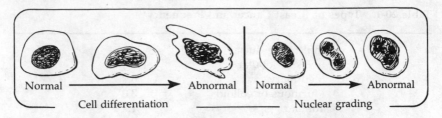

FIGURE 20-3

while the cells that look closer to normal ("well differentiated") are usually less aggressive (Fig. 20-3). The cells in between are called "moderately differentiated." Poorly differentiated cells, however, aren't a sign of doom—the fact that they look wild doesn't guarantee they'll act that way. It is important to realize that most breast cancers are either moderately or poorly differentiated but that many of these women do fine.

Another thing the pathologist will look for is how many cells are dividing, and how actively they're dividing. The most aggressive cancers tend to have a lot of cells dividing at the same time, because they're growing rapidly. Less aggressive cancers tend to have very few dividing cells. How many are dividing is indirectly measured by something called the *nuclear grade*. The nucleus of the cell is the part that goes through cell division, so the grade gives you an idea of the degree of cell division and how odd-looking the nuclei are. Pathologists usually grade on a scale of 1 to 3 or 1 to 4, with the higher number being the worst (Fig. 20-3).

The pathologist will also look to see if there are any cancer cells in the middle of a blood vessel or a lymphatic vessel. These are called vascular invasion, or lymphatic invasion, and suggest that the cancer is potentially more dangerous than if they're not there. In addition, the pathologist will sometimes count the number of blood vessels associated with the tumor. This is because tumors secrete a material that causes blood vessels to grow. If there are a lot of blood vessels, it may indicate that the tumor is especially well nourished and thus especially aggressive. I've noticed in my own work that if I'm operating on a lump I think is benign and there's a lot more bleeding than I would have expected, it's often the tip-off that the lump isn't benign but cancerous. Another ominous sign is "necrosis," or dead cancer cells. This usually means that the cancer has outgrown its blood supply, a sign that it is growing rapidly (Fig. 20-4).

All of these are methods of trying to get as much information as possible from looking at the cancer. None of them is 100 percent certain in predicting behavior.

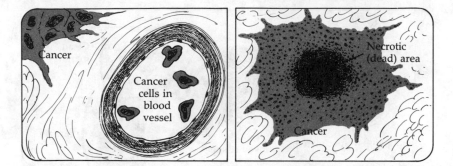

FIGURE 20-4

In addition, the pathologist will look to see whether there's cancer at the margins of the tissue that's been removed. This is done by a fairly imprecise technique. Ink is put all around the outside of the sample, before it is cut up and fixed and slides are made. If on the slides there are cancer cells next to the ink, this means that there's cancer on the outer border, and if there are cancer cells only in the middle, not next to the ink, there is a clean margin (Fig. 20-5). So the report might say, "The margins are uninvolved with tumor," or "The margins are involved with tumor," or "The margins are indeterminate." If the lump has been taken out in more than one piece, we usually can't tell if the margins are clear or not. Also, we can make only representative sections of the margin; to get them all, we'd have to make thousands of slides. So when we say the margins are clean, we're making only an educated guess—we can't be 100 percent sure. (See Chapter 16 for a discussion of margins and DCIS.) What we really are trying to determine is how much cancer might still be in the breast.

How clearly any of these things are seen depends on the expertise of the pathologist looking at them, and how hard the pathologist looks. Someone who makes only a couple of slides and looks at them very hastily is obviously more likely to miss things than someone who makes a lot of slides and looks at them carefully. If you are at all concerned about the quality of the pathology evaluation, or even if you are not, you might want to have your slides sent to another pathologist in another institution (see Appendix D). There is a breast pathologist I work very closely with, Dr. Sanford Barsky, who reviews the slides of all of the women we see in our Multidisciplinary Cancer Program at UCLA. Sometimes we end up changing the diagnosis, or at least reinterpreting a finding that might affect treatment. Some of the things we've discussed aren't always easy to see on the slides. It can be somewhat subjective: are these cells bizarre-looking enough?

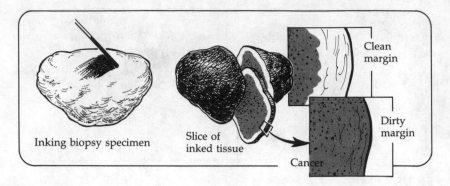

Inking biopsy specimen

Slice of inked tissue

Cancer

Clean margin

Dirty margin

FIGURE 20-5

Are they invading other structures? It's worth getting a second opinion.

Often pathologists themselves will ask other pathologists on the staff to look at the slides and give their opinions. If you live in a small town with a small hospital, you might want your slides sent to a big university center, where someone sees a lot of breast pathology. You can call the university hospital's pathology department and arrange to have them look at your slides, then call your hospital and have the slides sent. Make sure it is the slides themselves they send, since that's what the second pathologist needs to see—not just the first pathologist's interpretation. You need to get the clearest information possible to decide what course of treatment to embark on.

Biomarkers

More and more we are trying to identify characteristics of the tumor cells that we cannot see under the microscope but can measure with sophisticated molecular tests that will tell us how the tumor is behaving. We use a number of biological characteristics of the tumor to help us understand this. Unfortunately, we haven't yet figured out the best ones. We have an enormous list. Every time there's any new fact discovered about cancer, somebody will do a test to see whether it can be a good indicator of the tumor's behavior. I'll discuss here the ones most frequently used.

The most common is the *estrogen-receptor test*, done to find out whether or not the tumor is sensitive to hormones. A hormone is a chemical substance secreted into the bloodstream by a particular gland. Its function is to stimulate a physiological process. It travels till it reaches a cell that's equipped with a matching receptor. The hormone functions a little like a key, and the receptor is the lock to a cell, which opens only to the right key. When, for example, an estrogen molecule finds a cell with an estrogen receptor, it attaches itself to the receptor and forms a complex, which then brings about a number of cellular changes (Fig. 20-6). Once inside, it can do its job in the cell. Not all cells have hormone receptors, and those that haven't will never respond to a hormone—there's no lock for the key to open. Similarly, a specific hormone can't get into a receptor for another hormone—it's the wrong key for that door.

Like an apartment door in a big city, a cell can have a number of locks—or different hormone receptors. The number and types of receptors a cell has are variable, depending on the hormonal environment and on the type of cell itself. For example, a breast cancer cell may have receptors for both estrogen and progesterone, estrogen alone, or progesterone alone. We determine if a particular cancer is sensitive to estrogen (estrogen receptor positive) by doing a test on the tissue. If it's estrogen receptor negative, it isn't sensitive to estrogen. Similar tests are also done for progesterone.

The implications of the hormone receptor tests are twofold. In general, tumors that are sensitive to hormones—that have receptors—are

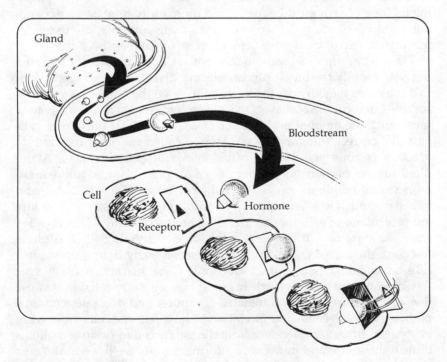

FIGURE 20-6

slightly slower growing and have a slightly better prognosis than tumors that aren't.[3] Generally, postmenopausal women are more likely to be estrogen receptor positive and premenopausal women are more likely to be estrogen receptor negative. Second, the test tells whether the tumor can be treated with some kind of hormonal therapy. If it's not sensitive to hormones, it rarely responds to hormone treatments. (See Chapter 28.)

We sometimes oversimplify the notion of estrogen receptors and convey the idea that if you're estrogen receptor positive and are given estrogen your tumor will grow rapidly, while if you're estrogen receptor negative it won't. For example, after you've been treated for breast cancer, your gynecologist might be treating you for menstrual irregularities or menopausal symptoms, and may be considering putting you on estrogen replacement therapy (see Chapter 15). Often in this situation gynecologists erroneously base their decision on whether or not your tumor was estrogen receptor positive, deciding against giving you estrogen if it was. Or, if you're considering pregnancy, your gynecologist may advise against it because it will increase your hormones. But in both situations the gynecologist is overestimating our knowledge of how estrogen receptors work. We really don't fully understand these hormone receptors and what stimulates them or blocks them. The decision must be made on a more individual basis, depending upon how severe the woman's symptoms are. (See discussion of menopausal symptoms after breast cancer in Chapter 30.)

The next group of measurements that we do is an attempt to figure out how rapidly the breast cancer cells are dividing, based on the idea that the more they divide, the more aggressive they must be. We measure this in a couple of ways. One is *flow cytometry*,[4] which is a way of measuring the amount and type of DNA in a cell. If the tumor cells have the correct amount of DNA, they're called *diploid*; if the amount of DNA is abnormal, they're called *aneuploid* (see Glossary). Aneuploid tumors account for 70 percent of all breast cancer tumors. Tumors that are diploid—that is, have the correct amount of DNA—tend to behave much less aggressively. In addition, these tests can measure the percentage of cells that are dividing at any one time. This is called the *S phase fraction*. If there are a lot of cells dividing (high S phase fraction), the tumor may behave more aggressively than if only a few cells are dividing (low S phase fraction). These markers actually give the same information as nuclear grade but are more reliable because they are measured by an automated computer and don't depend on a pathologist's subjective interpretation of how bad the cells look. As in every test, however, there are limitations. For node-positive patients these tests do not add much new information. As we'll see in the next chapter, their main use appears to be in deciding which node negative tumors need treatment and which ones don't.

Another measurement is the overexpression of the *Her 2 neu oncogene.* Her 2 neu is an example of one of the dominant so-called oncogenes, genes that contribute to cancer (see Chapter 14). Instead of being mutated, however, Her 2 neu is frequently overexpressed and amplified.[5] This means that more than two copies of the gene are present in cancer cells. The mechanism behind gene amplification is generally poorly understood. Her 2 neu is overexpressed in about one third of invasive cancers. At first we thought that this always indicated that the cancer was more aggressive. Interestingly, however, Her 2 neu is also overexpressed in precancer, which isn't yet invasive at all.

Another factor we are studying is *cathepsin* D.[6] This is an enzyme thought to help cells break into blood vessels. Therefore a high level of caphepsin D might indicate a cancer is more likely to have spread.

Up until now we have focused on information obtained from biomarkers that can predict which cancers are more aggressive and therefore more likely to have spread. Recently, however, we have become aware of a different use for these markers. It appears that some of these biomarkers may also be useful in predicting which treatment will work better, and how it will work. Examining Her 2 neu is a good example. It may predict which patients are more likely to respond to high doses of chemotherapy and which are not. We have some evidence to suggest that overexpressers will respond to high dosages while underexpressers won't.[7]

There are many other markers that have been described: epidermal growth factor, heat shock protein, nm23, p53.[8] Some of these were mentioned in Chapter 14. Our hope is that they will also help predict the prognosis of a particular cancer. Research is now going on to determine whether or not combining the information from all of the biomarkers would be more accurate than using one alone. The advance of computer technology makes this a feasible approach. So far this is still more of a hope than a reality. But in the future these biomarkers, or new ones, will provide our most important information and give us much more reliable information about prognosis.

21

Staging: How We
Guess If Your Cancer
Has Spread

The most important question regarding breast cancer is whether it has spread to other organs. This is what ultimately determines who lives and who dies of breast cancer. Unfortunately we have no test or scan that will reliably tell us whether breast cancer cells have gotten into, and begun growing in, other parts of the body. Therefore we have had to use circumstantial evidence to guess how likely it is that this has happened. Our hope is that this knowledge will help us determine the best therapy for any one woman—that is, we can just do surgery for those with localized disease and save chemotherapy for those women who we know have microscopic spread. Since we still don't have a method that works well, there are different approaches to this problem.

One approach is to categorize cases so that statistics can be kept and the long-term survival rates for various treatments determined. This classification system, the TNM (short for tumor, nodes, and metastases) system, is still used, but it is actually a holdover from the past. It doesn't fit very well with our current knowledge of biology, because it is based only on the size of the tumor in the breast and the number of lymph nodes involved as well as obvious spread to other organs. It does not take into consideration the behavior of the tumor or the fact that the lymph nodes are probably not the main route of spread. We have yet to develop a biological staging system based on biomarkers (see Chapter 20) that will more accurately reflect the behavior of the tumor. Since the TNM system is still being used and you might be exposed to it, I'm including a detailed explanation here.

In this system (Fig. 21-1), the tumor is judged by how large it feels to the surgeon who initially diagnosed it. If it's between 0 and 2 centimeters, it's T-1; between 2 and 5 centimeters, T-2; above 5 centimeters, T-3 (one cm. is .39 inch). If it's ulcerating through the skin or stuck to the chest wall it's T-4.

Then the lymph nodes are examined. If there are no palpable nodes, it's N-0; if the surgeon feels nodes but thinks they're negative, it's N-1a; if they're positive it's N-1b. If they're large, and matted together, it's N-2; if they're near the collarbone it's N-3. Finally, if obvious metastasis has been discovered by any of the gross tests we'll describe shortly, it's M-l, and if not it's M-0.

Then all this information is combined into stage numbers. Stage 1 is a T-1 tumor with no lymph nodes. Stage 2 is a small tumor with positive lymph nodes, a tumor between 2 and 5 centimeters with positive or negative lymph nodes, or a tumor larger than 5 centimeters with negative lymph nodes. Stage 3 is a large tumor with positive lymph nodes or a tumor with "grave signs" (Fig. 21-3). Stage 4 is a tumor that has obvious metastasis. This staging system is continually being altered to reflect new information. The stages are calculated twice. First the surgeon does it, making a clinical estimate, and then later the pathologist looks at the tissue that has been removed under the microscope and determines the pathological stage. It has been shown that when the surgeon who has felt the lymph nodes thinks they're negative, there's about a 30 percent chance that the surgical guess is wrong, so they have to be removed and studied under the microscope to be sure of the actual stage.

In spite of the limitations of the TNM system, it still gives us a conceptual framework for categorizing each case of breast cancer so that different treatments can be compared in the same types of patients. So we still use the general stages 1 through 4 categories when describing newly diagnosed cancers.

There is a series of tests that are useful for finding large chunks of breast cancer in other parts of the body. These are called staging tests and shouldn't be confused with the stages of breast cancer just described. It is important to keep in mind that a cancer that starts out as a breast cancer is still a breast cancer no matter where it travels, and that treatments used for the cancer are breast cancer treatments, not liver cancer or lung cancer treatments. A breast cancer that travels to the liver will retain all the characteristics of breast cancer, which are very distinct from those of liver cancer (very few cancers travel *to* the

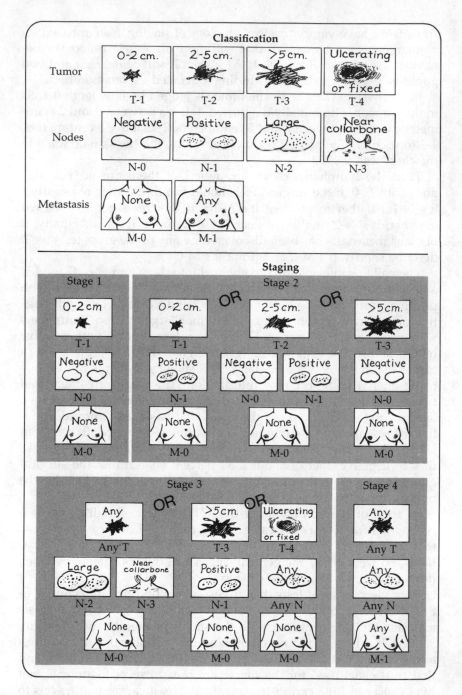

FIGURE 21-1

breast, by the way). It's a bit like what happens when a Californian moves to Paris. She's living in a new environment, but her language, her personality, her basic approach to life are still those of a Californian. She hasn't become a *Parisienne*.

To check the lungs, liver, and bones for breast cancer we do "gross" tests—so-called not because they're gross to have (although most medical tests are) but because they're used to find large chunks of breast cancer in other parts of the body. We can do a chest X ray to find cancer in the lungs. We can do a blood test to see if the cancer has spread to the liver. To learn if the cancer has spread to the bones we do a more complicated test called a bone scan. A bone scan is what we call a nuclear medicine test. A technician injects a low level of radioactive particles into your vein where they are selectively picked up by the bones. After the injection, you wait a few hours while the particles travel through the bloodstream; then you go back to the examining room where you are put under a large machine that takes a picture of your skeleton (Fig. 21-2). The machine whirs above you, reading the number of radioactive particles in your body. (The husband of one of

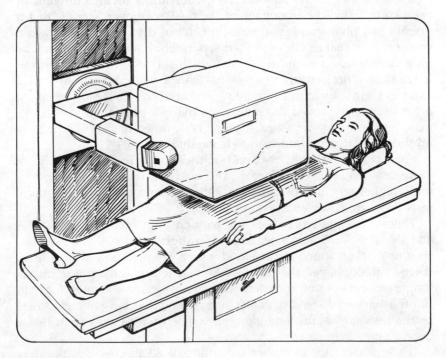

FIGURE 21-2

my patients wears a Geiger counter, and right after her bone scan it started clicking whenever she came near it.) In the areas where the bone is actively metabolizing—that is, doing something—the radioactive particles will show up much more strongly than in the more inert areas.

This doesn't necessarily mean that what the bone is doing is dealing with cancer cells, however. It can mean there's arthritis (which most of us have in small amounts, anyway), a fracture that's in the process of healing, or some kind of infection. All the scan will tell us is that something's happening. If there is, the next step is to X-ray the bone. This will help tell us what it is. We could just X-ray the bone to begin with, but we don't want to expose you to any more radiation than we have to.

There's a similar test for the liver, which is used if the blood test is abnormal. It's not quite as clear as a bone scan, however, because fewer radioactive particles show up in the liver when there's a metastasis. Sometimes we'll do an ultrasound test, in addition to the liver scan, to help confirm our findings.

If more information is needed, we can do a CAT scan (computerized axial tomography) on your liver, your lungs, an area of bone, or even your brain. The advantage of the CAT scan over X ray is that it doesn't just photograph you straight on, but divides your body into cross-sections that can be examined separately. For a CAT scan, you lie on a table inside a round machine, which rotates and takes pictures. It's a little more sensitive to lesions than a plain X ray, but it also exposes your body to much more radiation, so we do it only when the other tests have proved inconclusive. Finally a test called MRI (magnetic resonance imager) (see Chapter 11) is sometimes used, especially on the brain, if more information is needed.

Some women ask why we don't do these other tests first if they are more sensitive. For some doctors, the reason is that they use increasingly higher amounts of radiation. Others avoid them because these tests are more costly and less available.

There are some blood tests for women with breast cancer—CEA and CA 15-3. CEA (carcinoembryonic antigen) and CA 15-3 are nonspecific markers found in the blood which can be followed over time. It was initially hoped that the tests would tell us if there was microscopic growth but unfortunately they're not sensitive enough for that. But the markers do tend to go up in people with extensive metastases, so the tests are useful for following women with metastatic disease because they help us adjust treatment.

It's important to remember the limits of all the tests. A negative finding doesn't give you a clean bill of health; it simply tells you that there are no large chunks of cancer in those organs. Most people who are newly diagnosed don't have spread of this magnitude. So we no longer do these tests in the usual stage 1 or stage 2 breast cancers. If you have stage 3 or locally advanced breast cancer, or if you have symptoms in any of the organs breast cancer typically spreads to—like low back pain that started right after you found your lump and hasn't gone away—we might do these tests. But we don't routinely do them anymore without a reason. They're expensive, they involve radiation, and the chances of their finding anything in a woman with early (stage 1 or 2) breast cancer is so low that they usually just aren't worth it.[1] Some doctors still prefer to do them because testing does give them a baseline for comparison. They can see what those organs look like in you, and if later on you develop symptoms and something shows up on the blood test or X ray, the doctor can say, "Oh, yes, that's just her old arthritis" or "This is new, let's look into it more." But their utility is limited. If your doctor wants to do the test but you don't want the radiation to your body, you can say no; if your doctor doesn't want to do them and you feel more secure getting them, you can demand them.

Most cancers are found in stage 1 or 2, when the "gross tests" are almost always negative. Yet, though more women with stage 1 breast cancer will be cured than will women with stage 2 cancers, some will still die of their disease. This is where the TNM staging system breaks down (Fig. 21-1). You can have a stage 1 cancer and still have microscopic cells elsewhere in your body, or you can have a stage 2 cancer and be clear.

We desperately need a test or a scan that will determine for certain whether the microscopic breast cancer cells have spread to a particular organ. It would simplify treatment if we could say, "Yes, there's a breast cancer cell and it's in your left hip." Then we could do radiation, or chemotherapy, and afterward do the test again to make certain we'd gotten all the cancer. But to date, no such test exists.

There's no foolproof method for determining the early (microscopic) stages of a cancer's spread, so we have to approach it differently. We do have a number of methods of finding the likelihood of early spread—sort of trying a case on circumstantial evidence. We do this by looking for other conditions that often occur when a cancer has spread. If these conditions exist, we can guess that the cancer has spread; if they don't, we can guess that it hasn't. We go through a series of tests in different sequences to try to determine what the chances are.

The first level is based on how the cancer appears when it's diagnosed. There are certain signs and symptoms that statistically indicate a much higher chance that there are microscopic cells elsewhere. These have been incorporated into stage 3 (T-4 lesions) of the TNM

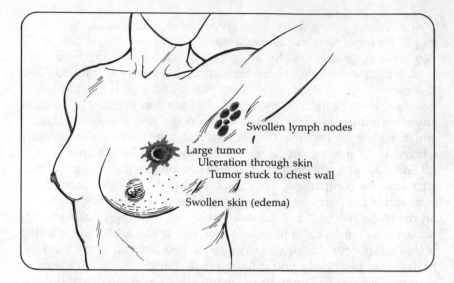

Swollen lymph nodes
Large tumor
Ulceration through skin
Tumor stuck to chest wall
Swollen skin (edema)

FIGURE 21-3

system. Cushman Haagensen[2] first described what he called the "grave signs"—findings on physical exam that indicate the likelihood that microscopic cells have spread to other areas of the body (Fig. 21-3). His work was done in the 1940s before chemotherapy was used in early-diagnosis cancer. Haagensen's plan was to determine which women could really benefit from a radical mastectomy. If there was no hope of saving a patient's life, he didn't want to cause needless suffering and destroy the quality of whatever life she had left. His system is still useful in a general way.

One of the signs that a cancer has probably spread is a large tumor—more than five centimeters (about 2 inches). If it's that big, there are probably microscopic cells elsewhere.

Another danger sign is swelling of the skin (edema) where the tumor is. As the skin swells, the ligaments that hold the breast tissue to the skin get pulled in, and it looks like you've got little dimples on the area. Because this can create an appearance similar to that of an orange peel, it's known as *peau d'orange* (Fig. 21-4). If the tumor is ulcerating through the skin, it's ominous. If it's stuck to the muscles underneath so it doesn't move at all, that's also a bad sign. If there are lymph nodes you can feel above your collarbone (supraclavicular nodes), or walnut-sized lymph nodes in your armpit, that's also dangerous. And if the skin around the lump appears red and infected, it can be inflammatory breast cancer (see Chapter 24), which is also likely to have spread.

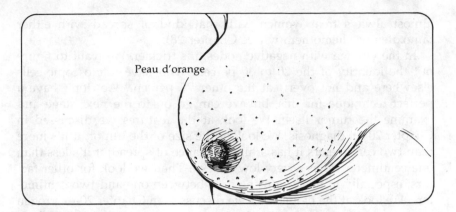

Peau d'orange

FIGURE 21-4

Any one of these signs suggests a high probability that there are microscopic cancer cells elsewhere in the body. If they are present, we plan a systemic treatment (see Chapter 23) as well as a local treatment for the cancer. These tumors are called locally advanced and are often treated with chemotherapy rather than surgery as a first step (see Chapter 28).

Many people haven't any of these grave signs, and for them we need to go on to the next step to try and figure out the likelihood of microscopic cancer cells existing in other organs. The way we do this is to remove some axillary (armpit) lymph nodes. There are between 30 and 60 lymph nodes under the arm, and of these we remove about 10–15, and examine them under a microscope. (See Chapter 25 for this surgery.) We look at these lymph nodes because they are a good reflection of what is going on in the rest of the body. If they reveal cancer cells, we assume there's a high probability that there are cancer cells in other parts of the body. If the lymph nodes don't show cancer, it means there is a lower probability that there are microscopic cells elsewhere in the body.

The lymph node evaluation doesn't give us a foolproof answer, either, however. In about 30 percent of cases, a woman with positive lymph nodes doesn't have microscopic cells elsewhere. In addition, with negative lymph nodes, 20–30 percent of breast cancers will have spread. To a certain degree the number of positive lymph nodes gives us a sense of the probability that there's spread elsewhere. With one or two positive nodes, you're less likely to have more cancer than with 10 or 15. We sometimes look at it in terms of 1 to 3, 4 to 10, and more than 10 to help us guess. However, because with any positive lymph nodes there's a pretty high chance that there are cells elsewhere, we almost always treat women with that kind of spread with either tamoxifen or chemotherapy (see Chapter 28).

In the women with negative nodes, it's trickier. We want to figure out the identity of the 20 to 30 percent who have microscopic cells elsewhere and not overtreat the other 70 percent. We don't have a perfect technique for this, but we can go on to the next stage and examine the tumor itself. We look at the features we discussed in Chapter 20 on diagnosis. We look at the size of the tumor; if it's more than two centimeters it has a higher chance of spread; if it's less than one centimeter it has a very low chance. Then we look for other factors, especially in that confusing area between one and two centimeters. We look at the biomarkers we discussed in Chapter 20—estrogen receptor, S phase, ploidy, and Her 2 neu oncogene.[3] We put all of these together and make our best guess. If this looks like it's probably a fairly aggressive tumor and there's a significant chance of a microscopic cell somewhere in the body, then it may be worth doing chemotherapy or hormone therapy. If it looks like there's a low chance, it may not be worth it.

All of these tests are only tools which, added together, help to give us a picture of the cancer and decide what to do. (See Table 21-1.) All that any of these tests, and others that are being developed, can do is to give a picture of that particular tumor at one particular time—sort of like a snapshot. They cannot tell anything about how it actually acts in a particular woman.

At the end of these tests your tumor will be characterized in a description something like the following:

This is a stage 2: two-centimeter, node-negative, estrogen receptor positive, S phase 10%, aneuploid, Her 2 neu amplified tumor.

Table 21-1. Breast Cancer: Clinical Stages and Prognosis*
(treated with local treatment only)

	Approximate Survival (%)	
Stage	5 years	10 years
0	>98	~90
1	95	65
2	70–85	45–55
3	50–52	20–40
4	17	5

*Based on Table 26-7 in *Cancer Treatment*, Fourth Edition. Edited by Charles M. Haskell M.D. Philadelphia: W.B. Saunders Co., 1995, and reprinted with their kind permission.

This kind of evaluation is what we use to make decisions about treatment because it encompasses as much as we are able to know about the natural history of the disease and the biology of the tumor itself.

None of this gives us absolute knowledge. All it means is that we look at large groups of patients and say, "The majority of women with these signs have this prognosis, and are likely to have this response to this treatment." But you, the individual patient, may or may not fall into the majority category. This has a number of implications. If 80 percent of patients in your cancer category survive, you have reason for optimism—but not, unfortunately, for total rejoicing. You'll probably be in the 80 percent, but you might be in the 20 percent who don't survive. You need to be optimistic, but careful. Do everything possible to keep your advantage—careful follow-up and perhaps some of the adjunct, nonmedical techniques discussed in Chapter 29 to complement your treatment.

By the same token, if 80 percent of women in your category die, that doesn't mean you have to die. While it would make sense for you to think seriously about the possibility of your upcoming death and how you'd best want to prepare for it, it also makes sense to think in terms of being part of the 20 percent who survive. Again, it may be worth looking into nonmedical attitudinal and nutritional therapies to complement your treatment.

It's also important to note that most of the survival statistics were compiled in pre-chemotherapy days, when the only treatment was local surgery. Chemotherapy is aimed at the entire system, so it's very likely that its use will have a positive impact on the stage 3 and 4 cancers. However, since we've only been using it widely in the past 10 to 15 years we don't yet know.

Knowing what stage your cancer is in will help your doctor suggest the treatment that seems most medically useful. It will also help you decide the treatment you want—and the two may or may not be the same thing. If, for example, you have stage 4 cancer, you might decide that painful chemotherapy treatments will ruin the time you have left to live, and therefore to risk a shorter but more comfortable life span. The writer Audre Lorde, who died in 1992, explained her own reasons for making this choice in her book *A Burst of Light*: "I want as much good time as possible, and their treatments aren't going to make a hell of a lot of difference in terms of extended time. But they'll make a hell of a lot of difference in terms of my general condition and how I live my life."[4]

On the other hand, a year or two might feel like "a hell of a lot of difference" to you. You might decide that the possibility of living a little longer is worth the limited suffering chemotherapy entails. There are no right or wrong decisions here; there is only your need, and your right, to have the most accurate information possible, and to decide, based on who you are, what choices make the most sense for you.

22

Fears and Feelings

The first thing a woman thinks of when diagnosed with breast cancer is, "Will I die?" This is quickly followed by "Will I have to lose my breast?" Obviously breast cancer is a disease with a major psychological impact. In fact, whenever you think you have a lump, or get a mammogram, or have a biopsy you rehearse the psychological work of having breast cancer. Although, as I have pointed out, many women don't die of breast cancer, and most do not have to lose their breasts, these remain the major fears.

How does the average woman react to this terrifying diagnosis? In my experience, women go through several psychological steps in learning how to deal with breast cancer.

First there is shock. Particularly when you're relatively young and have never had a life-threatening illness before, it's difficult to believe you have something as serious as cancer. It's doubly hard to believe because, in most cases, your body hasn't given you any warning. Unlike, say, appendicitis or a heart attack, there's no pain or fever or nausea—no symptom that tells you something's going wrong inside. You or your doctor have found this painless little lump, or your routine mammogram shows something peculiar—and the next thing you know we're telling you you've got breast cancer.

Along with shock there's a feeling of anger at your body, which has betrayed you in such an underhanded fashion. In spite of the horror you feel at the thought of losing your breast, often your first reaction is to want to get rid of it: take the damn thing off and let me get on with my life!

While this is a perfectly understandable emotional response, it's not one you should act on. Getting your breast cut off will not make things go back to normal; your life has been changed, and it will never be the same again. You need time to let this sink in, to face the implications cancer has for you, and to make a rational, informed decision about what treatment will be best for you both physically and emotionally.

Unfortunately, not all doctors agree with this philosophy, and some may try to talk you into signing a consent form for a mastectomy right away. This kind of authoritarianism can have a certain appeal: you're scared and stunned and there's daddy or mommy to tell you what to do and make it all better. It doesn't matter how intelligent and rational and well-educated you are; sudden fear can turn anyone into a four-year-old. What you need to do is recognize your response for what it is; if you're tempted to sign the consent form right away, don't. As I said earlier, a few days or even weeks won't make the difference between life and death, but they can make the difference between a decision you'll be comfortable with and one you'll regret.

Because patients are so vulnerable, I don't like to tell them about all their options at the same time I tell them they have cancer. I prefer to say that there are a number of treatment options that we'll discuss the next day at my office.

I begin this process early on. When a patient comes to me with what I think may be a malignancy, I start talking with her right away about the possibilities, from the most hopeful to the most grim, and ask her to consider what it would be like for her in the worst possible scenario. We use the scary word: cancer. We discuss the general range of treatments we'd be likely to choose from. Then we talk about when I'm going to call her with the results of her biopsy, so she can decide where she'll be and who will be with her. I was taught in medical school that you should never tell a patient anything over the phone, but I've found that it works better if I do. If the patient doesn't have cancer, why keep her in suspense any longer? And if she does, I prefer that she find out in her own home, or in whatever environment she's chosen to be in beforehand.

Then if it's bad news, she doesn't have to worry about being polite because she's in my office and there are all these other people around. She can cry, scream, throw things, deal with the blow in whatever way she needs to. And she won't have to lie awake all night hoping I'm not going to tell her something awful the next day but knowing the worst already. So I'll tell her on the phone, and then make an appointment to see her within 24 hours. By that time, the shock will have worn off a little bit, and she can absorb information about her options a little better.

Even then, it can be very difficult for a patient to take it all in. For this reason, I suggest that if you've been told you have breast cancer, you bring someone with you when the doctor explains your options—a spouse, a parent, a close friend. Sometimes the friend is the best idea: someone who cares a lot about you but who isn't close enough to be as devastated as you are by the news. The person is there partly to be a comfort and support, but also to be a reference later, so it's good if it's someone detached enough to remember everything said at the meeting. It's also a good idea to bring along a tape recorder. Then you can go over the options your surgeon has discussed with you again later on and as many times as you need to.

These days, my approach isn't all that unusual. In the past, surgeons were almost always very paternalistic: they told a woman she had cancer and she had to have a mastectomy but that when it was over she'd be cured and everything would be fine from then on. It was a lie, of course, but the patient usually believed it because she wanted to—who wouldn't?—and for the time being, at least, she was reassured.

Today there's much more emphasis on doctor and patient sharing the decision-making process, and there are more options to choose from. There's also a lot more knowledge available—there are articles about breast cancer and its survival rates in both the medical and the popular press; you *know* you have no guarantee that everything will be fine once "daddy doctor" makes you better. All this is good, of course, but it's also very stressful. In the long run, I'm convinced that you're better off when you've consciously chosen your treatment than when it's imposed on you as a matter of course. But in the short run, it's more difficult. The end result is a little more anxiety ahead of time, but less depression later.

Of course, different patients have different needs. Some women still want an "omniscient" doctor to tell them what to do. I was involved in a pilot study on how patients decide their treatments, and what kinds of decision making had the best psychological results. I expected to find that women coped better when they got a lot of information from their doctors and learned all they could about their disease, its prognosis, and the range of available treatments. But we found that this wasn't always the case. What was far more important was whether the doctor's style matched the patient's. Some women preferred to deny their cancer as far as possible, and have their doctor take care of it for them. They did better with old-fashioned paternalistic surgeons who told the women what was best for them, giving them minimal information. Others liked to feel in control of their lives, and to know all they could about their illness and its ramifications. They did better with surgeons like me, who wanted to discuss everything with them. And some women want a great deal of information but still would rather defer to the doctor for decision making. There is no right or wrong style, so don't feel guilty if your needs are not the same as your friend or neighbor.

I've experienced this in my own practice. There was a well-respected, excellent breast surgeon in Boston when I was at the Faulkner, who was much more in the old-fashioned mode, and he and I would lose patients to each other all the time—sometimes we referred patients to each other. It worked out very well, and we were both happy about it, since we were both able to help people while remaining true to our own styles and philosophies.

Sometimes I get a patient who clearly prefers not to know a lot, and over the years I've come to recognize the signals such a person sends and to respect them. I'll give such a patient enough information, but not in as much detail as I usually do, and then try to hear what she is choosing and say something like, "It seems to me that you're leaning toward mastectomy, and maybe that's the best decision for you." I still won't tell her what to do, but I'll give a little more guidance than usual.

So if the first stage is shock, the second is investigating the options. (Sometimes, however, it works in reverse. These stages can vary in order and intensity.) How extensive this investigation is varies enormously among women. For some patients, it consists simply of going over what I've told them and discussing it with a friend. For others it involves research in medical libraries and going for second and third and fourth opinions. You can't take forever, but you don't want to hurry yourself, either. In my experience, most patients can't handle prolonging this stage for more than three or four weeks.

Exploring the options often means getting a second opinion, and I think it is important to get it from a completely different institution. Talking to the partner of your surgeon or the oncologist to whom your surgeon always refers patients is not likely to be a real second opinion.

Some women assume that a second opinion is just a confirmation of the treatment plan chosen. They come to see me with their surgery scheduled for the next day and are often very upset if I disagree with their doctor's plan. But that is the risk you take. Breast cancer treatment is far from straightforward. If you go for another opinion you may well get one. When the second opinion is different from the first, a patient often assumes it must be the right one. Furthermore, having to think about what both doctors said and make a decision between them can be extremely stressful. You feel very insecure because it is your life on the line and no one seems to know what to do. But the truth is, there are choices. There are different ways to approach the problem and no right answer. And it's your decision: both opinions can be right. You would like to believe that there is some objective truth: one right way to treat your disease. Unfortunately, as you are finding from reading this book, this is often not the case. You have to keep exploring all of the possibilities and opinions until you find the one you're most comfortable with.

When you're exploring the options reflect seriously on what the loss of a breast would mean to you. Its importance will vary from woman to woman, but there is no woman for whom it doesn't have some significance. Although many women will say, "I don't care about my breast," deep down this is probably not true for most of us. A mastectomy may be the best choice for you, but it still will have a powerful effect on how you feel about yourself. For many women, the loss of a breast can mean feelings of inadequacy—she's "no longer a real woman." In her book, *First, You Cry*,[1] Betty Rollin talks about the first party she went to after her mastectomy, where she felt that, although she looked pretty with her clothes on, she was like a transvestite, only playing at being a woman.

The fear of feeling this way may start long before the mastectomy—indeed, it plays a part in how the woman copes with her breast cancer from the first. Rose Kushner[2] surveyed 3,000 women with breast cancer and concluded that most women "think first of saving their breasts, as a rule, and their lives are but second thoughts."

My experience has been different. The first reaction of most of my patients has been, "I don't care about my breast—just save my life." Later, when the first shock has worn off and they've had time to think about it, their priorities remain the same, but they realize that they do in fact care very much about their breast. Many women feel robbed of their sexuality when they lose a breast. Betty Rollin found that while her husband still desired her after her mastectomy, her own sexual feelings were gone. "If you feel deformed, it's hard to feel sexy," she writes. "I was dark and dry. I no longer felt lovely. Ergo, I no longer could love." Holly Peters-Golden,[3] on the other hand, points out the importance of distinguishing between the distress caused by mutilating surgery and the distress that comes from having a life-threatening disease. Certainly, my experience with patients has been that for them the latter far outweighs the former. The fear of the loss of a loved one can stress a relationship and affect one or both members sexually.

Anne Kaspar[4] studied 29 women between the ages of 29 and 72, 20 of whom had had mastectomies, and nine who had had lumpectomies. As she hastens to explain, she had no illusions that 29 women constituted a definitive study, but her findings are nevertheless interesting. She found that most of the women with mastectomies were deeply concerned before their surgery that the mastectomy would "violate their femininity." Yet, with one exception, they reported that after the surgery it was much less traumatic than they'd anticipated and that they'd realized that being female didn't mean having two breasts. "They got in touch with their identity as women, separate from social demands. Even the ones most determined to get reconstruction didn't feel that the plastic surgery would make them real women—they knew they already were real women," Kaspar says. She did find that anxiety was higher among the single women in her study, especially the single heterosexual women, who worried that "no man will ever want me." The women already in relationships usually found their partners were still loving and sexual, and more concerned with their health than their appearance.

Although the experience of these young, single, heterosexual women is consistent with my experience, I've also had many other patients with different reasons for wanting to keep their breasts. Often middle-aged women who are approaching or just over menopause have very strong feelings about their breasts. They've experienced the loss of their reproductive capacity with menopause; often their children have left home and they are rediscovering their relationship with their spouse. This is no time for a woman to experience yet another loss around her womanhood. Also, elderly women will often want breast conservation. They're experiencing many losses and may well not want to add the loss of their breasts, which have been a part of them for such a long time. Nothing makes me more angry than hearing of an elderly woman who has been told by her surgeon, "You don't need your breasts anymore; you may as well have a mastectomy." Different choices may make sense at different stages in a woman's life. Your choice should be based not only on the best medical information you can gather but also on what feels right to you. Don't let any generalizations about age, sexual orientation, or vanity get in your way.

Many studies have been done recently comparing conservative surgery and mastectomy with or without immediate reconstruction, looking for differences in psychological adjustment. Interestingly, the important factor often appears to be the match between the woman and her treatment.[5] That is, the way she feels about her body, about surgery, about radiation, about having a say in her treatment, and about a multitude of other factors will affect how she reacts to this new and enormous stress.

Most important for any woman faced with these decisions is the fact that she cannot make a "wrong" decision. If she is being given options it is because there are reasonable options for us to offer. According to our present knowledge both mastectomy and lumpectomy with radiation will work equally well (see Chapter 23). It is not as though if she chooses wrong she'll die, and if she chooses right she'll live.

Having explored the options, most women move into a "get on with it" stage. You know all you want to know, you've decided what you want to do, and now it's time to do it. This is the time to make your decision—you understand that you have cancer; you know the pros and cons of the different treatments; you're not happy about it but you're not still in shock.

How long this stage lasts depends on the treatment. If you're getting a mastectomy, without immediate reconstruction, it may just be one or two days. If you have reconstruction, it will be a few days in the hospital and a few weeks recuperating at home. If you're having wide excision and radiation, it will go on for six weeks, and if you're having chemotherapy in addition to your other treatments it can go on for another six to eight months. However long the treatment process lasts, it's important to have a lot of support around you, and it's important to allow yourself to feel lousy. Cancer is a life-threatening illness, and the treatments are all emotionally and physically stressful; you need to accept that and pamper yourself a bit. You don't have to be Superwoman. Get help from your friends and family—throughout the treatment. Sometimes, when you're having chemotherapy, the people who were supportive in the beginning start to drift off. At that point, you may want to get into a breast cancer support group, where there are women going through experiences similar to what you're going through, or who have been through it. Such a group can be of enormous help to you. In some parts of the country, away from big cities, it might be hard to find one, and you may feel uncertain about mixed-gender, mixed-cancer groups. It's worth checking out, however; sometimes such groups can work well, and often many of the members are in fact women with breast cancer (see Appendix C for some groups). Call the leader and ask about the others in the group, and if your situation will allow you to relate to them.

As stressful as the treatment period can be, it is an improvement on the earlier stages: you're actually doing something to combat your disease. (This feeling is often stronger when you're doing meditation, visualization, diet changes, or one of the other techniques we'll talk about in Chapter 29.) But when the treatment period is done, you're likely to find yourself in a peculiar sort of funk. This is what I see as the fourth stage, a post-treatment recovery stage, which often lasts as long as the treatment itself. You're experiencing separation anxiety because the experience and preoccupation you've lived with so intensely is over, and where are you now? The routine established during your treatment has helped you feel supported, protected, and active against your cancer. Losing that feeling is hard. It's a little like being fired from a job—even one you didn't like. Rationally, you're glad it's over, but emotionally you feel lost. The caretakers (nurses, doctors, and technicians) you've come to depend on are no longer a daily part of your life. Compounding this feeling is a reasonable fear. There's no more radiation going into your body, no more chemotherapy; without them, is the cancer starting up again? It's a scary time. This anxiety may well progress to depression, which is very common and can sneak up on you when you least expect it. You find yourself feeling sad and anxious; you can't sleep, or you want to sleep too much; you find you've lost interest and pleasure in people and activities that you used to enjoy. These symptoms are very normal and will often last a few weeks or months, but if they seem to drag on you may well want to see a therapist or counselor to help you get unstuck and enable you to go on with your life. Barbara Kalinowski, a nurse and former colleague of mine, runs two support groups at the Faulkner in Boston. She has found that this can often be one of the most helpful times for a woman to get involved with a support group. "Sometimes it can be too much for a woman before this: she's working at her job, she's taking care of her kids, and she's going for treatment. Adding the extra time commitment of a support group can create even more stress. But when it's done and the depression sets in, you may really need the group."

Many women find that this period of intense feelings can be a time of emotional growth. They see it as a time to reevaluate their lives; they know their own mortality in a way they never did before. How are they living? Are they doing what they want to do for the rest of their lives? I've seen fascinating changes in some of my patients' lives during this period. One of my patients finally left a bad marriage she'd stuck with for years. Conversely, another decided it was time to make a commitment she'd avoided before—she married the man she'd been living with for a long time. A minister who lost her job because of her cancer left the ministry and got a job selling medical equipment. Another, a breast cancer nurse, left her job to work at a holistic health center. A patient whose husband had had Hodgkin's disease had her first child: faced with life-threatening illnesses, the couple wanted to confirm their faith in life and bring a new life into the world. Several of my patients have begun psychotherapy, not only to deal with their fears around their cancer, but also to look into issues they'd been coasting by with for years. They want to make the best of the time they have left, whether it's five years or 50 years.

This period of preoccupation and turning inward can last a long time. It's not that you're always completely depressed and out of it; you're just tired, a bit listless. Your body and mind still haven't fully healed yet.

For many women the cancer never returns and they begin gradually to rebuild their lives. But sometimes cancer does return. Because the emotional issues of recurrence are so profound and complex, I've saved the discussion of these issues for Chapter 31.

What I've given is a general overview of the emotional recovery process. It's not a formula. You may not go through all these steps, and you may not experience the steps you go through in the way I've described them. Each person's recovery is individual, and there's no right or wrong way to cope with it. I've had patients tell me they're worried because they haven't started to cry yet! Some people cry a lot about their cancer and some don't cry at all. If you think you're holding back feelings that you're afraid to face, perhaps you'll want to see a therapist to help you face the feelings. But don't assume that you're not facing your feelings because you're not expressing them according to someone else's script.

Along with these fears and the process of recovery, there are a number of related issues. One is the tendency to feel guilty for having cancer—a sense that you've somehow done something wrong. I found it sad and interesting that when Nancy Reagan was interviewed on TV by Barbara Walters about her breast cancer, the First Lady admitted that after her breast surgery the first thing she said to her husband was, "I'm sorry." People have a tendency to blame themselves for being ill, and, irrational though she knows it to be, a woman often feels she's betrayed her function as a caregiver by getting breast cancer.

In this connection, the holistic methods we discuss in Chapter 29 can have their negative side. The mind-body connection is real, and its validation is very important, but it's not the only force at work in any disease. You didn't create your own cancer by eating too much sugar or thinking negative thoughts or allowing yourself to be too stressed out. I was appalled by a study that showed that 41 percent of women with breast cancer think they brought it on themselves because of the stress in their lives.[6]

In reality, most of the studies on the relation between stress and cancer have been done on rats, and are equivocal at that—some studies show that stress is a factor in cancer, others that it's a factor in *preventing* cancer. In any case, it's only one factor, not a significant cause. I wish there *were* some simple, clear cause of cancer so I could say, "Don't do this and you won't get breast cancer." Unfortunately, it doesn't work that way. We don't have total control over our own bodies; we don't always, to use the popular New Age phrase, "create our own reality." You didn't give yourself breast cancer, and you won't help your healing by feeling guilty about something you didn't bring on yourself.

It's true that studies have shown that survival rates of those who already have cancer can be affected by personality. People with a fighting spirit appear to have a somewhat better survival rate than passive victims. But the same studies also show that the people who try to pretend their cancer isn't there, who just get what treatments they have to and don't think about it, do just as well. It's the ones who admit they have cancer but assume they haven't got a chance and just give up who succumb sooner. I'm not sure how useful these studies are to someone who has cancer. It might be reassuring to a fighter, but not everyone has the goal of survival at any cost. Should anyone be expected to change personality overnight?

A particularly trying issue people face is the question of what to tell their children. Again, it's an individual decision, and there are no hard and fast rules. I do think, in general, it's wiser to be honest with your kids, and to use the scary word "cancer." If they don't hear it from you now, they're bound to find it out some other way—they'll overhear a conversation when you assume they're out of the room, or a friend or neighbor will inadvertently say something. And when they hear it that way, in the form of a terrible secret they were never supposed to know, it will be a lot more horrifying for them. By talking about it openly with them, you can de-mystify it. In addition, if all goes well, your children gain an opportunity to learn about survival after cancer.

How you tell them, of course, will depend on the ages of the children and their own emotional vulnerability. With a little child, you can say, "I have cancer, which is a dangerous disease, but we were lucky and caught it early, and the doctors are going to help me get better soon." What younger kids need to know is that you're going to be there to take care of them, that you're not suddenly going to be gone. They also need to know that the changes in your life aren't their fault. All kids get angry at their mothers, and they often say things like "I wish you were dead." When suddenly Mom has a serious illness, the child may well see it as a result of those hostile words or thoughts. They must be told very directly that they did not cause the cancer by any thoughts, words, anger, dreams, or wishes. Your children will also be affected in other ways. You're going to be gone for a few days in the hospital, and will need to rest when you come home. You may be getting radiation treatments, which consume a lot of your time and will leave you tired and lethargic. You may be having chemotherapy treatments that make you violently sick to your stomach. Your children need to know that the alteration in your behavior, and the decrease in your accessibility to them, aren't happening because you don't love them or because they've been bad and this is their punishment.

Some surgeons encourage their patients to bring young children to the examining room with them. I find it can be very helpful for a daughter in particular to see me examining her mother. If you're being treated with radiation or chemotherapy in a center like Dana Farber or Beth Israel in Boston, where your children are permitted to see the treatment areas, it's a good idea to bring them along once or twice. The environments aren't intimidating, and a child who doesn't know what's happening to you can conjure up awful images of what "those people" are doing to mommy.

It is also important to be careful about changes in your older children's roles at home. You don't want to lean too heavily on them to perform the tasks you are unable to do; instead, give them things they can do that will make them feel useful. Wendy Schain, a psychologist and breast cancer survivor, and David Wellisch, a psychologist I work with at UCLA, did a study on daughters of women who had had breast cancer. They found that the daughters who had the most psychological problems in later life had been in puberty at the time of their mother's diagnosis. This was partly because their own breasts were developing at the same time, but, interestingly enough, that wasn't the major reason for their problems. Far more damaging was the fact that they were expected to perform many of the mother's traditional household tasks. They were physically capable of this work, but they were not psychologically able to cope with the responsibility and they felt guilty about their resentment.[7] Also, it is a good idea to let your children's school know about what's going on at home.

Most important is addressing children's two main fears: assuring them that they will not be abandoned and that they will be cared for. Hester Hill, a social worker I know who works closely with women with breast cancer, points out that it is also important not to make promises that you may not be able to keep. It is a mistake to promise, for example, that the cancer won't kill you. Instead, if you're asked, "Will you die?," you can reply to your children, "I expect to live for a very long time and die as an old lady. The doctors are taking good care of me, and I am taking good care of myself, and I hope to live for years and years."

Frightening as it can be for kids to know their mother has a life-threatening illness, if you're honest and matter-of-fact with them, the chances are it won't be too traumatizing. One of my patients decided when she learned about her breast cancer that she would de-mystify the process for her seven- and ten-year-old daughters by showing them a prosthesis (artificial breast) and explaining what it would be used for. The next day she came into my office for her appointment. When I asked her how her experiment worked, she started to giggle. "Well, they certainly weren't intimidated by it. They listened very carefully to my explanation—and then started playing frisbee with it!"

Breast cancer has particularly complex ramifications for a mother and her daughter. Aside from all the normal fears any child has to deal with, a daughter might well worry about whether this will happen to her, too. It's not a wholly unfounded fear. As we discussed in Chapter 14, there is a genetic component to breast cancer. You need to reassure your daughter, explain to her that it isn't inevitable but that as she gets older she should learn about her breasts and be very conscious of the need for surveillance.

Often teenage daughters of my patients come and talk with me about their mothers' breast cancer and their fears for themselves. It can be very useful to a girl to have her mother's surgeon help put the dangers she faces into perspective, and it might be worth asking your surgeon about the possibility of such a meeting with your daughter. This may also be useful years later, if your daughter does develop problems; she's already built a good relationship with a breast specialist, and she's more likely to seek treatment with confidence and a minimum of terror.

Often daughters will find themselves feeling angry at their mothers, as though the mother created her own breast cancer and in so doing made the daughter vulnerable to it. And mothers themselves often feel the same way; their feelings that they caused their own cancer escalate into guilt over their daughters' increased risk. Often a patient will say to me, "What have I done to my daughter?" These feelings need to be faced, and dealt with. Without openness, the cancer can become a scapegoat for all the other unresolved issues between the mother and daughter, putting the relationship at risk.[8]

Husbands or lovers of women with breast cancer also have feelings that need to be acknowledged. They worry that she might die; they worry about how best to show their concern. Should they initiate sex, or will that be seen as callous and insensitive? Should they refrain, or will that be seen as an indication that she's now no longer sexually attractive?

It's important to realize that the cancer is affecting your whole family, not just you. While you're in treatment, you're usually focused chiefly on yourself, because you have to be. But as soon as you can you need to deal with how it's affecting those closest to you. If this is difficult, sometimes it helps to go into couples therapy with your spouse, or family therapy with your spouse and children. They too are feeling frightened, angry, depressed, maybe even rejected, if all your attention is going to your illness, and they may not have as much support for their feelings as you do for yours. It's crucial to communicate with each other at this time, to work through the complex feelings you're all facing.

At the same time, you might be feeling a little apart from the people you love. You're going through something they can't really understand—only somebody else who's been there can. Breast cancer support groups can be wonderful during this time. You'll meet other women who are at various stages of the disease—including some who had it 10 or 15 years ago and are living happy, healthy lives. Often the only people you've known with breast cancer were in an advanced stage—the ones who get better often don't talk about their disease with anyone. Knowing long-term survivors can help you to realize that you're not necessarily doomed. And knowing other women who are at your stage can give you a sense of shared problems, of comradeship with people who understand what's happening to you because it's also happening to them. (See Appendix C for a list of support groups and how to find them.) Indeed, you might want to look into a group even before your treatment. My former colleague Barbara Kalinowski whom I mentioned earlier has had women in her group who came before their surgery so that they could learn about it from women who had already been through it.

Above all, you need to be patient with yourself. Healing, both emotionally and physically, takes time. You're entitled to that time.

PART SIX

TREATING BREAST CANCER

23

Treatment Options:
An Overview

Once you've been diagnosed with breast cancer you are faced with a number of decisions about which treatment—or treatments—to undergo. All these treatments are described later on in more detail. In this chapter we offer an overview.

To evaluate the information we have from available studies and to help you understand the figures your doctor may quote you, we need to spend a moment looking at what the numbers mean. Research studies about cancer therapy can be very confusing. Some talk about the "percentage reduction in mortality," which refers to the percentage of patients who died compared to the number of deaths that were expected. For example, if a study showed that eight patients died in the control group and only six in the study group, there were two fewer deaths than expected. This is then reported out as a 25 percent reduction in mortality. A similar study with more patients might show that 40 patients died in the control group compared to 30 in the study group. The reduction of 10 deaths over a possible 40 is still 25 percent. In the second study, 10 patients' lives were saved, while in the first it was only two. So these percentages are only helpful if you know the expected mortality.

In breast cancer studies things can be even more complicated. Since breast cancer is a slow disease, even the women who are going to die of it often don't do so for many years. Therefore any study has to follow patients for 10 or even 20 years to be able to determine with confidence the effect of a treatment on the death rate (or, conversely, the cure rate). Many investigators, and indeed many patients, don't want to wait that long to look at the results of studies, so they look instead at the "time to recurrence"—the time between the diagnosis of the disease and the first recurrence (if there is one).

This still has much value. Although lengthening the time to recurrence isn't the same as cure, it is very important. For example, let's say you were diagnosed with breast cancer that, with the old treatment, would have killed you in one year. A new treatment increases your time to recurrence, or disease-free survival, by three years. You die four years after your diagnosis. You would not have reached the five-year mark, which is regarded (erroneously) as a cure, but you would have had three extra years of quality time.

Some studies will report out the "median," or middle, time to recurrence. Using a middle time is actually better than using an "average" time to recurrence. An average adds up all times and divides by two. Since many women will never recur, it is impossible to do that. The median is the middle of the times to recurrence at the time the study was done. Some women will have a longer time to recurrence and some shorter. And, of course, some will never recur at all. It is a helpful way to look at early data in a study. It also points out that cure may not be the only goal. Extra years of disease-free survival may well be worthwhile even if the treatment doesn't totally eradicate the cancer.

Treatments are divided into two categories: local (treatment of the breast itself) and systemic (treatment for the rest of the body).

Local Treatments

The first question usually addressed is what to do about local treatment. Until recently, most surgeons did mastectomies, assuming that this drastic procedure is the most effective way to save lives. But, as we discussed in Chapter 19, studies have proven them wrong.

The goal of surgery in the breast is to remove or reduce the cancer. This can be done by removing as much of the cancer as possible in a lumpectomy and letting radiation take care of what's left. Radiation can handle a few microscopic cancer cells; it just can't handle a lot of them. The cancer can also be removed by doing a total mastectomy, which, if the tumors are small, often takes out enough tissue to prevent recurrence. Finally, with very large tumors, we use both mastectomy, to remove as much of the tumor as possible, and radiation therapy, to take care of leftover cells. The various kinds of surgery and the terms used for each are discussed in Chapter 25.

You can have a local recurrence either way—whether you have a mastectomy or a lumpectomy and radiation. People often have the misconception that if they have a mastectomy the cancer will never come back again because there's no breast left. But, as I said earlier, we can never be sure if we've gotten all of the breast tissue. It can come back again in the scar or the chest wall. I saw one patient who had a very small cancer and had bilateral mastectomies because she never wanted to deal with it again, and a year later she had a recurrence in her scar. She was very angry and felt like she had been betrayed because no one had told her that this was a possibility. Patients are often amazed when I explain that they can still get a local recurrence after a mastectomy.

The first study to compare mastectomy and breast conservation began in Italy in 1973, comparing radical mastectomy to quadrantectomy (the removal of a quarter of the breast) followed by radiation. Researchers found no difference in the survival rate between the two methods of treatment.[1] Since then, the NSABP (National Surgical Adjuvant Breast and Bowel Project) did a study in the United States comparing lumpectomy alone, lumpectomy and radiation, and mastectomy, and had similar results: lumpectomy and radiation had almost the same survival and local control rate as mastectomy. After eight years, lumpectomy alone had a 39 percent local recurrence rate; lumpectomy and radiation had a 10 percent local recurrence rate; and mastectomy had a 8 percent rate. (These treatments are, of course, very different and are described at length in Chapters 25 and 27.) The study reported results at eight years,[2] and it's possible that there will be more recurrence and death in the next five or ten years, but so far, it seems likely that the study will confirm the Italian study's finding. There was a major scandal around this study involving falsification of data by one of the participating researchers. But the findings were reevaluated, with the erroneous data removed, and the outcome remained exactly the same (see Chapter 33).

These studies are important because they were randomized. Other, nonrandomized studies have shown similar results. The Joint Center for Radiation Therapy (JCRT),[3] where I sent my patients when I worked in Boston, has a series with one of the longest follow-ups in this country, and their results for local control are similar to those of the randomized data.

The NSABP study conclusively demonstrated that in most kinds of breast cancer radiation and lumpectomy are as good as mastectomy. And finally, in June 1990, a National Cancer Institute Consensus Conference concluded: "Breast conservation treatment is an appropriate method of primary therapy for the *majority* of women with Stage I and II breast cancer and is *preferable* because it provides survival equivalent to total mastectomy and axillary dissection while preserving the breast" (emphasis mine).

There are some special situations in which lumpectomy and radiation might have an edge over mastectomy; for example, if the cancer is right near the breastbone. Even with a mastectomy we can't get a normal rim of tissue around the lump. However, the surrounding tissue can be treated with radiation. If your cancer is located there, and you've had a mastectomy, you might consider following it with radiation.

On the other hand, in some situations, you're better off with a mastectomy—for instance, if you have a large cancer in a small breast (although Dr. Gianni Bonadonna's studies with preoperative chemotherapy, discussed later in this chapter, may help here), or two separate cancers in the same breast, or microcalcifications spread throughout your breast.

There's a lot about local treatment that we've learned, and a lot we still don't know. For example, are there patients who do better with radiation and patients who do better with mastectomy? In Boston I was working on a study with the JCRT, trying to learn more about this. In our study we were looking at the patients who had a recurrence to try and figure out if there was something special in their cases that we could use to predict who is at risk for recurrence. When we restudied the tissue taken out at the time of the lumpectomy we found an important clue: most of these women had a lot of ductal carcinoma in situ—DCIS—in the area surrounding the tumor and in the tumor itself, along with invasive cancer cells. (See Chapter 16 for a discussion of intraductal cancer.)[4] We called this extensive intraductal component (EIC). Strictly speaking, we define a biopsy as showing EIC if more than 25 percent of the lump is precancer and there's extensive precancer in the surrounding area, or if there is extensive DCIS with foci of invasion.

In fact we noted that women who had EIC in their original biopsy had a 25 percent risk of local recurrence compared to 6 percent for those women without EIC. This observation has been confirmed both by the Institute Curie[5] and by the surgical group at Westminster Hospital in London,[6] as well as others.

When we first found this out, we thought that the presence of EIC might indicate a particularly bad cancer, making radiation inadequate. But if this were the case, these people should have been dying at a faster rate than those whose cancer didn't recur, and this wasn't happening.

Then we asked ourselves whether EIC indicated that all the cells in the breast were predisposed to become cancer cells. But if this were the case, the cancer would recur throughout both breasts, and the recurrences we were looking at were all in the same area of the breast the tumor had been taken from.

So it began to appear that it wasn't a question of whether or not this cancer responded to radiation—there was obviously another element involved. One of the things we discussed was the fact that precancer is usually not visible or palpable (see Chapter 16): it's in the ducts and it rarely forms lumps. So the surgeon was probably taking out the lump and what appeared to be a rim of normal tissue, but the tissue actually contained a lot of intraductal cancer that was visible only under the microscope.

To test this hypothesis, we went back and did another study.[7] We looked at women who had had a re-excision after their first biopsy because of dirty or unknown margins. We found out that indeed the women who had EIC often had cancer left in their breasts after the first biopsy, whereas the women who didn't have EIC rarely had any cancer left (Fig. 23-1).

The reason that the people with EIC were having worse local control probably wasn't that radiation didn't work for them, but that we were leaving in too much cancer for the radiation to control. If we could get it all out and had clean margins, they should be okay. Stuart Schnitt and the Boston group recently demonstrated that this was indeed the case.[8]

We now feel that if a woman's lumpectomy reveals a lot of EIC (and this will be the case in about 30 percent of breast cancer patients), the surgeon needs to be sure the margins are clean. This is done by carefully examining the mammogram as well as the margins. It is vital that a post-biopsy mammogram be done to demonstrate if there are any residual calcifications after the first excision. If there is any question, the surgeon should do a second operation and get more tissue out to make sure all the DCIS is gone and the margins and the mammogram are clear before sending the patient for radiation. If the pathologist still finds cancer at the margins, the patient may need a mastectomy. We do know, from studies done by Peter Paul Rosen at Sloan Kettering, that a mastectomy—which is really just a very wide excision—does prevent the cancer from returning locally in most EIC cases (as with all mastectomies there will be a 5–10 percent chance of local recurrence, but not higher).[9]

Meanwhile we are investigating another option for these patients. We are removing the whole area involved (often a quarter or third of the breast) and immediately reconstructing the missing section with some skin and tissue from the back (see Chapter 26). They then will undergo radiation therapy as before. I did a pilot study of 18 cases in Boston and the cosmetic results were excellent. The women had breasts that for the most part retained sensation and looked very

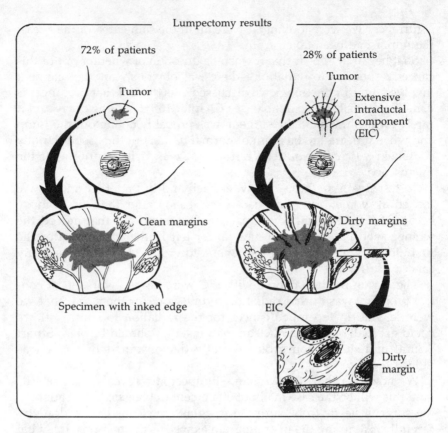

FIGURE 23-1

good. The reason we are doing this as a research project is that we will not be able to examine all of the margins at the time of surgery and there is a risk that we will still have dirty margins even after this large resection. If that happens, we will not go back and remove the reconstruction at that point but continue with radiation. We think that the radiation therapy should be able to handle any small residual disease but this has not yet been proven. The study is taking place in Boston at Beth Israel Hospital as well as at UCLA and we hope it will give us yet another option for local control.

Infiltrating lobular carcinomas also have a tendency to be sneaky and difficult for the surgeon to feel (see Chapter 16). These also need a wider excision and clean margins if they are to be treated with breast conservation.

Apart from these two types of pathology, however, margins are probably less important than we had previously thought. If the cancer is a distinct lump without any of the "tentacles" which are the hall-mark of EIC or lobular carcinoma then just barely removing it is fine. Even involvement of the margins at one or two points is acceptable in this situation.[10] The key is what is the chance that there is cancer left behind. In that type of cancer the chance is very low and radiation therapy can well accommodate it. In our early series from the JCRT before we were not attending to margins the recurrence rate was only 4 percent for these tumors.

The NSABP also discovered that with lumpectomy alone, a woman has a 37 percent greater chance of a local recurrence of her cancer.[11] This brings up the question of whether all women with breast cancer need radiation. If 37 percent of women who have wide excision alone will have a recurrence, we're radiating 63 percent of women who don't need it—whose cancer wouldn't recur anyway. If we could find a way to determine which women are in the 37 percent who need radiation and which are in the 63 percent who don't, we could save those who don't need it the discomforts and risks of radiation.

In the hope there might be a group of women on whom we could stop doing radiation, a study[12] that I was involved in looked at women who fit very strict criteria and offered them the opportunity to be treated without radiation in a very controlled context. To qualify for this study, the woman had to have a tumor less than two centime-ters (3/4 inch), negative lymph nodes, no EIC, no vascular or lym-phatic invasion, and at least a centimeter of normal tissue around her tumor. We felt that by selecting out these women with relatively less dangerous cancers, we were choosing those patients who might not need radiation. We followed these women very carefully, and at the first sign of a recurrence we added further treatment. Unfortunately, we found that even in these carefully chosen women there was a 9.2% local recurrence rate in 3 years compared to a 2% local recurrence rate in comparable patients treated with lumpectomy and radiation. Be-cause this rate of recurrence was higher than we felt was acceptable, we actually had to stop the study prematurely. So at least so far, we haven't been able to figure out a category of women who can safely go without radiation.

Finally the question has come up regarding the need to remove the lymph nodes under the arm. As we mentioned in Chapter 19, there is no evidence that axillary surgery affects survival, and our main pur-pose in doing it is to decide about adjuvant therapy and to prevent recurrence in the armpit. Some surgeons argue that if we are going to give systemic therapy to all women, node negative as well as node positive (a philosophy we discuss later in this chapter), there is no reason to dissect the lymph nodes. They feel they can save women the potential complications of this operation (see Chapter 25) by radiating the axilla instead. The fallacy in this argument, at least at the time of this writing, is that we are not at all sure that every woman should be treated with systemic therapy. Until we know whom to treat or have a better marker of prognosis than lymph nodes, I still feel a lymph node dissection is an important operation for most women. There probably is a subgroup of women, however, in which the possibility of finding positive nodes is so low that it is not worth doing a lymph node dissection, women with DCIS with or without microinvasion and women with invasive tumors less than five millimeters. Silverstein has shown that the chance of positive nodes in this group is less than 3 percent,[13] and many surgeons are beginning to admit that the surgery is probably not necessary. Certainly women need to weigh the pros and cons for themselves. If a woman is going to wonder if she was the 1 out of 100 who had a positive node and would have needed chemotherapy, maybe she should indeed have the surgery. On the other hand, if she can live with the uncertainty and less surgery, then I think it is reasonable to forego the dissection.

There's an international study going on to see whether in women over 70 we can eliminate the axillary dissections and the debilitating effects of general anesthesia, and just put all of them on tamoxifen. This is an important study, and I think it is a question we need to address. Outside of the study, however, postmenopausal women with hormone receptor positive tumors have an option regarding axillary dissection. If they and their doctors have decided that they will be treated with tamoxifen regardless of their nodal status, they may well forego the operation and include their nodes in their radiation. On the other hand, if their tumor is less than 1 cm and they would rather not take a drug for five years, they may choose to have the surgery to find out if their nodes are negative.

In some patients with severe health problems, the risks of general anesthesia may outweigh the advantage of knowing the lymph node status, and in these women it may be reasonable to forego this operation in favor of axillary radiation.

The discussion regarding axillary dissection is an ongoing one. I think in the future we'll be able to stop axillary dissection altogether. Once we've got a better biomarker so we can say, "This is your prognosis," we'll no longer have to subject women to the extra surgery of lymph node removal, with its side effects. At this point, however, I think it is important for every woman to question her surgeon about the necessity of the axillary dissection and make sure she is comfortable with the explanation before proceeding.

In my current position as director of the Revlon/UCLA Breast Center, I've spent the past year reviewing all the data with my colleagues.

We have come up with practice guidelines that suggest we look at every woman as a candidate for breast conservation, unless she strongly prefers a mastectomy. Any woman whose cancer was picked up on a mammogram should have a post-biopsy mammogram to demonstrate that the whole tumor has been removed. If she has had a lumpectomy and the margins are involved, the post-biopsy mammogram shows residual disease, or if she has EIC or infiltrating lobular carcinoma we suggest a re-excision. This step gives us further information. If the new margins are clear she is a candidate for radiation therapy. If not, she may well need a mastectomy. All women who choose mastectomy are offered the option of immediate reconstruction (see Chapter 26). We do not recommend an axillary dissection if the tumor is less than 5 mm, in cases of DCIS with or without microinvasion, or in postmenopausal women where the nodal status will not change our recommendations for adjuvant therapy. Otherwise the nodal surgery is done at the same time as the re-excision or mastectomy and helps us determine the need for systemic therapy.

MAKING THE CHOICE

What are some of the factors that influence women's choices? There's a tendency to think that mastectomy is more aggressive, because it's more mutilating. Actually, lumpectomy and radiation are more aggressive. If I do a lumpectomy and radiation, I can radiate all the breast tissue. The field of radiation can encompass all that tissue that the most extensive surgery misses. Some women choose mastectomy because they want to get it all over with as soon as possible and get back to their lives as though it never happened. It's understandable, but it doesn't always work that way. You can never go back to your life exactly the way it was. Your life will be irrevocably changed. You need to face the problem, deal with it, decide, and then go on to the next, new phase in your life. And don't rush into a decision. As we've said before, a few weeks' time isn't going to make the difference between life and death. But giving yourself that few weeks can make a very large difference in the quality of your life.

There are important drawbacks to mastectomy. It's less cosmetically appealing, and, even with reconstruction (see Chapter 26), it leaves you without sensation in the breast or breast area. Lumpectomy and radiation leave you with a real breast that retains its sexual sensation.

Sometimes a patient asks me what I'd do if I had breast cancer. I never tell her. I couldn't, because what I think I'd do now might be very different from what I'd actually do if I were faced with the reality. But even if I did know, what difference would it make? My choice would be based on who I am—my values, my feelings about my body, my priorities, my neuroses. It would be valid only for me. My patient comes to me for my medical expertise, but she is the expert on herself.

One of the bad things we were taught in medical school was to put ourselves in the patient's position. "If I were you I would . . ." But I'm not you and that attitude encourages me to impose my values on you. My job isn't to second-guess what you want or need. My job is to educate you and help you figure out what's best for you.

There have been studies that show that 30 percent of women with breast cancer need mastectomies, because the tumors are so large or the breast is so small, or for one or two other reasons we discuss earlier in this chapter. Seventy percent would do as well or better with lumpectomy and radiation. And yet, in the United States overall, 30 percent are getting lumpectomy and radiation. In the southeast it's only 10 percent.[14] The rest are getting mastectomies. Part of that reflects the patients' choices. But a larger part represents the failure of doctors to explain the choices thoroughly to the women—or the doctor's projection of their own biases: "If you were my wife, I'd want you to have a mastectomy." I always wonder when I hear those things what the guy's relationship with his wife is like. It seems to me that he'd want her to do what she thinks is best. In any case, you're not his wife. And you're not me—or your sister or your best friend or anyone else. Making assumptions for you isn't appropriate. What's appropriate is to give you all the information and then help you figure out what you want.

Many doctors seem to feel that the older a woman is, the more likely she is to choose mastectomy. This isn't what I've experienced among my older patients. Many of them would just as soon live the rest of their lives with their breasts. One of my patients was an 85-year-old woman who came to me for a second opinion after her surgeon had said to her, "You're not really vain, so you don't need your breast." Leaning over toward me, out of earshot of the niece who had accompanied her, she whispered, in a conspiratorial voice, "I really am vain, you know." She had bought a new hat and a new bra for this visit. When the surgeon talked to her, she felt she had to agree with him, because he made her "vanity" sound petty. But it wasn't petty. She wanted to keep her breast, just as much as any 35-year-old woman did. So she had lumpectomy and radiation, and she did fine. Another patient who had had some form of mental illness had been cavalierly told that a mastectomy would be better for her in her mental state. But, in fact, for her, it was even more important to keep her body intact, because she had a terrible self-image. Fortunately she had a daughter who supported her and brought her to me for a second opinion.

Conversely, many doctors assume that young women, especially single young women, want to keep their breasts—to help them "catch" a man. But some young women don't necessarily want to catch a man, and others feel that a man worth catching is one who won't choose his mate on the basis of her breasts. Furthermore, some of my younger patients point out that we know the effects of radiation over a 20- or 30-year period, but not over a 40-year period: they don't want to risk a radiation-associated cancer in their old age. I've had patients of all ages make different decisions, and I think it's ludicrous to assume that older women should have mastectomies and younger women shouldn't. The real factors vary as much as women and their lifestyles vary. I'm sure there are many factors that I haven't come across, but I can discuss a few I'm familiar with.

Some women choose mastectomy because of their jobs. Nancy Reagan explained in a television interview with Barbara Walters that her work as First Lady was too demanding to permit her to take off any more time than was absolutely necessary. A friend of mine who's a breast surgeon in rural Pennsylvania finds that her breast cancer patients almost always choose mastectomy: they're farmers who can't afford to take off six weeks for radiation treatments.

On the other hand, six weeks isn't such a long time if you really want to keep your breast for the rest of your life: you may be measuring six weeks against 20 or 30 years or more. It might be worth investigating all the ways you can manage to find those six weeks—the friends who can drive you to the hospital or babysit for you, all the resources you may not even realize you have until you try to figure them out.

The availability of one kind of treatment or another is also a factor. In some areas there's no place nearby that offers radiation. In others, there's radiation available, but it's not especially good: a radiation therapist really has to know the technique to get good results.

For some women, their breasts are an integral part of their sexuality and identity and they are willing (and able) to go to great inconvenience to save them. One of my patients lived in a small town in the central valley of California, too far to commute to my breast center in L.A. So she and her husband drove down in their mobile van and lived in the hospital parking lot until her six weeks were over.

I've had other patients whose cancer has recurred after lumpectomy and radiation, and even though they've then had to have a mastectomy, they're grateful that they've had an extra few years with both breasts. I've had other patients who have lumpectomy and radiation and then wake up every morning afterward sure that the cancer's come back—they probably would have been better off with mastectomies in the first place. Regardless of the medical facts, however, you need to feel safe with your choice.

The possibility of reconstruction, which we discuss at length in Chapter 26, may also play a role in a woman's decision. You might be more willing to lose a breast if it can be "replaced." However, as we discuss in Chapter 26, a reconstructed breast is never exactly like a real one.

Remember above all that it's your body and no one else's. Don't decide on the basis of what anyone else thinks is best. By all means talk to your friends and your family and your husband or lover, and think about what they say. But make your own decision. Husbands and lovers come and go, but your body is with you all your life. A truly caring mate should support whatever course you think is best for you. In her book *Why Me?*, Rose Kushner tells a chilling story about then–First Lady Betty Ford's breast cancer surgery in 1974. Kushner had heard about Mrs. Ford's impending biopsy, and had been told by her friends in the Washington press corps that if the lump proved positive, they were going to do a Halsted radical mastectomy immediately. Alarmed that such a drastic operation would be done without Mrs. Ford having any time to consider, Kushner managed to get through to one of President Ford's speechwriters. She told him of her misgivings, only to be told firmly that "the President has made his decision." Kushner's indignant observation that the decision belonged to Mrs. Ford and not her husband was met only with a reiteration that the president had made his decision. The next day, Mrs. Ford had both her biopsy and her mastectomy. As Kushner notes, "the president's decision had indeed been made."[15]

Systemic Treatments

If microscopic cancer cells are found in the lymph nodes, or if the tumor has other bad prognostic signs, we know that cancer has a higher chance of being in other parts of the body, and we go after it with one of the systemic treatments. It's a bit like fighting a guerrilla war: you're in the forest, and you think there may be enemy soldiers lurking behind a bush, though you can't see them there. So you shoot into the bush, to kill them while they're still hiding, so that they don't get the chance to ambush you. There are two main approaches to systemic treatment: hormones and chemotherapy.

HORMONAL THERAPY

Doctors have always been interested in the hormonal manipulation of breast cancers. In fact, the first adjuvant therapies were based on changing the body's hormonal milieu. If a premenopausal woman had a "bad" cancer, her ovaries were removed (*oophorectomy*) in an attempt to decrease the total amount of estrogen in her system. The idea was good, and recent studies show an increase in the survival rate in the women who had had oophorectomy compared to the control group which is as good as that of current chemotherapy.[16]

Now we can actually predict who is likely to benefit from adjuvant hormonal therapy by using the estrogen receptor test mentioned in Chapter 20. In those women whose tumors are sensitive to hormones, we can use a hormonal treatment as adjuvant therapy. We remove the ovaries, or we use tamoxifen, which is an estrogen blocker. Since it's not a male hormone, it doesn't have any of the side effects often suggested by the words "hormone therapy"—you won't grow a beard, or develop a baritone voice. (See Chapter 28 for actual side effects.)

Tamoxifen is a very peculiar drug. In some ways it blocks estrogen, as it does in the breast, but in other organs like the liver, bones, and uterus, it acts like estrogen. Some studies show that tamoxifen changes the cancer cell's normal growth factors as well. A normal cancer cell produces a factor called transforming growth factor alpha (TGF alpha), which induces growth, and an opposing factor called transforming growth factor beta. TGF beta is a suppressor—it acts as a brake, while TGF alpha acts as an accelerator. TGF alpha is depressed in estrogen receptor positive patients who get tamoxifen. At the same time, TGF beta is increased.[17] (Interestingly, TGF alpha isn't decreased in estrogen receptor negative patients who get treated.) So tamoxifen tends to lighten up on the accelerator and press on the brakes—at least in estrogen receptor positive tumors.

There's some evidence that tamoxifen also affects the immune system by increasing natural killer cells, though we need to be cautious about making too many assumptions here, since we don't know what the role of natural killer cells is in terms of breast cancer.

Though it's more effective in estrogen positive tumors, tamoxifen works in about 5 to 10 percent of estrogen negative cancers, again showing that it has some way of working apart from blocking the estrogen receptor.

We used to believe that tamoxifen didn't kill cells the way chemo did—it just blocked them and held them in static. We still call it a "cytostatic drug" instead of a "cytotoxic drug" for that reason. We thought that if you took tamoxifen for a period of time and then stopped, all those cancer cells that were at rest would start growing again. But the most recent overview study (a pooling of data from smaller studies), which looked at the 10-year results after treatment with tamoxifen, found that in all women who had taken tamoxifen for two to five years, the reduction in death rate after five years was maintained at 10 years—10 percent.[18] So, in addition to keeping some cells static, tamoxifen clearly kills some cells as well, and it does cure some people.

One sometimes hears the simplistic notion that tamoxifen throws premenopausal women into menopause. Actually it doesn't. It causes a big increase in estrogen and progesterone levels.[19] The questions are, are those increases significant, and are they harmful in terms of breast cancer? We don't really know. Most of the data on tamoxifen is on postmenopausal women, whether their menopause was natural or induced by chemotherapy. But it's currently being given to many premenopausal women on the tamoxifen prevention study (see Chapter 17), so we're on our way to getting information on its safety in premenopausal women. At this point it is still not clear that, in premenopausal women, it adds anything to chemotherapy or works as well as an adjuvant treatment.

In postmenopausal women with estrogen receptor positive tumors, however, tamoxifen is an effective agent in controlling cancer. As we saw in the overview study just mentioned, tamoxifen in postmenopausal women was shown to improve overall survival by about 10 percent compared to those women not given tamoxifen; about one fifth to one third of the women who would have had a recurrence in the first 10 years lived beyond them without a recurrence, or an average of two years was added to these women's life span.[20] The overview study showed and recent studies confirmed that tamoxifen works as well as chemotherapy for postmenopausal women with positive nodes and positive estrogen receptors.

The effects of tamoxifen are also age related, with the least effect in women under 40, some effect in women between 40 and 50, and maximal benefit in women over 50.[21] Currently tamoxifen is being given for three to five years, but the optimal duration is not yet known (see Chapter 28).

CHEMOTHERAPY

Chemotherapy was initially used to treat leukemia, a cancer which, by definition, is present throughout the bloodstream. Later it was used to treat any metastatic cancer. The idea was that drugs circulating through the bloodstream could get to all the places a cancer cell was likely to hide. Unfortunately, it didn't always work. On further study, the researchers came to understand that the failure stemmed from two problems: there were too many cancer cells for the drugs to handle, and some cancer cells became resistant to the drugs. They then began to consider giving chemotherapy earlier and earlier, and the concept of adjuvant chemotherapy was born. The time to give chemotherapy may be right after the primary local treatment—either surgery alone or surgery and radiation—when any spread would still be microscopic. And indeed this approach seemed to work. The first studies by Gianni Bonadonna[22] and the NSABP[23] showed that, as we mentioned in Chapter 19, premenopausal women with positive nodes had a significant decrease in breast cancer mortality when given adjuvant chemotherapy. This set the stage for the now common practice of giving systemic treatments at the time of initial diagnosis.

Chemotherapy reduces the risk of recurrence by about a third.[24] That means the higher the chance of recurrence the larger the difference that chemotherapy will make for you. If you have a 60 percent chance of recurrence it will reduce it by 20 percent, but if you have a 9 percent chance of recurrence the reduction in mortality is only 3 percent. We now give adjuvant chemotherapy to all premenopausal women with positive nodes and many with negative nodes.

There is still controversy, however, over the use of adjuvant chemotherapy in postmenopausal women. We are still wondering why there is a difference between postmenopausal women and premenopausal women. One thought has always been that chemotherapy causes a chemical menopause in the younger woman and therefore acts much the same way that tamoxifen or removal of the ovaries do. This wouldn't account for the total effect, however. The other possibility is that, in the premenopausal women, there is a small effect of cell kill (the same small percent seen in the postmenopausal woman) and an additional hormonal effect, but only the cell kill effect in the postmenopausal woman. In conflict with this theory is the fact that the chemotherapy effect appears not to disappear abruptly with the onset of menopause but decreases as a woman ages. Like aging itself, it's a gradual process. The older you get, the farther into menopause, the less effective it becomes. When you're newly menopausal, it's still very likely to have some effect.

Studies have shown that when we give chemotherapy to premenopausal women with positive lymph nodes at the time of diagnosis, we can improve their overall survival rates by about 10 percent compared to women not given chemotherapy. Another way to state this is that about one fifth to one third of the women who would have had recurrences in the first 10 years after diagnosis will live beyond 10 years.[25] It is too soon to tell how many women we are curing, if any, but for those we don't cure, it is safe to say that we are prolonging their life

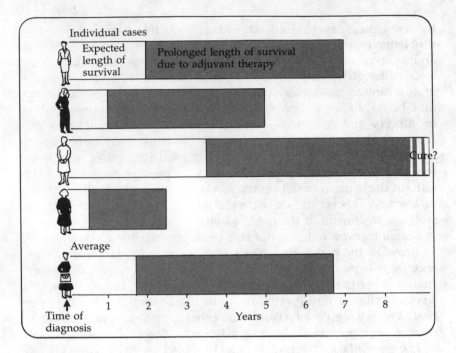

FIGURE 23-2

span two to three years beyond what they would have had without chemotherapy (Fig. 23-2).

If it is clear that a woman should get chemotherapy, there arises the issue of what drugs she should get. One of two combinations are usually given as adjuvant therapy for node-positive women. One is CMF—Cytoxan (cyclophosphamide) methotrexate 5 fluorouracil. The other is CAF, in which Adriamycin replaces the methotrexate.

Adriamycin is the strongest drug we have for metastatic breast cancer. So some doctors have concluded from this that it will probably work the best as adjuvant treatment. Although both CMF and CAF work, they have not been compared well enough for us to know if one works better. An NSABP study suggests that four cycles of CAF are equal to six cycles of CMF.[26] This doesn't mean that CAF is necessarily better, only that it is at least the same and you can get it over with faster. There are studies going on right now that will eventually tell us if CAF works better than CMF. Most oncologists, however, have made a leap of faith and decided that it must be better. We tend to think that if you have a lot of positive nodes or for some other reason have a very bad cancer, we should give you Adriamycin. If we think the cancer is less bad, we give you CMF. It is important for women to realize, however, that although many variations of CMF and CAF have been developed, we still don't know which if any is the best for any given situation.

Until the studies are finished and we have more certainty about this, I think it's particularly important for the patient to enter into the decision-making process. Ask your doctor why he or she has chosen a particular treatment and to show you studies that back it up. Find out exactly what the differences are in efficacy and in side effects. For example, some drugs are more likely to put you into menopause and thus render you infertile than others. Some, like Adriamycin, can be more toxic to the heart. So you may prefer to stick with the CMF. Or you may be willing to suffer more in the hope that the stronger drug will be better. If you don't feel that you are getting straight answers from your oncologist, get a second opinion. If it is available, consider participating in a clinical trial so that we will get some answers (see Chapter 33). It is your right to take control of this decision.

Additional studies are looking into the combination of tamoxifen and chemotherapy. Although it would seem that if one is good both would be better, this may not be true. Tamoxifen keeps cells from dividing and therefore may block the effect of chemotherapy and radiation.[27] As of yet there is no proof that tamoxifen adds anything to chemotherapy in curing breast cancer, although this issue is being currently studied.

MAKING THE CHOICE

Should you always choose chemotherapy if you're node positive? If you're premenopausal, I think you should; if you're postmenopausal and hormone receptor negative, maybe. In this case it is not clear that it will improve your survival at all. If it does, it will decrease the risk of dying from breast cancer by about 10%. That means if your risk of dying of breast cancer is 30–90%, your maximum benefit will be 3–9%. For most women there are many issues which enter into this decision, like the quality of life. If you're 80, for example, and have positive nodes, which means the cancer may come back in the next 10 years, you may decide it's worth the gamble not to do chemotherapy and live out your life in comfort—or you may decide that any chance of extra time to live is worth it. If you're relatively young and have another life-threatening condition that could be exacerbated by the chemotherapy, such as a heart condition or severe kidney disease, maybe you won't feel the risk is worth it. On the other hand, you may be 50 and just postmenopausal and feel that even the chance of an extra 1 percent is worth it to you. Many women in this situation will, of course, do quite well, in spite of the positive nodes and the fact that

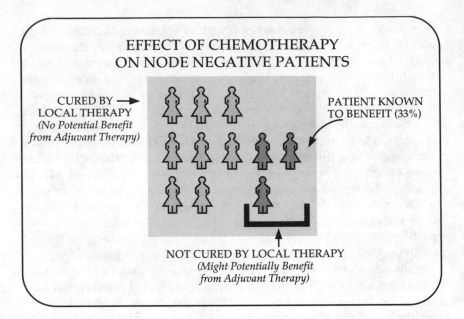

FIGURE 23-3
Reprinted with permission from *Cancer*, Vol. 65, No. 9, May 1, 1990. Copyright © 1990, by the
American Cancer Society, Inc. J. B. Lippincott Company.

taking an adjuvant treatment that holds little promise of increasing
those odds may not be worth it. For women who want to try something, we would use tamoxifen, which has been shown to have some
effect in 5–10 percent of estrogen receptor negative women. Your values and beliefs will play a large part in your decision.

In cases where the tumor is sensitive to hormones, tamoxifen is
now used as an adjuvant treatment in postmenopausal women with
positive nodes or poor prognostic indicators.

If choices around chemotherapy are confusing for women with positive nodes, those for women with negative nodes are even more so.
We know that between 20 and 30 percent of women with negative
lymph nodes will still get metastatic breast cancer and sooner or later
die of it (Fig. 23-3). If we give these women chemotherapy for their
primary cancer, some of them will have at least a delay in recurrence.
But 70–80 percent of women with negative lymph nodes won't ever
have a recurrence, and if we give them chemotherapy we subject them
to an extremely unpleasant process that can have severe and permanent side effects—including, possibly, other cancers. The side effects,
even the cancers, are worth it for women whose alternative is to die of
breast cancer: it doesn't much matter that you'd get a second cancer at
60 if your breast cancer kills you at 40. But when there's a 70–80 per-

cent chance that your cancer won't metastasize, should we expose you to the dangers of chemotherapy? Unfortunately, we do not yet know how to tell these two groups of women apart.

It is likely that chemotherapy does work some in node-negative women but that the magnitude of the benefit is limited. In the most recent overview of adjuvant chemotherapy, across the board, with both node-negative and node-positive patients, treatment seemed to improve things by a third. As we saw earlier, that means that if you have a lot of positive nodes, and your chance of recurrence is 60 percent, then chemo will improve it by 20 percent. If your chance of recurrence is 30 percent, like the average patient with negative nodes and a tumor over two centimeters, then chemo improves your chance by about 10 percent. And if your chance of recurrence is 9 percent, like the average node-negative woman with a tumor less than two centimeters, it will improve it by 3 percent. So the amount of difference in recurrence depends on what your chances of recurrence already are.

Some oncologists suggest women take chemotherapy as "insurance." The patient thinks this means it will ensure she will live. That is not true, but it is a good analogy. If you were one of the women who would have been cured by surgery and radiation alone, the chemotherapy would not be a good investment—sort of like buying earthquake insurance when you live in New Jersey. On the other hand, if you have a higher chance of recurrence, the investment may prove worthwhile—as those of us in Los Angeles learned during our recent earthquake.

This uncertainty is the reason we put so much time and energy into biomarkers like estrogen receptors, flow cytometry, and DNA (see Chapter 20)—to try and figure out who is most likely to benefit from systemic therapy. But so far, we still haven't found the answer.

So your decision about systemic treatment may be difficult. After you've received your local treatment your doctor will probably bring up the question of chemotherapy or hormone therapy; but which drugs, how long, and how much are very much in question. There's a lot of controversy, and there's currently no "right" answer. Ask questions, get second opinions, and find out about clinical trials.

Some of my patients say, "If there's the slightest chance this will help, I want to do it." Back in 1984, one of my patients, who had node-negative cancer, decided to have chemotherapy. As she explained it to me recently: "They told me at the time it was a small tumor and there was an 80 to 90 percent chance I'd be alive in 10 years. That wasn't very reassuring to me at 34. My mother had died of breast cancer years before. No one suggested chemotherapy to me, but I pursued it on my own. I know that cancer's a systemic disease, and it just made sense to me to pursue a systemic treatment. I'm glad that with this new focus on node-negative chemotherapy, women will at least be told about it as a possibility."

Other patients feel that unless they have proof that chemotherapy will make a difference, they don't want to risk it. "I decided against chemotherapy because there doesn't seem to be anything definite one way or another about it in my kind of case," says one of my node-negative patients. "They said it was 'just a precaution.' But that's six months of chemotherapy, with all the possible side effects. It seems sort of drastic, as a precaution, and there's no guarantee even with the chemo that the cancer won't spread. If I definitely needed it, okay, but not 'just in case.'"

HIGH-DOSE CHEMOTHERAPY

As you can see, chemotherapy has improved the cure rate of breast cancer, but certainly not to the extent we would like. There's a theory now that the reason we don't do very well in curing women with a lot of positive lymph nodes is that we aren't giving strong enough chemotherapy. The theory is that if a little chemotherapy is good, more must be better. Some doctors believe that high-dose chemotherapy with stem cell rescue (the most recent form of bone marrow transplant—see Chapter 28) is the answer. Actually, when it comes to breast cancer treatment, the term "bone marrow transplant" is a misnomer. It is not a "transplant," since the patient receives her own cells back and not someone else's, and the cells are now usually taken from the blood, not the bone marrow. However, the term has stuck.

The limiting factor in how much chemotherapy we can do is the patient's bone marrow. What chemo does is to block rapidly dividing cells. But cancer cells aren't the only ones that divide rapidly. There are also the cells in your bone marrow. Your bone marrow is constantly making red blood cells, white blood cells, and platelets, churning all of them out in its own little "factory." Most of the chemotherapy drugs will depress your bone marrow. That's why we have to do your blood counts constantly, to see how the product of the "factory" is doing under the assault. This product is vital to your survival. Red blood cells carry oxygen to all parts of your body, white blood cells fight infection, and platelets help in clotting. So it occurred to some doctors that we could take bone marrow out, stick it in a freezer for a while, and blast you with very high doses of chemotherapy, which would normally destroy the bone marrow. Then when the treatment was over, we would take the marrow out of the freezer and put it back in you. That's the idea of the autologous bone marrow transplant—the one that uses the body's own marrow (Fig. 23-4).

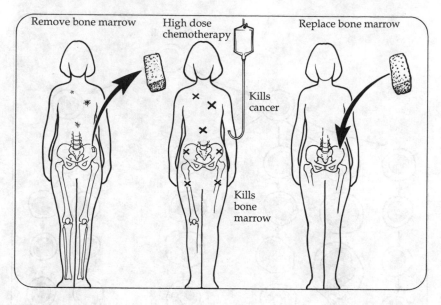

FIGURE 23-4

When researchers first started doing bone marrow transplants for breast cancer, shortly before the first edition of this book, they would harvest the patient's bone marrow, and she had to be in the hospital for a month to six weeks. First she had to get the chemotherapy. Then they replaced her bone marrow, but it took a while for the marrow to "reconstitute" (somewhat like what happens with instant potatoes, but far more complex: instant potatoes are dried out and processed, then need water to reconstitute; bone marrow needs time to reconstruct into its original form. With bone marrow transplants, there were different stages in the process. The marrow had to make the first cells (the progenitor cells), and then differentiate into various white cells (Fig. 23-5).

During this recovery time the patient had to remain in the hospital, in isolation, on antibiotics, and at high risk for infection. If she got an infection, she had no blood cells to fight it, and could easily die. The mortality rate of the treatment—apart from the disease itself—was 20 percent. But they also found that there was some response in the 80 percent of women who survived it. The response was initially higher than the response to conventional chemo. Unfortunately, in these women with very advanced breast cancer, the responses didn't last long.

As they continued to experiment with bone marrow transplant, they realized that some of the body's normal growth factors help it to produce these white cells more quickly. GCSF, the granulocyte cell

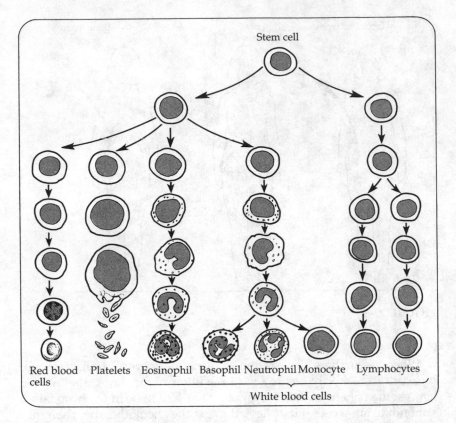

Red blood cells   Platelets   Eosinophil   Basophil   Neutrophil   Monocyte   Lymphocytes

White blood cells

FIGURE 23-5

stimulating factor we discuss in Chapter 28, comes into play here. If we return to our factory metaphor, we've got the factory running along quietly, and suddenly it's heading into the Christmas season and we've got to produce a lot of stuff very quickly to get our product in the store for Christmas. So we do whatever high-powered stuff we need to do to get everyone working overtime to get the product out in time. GCSF is that high-powered mechanism. The researchers found that, when they gave the bone marrow back to the patient, they could give some GCSF following it and reduce the time it took to reconstitute. You didn't have to stay in the hospital as long. But it was still three weeks or more, and the mortality rate was still 10 percent.

The most recent innovation in this field is being studied at UCLA. We can now harvest the progenitor cells, the grandmother cells, from the blood itself (Fig. 23-6). This enables us to remove less bone marrow. When we give back the smaller amount of marrow we've now

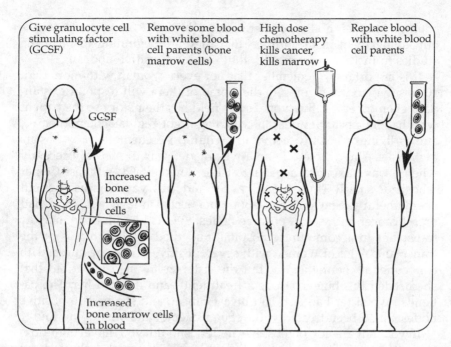

| Give granulocyte cell stimulating factor (GCSF) | Remove some blood with white blood cell parents (bone marrow cells) | High dose chemotherapy kills cancer, kills marrow | Replace blood with white blood cell parents |

GCSF

Increased bone marrow cells

Increased bone marrow cells in blood

FIGURE 23-6

taken, we also give progenitor cells with it. That helps reconstitute the blood even faster. Patients are in the hospital for two weeks, and mortality rates are further diminished.

In the next step, while the patient is getting her chemo, we mix the progenitor cells with combinations of growth factors in a test tube; there, it will turn into white cells. The factory, in effect, contracts its work out to another factory, and the product is returned whole to the original factory—the patient's own body.

All this has made high-dose chemotherapy easier to do, safer, and less expensive, since it's not as long a hospital stay. The mortality rate across the country is still, however, around 3–5 percent.[28] And, as I mentioned in the beginning, we still don't know if it works. Nonetheless it is being tried increasingly in women with a high chance of microscopic spread to try and alter the mortality rate. There are studies going on with women who have more than 10 positive nodes or who have locally advanced disease (see Chapter 24). They're given some standard-dose chemotherapy for three to four cycles and then are put into a bone marrow transplant program. The studies are ongoing and as yet the follow-up is short, so it's too soon to know whether this adds to their lives or not. The transplanters, however, are so encouraged at their ability to "get women through" the treatment without killing them in the process that they are beginning to push the studies to include women with four or more positive nodes.

It is important to remember that not every woman with more than 10 positive nodes is going to die. Some of them will respond to standard chemotherapy. Everyone in my field has their story of the patient who had 17 positive nodes 10 years ago, got regular chemotherapy, and is living a healthy, active life. High-dose chemotherapy has its own risks. This whole dilemma was made clear to me very recently when I was talking to a patient at the Revlon/UCLA Breast Center who had a fairly early breast cancer and was very confused about chemotherapy. She told me about her sister-in-law, who had had breast cancer with seven positive nodes. She had had a bone marrow transplant in a community hospital, and died in the process of the transplant. A lot of women with seven positive nodes are cured with conventional chemotherapy. But the sister-in-law had been told that she needed this bigger, stronger treatment—and it killed her. The patient's own sister had also had breast cancer, and she had 10 positive nodes. She'd been treated with regular chemo, and was doing fine.

If you have a lot of positive nodes, should you have high-dose chemotherapy? This is a very difficult question which only you can answer. Make sure you investigate it thoroughly and clearly understand what you are getting into. Ask questions about the data and lack thereof, and know clearly the risks and complications. If at all possible, participate in a randomized clinical trial so that future generations of women will know whether it indeed works.

TIMING

Studies are also being done on the timing of chemotherapy. Generally speaking, we tend to do the chemotherapy first and the radiation afterward—particularly with somebody who has a high risk of recurrence, because we want to save her life, and radiation is more of a local cleanup. But it's not clear that delaying the radiation won't add to the risk of recurrence in the breast. There was a study done recently in Boston in which one group of women was given radiation first and the other chemo first: the data from that study should be out soon, and will help to answer that question. Another issue being aggressively studied is the concept of neoadjuvant chemotherapy. This means giving the chemotherapy first, before surgery, after making the diagnosis with a needle biopsy. This helps us shrink the tumor and allow for less drastic surgery. There are several studies around this. Dr. Gianni Bonadonna[29] has found that three cycles of chemotherapy before surgery can shrink some medium-sized (greater than 3 cm.) tumors and allow breast conservation for women who might otherwise need a mastectomy. Dr. Bernard Fisher and the NSABP are also looking at the effects of preoperative chemotherapy. We routinely do preoperative chemotherapy in women with locally advanced breast cancer (see Chapter 28), but we may see more and more use of this technique in women with stage 1 and 2 breast cancer.

There are certain drugs we can give you at the same time as radiation. If we use CMF we can do both at the same time, but we can't with CAF, because Adriamycin compounds the skin damage of the radiation.

GUIDELINES

All this means that a woman's decision about whether or not to have systemic treatment, and if so which treatment, is complicated. In the practice guidelines mentioned earlier that we have prepared at the Revlon/UCLA Breast Center, we have outlined what we feel is a reasonable way to treat women with breast cancer who need systemic treatment. It's not the only way: many of these areas are controversial, and the data are inadequate. But it will give you an example of one approach. (See Table 23-1.)

If a woman is premenopausal and has positive nodes, we give adjuvant chemotherapy for four to six months; if she's postmenopausal and estrogen receptor positive, we'll use hormone therapy (tamoxifen) for three to five years.

In node-negative women for tumors of less than a centimeter, the risk of recurrence or death is so low, and the advantage of adjuvant chemotherapy or tamoxifen so slight, that it's not worth giving systemic treatment. If the tumor is greater than two centimeters it probably is worth having one or the other systemic treatment. If it's between one and two centimeters, it's a gray area, and that's where we use all the biomarkers we discuss in Chapter 20. Unfortunately, we don't know how to add all the factors together, and still end up having to make our best guess based on the information we have.

Many unanswered questions remain, and we are studying them. For instance, the best treatment for hormone receptor negative postmenopausal women is still unclear. And the answer as to whether to give chemotherapy or not to these women may well be related to age and overall health. If the person is healthy and can tolerate it we might give her chemo; if she's feeble and has other problems we might not. Other questions include the use of tamoxifen in

Table 23-1. Adjuvant Therapy

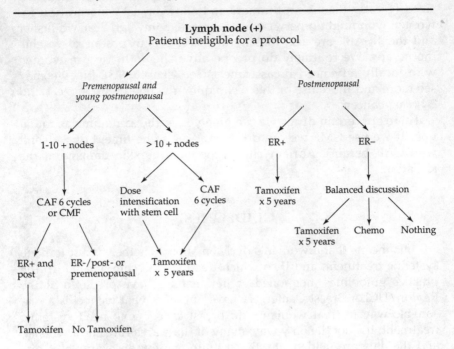

Lymph node (+)
Patients ineligible for a protocol

*Premenopausal and
young postmenopausal*

Postmenopausal

1-10 + nodes

> 10 + nodes

ER+

ER–

CAF 6 cycles
or CMF

Dose
intensification
with stem cell

CAF
6 cycles

Tamoxifen
x 5 years

Balanced discussion

ER+ and
post

ER–/post- or
premenopausal

Tamoxifen
x 5 years

Tamoxifen
x 5 years

Chemo

Nothing

Tamoxifen

No Tamoxifen

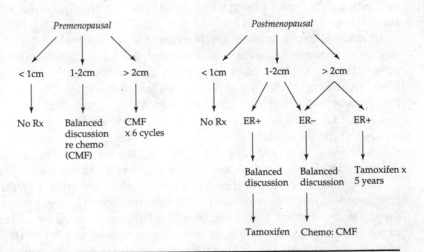

Lymph node (–)
Patients ineligible for protocol with 8 or more nodes sampled

Premenopausal

Postmenopausal

< 1cm

1-2cm

> 2cm

< 1cm

1-2cm

> 2cm

No Rx

Balanced
discussion
re chemo
(CMF)

CMF
x 6 cycles

No Rx

ER+

ER–

ER+

Balanced
discussion

Balanced
discussion

Tamoxifen x
5 years

Tamoxifen

Chemo: CMF

premenopausal women (see Chapter 28) and the combination of tamoxifen and chemotherapy. Again, it is vitally important that women participate whenever possible in clinical trials which can help to answer these questions for the next generation of women (see Chapter 33).

We really don't have the perfect formula. I had one patient back in Boston who had a small tumor, negative nodes, and good biomarkers. But she wanted chemo. Her oncologist and I both argued with her. She was adamant, and got chemotherapy. Yet a year later the cancer metastasized and she died. By all statistical predictions she should have survived, even without the chemo, and the chemo should have guaranteed her survival. This isn't meant to depress you: it often works the other way. I have a patient who was diagnosed with 17 positive nodes 13 years ago and had conventional chemotherapy; she's alive and well and living in Maui. It just illustrates that we really have no certainty; to some extent, it's a crap shoot. You have to just search your heart and make your own choice.

Complementary Treatments

We've talked about two components of treatment, systemic and local. There's a third component, which I'll touch on briefly here.

Breast cancer, like any cancer, is a fight between the cancer cells and your body's immune system (see Chapter 19). The techniques we've just discussed are methods to decrease the total number of cancer cells. But other approaches take it from the opposite end—they try to boost your immune system and make it better able to fight the cancer off. Unfortunately, in science we haven't yet figured out a good method to do that. But the hope that we can boost the immune system through a mind-body connection is the basis of many of the so-called complementary treatments we discuss in Chapter 29. These range from visualization to diet to prayer, and it's worth your while to think about looking into these to complement whatever medical treatment you embark on. While we're not certain yet if they can actually help you physically, they will often empower you psychologically by giving you something that you can do as part of your own treatment.

Second Opinions

Before you decide on which treatment, or treatments, you want, I think it's always wise to consider getting a second opinion, no matter how much you trust your surgeon or oncologist's advice. The prefer-

ence for a treatment is always somewhat subjective, and you're entitled to consult with more than one expert. Furthermore, special kinds
of cancer might require a different approach than your doctor's, and
different institutions may be involved in different research with new
treatments that might be relevant to your situation.

At UCLA I've created a structure in which women who have been
diagnosed elsewhere can get second opinions and get all the information they need. Anybody who's newly diagnosed with breast cancer
comes to our multidisciplinary program, which occurs twice a week.
They all arrive at the same time. We see up to 12 patients at a session.
We encourage them to have their family members or a close friend
there. We also encourage them to bring a tape recorder to make a
record of everything we tell them; we also have tape recorders to lend
them, and free tapes. They're seen by a surgeon, a radiation therapist,
an oncologist, a plastic surgeon, and a mental health professional, all
in one afternoon. We give the patients a break between 3 and 4, while
we have a conference. Then we as a team review every case—look at
the X rays with a radiologist, look at the slides with a pathologist, and
make a recommendation. Meanwhile the patients are either going to
the drop-in support group or going off by themselves for a while—
however they deal with stress.

At 4 o'clock one of the doctors they had seen earlier sits down with
them and reviews our recommendation, making sure they understand. By the end of the afternoon they've seen all the specialists, had
everything reviewed, and have an answer. So they've only had to take
a half day off from work instead of six days running around to different specialists. It's very efficient for both patients and doctors. There
are several breast centers in the country that have similar programs. In
most of them you can be self-referred—you don't have to be referred
by a doctor. I would recommend that any woman with breast cancer
research the possibilities of hooking up with one of these centers.

But if you can't, don't let that stop you from seeking a second
opinion. Sometimes patients are shy about doing this—as though
they're somehow insulting their doctor's professionalism. Never feel
that way. You're not insulting us; you're simply seeking the most precise information possible in what may literally be a life-and-death
situation. Most doctors won't be offended—and if you run into a doctor who does get miffed, don't be intimidated. Your life, and your
peace of mind, are more important than your doctor's ego.

24

Special Cases

So far, I've been discussing the "typical" breast cancer—the small lump that forms inside a woman's breast, usually discovered by the woman herself or by her doctor, or detected in a screening mammogram. Sometimes, however, we find a cancer that manifests itself differently, or is unusual in its behavior.

Locally Advanced Breast Cancer

Once in a while, a breast cancer won't be discovered until it's fairly big—a stage 3 cancer. It will be a large tumor—larger than five centimeters (2 inches), with positive lymph nodes. Or it will have one of the other features that we think give it a bad prognosis, like swelling (edema) of the skin, or a big, matted cluster of lymph nodes. It might be stuck to the chest muscle, or be ulcerating through the skin (Fig. 21-4).

These are all indications that the cancer is likely to have spread elsewhere in your body, at least microscopically, and so when we find them we often don't do surgery as a first step. We don't need to sample your lymph nodes: we already have the information we need. There is often a question of whether a wide excision is even possible.

If you've got very large breasts, it might be, but if your breasts are small, it may be impossible to get enough surrounding tissue out without a mastectomy. If the tumor is stuck to the muscle or ulcerating through the skin, an immediate local treatment might not be feasible at all: removing the muscle or all the skin that's ulcerated might not leave sufficient tissue to sew back together again.

All this generally suggests that we should start with a systemic rather than a local treatment, usually chemotherapy (see Chapter 28). Normally the drugs used are CAF—Cytoxan (cyclophosphamide) Adriamycin 5 fluorouracil. This may not eradicate the whole tumor, but if it doesn't, it can still do two important things: it can work on the cells that have spread, and it can shrink the tumor to a size that can be more easily managed with surgery or radiation.

Usually we'll continue with the chemotherapy for three to four cycles, and then reevaluate the situation. If the tumor has shrunk, we'll do a lumpectomy. Even when the tumor seems to have disappeared, as far as feeling it or seeing it on a mammogram is concerned, there may still be some cancer cells present. So we always want at least to do a lumpectomy on the spot where the tumor had been to see what's actually left. (With more imagination than we usually find in surgical terminology, this procedure is called a "ghostectomy.") If the ghostectomy is clear or shows clear margins then you're a candidate for radiation. Similarly, if we can do a lumpectomy and get clear margins because the lump is small, then that plus radiation is a sensible treatment. If there is still a large lump or a lot of cancer at the margins, it may be best to do a mastectomy with or without immediate reconstruction. In the case of an ulceration that doesn't leave enough skin to sew together, breast reconstruction has not only a cosmetic but also a medical advantage: reconstruction provides skin from another part of the body (see Chapter 26).

After lumpectomy or mastectomy some women with stage 3 breast cancer may be offered high-dose chemotherapy with bone marrow rescue (bone marrow transplant—BMT) at this point. (See Chapter 28 for a description of this procedure.) We know that many of these locally advanced cancers are very aggressive and therefore many doctors feel that higher doses of chemotherapy may be better. There are several experimental protocols looking at the use of high-dose chemotherapy in this setting. If a woman isn't a candidate for BMT, or doesn't want to try an experimental protocol, she will have an additional three cycles of chemotherapy. Finally at the end she will get radiation therapy.

Different hospitals have different preferences in treatment order and combination. Most centers do chemotherapy first, and many of them will then do a mastectomy no matter what.[1] Some of them will consider breast conservation if the lump becomes small enough. Then they usually follow with radiation. As we're using these combinations of treatments in this kind of breast cancer, we're actually seeing better response rates.

In many areas of the country there are protocols studying locally advanced cancers, trying to determine whether different combinations of drugs, or different combinations of chemotherapy, radiation, and surgery, affect survival rates. I think it's well worth considering participating in one if it's available to you (see Chapter 33).

Cancers of this sort usually fall into one of two categories, though both are generally treated the same way. Sometimes it's a very aggressive cancer that seems to have come up overnight as a large and evidently fast-growing tumor. At other times, the tumor has been there for several years, and the woman tries to pretend it isn't there, until it gets huge or begins ulcerating through the skin and she finally gets to a doctor. This latter case we call a "neglected primary"—it's not an especially aggressive cancer, just an especially frightened woman. Patients with a neglected primary cancer often do better than you might expect: if you've had a palpable but untreated cancer for five years and it hasn't killed you or obviously spread anywhere, it's clearly a slow-growing cancer.

Few studies, however, have differentiated between aggressive cancers and neglected primaries. Studies of these types of cancer taken together show a five-year survival of around 35–40 percent—which isn't great, but it isn't absolute doom either.[2] So if you've been putting off seeing your doctor about a lump that's been growing, or if you're suddenly faced with a new large or ulcerating tumor, don't ignore it and assume you're dying—get it diagnosed and start your treatment right away. Your prognosis may not be as good as it would be with a smaller tumor, but it's not hopeless, and the sooner you begin to take care of it, the better your chances are.

Inflammatory Breast Cancer

"Inflammatory breast cancer" is a special kind of advanced breast cancer, and it's a serious one. Fortunately, it's also rare—it accounts for only 1 to 4 percent of all breast cancers. It's called "inflammatory" because its first symptoms are usually a redness and warmth in the skin of the breast, often without a distinct lump. Frequently the patient and even the doctor will mistake it for a simple infection and she will be put on antibiotics. But it doesn't get better. It also doesn't get worse, and that's the tipoff: an infection will always get better or worse within a week or two—it won't ever stay the same. If there is no change, the doctor will perform a biopsy of the underlying tissue to see if it's cancer. Two of my patients who have had this cancer had similar stories. One had been breast-feeding and developed what her doctor thought was lactational mastitis (see Chapter 8). It never cleared up and didn't hurt much—there was no fever or other sign of infection. It hadn't gone away or gotten worse in six months. The other patient, not breast-feeding, noticed that one breast had suddenly become larger than the other; there was also redness and swelling. Her doctor also at first thought she had an infection. It's important for the doctor to recognize the possibility of cancer, however, and if the symptoms continue after treatment, you should ask to have a biopsy done of the breast tissue and of the skin itself. With inflammatory breast cancer, you have cancer cells in the lymph vessels of your skin, which is what makes the skin red; the cancer is blocking the drainage of fluid from the skin.

Inflammatory breast cancer is the only form of breast cancer that virtually everyone agrees doesn't call for mastectomy as its *only* primary treatment. Because it involves the lymphatic vessels of the skin as well as the breast tissue, and the skin is sewn back together after a mastectomy, doing a mastectomy will leave a great chance of a recurrence in the skin. So we go directly to chemotherapy before we even think about local treatment.

Statistics in the past suggested that most women with this aggressive cancer had a survival rate of about 18 months, with only 2 percent surviving five years.[3] With the advent of systemic treatments, we're trying all kinds of different techniques and we're getting much better results. The five-year survival rate is now about 40 percent.[4]

Like advanced cancers, we start with three or four cycles of CAF. Then we'll do a local treatment—usually mastectomy. Then, if the patient is interested in and eligible for a protocol of high-dose chemotherapy with stem cell or bone marrow rescue, she will go on to that. If not, she will receive three to four more cycles of chemotherapy followed by radiation therapy to the chest wall. We don't have any statistics yet about whether the bone marrow transplant improves the odds, but our hope is that since inflammatory breast cancer is such an aggressive, rapidly growing cancer, it might be just the case where BMT could have its greatest use (see Chapter 28).

Grim though it can be, inflammatory breast cancer is still an extremely variable disease. Several years ago, I diagnosed three cases of inflammatory breast cancer. Two were unusually young—26 and 29. They both had chemotherapy first, followed by radiation, and both did fine for a couple of years. Then the 29-year-old had a recurrence in her breast: she had experimental chemotherapy but the cancer had spread and she died within the year. The other woman also had a recurrence in the breast; she had a mastectomy (with immediate re-construction) and did well for a while. Then it recurred in her liver. After that she had several recurrences which were treated with a variety of chemotherapies and hormone therapies. She finally died six years later, but she had a longer life than statistics would have predicted. The third patient, an older woman, had inflammatory breast cancer and was treated for it, and when I left Boston seven years later she had had no recurrences.

The Unknown Primary

"The unknown primary" sounds a bit like the title of a murder mystery; actually, it's the name we give another kind of mystery—a breast cancer that we can't find in the breast. Someone shows up with an enlarged lymph node, usually in the armpit. It's biopsied and we find breast cancer cells, but there are no breast lumps. So we send the woman off for a mammogram, and it doesn't show any questionable areas. We know the cancer's there, but how do you treat a cancer you can't find?

In the old days, the doctors simply did a mastectomy on everyone in this situation, and discovered cancer in the breast in between 60 and 70 percent of the cases, depending on how thoroughly they examined the breast tissue.[5] Now mammography is likely to show a density in the breasts of such patients, and there are fewer women with truly unknown (or undetected) primaries. In those that do occur, the treatment is controversial. There's no doubt that a mastectomy would get rid of the cancer, but we have to ask if a mastectomy is necessary, given that the primary cancer is so tiny we can't even detect it. Shouldn't radiation be sufficient? Many doctors think it should be,[6,7] but others strongly disagree, saying that a mastectomy is called for, since there's no way to pinpoint the exact location of the cancer. And many radiation therapists don't like doing radiation in these cases, because they can't give a boost of radiation (see Chapter 27) to the actual site of the tumor.

If a mastectomy is overkill and radiation is chancy, what can you do? Some doctors think you should have chemotherapy, then wait and see if something shows up, rather than do a primary therapy right away. But that's a little scary. Others recommend an upper-outer quadrantectomy.[8] Since many cancers are located in that area of the breast, there's a possibility that the mysterious tumor is there. Others favor doing multiple fine-needle aspirates to try and find the tumor—truly a needle-in-the-haystack approach, but sometimes an effective one.

Every case of unknown primary is different. I've had two interesting cases. One was a woman with a strong family history of breast cancer. She was very thin and small breasted, and her breasts weren't lumpy: it would seem that any lump, however small, would be easy to find. She had an enlarged node in her armpit, and the node was found to be cancerous. I did nine fine-needle aspirates in different areas of her breast, and found cancer in four of them. I did fine-needle aspirates in the other breast as well, and one of these revealed cancer, so we decided to remove both breasts. It turned out that in the breast on the side with the enlarged node, she had a fairly widespread cancer that hadn't formed lumps but had snaked through the breast tissue.

In the other case, I did fine-needle aspirates again. This time they were negative, but the patient had had a positive lymph node, so we had to do something. My patient emphatically didn't want a mastectomy. She was somewhat psychic, and was convinced that the cancer was in the upper-outer quadrant. Since that's the site of many cancers anyway, a quadrantectomy seemed a good idea to both of us. After removing the tissue, I turned it upside down, and there, on the undersurface, was the lump. Both she and I were greatly relieved. Because we'd found the location of the cancer, she was able to have radiation, and to keep her breast. In other women I've treated we have never found the primary at all.

It's unlikely that you'll have this kind of cancer, but if you do, it's important to think about what treatment you'll be most comfortable with. If your surgeon comes down with a hard line and tells you there's one sure way to deal with it, be suspicious and insist on a second opinion.

It's interesting to note that, contrary to what you might expect, the survival rate in cancers that show up in the nodes but not in the breast is actually a bit better than it is for cancers that show up as both a breast lump and an enlarged node.[9]

Paget's Disease of the Breast

Dr. Paget was an active gentleman, and he's gotten his name on any number of diseases: there's a Paget's disease of the bone and a Paget's disease of the eyelids, as well as a Paget's disease of the breast. The diseases have no relation to one another, except for their discoverer.

Paget's disease of the breast is a form of breast cancer that shows up in the nipple as an itchiness and scaling that doesn't get better. It's often mistaken for excema of the nipple—a far more common occurrence. Paget's disease is almost never found in both breasts (bilateral), so if you've got itching and scaling on both nipples, you've probably got a fairly harmless skin condition. However, if it doesn't get better, you should get it checked out, whether it's on one or both nipples.

First you'll need to get a mammogram to make sure there's no cancer in the breast itself. Then you should get the skin on the nipple biopsied. This can be done in the doctor's office with local anesthetic; it's called a "punch biopsy," and involves removing only about a millimeter or two of tissue. If it's Paget's, the pathologist will see little cancer cells growing up into the skin of the nipple—that's what makes the skin flake and get itchy. Sometimes it's associated with a cancer inside the breasts; sometimes not. It's often associated with ductal carcinoma in situ (see Chapter 16).

There are probably two variants of Paget's disease: one associated with an invasive cancer in the breast and one that involves only the nipple. The former would be treated as any invasive cancer. If the invasive cancer lump is far from the nipple, a mastectomy may be necessary to get both areas out; otherwise wide excision and radiation is a reasonable alternative.

Paget's disease that involves only the nipple has a better prognosis than regular breast cancer.[10] It tends not to be too aggressive, and usually the lymph nodes turn out to be negative. Until recently most doctors assumed that you needed a mastectomy—they seemed to think that if you couldn't keep your nipple, your breast didn't matter.[11] Most women, of course, know better.

This has been a campaign of mine, and recently some of us have managed to convince the rest of the medical establishment that all that's needed is to remove the nipple and areola, and that many women prefer to keep the rest of the breast if they can.[12,13]

True, your breast looks a bit funny after the nipple's been removed—somewhat like a football. An artificial nipple can be made by a plastic surgeon (see Chapter 26), so some of my patients with this kind of Paget's disease choose plastic surgery, but others don't bother with it. Many women don't mind the way the breast looks, as long as they look natural in a bra.

Cystosarcoma Phylloides

The most dramatic thing about cystosarcoma phylloides is its name. It's usually fairly mild and takes the form of a malignant fibroadenoma (see Chapter 9). It shows up as a large lump in the breast—it's usually lemon-sized by the time it's detected. It feels like a regular fibroadenoma—smooth and round—but under the microscope some of the fibrous cells that make up the fibroadenoma are bizarre-looking, cancerous cells. It's usually not a very aggressive cancer. It rarely metastasizes; if it recurs at all, it tends to recur only in the breast. It can be treated with wide excision, removing the lump and a rim of normal tissue around it.[14] It doesn't require radiation, and we usually won't check the lymph nodes since it so rarely metastasizes. We'll watch you closely to see if it recurs, and if it does, another wide excision will usually take care of it. I had one patient who came to see me because her cystosarcoma phylloides had recurred three times, and her surgeon told her she'd have to have a mastectomy because it kept coming back. I told her I thought we should wait and see if it did come back, and in the six years I followed her, it hadn't.

The medical literature will sometimes talk about a "benign" versus "malignant" cystosarcoma phylloides, based on a subjective interpretation of how cancerous they think the cells are. The implication is that malignant cystosarcomas will behave more aggressively. Although there are rare cystosarcomas that do metastasize (5%) and ultimately kill the patient, it is hard to predict this accurately in advance. Most surgeons will suggest a more aggressive approach (mastectomy) if the pathologist feels that it's "malignant." These cancers are sufficiently rare that you may well want a second pathologist's opinion before embarking on any therapeutic approach.

Cancer of Both Breasts

Once in a great while, a woman will be diagnosed as having a cancer in each breast at the same time. Typically this is discovered when, finding a lump in one breast, she gets a mammogram to find out what's going on there, and learns there's also a lump in the other breast. A biopsy shows them both to be cancer.

They're probably both primary cancers; one isn't a metastasis of the other. So they're both treated the same way: we do a lumpectomy, or mastectomy, and lymph node dissection on one and then the other side. Usually the surgeon will first dissect the lymph nodes on the side that appears worst, so that, if the nodes are positive and will require chemotherapy, the other nodes won't have to be dissected. Unfortunately, the surgeon's guess isn't always right. I recently had a patient who had three cancers: she had a lump in the top of her right breast, and the mammogram showed two densities in the bottom of the left breast. They'd all been biopsied with needles. She really wanted to keep her breasts, so I did a wide excision of the right breast and sampled the lymph nodes, and they were fine. Then I did a wide excision of the two cancers in the left breast, and on the left side she had positive lymph nodes. Had I been able to guess better, I'd have started on the left side and wouldn't have had to do the extra surgery.

You can have radiation treatment on both breasts at the same time, but the radiation therapist has to be very careful that the treatment doesn't overlap and cause a worse burn in the middle area.

It isn't necessary to do the same treatment on both breasts. You might decide on a mastectomy on one side and wide excision plus radiation on the other, for example. It is important to note that your prognosis is only as bad as the worse of the two tumors—not doubly as bad as either one.

Cancer in the Other Breast

Sometimes a woman who has had cancer in one breast will turn up with cancer in her other breast. Usually this isn't a recurrence or a metastasis; it's a brand new cancer. It's possible for breast cancer to metastasize from one breast to the other, but it's rare. A new primary cancer has a different significance than a metastasis. What it suggests is that your breast tissue, for whatever reason, is prone to develop cancer, so you developed one on one side and then several years later the other side followed along. As with any new cancer, it's biopsied, your lymph nodes are dissected, and you're treated. Your prognosis isn't made any worse because you developed the second breast cancer; it's as bad as the worst of your two cancers. You can still have breast conservation; you don't have to have a mastectomy if you don't want it. People who have second cancers are more likely to have a hereditary predisposition.

Some women are so scared of getting cancer in the other breast that they consider having a prophylactic mastectomy to prevent that. Unfortunately, the most thorough mastectomy in the world can't assure you that all of your breast tissue is gone and that therefore all the risk is gone (see Chapter 17).

Breast Cancer in Very Young Women

Sometimes a cancer is unusual, not in itself, but in the situation in which it occurs. As we noted earlier, breast cancer is most common in women over 50, and there are many cases in women in their 40s. It's far more rare in women under 40, but it does occur. We tend to be particularly shocked when it occurs in a young woman. Usually in a young woman it's detected as a lump, since we don't do screening mammography because it isn't very accurate, for all the reasons we discussed in Chapter 18.

Very often, a young woman gets misdiagnosed. She detects a lump, or a thickening, and she's told it's just lumpy breasts, or "fibrocystic disease," and it's followed for a while until they realize it's something serious. Although this can be frightening, in fact, it's quite understandable, because most lumps in women under 35 are benign, and the risk of cancer is very low. So if we were to biopsy everyone who thought she had a lump, we'd never get out of the operating room. The fact that cancer is not diagnosed immediately doesn't mean that she'll die: as we've said, most breast cancers have been around eight to ten years, and whether it's diagnosed the minute you find it or six months later isn't the critical factor. I think we're so horrified when a young woman gets breast cancer that there's a disproportionate number of lawsuits against doctors for failing to find breast cancer in this population, because they're often misdiagnosed and because it's such a gut-wrenching situation. But in most cases, the doctors are not negligent.

I know of a case of breast cancer that occurred in a 19-year-old. The youngest patient I diagnosed was 23. She was on her honeymoon and discovered a lump. We diagnosed her as having cancer; she had a positive node, and underwent radiation and chemotherapy. That was more than 10 years ago. She's had three daughters and just developed a local recurrence requiring a mastectomy now 10 years later.

Many doctors believe that breast cancer in young women is more aggressive than that in older women. Two studies have recently shed some light on this theory. Both studies showed that the mortality from breast cancer was higher in women who had been pregnant in the past four years.[15,16] The risk was highest right after a pregnancy, and decreased with each year, going back to normal after four years. Since young women are more likely to have been recently pregnant, they will show more of this effect. This suggests that it may not be the woman's age itself that affects aggressiveness, but the immune system changes (necessary so that you won't reject your fetus) and hormonal changes that go with pregnancy.

Another interesting fact about breast cancer in younger women is that it's more likely to be hereditary.[17] That makes sense—if you've inherited a mutation, and you only need one or two more mutations to get cancer, you're one step closer, and you're likely to get there faster, whereas if you "acquire" breast cancer, you still need to get all of the mutations. That doesn't work all the time: like older women, the majority of younger women with breast cancer have no family history. But if you have breast cancer in your family, you're more likely to get it at a younger age than if you don't.

With younger women, there's some question about whether it's safe to do lumpectomy and radiation. The concern is twofold: we don't know what the 40- to 60-year risks of radiation are; and women in their late 20s and early 30s are more likely to live another 40 or 50 years than are women in their 50s and 60s.

Furthermore, there appears to be a higher local recurrence rate reported in young women who get lumpectomy and radiation than in women in their 40s and 50s.[18] We don't know why this is, but recent studies show that there's also a higher local recurrence after mastectomy in that group.[19] So it is not a real issue and the treatment for breast cancer in young women is pretty much the same as for older women, with the option of either breast conservation or mastectomy, with or without reconstruction.

Interestingly, chemotherapy works better in younger than in older women. We've decreased the death rate for breast cancer through our treatment in this subgroup more than in any other. There are problems with chemotherapy, however. Often it will put a young woman into menopause. The really young woman—in her 20s or early 30s—is less likely to have that happen than the woman in her late 30s or early 40s. The closer you are to your natural menopause, the more likely it is that it will push you over. So the much younger woman will probably get her period back after the treatment course is finished. If that happens, she'll still be fertile.

Because of the likelihood of chemotherapy-induced menopause, some women have considered preserving their eggs before the treatment, so they can still have children later. There are problems with that, however. With the current state of technology, you can't preserve an egg alone, but can only save an embryo. Unfertilized eggs won't keep frozen, but the fertilized egg will. So you must choose a sperm donor whether or not you already have a partner.

The second problem is that in order to make the eggs grow and harvest them, you have to be given a lot of hormones. And doctors are often reluctant to give those high doses of hormones to someone with breast cancer. I generally don't encourage doing that, unless my patient is so anxious to have her own baby that she's willing to risk anything. Several of my patients have looked into it, but it's so daunting that none of them have gone through with it. Most women feel that their survival is of utmost importance and that they can explore other modes of parenting once their treatment is done.

When a young woman has breast cancer, there's an increased risk for her mother, as well as her sisters and daughters, and they should all be monitored closely.

Finding the right support group can be difficult for the younger woman. Such groups are usually made up of women in their 50s and older, and she can feel very out of place. Most hospitals are making an effort to have support groups for young women, because the issues are often quite different. There are several books now on dating after a mastectomy, which is a concern to single women of all ages, as are all the psychosocial issues we discuss in other chapters.

The incidence of breast cancer in the other breast is about 1 percent per year, which usually maximizes out to about 15 percent. Since younger women have many more years to get cancer in the opposite breast, their risk is slightly higher than that of older women. Because of this, doctors often advise young women to have prophylactic mastectomy of the other breast. Generally I'm not in favor of that because even double mastectomies don't guarantee that you'll never get cancer again. (See Chapter 17.)

Breast Cancer in Women Over 70

Just as very young women can get breast cancer, so can very old women—women over 85—and they have some of the same issues very young women do. Neither end of the extreme, however, always fits our general approach. There are studies[20] showing that older women aren't treated as aggressively—there's a tendency not to give them all the options for treatment: "Well, they're old; they don't really want chemotherapy." I think a special effort has to be made to make sure that that's what the patient wants, and that the physicians don't make their own assumptions.

In addition, there's a tendency to do mastectomies on older women without offering them breast conservation, assuming that at that age a woman doesn't care as much about her looks. But that's not always the case: a woman who's lived with her breast for 85 years often wants to keep it till she dies—it's part of her, and she's used to it.

Some doctors will tell an older woman that six weeks of radiation therapy will be too much for her, making mastectomy sound less arduous than lumpectomy plus radiation. But radiation isn't really all that hard to go through, and for some older women, just as for their younger friends, it's far better than the emotional trauma of mastectomy.

Not only do many doctors neglect to mention lumpectomy/radiation, they also neglect to offer reconstruction to the older woman upon whom they've foisted mastectomy, again assuming that she won't care enough about her looks to want it. And again, that assumption may be totally off base. I can remember one patient in her mid-80s who had very large, droopy breasts, and she'd always wanted to have reduction, but she thought it was too dangerous. She got a cancer at the upper end of one of her breasts. She wanted breast conservation; she didn't want a mastectomy. But it seemed foolhardy to us to radiate all this breast that didn't show cancer. So after discussing it with her, we did a lumpectomy, and bilateral reductions, and then did radiation. She was delighted; when the radiation was done she went off on a cruise and found a new boyfriend.

So you can't make assumptions.

There's a move, particularly in the United Kingdom, to treat older women with breast cancer—women 70 or over—with tamoxifen alone, rather than with surgery. There are two studies in which women were divided into groups getting either surgery and tamoxifen or tamoxifen alone. They found that about a third of the women responded to tamoxifen alone: their tumors shrunk and sometimes even disappeared. In one study of 113 women[21] the cancer disappeared in 38 women, got smaller in 17, didn't change in 34, and got worse in 24. Thus, almost a third of women might be spared a mastectomy. The long-term data regarding local recurrence and metastasis is not yet available.

The other study[22] found that in 34 months there was no difference in survival rate or quality of life between women who had surgery plus tamoxifen and women who had tamoxifen alone. More of the women who had tamoxifen alone had to have surgery later, in contrast to those who had had surgery in the first place. The doctors who did the study argue that when an older woman has breast cancer she should be put on tamoxifen alone, and then if that doesn't work at the end of three to six months she can be operated on. That saves a third of the women from the dangers and discomforts of surgery. It also suggests that if you're older and are fragile, and you don't want to go through surgery, it's reasonable to start you off on tamoxifen alone and hope you can continue to avoid surgery.

Part of the problem in studying women over 70 is that we really can't evaluate long-term survival, since there are so many other illnesses that elderly people die from. And not all elderly women are frail. I had a 95-year-old patient in Boston who wasn't especially frail at all—in fact, she was very active. She developed breast cancer. I did a lumpectomy and put her on tamoxifen. Unfortunately, she couldn't tolerate the tamoxifen, and she stopped it. She was fine for about a year and a half; then her cancer recurred locally. I did another lumpectomy, and this time I really tried to get her to stick with the tamoxifen, and she did for a while. The last I heard she was still going strong. So when we look at how to treat "old" women, we need to look at how frail they really are: it will vary greatly. People who live into their 90s tend to be pretty healthy, or they wouldn't live to that age. We can't just assume, as many doctors do, they'll be dead in a year or so, and forget it—sometimes they live to over 100.

Cancer in Pregnancy

Once in a very great while, a patient develops breast cancer while she's either pregnant or breast-feeding. We used to think that such a cancer was especially aggressive, and that the pregnancy-related hormones fired the cancer up and made it worse.

The studies are contradictory. Most studies have shown that, stage by stage, it's no worse than any other breast cancer. The problem is that it usually isn't discovered right away. When you're pregnant, your breasts are going through a lot of normal changes, which can mask a more dangerous change. For one thing, they're much lumpier and thicker than usual. Similarly, when you're breast-feeding, as we discussed at length in Chapter 3, you tend to have all kinds of benign lumps and blocked ducts, and you may not notice a change that ordinarily would alarm you. Infections are common when you're breast-feeding and can mask inflammatory breast cancer, so the physician may find diagnosis of inflammatory breast cancer difficult.

Two recent studies discussed earlier in this chapter suggest that there may be something to the old theories. They found that women who were diagnosed with breast cancer while pregnant or within four years thereafter did indeed have a higher mortality rate.[23,24] As more women are having later pregnancies at the age when breast cancer becomes more common, this may become a bigger issue.

Treatment is also a problem. What we can do about your cancer depends on what stage of pregnancy you're in. If you're in the first, or early in the second, trimester, you might want to consider therapeutic abortion, depending on your beliefs about abortion and the importance this particular pregnancy holds for you. It is important to add, however, that there is no evidence that women who abort their fetuses have a better prognosis: it is just easier to proceed with treatment. If you continue with the pregnancy, treatment options are somewhat limited. We wouldn't give you radiation in the first trimester because it can injure the fetus, and we're a little leery about chemotherapy, since the fetus's organs are being formed at this time. For the same reason, we don't want to give you a general anesthetic, which rules out a mastectomy. We can do a biopsy or a wide excision under local anesthetic. But if further treatment is called for, we usually try to wait until the second trimester.

In the second trimester, since the fetus's organs are already formed and it's safer to use general anesthetic, we can do a mastectomy. We would rather not risk radiation or chemotherapy: we don't yet know what effects the chemicals can have on the fetus. There are some reports of women who have received chemotherapy while pregnant and the babies have been healthy. It is possible but worrisome.

If you're in your third trimester, we could do a lumpectomy, or, if need be, a mastectomy, then wait for further treatment until the child is born. If it seems necessary to do treatment right away, your obstetrician can keep testing, and, as soon as the baby can be expected to survive outside the womb, do a cesarean section and then start you on chemotherapy and radiation. Chemotherapy has been given in the third trimester to women with leukemia and Hodgkin's disease. Although it appears safe, the numbers are small and the follow-up is still short.

I recently saw a woman who was diagnosed when she was seven months pregnant. She underwent a radical mastectomy (this was 20 years ago) and then had radiation with cobalt while pregnant. She said she had to have a dose monitor in her vagina to monitor the amount of radiation her fetus was receiving. Nonetheless she carried the baby to term and both are fine 20 years later. Two other patients have recently been treated with chemotherapy while pregnant, so far with no untoward effects to their children.

Breast cancer during lactation isn't quite as complicated, since you can always stop breast feeding and start your child on formula. Radiation will probably make breast feeding impossible, and you won't want to breast-feed if you're on chemotherapy, since the baby will swallow the chemicals.

We're not sure yet if lactation affects the cancer itself. I've had two patients whose breast cancer showed up while they were lactating. Both were treated, both stopped breast feeding, and both did well without a recurrence for several years. After much debate, both women decided to get pregnant again. One had a recurrence during the second pregnancy; the other had a second primary develop while lactating. This leads me to the question of whether, if a cancer shows up while a woman is pregnant or lactating, there is a higher risk of a recurrence in another pregnancy. Obviously we can't do a randomized study, and it's too unusual an occurrence to draw any conclusions. Our evidence is purely "anecdotal." For now, all I can suggest to someone who has developed breast cancer while pregnant or lactating is to consider seriously not having another pregnancy, in case it affects the chance of a recurrence. (See Chapter 30 on the question of pregnancy after having breast cancer, and Chapter 3 in regard to breast-feeding after breast cancer.)

Women with Implants

There's no evidence that women with implants have a higher vulnerability to breast cancer than other women, and some evidence that it may actually be lower.[25] Sometimes it's detected on mammogram, and sometimes the lump is palpable. It's diagnosed in the same way as any breast cancer—with a biopsy. Sometimes we can do a needle biopsy, depending on where the lump is—we don't want to stick a needle into the implant and spread the silicone, or saline, loose in the breast.

The treatment options are the same. You can have lumpectomy and radiation.[26] You can radiate with the implant in place. There is a slightly higher incidence of encapsulation, but other than that there's no problem. You might think that cutting into the breast could break the silicone envelope, but there are a couple of ways around that. One of the things we can do is use electrocautery instead of the scalpel, and that can't cut into the implant. Even in a biopsy, we know you've got an implant, and we're careful.

If you had injections back in the 1960s when they were legal, the same applies. It's even harder with injections than it is with implants to detect cancer on mammogram, since it's hard to tell what's silicone and what's something else. So you need to go to a good place where they can monitor you very carefully. And it's very important to have the mammograms serially, so as to compare one year to another, because that's what can tip you off: one of these lumps that you were calling silicone is growing. You can then have lumpectomy and radiation.

Breast Cancer in Men

This book mostly addresses breast cancer in women, and there's a reason for that. It is the most common malignancy in women, and very rare among men, accounting for less than 1 percent of male malignancies. Many of the men who get it seem to have a family history, on either the father's or the mother's side.[27] There's also a theory that it's connected to gynecomastia—femalelike breasts (see Chapter 1), either in the present or during the man's puberty, but so far we have no proof of this. We do have proof that men with Klinefelter's syndrome, a chromosomal problem in which not enough testosterone is produced, are susceptible to breast cancer.[28]

For a time there was some concern that men who got estrogen treatments for prostate cancer would be more vulnerable to breast cancer, but this doesn't seem to be the case. What can happen is that the prostate cancer itself can metastasize to the breast.[29]

Breast cancer in men shows itself in all the ways it does in women—usually as a lump—but it tends to be discovered at a much later time because men aren't usually as conscious of their breasts as women are of theirs. The treatments are the same. The cosmetic implications are somewhat different for them. On the one hand, they don't tend to be as invested in breasts as crucial to their sexuality as women are. On the other hand, they're far more often in situations where their naked chests are visible: it can be more awkward for a man to have a scar, to lack a nipple, or to have a deformed chest—than it is for a woman. So, like a woman, a man might prefer lumpectomy and radiation to mastectomy. The one extra consideration is hair. After radiation therapy a man will lose most of his chest hair on that side. If he is very hairy, a mastectomy with the scar hidden in hair might prove more cosmetic. Depending on where the tumor is, the nipple can often be conserved. If he loses the nipple, a plastic surgeon can give him an artificial nipple. We had a golfer come to UCLA recently with a small breast cancer. He was very distressed that the only option he had been given was a mastectomy. After a lumpectomy and radiation, he was very happy and felt more normal on the course.

Treatment in terms of chemotherapy and axillary nodes are exactly the same as for women. And, interestingly, tamoxifen works in men. Why an estrogen blocker works in a man, I don't know. But it does tell us that the way tamoxifen works isn't as simple as it once seemed to be.

Usually, when a man has a breast lump, it isn't cancer, it's unilateral gynecomastia, which can happen anytime in a man's life, especially if he's been on some of the drugs used to treat heart conditions or hypertension or smokes marijuana. It's never a cyst or fibroadenoma—men don't get those.

Other Cancers

When I arrived at UCLA in 1992, within the first week or two I got a call to see a patient who had a breast lump. It was soft and smooth, and on the side of her breast. It felt like a cyst, but I tried to aspirate it and that didn't do any good. Then she had a mammogram and an ultrasound, which confirmed that the lump was solid. We took the lump out under local anesthesia, and indeed it was malignant. When I talked to her afterward, I broke one of my cardinal rules—never make absolute promises. I told her that, though it was unfortunate that her tumor was malignant, it was a small tumor and I could guarantee that she wouldn't have to get chemotherapy: since she was postmenopausal, the most she'd need would be tamoxifen.

Then we looked at it more closely under the microscope, and it turned out that it wasn't a breast cancer at all—it was lymphoma, in a lymph node in the breast. The way to treat lymphoma is with chemotherapy. The tale has two morals. One, never break your own wisest rules. And two, things aren't always what they seem. It's ironic that my first breast cancer patient at UCLA didn't have breast cancer at all. (I'm glad to report that she responded well to the treatment and is doing fine.)

So occasionally you can have other kinds of cancer in the breast. Since the breast contains several kinds of tissue besides breast tissue, any of the cancers associated with those kinds of tissue can appear in the breast. In addition to lymphoma (since there are lymph nodes), these include a cancerous fat tumor (liposarcoma) and a blood vessel tumor (angiosarcoma). You can also have a melanoma—a skin cancer. Connective tissue in the breast, as elsewhere, can become cancerous. Usually these cancers are treated the same way they'd be treated in any other part of the body—the tissue is excised, and radiation and chemotherapy follow (the chemicals are different from those used to treat breast cancer).

When another form of cancer shows up in the breast, we learn it isn't breast cancer from the pathologist's report. As I discussed earlier, each kind of cancer has its own distinct characteristics, and we rarely mistake one kind for another. We choose treatment for the particular cancer rather than breast cancer treatment. We didn't, for example, do an axillary dissection on my lymphoma patient.

It's important to remember that having breast cancer doesn't immunize you from other forms of cancer. You have the same chances as anyone else of getting other cancers. I've had a couple of patients with breast cancer who were also heavy smokers: they were treated for their breast cancer, continued smoking, and ended up with lung cancer. A bout with any kind of cancer can provide a useful time to consider altering your lifestyle in ways that promote overall health.

25

Surgery

Almost every form of breast cancer will involve some surgery—the initial biopsy, and probably a mastectomy or a partial mastectomy (lumpectomy) as well. It's always a frightening thought, but demystifying the process can be helpful. For one thing, the old theory that surgery would "let the air get to the cancer" and thus cause it to spread all over is a myth. This misconception may have arisen at a time when surgery was done only on very late cancers. When the cancer inevitably spread, it was blamed on the surgery instead of the cancer. No one should be afraid to have an operation for cancer. As we mentioned in the previous chapter it may not cure you by itself but it is an important part of the overall treatment.

We've already discussed some surgery in previous chapters (5 and 12). In this chapter we will go over what you can expect from your surgeon and your operation for breast cancer. I will be fairly explicit because I think the more information you have, the less scared you will be. If you find surgical details unpleasant, you may want to skip some parts.

In my own surgery practice, I talk with the patient a few days ahead of time and explain exactly what I'll do in the operation, and what risks and possible complications are involved. I draw her pictures and show her photographs, so she'll know what to expect. As with any operation, patients are asked before the surgery to sign a consent form. This can be a little scary, especially if you read all the fine print, because it asks you to state that you're aware that you can die from the surgery or suffer permanent brain damage from the anesthetic. This doesn't mean that these things are likely to happen, or that by signing the form you're letting the doctors off the hook if something *does* happen. What it does is guarantee that you've been told about the procedure and its risk and that you still want to have the operation. (Obviously you have to balance for yourself the risk involved in the operation against the risks of not having the operation.)

It's very important that you do know the risks. You should never permit yourself to be rushed through the signing of the consent form. You should be given the form well before you go in for surgery—it's hard to read small print when you're about to be wheeled into the operating room. You should have plenty of time to ask the surgeon any questions about risks and complications. If anything confuses you at all, be sure to ask.

For the bigger operations (mastectomies) I often recommend that the patient donate a couple of pints of her own blood a week or two prior to the operation. I don't often have to transfuse a patient, but it is a nice secure feeling for the patient to know that if she does need blood she can get the safest type possible, her own. If your surgeon doesn't offer this you should ask. The Red Cross is more than happy to assist in this procedure.

Finally, like other surgeons, I tell all preoperative patients to stop taking aspirin, aspirin-containing products, and any nonsteroidal anti-inflammatory drugs at least two weeks before surgery. All of these will interfere with blood clotting and will therefore cause more bleeding in surgery. If someone has taken a drug of this type we will do a "bleeding time" (a test that tells how fast your blood clots) prior to surgery to make sure it is safe to proceed. If not, we postpone the surgery for a week or two until the clotting returns to normal.

There have been several studies looking at the timing of surgery in relation to the menstrual cycle.[1] These studies have been retrospective: the researchers went back to records of women operated on 10 years ago and tried to figure out where they were in the menstrual cycle at the time of surgery by looking at their last period and calculating a 28-day cycle. These studies were obviously done by men: any woman knows that we have varying and often irregular menstrual cycles, and that furthermore, the stress of surgery is likely to throw the most regular of women off. Nonetheless they found that women who were operated on in what appeared to be mid-cycle, rather than at the beginning or end, did better. Recently a larger study from Italy[2] looked at 1,175 women who had been followed up for an average of eight years after surgery for breast cancer. They found a difference in survival at five years in those women with positive nodes, but not in those with negative nodes. Those who had positive nodes and were operated on during the first part of the cycle had a worse survival (63.3%) than those operated on in the second half of the cycle (75.5%). The reasons for this finding are not clear, and we need more research. In this country, there is an added complication with such studies. In Italy, they still use a one-step procedure with the biopsy and surgery. Here we usually do surgery in two and sometimes three steps. We'd need to time each stage of the surgery—the biopsy, the partial mastectomy, and the mastectomy. At this point I think these data are provocative and I am starting to change my practice. After all, there are no side effects to changing the date of surgery, and only potential benefits.

Anesthesia

There are a variety of anesthetics that we can use in various procedures. There's local anesthesia, which we described in Chapter 12; there's general anesthesia, which we describe below; and there's a kind that falls between, that puts you into a kind of twilight sleep in which you're somewhat aware of what's happening but you really don't care. (This is also described in Chapter 12.)

There are other anesthetics that are midway between local and general. A nerve block can sometimes be useful. The anesthesiologist finds the nerve that feeds into the area the surgeon will operate on, and anesthetizes the nerve itself, so that everything it feeds goes numb. This is what dentists usually use, which is why the whole side of your mouth goes numb and you end up chewing the inside of your cheek. But a nerve block works only in an area controlled by a single nerve and in which the controlling nerve is easily accessible. Since the breast area involves a number of nerves, we can't use it for major breast surgery.

There's also the spinal—more extensive than the nerve block, but less extensive than general anesthetic. Local anesthetic is put into the spinal fluid where it bathes the spinal column, making all the nerves below the area go numb. It's good for a number of operations done below the waist, like hemorrhoids, gynecological surgery, and hernia. Unfortunately, it can't be used above the waist, since it would numb the nerves that control breathing and heartbeat. The epidural works similarly, and has similar limitations.

Local anesthesia doesn't work for extensive breast surgery, either: the amount of local anesthesia you'd need to block out the pain would be toxic. This is because most breast cancer surgery beyond the biopsy stage requires that we take out lymph nodes in your armpits, and all the nerves that go to your hand go to your armpit.

In the old days, general anesthesia just meant ether, but in recent years it's become a very complex and sophisticated combination of drugs. The first element in any general anesthetic combination is something to induce sleep quickly—usually sodium pentothal or propophol, a new, faster-acting drug. Both sodium pentothal and propophol are given intravenously, and they put you out immediately. The effects of sodium pentothal last only about 15 minutes, so it's followed with a combination of other drugs. Sometimes the anesthesiologist will use a combination of narcotics to prevent pain, nitrous oxide ("laughing gas") to keep you unconscious, and a muscle paralyzer to keep you from coughing or otherwise moving during the operation. Since the muscle paralyzer prevents you from breathing, it is necessary to put a tube down your throat and into your windpipe to keep your airway open, and hook you up to a breathing machine to assure that you get enough oxygen into your body during the operation. Sometimes, rather than use the narcotics, they'll just use gas: some kinds of gas can keep you asleep and get rid of pain.

Which of these various agents are used, and in what combination, will be chosen only after consultation with the individual patient. Your medical history will make a big difference here. If you have asthma, for example, a drug that opens up the airways is more suitable so that you don't get an attack under anesthesia. If you have a heart condition, a drug that doesn't aggravate the heart but has a calming effect on it will be chosen.

There are also drugs more suitable for different kinds of operations. If you're having your gall bladder removed, a drug that keeps your stomach muscles relaxed allows the surgeon to reach the gall bladder more easily. In a breast operation, that's not much of a problem, since the breast is on the surface of your body.

Since anesthesia and its administration are so sophisticated and precise, most hospitals will have you meet with the anesthesiologist before the operation. Anesthesiologists are well-trained doctors who've gone through at least three years of specialized training after their internships. Your anesthesiologist will take your medical history, looking for things in that history that might suggest using, or not using, various of the anesthetic agents. She or he will ask about chronic diseases you may have, past experiences with anesthetic, and so forth; and only after thoroughly exploring all this with you will decide what to use in your operation. This interview is very important, since as much of the risk of any operation is in the anesthesia and its administration as is in the surgery. When you talk to the anesthesiologist, ask questions, and give any information you think might be of importance. Many hospitals also have nurse anesthetists who help administer anesthesia under an MD's supervision.

Before you're put to sleep, you're hooked up to a variety of monitoring devices. There's an automatic blood pressure cuff. There's an EKG monitoring your heart rate. Sometimes a little clip or piece of tape is put on your finger, toe, or earlobe to measure the amount of oxygen in your blood. If the operation is a lengthy one, a catheter is put in your bladder to measure the amount of urine output and to make sure you're not dehydrated. So your bodily functions are all carefully monitored.

Once you're on the operating table, you're asleep very quickly. Many people who haven't had surgery for 20 or 30 years remember the old days of ether, and are nervous about unpleasant sensations they recall going under. But sodium pentothal works much differently, and most patients report it as a very pleasant experience. You may experience a garliclike taste at the back of your mouth just before you go under, and you may yawn. Propophol may burn as it goes into your arm. Then you're asleep. Don't worry: in spite of all the television melodrama, you're not likely to reveal all your deep, dark secrets under sodium pentothal. You might mutter something just as you go under, but when you're asleep, you're quiet.

How you wake up from the operation will depend, again, on what drugs have been used. With some drugs an antidote can be given to end the drug's effects. So if, for example, you've been given a muscle paralyzer, a drug can restore your muscle mobility. But if you've been given gas to put you to sleep, you have to wait till the gas wears off. As soon as they think you're awake enough to breathe on your own, the tube is removed. Occasionally you'll be vaguely aware that this is happening, but usually you're still too out of it to notice. You stay a little fuzzy for a while. When the surgery is over, you're taken to the recovery room, where a nurse remains with you, monitoring your blood pressure and pulse every 10 or 15 minutes until you're fully awake and stable.

Patients often feel cold when they first wake up. Particularly in a big operation, when you haven't been covered up, you've lost body heat; in addition, the intravenous (IV) fluids going into you are cold. Some of the drugs can create nausea, and you may feel sick when you first wake up. This was succinctly described by a recovery room nurse I once saw on a TV show. She was asked what patients usually say when they first come out of anesthesia, and it was clear the host was expecting something profound or moving. Instead, she replied, "They say, 'I think I'm going to be sick'—and then they are."

You may find that you wake up crying, or shivering, but only rarely do patients wake up in great pain. You'll probably fade in and out for a while, and then you'll be fully awake. But expect to be groggy and out of it for a while. It's several hours before most of the drugs are out of your system, and a day or more till all of it's gone. If it's day surgery, you'll probably just want to go home and go to bed; if you're still in the hospital, you'll sleep it all off there.

Even apart from the surgery, anesthesia itself is a great strain on your body, and it will cause some degree of exhaustion for at least four or five days. People often don't realize this, especially if the effects of the surgery itself are very painful: they attribute all their exhaustion to the pain caused by the operation. But anything that puts great stress on your body—surgery, a heart attack, an acute asthma attack, or anesthetics that interfere with your body's functions—will have a lingering effect. It's as if your body takes all its energy to mobilize for the big stress, and doesn't have any left over for everyday life for a while. You need to respect that, and give your body time to recuperate from the stress of both the surgery and the anesthetic.

There are, of course, risks involved in using general anesthetic, but it's important to keep them in perspective. With the refinements in anesthesia in recent years, the risks are extremely low (about one death in 200,000 cases).

Depending on how complicated the operation is, you can now have surgery in which you're admitted to the hospital the day before, or on the same day you have your surgery. In some cases you can even have day surgery—"outpatient" surgery. Nowadays I do lumpectomy with axillary dissection only on an outpatient basis, so my patient has her two hours of surgery, spends another few hours in the recovery room, and then gets to go home. I'm moving toward doing mastectomies as day surgery or just an overnight stay. Many women prefer this, while others prefer to stay in the hospital for a couple of days. If a patient has a mastectomy and immediate reconstruction, she'll be in the hospital for about a week.

If the surgery is being done under general anesthesia, then all the pre-op procedures are the same, whether it's day surgery or you stay in the hospital for a number of days. "Twilight sleep" procedures still require the same pre-op preparations, since they need to be monitored, just as general anesthesia does.

Preliminary Procedures

In the operating room, before you are anesthetized, the anesthesiologist will be setting up, and the nurses will put EKG leads and an automatic blood pressure cuff on you. Often we use something called "pneumatic boots"—plastic boots that pump up and down massaging your calves during the operation to prevent clots from forming (Fig. 25-1). A grounding plate is put on your skin to ground the electrocautery. The IV is put in, and then you're given pentothal (or propophol). During this time, your surgeon may or may not be with you. Some surgeons prefer a more personal contact beforehand; others maintain a professional distance. I like to establish a connection with my patient

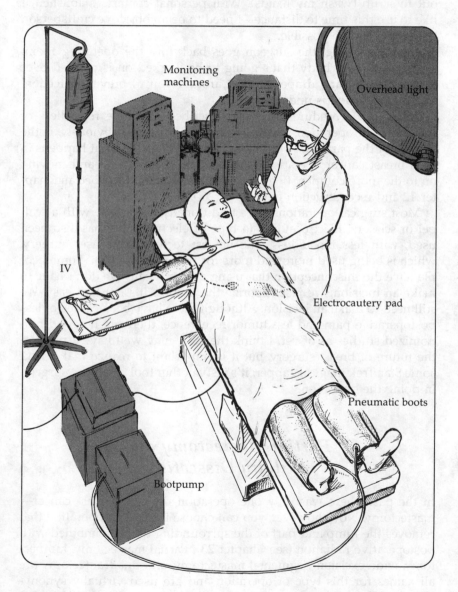

FIGURE 25-1

beforehand, so I go into the operating room and, while all these procedures are taking place, I'll stay there with my patient and hold her
hand. My patient is scared, and usually I'm the only person there she
knows. This contact also helps me confirm my commitment to the
patient as an individual who has offered her trust to me.

Once my patient is asleep, I do what every other surgeon does: I go
out to scrub (wash my hands). With personal contact established, I
like to use this time to distance—I need to be an objective craftsperson
to do the best job possible.

After scrubbing, the surgeon goes back into the operating room.
The area of your body that's going to be worked on is painted over
with a disinfectant, drapes are put around you to prevent infection,
and the operation is under way.

All of the procedures I've just described are done regardless of
what kind of operation you're having. What varies, obviously, is the
process of the particular operation. Now I'll describe what happens in
each breast cancer operation, starting with the simplest and moving
on to the more complex (Fig. 25-2). (Biopsies were described in Chapter 12 and reconstruction in Chapter 26.)

Most surgical operations have traditionally been done with a scalpel or scissors. Electrocautery (a type of electric knife) has also been
used, with less blood loss. The newest technique is laser surgery,
which is being used more and more for breast operations.[3] Some people have the misconception that using a laser means we don't have to
make an incision; we just vaporize the tissues. It's not that easy. We
still need to make an incision. Although there have been claims of less
postoperative pain and less tumor recurrence, there are no good randomized studies as of yet. I think the laser may well have a place in
the future of breast surgery, but it is important to realize that it isn't
some Star Trek magical zapper: it's just another tool to aid the surgeon
in doing the operation.

Partial Mastectomy and Axillary Dissection

In the past, there was only one operation done for breast cancer—
mastectomy. Now, however, you can choose instead an operation that
removes the lump and part of the surrounding tissue, combined with
postoperative radiation (see Chapter 23). Partial mastectomy, lumpectomy, wide excision, segmental mastectomy, and quadrantectomy are
all names for this type of operation and are used virtually synony-
mously. What each term means depends on the surgeon who's using

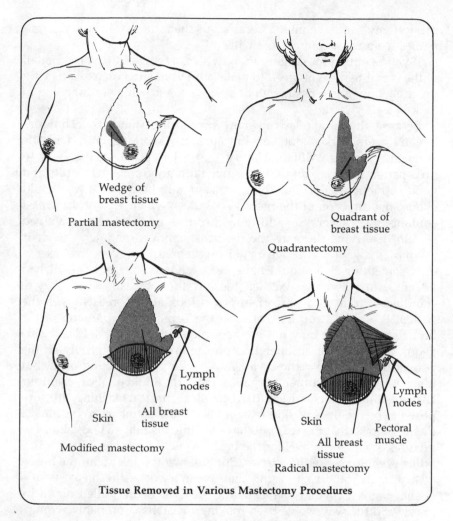

Wedge of
breast tissue

Partial mastectomy

Quadrant of
breast tissue

Quadrantectomy

Lymph
nodes

Skin   All breast
tissue

Modified mastectomy

Lymph
nodes

Skin   Pectoral
muscle
All breast
tissue

Radical mastectomy

Tissue Removed in Various Mastectomy Procedures

FIGURE 25-2

it. Except for quadrantectomy, none of the terms suggests how much tissue will be removed, and often surgeons use "quadrantectomy" when they don't necessarily mean they'll remove a fourth of the breast. With a partial mastectomy, the "part" removed can be 1 percent or 50 percent of the breast tissue. "Lumpectomy" depends on the size of the lump. "Wide excision" just says that you'll cut away tissue around the lump—it doesn't say how much you'll cut. "Segmental" sounds like the breast comes in little segments, like an orange. But it doesn't, and the segment removed can be any size. Your surgeon will use whatever term appeals most to her or him: I use "partial mastectomy" at the moment, because it's the term that insurance companies seem most comfortable with.

If you're opting for surgery that involves taking out part but not all of the breast tissue, you need to make sure your surgeon explains very precisely how much tissue will be removed, and what you're going to look like afterward.

Because this is a relatively new procedure, standard techniques haven't been worked out yet. I'm currently working with a plastic surgeon colleague, William Matory, Jr., to determine the best way to do a partial mastectomy that will give both good medical results and good cosmetic results. One thing we've determined is that we should choose the direction of the incision based on which area of the breast contains the cancer.[4] In addition, the area of the breast involved should determine the way the tissue is removed and whether it is sewn back together. After years of being a breast surgeon, I've discovered something that should have been obvious long ago, but it had never occurred to me. Women look at their breasts when they're standing in front of a mirror; surgeons look at the breasts when the patient is lying flat on her back. So the surgeon's impression of the best cosmetic effect may not be the same as the patient's. Plastic surgeons, at the end of an operation on the breast, will typically sit the patient up to see how the breast looks with gravity acting on it. But it's not something other surgeons tend to think of. For example, Langer's lines, which are standard classical surgical teaching, are supposed to be the lines of skin tension that show us where to best make the incision so that the scar will have as little visibility as possible. The pictures of Langer's lines for the breast look like a target (Fig. 25-3), a bull's-eye with concentric circles. But when you think about the breast of a woman standing upright, that doesn't work—the breast is in a U-shape, not a circular shape, as the breast is being pulled down by gravity. So the way we've been making incisions is probably wrong. .

When I was at the Faulkner Breast Centre in Boston, we did a study asking patients what they felt were the most significant aspects of the cosmetic results. My bias going into the study was that the most important thing for the patient would be that we sew her breast tissue back together again in such a way that her breast wouldn't have a dent. It would be a smaller breast, but it would be the right shape. The study showed that I was wrong. What was most important to the patient was size of the breast and the nipple placement. Shape was less important.[5]

When you think about it, it makes sense. If you have a breast one size smaller than the other, it's hard to buy a bra that fits, or clothing that fits properly. If you've got a breast that's the right size but has a dent in it, you can push the edges of the dent together inside the bra

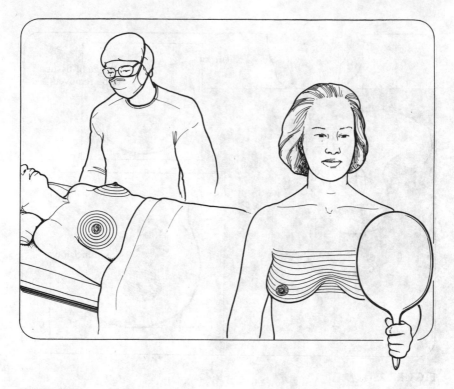

FIGURE 25-3

cup. So I no longer sew the breast tissue together: I sew just the subcutaneous tissue—the fat—and the skin. That leaves it the right size, as close as possible to the other breast.

Another thing we realized is that if the surgeon does a horizontal incision, above or even below the nipple, it changes the nipple position, pulling it in the direction of the incision. The same thing happens with a vertical incision: the nipple gets pulled to the side, or toward the middle of the chest. A radial incision will leave the nipple position unchanged. But that too is imperfect. Radial incisions are likely to be very visible in a bathing suit or a low-cut blouse, particularly if they're on the upper part of your breast. So as the patient, you have to decide which is more important: would you rather have your nipples lined up symmetrically, or would you rather have a scar that won't show above your bathing suit? The answer to that varies from woman to woman. These are the kinds of questions that we're just starting to look at in terms of breast conservation. We now have an atlas which demonstrates for all surgeons the best techniques.

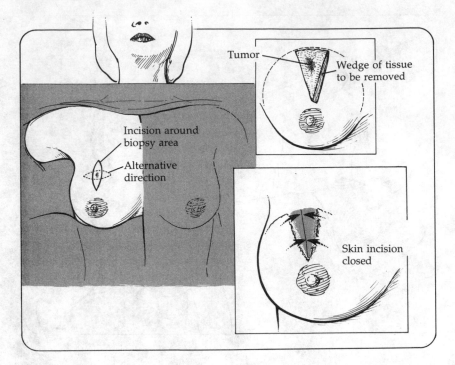

Tumor

Wedge of tissue to be removed

Incision around biopsy area

Alternative direction

Skin incision closed

FIGURE 25-4

With partial mastectomies, as with most surgical procedures, different surgeons will have slightly different approaches. Some like to keep the patients in the hospital for one or two days. I prefer to do a partial mastectomy and lymph node surgery as day surgery.

The operation itself, however, is pretty standard. It begins with carefully monitored general anesthetic. The surgeon usually starts by taking out the breast tissue in a wedge, like a piece of pie, all the way down to the level of the muscle (Fig. 25-4). That piece is given intact to the pathologist. Then the tissue and skin are sutured together. Some surgeons put drains into the breast to collect fluid afterward. I find this unnecessary, and rarely do it.

When the breast surgery itself is finished, the surgeon will begin operating on the lymph nodes (Fig. 25-5). An incision is made about two inches across the armpit, and the surgeon removes the wad of fat in the hollow of your armpit that contains many of the lymph nodes. The lymph nodes, as I said earlier, are glands—sometimes they're swollen and big, but usually they're very small and embedded in fat. We take out a section of the fat, defined by certain anatomical boundaries, that usually contains at least 10 to 15 lymph nodes. The tissue is

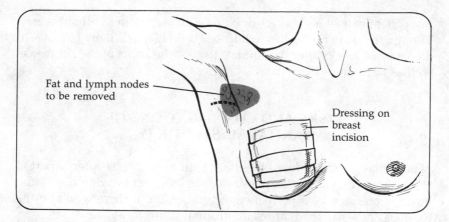

Fat and lymph nodes
to be removed

Dressing on
breast
incision

FIGURE 25-5

sent to the pathologist, who examines the fat and tries to find all the lymph nodes in it.

Some women will have more nodes than others. Every now and then a patient will ask me, "How come you got seventeen lymph nodes in me and only seven in my friend?" We are all built differently. The existence of that difference was recently brought to my attention, after I'd done a routine axillary dissection. A new pathologist was dissecting out the nodes. She amazed me by finding 40 in a specimen that usually would contain 15. She had just looked harder than usual. The total number of nodes is less important than the number that are positive. The most important thing for the surgeon to do is to remove the tissue which should contain the nodes. There have been studies showing that the chance of missing a positive lymph node if we remove the tissue in the lower two levels of the armpit is less than 5 percent.[6]

Many surgeons put a drain in the axillary incision afterward, but again, I prefer not to—there's not enough fluid to worry about in my experience.[7] I put a little long-acting local anesthetic into the wound, so my patient won't wake up in pain later, and then sew up the incision.

The operation takes from one to three hours altogether. You wake up in the recovery room and, according to your surgeon's preference, you can go home that night or in a day or two. I prefer to send you home that day, unless you have some medical condition that might be aggravated by anesthesia—severe asthma or heart problems, for example.

When you go home you'll have a small dressing on your incision. I use dissolvable sutures inside the skin and Steristrips on the skin, so

369

my patient can take a shower or bath or go swimming without worry. Though there are no sutures to take out, I do like to see my patients 10 days to two weeks after the surgery to trim the knots of the sutures as well as to monitor the patient's progress.

RISKS AND COMPLICATIONS OF
PARTIAL MASTECTOMY

There may be some loss of sensation in your breast after a partial mastectomy, depending on the size of the lump removed. If it's a large lump, there may be a permanent numb spot, but there won't be the total loss of sensation that results from a mastectomy.

Your breast will be different in size and shape than it was before, and consequently it will probably be somewhat different from your remaining breast. How great the difference is depends on how much tissue was removed and how skillful the surgeon is. If your breasts have become asymmetrical to an extent that disturbs you, you can get partial mastectomy breast pads called shells to wear in your bra. You can also get reconstructive surgery: you can have a small flap of your own tissue put in to fill things out (see Chapter 26). Or, depending on how large your breasts are to begin with, you can get the other breast reduced to create a more symmetrical appearance. Usually, however, that won't be necessary. If you have a small lump, and medium or large breasts, it's often hard to tell afterward which breast was operated on, except for the scar.

The possible complications resulting from lymph node surgery are more serious. There's a nerve—and sometimes two or three nerves—going through the middle of the fat that has been removed. This nerve gives you sensation in the back part of your armpit. It doesn't affect the way your arm works, but it does affect sensation. If that nerve is cut, you'll have a patch of numbness in the back part of your arm (Fig. 25-6). Most surgeons do cut the nerve, because it's difficult to save, and they don't think sensation in the armpit is very important anyway. Of course, most surgeons are men—they generally don't shave their armpits, and they don't know how awkward it can be when you can't feel the area you're shaving. I always try to save the nerve, though I'm more successful in some cases than in others. Even if the surgeon does save it, it may get stretched in the process and give you decreased sensation either temporarily or permanently. If the sensation is gone for more than a few months, the loss is probably permanent. (If this happens to you, you might want to give up shaving your armpits, or to use an electric shaver rather than a razor, which is more likely to cut the skin and cause bleeding.)

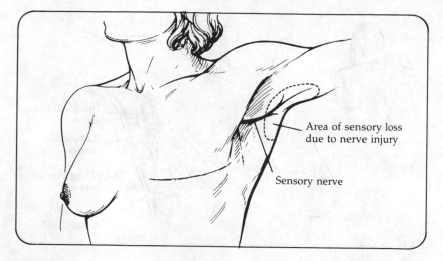

Area of sensory loss
due to nerve injury

Sensory nerve

FIGURE 25-6

Another complication, one that's unusual, is fluid under the armpit. Most women get some swelling, but some will get so much that it looks like they've got a grapefruit under their armpits. When it gets to this point, the fluid usually is aspirated (drawn off).

Another early problem can be phlebitis in one of the arm veins. This usually shows up three or four days after surgery. The woman says, "I felt wonderful after the operation and now I have this tight feeling under my arm that goes down to the elbow and sometimes even to the wrist. The pain is worse and I can't move my arm nearly as well as I could before." This is an inflammation of the basilic vein. It is not serious but it's bothersome. The best treatment is ice and aspirin. It will go away within several days to a week.

The major complication, but fortunately an uncommon one, is swelling of the arm, a condition called lymphedema which we discuss later in this chapter.

Another rare complication of lymph node surgery involves the motor nerves (Fig. 25-7). These are different from the sensory nerves. Two motor nerves can be injured by lymph node surgery. One of them—the long *thoracic nerve*—goes to the muscle that holds your shoulder blade against your back when you hold your arm straight out. If that nerve is injured, your shoulder blade, instead of remaining flat, will stick out like a wing when you hold your arm out. Hence it's called a "winged scapula." (There are other causes of winged scapula as well; sometimes it's a congenital condition.) If you're not athletic, it probably won't affect you very much in your daily activities, but it affects activities like serving in tennis or pitching a baseball.

371

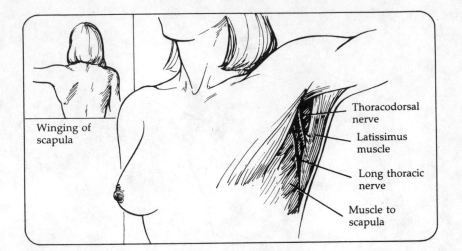

Winging of scapula

Thoracodorsal nerve

Latissimus muscle

Long thoracic nerve

Muscle to scapula

FIGURE 25-7

Permanent winged scapula cases are extremely rare; if the condition is temporary, it should go away in a few weeks or months. In order to cause a permanent winged scapula, the surgeon would have to cut completely through the nerve.

The other nerve is called the *thoracodorsal nerve*, and it goes to the latissimus muscle. Damage to this nerve is rare and less noticeable than the winged scapula. It will probably give you some sensation of tiredness in the arm, which won't work quite as well as it did before, but it won't give you any glaring problem.

AT HOME AFTER PARTIAL MASTECTOMY

Your surgeon may put your arm in a sling to prevent your moving it around and pulling the incision apart. I don't like to do this; I think the earlier you start moving your arm around normally the less chance there is that your arm will get stiff. Keeping the arm in a sling will cause it to stiffen, even if you haven't had an operation. If your arm is kept immobile for any length of time, you'll need physical therapy to help you start using it again. If you do use your arm normally right away, you probably won't need physical therapy (see Chapter 30). I have found that my patients are sufficiently sore that they don't tend to fling their arms about anyway. You shouldn't lift anything more than about five pounds with that arm for several days, but then you can use it pretty normally afterward.

Once you're sent home, the biggest problem, as we said, is that you're exhausted. Respect that tiredness: you've just been through major surgery, anesthesia, and an emotionally difficult operation. The exhaustion often comes and goes suddenly: you'll feel fine, and go out shopping; when you get home you'll suddenly feel completely wiped out and need to sleep. It will take several days before you feel fully recovered.

You'll have some pain, but probably not a lot. Like most doctors, I give my patients pain medication—usually Percocet or codeine—when they go home, but the majority of them don't even finish off the prescription. There are occasionally people who have a lot of pain, and if that's the case it's a good idea to let the doctor know, because it's often a sign of something wrong, like postoperative bleeding or a hematoma.

After a lumpectomy, you should wear a good, strong support bra day and night for about a week—it hurts when your breast jiggles. Another trick my patients have taught me, particularly my patients with larger breasts, is that if you want to lie on your side in bed, you can lie on the side that wasn't operated on and hold a pillow between your breasts: the pillow cushions the breast that's been operated on (Fig. 25-8).

The pathology results will usually be available within a couple of days. I can then tell my patient what the margins were like and what was actually in her breast tissue, and, more importantly, whether there was any cancer in the lymph nodes. On the basis of the pathology report, we'll discuss the next steps, and whether there is a need for adjuvant therapy.

FIGURE 25-8

Total Mastectomy

In spite of the availability of partial mastectomy and radiation, which conserve the breast, most women in this country still get total mastectomies as their initial therapy for breast cancer.

"Total mastectomy" should not be confused with "radical mastectomy." The latter, once the norm, is of interest now for historical reasons only. The surgical procedure was basically the same as that for the modified radical (described below), but, obviously, more extensive. In addition to removing the whole breast the surgeon removed the pectoralis major and pectoralis minor muscles (Fig. 25-9). All of the lymph nodes in the axillary area (up to the collarbone) were removed as well. It was far more deforming than the mastectomy we do now. There's virtually no situation anymore in which it's necessary. For very large tumors we almost always use neoadjuvant chemotherapy to shrink them before we do surgery (see Chapter 28). In other cases, the tumor is stuck to the muscle, so the muscle has to be removed in order to get the tumor out. (In very rare cases, the cancer will actually have spread into the muscle itself.) We used to do radical mastectomies in all of these cases, but now we just take a wedge of muscle right under the tumor and leave the rest.

"Total mastectomy," the name we usually give the form of mastectomy used today, is a bit of a misnomer, since we can never be certain the operation is total. Our goal is to remove all the breast tissue, but

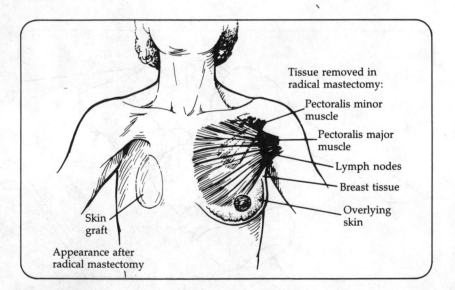

Tissue removed in radical mastectomy:

Pectoralis minor muscle

Pectoralis major muscle

Lymph nodes

Breast tissue

Overlying skin

Skin graft

Appearance after radical mastectomy

FIGURE 25-9

we can't ever do that. What we do in this operation is to remove as much of the breast tissue as we can and some of the lymph nodes. It usually takes between two and five hours.

The breast tissue, as we discussed earlier, extends from the collarbone down to the edge of the ribs and from the breastbone out to the muscle in the back of the armpit. The surgeon wants to get as much of that breast tissue out as possible. So we start with an elliptical incision that includes the nipple and whatever scar you have from the biopsy: exactly where it is depends on where your biopsy scar is (Fig. 25-10). We take that skin out. Next we tunnel underneath the skin all the way

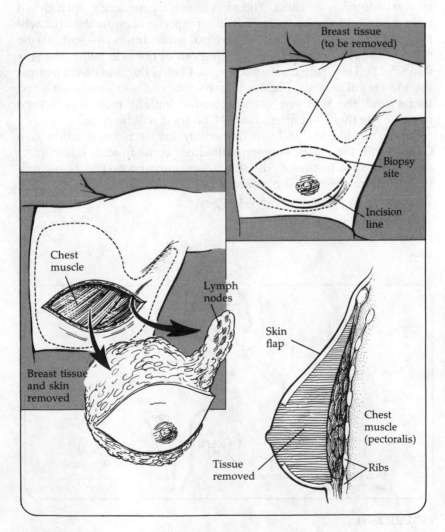

Breast tissue (to be removed)

Biopsy site

Incision line

Chest muscle

Lymph nodes

Breast tissue and skin removed

Skin flap

Chest muscle (pectoralis)

Tissue removed

Ribs

FIGURE 25-10

up to the collarbone, then down to the border of the ribs, from the middle of the sternum, and out to the muscle behind your armpit. Once the dissection is done, we peel the breast off, leaving the muscle behind.

When the breast is fully removed, we reach up under the skin to the armpit and remove some of the lymph nodes, as we do for the axillary dissection described earlier. We send the breast tissue and the attached fat with nodes to the pathologist, who examines it and begins the process of fixing it to make slides. Meanwhile we sew together the flaps of skin around the incision. You end up completely flat (or, if you're very thin, slightly concave), with a scar going across the middle of that side of your chest. The skin doesn't completely stick down right away, and the body doesn't like empty spaces, so the area will fill up with fluid. To prevent this, we put some drains in—soft, plastic tubes with little holes in them, coming out of the skin below the scar (Fig. 25-11). They help create suction that holds the skin down against the muscle till it heals. Fluid will come out of these drains—it's just tissue fluid, the kind you get in a blister. Initially there'll be a little blood in the fluid, but after about 24 hours it will be clear.

If you've decided to have immediate breast reconstruction (see Chapter 26), the plastic surgeon will either come in after the mastectomy is finished but before the skin is sewn up and do the reconstruction, or be part of the team from the beginning, raising the flap while the surgeon is doing the mastectomy.

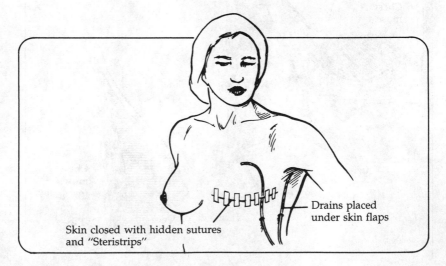

Drains placed under skin flaps

Skin closed with hidden sutures and "Steristrips"

FIGURE 25-11

As in other operations, the pathology results will be available in a couple of days. This tells you what the breast tissue looked like and, more importantly, if there is any cancer in the nodes. If there are any indications of systemic spread you will want to discuss adjuvant systemic treatment (see Chapter 28).

Different surgeons have different styles in postoperative treatment. I usually put a big, bulky wrap-around dressing on my patients because it helps them feel protected from the world for a while. You'll probably stay in the hospital at least overnight. When there's no longer much fluid coming out of the drains—in about three or four days—we'll take the drains out and change the dressing. We used to keep people in the hospital till all the drains came out—nowadays patients sometimes go home and come back later to get the drains removed.

While you're in the hospital, someone from Reach to Recovery or a similar support group may come to see you with what's called a "going-home prosthesis." Some insurance companies will pay for it if it's ordered while you're still in the hospital, but not if you wait till you're home. Insurance policies vary; make sure you check out what yours will cover. (See Chapter 26 for a discussion of prostheses.)

Some women want to see the wound right away; some prefer to put off looking at it for a week or two. Either way is fine; you need to decide what will make you feel best. But it's important that you look at it at some point. It's amazing how, if you're determined to avoid looking at your body, you can do so when you shower, get dressed, even when you make love. That's okay for a while, but this is the body you're going to be living with, and you need to see it and accept it.

Many of my patients like me to be with them the first time they see their scar. This way I can offer emotional support and also answer any questions they have right away. If you feel comfortable with your surgeon and would like her or him with you when you first look at your chest, ask.

Others prefer to be alone when they first look at the scar. Some want to see it alone before showing it to their husband or lover. Again, there's no right or wrong way to face it, as long as you do face it. In my experience, most women are relieved that it doesn't look as bad as they feared it would.

Numbness around the chest wall is one of the more unfortunate results of the operation. The breast's nerve supply has been cut. So the area around the scar of the mastectomy will be permanently numb. Some sensitivity remains around the outer borders of the area on which your breast was located. Sometimes the breast is not entirely numb, however; you can tell if someone's touching you. Unfortunately, this usually isn't a pleasant sensitivity. It can be very uncomfortable, like the sensation that you feel when your foot's asleep and starts coming back again, with a tingly feeling. This is known as dysesthesia, and, while it may lessen in severity, it will remain with you. Often people who've had mastectomies don't like their scars being touched because it brings about this slight unpleasant sensation.

Some women also experience phantom breast symptoms—like the amputee who still feels itchiness in the toes that are no longer there. Similarly, the mastectomy patient may feel her nipple itch, or her breast ache, as though it were still there. This simply means that the brain hasn't yet realized what's happened to the body. The nerve supply from the breast grows along a certain path in the spinal cord and goes to a certain area of the brain. The brain has been trained over the years that a signal from this path means, for example, that the nipple is itching. When the nipple's been removed, the signal may get generated in a different place further along the path, but the brain cells think it should be coming from the nipple, and that's the information they give you. This will gradually improve as your brain becomes reprogrammed.

Audre Lorde described some of the feelings wonderfully well in her book *The Cancer Journals*: "Fixed pains and moveable pains, deep pains and surface pains, strong pains and weak pains. There were stabs and throbs and burns, gripes and tickles and itches."[8] In addition, some women feel a tightness around the chest as the healing starts. This will ease up over time, and all the weird sensations will start to settle down.

RISKS AND COMPLICATIONS
OF TOTAL MASTECTOMY

Like any operation, the mastectomy has a certain number of risks. In the process of removing the breast tissue, we sever a number of blood vessels. The only ones remaining are those that go the whole length of the flap of skin left when the tissue underneath is removed. These vessels can barely get to the ends of the flap. Sometimes this doesn't give enough of a blood supply, and the flap doesn't heal right; a little area of skin dies and forms a scab (Fig. 25-12). Once the wound has healed, the scab falls off. It's usually not a very serious complication. If a big enough area of skin is involved, or there's an infection, the surgeon may have to trim the dead tissue so that the body can heal the wound.

A second possible complication occurs when fluid continues to collect under the scar after the drains are removed. You'll know this is happening because there's a swelling around the incision; sometimes

Two possible complications . . .

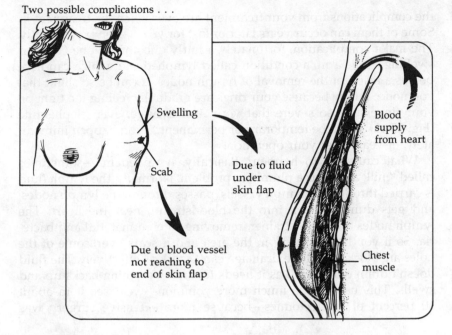

FIGURE 25-12

you'll hear a splash when you're walking, or you'll simply feel the fluid on your chest. If it's a small amount of fluid you can just leave it alone and it will eventually go away by itself. If there's a lot of fluid, you can have it aspirated with a needle: it won't hurt, since the area's numb, and it usually doesn't require even local anesthesia. (We try to avoid too many aspirations, though, since there's always the slight risk of transmitting infection through the needle.) Again, this isn't a serious complication, but it can be an annoying one.

The risks from lymph node removal are exactly the same as those in the partial mastectomy—loss of sensation, phlebitis, swelling, and winged scapula. It's important to move your arm around and keep it from stiffening.

Surgery is never fun. But it's often necessary, and if you know what to expect ahead of time, you can reduce the stress and fear surrounding it.

LYMPHEDEMA

Aside from the cosmetic implications of mastectomy, there are other problems you may have to deal with. Unfortunately, not all of

379

the complications from your treatment are over when the treatment is. Some of them can occur years later or last for years, even permanently. The major complication, fortunately a fairly uncommon one (10%), is swelling of the arm, a condition called lymphedema, which can happen as a result of the removal of lymph nodes. It can be so slight that you notice it only because your rings are gradually feeling too tight on your fingers, or so severe that your arm is huge, even elephantine (Fig. 25-13). It can be temporary or permanent. It can happen immediately, or years after your operation.

What causes it to happen? Basically, lymphedema—sometimes called "milk arm"—is a plumbing problem. Normally, the lymph fluid is carried through the lymph vessels, passes through the lymph nodes, and gets dumped back into the bloodstream, near the heart. The lymph nodes act like a strainer, removing foreign material and bacteria. So if you have surgery in the area and it scars over, some of the holes are blocked and the drainage can't work as effectively. The fluid doesn't drain out as well as it needs to, and everything backs up and swells. This used to be much more common—we'd see it in about 30 percent of mastectomies—because more extensive surgery was

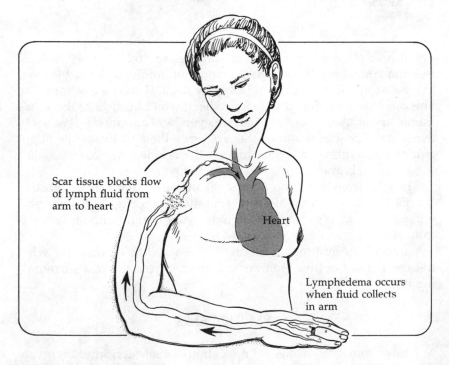

Scar tissue blocks flow of lymph fluid from arm to heart

Heart

Lymphedema occurs when fluid collects in arm

FIGURE 25-13

done. Nowadays, since we remove less tissue, it happens only in about 10 percent of mastectomies. I think, however, that this figure is a bit low, and that if we measured every patient carefully in the follow-up visits we'd find the mild cases are a lot more common, and for whatever reason the women don't tell their doctors about it.

If you get lymphedema, there's not much you can do about it. Many doctors and nurses will send you home with extensive instructions regarding care of your arm after surgery. They are trying to prevent infections since infection is thought to increase the chances of lymphedema. Since your lymph nodes have been removed you're more susceptible to infections. They will insist that you never garden without gloves because you might get pricked by a thorn, or that you never reach into a hot oven, or cut your cuticles, or have injections in that arm. Be sensible: you want to reduce the risk of infection, but you're not going to die if you get a minor infection, and there's no need to live your life in terror of pin pricks. Be reasonably careful, and if you do get an infection, get to your doctor as soon as possible and have it taken care of. Nonetheless, it is important to try and prevent lymphedema. Although you should try to avoid significant trauma to the involved arm (having blood drawn, blood pressure cuffs), this is not as vital as it was in the days of a radical mastectomy. Probably the most important prevention is avoiding heavy lifting with your arm hanging down for a period of time, that is, carrying a suitcase or briefcase. Try to get your groceries delivered instead of carrying them yourself; if that's not feasible, get one of those little grocery carts and wheel them home. Get suitcases with wheels if you do any traveling.

Once lymphedema develops, treatment has been difficult until now. You can elevate your arm to help reduce some of the swelling. Physical therapy and exercise can help in early cases. There are long support gloves similar to the stockings they make for varicose veins, which are unaesthetic but can reduce the swelling. For extreme cases, you can pump out the fluid daily with an electric pump, which will keep the swelling down to a manageable level—you can rent or buy them from a medical supply store. More recently our physical therapists have started doing manual massage as a technique for reducing lymphedema.[9] When combined with pumping and bandaging it works quite well to keep things under control.

There are few well-trained manual lymphatic drainage specialists in this country. In Australia they have shown good results with benzopyrones.[10] These drugs have very few side effects and result in a slow but steady reduction in edema. Unfortunately the FDA has not made the drug available in this country. (Contact the National Lymphedema Network for updated information on its status.)

My theory about lymphedema is that we're probably approaching it backwards. The tendency has been to tell you to go home and elevate the arm if you have a little bit of swelling, to put on a elastic arm-stocking if you have a lot of swelling, and to use the pump if you have an extreme amount of swelling. But by the time you use the pump, your tissues have been so stretched out they've lost all their normal elasticity. It's like putting on a pair of panty hose you wore all day yesterday. What then happens is that as soon as you get off the pump, the fluid returns.

I think we should act aggressively when we find a small amount of swelling—use physical therapy, manual massage, the pump—and try to reverse it. Then we'd probably be able to reverse the process in more people, because they'd still have the elasticity in their skin. I'm planning to do a study in which the participants will have their arms measured at every follow-up visit, and as soon as somebody shows clear signs of lymphedema we'll randomize them to the standard treatment or aggressive therapy. Then we can see if the long-term results are any better.

There have been a number of operations that have been used on lymphedema, but none of them have been very effective.

You should never take lymphedema lightly. Not only is it uncomfortable and aesthetically displeasing, but in about 10 percent of cases it can develop into a rare form of cancer called lymphangiosarcoma, which shows up as red nodules on the arm. This occurs eight to ten years following the development of lymphedema and can be fatal. (See Appendix B for further help and information.)

This problem has been vastly underestimated by the medical profession. The psychological and physical difficulties of women with lymphedema are enormous. We have started what I think is the first lymphedema support group at UCLA in an attempt to address some of the problems. The only true way to prevent lymphedema will be to stop doing axillary dissections. Luckily, that day is on the horizon. (See Chapter 21.)

EXERCISE

Exercise is important after your treatment, and not only in terms of lymphedema. Again, doctors can often be over-restrictive. After you've had a mastectomy or a lymph node sampling, your surgeon may tell you not to move your arm at all. As we said earlier, there's controversy over how protective of the area you should be.

If you do keep your arm very still at first, you'll probably find your shoulder extremely stiff when you do start moving around. That's to be expected—if you take someone who's in perfect health and put her arm in a sling for a week, she'll end up with a stiff shoulder.

Certain exercises, however, can help your shoulder (Fig. 25-14). One is called "climbing the walls." It involves walking your fingers up the wall, stretching a little bit farther each time. You can do it while you're watching TV or talking on the phone. The other one involves leaning over and making bigger and bigger circles with your arm. Swimming is also an excellent exercise.

If your arm remains very stiff, after two or three weeks, ask your doctor to refer you to a physical therapist. I find that only about 10 to 15 percent of my patients need physical therapy. It's very important to get your shoulder flexible again, and soon; otherwise you can end up with a condition called "frozen shoulder," which is difficult to treat successfully.

Any sport or exercise you did before your cancer you can do now—and you should, if you want to. If you've been a fairly sedentary person, you might want to change that. You might also want to examine your eating habits, and health habits in general. Often people who have suffered life-threatening illnesses are more aware of the importance of health than they were before, and want to invest energy into maintaining their health as much as they can.

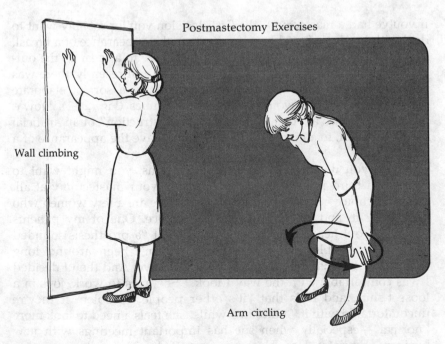

Postmastectomy Exercises

Wall climbing

Arm circling

FIGURE 25-14

26

≡

Prosthesis and Reconstruction

If you've had a mastectomy, the first decision you'll probably want to deal with is whether, and how, to re-create the appearance of a breast. Most women take it for granted that they have to appear to the outside world as though they had both breasts. Until recently, there was only one way to do that—through a prosthesis, a sort of elaborate "falsie" designed for women with mastectomies (Fig. 26-1). Nowadays, there is also another option, the "reconstruction" of an artificial breast that will, to a greater or lesser extent, have the appearance of a real breast.

Before you decide on one of these options, you might want to consider a third possibility—not disguising your mastectomy at all. It's not a choice many women make, but there are a few women who do choose it, and are happy with the choice. One of my patients thought about her options, then decided that "a prosthesis sounded too uncomfortable, and reconstruction hasn't been around long enough to see what long-term effects it can have. And then I decided I was comfortable with the way I look." She goes to work, jogs in a loose t-shirt, and feels that "it's other people's problem if they're uncomfortable with it." Once in a while, she feels a need to look more "normal"—especially when she has important meetings with new business associates. Her solution is to stuff shoulder pads from other

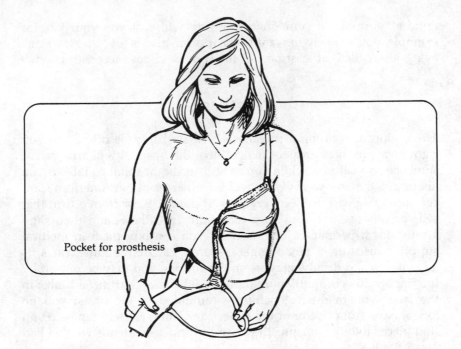

Pocket for prosthesis

FIGURE 26-1

dresses into her bra. "I never liked shoulder pads anyway," she laughs. "Now I get to put them to good use!" For other women, refusing to create the illusion of a breast is part of their feminist beliefs. The poet Audre Lorde wrote in *The Cancer Journals* about her rejection of "cosmetic sham": "I believe that socially sanctioned prosthesis is merely another way of keeping women with breast cancer silent and separate from each other."[1] Artist Matushka has created photographs of herself in a cutaway gown, showing not her remaining breast but the mastectomy scar. The photograph was on the cover of the *New York Times Magazine*. The effect is harsh and defiant, choosing to show the world what the disease of breast cancer does to a woman's body. Writer Deena Metzger,[2] whose book *Trees* addresses her cancer, has a photograph with a different approach: she softens the effect of the amputation by covering the scar with a beautiful, evocative tattoo of a tree, creating a new beauty where the beauty of her breast once was.

Having the self-confidence to feel comfortable without the appearance of a breast is wonderful, but most of us are products of our culture and need to feel that we are cosmetically acceptable to the outside world. In some cases there are actual penalties for failing to appear "normal." If your nonconformity will cost you your job, for example, you're likely to want to wear a prosthesis (or "breast form," as it's also called) at least part of the time or choose reconstruction.

Prostheses

The option of wearing a prosthesis will probably be offered to you right away. In most areas of the country the hospital will arrange for someone to visit you while you're still in the hospital to talk to you about prostheses—your visitor will be either from the American Cancer Society's Reach to Recovery (see Appendix B) or from a firm that sells prostheses. You can get a temporary prosthesis and then shop around for a permanent one. Usually you can buy them in medical supply houses or in fancy lingerie stores. Each environment has its advantages and disadvantages—in the former, you may be put off by the implications of mutilation, the wheelchairs and artificial limbs; in the latter you might feel painfully reminded of the breast you no longer have. Your doctor or the American Cancer Society can help you find places to buy your prosthesis, or you can ask friends who've had mastectomies.

There are stores that will custom-make a prosthesis for you; it's expensive, and your insurance company may not pay for it, but it might be worth it to you to get a totally precise match. (In general, it's a good idea to check with your insurance company before buying your prosthesis anyway; different companies have different quirks, and you want to be sure of what your own expenses will and won't be. If you're on Medicare, they'll pay for a prosthesis every year or two years—with a prescription. Why you need a prescription for a prosthesis, I don't know—I've never met a woman who bought one for the fun of it—but the ways of bureaucracies are mysterious.) There are also prostheses made for swimming, though most of the better prostheses are made of silicone and thus waterproof to begin with.

If you live in a rural area where there are no lingerie shops or medical supply stores that carry prostheses, or if you find it too painful to approach a salesperson about buying one, several mail order catalogues also offer them, at a range of prices. I've seen them advertised in both women's wear catalogues and in catalogues that specialize in health products for older people. The catalogues also sell mastectomy bras that hold the forms.

Prostheses come in a range of prices, with varying quality. If you don't have insurance to pay for your prosthesis, or if you're undecided yet as to whether you want a prosthesis or reconstruction, you'll probably want the least expensive form available, at least temporarily.

Catalogues and many stores offer forms for as low as $15, and mastectomy bras for around $10.

Why Me?, a volunteer organization of breast cancer survivors (see Appendix C), will send prostheses, as well as wigs, to women who need them to deal with chemotherapy-induced hair loss, if they have the size required in stock, for a nominal fee.

Prostheses, of course, are made in different sizes, and they're also made for different operations. If you've had a radical mastectomy you can get a fuller prosthesis than if you've had a simple mastectomy. If you've had a wide excision that's left you noticeably asymmetrical, you can get a small "filler" or shell that will fit comfortably in your bra. In the past, prostheses didn't have nipples, and this has caused some problems for women whose remaining breast had a prominent nipple (Betty Rollins, in her book *First, You Cry*,[3] has a very funny description of her efforts to make her own "nipple" out of cloth buttons). Fortunately, that's changed: any prosthesis you buy will have a nipple, and you can get a separate nipple to attach to it if your own nipple is more prominent than the one on the prosthesis.

Reconstruction

Another option is reconstruction—the creation, by a plastic surgeon, of an artificial yet natural-appearing breast. Breast reconstruction has made a big difference both physically and emotionally for many women who have had mastectomies. But it's important to understand its limits before you decide to have it done.

What's constructed is not a real breast. When it's well done, it will look real, but it will never have full sensation, as a breast does. Any surgeon who tells you, "We're going to take off your breast and give you a new one, and it'll be as good as new" is either naive or dishonest. Sometimes a doctor will tell you that the new breast "will feel normal"—at best, a half-truth. It will feel normal to the hand that's touching it, but it will have little sensation itself. Also, feeling is only about one-half skin sensation and at least one-half cerebral. You may have some "feeling" return, but it will never feel completely normal to you. As one of my patients told me, you need to have time to bond with your new breast.

Is it worth doing, then? For most women, yes. It can make you feel more normal, to yourself and other people, since it looks like a breast. And it can make your life a little easier—you can wear a t-shirt or a housedress and not worry about putting on a bra. If the doorbell rings while you're still in your bathrobe, you don't have to deal with whether or not you want the mail carrier to see your unevenness. It makes it easier to buy bathing suits and other "revealing" clothes. In *Why Me?*, Rose Kushner explains why she decided to have reconstruction done. She was alone in a hotel room one night when she was awakened by the sound of the fire alarm and the smell of smoke. She jumped out of bed, threw on her clothing, grabbed her glasses, and ran. Downstairs in the lobby with the other guests, she realized that only she had gotten dressed; the others were all in their robes. Then she realized why: "This 'well-adjusted' mastectomee wasn't going anywhere publicly with one breast."[4]

A reconstruction can help some women put their cancer experiences behind them. As one of my patients said, "When I was wearing my prosthesis every day, when I looked at my body and it was concave where there had been a breast, I felt that I was a cancer patient, that I was living with that every single day. With the reconstruction I feel that I'm healthy again, that I can go on with my life." Another patient says that after her mastectomy, "I always felt the hollows under my arm. After my reconstruction, I put my arms down, and something was there. That's when the tears came; it was splendid to have that back."

On the other hand, it isn't necessarily right for everybody. One of my patients regrets her decision to have reconstruction. Displeased with the appearance of her reconstructed breast, she also feels that getting the reconstruction functioned as a form of denial. "It caused me to postpone the mourning I had to do over losing a breast," she says. "Instead of mourning the loss of a breast, I was thinking in terms of getting a breast. So it wasn't until the process was over, and I saw my new breast, which wasn't like my other breast, that it hit me that I'd lost a breast. If I had the decision to make now, I don't think I'd have reconstruction." The best reconstructions look like real breasts— but not all operations are the best, and some look real only through bras or clothing.

Reconstruction surgery is done in a number of ways. There are two basic kinds—those using artificial substances and those using your own body. Within these categories there are also variations. In the first category is the implant, which can be either silicone or saline (salt water). There has been much controversy over silicone, which we discussed at length in Chapter 5. Although it was banned in 1992 by the FDA for use in cosmetic breast enlargement, women who choose to use it for breast reconstruction have, as of this writing, access to it.

Although there have been two million implants used over the past 30 years there is still very little information about its long-term effects. The new government study discussed in Chapter 5 is designed to change that. When the implant is done for breast reconstruction, there is no fear of interfering with mammography, and there is no evidence that implants interfere with the detection of recurrences.[5]

The procedure for both silicone and saline is the same. The disadvantage of the saline is that it may feel more like water than flesh and when it leaks the reconstruction completely collapses. The advantage is that when it does leak, it's harmless saline going into your body, and not silicone, with its possible dangers. We should note, however, that it is still encased in a silicone envelope. If the solid silicone is a problem (as of now we have no data) changing the contents to saline will not eliminate it. The same holds true for other substances now being used to fill implants in experiments.

The implant is placed behind the pectoralis muscle and the skin is sewn together, which will give you a bulge (Fig. 26-2). The silicone has some weight and bounce to it, which helps it feel real. The problem is that it can't give you a very large breast because it's behind the muscle, pushing everything forward, and everything has to close over the top of it, so you're limited in size. Also the implant-reconstructed breast tends to stay firm, while your other breast may not. The implant won't gain and lose weight with you, either. It works best in

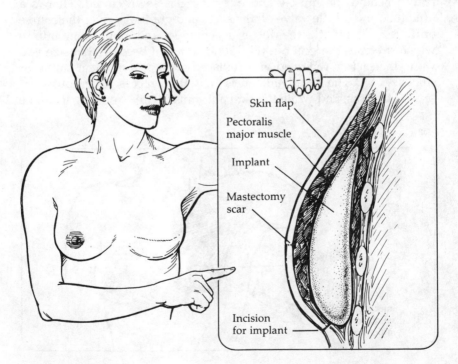

Skin flap

Pectoralis
major muscle

Implant

Mastectomy
scar

Incision
for implant

FIGURE 26-2

smaller-breasted women, or on women who have had bilateral mastectomies and are happy with small breasts. It's easier to do than any of the other operations. With the implant, your hospital stay won't be longer than usual. If you're having it done some time after your mastectomy, the hospital stay will be about one to two days.

My plastic surgeon colleague, William Shaw, has found in his practice that there are certain categories of women for whom implants are often a better choice than the other forms of reconstruction we discuss later. "For an elderly woman who wants something better than a prosthesis, something she can comfortably wear a bra and clothes over, it may make more sense. She is unlikely to be concerned about the problems 15 or 20 years down the line, and it's an easier operation than the others." At the other end of the spectrum is the younger women with preschool children at home. "Often I find that a woman in this situation is most concerned with spending all the time she can with her family—and five days longer in the hospital plus the recovery from a flap surgery can make a big difference. Five or ten years later, she may want to come back and have a flap operation—but for now she just wants something to get by with."

A variation on the implant is the expander. A hollow, empty sack is placed behind the muscle and everything is sewn closed. There's a little tube and a little valve on the sack, and gradually over the course of three to six months the doctor injects more and more saline into it, which stretches the skin out (Fig. 26-3). When it becomes the size you want, the sack is removed and replaced with a permanent saline or silicone sack. The disadvantage is that the process drags out over several months, and while the skin and muscle are stretching it can be

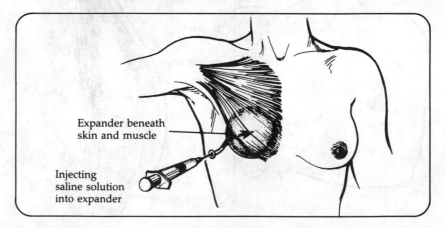

Expander beneath
skin and muscle

Injecting
saline solution
into expander

FIGURE 26-3

uncomfortable. The expander will probably add no extra days to your hospital stay. If done at a separate time from the operation, it will keep you in the hospital about two or three days.

In surgery there's always a danger of postoperative infection. With expanders and implants it's especially serious because they are foreign to your body and an infection will not heal. One of my patients had a very bad infection and had to have the expander removed. Moreover, implants and expanders are more likely than other procedures to necessitate your having something done to the other breast to make it match. They're going to give you a perfectly shaped 17-year-old's breast, and you're probably not a perfectly shaped 17-year-old. The reconstructed breast doesn't sag much so it may be higher than you want it to be. One of my patients who has been very unhappy with her operation found this particularly displeasing. "The reconstructed breast didn't look like my real breast, and it was much higher," she says. "I had to start wearing a bra, which I don't like at all." So when plastic surgeons tell you implants are the easiest form of reconstruction, requiring the least amount of surgery, it's true as far as it goes, but you need to consider that you may end up choosing more surgery, on the other breast.

Because of this, it's important to let the plastic surgeon know what size you want to be. I had a fairly flat chested patient who wanted an implant. She wanted to stay pretty flat chested; that was what she was used to being. But the plastic surgeon had a difficult time believing that. He was so conditioned to thinking that all women wanted large breasts. He kept trying to persuade her to let him give her a larger implant and to enlarge her other breast to match it. Another of my patients had had silicone implants and the implant on one side had encapsulated. But she liked the firm, rocklike texture of that breast, and when she had a mastectomy on the other breast, she wanted the reconstructed breast to match the encapsulated one. The plastic surgeon again had a hard time with that—it wasn't what women were supposed to want. If you know what you want and your plastic surgeon argues with you, argue back, or change plastic surgeons. It's your body, not the surgeon's, and it's you who will live with that body.

When the operation works well and the patient's expectations are realistic, implants can make a wonderful difference in her life. As one of my patients says, "I forget it's there—it's a part of me now. It's a little harder than my other breast, but otherwise great: I don't have to worry about what I wear."

Dr. Shaw warns of one other hazard. As we discussed in Chapter 5, implants don't always last forever. For the woman who has had implants to enlarge her breasts, needing them replaced can be upsetting enough. For the woman with a mastectomy, it can be devastating. "It's like losing the breast all over again," Dr. Shaw says. Such patients almost always need the flap reconstruction (described below) because they have had problems with the implant and are likely to have problems later on. "If you have problems with implants, I might take the implant out and do it again. I might even do it a second or third time. But the fourth time, I wouldn't. I don't think I can be any smarter the fourth time than I was, or the other surgeon was, the first three times." So patients need to weigh the comparative ease of the implant surgery against the inconvenience and emotional consequences of possible later surgeries.

I don't particularly favor either the implants or the expanders, although of course I will support whatever my patient wants. Because of the inferior cosmetic effects, the mismatch with the other breast, the possibility of needing them replaced in the future, and the possible health problems with silicone, I don't personally think it's the wisest choice.

There are several procedures that use your own tissue, and that's what I tend to favor. In the *myocutaneous flap*, a flap of skin, muscle, and fat is taken from another part of your body. It's better than the silicone implant in the sense that it's your own tissue, and because you've got extra skin, it can make a bigger breast and a more natural droop. You may feel more normal externally, since it's real tissue, skin and fat, though it will still have little sensation.

There are two different techniques for the myocutaneous flap. One is the pedicle, or attached flap (Fig. 26-4). Here the tissue is removed except for its feeding artery and vein, which remain attached, almost like a leash. The site from which the tissue was removed is sewn closed. The little island of skin and muscle is then tunneled under the skin into the mastectomy wound. Since the blood vessels aren't cut, the blood supply remains.

The more recent operation is the "free flap," one of whose pioneers is Dr. Shaw. "Like all the other plastic surgeons, I did the tunnel procedure in the beginning. But then there were patients I couldn't do the tunnel procedure on, because they'd had a gall bladder operation that cut across the upper muscle, or something like that. With the free flap, you don't have to disrupt the abdomen as much." In the free flap, the tissue is removed and the feeding artery and vein are cut. Then the tissue is moved to a new location and the artery and vein are sewn to an artery or vein in the armpit, with a microscope to allow the surgeons to see what they are doing.

The advantage of the pedicle flap is that it's easier to do, so there are more plastic surgeons who can do it. A disadvantage is that we can only use tissue from locations that can stretch to the breast—the

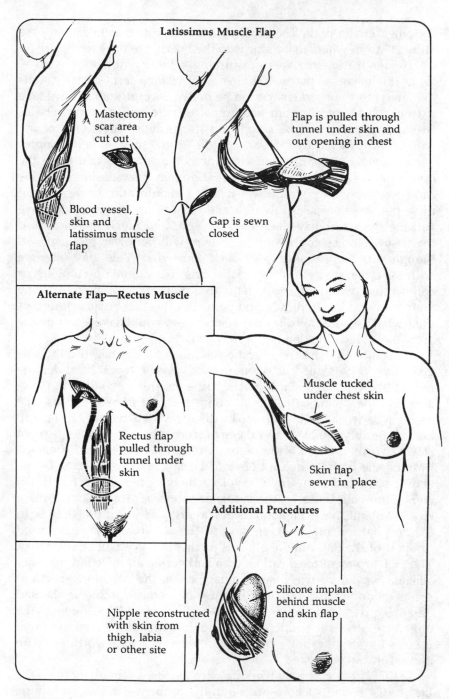

Latissimus Muscle Flap

Mastectomy scar area cut out

Blood vessel, skin and latissimus muscle flap

Flap is pulled through tunnel under skin and out opening in chest

Gap is sewn closed

Muscle tucked under chest skin

Skin flap sewn in place

Alternate Flap—Rectus Muscle

Rectus flap pulled through tunnel under skin

Additional Procedures

Nipple reconstructed with skin from thigh, labia or other site

Silicone implant behind muscle and skin flap

FIGURE 26-4

abdomen or the back. The other disadvantage is that in making the "tunnel" from where that tissue is to the breast, we have to disturb all the tissue en route, so we're disturbing a lot of your body surface. What this means is that you'll have a lot of long-term complications that aren't terribly serious but can be pretty uncomfortable. If we take it from the abdomen, your abdominal muscle will no longer be as strong and you won't be able to do things like situps. One of my patients now has to wear a panty girdle all the time, to help support her weakened abdominal muscle. Another has found that since the operation the area around her upper abdomen is so sensitive that she can't wear anything with a waistband. I should add, however, that these problems are relatively rare, and most of my patients who have had the procedure have had few problems, and much satisfaction. If the tissue is taken from your back there will be fewer problems, although you may weaken your back somewhat. This may interfere with shoulder strength for special sports like mountain climbing or competitive swimming. It also may need more physical therapy. Some women have a lot of stiffness and pain after this flap because it throws their whole shoulder girdle off. In either case, you'll have a scar on the area from which the flap has been taken.

With the free flap, the operation is much harder because the surgeon has to be skilled at sewing blood vessels together under the microscope (Fig. 26-5). Most plastic surgeons aren't expert at it. However, in expert hands, the complications are much fewer, because the tissue in between doesn't have to be disturbed: less tissue is taken out, and it's simply removed and the area from which it is taken is sewn closed. Further, because the tissue is removed rather than tunneled through the body, it doesn't have to be taken from the back or the abdomen; it can come from anyplace there's anything extra. It can come from your buttocks, the saddle bags on your thighs, or anyplace else. It's about five to eight hours of surgery, and you'll probably be in the hospital for four to seven days. If the blood supply gets messed up, part of the flap can die off, and further surgery will be necessary. The patient I mentioned earlier, who had gotten an infection from her silicone expanders, was unable to have either the latissimus (back) or rectus (abdominal) procedures because of medical problems she had had in her back and abdomen. The free-gluteus flap (Fig. 26-6) was the only alternative she had left, and, though it was difficult surgery that involved a long healing period, she feels it was well worth the pain and inconvenience.

At UCLA I'm currently working with Dr. Shaw—in my opinion the best breast reconstruction surgeon in the country—on this procedure, and we have had great results. In this kind of situation, I favor free flaps for reconstruction. It's really been the "Cadillac" operation, and

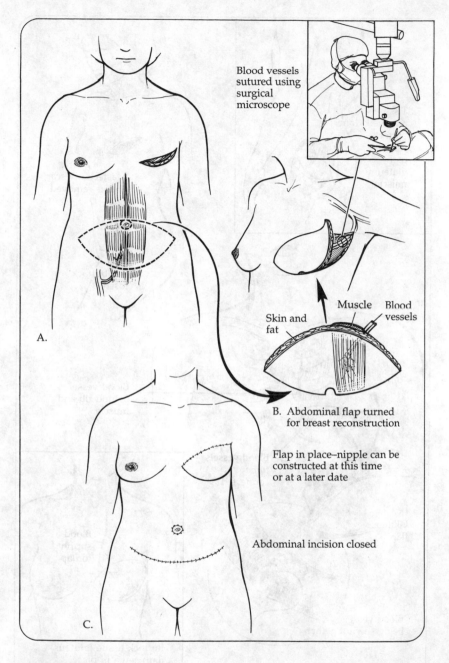

Blood vessels sutured using surgical microscope

Skin and fat   Muscle   Blood vessels

A.

B. Abdominal flap turned for breast reconstruction

Flap in place–nipple can be constructed at this time or at a later date

Abdominal incision closed

C.

FIGURE 26-5

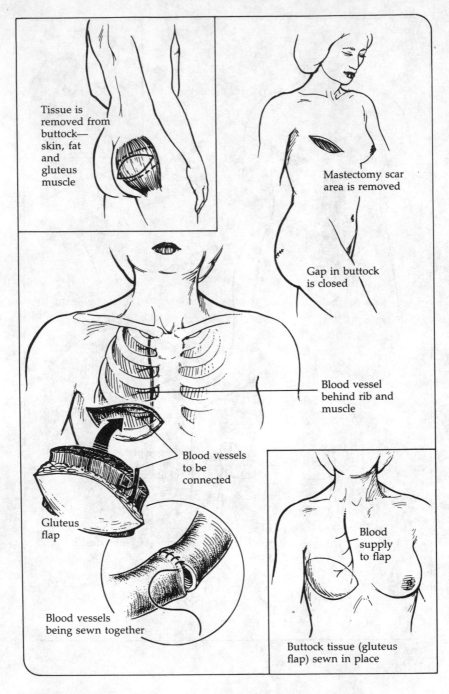

Tissue is removed from buttock—skin, fat and gluteus muscle

Mastectomy scar area is removed

Gap in buttock is closed

Blood vessel behind rib and muscle

Blood vessels to be connected

Gluteus flap

Blood vessels being sewn together

Blood supply to flap

Buttock tissue (gluteus flap) sewn in place

FIGURE 26-6

it's not available everywhere. But this is beginning to change. Dr. Shaw says that "in the last two or three years, the free flap is being used more around the country."

Another alternative is to do a combination operation, using the latissimus flap and a silicone implant behind it (Fig. 26-4). This can be useful when there are problems with the abdominal area—for example, abdominal surgery that's left a lot of scarring. Also, abdominal flaps can throw your posture off if you have back problems.

With this free flap, you'll probably be in the hospital for four or five days; the stitches will be out in two to three weeks, and by five or six weeks, you'll be ready for a fully active lifestyle again.

As I noted earlier, both versions of the flap procedure require highly trained plastic surgeons. There aren't that many around, and it might be very difficult for you to find the one you need. There are far more plastic surgeons in the country who can do the simpler procedures of the implant or expander.

To decide what's best for you, discuss it with your surgeon and then separately with a plastic surgeon. They will look at you and your body, see how your body hangs together and how your breasts look before your surgery, and tell you what kind of procedure they think would be best for you. Make sure you ask them which procedures they are familiar with and do regularly. Often a woman has come to me who has been told she's not a candidate for a flap, when in reality the plastic surgeon she saw just doesn't know how to do the operation.

My Boston colleague Robert Goldwyn, who has done many reconstructions, points out something crucial: your plastic surgeon should show you pictures of the best and the worst results he or she has had. Some doctors will show women only the best results—an act he compares to false advertising. It's important for you to know the limits of what the procedure can do for you, and the risks you run of having far-from-ideal results. Dr. Shaw concurs, and emphasizes the importance of demanding absolute honesty from your plastic surgeon.

Any of these procedures can be done immediately, or at some later time. The advantage of having it done immediately is that you don't have to face another operation later: your regular surgeon performs your mastectomy; then, while you're still under anesthesia, the plastic surgeon comes in and does the reconstruction. In my experience, many women don't have reconstruction because they don't want to go through another bout of surgery. The disadvantages are that it's a longer time in the operating room (usually about six to eight hours), and that it's harder to schedule, since you have to get the surgeon and the plastic surgeon at the same time.

The way we do it now at UCLA is to have the plastic surgery team work on the flap in the abdomen while I am doing the mastectomy. (If the tissue is taken from the buttocks or back, I operate with the patient lying on her side.) By the time I'm finished they're ready to start moving the flap up. Through this teamwork approach we've gotten the time down to about four to five hours.

When we're done, the patient is taken to the "flap room," a three-bed room that's sort of an intensive care unit for the flap—not for the patient, for the flap. The concern is that something will happen in the area where the blood vessels are sewn together, and the blood supply will get blocked, which will cause the flap to turn black and die. So they carefully monitor the flap with temperature probes that are taped to it, and if the flap starts getting cold, the probes alert the surgeons that the blood supply may be compromised.

Whether or not you've had your surgery at a facility like UCLA, you come out of anesthesia feeling like a Mack truck just hit you. You've had hours of surgery on both your breast and your abdomen, back, or buttocks. At UCLA and most other hospitals, there's continuous pain medication you can get through an IV with a button you can press so that you can control the timing. We keep you in bed rest for a couple of days, and you have a catheter so you don't have to get up and go to the bathroom. By about the third or fourth day you start feeling a little better, and we get you out of bed and walking around a bit. You're usually in the hospital about six or seven days altogether. There are drains placed in the abdominal or back or buttock scars as well as in the chest. Usually you won't have much pain in your chest, which will feel numb, but the area the tissue has been taken from will hurt a lot.

So it's certainly an ordeal to go through. And the ordeal continues for a time, in a milder form—you'll probably end up getting a second operation for final touch-ups, and to make a nipple if you want one. Sometimes after the operation there will be a little too much tissue one place or another, so the surgeon does some fine tuning. (This doesn't hurt because the area is numb.) But the operation is usually worth the ordeal you go through. You do recuperate after a while. We've even done the operation on elderly women who have other medical problems, and it's worked for them. The cosmetic effects are superior.

If the free flap operation is the one you want, take the time to do research. Find out who in your area can do it. If there's no one, and you still want that form of reconstruction, you can always wait, have the mastectomy first, and then find the right plastic surgeon when your treatment is done.

It's also possible that you won't be sure at first whether you want reconstruction. Both Dr. Shaw and Dr. Goldwyn say that many pre-mastectomy patients they see are too upset by the cancer and the prospect of a mastectomy to make yet another major decision at the time. When they come across this kind of ambivalence, they suggest the patient have her mastectomy, take whatever time she needs to deal with it, and then, when she feels ready, come back to them if she still wants reconstruction.

Many plastic surgeons don't like to do immediate reconstruction because it's a new procedure and they're leery of it. If you want it done and the surgeon tries to argue you out of it, don't give up—just look for a surgeon who's had experience and is comfortable with it.

There is no time limit for reconstruction. In fact, current techniques have made it a better option than it used to be. If you had a mastectomy in the past and are now thinking about reconstruction, you should feel encouraged. Even with a radical mastectomy, reconstruction is still possible. Or, if you've decided against reconstruction, and now want to reconsider, that's also fine. (I've had patients who have had their mastectomies in the winter and didn't want reconstruction, and then decided in the summer, when they want to wear bathing suits and sundresses, that maybe it's a good idea after all.) Women with bilateral mastectomies can have both sides reconstructed—and to any reasonable size they like. If you were an A cup and always wanted to be a C, now you can do it!

Once the new breast is on, you can also get a nipple made. We don't do it right away, because the surgeon needs to be sure it's in the right place. There's a lot of swelling after reconstructive surgery, so we need to wait till that's gone down and the nipple is placed on the breast as it will look permanently. It will look "real," and match the color of your original nipple. Sometimes the skin from your inner thigh is used, since it's darker than breast skin. Sometimes a nipple can be made from the tissue in the flap and an areola tattooed on. Whether or not you want to bother with the nipple depends on why you want the reconstruction. If it's just for convenience, you may decide against it. If you want the new breast to look as real as possible, you'll probably want the nipple. Again, it's your decision— you're the one who'll go through the surgery, and you're the one who'll live with the results. I've had a couple of patients who, before they had the nipple put on, showed their reconstruction to anyone who was curious—then, once the nipple was on, they didn't want to show it. Somehow it felt more like a real breast, and displaying it seemed suddenly immodest.

Breast reconstruction depends on the patient's goal. Some women are concerned about symmetry; others aren't. Do you want to look good in your clothes, or is it important that a new lover doesn't know you've had surgery? Do you want to have your remaining breast altered to achieve a more perfect match? None of these are foolish concerns, and you should never hesitate to look for what you want.

There's nothing wrong with being vain. You've been through a very unpleasant and life-changing experience; you're entitled to do what you can to make its aftermath as comfortable as possible for yourself. Talk with your plastic surgeon about all the possibilities and decide what's best for you. Dr. Shaw warns against looking for one universal operation that's best for every patient: "One of the mistakes surgeons and patients both make is to act as if breast reconstruction is some kind of product you can compare objectively—what's the best airplane? But one thing I've learned over the years is that there's no one operation that's best for everyone."

Whatever you decide, check with your insurance company. Some companies will pay for either a prosthesis or reconstruction but not one and then the other, and that might affect your decision.

Partial Reconstruction After Lumpectomy

Women who have had a large amount of tissue removed and have a poor cosmetic result can have a delayed partial reconstruction. The cosmetic results are good, and we have found that the flap tissue doesn't obstruct a mammogram. The one thing that you shouldn't do—and we need to be very clear about this—is to put a small silicone or saline implant in the remaining breast tissue. We can't mammogram through an implant. If the woman has a recurrence it's likely to be in the same area—the area that's obscured by the implant. When women have an implant for augmentation there are techniques we can use to push the implant back and take a mammogram. After lumpectomy, the implant is in the middle of the breast tissue so it is always in the way. Since the flap uses the body's own tissue, which is mostly fat, it won't block the mammogram.

I'm involved in a research protocol working on partial reconstruction immediately, taking some tissue from the back as a latissimus flap and filling the hole where the tissue's been removed. Unlike complete breast reconstruction, this will preserve a normal breast, with normal breast sensation—it's sort of a patch. We did a pilot study on 18 patients in Boston and it worked very well. The cosmetic results were good. Then those patients went on to have radiation. What we don't know yet, and the reason this is only in study form, is whether or not the recurrence rate will be higher than it is in women who have had mastectomies, since the tumors were large to begin with. We need to follow these patients for a while before we can see that. But it will give us a middle road between mastectomy and reconstruction and lumpectomy without reconstruction in terms of the best cosmetic results for women with extensive tumors.

Contralateral Mastectomy for Symmetry

There is another alternative, one that some women request. If your only aesthetic concern is symmetry, you can have both breasts removed. While this destroys a perfectly healthy breast, it does make it possible for you to wear loose shirts without wearing a prosthesis or looking conspicuous, and it's easier surgery than reconstruction. I've had only one patient who's chosen this route, and she had to fight with her insurance company to get them to pay for the removal of the healthy breast. She told them that since they paid for reconstruction for symmetry they should pay for a contralateral mastectomy for symmetry. I would warn any woman considering this option that she should think of it only in cosmetic terms: it won't guarantee that she'll never again have breast cancer (see Chapter 23).

27

Radiation Therapy

The idea of radiation therapy may make you nervous. After all, radiation can cause cancer, and the last thing you want is to find yourself in danger of even more cancer: you've got quite enough now, thank you. But the doses given in radiation therapy rarely cause cancer, and often cure it. We've discussed this at length in Chapter 23.

As a form of local control (treatment of an original cancer), radiation is more effective in some forms of cancer than in others; it's been very effective with breast cancer.

Radiation is often used in conjunction with surgery, so you may have had a lumpectomy (or even a mastectomy) before receiving radiation treatment. Radiation works best when it has comparatively few cells to attack—it's least effective on large chunks of cancer. So we try, if possible, to do the surgery first, getting rid of most of the tumor surgically and then cleaning up what's left with radiation.

In the old days, we used a cobalt machine that was aimed at the general area instead of a carefully plotted site, and the radiation scattered a lot. One of my patients had been treated with a cobalt machine for Hodgkin's disease in the 1960s. While it cured the Hodgkin's, it scattered a lot of low-dose radiation into her breasts, and she now has breast cancer. At the time, the cobalt machine was the best form of radiation therapy we had, and if the Hodgkin's had gone untreated, she probably would have died long ago.

In the early days of radiation, women who were radiated after a mastectomy for breast cancer often developed other problems because of the radiation. If the machine is aimed straight-on at the breast, you also radiate the lungs, and, if it's the left breast, the heart. Some studies show that women whose left breasts were radiated after they had mastectomies had a higher incidence of heart disease 20 years later than other women—including women whose right breasts were radiated.[1]

We've come a long way since those days. We've refined the process of administering radiation so that it's much more precise. We're much better able to hone in on the specific site we want to radiate. We administer the radiation in tangents, as well as straight on, so that the radiation goes through a particular breast area and out into air, and less into your heart or lung (Fig. 27-1). At the same time we shield other body parts to prevent scatter radiation.

Radiation, like surgery, is a localized treatment. (Chemotherapy, given through an injection or a pill, goes through your bloodstream and affects your entire body.) Radiation is aimed at a very specific area and affects only that area. It's usually administered by a machine called a linear accelerator, which accelerates radioactive particles and shoots them directly at the body part they're intended for, like a gun.

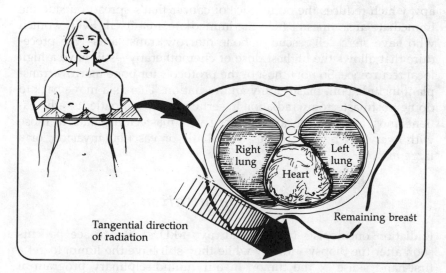

Right lung

Left lung

Heart

Remaining breast

Tangential direction
of radiation

FIGURE 27-1

As we discussed in Chapter 23, radiation is often used as an alternative to mastectomy. Sometimes, it is also used with mastectomy. The first treatment used for breast cancer was mastectomy. But those early surgeons soon began to notice that there were still some patients who didn't do well. There were certain predictors for which patients did badly, based on the "grave signs" we discussed in Chapter 21: very large tumors, a lot of positive lymph nodes, involvement of the skin. So in these cases, postoperative radiation was used after the mastectomy. For a long time, in the 1960s and 1970s, most women who had danger signs following a mastectomy, especially positive lymph nodes, would get cobalt—the form of radiation used in the early days. You hear some real horror stories from those days—burns to the esophagus, skin burns, and so forth. Then a study was done to see how well it was working, which showed that it wasn't: the survival rate remained the same. Local recurrence—recurrence in the chest wall or the scar—decreased, but this didn't seem to cure anyone: the cancer had already spread.

When it became clear that the problem was really systemic, we began using adjuvant chemotherapy, and that did affect cure rates. So postmastectomy radiation was dropped. We decided to only radiate women who actually had a recurrence in the chest wall. It was thought that in most women, chemotherapy itself would work to prevent local recurrence.

But over the past 10 or 15 years, as adjuvant chemotherapy has improved survival, we're seeing more local recurrences. Chemotherapy, which reduces the occurrence of cancer that's spread outside the immediate area, doesn't help the immediate area itself. Even women who have stem cell rescue or bone marrow transplants—the procedure that allows the highest dose of chemotherapy—still have a high local recurrence. So now most of the protocols for bone marrow transplant include both mastectomy and radiation. There's a move back to doing postmastectomy radiation in certain groups of patients—the patients most at risk for local recurrence after mastectomy, such as those with over four positive nodes, lymphatic or vascular invasion, or a large tumor.

Initial Consultation

Radiation oncologists (who are always M.D.'s) like to see patients soon after the biopsy—ideally while they still have the lump, to get a first-hand sense of the tumor. In our multidisciplinary program at UCLA we all see the patients as a team. Sometimes the initial consultation is in the radiation therapy department and involves a team approach, including a specially trained radiation nurse, who will inquire into the patient's needs, taking into account her emotional response to her cancer. The consultation involves a physical exam as well as conversation with the patient.

This first visit to a radiation oncologist doesn't mean you'll necessarily have radiation treatments. The radiation oncologist will talk with you and get your medical history, do an examination, review your X rays and slides from any surgery you may have had done, and talk with your primary doctor, your surgeon, and your medical oncologist if you have one. They will then come up with a recommendation. If radiation does seem appropriate, you'll be sent for a planning session and whatever X rays are needed after surgery (see Chapters 25 and 26), if any has been done.

There are issues that may enter into the decision about whether or not to use radiation. One is that if you have large breasts the equipment they have may or may not be able to accommodate them. You may need to find a center that has the correct equipment.

Another issue is that a bit of the lung gets radiated, and if you have chronic lung disease, that can be dangerous. So with patients who have conditions like asthma or emphysema, we often do the planning session (see below) just to do the measurements—to see how much lung will be affected and whether or not it is safe for them to have radiation therapy.

In women who have collagen vascular diseases like lupus or scleroderma, the skin response to radiation is increased, so they're not good candidates for radiation, either.

In any of these cases, when the potential risks of radiation are greater than the potential gains, a mastectomy would be done rather than lumpectomy and radiation.

Since radiation therapy after mastectomy is done primarily to prevent a recurrence in the chest wall or scar, there is a choice as to whether to do it now or later. In those women who have conditions precluding radiation therapy, it is better to wait and attempt it only if there is a local recurrence.

The Planning Session

Usually you'll wait at least two weeks after surgery before the planning session, to make sure everything's healed and you can get your arm up over your head comfortably.

The session takes about an hour. You put on a johnny and lie on a table with your arm lifted and resting on a form above your head. Over you there's a machine, similar to the radiation machine, called a

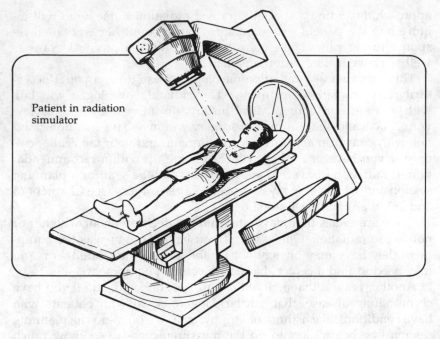

Patient in radiation simulator

FIGURE 27-2

"simulator" (Fig. 27-2). It doesn't actually give radiation, but follows the identical positions and motions as does the machine that gives the radiation treatments. A lot of measurements and technical X rays are taken to map where your ribs are in relation to your nipple, where your heart is in relation to your ribs, and so on, figuring out precisely how that area of your body looks. Depending on what area of your body is going to be radiated, you may also be sent for X rays, a CAT scan, or ultrasound to get more information. In some centers a *lymphoscintogram* is used to help in the planning. This is a type of scan similar to the bone scan (see Chapter 21) which is done to show the lymph nodes under your breastbone. It helps the radiation oncologists see where the nodes are in relation to other organs and therefore direct the radiation more specifically. Then all the information is put into a computer, which calculates specifically the angles at which the area of your body should be radiated. In some cases they actually make a mold for you to hold your arm in, so that you'll be in the same position every day. In women with very large breasts they sometimes put a sort of fishnet halter on the breast so it will always be in the same position.

Before the treatments start, the radiation oncologist marks out the

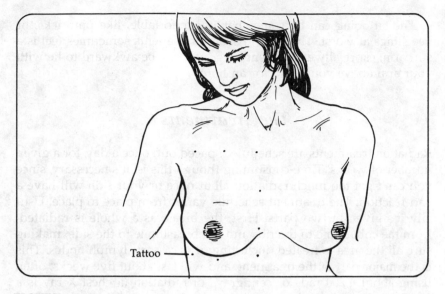

Tattoo

FIGURE 27-3

area of the breast that's going to be treated. You should be aware that the breast and the lymph node areas will be treated from different angles, which means covering a fairly large area of your chest. Many doctors use tattoos, which are permanent little blue dots, to outline the area to be radiated (Figure 27-3). There are a couple of reasons for that. One is to be sure that during treatment they use the same "landmarks" and measure exactly the same way every time. The other is to make sure that in the future any radiation oncologist will know you've had radiation in that area, because you can only be radiated once on any given spot. So if, for example, you were to get cancer in the other breast, and the area was near the area of the previous cancer, the tattoo mark would tell the radiation oncologist where the field that could be radiated ended. I find them useful because often when I'm doing a follow-up exam on a patient whose surgery wasn't terribly extensive, I can't remember which breast was treated—it can be a year or so after the last exam. So I look for the tattoo, and that lets me know.

Although the dots may be cosmetically displeasing, they're not going to turn you into Lydia the Tattooed Lady—they're tiny and, depending on your skin coloring, can be invisible. One radiation nurse I know says, "I've had patients call me up and say, 'I've washed my tattoos off—I can't find them!' " Some doctors use Magic Markers, especially if the patient is adamant about not having tattoos; the problem with this is that the markings can be washed off, and doctors working with you in the future will not have this information.

The tattooing can be somewhat uncomfortable, like pinpricks, or bee stings at worst. The other discomfort patients sometimes feel is a stiff arm; especially after recent surgery it can be awkward to lie with your arm above your head for an hour.

The Treatments

Radiation treatments are scheduled, paced out, once a day, for a given number of weeks. Time-consuming though this is, it's necessary, since you can't get too much radiation all at once or your skin will have a bad reaction. The treatment schedule varies from place to place. Usually it's given in two parts. First, the breast as a whole is radiated, from the collarbone to the ribs and the breastbone to the side, making sure all the area is treated, including, if necessary, lymph nodes. This is the major part of the treatment, and will last about five weeks, often using about 4,700 rads or centigrays of radiation (a chest X ray is a fraction of a rad). If there are microscopic cancer cells in the breast, this should get rid of them. After this, the boost (described later) is given.

How soon after the simulation the treatment begins varies from hospital to hospital, depending on how many radiation patients there are, how much room is in the radiation department, and how large the staff is. Sometimes it will be between two weeks and a month, and often patients worry that the delay will cause the cancer to spread. Though the wait doesn't pose any real danger of the cancer worsening, it can be emotionally hard on the patient.

There may be delays for other reasons. Depending on the status of the lymph nodes, you may be getting chemotherapy first, and your doctors may not want you to get them both at the same time. As we mentioned earlier, with some drugs, such as CMF (see Chapter 23), you can have chemo and radiation together; with others, like Adriamycin, you usually have the chemo first and then the radiation. Sometimes they're given in a sandwichlike sequence: chemotherapy, then radiation, then more chemotherapy.

There are important skin care guidelines to follow during your treatment. You should use a mild soap, such as Ivory, Pears, or Neutrogena. During the course of your treatment avoid all soaps that use fragrance, deodorants, or any kind of metal. All of these can interact with the radiation, and it's very important to avoid them. Don't use deodorant on the side that's being treated; deodorants have lots of aluminum. Through the course of the treatment you can use a light dusting of cornstarch as a deodorant; it's usually pretty effective, though it varies from patient to patient. But don't use talcum powder.

You can check the health food store for natural deodorants, some of which don't use aluminum—but read the label very, very carefully.

When you go for your first treatment, it's wise to bring someone with you for support. You're facing the unknown, and that's usually scary. Most patients don't feel the need to have someone with them after the first session.

For the treatment itself, you'll change into a johnny from the waist up. It's wise to wear something two-piece so you have to remove only your upper clothing. You can wear earrings or bracelets, but no neck jewelry. After you've changed, you'll be taken into a waiting room; the wait may be longish, and varies from place to place and day to day, so you may want to bring a good book or your Walkman. Then you're taken into the treatment room. You're there only for about 10 minutes, and most of that time is spent with the technologist setting up the machine and getting you ready. There's a table that looks like a regular examining table, and, above it, the radiation machine (Fig. 27-4). You lie down on the table, and a plastic or styrofoam form is placed under your head. This has an armrest above your head, in which you'll hold your arm during the treatment. When you're set up, the technologist leaves the room and turns on the machine. The radiation isn't given all at once; it's done a number of times from different angles—twice if

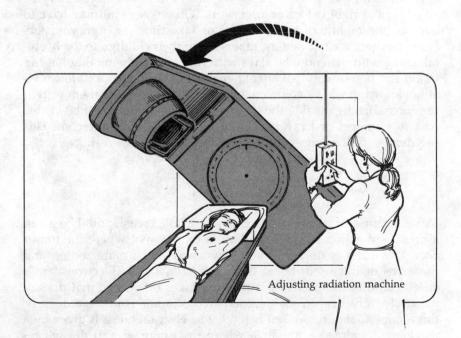

Adjusting radiation machine

FIGURE 27-4

409

only the breast is radiated, more if lymph nodes are also being treated. After repositioning you the technician will leave, turn on the machine for a little less than a minute, come back in, reposition the machine, and go out again. If you're claustrophobic, you may find lying under the machine a little uncomfortable, but it doesn't last long, and the machine itself never moves down toward you.

Radiation therapy units have cameras, so that they can see you while you're being treated, and an intercom system so that if you're anxious and need to talk with the technologist, you can. If a friend or family member has come with you, many hospitals will allow them in the room outside the treatment area, watching on the monitor and able to hear you through the intercom. The most important thing for you to do during the treatment is to keep still. You can breathe normally, but don't move otherwise.

Your blood will be drawn routinely during the course of the treatments—once at the beginning of the therapy process, once a few weeks later, to make sure there's no drop in your blood count. This usually isn't a problem with breast cancer, since there's not much bone marrow treated, but we do it to be safe.

What most people find hardest to deal with is the time that the treatments take. They last for six and a half weeks, five days a week. If your workplace and home are fairly near the hospital, you may be able to come right before or after work. Otherwise, you may have to cut into the middle of the workday, or take time off from your job. Some mothers use babysitters, others bring their children to the hospital, along with a friend who stays with them while the mother has her treatment. If your children are old enough to be curious, or are scared at not knowing what's going on, you might want to have them wait in the room directly outside the treatment room, where you'll be visible on two monitors and can talk with them through an intercom. This can demystify the process and alleviate the children's fear.

The Boost

After a course of radiation to treat your whole breast, you'll be given a boost—an extra amount of radiation on the spot where the tumor was. The boost is done in one of two ways. The more recent, and more frequently used, boost is the electron beam. Electrons are a special kind of radioactive particle that gives off energy that doesn't penetrate very deeply, so it's good if the tumor isn't very deep or there's not a lot of tumor left behind. The electron boost is given by a machine; it's aimed at the area where the tumor was. It doesn't require hospitalization.

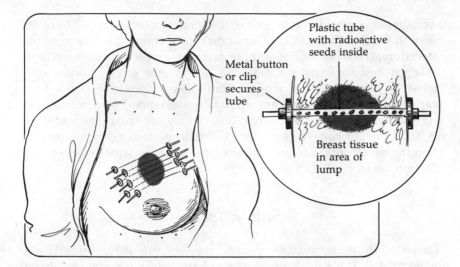

Metal button or clip secures tube

Plastic tube with radioactive seeds inside

Breast tissue in area of lump

FIGURE 27-5

The other type of boost is a radioactive implant, done under either general anesthetic or local anesthetic and some kind of sedation (Fig. 27-5). Thin plastic tubing hooked like thread into a needle is drawn through the breast where the biopsy was done. Then the tubing is left in and the needle withdrawn. The number of tubes varies; sometimes they are inserted in two layers. Small radioactive pellets, called iridium seeds, which give off high energy for a very short distance, are put into the tubes, "boosting" the immediate area of the biopsy. This implant is left in for about 36 hours. The time depends on how active the seeds are, how big your breast is, and how big the tumor is.

This radiation can be picked up by people around you, although not in large doses. If you sit across the table from someone for four hours they'd get about the same amount of radiation they'd get in a chest X ray. Normally, that's no problem, but for some people, like pregnant women, exposure even to that much radiation could be dangerous, so you can't be out in crowds during the time the tubing is in. Thus you're usually kept in the hospital with a sign on the door saying "Caution: radioactive." (Your friends, unless they're at risk, can visit you; they can sit a distance across the room and chat with you.) At the end of about 36 hours the tubes are removed, a process that requires no anesthesia, and, unless there's some other reason for you to stay hospitalized, you can go home.

Whether the electron boost or the implant boost or no boost is used depends on a variety of factors—the amount of surgery you had, the size of your tumor, the size of your breast, and the equipment

411

available to your radiation oncologist. Some oncologists don't have an electron machine available; others don't have training in the implant procedure; some oncologists simply prefer one treatment to the other.

When both options are available, the doctor often chooses one based on the amount of surgery that's been done. When we first started doing lumpectomy and radiation, we tended just to take out the lump and then radiate the breast to clean up the margins, and then we used the implant. Now the trend is to do more surgery, taking out more tissue to obtain clean margins, and to use a smaller boost, the electron beam.

Side Effects

The side effects of radiation depend on the part of the body that's being treated. If it's the breast and you have soft bones you may have asymptomatic rib fractures, which you won't feel but which will show up on X ray. Depending on how your chest is built, a little of the radiation may get to your lung and give you a cough. If you're being treated for cancer in the brain, your hair may fall out. If an area near the stomach is treated you may have nausea; if the area is lower, you may have diarrhea. Your radiation oncologist will tell you about all the possible side effects before your treatment starts.

You'll usually have some kind of "sunburn" effect. The severity varies considerably from patient to patient—one person will get a severe skin rash, while another will barely be bothered at all. Unlike the case with sunburn, fairness of skin isn't relevant.

The other major symptom virtually every radiation therapy patient has is tiredness. I used to think that this was because of the amount of time involved in the treatment, but there's more and more evidence that, like anesthesia (see Chapter 25), radiation in the body itself creates tiredness: the body seems to be using up all its resources to cope with the radiation, and doesn't leave much energy for anything else. The fatigue usually gets worse toward the end of the treatment, and its severity depends on what else is going on in your life. You'll probably want to cut back on your activities if it's at all possible. The fatigue may last several months after the treatment has finished, or may even begin after the course of treatment is over.

The extent of the fatigue varies greatly. One of my patients, a lawyer, had no problem working a full day, but says she "didn't feel like going out for dinner after work." For others, the fatigue is extremely unpleasant. One of my patients compares hers to the effects of infectious hepatitis, which she'd had years before. "The symptoms sound very nondescript," she says, "but I felt really rotten. I was tired all the time—not the tiredness you feel after a hard day's work, which I've always found fairly pleasant. My body just felt wrong—like I was always coming down with the flu. Some days I couldn't function at all—I had to keep a cot at my job." She also experienced peculiar appetite changes. "My body kept craving lemon, spinach, and roast beef—I ate them constantly, and I couldn't make myself eat anything else; food just didn't interest me."

When the breast is being radiated, it may sometimes swell and get more sensitive; if you're used to sleeping on your stomach, you may find that uncomfortable. As we discussed in Chapter 25, one trick is to hold a pillow between your breasts and sleep on the side that hasn't been treated. This sensitivity, like the other side effects, can take months to disappear, and you may find that breast especially sore or sensitive when you're premenstrual.

Interestingly, few of my patients get depressed during radiation, but many get depressed afterward—possibly because, time-consuming as the treatments are, there is a sense of activity, of doing something to fight the cancer, and when it's done, there's a sense of letdown. This really shouldn't be too surprising. It happens in dozens of other intense situations, like the classical postpartum depression, or the feelings that occur when any time-consuming structure in your life is over—a job you've worked at, or the end of a school term. This may be the time to get involved in a support group, if you haven't already done so. You'll have a little more time since you're not going to the treatments, and the company of others who know how you're feeling may help you get through these feelings.

Often the skin feels a little bit thicker right after radiation, and sometimes is darker colored: that will gradually resolve itself over time. The nipple may get crusty, but that too will go away as the skin regenerates. This can take up to six months, and in the meantime you'll look like you've been out sunbathing with one breast exposed.

If there's been a lot of radiation to the armpit, it will compound whatever scarring the surgery caused, and the combination can also increase your risk of lymphedema (see Chapter 25). Another, rare, side effect of radiation to the armpits is problems with the nerves that go from the arm to the hand, causing some numbness to the fingertips.

Aside from skin reaction and tiredness, there are some later side effects. Some women get costochondritis, which is a kind of arthritis that causes inflammation of the space between the breasts where the ribs and breastbone connect (Fig. 27-6). The pain can be scary—you wonder if your cancer has spread. It's easy to reassure yourself, though. Push your fingers down right at that junction; if it hurts, it's costochondritis, and can be treated with aspirin and anti-arthritis medicines.

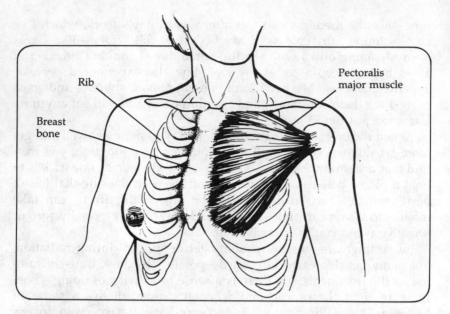

Rib

Pectoralis
major muscle

Breast
bone

FIGURE 27-6

When the treatments are over you'll continue to get some tenderness and soreness in your breast, which will gradually go away. But it will never feel completely normal again: you'll continue to have some sharp, shooting pains from time to time—how often varies greatly from woman to woman.

Often patients worry about being radioactive—that they'll harm other people. They ask, "Can I hug my grandchild? Can I pick up my kids?" Once each treatment is over, the radioactivity is gone and you can be close to anyone (the implants described earlier are an exception). It's like lying in the sun—once you're out of it, the effects remain, but the sunlight isn't inside you, and can't be transmitted to anyone else.

Finally, but thank goodness, rarely, radiation can cause second cancers. These are usually a different kind of cancer, a sarcoma, and don't occur for at least five years after radiation therapy. Our best guess is that, for every 1,000 five-year survivors of wide excision and radiation, about two will develop a radiation-induced sarcoma over the next 10 years.[2] As we mentioned in Chapter 25, a rare kind of sarcoma can develop after a mastectomy if a woman develops a badly swollen arm. Both situations are unusual: I've never seen either one myself.

Above a certain dosage, radiation given again will damage normal tissue. So if you have breast cancer and it recurs in the same breast, you can't have it radiated again. If you have the tattoos we mentioned previously, they will make sure future doctors know you've had radiation treatment in that area.

The decision on how best to use radiation depends on which procedure will have the best medical results, as well as the best cosmetic results. Sometimes a patient will have a tumor that's extremely large in comparison to her breast. In that case, removing the whole tumor surgically will cause severe asymmetry, so we'll sometimes start with radiation to shrink it, and then do a lumpectomy; if the radiation eliminates the tumor completely, we'll skip the lumpectomy and just do a boost. The problem is that a large amount of radiation will always be somewhat cosmetically displeasing, since it can cause permanent swelling in the breast as well as thickened skin. Usually lumpectomy followed by radiation creates the best cosmetic results.

After your treatment is completed, your radiation oncologist will continue to see you, as will your surgeon. In addition to making certain there are no new tumors, the radiation oncologist is watching for signs of complications from the radiation, and the surgeon for signs of surgical complications. These complications are rare, and radiation remains one of our most valuable tools in the treatment of local breast cancer.

28

≡

Systemic Treatments

The hallmark of systemic therapies is their ability to affect the whole body and not just one local area. The systemic treatments used in the treatment of breast cancer include chemotherapy and hormonal therapy.

Chemotherapy has gotten a lot of bad press, and it's a pity, because it's one of the most powerful weapons against cancer that we have. It literally means the use of chemicals to treat disease. As we use it, however, it usually refers only to the use of cytotoxic chemicals (those that kill cells).

How does chemotherapy work? Each cell goes through several steps in the process of cell division, or reproduction. Chemotherapy drugs interfere with this process so that the cells can't divide. As a result, they die. Different drugs interfere at different points, so often more than one kind of drug is used at a time (Fig. 28-1). Unfortunately, this effect on cell division is not very selective. It acts on all cells that are rapidly dividing—including hair cells and, more important, bone marrow cells, as well as cancer cells. The bone marrow is a factory that produces red blood cells, white blood cells, and platelets on a continuous basis (Fig. 28-2). Chemotherapy slows this production down. When we give chemotherapy, then, we have to be careful not to stop the production altogether. This is one of the reasons that chemother-

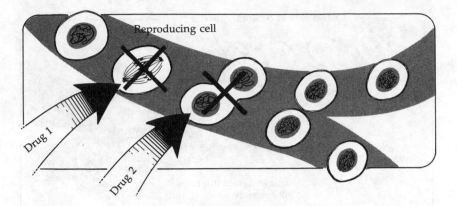

FIGURE 28-1

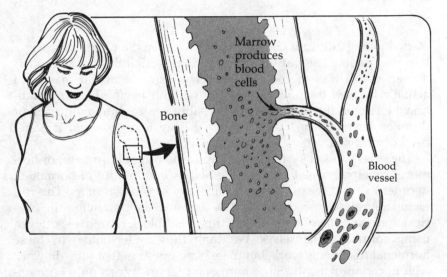

FIGURE 28-2

apy is given in cycles, with a time lapse between treatments to allow the bone marrow to recover.

Another reason the drugs are given in cycles is that not all the cancer cells are dividing at any one time. The first treatment will kill one group of cells; then three weeks later there will be a new set of cancer cells starting to divide, and the drugs will knock them out, too (Fig. 28-3). The idea is to decrease the total number of cancer cells to a number small enough for your immune system to take care of, without wiping out the immune system while we're at it. When we first

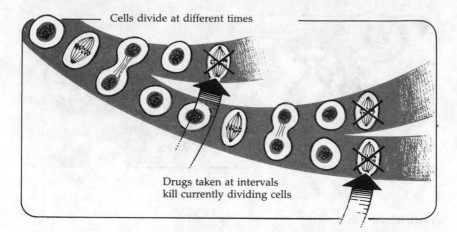

Cells divide at different times

Drugs taken at intervals
kill currently dividing cells

FIGURE 28-3

started giving adjuvant chemotherapy, we gave the treatments over a two-year period. Later, studies showed that six months was as good as a year, which was as good as two.[1] The extra treatment may have actually harmed the immune system, without having had any additional effect on the cancer. There probably is a certain key dosage or duration beyond which any additional drug is useless, but it hasn't been determined yet.

The other kind of systemic therapy is the use of hormones, or hormonal manipulations to change the body's own output of hormones, in order to affect the growth of hormonally sensitive tumors. This can include surgical procedures such as *oophorectomy* (removing the ovaries), radiating the ovaries, using drugs that block hormones, or even using hormones themselves. We don't fully understand why these hormonal treatments work, but there is no question that they do work well in certain patients. Since hormone therapy affects only hormonally sensitive tissues, its side effects are more limited than those of chemotherapy. It hasn't the same effect on other growing cells, such as hair and bone marrow. The goal, however, is the same: to kill cancer cells or prevent them from growing.

Systemic therapies are used at two different points in the natural history of breast cancer. The first is at the time of diagnosis, when it's called adjuvant therapy. The second is at the time of recurrence elsewhere in the body, when the cancer has metastasized. We will discuss the latter in Chapter 31.

When there is a possibility that you'll need systemic therapy, you'll want an appointment with a medical oncologist, or cancer specialist, who specializes in systemic treatment. After talking with you at length, and reviewing your records, the doctor will decide what systemic program you need and what your options are. These options may vary from place to place. There are general guidelines for breast cancer treatment, drawn up by a group of nationwide breast cancer specialists. At UCLA we have developed our own specific guidelines to cover many situations. The field is always changing, however, and it is important that you check with several doctors before you settle on a treatment. You'll want the advantage of the most up to date information. You may also want to become involved in a protocol or clinical trial (see Chapter 33).

There are many well-trained medical oncologists throughout the country now, and you can usually get very good treatment close to home. You may, however, want to get a second opinion about chemotherapy or hormone therapy at a cancer center prior to starting (see Appendix D for a list of comprehensive cancer centers). Sometimes the cancer center and your local medical oncologist can work together in designing and supplementing your treatment, giving you the best of both worlds.

Your doctor or medical team will also discuss with you the role of systemic treatment in your overall treatment, the expected toxicity (side effects), and how the side effects will be managed. Before you make a decision together with the doctor and sign a consent form, all these things must be made very clear to you.

The time spent on this depends on the institution and the particular doctor or nurse you're dealing with. Ideally, you'll spend an hour or so, since the information is extremely detailed. Susan McKenney, a nurse practitioner I used to work with at the Dana Farber Cancer Institute, also gives the patient a written description of everything she needs to know. "I like to translate the information from a didactic, medical form to a written, easily understandable explanation that she can take home and look over at her own convenience; often this is the consent form for a protocol. It's hard to take that much in at one time, and the patient is often overwhelmed—she's dealing with the unknown. I've had a patient sit with me for a hour and the next week when she comes in for her treatment she can't tell me the names of the drugs she's going to get." Often oncologists will spend a lot of time explaining chemotherapy and very little on the side effects, risks, and complications of tamoxifen. Make sure you understand exactly what drugs you are getting, how you will be getting them, and what side effects you can expect.

In addition, says McKenney, it's difficult for a patient to feel that chemotherapy or hormone therapy is really going to help her, because she's being told about all the unpleasant things it may do to her in the process. She needs time to assimilate the information about the side effects she'll have to deal with, and written information helps her do this.

You might also want to review the Wellness Community Physician/Patient Statement in Appendix F and discuss it with your doctor.

We have discussed the decision-making process and options for adjuvant therapy at length in Chapter 23. Now we will look at the actual experience of receiving chemotherapy or hormone therapy.

Adjuvant Chemotherapy

Once you've signed a consent form for chemotherapy, you'll be scheduled to come in for your treatment. It may be in a hospital, a clinic, or your doctor's office. A blood sample is usually taken to check your blood count before your treatment, to help the doctor or nurse know whether or not your body is capable of taking chemotherapy—and as a baseline for comparison later. Your initial dose is determined by your body surface area (height and weight). This is a good guess, but it's rarely perfect.

The bone marrow's recovery rate helps the doctor adjust the dosage of drugs—a process known at titration. We check to see if the marrow has recovered by doing a blood count. A high blood count means that the dose of chemotherapy is probably too low for you and you will be given more. If your count is too low then the dose is probably too high and needs to be lower. Sometimes when the count is too low you will have to wait for a day or two before treatment to allow your bone marrow more time to recover.

Think of the bone marrow as a factory churning out red blood cells, white blood cells, and platelets. Chemotherapy injures half the factory's employees, and the factory doesn't work as well till they're all recovered. Recently, however, we've discovered some drugs that help accelerate the recovery of the patient's bone marrow—keeping all the workers healthy so the factory can get back on track.

The major drug we have for this is GCSF (granulocyte cell stimulating factor). GCSF is a natural product that you normally have in your blood. Its function is to stimulate the bone marrow to make more white blood cells in times of stress or infection, when you need to build up your immune system. Now we've found a way to utilize this in chemotherapy treatment.[2] It's a natural product, which we made from bacteria through genetic engineering. We found when we give it to someone, it whips their bone marrow, so that instead of having a normal white blood cell count of 10,000, they have forty or fifty thousand. So now, when a woman's white blood cell count becomes too low, we give her GCSF in an injection and it hastens the bone marrow's recovery. So it's like operating on those factory workers with the injury and getting them back to work. GCSF is thus able to reduce the time it takes your bone marrow to recover following chemotherapy.

Blood counts are taken throughout the course of your therapy, generally once a week, before and after therapy. When your white blood count is low you have an increased risk of infection, although interestingly enough this doesn't usually include colds; if your platelets are very low you are at an increased risk of bleeding (this is actually quite rare).

If your treatment begins the day the blood count is taken, you'll have to wait for 15 to 45 minutes for the treatment to begin. In any event, you'll probably have to wait while the drugs are being mixed. Again, this depends on the practice in your institution. Though the wait may be annoying, it can also be an advantage: often this is an opportunity for women to talk to each other and find support in being together. (Or, if you'd rather, bring along a book or magazine.)

Chemotherapy treatments are usually given in 21-day cycles or in 28-day cycles. If it's a 21-day cycle you come in for an injection every three weeks. On a 28-day cycle you come in for treatment on day 1 and day 8, and then go two weeks with no therapy. That's two weeks with therapy and two weeks off. During this time, your treatment may be all intravenous, or a combination of intravenous medicine and pills, taken orally at home. The treatments can last anywhere from 12 weeks, to six months, to a year of chemotherapy.

Treatment areas vary from hospital to hospital. Sometimes there's an entire floor for oncology patients, sometimes just a separate area of a larger floor. Chemotherapy can also be given in a private doctor's office. Everyone is aware of the anxiety level of patients, and will try to make the area as comfortable as possible. Since the process doesn't involve any machines, it doesn't look as intimidating as the radiation area. The room will be comfortably lit, and often has television sets or stereos in it. You may have a room to yourself, or be sitting with several other patients who are getting their treatments. You'll sit on a comfortable lounge chair for the procedure (Fig. 28-4). Many patients bring a book or a Walkman. If your treatment is a long one, and there are no TV sets, you might want to invest in one of those tiny, checkbook-sized TV's and watch your favorite talk show or soap opera during your treatments. Or, if you have easily transportable paperwork for your job, you can work while the treatment is in progress. If you like to have a friend or family member with you, most hospitals and doctors will permit that.

The length of time a treatment takes, and the intervals at which treatments are given, will vary depending on the type of drugs being used, the institution giving you the treatment, and the protocol. Many

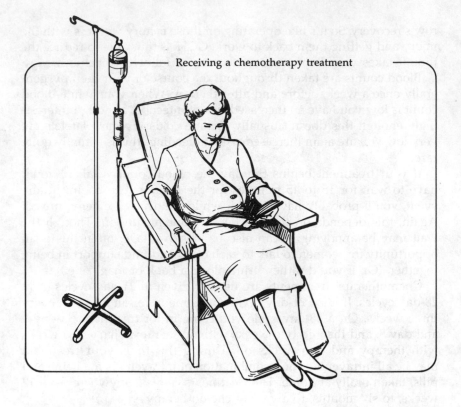

Receiving a chemotherapy treatment

FIGURE 28-4

different combinations of drugs may be used, each requiring a differ-ent time length for administration; in addition, you may be given extra fluid to control nausea and vomiting. All of this affects how long a treatment takes. Sometimes a treatment will last 10 minutes; some-times it will last three or four hours.

The treatments are given either by your medical oncologist or by a specially trained nurse. There's nothing particularly painful about the treatment itself, which feels like any IV procedure. The chemicals come in different colors—in breast cancer, the drugs we use are usu-ally clear, yellow, and red; there's a blue drug we also use sometimes.

You usually don't feel the medications going inside you, though some patients do feel cold, if the fluids are run very fast or if they're cold to begin with, and if the patient's body is especially sensitive to cold. The doctor or nurse will always be there with you, and they're both highly trained specialists in chemotherapy. Sometimes the drugs irritate veins and cause them to clot off and scar (sclerose) during the course of the treatment. This will make it very hard to get needles into the veins.

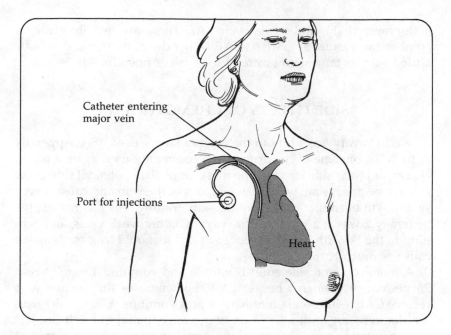

Catheter entering
major vein

Port for injections

Heart

FIGURE 28-5

There's a procedure that has existed for some time, but lately we're doing it far more frequently than we used to. This is the use of what we call a central access device, either a portacath or a Hickman line—a catheter-type device placed under the skin into a major blood vessel (Fig. 28-5). Needles can go in and out of the device and spare the patient the discomfort of having peripheral veins (the ones close to the surface, that are normally used for needles) stuck. It's important to make sure the catheter is inserted in the side of the body away from the affected breast, in case you eventually have a mastectomy. This involves a surgical procedure, usually done under local anesthetic. It can be quite uncomfortable, but it's a trade-off. Patients like the fact that they don't have to get stuck with a new needle each treatment, but on the other hand it can feel fairly strange to have the catheter sticking out of your body for several months. The other problem is that the catheter is a foreign body, and on rare occasions can cause an infection. It needs to be flushed every so often with a blood thinner, so it doesn't clot. For most women, the decision to use or not use a catheter is reasonable either way, but it is essential for a patient who has a lot of trouble with her veins, and for a patient who is getting a bone marrow transplant (discussed later in this chapter).

There are four drugs commonly given in adjuvant chemotherapy for breast cancer: cyclophosphamide (Cytoxan) (C), methotrexate (M),

5 fluorouracil (F), and Adriamycin (A). These are usually given in combinations either as CMF or CAF. Other drugs (hormones) may be added such as tamoxifen or prednisone (see Appendix A).

SIDE EFFECTS OF CHEMOTHERAPY

Side effects vary according to the drugs that are used. (See Appendix A for a list of some of the drugs most commonly used against breast cancer and their side effects.) The most immediate potential side effect concerns Adriamycin, which can leak out of the vein and cause a very severe skin burn that could require skin grafting. For this reason, it's generally given in a very specific way: avoiding weak veins, and running in the IV with lots of fluids, so that if it should leak out it won't cause as much harm.

A more common side effect is nausea and vomiting. Overall about 20 percent of women who get CMF, and more of the women who receive CAF, will complain of nausea and vomiting. Usually the nausea doesn't start until four to six hours after the injection. It can last anywhere from a few hours to two days, and can come in waves at varying time intervals, or remain constant the whole time—again, this happens differently for each person, and we can't predict in advance how it will work for you.

We've got a lot of new drugs to treat nausea, one of which is Zofran. Zofran works extremely well for most people, so the days of constant horrible nausea and vomiting are becoming history. Unlike the older anti-nausea drugs, Zofran doesn't make you feel spacey or depressed and out of it. I used to have patients who felt so awful on the anti-nausea drugs that they felt better toughing it out, so they could be functional when they weren't throwing up. One of my own patients who underwent chemotherapy several years ago still gets waves of nausea when she runs into any of the doctors or nurses who worked with her, though she found them very helpful and supportive.

Because the thought of chemotherapy can be frightening, it is a good idea to bring someone with you for your first treatment to see how well it goes and, if you've come by car, to do the driving if necessary. Then if the first treatment goes well and you feel all right afterward, you may not need anyone for the following ones. Usually, if you start off feeling all right and your anti-nausea drugs are effective, you'll probably get through the rest of the treatments with relative comfort.

In addition to the drugs, some hospitals, like the Beth Israel in Boston, incorporate such anti-stress mechanisms as visualization, imagery, and relaxation techniques into their treatment program. They have found that these techniques are often very effective. If your hospital or doctor doesn't offer such techniques, you might want to try some of the techniques discussed in Chapter 29 or read some of the books suggested in Appendix B. Many of the techniques are simple and easy to teach yourself. In addition, many adult education centers and holistic health institutes in cities and towns all over the country have visualization programs. Acupuncture and Chinese herbs, also discussed in Chapter 29, have proven effective in nausea relief.

Sometimes chemotherapy causes you to lose your appetite (anorexia, which is different from anorexia nervosa). In spite of this and the nausea, 21 percent of women will have some weight gain while on treatment—gains of between 5 and 15 pounds.[3] Food may taste different to you, and some chemicals interact badly with certain foods, though both loss of appetite and chemical interaction are less common with breast cancer drugs than with others. The National Cancer Institute puts out a helpful recipe booklet for people whose eating is affected by their chemotherapy. You may also experience peculiar odors. Barbara Kalinowski, who co-facilitates a support group for women with breast cancer in Boston, describes one woman who talked of constantly walking through her house opening windows so she could get rid of the odor, which she described as similar to the smell of a new car.

Fifty-seven percent of premenopausal women will have hot flashes while on treatment. The drugs can create a chemically induced menopause, with hormonal changes, hot flashes, emotional mood swings, and no period. If you're under 40 your period will probably come back, but if you're close to menopause to begin with, it may not. If you do experience early menopause, you will of course be infertile. If your period comes back you can still conceive. Since it is difficult to tell which group you are in it is wise to use mechanical birth control while on treatment. (See Chapter 30 for a further discussion of the treatment of menopausal symptoms.)

Chemotherapy treatments used in breast cancer, as in many other cancers, often cause either partial or total hair loss. This is somewhat predictable according to the drugs used and the duration of treatment. Those women who get Adriamycin as part of their treatment will always lose their hair, usually fairly soon after the onset of the treatment. On the other hand, those women who receive CMF will only sometimes lose their hair; it will occur about three weeks after treatments have begun, and it won't fall out all at once. You'll wake up one morning and find a large amount of hair on your pillow or in the shower, or you'll be combing your hair, and notice a lot of hair in the comb. This is almost always traumatic for patients, and it is probably wise to buy a wig before your treatment starts. It's best to go to a hairdresser or wig salon at the start of the treatment, so that the hairdresser can know what your hair usually looks like and how you like to wear it—it makes for a better match. Often, women don't end up having to use the wigs they've bought. But patients who haven't prepared in advance for the hair loss have a difficult time emotionally if their hair does fall out.

Remember, though, it isn't only the hair on your head that falls out. Pubic hair, eyelashes and eyebrows, leg and arm hair—all the hair on your body will fall out. Most of the time that isn't too much of problem cosmetically—you can draw eyebrows on with pencil, for example—but it can be startling if you're not prepared for it.

It may take a while after the treatments have ended for your hair to grow back. Usually a little down begins to form even before your treatments have ended, and within six weeks you should have some hair growing in, though the time depends on how fast your hair normally grows. Sometimes, though rarely, it will come back with a different texture—curly if it's been straight, or straight if it's been curly. It may come back in a different color, most commonly gray or black.

Some women experience sexual problems, often related to the frequently occurring vaginal dryness. Some of the chemicals can interact badly with an IUD, causing infection. And you may suddenly encounter problems with your diaphragm, if that's the birth control form you're using. In addition there are the physical and psychological effects of the treatment. It's hard to feel sexy when you are throwing up and bald. This is a time when it's important for you and your partner to communicate your feelings and needs and to try and find a comforting compromise. (See Chapter 30 for a discussion of sexual issues and breast cancer).

Other common side effects include mouth sores, conjunctivitis, runny eyes and nose, diarrhea, and constipation. You may have bleeding from your gums or nose, or in your stool or urine, though this is unusual. You may get headaches. Any of these can be mild or severe, or anything in between.

The long-term side effects include chronic bone marrow suppression and second cancers, especially leukemias. This risk is certainly small—.5 percent in the NSABP series—and probably worth the benefit of the treatment, but it's important to remember that no drug is without its long-term effect.[4]

Adriamycin in particular can be toxic to the heart. We assume that it's dose-related. It's possible that there are also long-term cardiac effects that we don't yet know about. For example, some of the people who were treated with Adriamycin several years ago[5] for childhood cancers are experiencing heart failure and need heart transplants. We're only beginning to consider this now because in the past we used Adriamycin only for metastatic cancers, and those patients usually died of the cancer within a few years. Now that we're using it more frequently for women with negative lymph nodes, the patients may well be alive in 20 or 30 years, and we may see more side effects than we did before. It is important not to assume that a drug or treatment that is relatively safe at the time will be safe over the long haul. We saw this in the radiation studies discussed in Chapter 27: radiation treatments that seemed safe at the time turned out to cause serious health problems in later years. The same thing might well happen with drugs like Adriamycin. I've seen at least one patient who ended up with a heart transplant because of heart disease she'd developed after being treated with Adriamycin. I'm not suggesting that we abandon all use of Adriamycin for adjuvant treatment—my patient, after all, survived long enough to get her heart ailment. Adriamycin is one of the best drugs we have to treat breast cancer. If it is indicated it should certainly be used. But we should not use it indiscriminately in women who are not at such high risk.

Though there's no way to know in advance for certain how you'll react to your treatments, your doctor or nurse can tell you how people who've been treated with the drugs you're on have done in the past.

While it's important to be prepared for the possible side effects, it's equally important not to assume you'll have all, or even any, of them. This assumption can intensify, and sometimes even create, the symptoms. Often people will see your side effects from the chemotherapy as signs that your illness is getting worse, and contribute to your own negative feelings. Bernie Siegel,[6] the doctor who has worked so intensively with mental techniques to reduce pain and help heal diseases, reports in his book *Love, Medicine, and Miracles* on a study done in England, in which a group of men were given a placebo and told it was a chemotherapy treatment. Thirty percent of the men lost their hair.

Most chemotherapy treatments are given on an outpatient basis. You will soon know whether you are going to feel sick and, if so, on which day the nausea hits and how sick you will feel. Many women are able to continue their normal lives with minor adjustments while receiving treatments. You won't feel great, but you'll be functional.

It may, however, be a good time to take up your friends' offers of help. A ride to your treatment can be wonderful: both for the company and the release from worry about traffic and parking. Child care may well give you a breather in a stressful time, as can offers to cook dinner or clean the house. Most friends and family members really do want to help, and this may well be the best time to use all their support.

Don't expect to feel perfect the minute your last treatment is over. Your body has been under a great stress and needs time to recuperate.

It often takes six months or even a year before you feel perfectly normal again. It will happen, however, so don't despair. (See Chapter 30 for a discussion of rehabilitation after breast cancer.)

Bone Marrow Transplant

Although adjuvant chemotherapy has had some success in reducing the mortality of breast cancer, there are still some subgroups of patients in whom it has worked less effectively. These are women with very large tumors (larger than 5 cm.), locally advanced cancer, or cancer with more than 10 positive nodes. For such women, the treatment of high-dose chemotherapy with *stem cell rescue*—still popularly known as bone marrow transplant—has been used experimentally. Although the use of this treatment has yet to be proven better than standard therapy, it is being used now in a variety of experimental protocols. Therefore we will explain what it is like here.

As we mentioned in Chapter 23, there have been many advances in the delivery of high-dose chemotherapy with stem cell rescue, but even with these improvements the process isn't a comfortable one. According to Stephanie Chang, a clinical nurse specialist who works with stem cell rescue protocols at UCLA, the process is always extremely difficult for the patient.

At every center that does the procedure, pre-screening workups are done on the patient to make sure she has no problems with her heart or other vital organs, so that her body can withstand the assault it is about to go through. Once it's determined that she's in good enough health, the process begins. Depending on the particular protocol, details may differ, and if you're getting an actual bone marrow transplant, which can happen on certain protocols, the difference is probably particularly notable, especially in terms of time lengths.

In the UCLA program run by Dr. John Glaspy the patient begins with seven days of growth hormone injections which will cause the bone marrow's stem cells to be produced extremely quickly. With this rapid growth, the cells will spill out from the marrow itself into the periphery of the bloodstream. During the last three days of injections, they collect these stem cells through a special apheresis catheter located on the chest wall. Lisa, one of my patients who had stem cell rescue in 1993 in one of the UCLA protocols, describes this part of it as "like a transfusion—your blood goes out of one arm [actually the port of the catheter] and into another [port], and on the way out the stem cells are culled and saved in bags."

All this is done on an outpatient basis, and no general anesthetic is needed since they're not going into your bone marrow itself at this stage. You do have some side effects, Chang cautions. These may include headache and back pain. You're also likely to be very tired. While some patients continue going to work at this time, Chang advises against it.

On the eighth day of the program, after the collecting is finished, you're admitted to the hospital (again, this will vary depending on the institution and on the specific chemicals being used). At this stage, you're in a private or semi-private room, but not yet in isolation. The next morning, the chemotherapy treatments begin. The drugs used at UCLA are cyclophosphamide (Cytoxan), cisplatin, and carmustine (BCNU). They may last between three and eight days, again depending on the institution and the particular drugs. "Patients often ask me if the duration of the chemotherapy has any effect on survival rates," Chang says. "It doesn't. You won't live any longer if you get a drug for eight days. It depends on what the drug is and how effective it is against the tumor."

When the chemotherapy is finished, there is a day when nothing is done, because they need to make certain the chemicals are all excreted from your body. Your stem cells are given back to you 24–48 hours after the last date of chemotherapy. They can be given over one day or multiple days depending on the protocol. At about this time, you're moved into an isolation room. The room itself can be depressing, no matter how cheerful the staff and the patient herself try to make it. "I was relieved to get into the hospital itself," Lisa says. "But I hated that little room. Weeks without fresh air, just being in this little room all the time."

It takes a little while for the blood counts to start dropping, but when they do, many patients begin to experience symptoms. "Not all women get all the same symptoms," Chang says, "and there's no way we can predict who'll get which." Some women have nausea or diarrhea. They begin to feel a fatigue, which intensifies as the days go on and their blood count begins to drop. It's much worse than the fatigue associated with standard chemotherapy, says Chang, because it involves between five and ten times the dosages. Most begin to feel severely depressed, probably in part a physical reaction to the chemicals and in part an emotional reaction to the whole process. "They're very tearful, very depressed, very frightened."

Most institutions permit the patient to have someone sleep in the room with them, and provide a cot or a lounge chair for that purpose. Chang emphasizes the importance of this, especially at this stage of depression and fear. It can be a spouse, a relative, or a friend—whomever you feel close enough to lean on for support at this stage.

When the bone marrow is finally all wiped out and your counts are at their lowest, about seven to ten days into the process, you feel completely drained. "I wasn't in pain at all," Lisa says. "It's just like this overwhelming flu. You have the biggest case of the blahs. I couldn't read. My husband brought videos and we watched some of those, but I couldn't concentrate even on those. " She lost her appetite, as most patients do by this stage, and the food she was permitted didn't help. "It's all tasteless, bacteria-free food out of a can—nothing fresh because it might have bacteria. But it's important that you eat, so you force yourself."

Most patients have a fever during this time, anywhere up to 104 degrees. Many have bleeding problems because their bone marrow isn't producing platelets or red blood cells. They may have nose-bleeds, they may bleed from the bladder or rectum; even, rarely, internally in the brain. With some chemicals, there are ulcerations in the mouth that prevent the patient from being able to eat or talk.

Even without painful or frightening symptoms, however, all patients experience the fatigue, and with it, extreme boredom. "You're climbing the walls," my patient says. "There's a chart on the wall, and every day they count your white blood cells. Each day they take your blood and record it on the chart, and so the highlight of the day is when they take your blood, because you know that when it's high enough you'll get to go home." Other women, says Chang, are "so fatigued, they don't care about the isolation."

Again depending on the hospital, your room may have cheerful pictures on the wall, and a television and VCR. At UCLA and some other programs, the VCR has more than just an entertainment function. They suggest you listen to relaxation tapes, and there are specialists who work on relaxation techniques with the patient.

There are some practical things you can do to make your experience easier on you. Chang recommends having an answering machine on your phone in the isolation room, with a message saying something like, "Hi, I'm grateful for your call, but I'm not answering the phone right now. Someone will call you later with a progress report." It's also wise, says Chang, for your family to put a message on the answering machine at home, giving updates on your condition and letting people know you'll get in touch with them after you leave the hospital.

You may have a plastic catheter in your hip, like my patient did. There is a large vein in the groin; the chemo goes through this vein and the blood comes out through it.

During this time, you can have visitors—the number of visitors and length of visits permitted will vary according to the institution's policy, but most patients want short visits from a few people anyway. "The visitors you want are those you don't have to thank for coming,"

Chang says. "You should be able to be nasty or fall asleep on them, or whatever." They can't bring live flowers, but silk flowers, balloons, and other gifts are fine. At UCLA, patients are encouraged to have their children visit, and Chang thinks it's important to allow your children to see the room and get a sense of the process at least once, to demystify things for them.

At UCLA, visitors must wash their hands, but no other sterilization procedures are required. Other institutions may make visitors wear masks and gowns, or even be in laminar flow rooms—"You know, like the boy in the plastic bubble," Chang says.

You'll be in the hospital for about three weeks, depending on how soon your blood count rises to normal rates again and on what symptoms you've developed. When you go home, it will take a while to recover. "The first few weeks can be hard," Chang says. "You're still very fatigued; it's still hard to concentrate. And after all that time in isolation, you feel bombarded by normal stimulation. It's like shell shock." You may also have complications—Lisa had a lung infection that affects 30 percent of patients on the chemicals she was given. Even without complications, it will take about three weeks to begin feeling better, and three months to be back to normal. In addition, depending on the particular program you're on, you may have further treatment—radiation and/or surgery.

Eventually, however, you do recover from the chemotherapy. A year after her transplant, as this book was being written, Lisa was living a normal, comfortable life. "It's hard to believe I was going through that hell a year ago," she says.

You also continue to live, as every woman with breast cancer does, with the understanding that the cancer may still recur. "There are no guarantees," as my patient says. "But for me, for that 15 percent improved chance of survival, it was worth it."

Adjuvant Hormonal Therapy

In terms of its administration, tamoxifen is the simplest of the breast cancer therapies. You don't need to go anywhere or have anything done to you—you simply take a pill. Tamoxifen is usually taken twice a day, 10 milligrams in the morning and another 10 at night, but there's no reason they have to be taken that way. If it fits better with your lifestyle, you can take the two pills together.

Because we tend to look at tamoxifen in relation to chemotherapy, we often say that it has no side effects. And indeed, compared to chemotherapy, its side effects are fairly mild. But it does have side effects, and for some women these can be quite significant: phlebitis, pulmonary emboli, visual problems, depression, nausea and vomiting, hot flashes, and others. A lot of women who have these symptoms ask me if they could be from the tamoxifen. When I say yes, they say, "Thank God—I thought I was going crazy because my doctor said I wouldn't have side effects."

It's wrong to assume tamoxifen should always be used because it is comfortable and risk-free. First, as my colleague Dr. Craig Henderson is fond of saying, a nontoxic therapy is not justified just because it's nontoxic. Second, and probably more important, we don't actually know that it is nontoxic. It doesn't have many immediate side effects, but the potential for long-range problems is real.

The most common of the side effects are hot flashes—and they occur in about 50 percent of women on tamoxifen. They can be severe or mild, just like any hot flashes. They eventually go away, but "eventually" may be years.

About 30 percent of women on tamoxifen will get major gynecological discomfort—anything from vaginal discharge to severe vaginal dryness.

A small percentage of women get severely depressed. It can be insidious, very slow in onset, so you don't realize it's happening until you're in the midst of a horrible depression. When you get off the tamoxifen, the depression lifts. It may be that this is more prevalent in women who are prone to PMS and postpartum depression—susceptible to hormonal mood swings.

There's some evidence that tamoxifen may, in unusual cases, increase thrombophlebitis, a form of phlebitis in the leg in which the vein gets irritated and forms clots.[7]

The most serious side effect of tamoxifen has recently been identified—uterine cancer. A large NSABP study looking at the use of tamoxifen has reported eight deaths from uterine cancer that developed in the women on tamoxifen.[8] The risk is higher the longer the women are on the drug. This is not surprising, since the uterus is one of the places where tamoxifen acts like estrogen, and thus, like estrogen alone, can cause uterine cancer. For women who have had hysterectomies this isn't a problem, but it's a risk to others. There has been much discussion in the breast cancer field about how this new risk should be dealt with. Some are recommending endometrial biopsies or vaginal ultrasounds on all women on tamoxifen. I think this is a bit much. The risk is only 1 in 1,000, and is usually indicated early by abnormal bleeding. I think that a routine gynecological exam once a year is probably adequate. Some gynecologists prescribe progesterone with tamoxifen on the theory that since progesterone protects the uterus from cancer in women on Premarin it should be used here as well. The trouble is that we have no data on the safety of progesterone in women with or without breast cancer. I would be very reluctant to add yet another unknown drug to the mix. But anybody who is on tamoxifen who has any kind of vaginal bleeding should get it checked out.

In rats, tamoxifen causes liver cancer. But that doesn't tell us too much, since in rats almost any estrogen causes liver cancer. Many women on tamoxifen experience some eye problems, including blurry vision, as well as headaches and loss of appetite. There's some concern that in premenopausal women, because tamoxifen stimulates the ovaries and increases estrogen and progesterone levels, it may increase the incidence of ovarian cysts and stimulate ovulation while blocking estrogen in the breast. This means that if you're heterosexually active you should consider using some type of barrier contraceptive while taking the drug.

It's interesting to note that for all of these bad effects, there are a few bonuses. Tamoxifen improves your high-density lipoproteins and your low-density lipoproteins, which may make you less likely to get heart disease.[9] For women between 50 and 94 the cumulative risk of heart disease is 31 percent; the cumulative risk of breast cancer is 2.8 percent. (See Chapter 14 for an explanation of risk statistics.) Put another way, scary as the 1-in-9 statistic for breast cancer is, the lifetime risk of heart disease for women is 1 in 3. So while treating your breast cancer, you may also be lowering your chance of heart disease. Tamoxifen certainly doesn't make osteoporosis worse—sometimes it makes it better, and sometimes it stabilizes it.[10]

The third good thing about tamoxifen is that, while it treats the cancer you have, it reduces your chance of getting cancer in the opposite breast from 15 percent to 10 percent. So considering all these pros and cons, you need to weigh the risk of uterine cancer, depression, and other side effects versus the risk that your breast cancer will recur and that you'll acquire heart disease.

One of the questions about tamoxifen is when to stop taking it. Initially people were saying you should take it for five years, but the more recent thinking has been that you should continue it for the rest of your life, with the idea, noted earlier, that it only temporarily stops cancer growth. But there's the worry that we may be setting ourselves up for cancers that are resistant to tamoxifen, so that then if you develop a second cancer or a recurrence, and you've been taking tamoxifen continuously, you develop a worse recurrence. Now, with the recent data on uterine cancer, many specialists are opting for only five years of tamoxifen. This remains a controversial area. In this country tamoxifen is a very expensive drug. However, a generic variant has just come on the market.

At one time there was the suggestion in premenopausal women that, to be effective, tamoxifen had to induce menopause. If their periods didn't stop we'd double the dose. There's no evidence, however, that a higher dose works any better. In fact, tamoxifen doesn't put premenopausal women into menopause—it increases estrogen and progesterone.[11] I had one poor woman who came in to see us at UCLA. She had had chemotherapy and then her oncologist had started her on tamoxifen. When her period didn't stop he'd doubled and then tripled her dose. Her side effects were horrific and her period got heavier. He told her she would just have to have her ovaries out since they were not responding to the tamoxifen. Since tamoxifen is a stimulant and not a depressant to premenopausal ovaries, it was he who was confused. We just stopped her tamoxifen and she did fine.

It takes six weeks for tamoxifen to get out of your system when you stop. So if you miss a pill one day, it isn't the end of the world. This also means that if you're going to have a biopsy for a breast lump, you need to stop taking it for six weeks to get an accurate measure of the estrogen receptor status.

There are other hormonal treatments, but they are not usually used as adjuvant treatment. They will be discussed at length in Chapter 32 on metastatic disease.

29

<hr>

Complementary
and Alternative
Treatments

Twenty years ago, if you told people you were doing daily meditation to help cure your cancer, or closing your eyes and pretending your cancer cells were dirt stains and your immune system was a scrub brush washing them away, they'd have assumed your disease had driven you completely crazy. Some people still would. But thanks to the work of physicians like Herbert Benson, Carl Simonton, and Bernie Siegel, psychologists like Stephanie Mathews-Simonton and Lawrence LeShan, and informed laypeople like Norman Cousins, there is increasing evidence that these mind-body techniques can help the body cope with the side effects of medical treatment, and in some cases, may help prolong life and even cure cancer. Many cancer patients are now combining these techniques with their regular treatments, often with their doctors' blessing, and sometimes with their doctors' participation.

Therapies involving particular diets, vitamins, and the use of herbs are also becoming increasingly popular. Almost all of these therapies are based on theories about the role of the immune system in fighting off disease, and the need to strengthen that system (see Chapter 19). Unfortunately, up to now, it hasn't been shown conclusively that any of these therapies have an effect on the immune system, but they do bear examining.

In a single chapter I can't do much more than give you a brief description of some of the most commonly used techniques, and I have drawn on the expertise of some of my colleagues to do this. If you're interested in pursuing any of these techniques further, you'll find a list of useful books in Appendix B.

Mental Techniques

There are a number of techniques that seem to work because of the "placebo effect." The placebo effect is what takes place when your mind, in effect, tells your body that it's getting a certain healing substance, and your body responds as though it were true.

For years, placebos have been used to test the effectiveness of new drugs. If, for example, we're looking to see if substance X relieves symptom Y, we take 100 randomly chosen subjects, and give 50 of them pills containing substance X and 50 of them apparently identical pills without substance X. None of the subjects knows who is really getting substance X. When we look for the results, we discover that 49 of the 50 subjects who took the substance X pills no longer suffer from symptom Y, while only 10 of the other 50 are relieved of their symptom. We now have good reason to believe that substance X indeed does cure symptom Y. But what accounts for the 10 subjects who didn't really take substance X and yet were cured? They thought they were taking it, and it had the same effect on their symptom as if they were actually taking it. In other words, your belief that a particular substance, or withdrawal from a particular substance, will relieve your condition may, in itself, cause it to do so.

This doesn't mean you're gullible or stupid or imagining things; it means that the mind affects the body in ways we don't yet fully understand, and that you're fortunate enough that the body-mind interaction is working in your favor. Norman Cousins, a pioneer in this area, and the *Saturday Review* editor whose *Anatomy of an Illness* recounts his recovery from a connective tissue disorder, devoted much of the book to the placebo effect. "The history of medication," he writes, "is far more the history of the placebo effect than of intrinsically valuable relevant drugs," pointing to the success doctors in ancient times had with such "treatments" as bloodletting with leeches and giving their patients powdered unicorn horns. He calls the placebo "the doctor who resides within," who "translates the will to live into a physical reality."[1] If a sugar pill can reduce swelling and eliminate pain in substantial numbers of people, perhaps that ability can be used directly and consciously by the mind. This is the theory behind most mental healing techniques.

There is increasing evidence of this mind-body connection. David Spiegel at Stanford ran a support group for women with metastatic breast cancer and showed that the women who participated in the support group lived on average 18 months longer than those who did not.[2] Fawzy Fawzy at UCLA did an experiment with people who had melanoma. He randomly assigned half of them to participate in a six-week group with stress reduction and support. He was able to show that the immune system's weapons, natural killer cells in the blood, were higher in the patients who were part of the support group. He also found that these patients had fewer recurrences at six years.[3]

PRAYER

The most obvious mental technique is one that's probably very familiar to you—prayer. For centuries, people of all religions have believed in the power of prayer—and for some of them, it seems to have worked. In spite of the fraudulence of some charismatic healers, many are sincere; more to the point, the deep faith people bring to these services may have an effect on their actual ability to heal. Estelle Disch, a Boston-area therapist who has worked with many cancer patients, is not herself a believer in Christian theology, but she has seen the belief work for others. "A deeply religious Catholic woman I know has bad colon cancer," she says, "and she goes to every charismatic healing service she can find. I firmly believe her faith has kept her alive. If you're praying for health, on some level you're seeing yourself as healthy, and I believe that makes a difference." I know that many of my patients pray for their recovery and I am certain it helps them. Believing that there is a power that can make you well—whether that's God, or your surgeon, or your own will—can help you to get well. Soliciting others to pray for you as well can only increase your confidence. One of my recent patients was debating how many of her friends to tell about her impending breast cancer surgery. She told me that she had decided that "the difference between bad luck and good luck is the number of people who are praying for you." Against the odds her surgery not only went well but showed that her cancer had been much more limited than anyone expected. History is full of accounts of miracles, and while we have no laboratory proof that these accounts are accurate, there are simply too many of them to dismiss. No doubt some "miracles" are fraud, and some self-delusion, but I'm convinced that some are indeed exactly what they claim to be, and that faith, of whatever sort, has played a part in their occurrence. I often pray for my patients, hoping to harness whatever forces I can to help them achieve the result which is best for them.

Recently, two separate groups of researchers have pulled together collections of scientific studies on the effectiveness of prayer, and the results are thought provoking, to say the least. Paul N. Duckro, a professor of psychiatry and human behavior at the Saint Louis University School of Medicine, looked at experimental studies conducted over 20 years and found striking examples of the effectiveness of prayer. One study looked at 18 children with leukemia, divided into two groups. Families from a distant Protestant church were given the names of 10 of the children and asked to pray for them. Fifteen months later seven of the 10 were alive, while only two of the eight children in the control group were alive.[4] *Healing Words*, a recent book by Larry Dossey,[5] former chief of staff at Medical City Dallas Hospital, reports on similar studies. In one study discussed in both works, a randomized double-blind trial of 393 heart patients at San Francisco General Hospital, half the patients were prayed for daily and half weren't. None of the patients, their doctors, or their nurses knew who were being prayed for and who wasn't. The patients who received the prayers had fewer complications and needed fewer antibiotics.

MEDITATION AND VISUALIZATION

To many people, the word "meditation" conjures up images from sitcoms: the dippy heroine sitting cross-legged on the floor, with her eyes closed, chanting "om" while her bemused friends stare at her. But meditation has been a very serious part of almost every major religion in history—Buddhism, Catholicism, Native American religions. And while there are many forms of meditation, the ones most commonly used in conjunction with healing work are variants of the very simple form in which the person sits in a comfortable position, eyes closed, focusing on the inhaling and exhaling of breath, and chanting a "mantra," a particular word or phrase. The Eastern "om" is fine if you like it, but it usually doesn't have much meaning for Americans, and you might do better to use a phrase consistent with your own beliefs—"peace," for example, or a brief phrase from a prayer used in your religion.

Herbert Benson, an M.D. who has extensively studied various forms of nonmedical healing, describes this particular form of meditation as "the Relaxation Response." He uses it as the basis of his work as director of Behavioral Medicine at Boston's Deaconess Hospital. He and his colleagues run a number of groups for people with a variety of diseases. In the late 1980s their cancer group was co-led by oncologist Leo Stolbach. "What the relaxation response can do," says Dr. Stolbach, "is to slow down or even stop the continuous chatter the mind is constantly putting us through. It gives the mind a rest from those thoughts and then a chance to deal with the issues they raise. Physiological responses occur when you elicit the relaxation response. These include a decrease in pulse, blood pressure, respiration rate, oxygen consumption, and overall metabolism. These physiological responses contribute to stress reduction."

Most programs that use meditation combine it with visualization, or imagery. This too is an ancient technique, discovered in recent years by "New Age" devotees. It's used for a variety of purposes, from finding a parking space to curing cancer. Its basis is the belief that if you create strong mental pictures of what you want, while affirming to yourself that you can and will get it, you can make virtually anything happen.

The pioneers of visualization in disease treatment were the then husband and wife team of Carl and Stephanie Simonton (an oncologist and a psychologist). Their 1978 book, *Getting Well Again*, has influenced many cancer patients as well as doctors and psychologists. In it, they recount their experiences with "exceptional cancer patients"—those who recover in spite of a negative prognosis—and maintain that their visualization techniques have significantly extended patients' lives. Equally popular has been the work of Bernie Siegel, a surgeon who has also used visualization and meditation techniques as part of his cancer treatment approach.

Though Siegel, the Simontons, and others claim their techniques have cured cancer, the evidence is chiefly what we call "anecdotal"— that is, stories of individuals or groups of individuals, rather than studies set up in controlled situations. This doesn't mean visualization can't cure cancer or prolong cancer patients' lives; it simply means that so far we have no firm proof that it does.

What studies have proved, however, is that visualization and meditation combined can reduce pain and the uncomfortable side effects of cancer treatments—we've already discussed this a bit in Chapters 27 and 28. This in itself is impressive, and combined with the possibility that it might affect the outcome of the disease itself, makes a meditation-visualization program well worth trying.

How does visualization work? Typically, you do a meditation/ relaxation exercise first, to become fully relaxed and receptive to the imagery that comes to you. Then you begin to visualize your cancer cells in terms of some concrete image—gray blobs inside your breast (or whatever area you're dealing with). Then you picture your white blood cells, or your radiation or chemotherapy treatments, as forces countering the cells (Fig. 29-1).

The Simontons have favored violent images—soldiers attacking the cells, or sharks destroying them. These images, however, aren't

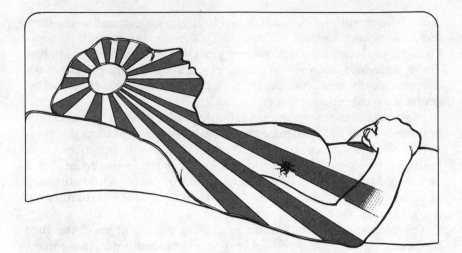

FIGURE 29-1

always right for everyone. Therapist Estelle Disch, who works with cancer patients individually and in groups, says that "many people I work with don't like violent imagery. They do better with beams of light drying up the cells, or water flowing through the area and washing the cells away." Leo Stolbach also emphasizes the importance of patients' finding the imagery that works best for them.

To help her clients find the best images for themselves, Disch works with each client separately, helping them create the imagery that feels best to them, and then makes a tape based on that discussion. This is especially helpful when people have problems with certain relaxation images. Some people relax deeply while paying attention to their breathing; others find the idea of climbing slowly down a staircase effective, and others prefer to imagine drifting or floating gently on air or water. "Obviously if someone has a fear of water, or heights, or something else, then I'd avoid using those images on the tape," she says.

Most people do relaxation and visualization images as part of a group, working on a regular basis with the group, and doing the exercises daily between group meetings. Such groups exist in different parts of the country, and in Appendix C you'll find a list of places to call to locate a group. If there is no such group near you—and even if there is—you can learn the techniques on your own. I've had patients who've used the techniques in groups and by themselves. One of my patients started off in Dr. Stolbach's group, and found it helpful in the beginning. "But what I got out of it mostly was the techniques, which I use at home on my own. I'm not much of a joiner, I guess." She is convinced that the techniques have been a useful part of her healing, and have helped her deal with the anxieties her cancer caused. "Cancer is no longer the first thing I think of in the morning, and the last thing I think of when I go to bed."

If you want to try working with the techniques on your own, there are a number of relaxation and imagery tapes you might want to try out. "I'd recommend Bernie Siegel's tapes," says Disch. "But with so many available, you might want to buy three or four, check them out, and see which feels most comfortable to you." If none of these tapes are exactly right for you, you can try creating your own. In his book *The Road Back to Health*, psychologist Neil Fiore suggests a model for creating your own visualization tape.[6]

Similar to visualization, and often used in conjunction with it, are affirmations. These are statements affirming one's value and one's intentions, recited aloud if possible, mentally if necessary. Like visualization, they can be used for any goal, from wealth to spiritual growth, and they're often used for health. One of my patients has a list of her favorites, which include "I am now willing to become free of all pain and illness," "I am now renewing my body's ability to heal itself," and "I now let the light from above heal me with love." Others prefer to frame their affirmations in terms of choice: "I choose health."

I'm told by people who work with affirmations that it's important to frame them positively rather than negatively—not "I am not staying ill," but "I am growing more and more healthy each day."

They also suggest that affirmations should be repeated regularly, and frequently. You can say them while you're taking your shower, walking to your car, or unloading your groceries. Unlike many of the other mental practices, they needn't take time from a busy schedule.

LAUGHTER

Reader's Digest has for many years had a section of humor called "Laughter, the Best Medicine." They mean it metaphorically, but when Norman Cousins set about to cure himself of his degenerative illness, he took it literally. "I discovered that ten minutes of genuine belly laughter had an anesthetic effect and would give me at least two hours of pain-free sleep," he wrote.[7] There appears to be some medical basis for this: laughter can stimulate endorphins—chemicals that act like narcotics in the brain.

Some of my patients have found that laughter is an important part of their healing process. One woman had breast cancer twice, and, along with her medical treatments and her meditation, she has worked laughter into her regime. "I told people I wanted to laugh.

Friends send me funny books, cut out cartoons, call me and say funny things," she said. Though she eventually died from her cancer, her multileveled approach to fighting it gave her the strength she needed to live her life fully to the end—including helping launch the breast cancer political movement we discuss in Chapter 34.

Certainly giving yourself time not to think about your cancer, just to escape into zany humor, can be emotionally very healing. Be sure to pick the things that make you laugh. Cousins enjoyed Marx Brothers movies and "Candid Camera" TV shows. You might prefer stand-up comedians such as Elaine Boosler, or P.G. Wodehouse novels, or "I Love Lucy" reruns—whatever makes you laugh out loud and hold your sides, totally absorbing you into its delightful nonsense.

PSYCHIC HEALING

Before you scoff at the idea of psychic healing, remember that it's been respected by some intelligent people. In his hospital in the African jungle, Albert Schweitzer often consulted with a witch doctor whose work he respected.[8] Much of charismatic Christian healing involves laying-on-of-hands, a classical psychic healing technique. And the relatively new "therapeutic touch," designed by nurses in the U.S., uses a similar approach.

I haven't had much experience with psychic healers, in terms of my own patients, but there is a fair amount of anecdotal evidence about cures through psychic healing, and a friend of mine, severely asthmatic, had a brief but dramatic improvement after a few sessions with a healer. She's not certain whether this is the result of the healer's power or of her own mind, and she doesn't care. "What I care about is breathing, and he helped me do it," she says.

Certainly if the placebo effect has any validity, there's no reason why psychic healing can't trigger it off. As long as you're not paying exorbitant sums to a psychic who guarantees a cure, a few sessions with a psychic healer won't do you any harm—and it might do some good.

Sometimes psychic healing isn't even done in person—healers and even ordinary people "send healing energy." And again, as with prayer, according to anecdotal evidence, it sometimes seems to help. One of my Jewish patients had a Catholic nun as a fellow patient at the time of her mastectomy. "Sister Cecile got all the nuns in her convent praying for me," recounts my patient. "I know that helped. Every time I've had surgery I've gotten people from every religion, every belief system, working for me—prayer, positive vibrations, whatever. I'd say, 'I'm going into surgery at 8 o'clock this Thursday, and I need your positive thoughts.'"

Whatever else such healing thoughts can do, they can achieve a twofold benefit. For the patient, it is a reminder of all the love and support that's out there for her—from friends, from loved ones, even from strangers. And for those who love her, it can alleviate some of the terrible sense of helplessness they feel in the face of a loved one's suffering. For the most part, your friends can't operate on you or administer your chemotherapy, but they can pray or send healing thoughts.

Unfortunately psychic healing has barely been studied at all by scientists, but Herbert Benson, in his *Beyond the Relaxation Response*, cites studies done in Canada by Dr. Bernard Grad that suggest the possibility that such healing, even when the subject isn't aware it's being done, may actually have an effect on illness.[9] (This echoes the studies on prayer mentioned earlier, and suggests that the placebo effect alone isn't enough to account for the effects of either prayer or psychic healing.) Hopefully, when doctors become less territorial about their healing abilities, more and more research will be done in this area.

Something else in the psychic realm to which people attribute healing powers are crystals and other stones. Many believe that these can affect different parts of your physical and emotional health, and that using them to meditate, wearing them as jewelry, or simply keeping them around can help you remain healthy, or restore health if you're ill.[10] As far as I know, no scientific studies have been done on the healing power of stones, but that doesn't mean they can't work. Some of my patients have great faith in them, and I like to keep a small collection of amethysts in my office.

My co-author, who has done some research on the popularity of healing stones, speaks of them this way: "In an age when many people don't believe in a personal God, but do believe in some kind of higher power, crystals can function like the Catholic rosary or the Jewish mezusuh. They provide a concrete symbol of your own belief in your ability to heal, but they don't tie that belief into a particular theology. And the fact that different stones are connected to different healing functions links them with the Catholic saints." According to her research, amethyst is seen as an all-purpose healer. Sugalite and tiger's eye are considered particularly effective with cancer, and moonstone with women's cancers. "But almost everyone who works with stones will tell you that the most important thing is that you feel strongly drawn to a particular stone, and that its power comes as much from your connection to it as from any outside definition of its particular function."

Some patients bring their healing stones to radiation, chemotherapy, or other frightening or unpleasant treatments; they can be very soothing. One of my patients had her favorite crystal taped to her hand during surgery. Another carried her sugalite with her to her chemotherapy treatments, and held it to the parts of her body that the chemicals most negatively affected.

My co-author recommends a touch of common sense in regard to healing stones. "If a salesperson tells you that a $100 crystal is more powerful than a $10 one, you might want to take your business elsewhere. Stones aren't capitalists; if they really can heal, I don't think their ability will be limited by their price-tag or their karat count."

As the evidence of the effectiveness of all of these mind-body techniques accumulates, this section of our book will undoubtedly enlarge and the holistic (involving the whole person) approach to treatment will become the norm rather than the exception.

Diet, Vitamins, Herbs, and Acupuncture

All the treatments I've discussed so far use purely mental or spiritual techniques—they don't involve putting any physical substance into the body. Some forms of nontraditional treatments use herbs, vitamins, or other substances, as well as particular diets believed to heal cancer.

Studies show that women who eat a low-fat diet may have a decreased occurrence of breast cancer, and others show that women who are obese at the time of diagnosis have a poorer prognosis (see Chapter 15). So there's scientific evidence to support changing your diet to a low-fat diet, and also losing weight once you are diagnosed. When I worked in Boston, I participated in a pilot study, working with a nutritionist, to see if postmenopausal women with breast cancer could reduce the amount of fat in their diet to less than 20 percent of their calories. We found that indeed they could.[11] Now I'm participating in a large national study called the Women's Intervention Nutrition Study (WINS). We have one group of postmenopausal women with breast cancer who are being put on a long-term, very low fat diet. They meet regularly with a nutritionist and have their diets monitored carefully. There is a control group of women who continue to eat whatever appeals to them, which in our culture means a very high fat diet. The patients in the study are having all the regular treatments that they would normally have; we're simply adding this dietary aspect. I think any postmenopausal woman with breast cancer who's interested in exploring this should call the PDQ (Physician's Data Query, 1-800-4-CANCER, at the National Cancer Institute) and find out whether there's a center near her that is participating in this study.

Even if you're not on a study, you can decide to integrate diet changes into your own healing work. There are many diets recommended for cancer in general, and some for breast cancer in particular, most of which are low in fat. If you decide to attempt a nutrition approach to healing your cancer, you should work very closely with your nutritionist and your physician both to create your particular diet and to coordinate it with your other treatments.

One physician who combines dietary treatment with conventional treatment is Dr. Jeanne Hubbuch, a Boston-area physician who has treated patients with a number of cancers, including breast cancer. Some of her dietary suggestions are basic ones that most nutritionists agree are helpful in preventing a number of diseases. "I try to get people to cut down on fats, especially fried food and margarine, and decrease dairy foods, sugar, and white flour. For patients with breast cancer, it's especially important to eliminate meat or chicken that's been fed hormones, because breast cancer can be estrogen dependent. Also, I try to get them to eliminate caffeine, alcohol, soda, anything with additives or chemicals. And I put in their diet vegetables, fruits, whole grains, fish, chemical-free sources of chicken." If a patient with breast cancer is overweight, she includes a reducing component to the diet, "because of the estrogen effect of stored fat. In addition, people who are lean have much more resistance to chemical toxins, probably because pesticides and other pollutants are stored in the fat, so the more fat you've got the more places you have to store them and the more burden there is on your body to detoxify them."

Hubbuch also uses a variety of vitamin supplements with her patients. She favors antioxidants like vitamin C, vitamin E, selenium, vitamin A, and beta-carotene, particularly for patients undergoing radiation or chemotherapy. She does not advise abandoning standard treatments in favor of diet and vitamin treatment, although if patients are adamant about doing only nutritional or other nonmedical treatments, she is supportive. "If a patient wants to go that route, I explain the data from different studies, and tell her that she must understand the risk she's taking by working only with nutrition—that there's a real possibility that it won't work. If a woman wants to avoid all treatments and toxic effects—chemotherapy and radiation—and only use nutritional and immune-enhancing methods, I try to help her evaluate the risks of standard treatment versus the risks of relying solely on natural methods. I think the decision about which treatments to use is intensely personal, and can only be made by the woman facing her own situation with cancer. I try to support each woman in her choice of treatments, and encourage her to include immune-enhancing methods." Hubbuch recommends that anyone interested in exploring a dietary component for her breast cancer treatment read Carlton Frederick's *Winning the Fight against Breast Cancer: The Nutritional Approach*.[12]

Macrobiotic diets have also been extremely popular with many who believe that cancer can be cured or prevented through nutrition. Based on a Zen philosophy too complex to begin to describe here, macrobiotics emphasizes whole grains, miso soup, fresh vegetables, and beans, with little fruit (only the fruit grown in your own region), and no sugar. Michio Kushi's *The Cancer Prevention Diet*[13] explains the diet in detail, and has specific suggestions for breast cancer patients, including 50–60 percent of whole-grain cereals, 5–10 percent of tamari or miso soup, 20–30 percent of cooked vegetables, 5 percent of small beans, and 5 percent of "sea vegetables." He rules out fats, iced foods or drinks, and a number of fruits. Unfortunately, unlike Jeanne Hubbuch, Kushi recommends that patients refrain from chemotherapy, radiation, or surgery. This, especially in cancer that is not yet metastatic, can be dangerous, even tragic.

The diet itself, while generally a healthful one, can, if too strictly followed, cause some problems for a patient undergoing chemotherapy or radiation, or recovering from surgery. It's low in calories and in protein, and when your body is depleted from these processes, that can be dangerous. If you're on a macrobiotic diet while undergoing medical treatments, make certain it's not causing medical problems— and perhaps, at least while you're being treated, you might want to modify the diet somewhat.

For many Western palates, a macrobiotic diet can be odd and unappetizing. If it's unpalatable to you, it probably won't do you any good. If a state of well-being is an essential part of getting well, as the concepts I discussed earlier in this chapter suggest, regularly eating foods you loathe can be counterproductive.

Changing one's diet, however, can be an active way to participate in one's own recovery. A patient of mine who started her macrobiotic diet when she was diagnosed with cancer is certain it played some part in her healing, and continues on a modified macrobiotic diet. "It's part of how I changed my life around in the wake of learning about my cancer, part of taking control of my body again," she says. She finds the diet comfortable and helpful.

Some branches of complementary healing involve procedures and substances not usually defined as medicine. One of these is the ancient Chinese science of acupuncture, which sees healing in terms of "meridians," energy channels that run through the body. Special needles are inserted into the meridians. Acupuncturists have worked with breast cancer patients, usually in conjunction with Western medical treatments.

Marie Cargill, a Boston-area practitioner of traditional Chinese medicine (TCM), has used acupuncture with breast cancer patients.

"What they've been using in China is a combination of Western treatments—surgery, radiation, chemotherapy—and traditional Chinese medicine," she says. "The oncologist sees a limited part. The patient is in and out, in and out, and then at the end, the patient is let go except for periodic follow-up. But meanwhile, we have a patient trying to survive. What patients do in China—and what I try to encourage here—is to put themselves under the care of a TCM practitioner all the way through the whole process." Acupuncture, she says, can strengthen the body overall, as surgery, radiation, and systemic treatments are weakening.

Cargill and many other practitioners of TCM like to combine acupuncture with Chinese healing herbs. "We usually recommend the person start herbs a few days to a week before chemotherapy or radiation, which will allay almost all the side effects, and then continue all the way through, and stay under the care indefinitely." That way the herbs can fight whatever cancer cells may still be in the body. If the cancer is advanced, or there are other health problems as well, Cargill especially recommends combining acupuncture and herbs—"acupuncture two or three times a week, at least to begin with." She tells of a patient who had both AIDS and metastatic breast cancer. "We had no illusions at that point that we could save her life, but the acupuncture and the herbs helped the quality of her life enormously." Both acupuncture and herbs, she says, can work in a threefold level. They can help all the side effects of radiation and chemotherapy—nausea, hair loss, fatigue, loss of appetite. "Cracking toxin herbs" fight the cancer itself and supplement the work of the other treatment.

Other herbs help build the immune system, which chemotherapy breaks down. There are particular herbs for breast cancer, which are different from herbs for other cancers. In addition, there are herbs to work on the depression and anxiety that often accompany life-threatening illness.

Unfortunately, it can be hard in this country to find Chinese herbs and herbal practitioners outside of a big city. Some patients find a practitioner through a friend or acquaintance, visit the practitioner once for an initial examination, and then work with the practitioner over the phone. Though Cargill feels the combination of acupuncture and herbs is the best approach, she says that acupuncture alone can work well, if it's used frequently enough.

She also suggests that women with a family history of breast cancer should start taking herbs when they're young, and should take them throughout their lives.

Another area of holistic healing often used in conjunction with acupuncture is homeopathy, which practitioners describe as a method of self-healing stimulated by very small doses of those drugs that would produce in a healthy individual symptoms like those of the disease being treated. The drugs are chosen by the patient with the assistance of a homeopathic practitioner, who may or may not also be an M.D. The substances are all legal, and over-the-counter; you can take them on your own, but it's wiser to consult with someone who's trained and can suggest remedies suited to your problem and your overall health history. Common homeopathic substances include belladona and bryonia. Ted Chapman, a homeopathic M.D. in Boston, has worked with patients who have breast cancer. He emphasizes that homeopathy doesn't cure cancer, and he doesn't recommend it in place of medical treatment. "Doctors work on the end product of the disease, and they come in from the outside. We're working from the inside, on what makes you vulnerable to your disease in the first place." Like many other adjunctive therapies, homeopathy is thought to work on the immune system, working to strengthen the patient's mind and body. It's helpful in alleviating some of the side effects of radiation or chemotherapy. The only negative side effect of homeopathy, says Dr. Chapman, is a brief aggravation of your symptoms— pain, fever, etc.—before they begin to regress.

Alternative Treatments

Some treatments have been proposed to take the place of medical treatments. Most of them have not been studied in any scientifically rigorous way and their risks and complications are largely unknown. We mention them to be complete, but I do not endorse their use.

The best known of these is laetrile, a substance made from apricot pits. It hasn't been shown to work in randomized, controlled studies, but it has a fair amount of nonscientific support. It's illegal in the U.S., and is currently being used in clinics in Mexico. Unfortunately its method of action has been misrepresented. Those who advocate its use claim that the cyanide it contains will be broken down by normal cells and not by cancer cells, thus causing the latter to die. This is not true, since neither type of cell can break down the cyanide. There have been reports of deaths from cyanide poisoning in patients taking laetrile.[14]

Another treatment is immuno-augmentative therapy, which was invented by Lawrence Burton, who practices in the Bahamas since the therapy is illegal in the U.S. It is an individualized treatment that is considered by its advocates to restore natural immune defenses against all forms of cancer.

If you are interested in researching any unproven cancer therapy I suggest that you go to your local American Cancer Society Division

Office and get statements on these treatments. These are fair and will describe exactly what is involved, as well as the known risks, side effects, opinion of the medical establishment, and any lawsuits that have been filed. Get these in addition to the material you get from the therapy's advocates. Make sure you are fully informed. Many of the alternative practitioners will say that they do not have the money to do studies. They do, however, charge a lot for their treatments. The National Institutes of Health will help them with the necessary studies if they are truly interested. It now has a Division of Alternative Medicine set up to help study some of these techniques. I do believe strongly that all treatments—be they bone marrow transplants or laetrile—need to be held to the same standard and need to be studied adequately in a randomized controlled trial.

While I don't recommend that patients take on a treatment that excludes the use of traditional treatments, I do feel that this is a highly personal decision. What risks any of us will take for what reasons depends very much on who we are and what our values are.

There are, in fact, situations when refusing traditional treatment isn't really much of a risk. There are some cancers, and some stages in the development of other cancers, when the treatments we have simply aren't very helpful. If your prognosis isn't good, and chemotherapy isn't likely to extend your life for any length of time, you may well consider that the discomforts of the treatment aren't worth the slight chance that it will cure you, and that an alternative treatment offers both better survival hope and more comfort during the remainder of your life. Audre Lorde, the poet and political activist whose *Cancer Journals* described her experiences with breast cancer, later published a book of essays, *A Burst of Light*.[15] In the title essay she describes how, when she learned her cancer had metastasized to her liver, she decided to forego chemotherapy and use "homeopathic" methods instead. When the tumor in her liver was first discovered, in February 1984, she refused even to have it biopsied, fearing the surgery would spread the cancer cells—a common, although not very realistic, fear. Instead, while in Berlin teaching classes, she went to a homeopathic doctor who treated her with injections of Iscador, a substance made from mistletoe that is believed to strengthen the immune system. Later, she continued this treatment at a homeopathic clinic in Switzerland. When a sonogram later demonstrated that she did indeed have metastatic cancer, her doctor told her, accurately, that chemotherapy could add only about a year to her life. She decided to stick with her homeopathic healing, adding visualization and meditation to the process, and determinedly living her life to the fullest. She lived until November 1992—an impressive achievement with liver metastasis, and who's to say that it wasn't because she chose a treatment that she believed in, and that

449

allowed her to remain as active as possible, doing the work to which she was so passionately committed?

As much as I wish it were otherwise, traditional medical treatments are imperfect. They are often successful, and should not be lightly discarded. But they can be supplemented, in ways we have good reason to believe may increase some patients' survival rates. Whether any of these ways is right for you, I can't say. But I recommend that you look into them, and take from them what seems helpful to you. I like the attitude of one of my patients, a 46-year-old woman whose cancer metastasized to her bone marrow, and who did remarkably well for several years. A devout Catholic, she cherished the advice of a nun who told her to "work as though everything depended on you, and pray as though everything depended on God." She had surgery and tamoxifen therapy. She also went on a macrobiotic diet, later reinforcing it with a diet of linseed oil and cottage cheese recommended by a holistic doctor in Germany. She took Dr. Stolbach's course at the Deaconess Hospital, and one of Bernie Siegel's workshops, and continued a regular meditation and visualization program. Whenever a church has a healing service, she went to it—"Catholic or Protestant, I go wherever I'll get healed," she said. She went to Lourdes with her aunt, who also had cancer ("I stayed for three days," she says. "It was a very emotional, very draining, experience—my aunt's tumor disappeared.") She carried an amethyst with her, and was interested in crystals. "Because I'm Catholic, my friends gave me a rosary made of crystal, which I carry with me all the time, so I've got the healing power of the rosary and of the crystal combined. I'm not settling for just one thing."

Though she ultimately died from her cancer, her health improved during the year she began integrating these methods into her healing work. In spite of the cancer in her bones, she went mountain climbing and cross-country skiing—and dancing.

I don't know which component of this patient's healing work did the most good, but I do know that her commitment to taking control of her healing process turned a terrifying experience into a triumphant challenge. She gave herself every chance to survive, and to live a quality existence—which she did to the end. Not everyone, of course, will have the time or energy to follow all the routes she has, but everyone can learn from her example, and use whatever techniques best suit them to make a wholehearted commitment to life.

PART SEVEN

LIVING WITH BREAST CANCER

30

Life After
Breast Cancer

You've had breast cancer, you've been treated for it, and now it's time to get on with your life. But your life has changed now, and you have to adjust to your new situation on a number of levels.

The Follow-Up

For one thing, you'll have to be dealing medically with the fact of your cancer for a long time. Usually the surgeon and/or other specialists who did your primary treatment—your mastectomy or wide excision—will follow you at regular intervals for a period of time.

At UCLA we have a follow-up program in which patients are seen every six months for the first two years and every year after that. The program includes not just exams and mammograms, but also physical therapy, nutritional counseling, psychosocial support, and involvement in research.

When we do follow-up examinations, there are a few things we're looking for. In the breast or mastectomy scar we look for lumps. We check the neck and the area above the collarbone for lumps that might indicate an enlarged lymph node, and we feel under both arms. Once a year or once every six months we do a mammogram.

In addition, I question the woman very carefully about how she is feeling physically. We check to see if she's had persistent and unusual pain in her legs or back, or a persistent dry cough, or any of the other symptoms described at length in Chapter 31. In general, if you have any new symptom that doesn't go away in a week or two, check it out. Usually, that's what my patients do anyway.

Patients are often surprised when we don't find anything on their follow-up exam. They've been waiting for the cancer to pop up again, and tend to be very anxious about examinations. Often they're especially worried on the anniversary of their original diagnosis—and my examination serves a psychological purpose as well as a medical one. We seldom find something on a follow-up that the patient hasn't already noticed.

Not all symptoms mean the cancer has spread. Women who have had cancer may also acquire other diseases as they age. Having had cancer does not make one immune to arthritis or diabetes, for example. Aside from ordinary, nonrelated problems, patients can experience changes as a result of the treatment for their cancer. Part of the reason it's important to have frequent checkups is that a breast that's been radiated undergoes a lot of changes. There will be a lumpy area under the scar and perhaps some skin firmness and/or puckering. By keeping regular track the doctor can assure the patient that the changes she's experiencing are related to the treatment—and if there's a different, more ominous change, the doctor can distinguish it from the others.

For the same reasons, your surgeon will probably want you to have mammograms every six months for a year or two, and then once a year. In addition to monitoring the treated breast, we watch your other breast for the possible development of a new cancer. Women with cancer in one breast have an increased risk of getting it in the other. This is not an inevitability: this risk is about 1 percent per year or an average of 15 percent over a lifetime.[1] (See Chapter 24 for a discussion of the second primary cancer.) There are some types of cancer that indicate a greater propensity for second cancer to develop. Cancers with a lot of lobular carcinoma in situ (see Chapter 16) have been thought to fit into this category.[2] Even in this situation, however, the increased risk to the second breast is about double, or 2 percent per year; a cumulative lifetime risk of 30 percent. Obviously the younger you are and the longer you live, the more chance you will have to develop a second cancer. If this is too scary for you, you may want to consider a preventive mastectomy on the other side (total, not subcutaneous; see Chapter 17), but I find that most women prefer close follow-up to such a drastic step. If you're considering this, it's important to remember that a mastectomy almost never removes all the breast tissue in your body, and therefore can't provide a guarantee that you won't get breast cancer again.

In addition to your regular doctor, you may be followed by your whole team—your radiation therapist and/or your chemotherapist (oncologist) might also want to check on you regularly. Some patients find this a little overwhelming, and don't want to spend all that time trekking back and forth to doctors. More typically, you'll be followed by one of the members of the team, or even by your local family doctor, if she or he has some experience with breast cancer. Health care reform may affect which kind of follow-up is available. In the near future we'll be training primary care doctors in how to follow breast cancer patients, so if something occurs that may be dangerous, they'll know to refer you to a specialist.

Some doctors still do blood tests every three months, including not only your blood count but also specific blood tests, a CEA and a CA 15-3, that they hope will catch metastatic disease at the earliest point. They don't always succeed, and I'm not sure there's much point. Unfortunately there's no evidence that such detection does you any good.[3] As we note in Chapter 32, we have no means yet to cure metastatic disease—we can, however, relieve symptoms and perhaps add a few years to your life. But there's no evidence that treating metastatic disease before it shows symptoms will give you more time than treating it after the symptoms have surfaced.[4] And in terms of quality of life, it probably doesn't do you much good to be upset by the knowledge that you have a metastasis. So these tests may actually interfere with the quality of your life without affecting its length. And they don't provide any authentic security when they turn out negative. It doesn't mean you don't have a metastasis, only that any metastasis you might have is too small to show up on the tests. This also holds true for the routine use of bone scans, chest X rays, CAT scans, and liver blood tests. So unless you're taking part in a protocol that requires regular staging tests, you may not want to have them.

The only test that is useful in terms of affecting your longevity is the mammogram. This can tell if there's a local recurrence in the breast or a cancer in the other breast.

With breast cancer, unlike some other cancers, we can't be sure that if it hasn't recurred within a few years, it won't. It's usually a slow-growing cancer, and there are people who have had recurrences 10 or even 20 years after the original diagnosis. In some ways this is similar to a chronic disease. You are never quite sure if or when it will come back again.

Time does, however, affect the likelihood of recurrence—the longer you go without a recurrence, the less likely you are to have one. So going 10 years without the cancer coming back should give you reason for optimism, if not certainty.

Lifestyle Changes

Often people who have suffered life-threatening illnesses are more aware of the importance of health than they were before, and want to invest energy into maintaining their health as much as they can.

Any sport or exercise you did before your cancer, you can do now—and you should, if you want to. If you've been a fairly sedentary person, you might want to change that. As we mention in Chapter 17, exercise has been shown to help prevent breast cancer. It can't help but benefit women after their diagnosis. Not only will you feel better but it will help you regain a sense of control over your body.

You might also want to examine your eating habits, and health habits in general. We are currently participating in a national study looking at the effect of a very low fat diet on postmenopausal women who have been treated with breast cancer. As we discussed in Chapter 29, nutrition is an important component in healing.

Since problems resulting from treatment can come up years afterward, it's important to keep records of the treatment and to have continued contact with somebody who knows about the delayed effects of treatment. An oncologist colleague of mine from Los Angeles, Dr. Patricia Ganz, says, "I've seen women 10 or 15 years after their treatment who have no records of what happened years ago. And we've had to try and reconstruct their history. Survivors need to have knowledge about what they were treated with, so they can remind their family doctor or tell any new doctor about it, and have medical records to show them."

At the end of this period, you go back to your normal activities; you look fine and, physically, you feel fine. Everybody's relieved that things are back to normal again—everybody but you. You may still be very nervous. Little things that wouldn't have bothered you before now seem ominous. That slight headache that two years ago you would have dismissed as tension—has the cancer metastasized to your brain? And what does the bruise on your arm mean—have you got leukemia now? You're now in the "I can't trust my body" stage. Well, why should you trust your body? It betrayed you once, and you know it can do it again. Every time you go for a checkup, every time you get a blood test, you're terrified. In my experience with patients, this stage usually lasts two or three years, until you've had enough innocent headaches and bruises, enough reassuring checkups and blood tests, to feel somewhat trusting of your body again.

And then, just when you are settling down and starting to forget about it, something pops up in the paper or on the news about a risk factor or new treatment, and it all comes back to you. You start wondering: was it the alcohol or the birth control pills (or whatever happens to be on today's "hit list") that caused your cancer? Or you start to regret the decisions you made, thinking, "with this new information maybe I should have done things differently." Remember, what is past is past. You can't change the way you lived your life in the past based on new information just coming to light today. And you have to comfort yourself with the realization that you probably got the best treatment that was available at the time you were diagnosed. If there are improvements in treatments now, that's wonderful—but you can't waste your energy on what might have been. Read the newspapers and keep informed if you're interested, but don't use it to torture yourself about what might have been. Gradually your perspective will return.

Though your life will never be completely the way it was before, you'll stop living in terms of your cancer. The fears and memories will come back occasionally—maybe on your yearly checkups, maybe on the anniversary of your diagnosis, maybe when you find out a friend had a recurrence. But they'll be part of your life, not the center of it.

Physical Adjustments

Unfortunately, your body doesn't always feel like it did before your cancer began. One problem you may face as a result of your lymph node surgery is lymphedema. Because it can be such a serious problem, we've devoted a section of Chapter 25 to the condition and the exercises you can do to combat it.

Radiation can cause some delayed problems. There's a side effect that can occur between three and six months after you've finished your treatment. The muscle that goes above and behind your breast, the pectoralis major muscle (Fig. 27-6), will get extremely sore. That's because the radiation has caused some inflammation, and as the muscle begins to regenerate and get back to normal, it can get sore and stiff, just as it would if you strained it in some strong athletic activity. Again, most women think that it's the cancer spreading—especially since the radiation's been over for months and they're not thinking in terms of new side effects from it. If you grab that muscle between your fingers, it will feel extremely sore.

You may also experience problems as a result of chemotherapy. As we noted in Chapter 28, chemotherapy can bring about premature menopause. This can be extremely difficult. Women who are within 10 years of a natural menopause are more likely to find themselves in permanent menopause from the chemotherapy than younger women. This can be very disconcerting, and is especially hard for a woman who may not have finished having children yet.

Dr. Ganz has been researching the subject for several years. She says, "A woman who might normally transition into menopause over a 10-year period is suddenly menopausal, and in addition to dealing with the crisis of breast cancer and the side effects of chemotherapy and radiation, she's now dealing with hot flashes, mood disturbances, sweats, vaginal dryness—all of those things." Predictably with something as individual as menopause, the experiences range from unpleasant to intolerable. "Many women don't have incapacitating experiences," says Dr. Ganz, "and some who do only have them for the first year or two and then they get better." The suddenness of the menopause makes it worse, as does the fact that we don't like treating women who have had breast cancer with estrogen therapy.

What then can be done? "We do have a number of other medications," Dr. Ganz says. "A Clonadine patch can be useful. Megace can be used to control hot flashes. For vaginal dryness there are various vaginal lubricants, like Replens, you can buy over the counter. Some women use herbs like oil of primrose. Unfortunately we don't know what pharmacological agents are in them, so some of us are reluctant to suggest them. We need to research the herbs to see if they have estrogen-like contents."

It may also be worth looking into some of the alternative treatments mentioned in Chapter 29, Chinese herbs, acupuncture, and homeopathy, all of which have been used in treating menopausal symptoms. Bioflavinoids are being used by some holistic practitioners to help alleviate symptoms.

In women who have terrible symptoms that continue after the first few years, Dr. Ganz says, you might consider taking estrogen replacement therapy (ERT). "We don't have information that estrogen does for certain cause breast cancer, and the risk may be worth it. Do you live for today or for tomorrow? It's a very individual decision." Women who are at high risk for heart disease or osteoporosis might also still choose ERT. "We may be trading off one disease for another," Dr. Ganz says.

Even a woman who is already in menopause can experience heightened problems after breast cancer. If she's been taking estrogen for her symptoms, she'll be strongly advised to stop it, and the symptoms it's controlled will probably return. To make it worse, if she's given tamoxifen, her symptoms may worsen. Again, some of the remedies Dr. Ganz suggests, or some of the alternative remedies, may help.

Our approach to estrogen replacement therapy in breast cancer has taken an interesting turn.[5] It used to be felt that women with breast cancer could never take hormones because it would be "like pouring gasoline on a fire" and would immediately cause the cancer to flare up. This was in part because most breast cancers require estrogen to grow in a test tube. We really don't have any data regarding actual use in women. Recently the trend of putting all women on postmenopausal hormones (see Chapter 15) has led us to reevaluate this premise. Physicians are noting that there are no data and have done a 180-degree switch. We used to say, "No data so don't take it." Now we are saying, "No data so it's okay." Neither approach is sensible. We need a study to look at the safety of hormone replacement therapy and estrogen replacement therapy in women who have had breast cancer to answer the question of safety.[6] Some gynecologists will say that if the tumor is estrogen receptor negative it is okay to take hormones, and if it is estrogen receptor positive it's not It is not that simple. The estrogen receptor works in a complex manner—we can't assume that lack of an estrogen receptor will make estrogen safe to take. Also, some practitioners, having jumped on the everyone-needs-something-to-prevent-osteoporosis bandwagon, will prescribe tamoxifen on the theory that it is as good as estrogen. Again, this has not been shown in any studies, and in reality tamoxifen does not treat menopausal symptoms. I don't think that women with breast cancer—or women without breast cancer, for that matter—should take postmenopausal hormones for prevention (osteoporosis or heart disease) until we have data proving that they work (see Chapter 15). If women with breast cancer have terrible symptoms they need to weigh the risks and benefits for themselves. The quality of life is important, and I am not opposed to women taking hormones for symptoms as long as they realize that we have no idea whether they are safe or dangerous.

Healing the Mind

Obviously, not all the after-effects of breast cancer are physical. You've had a life-threatening illness, and one that affects your sense of yourself as a woman. Emotional healing techniques are more varied and individual than physical ones, but there are many that have proven helpful to my patients and other women with breast cancer.

Many women find it helpful to keep a journal of their experiences, to refer to later to help them cope with their feelings. Some take their healing out beyond themselves—reaching out to other women who are going through what they've been through. Writers like Audre Lorde, Betty Rollins, Rose Kushner, and many others have written about the experience (see Appendix B for a list of first-person books). Actress Ann Jillian wrote and starred in a TV movie about her battle with breast cancer, in the hope of helping other women. Years ago, when breast cancer was still considered somehow shameful, public figures like Shirley Temple Black, Happy Rockefeller, and Betty Ford spoke out in the mass media about their experiences, hoping to encourage women to examine their breasts and have suspicious lumps checked out immediately.

It's not only famous women, or women in glamorous occupations, who can turn their work toward helping other women with breast cancer. Two of my patients are psychotherapists who now specialize in breast cancer therapy. Another has begun doing breast cancer workshops at her corporation. A sales clerk might want to work in a store selling prostheses, since she now has a special understanding that might help her customers.

If your profession isn't one that can be adapted to some form of working with breast cancer, or if you don't feel drawn toward spending your work life dealing with the disease, you can still help other women—and thus yourself—on a volunteer basis. You can become involved with Reach for Recovery (see Appendix C) or similar groups that work with breast cancer patients. You know how frightened you were when you were first diagnosed. The presence of someone who's survived the disease can be enormously reassuring to a newly diagnosed woman who only knows of people who have died from it.

You can also become involved in political action, like the work done by the National Breast Cancer Coalition (see Chapter 34). You can define the level of your participation according to your own energy, time constraints, and degree of commitment: anything from an occasional letter to your congressperson to organizing demonstrations and fund-raising events. Jane Reese Colbourne, vice-president of the Coalition, found that in her own experience political activism has been "a very good way to channel anger at the fact that you've had this disease. For me, it was the next step after a support group. Talking about it with other women was important—but I wanted to do something about it."

Finally, make sure you don't feel ashamed of what you've been through. Cancer still carries a stigma in our culture, and breast cancer can have especially difficult associations. You need to demystify it to yourself, and to others. You don't have to dwell on it, but it's not a good idea to repress it, either. You need to have friends you can talk freely to about your disease and your feelings about it; you need to know you can include it in casual conversation, that you don't have to avoid saying, "Oh, yes, that was around the time I was in the hospital for my mastectomy."

Sex

One of the least discussed subjects about life after breast cancer is sexuality. Your surgeon won't bring it up if you don't, and in fact most surgeons assume that if you're not complaining, everything must be fine. Yet most women find sex hard to talk about—especially when it concerns feelings, perhaps only half recognized themselves, about losing both their sexual attractiveness and their own libidos when they lose a part of their bodies so strongly associated with sexuality. Doctors need to learn how to open the subject delicately, in a way that doesn't feel intrusive to the woman and yet makes it clear that she has a safe place to discuss issues around sexuality that have arisen for her. I remember one surgeon who had referred a patient to me on his retirement. He said that she had surprised everyone after her mastectomy with her rapid recovery and how well she had "dealt with it." I took over the case, and in my first conversation with her found out that, however well-adjusted she seemed on the surface, she had not yet looked at her scar five years after the operation. She had never resumed sex with her husband and even dressed and undressed in the closet so he couldn't see her.

Many women have difficulties with sex and intimacy following a breast cancer diagnosis. Aside from the feeling that your body has betrayed you, there is a feeling of invasion from the treatments. All these strangers have been poking and prodding you for weeks. You can feel almost as though you've been violated, and you forget that your body can provide you with pleasure. It takes a while to feel good and in control of your body again. You need to communicate these feelings to your partner so he or she can help you in your healing.

Some women find after surgery, whether mastectomy or lumpectomy, that a sexual relationship becomes even more important in helping them to regain their sense of worth and wholeness. There may, however, be changes. One patient of mine who had had bilateral mastectomies felt that all the erotic sensations she formerly had in her breasts had "moved south," and that her orgasms were doubly good. Other women miss the stimulation from a lost breast so much that they don't want their other breast touched during sex. Dr. Patricia Ganz, who has both worked with and studied the problems of women with breast cancer, talks about the problems women who have had lumpectomy and radiation may experience. "Especially with women who had radiation a number of years ago, they often find the breast isn't as soft and beautiful as it was before the radiation." These changes in the conserved breast can carry over into their sexual relationships.

Some of the changes may be more practical than emotional. Your arm or shoulder may not be as strong on the side of your surgery, and this can make certain positions more difficult during intercourse, such as kneeling above your partner. You may feel uncomfortable lying on the side of the surgery for many months. It is important that you communicate with your partner so that together you can explore new ways of lovemaking that you both enjoy.

The chemical menopause discussed earlier in this chapter can also affect a woman's sexuality. Menopause, and aging itself, often lessen sexual desire, and when that combines with the other issues around breast cancer, a woman can find that her libido is suddenly seriously lessened. "Sometimes ovaries fail, and you become testosterone deficient," says Dr. Ganz. There are studies in which women are being given extra testosterone to reawaken their libidos. Not all testosterone is lost, however, since the adrenal gland still produces some. Dr. Ganz is now involved in studies to see whether the libido loss of women with chemically induced menopause is more severe than that of women who have experienced menopause normally.

She also adds that it's difficult to separate out the physiological and emotional aspects of libido loss. "Sex is at least partly in the brain," she says, "and the hormones circulating in the body affect the brain and thus sexual arousal. Psychological distress can affect hormones; we've found in our work that women who have a lot of psychological distress have more sexual dysfunction.

It is important to note that there are no aspects of sexual intimacy that will cause cancer or increase the chance of recurrence. Nor can cancer be "caught" by sucking on a nipple. Barbara Kalinowski, who co-leads support groups at the Faulkner in Boston, finds that "sometimes women who have had lumpectomy and radiation have a fantasy that the breast still has cancer in it, and don't want it fondled because they fear it will shake things up and send the cancer cells through the rest of the body." Even when your intellect knows such fears are groundless, your emotions may still accept them—and that's bound to have an effect on your and your partner's sexual pleasure.

Sheila Kitzinger[7] in her book *Woman's Experience of Sex* says that some women have told her that an important part of their healing process was having a brief affair. They said it was all well and good for a husband of 35 years to still love them without a breast, but they needed the confirmation that they were still sexually attractive to feel whole again. That might work for you—though on the other hand, it is likely to put a severe strain on your marriage. At the very least, however, you'll want to be in touch with whatever feelings you're having about sex, and decide which ones to act on and which ones simply to fantasize about.

This brings up another issue. If you are single and dating, should you tell or not? Again, this is an individual issue. Some women will tell a prospective lover way in advance, preferring to have it out in the open before the moment of passion. Others will wait until the last instance when there is no turning back to disclose their secret (never a good idea). For the woman who has had only a small lumpectomy, or who has had mastectomy and a very attractive and natural-looking reconstruction, the need to tell a casual lover about her situation may or may not arise. However, the need to be honest about having had cancer may be an important part of the relationship. For the woman whose surgery leaves visible alteration, dating can be a matter of concern. However, it doesn't mean you have to resign yourself to a life of celibacy. Barbara Kalinowski has found that several women in her support groups have been able to form successful new romantic relationships shortly after the surgery is over. She recalls one woman who had never married and who had a mastectomy with reconstruction in her 50s. "I got a call from her a couple of years ago. She was as giggly and happy as a teenager. 'Guess what!' she told me. 'I'm getting married!' They were planning a honeymoon in Paris and she was ecstatic." Another woman from one of Kalinowski's groups had been happily married to a man who had been wonderful to her during her treatments. Two years after her treatments, he died of a heart attack. Soon after his death she met a widower and they fell in love. "They decided not to wait," Kalinowski says, "because they both knew how chancy life was. She told me, 'We both learned that we don't want to wait for anything anymore'."

Working out these issues and feeling comfortable with yourself are all part of the healing process. If you find it difficult or if you get stuck on some issue you may well want to try some counseling. A diagnosis of breast cancer reminds you that life can be short and you certainly want to live it as fully as you can.

Pregnancy

One question that comes up frequently with my younger cancer patients is whether or not they should get pregnant once they've had breast cancer. There are two areas to consider—the ethical implications and the health-related implications.

In the not-too-distant past, doctors (who were usually male) tended to impose their own value judgments on patients and to tell them not to get pregnant until at least five years after having breast cancer. If you'd survived five years, they reasoned, there was a good chance you'd won your bout with breast cancer; otherwise, they didn't want you bringing a child you couldn't raise into the world.

This is a moral decision for the patient, not the doctor, to make, and there are two equally valid ways to look at it. Some women do indeed feel that they don't want to have a child if they're not reasonably sure they'll be around to raise it. Others feel that, even if they do die in a few years, they'll be able to give a child the love and care it needs to grow up well, and that they want to pass on their genes before they die. Having a child is never a decision to make lightly, and having a life-threatening illness complicates it further. Think it through carefully and get the thoughts of people whose opinions you respect—and then make your decision.

Can getting pregnant decrease your chances of surviving breast cancer? I wish I knew. Although there are no randomized studies, some centers that have reported on the outcome of women who have had pregnancies following breast cancer have shown no difference in survival.[8,9]

We do know that getting pregnant won't cause the cancer to spread. Either it has spread or it hasn't before you've gotten pregnant. But if you had a tumor that left microscopic cells in your body, it's possible that pregnancy, with its attendant hormones, can make them grow faster than they would have if you weren't pregnant. This could decrease the time you have left, so that, for example, if you would have died of breast cancer four years from now, you'll die in three years instead.

So the question is, do you want to take that risk? If you've had a lot of positive nodes, or a very aggressive tumor, or some other factor that increases the likelihood of micrometastases, you'll want to take that into consideration. It may be worth the risk to you, or it might not. Again, that's a very individual decision.

If you get pregnant, how will your breasts react? If you've had a mastectomy, obviously nothing will happen on the chest area where your breast was, but your other breast will go through all the usual pregnancy changes we discussed in Chapter 3. If you've had lumpectomy and radiation, the nonradiated breast will probably go through the normal changes. Radiation damages some of the milk-producing parts of the breast, so the radiated breast, while it will grow somewhat larger, won't keep pace with the other breast, and will have little or no milk production. You can nurse on one side only, if you want. The only problem with that is increased asymmetry; the milk-producing breast will grow, and will stay larger even after you've finished breast feeding. If this disturbs you a great deal, you can have the larger breast reduced later through plastic surgery (see Chapter 5). One of my patients got pregnant shortly after she finished her radiation treatments, and successfully breast-fed the baby. But one breast is now twice as large as the other. Knowing she wanted another child, she waited till after her next pregnancy to have reduction surgery. She's pregnant now, and planning to have the surgery after she's nursed her new baby.

Chemotherapy presents another set of problems. As we discussed in Chapter 28, it depresses your ovaries and stops your period. If you're close to menopause, your period will probably never come back; if you're young, it probably will. Unlike the man's sperm, which is constantly being produced, the woman's eggs are all there at the time of her birth. It's probably a good idea to wait till a year or so after your treatment to get pregnant, because it's a stressful process and you won't want to add morning sickness to the nausea you're likely to get from the chemicals.

On the other hand, I had a patient who inadvertently got pregnant right after she'd finished her chemotherapy and, after talking it over with her husband and her caregivers, decided to have the baby— who's now a perfectly healthy little girl.

The decision is up to you. If the stress of dealing with cancer and its uncertainties is too great, you may not want to have a child. On the other hand, if you do want to have a child, and have the assurance of a partner or family to back you up in caring for the child, perhaps creating a new life can help you to cope with the knowledge of mortality that a life-threatening illness carries with it—a reminder that even death isn't the end.

Insurance and Getting a Job

Unfortunately, maintaining a healthy attitude isn't always easy, in the face of what often amounts to discrimination against people with cancer. There are some precautions everyone with cancer needs to take.

In the first place, be sure you don't let your insurance lapse. Your company can't drop your policy because of your illness, so you're safe on that score. But many insurance companies won't take on someone who's had a life-threatening illness, and others will take you on but exclude coverage in the area of your illness. If you change jobs and go from one company's coverage to another, you'll probably be all right (but make certain of this before you accept the new job). If you quit for a while, make sure you keep up your insurance on your own. It's costly, but not nearly as costly as not being covered if you have a recurrence.

Life insurance and disability insurance are also harder to get if you've had breast cancer. More and more cancer survivors are fighting to get this changed, and it should get better in the future. But for now, be very alert.

There's at least some good news in this area. California has just passed a law requiring insurance companies to cover preexisting conditions after you've had your insurance for a year. The health care reforms outlined by the Clinton administration contained provisions preventing discrimination against people with preexisting conditions. This would have prevented "job-lock"—being unable to leave your job because you'll lose your insurance. (As one cynic noted, it would also prevent "slob-lock"—being unable to leave your husband because you'll lose your insurance.) A reform worth fighting for.

One of the hardest questions is whether or not to tell employers and co-workers about your cancer. There are pros and cons either way. Federal law prohibits federal employers or employers who get a federal grant or federal financial assistance from discriminating against the handicapped or anyone mistakenly thought to be handicapped. The new Americans with Disabilities Act (ADA), which was passed in 1992 and amended in 1994, extends this concept to the private sector. Any employer with 15 or more employees is prohibited from discriminating against qualified applicants and employees because of disability. Cancer and other diseases are considered disabilities in the terms of this legislation. The employer must also make reasonable accommodations to the disability—for example, if you have trouble reaching a high shelf because of pain from your mastectomy, the employer must make material accessible on a lower shelf or even build you a lower shelf if that's at all feasible.

Still, many women fear that employers will find subtle ways to discriminate against them if their cancer is discovered. One of my fellow breast cancer activists tells a great story of how she handled the loss of her job after her mastectomy, before the ADA was passed. Furious, she stormed into the boss's office, reached into her dress, pulled out her prosthesis, and slapped it on his desk. As he gaped at her in horror, she snapped, "Sir, you are confused—I had a mastectomy, not a lobotomy!" Then she calmly walked out, leaving her boss to buzz his secretary and ask her to remove the prosthesis.

There is the possibility that your boss and co-workers will offer you increased support if you are open to it. It is a dilemma that is probably best solved on an individual basis. There is more and more attention being given to cancer survivors in the workplace, and you may well be able to find a career counseling center that can give you good advice.

If you are looking for a new job there is even more difficulty. Some companies are reluctant to hire someone with cancer. This too is illegal under the ADA, but there is always the fear that an employer will find another excuse not to hire you. You might want to be open about your cancer because you don't want to work for someone with that attitude. On the other hand, you might need the job too much to risk being turned down. But if you don't tell them and then end up missing a lot of time for medical appointments or sickness, you can run into problems that could have been avoided if you'd been frank in the beginning. It's a tough problem, and there are no easy answers. We have included some references and reading about cancer and the workplace in Appendix B.

31

When Cancer Comes Back

Since the first edition of this book came out, I have met many women who have told me they were unhappy about the lack of information on either local recurrence or metastatic disease. They said that my book had been their bible when they were first diagnosed, but when they developed a recurrence and went back to the book, they were disappointed to find very little on their new problem. They felt that I had betrayed them in some way and didn't care about them anymore now that they had "failed their treatment." That could not be further from the truth.

I think that my failure to include more on these topics reflects my own unconscious desire to avoid the hardest topic to deal with. In terms of metastasis, this was compounded by my background as a surgeon: metastatic cancer is usually treated by oncologists rather than surgeons.

In this edition I am trying to remedy the situation with additional information on the diagnosis and treatment of both local and distant recurrences.

We know that you have a recurrence when we find that breast cancer cells have reappeared in the area around the breast (local or regional recurrence) or in other areas of the body (metastasis). For the most part these are microscopic cells that presumably got out before your diagnosis and found a niche elsewhere in your body. The cells can get out through the bloodstream or the lymphatic system. They can remain there dormant for years. And then something happens to wake them up. (See Fig. 13-6.) If we could figure out what puts these cells to sleep and then what wakes them up, we'd be a long way toward eliminating breast cancer.

One way to conceptualize it is to say that the radiation or chemotherapy has injured the cells and knocked some of them out, and then after a long while they recover and begin doubling again. That's probably partially true, but it doesn't explain it all, and we need to keep doing research to get to the whole answer.

Being diagnosed with any kind of recurrence can be devastating. The process of psychosocial adjustment will start all over again; trusting your body may take longer when you've been doubly betrayed by it. All the feelings you experienced the first time around are back double because now you not only don't trust your body but you begin to wonder about your doctors and treatment in general. It is important to discuss these feelings with your caregivers or to get new ones if, after talking with them, you no longer feel you are part of a team that you have confidence in. In addition, it is important to get support and help from those around you: counselors, therapists, and support groups.

What kinds of support groups are available vary widely, depending on where you are. It may be that the only groups available are general cancer groups. Such groups can be very helpful, but most women with breast cancer find breast cancer groups more helpful. In big cities you might want to search out groups for women with recurrences, or, if your disease has metastasized, for women with metastasis alone. There are advantages to all three. Barbara Kalinowski, at the Faulkner Hospital in Boston, co-leads both a first-diagnosis group and a recurrence group, both of which have gone on for a number of years. In the recurrence group, the women all faced similar issues for three years, but after a time, the dynamics changed as the women with metastasis began to worsen. "The women who are sick are very happy for the women who are getting better, and the women who are getting better are very supportive of the women who are sick." One of the women who was well had lunch with one of the others whose metastasis was worsening. Jackie Onassis had just died, and the sick woman said she wanted white and pink flowers at her funeral, the way Jackie had. The next week the other woman sent her a gorgeous bouquet of white and pink flowers, with a note saying, "You don't have to wait until you die for your flowers."

At the same time, Kalinowski says, women with metastatic cancer have more in common with each other as the illness progresses, and she

469

would like to do a separate group for such women. At UCLA in the Rhonda Fleming Mann Center for Women with Cancer, we have addressed this, and our social worker Carol Fred leads just such a group.

In order to best deal with your recurrence, you need to know more about the nature of breast cancer recurrences. In the rest of this chapter we will discuss the types of recurrences and their symptoms. In the next chapter we will discuss the treatments.

Local and Regional Recurrence

There are several ways cancer comes back in the breast and node area, and they mean different things. Most commonly, it shows up in the area of the original cancer. If you've had a wide excision and radiation, it may come back in the breast itself (Fig. 31-1), and this is called local recurrence. In this case, we see it not as a spread but as leftover cancer inadequately treated in the first place (see Chapter 23 for a discussion of why and how this happens). We are just beginning to get some data on the significance of these recurrences and to develop a reasonable way of treating them. Studies of women who have had this kind of reappearance of cancer in the breast show that their likelihood of dying of the disease is not much greater than that of women at the same stage of disease and who have had mastectomies.[1]

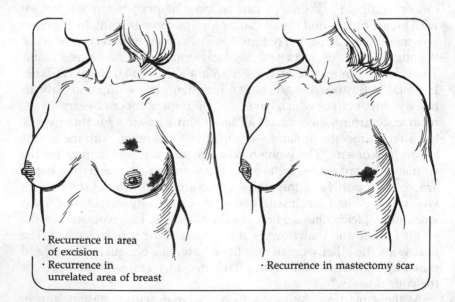

· Recurrence in area
  of excision
· Recurrence in
  unrelated area of breast

· Recurrence in mastectomy scar

FIGURE 31-1

What kind of disease recurs is important in terms of prognosis. If the recurrence is precancer (see Chapter 16), it is most likely left over and just needs to be cleaned up with further surgery. On the other hand, if the recurrence is invasive it may have had a second opportunity to spread. This is a million-dollar question, which is still unanswered: can tumor cells spread from the recurrent cancer into the bloodstream as they do from the original? Although intuitively it would appear to be possible, most evidence would indicate that this is not the case. It is, however, true that the women who have invasive local recurrences have more aggressive disease. Therefore, it may be well worth adding systemic therapy to the local treatment.[2] This is still unresolved at this time, but I would encourage anyone with a local invasive recurrence to get an opinion regarding chemotherapy or tamoxifen.

The first step to take if a local recurrence is detected is to do tests (see Chapter 21) to make sure there is no sign of cancer anywhere else in the body: bone scan, chest X ray, and liver blood tests. If the tests are normal (and they usually are), then we have to figure out what best to do to eradicate the tumor from the breast. Usually in these cases we do a mastectomy, since the less-drastic surgery and radiation didn't take care of it before. (In France they're experimenting with just doing another wide excision; so far we don't know how effective that will turn out to be.) Some doctors have argued against lumpectomy and radiation as a primary treatment on the theory that if you get a recurrence and need a mastectomy, the radiation means you can't get a reconstruction. But this isn't true. What is true is that you often can't have reconstruction with an expander (see Chapter 26), because the radiated skin can't tolerate being stretched out the way normal skin can. But expanders aren't the only form of reconstruction—or even, for that matter, the best one. The flap, as we discussed in Chapter 26, is better on a number of levels, and in this case it actually can be medically beneficial, because it brings new skin to the area.

There's something else we call a "local recurrence" that actually isn't a local recurrence at all—it's a new cancer in the breast. This typically occurs many years after the original cancer and in an entirely different area of the breast. Its pathology is often different—lobular instead of ductal, for example. These second cancers are not too common, but they remain possible as long as you have your breast. Though they are often counted as recurrences in the statistics for breast conservation, they have a different meaning. They should be treated as completely new cancers, much as with second cancers in the opposite breast. Most often the local treatment will be a mastectomy, since you can only receive radiation therapy once to that breast. The addition of chemotherapy will depend on the size and biomarkers of the tumor (see Chapter 20).

You can also get a local recurrence in the scar or chest wall after a mastectomy. Actually the term "chest wall" is inaccurate here, because it implies that the cancer is in the muscle or bone. But usually such a recurrence appears in the skin and fat sitting where the breast was before: only rarely does it include the muscle (Fig. 31-1). This can happen in one of two ways. The cancer can be in leftover breast tissue, since the surgeon was unable to get all the breast tissue out during your mastectomy. This is very similar to a recurrence after lumpectomy and radiation. It's residual, rather than metastatic. In this situation, we usually cut out the recurrence and perhaps radiate the chest wall, and you'll probably be fine.

The other type of recurrence appears not in residual breast tissue, but is spread through the bloodstream and lodges in the scar. That kind of a recurrence is more serious, because it often reflects microscopic cells elsewhere in the body. In 70 to 80 percent of those cases, the women will show an obvious metastasis elsewhere within two years.[3] Because of this, the doctor might then want to add systemic therapy to the surgery and radiation. A recent randomized controlled study from Europe has shown that adding tamoxifen to local excision and radiation for a postmastectomy recurrence significantly improved the 5-year disease-free survival.[4] Unfortunately we can't always distinguish between these two kinds of recurrences after mastectomy.

A local recurrence after mastectomy will usually show up as a pea-sized lump in your scar or under your skin. Sometimes it's in the skin itself, and is red and raised. It's usually so subtle the surgeon is likely to think at first that it's just a stitch that got left in after the operation. Then it gets bigger, and you need to get it biopsied. That can be done under local anesthesia, since the area is numb. It is important to note that reconstruction rarely if ever hides a recurrence. With implants the recurrences are in front of the implant. With a flap the recurrences are not in the flap (tissue from the abdomen) but along the edge of the old breast skin.[5]

To a certain degree we can predict which women will have a local recurrence. They are the ones whose initial cancer was particularly severe: women with inflammatory breast cancer, with cancer cells in the lymphatics of the skin, or the lymphatics of the breast. They may have a big tumor or many positive nodes. For these women we will suggest radiation therapy to the chest wall after a mastectomy to try and prevent this distressing type of recurrence. Although you would think that chemotherapy—and especially the extra-high-dose chemotherapy that we use with stem cell rescue (see Chapter 28)—would kill all of these cells, it doesn't seem to be true. The initial studies of high-dose chemotherapy were done with mastectomy as the only local therapy. To the surprise of the investigators many of the women had local recurrences in their scars in spite of all of the drugs and surgery.[6] Maybe it is harder for chemotherapy to be delivered to the scar. At any rate, now all adjuvant transplant patients receive radiation after their mastectomy.

On occasion, women will have extensive local recurrences after mastectomy, with myriads of nodules in the skin. They will ultimately merge together and act almost like a coat of armor across your chest and even into the back and the other breast. At this point we call it *en cuirasse*, a French word meaning "in casing." Other women can have large masses of tumor on their chest wall that weep and bleed. Both of these situations are rare but are very distressing because you are watching the cancer grow on the outside and slowly eat you away. There must be a different mutation for this type of local recurrence than for distant metastasis, because these women usually do not have extensive disease in the rest of their body for a long time. Unfortunately we don't have good therapy for this situation. Surgery cannot cut out enough tissue to clear it, and radiation therapy is limited in extent as well. Some have tried hyperthermia (very high heat) in an attempt to burn off the tumor, but its effect has also been limited. Sometimes chemotherapy will give some relief, but not always. These cases are very upsetting for the doctor and patient and we are still searching for the right approach to their treatment.

A *regional* recurrence is one in the lymph nodes under the arm or above the collarbone. Now that we are taking out fewer lymph nodes from the axilla (see Chapter 25), a cancerous node could be left behind. This is rare, occurring in about 2 percent of breast cancers. Further treatment to this area with either surgery or radiation will often take care of the problem. Regional recurrence in lymph nodes elsewhere, such as the neck or above the collarbone, has a more serious implication, since these are more likely to reflect spread of the tumor through the bloodstream. They are more akin to local recurrence following mastectomy and usually warrant a more aggressive approach.[7]

As physicians, we tend to downplay local and regional recurrences because they are not as life-threatening as metastatic disease can be. Nonetheless, for the patient they can be devastating. When a woman gets a local recurrence she finds it much harder than she did the first time not to think of herself as doomed. She gave it her best shot and it didn't work—how can she trust any treatment again? This became obvious to me when we first set up our support group for women with metastatic disease at the Faulkner Breast Centre in Boston. I wanted to exclude women with local recurrences because I thought their situation wasn't serious enough for this group. My co-workers and patients convinced me that this was not true, and they turned out to be right. The overwhelming feelings are the same. Barbara Kalinowski, who co-leads two support groups at the Faulkner, describes the difficulties women with recurrences have even around other women with breast cancer. "They find themselves being 'polite' in mixed groups. One woman was talking about having just had her sixth chemotherapy treatment, and the woman next to her said, 'Oh, good, you're almost through!' And she didn't have the heart to tell her this was her second time around." When a woman has gone through the tough round of surgery, radiation, and chemotherapy and has tried to put it behind her, knowing she'll have to go through it all over again can be desolating.

Distant Recurrence (Metastatic Disease)

As hard as it is to face a local recurrence, metastatic disease is even more devastating. There are the same feelings that go with any recurrence, compounded by the knowledge that the chance of cure is slim. Now you need to face the likelihood of dying sooner than anticipated, and to find the way to create the best quality of life for yourself in the time you have.

As we mentioned in Chapter 21, when breast cancer shows up in your lungs, liver, or bones, it's still breast cancer—not lung or liver or bone cancer. We can usually tell which it is by looking at it under the microscope. When a cancer spreads to a different organ, it's known as metastasis.

It's important here to differentiate "metastatic" from "micrometastatic." "Micrometastases" is the term we use when we discuss the likelihood of small cancer cells remaining in the rest of the body at the time of an initial treatment. They are cells that we presume are there, but are so small we can't detect them. We believe that such spread, if it exists, can be cured in many people (see Chapter 28). But when we talk about metastatic disease itself, we mean cancer cells that we can detect on an X ray or scan, not simply that we think are probably there. At the time we're writing this book, nothing that we know of can cure metastatic breast cancer.

The average survival of women with metastatic breast cancer from the time of the first appearance of the metastasis is between two and three and a half years, according to most studies. But 25 to 35 percent of patients live five years, and about 10 percent live more than 10 years. And 1 or 2 percent are cured.[8] There are cases in the medical literature, like the woman who had metastases throughout her bones, had hormone treatment, and was well 24 years later.[9] I wish we could take credit for such rare and wonderful cases, but we have no idea what has caused the cure in any of them. It could be a miracle, or good luck, or an extraordinary immune system. Or it could it be that the cells just go on lying dormant for an abnormally long time.

There are many factors that can help predict who will live a long time, but they're not absolute. One is the length of time between your original diagnosis and your metastasis. If the metastasis shows up six months after your diagnosis, it suggests that you have a much more aggressive cancer than if it's six years after your diagnosis.

Another factor is the aggressiveness of your original tumor. Still another is whether or not your tumor was sensitive to hormones. We also look at how many places it's metastasized to—if there's only one, or if you have multiple spots. Where it recurs is also a consideration. Metastasis to the bone or the scar is less serious than metastasis to the lung or liver.

All this is just statistics. What happens to an individual woman may or may not conform to the norm. I've had patients with metastatic disease who have far outlived the most optimistic prognosis. I had one patient who, while she was getting her adjuvant chemotherapy, developed lung metastasis. That means she had hardly any disease-free interval, and the cancer seemed resistant to chemo. Statistically, she should have been dead within months. She was treated hormonally and the cancer disappeared for two years. It came back at that point and another treatment made it disappear for another two years. When it came back that time we gave another hormone. Ten years after her initial diagnosis, she died of breast cancer. When she was diagnosed she had an eight-year-old son, and she was able to raise him almost into adulthood.

So we can't accurately predict the course of any individual's illness. This is true of initial disease, and metastatic disease is even more unpredictable.

Usually I find that women who have just finished breast cancer treatments don't want to think about the possibility of its spreading. They're busy dealing with the healing process and metastasis is too painful to think about. But, of course, it's always somewhere in the back of a woman's mind. Usually about a year after her initial treatments the patient will start asking me what the symptoms of metastasis are. (This is an observation, by the way—not a guideline. If you want to know right away, or two months later, talk to your doctor. There's nothing particularly brave about toughing it out when you're worried. Every woman's pace is different.)

In medical school, we used to be taught that we shouldn't tell people who had been treated for cancer what to look for if they were worried about recurrences, because they'd start imagining that they had every symptom we told them about. I've never liked that idea. It doesn't soothe people at all; it just means they'll be afraid of everything, instead of a few specific things. When you've had cancer, you're acutely aware of your body, and any symptom you ever had—or never noticed before—can take on new, terrifying significance for you. Anything unexpected in your body has you petrified. Inevitably, this will mean a lot of fear over symptoms that turn out to be harmless. But if you know that the symptoms of breast cancer metastasis are usually bone pain, shortness of breath, lack of appetite and weight loss, and neurological symptoms like pain or weakness or headaches, there are at least limits to your fear. You'll probably be frightened when anything resembling those symptoms comes up, even if it turns out to be nothing but a tension headache or a mild flu. But at least you won't get terrified by a sore spot on your big toe or an unexpected weight gain. Knowing what symptoms to look for reduces fear; it doesn't increase it.

Most women whose breast cancer has metastasized don't show any symptoms until the disease is quite extensive. It isn't a case of years and years of terrible suffering, the way TV melodrama likes to show it.

Like other cancers, breast cancer can spread anywhere, but it's more likely to show up in some places than in others, the most common being the lungs, liver, and bones. Why this is we don't know. There's a lot of research being done about it, and perhaps one day we'll have a better understanding of it. It must be that the environment of certain organs is more conducive to growth for this type of cancer cell.

In a quarter of the cases, the bones are the first site where metastatic disease is detected. This is true partly because it's more common there than in other places, and partly because it creates definite symptoms. Even if it first appears elsewhere, as the disease progresses, it will usually reach the bone at some stage.

The way metastasis to the bone is usually diagnosed is that the patient experiences pain. Sometimes it's hard to know if the pain is ordinary low back pain or some other disease, like arthritis. Usually the pain you get with breast cancer in the bones is fairly constant. With arthritis, you wake up in the morning and feel stiff, but get better as you move around during the day. With some muscular problems that cause bone pain, the more you do, the worse the pain gets. But the pain from cancer is steady, and usually remains even at night, when you're not doing anything. The pain is probably caused by the cancer taking up room in the bone and pressing on it, and so sometimes it can get worse in different positions. If you're standing up on the bone you might be compressing it more and causing more pain than if you're lying down. If you have pain that lasts for more than a week or two and doesn't seem to be going away, and isn't like whatever pains have been familiar to you in your life, you should get it checked out.

We usually check bone pain by doing a bone scan. This is a radioactive test, which we've described in Chapter 21. It's not very specific, because it can be positive for a lot of different conditions, but it's pretty accurate for showing when there's cancer.

If the bone scan doesn't give a conclusive answer, the next step is an X ray. If there's metastasis, it will show one of two things. It will either show lytic lesions, which are holes where the cancer has eaten away the bones, or it will show blastic lesions, which are an increase of bone where the growth factor of the cancer has caused the bone to get more dense.

CAT scans and MRI, which are described in Chapter 11, can also be used to diagnosis cancer in specific bones.

Most of the time, if you're diagnosed with bone metastasis, the major treatment will be geared toward alleviating the symptoms. If it's just one spot in one bone and the rest of your bone is okay, we can use radiation on that. It will kill the tumor cells, shrink the tumor, and give you relief. If there are several different spots in your bones that are causing pain, and we can't radiate them all, we'd probably begin with some form of systemic therapy.

The thing we worry about most in women with cancer in their bones is the possibility of fractures. If the cancer eats away enough bone, the bone will no longer be able to hold you up. Then you can get what's called a "pathological fracture," so named because it's caused not by a blow from outside—you've tripped on the stairs and the bone has been banged against the wood—but by something wrong in the bone itself (Fig. 31-2). It's similar to osteoporosis in that it doesn't take very much to cause this fracture, because the bone is so weakened. So a slight pressure on the bone, which usually wouldn't even cause a bruise, triggers off the fracture. (It's different from osteoporosis, however, in that it doesn't affect all your bones.)

One of the ways we deal with this is by trying to predict ahead of time which bones are likely to fracture, so we can help prevent it. The doctor will pay a lot of attention to what particular bones are involved. The ones to worry most about are the ones that hold you up—your leg or hip bones. The upper arm can also fracture, but it's less likely because you don't put as much constant pressure on it. You can also get a fracture in your spine. If we can see on the X rays that a bone in a critical place has metastatic disease that would be at risk for a fracture, we can do surgery ahead of time—pin the hip or stabilize the bone. Again, the idea is to keep you stabilized and functional, with as high a quality of life as possible for as long a time as possible.

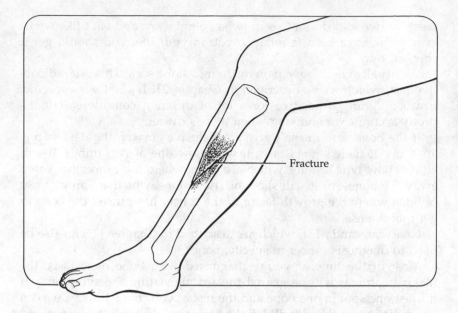

Fracture

FIGURE 31-2

A new treatment for pain caused by bone metastasis is strontium. This is a radioactive particle that is injected intravenously and is taken up by the bone. The radioactivity can then act directly on the metastasis. This is still experimental but worth looking for if you have diffuse bone disease.[10]

We also see breast cancer metastasis fairly often in the lungs (Fig. 31-3). Usually the symptoms for that are shortness of breath and a chronic cough. Sixty to 70 percent of patients who die of breast cancer eventually have it in their lungs. The lungs are the only site of metastasis in about 21 percent of cases. There are a few different ways it can form in the lungs. One is in nodules—usually several—that show up on the chest X ray. If a chest X ray shows one nodule, we can't tell if it's lung cancer or a breast cancer spread. So we do a needle biopsy or a full biopsy to find out. (Lung cancer usually starts in just one spot. Any other cancer that has spread to the lung through the bloodstream is likely to hit multiple spots.)

If your breast cancer has spread to your lungs, you may experience shortness of breath on slight exertion. It can be fairly subtle. It comes on slowly, since the cancer has to have used up a lot of your lungs before you get short of breath.

Another form of metastasis in the lung is called lymphangitic spread. Here the cancer spreads along the lymphatics, and so instead

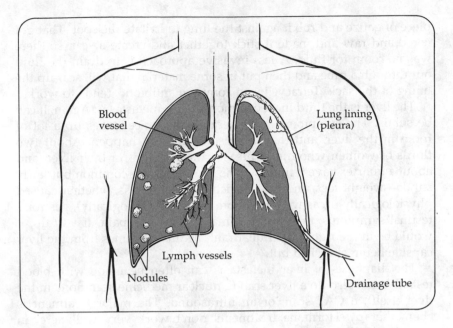

FIGURE 31-3

of being nodules it's a fine pattern throughout the lung. That's subtler and harder to detect on a chest X ray. It too will ultimately give you shortness of breath, since it takes up room and scars the lungs, making them less able to expand and contract.

The third way it can show is through fluid in the lung. That usually indicates spread in the lining of the lung rather than in the lung itself. (The lung sits in a sack with a smooth lining around it, so that it can move without sticking to your chest wall.) The cancer creates fluid in the lung, and the fluid causes the lung to collapse (Fig. 31-3). Here again, you'll experience shortness of breath. Usually breast cancer in the lungs doesn't cause pain.

If we think your cancer may have metastasized to your lung, we do a chest X ray. If the X ray doesn't show nodules, fluid, or any of the other signs, we can still do a CAT scan or even an open lung biopsy.

The treatment for lymphangitic and nodule symptoms is chemotherapy, because you want to make breathing easier quickly. Steroids such as prednisone can also help relieve the symptoms.

Fluid in the lung can be treated by sticking a needle into the chest and draining the fluid. This works immediately, but only temporarily. Often the fluid comes right back again. To prevent the reaccumulation of fluid, we need to scar down the lining of the lung. When I was in medical school we used to do an operation, open up the chest, take a piece of gauze and rub it against the lung to irritate the spot. That got it red and raw and made it stick together and create a scar, so there was no room for fluid. A less invasive approach is to drain the fluid out through a tube and then put in some material that will scar up the lining of the sack. Tetracycline, a common antibiotic, tends to work.

The liver is the third most common site for metastases. Again, it can be subtle. The symptoms occur because the cancer takes up a lot of room in the liver, and that takes some time to happen. About two thirds of women who die of breast cancer have it in their liver, and about a quarter have it initially. The symptoms are common but fairly subtle—weight loss, anorexia (which is appetite loss, whether caused physiologically or, as we think more often, psychologically), gastrointestinal symptoms, or fever. You may have some pain. If you do, it would be in the right upper quadrant, because it comes from the liver capsule being stretched out.

The diagnosis of liver metastasis can often be made with blood tests. We can also do a liver scan (a nuclear medicine scan done in the liver itself), a CAT scan, or an ultrasound. The major treatment is chemotherapy. Hormone treatments don't work very well here. In some kinds of cancer, like colon cancer, liver metastasis can be a single spot, and thus can sometimes be cut out. But with breast cancer, there usually is more than one spot involved and surgery becomes impossible. In the rare exceptions when there is only one spot, we can surgically remove part of the liver to relieve symptoms. Sometimes when patients have a lot of pain, we radiate the liver to shrink it. At one time we were working on putting chemotherapy into the liver directly through a catheter into the artery that went into the liver, thinking it would be a more direct treatment of the metastasis. But we really get just as good a response with less drastic and more comfortable forms of chemotherapy, so we don't do this much anymore.

Less common, but very serious, are neurological metastases. Breast cancer can spread to the brain and the spinal cord. It's fairly uncommon—about 6 percent. Predictably, the most common symptom is headache. I almost hate to say that, since most people get a lot of headaches during their lives, and I'm afraid any reader with breast cancer who gets a tension headache will be terrified. But if the headache doesn't go away in a reasonable time, check it out. In some patients it's the kind of headache that always occurs with a brain tumor. It begins early in the morning before you get out of bed, then improves as the day goes on, but then gets worse and worse over time. Ultimately you also have drowsiness and nausea. It usually comes on slowly, over a period of weeks.

Behavior or mental changes are sometimes, though rarely, caused by the tumor. You can have weakness or unsteadiness in walking, or seizures. It can resemble a stroke: you suddenly can't talk, or half your body is paralyzed, or you can't see out of one eye. Those kinds of symptoms come from a blocking of a portion of your brain, which the cancer growth can cause. The best way to diagnosis it is through CAT scan or MRI. About half the patients will have one lesion; the other half will have several. The treatment is usually radiation, which shrinks the metastasis. As in liver cancer, if there's only one lesion, surgery might work. You'll also be put on steroids—cortisone or pred-nisone—right away, to reduce the swelling of the brain. Since the brain sits within a hard bony shell (the skull) there isn't much room for swelling before important structures are injured. If you're having seizures, you'll also be put on antiseizure medication. Chemotherapy doesn't work very well on brain metastasis.

Another kind of brain metastasis you can get is a form of meningi-tis called *carcinomitis meningitis*. It affects the lining of the brain, rather than the brain itself. It causes headaches and stiff neck, the way any form of meningitis does. In that situation the treatment is surgical, to put a little reservoir into the lining of the brain and put chemotherapy directly into the spinal fluid which baths the brain. Radiation is also used.

Metastasis to the spinal cord is also very serious. The tumor can push on the spinal cord and cause paralysis. Sometimes this happens because the bone metastasis is in the vertebrae, and pushes against the spinal cord as it passes by (Fig. 31-4). Sometimes the tumor grows directly in the spinal cord itself. Before the paralysis, however, there are earlier symptoms—pain, weakness, sensory loss, and disturbances of the bowel or bladder. Pain is the most common—85 to 90 percent of patients with spinal cord metastasis have pain. It may be the only symptom for months. The problem is that you'll also have pain if your cancer is only in the bones in the back. So we have to be able to differentiate, or at least to be extremely alert, to be certain that the patient with bone metastasis in her back isn't on the verge of spinal cord compression. Most of the pain is aching and continuous. Its onset is gradual and it gets worse over time. And it's very localized: you feel it exactly on the spot where the tumor is. There is another kind of pain that goes downward the way sciatica does, when a disk compresses the nerves and goes down your leg and gets worse if you cough or sneeze. You might also feel pain in your shoulder or back from spinal cord compression. Seventy-five percent of patients with metastasis to the spinal cord have weakness in their muscles from the tumor push-ing against the nerves and about 50 percent will have spots of numb-ness. Anyone with metastatic breast cancer who has unrelenting pain in one spot, and neurological symptoms, should be checked. If you have no other signs of metastasis, it probably isn't spinal cord com-

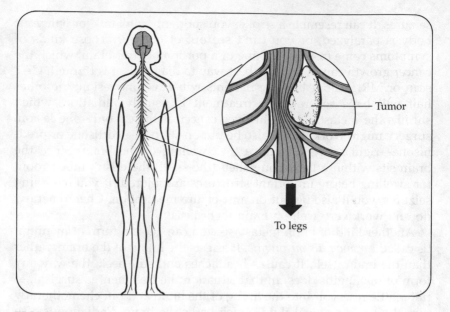

Tumor

To legs

FIGURE 31-4

pression, since that's rarely the first place breast cancer metastasizes. The way we diagnose it is with a CAT scan or MRI. We used to do a myelogram, in which dye was injected into the spinal column, but we rarely do that anymore. The treatment is emergency radiation and steroids—one of the few cases in which radiation is used as an emergency treatment. The radiation shrinks the tumor and the steroids prevent the spinal cord from swelling. It's possible that surgery is also called for. If it's one spot, we may be able to remove the tumor and decompress the spinal cord.

Breast cancer can also metastasize to the eye, though, again, it's rarely the first place breast cancer spreads. The first symptoms are double or blurred vision. It's diagnosed by CT scan or MRI. It's also treated with radiation, which can often prevent loss of vision.

Another area is bone marrow. The main symptom is anemia, caused by a decrease in the number of red and white blood cells and platelets. Though it sounds grim, metastasis to the bone marrow actually responds very well to treatment, either with hormones or chemotherapy. I have one patient who had had breast cancer in one breast, did fine, and got breast cancer in the opposite breast several years later. She decided to have mastectomy and reconstruction. Right before surgery, her blood count was a little low. So we went ahead with the surgery, but we also did a bone marrow biopsy, and found her cancer had metastasized. We put her on tamoxifen, and she did well for six or seven years.

Breast cancer in all its manifestations is an unpredictable disease. These are general descriptions. As I write, many women come to mind who didn't follow the rules. Use this information to help understand your own situation and to ask questions. Your situation will be unique to you no matter what happens.

Taking Care of Yourself Emotionally

David Spiegel at Stanford has recently shown how important the mind-body connection is in metastatic disease. As we mentioned earlier, he had two groups of women with newly diagnosed metastatic breast cancer. One participated in a support group while the other had only regular care. When he looked back at the data 10 years later he was amazed to find that the women who had participated in the support group lived, on average, double the time of those who had not.[11] And, in addition, they had a better quality of life. A diagnosis of metastatic disease is a time to reorder your life and pay attention to what is most important to you. You may not be able to change things but you can improve how you deal with them.

Spiegel tells the story of a woman who had always wanted to write poetry and started after her diagnosis of metastatic disease. She had a book of her poems published before her death. One of my patients, Susan Shapiro, was very distressed with the lack of analysis of breast cancer from a feminist political prospective. She wrote an article in the local feminist paper and called a meeting. As a result she started the Women's Community Cancer Project in Boston a few months before she died. I know she would be happy to know that her work sparked a national movement that continues today (see Chapter 34).

A diagnosis of recurrence or metastasis will remind you that you do not have control over your body. But you certainly do have control over your mind, emotions, and spirit. This is a good time to revisit some of the complementary treatments such as visualization, self-hypnosis, and imagery (see Chapter 29). And find a doctor to whom you can talk, and who will listen to you. Shop around if you have to. If you are in a small town and/or in an insurance plan with limited choice, then schedule an appointment with your oncologist so that you can talk about what you need from them as well as what they expect from you. (See Appendix F for the patient and doctor's rights.) You need to know as accurately as possible what to expect from your condition and your treatments so that you can plan. Ask for the information you need and tell your doctor if there are things you would rather not know. As in any relationship, frank communication about your needs will go far in having them met.

There are two main fears that accompany a diagnosis of recurrent breast cancer: pain and death. Pain is certainly not inevitable. The good news is that pain control has finally gone mainstream in the United States. There are pain centers and many methods which have been developed to deal with pain without clouding your mind and ruining your life (see Chapter 32).

Not everyone dies from a recurrence or metastatic breast cancer but it is certainly a possibility. David Spiegel's book *Living Beyond Limits*[12] is invaluable in addressing the needs of the heart and soul in the face of terminal illness. You may not be able to avoid death but you can control it. One of my patients was a great denier. From the first moment of her diagnosis she refused to let her cancer interfere with her life. Once she had metastatic disease this pattern continued. She continued to hurl herself through life: physically active, sailing, traveling, and enjoying herself. My first reaction was to be a little critical of her inability to face the reality of the situation, until I realized that that was what she had done. She knew exactly what she was doing and was determined to take control of whatever time she had left. She slipped into a coma on her sailboat among friends and died as she wanted, where she wanted, in control to the end.

When to Stop Treatment

Often people ask their doctor, "How long have I got to live?" I never answer that—not because I want to withhold information from my patient, but because I simply don't know. There are statistical likelihoods, but they never cover everyone. There are patients who, according to the statistics, should die in four months and they live four years; there are others who should last four years and die in four months. I'm always amazed at the variations. One of my patients had a small cancer and negative nodes, with what should have been a good prognosis, but when she finished her radiation we discovered the cancer had metastasized to her lungs, and she died in three months. It often works the other way, as in the case of my patient with the so-called galloping cancer. Another patient, a Chinese woman who spoke no English, had a cancer that was very bad and I privately thought she wouldn't live very long. I had to talk to her through her sons, who kept trying to get me to say how long she had. I wouldn't tell them. It's a good thing, because seven years later, she's still alive. Sometimes I think she's lived so long because she didn't know she was supposed to die!

At the same time, it's important for your doctor to be honest with you. I think it's sensible to say to a patient who has asked for a frank response, "This is serious, but we don't know how long you'll live until we see how you respond to treatment. You'll probably eventually die of breast cancer, and you probably won't live another 40 years, so you may want to plan your life with that in mind." If you insist on more specific predictions, a doctor may quote statistics—but you should always be reminded that there are exceptions to statistics. Even if 99 out of 100 patients in your condition die within a year, 1 out of 100 doesn't—and there's no reason to assume you won't be that one.

Eventually, however, there comes the hardest part, for the patient and for the doctor. We've tried all the available treatments, and we know that you don't have much longer. Even then, we don't know if it's days or weeks, and even then, there is still the possibility of a miracle. But there's a point at which you're clearly dying, and you have a right to know that. It used to be the prevailing belief that it was better not to tell patients they were dying. But this sets up an unhealthy climate of denial. Often you'll sense it yourself, but since no one else wants to talk about it you pretend it's okay in order to spare them, and they pretend it's okay in order to spare you. Such denial can keep you from finishing up your business—clearing up relationships, saying good-bye, saying the things you won't get another chance to say to the people you love, giving them the chance to say those things to you. I think doctors make a great error in denying death. We tend to look at it too much as a defeat, and to get caught up in our own denial, at the patient's expense.

While you're still feeling fairly well, you might want to talk with your doctor, and with your family members or friends, about how you want to die when the time comes. Do you want extraordinary measures taken, or not? Do you want to die at home, or in the hospital? Do you want to be heavily medicated or as alert as possible? No way is universally better, but one way might be better for you. If your wishes are clearly known—especially if they can be documented in a Living Will—you might be able to prevent those tragic situations where doctors and family members are fighting over whether to keep you on a life-support system.

These questions are important for every one of us to consider, since none of us are immortal, and death can come for anyone at any time. Of course, you may live another 10 or 20 years anyway—but you haven't lost anything by having those discussions, and you might even have gained a little peace of mind.

32

Metastatic Disease:
Treatments

The treatment approach to metastatic disease is different from primary breast cancer. As we said in Chapter 31, with metastatic cancer there isn't a reliable method of cure. Our goal is twofold: first, to control your symptoms and make you feel better, and second, to prolong your survival if we can.

Many people will say, "If I have metastatic disease I don't want any therapy—it will just make me suffer more." However, some of the best tools we have for improving quality of life are surgery, radiation therapy, hormonal therapy, and chemotherapy—the same tools we use to treat the initial cancer. This may come as a surprise to many readers, especially in terms of chemotherapy. For many, the very word "chemotherapy" conjures up images of violent and debilitating nausea. But in fact, with metastatic cancer, chemotherapy and hormone therapy can alleviate much suffering. As we discussed in the last chapter, a woman with metastatic breast cancer can experience severe discomfort as the disease progresses—pain in her bones, shortness of breath, or weakness and lethargy. By shrinking the tumor that creates these symptoms, therapy can make her feel dramatically better. That's not a small accomplishment. Death is inevitable at some point, though most of us prefer to think that point is always years away. But more than death itself, most people fear a prolonged, enfeebling illness in which life is too painful to enjoy and they have become a burden on those they love.

As we were working on this edition of the book, Virginia Kelly, President Clinton's mother, who had metastatic breast cancer and had decided not to have any type of "debilitating treatment," died. Her decision was probably right for her, since she seems to have had few, if any, symptoms. Three weeks before her death, she had spent Christmas at the White House, then went to Las Vegas for New Year's Eve with Barbra Streisand. But for somebody whose symptoms are themselves debilitating, the treatment will probably bring a better quality of life.

One of the things most difficult for patients with metastatic cancer is having no clear idea of what to expect—how soon they might die and how much pain they are likely to be in. Two things are important to consider. One is dealing with your own emotions, through counseling, a support group, religion—whatever works best for you. (We discussed this at length in Chapter 22, Fears and Feelings, and again in Chapter 31.)

The other important thing is to get as much information as your doctor has about the probable progress of your illness and what it entails. Some doctors are very uncomfortable with death; they see their job as fighting even the thought of death until the last minute, and therefore they deal with your fear of dying by pretending it won't happen. Sometimes doctors try to deal with the patient's fear by using every kind of therapy as rapidly and in as great a dose as possible, to try to ward off the inevitable. Often the patient herself goes along with this approach. But it's as dangerous as the opposite extreme of shying away from any treatment at all.

In this chapter we want to discuss more sensibly what treatments are available for metastatic disease and what you should expect from them.

During and after your treatment for metastatic disease you will be followed with staging tests—bone scan, chest X ray, and blood tests—as well as a few other tests. These will help to determine if you are indeed responding to treatment (see Chapter 21 and Chapter 31).

It would be nice to be able to tell you that treatment for metastatic disease would improve survival, but we simply don't know for certain. The studies are mixed. There have been a couple of studies comparing the survival of women in 1974, before we were using chemotherapy, to that of women treated after 1974 who had been given chemotherapy. They found that within that time frame, the survival rate remained fairly steady.[1]

However, a study at M.D. Anderson Cancer Center in 1985,[2]

showed that survival time between original diagnosis of metastases and time of death slightly increased—from 12 months in the 1960s to 22 months in the 1970s. Presumably it's even longer in 1995. A woman who died in 1950 five years after her original diagnosis would have survived five and three quarters years after diagnosis in 1965, and almost seven years after diagnosis in 1971. Since screening mammography was not yet commonly used in the 1960s, it's unlikely that this improvement can be dismissed as lead-time bias. The study also found that the better the patient's cancer responded to the chemotherapy in the beginning of her treatment for metastatic cancer, the longer she survived.

We speak about two kinds of responses to treatment for metastatic breast cancer—partial and complete. A partial response is when the tumor regresses by 50 percent, and a complete response means it regresses so far that we can no longer detect it. For us to measure a response like this, you need to have what's called "measurable disease." We have to be able to see it clearly enough to measure it.

We can't always do that. If you have a nodule of cancer in your lungs, we can take X rays to determine how well it's gone down. But if you have pain from bone metastasis, that's harder to measure. We know that treatments are working because your pain is reduced, but that isn't a scientific measurement: we can't say your pain went away 50 percent or 38 percent. So some symptoms are easier than others to measure, and we don't always get an exact estimate of your response.

For the doctor planning the most effective treatment, the job is to figure out what the symptoms are and match the treatment, with the least toxicity possible.

Endocrine Treatments

We've known for a long time that breast cancer in women is an endocrine disease—the endocrine glands are the ones that make hormones. We can test the cancer when the tumor is first removed and tell if it's sensitive to hormones by doing the estrogen receptor test described in Chapter 20.

So in women who have metastatic disease and a tumor that's sensitive to hormones, using endocrine treatments first often makes more sense than chemotherapy. When a patient has responded to one hormone therapy, we know she's likely to respond to all of them, so we use them serially.

The first hormonal treatment devised was used in premenopausal women and consisted of ovarian ablation—which meant surgically removing the ovaries. We can now do this by removing them surgically or by radiation or drugs. In menstruating women who are estrogen receptor positive, the response to oophorectomy is 35 percent.

Of course, removing the ovaries puts you into immediate menopause, complete with mood swings and hot flashes. But it also can almost immediately relieve your metastatic breast cancer symptoms, often by the time you leave the hospital. This approach has gone out of fashion with the introduction of chemotherapy but it can be just the right treatment for a premenopausal woman with bone metastasis and an estrogen-receptor-positive tumor.

Whether we remove the ovaries or radiate them, it's equally effective. We now have a technique for removing ovaries with a laparoscope, so we don't even have to do open surgery, with all its attendant risks. We are now doing studies on the use of chemical oophorectomy, by using some of the GnRH inhibitors (Lupron or Zoladex)(see Chapter 28), which are pituitary blockers that can put you into a reversible menopause.

Another approach is using estrogen. Interestingly, either giving or blocking estrogen can be effective in women whose tumors are estrogen receptor positive. DES—infamous for its damage to fetuses of women who were given it with the hopes of preventing miscarriage—can be beneficial in treating breast cancer. It works just as well as tamoxifen, which is an estrogen blocker. But we usually use tamoxifen because DES has more side effects. About 20 to 25 percent of women will respond to estrogen or estrogen blockers (tamoxifen).

Megace, a kind of progesterone, is the drug of choice after tamoxifen. The biggest side effect of Megace is an increase of appetite, which leads to weight gain. This occurs in about half the patients, and they gain somewhere between 10 and 20 pounds. Twelve percent of women gain more than 30 pounds. (In fact, Megace is so likely to cause weight gain that there's now talk about using it in treating people with AIDS and other wasting diseases.) Megace works for about 20 to 30 percent of women.

Since anti-estrogens work, some doctors have been looking at the possibility of using anti-progesterones as well. The most well known anti-progesterone is RU486, which is used outside the U.S. for early abortions. There's been a very small study showing that some breast cancers do respond to anti-progesterones. But we don't have any large studies to date. Provera has also been used as a progestin therapy.

Aminoglutethimide is the next drug in line. It blocks steroid synthesis. We used to take out the patient's adrenal glands, but now we use this chemical blocker instead. It's used more in postmenopausal than younger women. Again, the response is about 28 percent, and the duration averages about 18 months. Several new, similar drugs, aromatase inhibitors, with less toxicity, are being tested, and it is likely that at least one will be approved by the time this book is out.

You might think that if all these different hormones work separately, they'd work even better together. But we've tried that and the response rate doesn't change much, so it seems wiser to do them one at a time. Patients who respond to one therapy are more likely to respond to the next one. Once a woman stops responding to hormones she still has the option of chemotherapy.

Something called "flare" can occur in hormonal treatment of metastatic breast cancer. What this means is that within the first month of therapy, there is an exacerbation of the patient's disease. This actually indicates a good prognosis. Typically it occurs with someone who has bone metastasis, and is put on tamoxifen. Suddenly her pain is worse than ever. But then she's back to normal soon after. We don't understand why that happens. It may be normal tissue responding to the swelling, or tumor regression. But it is good to understand because it can be very scary.

Though overall response rates to hormone treatments are better in women who are estrogen receptor positive than in women who are estrogen receptor negative, there is some response in estrogen-receptor-negative tumors. For example, tamoxifen works for 54 percent of estrogen-receptor-positive women and 9 percent in estrogen receptor negative women. Ovary removal has a 62 percent response with receptor-positive women and 6 percent with estrogen-receptor-negative women. So when you look at the overall effectiveness of all the hormonal treatments, you'll hear that it's about 40 percent. But it isn't equal in all women: if your tumor is estrogen positive, you'll have a 60 percent response rate. That means in over half the cases, your symptoms will be alleviated for a significant amount of time.

Usually the effects of endocrine treatments last for about 18 months, but many women will stay in remission for two to five years with some free of disease as long as 10 years. The 24-year survivor mentioned in the previous chapter was treated with hormonal therapies only. A widely held belief of medical oncologists is that chemotherapy works faster than hormonal therapy in reversing symptoms. Not a scrap of evidence supports this notion. Patients may have dramatic relief of bone pain within a day or two of starting endocrine treatment. One reason for the belief that patients respond more rapidly to chemotherapy is that the patients who respond to endocrine therapy are usually those with the more slowly growing disease. There is probably a relationship between the rate at which the disease grows and the rate at which it disappears.

When the tumor does show up again, sometimes just stopping a drug can give a secondary response. It seems that whatever we do to change the hormonal environment helps throw the cancer's growth off and stop it for a while. If we continually change the environment around the cancer, we can keep putting people into remission for a long time. (It may even be that part of chemotherapy's value is in suppressing the ovaries in premenopausal women.)

As always, we urge all readers to consider participating in a clinical trial or at least finding out which trials you are eligible for (see Chapter 33). For premenopausal women not participating in a trial, at UCLA we try either tamoxifen or oophorectomy first. If that works, we stay with it until the symptoms recur and then go on to Megace or one of the other hormonal treatments. With postmenopausal women we definitely start with tamoxifen (since taking the ovaries out of a postmenopausal woman doesn't change much); if that works for a time the next step is tamoxifen withdrawal, then Megace, then amino-glutethimide, then possibly DES or halotestin (a male hormone), and finally chemotherapy. If a woman was on tamoxifen adjuvant therapy at the time of her metastasis we would start with Megace. Only when a woman stops responding to hormones do we go on to chemotherapy.

As weird as it sounds, the woman with metastatic breast cancer whose tumor is sensitive to hormones is comparatively lucky, because she has many more avenues of treatment that are less toxic than the women whose tumor is resistant to hormonal influence. Even some women with hormone-receptor-negative tumors will response to hormone therapy. Dr. I. Craig Henderson, my former colleague at the Dana Farber Cancer Institute and now head of oncology at the University of California in San Francisco, believes that every woman over age 60 or 65 should have endocrine treatment, regardless of her receptor status, unless there is evidence that her disease is progressive. All women with metastasis should question their medical oncologist about the possibility of hormonal treatment. Most medical oncologists are better trained in giving chemotherapy than endocrine therapy, and they derive a greater financial profit from it as well. It just may not occur to them to try a hormonal maneuver first unless you bring it up. Certainly the best quality of life is likely to be associated with the less toxic but successful hormonal treatments.

Chemotherapy

For the women whose tumors are not responsive to hormone therapy, the alternative is chemotherapy. The percentage of patients who respond to chemotherapy is often quoted as being twice as high as that of patients who respond to hormone therapy, but it is only because it doesn't depend on whether or not you're sensitive to estrogen. The percentage of patients who respond at least partially to the commonly used chemotherapy treatments is 42 percent to 82 percent, and 27 percent will have a complete response—their symptoms will totally vanish for six to twelve months. Usually it takes around six weeks for the response to occur. Sometimes, however, it can take longer—even a year. The duration of the response is between 5 and 13 months. The maximum duration reported so far is over 180 months—which means, in effect, that it's over 10 years and thus could almost be called a cure. (Unfortunately, this length of survival is very rare.) The average survival of the responders is 15 to 42 months. So chemotherapy, like hormone therapy, can help you to live comfortably for anywhere between one and four years, and there's a small chance that it can give you 10 or more years of quality life.

More than 80 cytotoxic drugs—drugs that kill cells—have been tested. Of these, 10 are used commonly in breast cancer treatment. Interestingly, breast cancer creates the kind of tumor that is responsive to the greatest array of drugs—most other cancers don't respond to as many chemicals. The standard drugs are the same ones we discussed in Chapter 28 in terms of adjuvant treatment—cyclophosphamide (Cytoxan) (C), methotrexate (M), 5 fluorouracil (F), and Adriamycin (A). Those four have the highest anti-tumor activity among all the patients studied, and they have only limited cross-resistance.

Usually CMF or CAF or Adriamycin are used. Since these are the same drugs that we use for adjuvant chemotherapy, some women will have built up a resistance to them. Fortunately there are other drugs as well. These include vinblastine, which is an alkaloid and a type of antibiotic. Mitomycin C is another standard drug although not approved by the FDA for this use.

The newest chemotherapy drug for breast cancer is Taxol, which comes from the bark of the yew tree. It acts a bit differently than the others: it blocks a part of the cell called the microtubules, which are necessary for cell division: basically it's a cell poison. The media have treated it like a miracle drug that would solve all cancer problems, but it's not. It's simply another form of chemotherapy. But that in itself is exciting enough—we haven't had a new chemotherapy drug in years. It works as well as Adriamycin, which was our best drug—not better, but as well. So it gives us another drug to use. However, it won't cure everybody, and it has risks and complications, such as neurological, side effects. Now we're in the process of seeing how it works in combination with other drugs.

Each drug has limitations. With Adriamycin, we can give only a certain dosage, and then it becomes toxic to the heart. Once you've reached that point, you can't ever use it again. Some of the other drugs you can take indefinitely.

We tend to use drugs together in chemotherapy, which we don't do in hormonal therapy. As we discussed in Chapter 28, chemotherapy drugs act at different points in the cell's cycle. Theoretically, when we give a drug we kill a certain fraction of the existing cancer cells. Though in reality you have millions of cancer cells, for the sake of simplicity let's say that you have a thousand. On the first hit of a cytotoxic drug we kill 200. Then there are 800 cells. We wait three weeks, during which time some grow back. When you hit the next cycle, you have 900: the chemo kills another 150 and you're down to 750. We keep doing this, and hopefully get you down to a small enough number that the immune system can fight them effectively for a time. We are not able to kill them all off, unfortunately, but we can get a lot. By using different combinations of drugs we may be able to increase the number of cells we kill. The cells don't all divide at the same time—one group divides now; another group divides the day after tomorrow. Some of the drugs will attack today's dividing cells, while the others will attack tomorrow's.

All of the chemotherapy drugs produce the standard side effects—vomiting, etc.,—and in combination the side effects tend to be worse. As we mention in the chapter on adjuvant therapy there are now terrific anti-nausea drugs which have almost eliminated this problem. Most drugs involve some hair loss. Several have the potential to cause leukemia down the road; however, since you're dealing with metastatic breast cancer, that's not a reason to eliminate them. Most will decrease your white cell count. Attempts have been made to test the tumor cells against a variety of drugs in a test tube to predict the right drug or combination of drugs. Although it sounds like a great idea, it hasn't worked as well as we would like in practice. What works in the test tube doesn't always work in a human being.

You won't always build up a resistance to the drug and need to have new ones. Sometimes we'll treat metastatic cancer with a particular drug and get a response: the disease recurs and we use the same drug again, and again it works. It always amazes me how often we find a drug that doesn't work for the majority of patients, but turns out to be exactly what one particular person needs. I had one patient with horrible lumps all over her chest. We treated her with just about everything, including experimental drugs, and nothing seemed to work. Then we went back and tried straight 5 fluorouracil with leukovorin rescue, which usually doesn't work that well in breast cancer—and everything disappeared. So we sometimes can't predict what the right drug is for a particular person, and if you have metastatic disease, you need to keep that in mind. You may feel discouraged if particular drugs don't seem to be working, especially if they're the standard breast cancer drugs. But you never know when we'll hit on the one that will alleviate your symptoms.

Once we've found a drug that works, we continue it for a time.

How long a time is something that doctors disagree about. There are two philosophies. One is that we'll get about as much response as we're going to get in about six months, so we should give the chemo for six months and then stop. The other philosophy is to give it continuously until the patient becomes resistant to it, and then move onto something else. There are arguments for both schools. It's something you should discuss with your doctor and be clear about before you start treatments.

You would think that adding chemotherapy and hormonal therapy might work better than either one alone. This is actually not the case. In women with hormonally sensitive tumors adding chemotherapy to hormones does not increase disease-free survival. However, chemotherapy works just as well after a hormonal therapy has been used. This may not be the case for hormonal therapy after chemotherapy. This is another argument for trying hormonal therapies first.

Any woman with metastatic disease needs to investigate the available clinical trials. There are new drugs and/or new combinations of drugs which are being tested all of the time and may be the best choice for someone with metastatic disease (see Chapter 33). It's important to talk with your doctor and get clear, precise information about what drugs are best for you, how long and in what combinations you can take them, and what their side effects are.

High-Dose Chemotherapy

Oncologists find it frustrating that they can't give higher doses of chemotherapy because of the damage it does to bone marrow. As we described earlier, this has led to a new form of treatment—high-dose chemotherapy with bone marrow or stem cell rescue, popularly called bone marrow transplant, or BMT. This has been tried as a last resort in women with metastatic disease. The notion of high-dose chemotherapy with BMT isn't simply to get rid of symptoms—it's far too drastic a treatment for that. The hope is that the extra high doses of chemo will actually cure the patient. At this point, that's all it is—a hope. We can't be sure that just because chemotherapy helps many patients, heavy doses will help more patients. It may be that what makes chemotherapy work isn't the amount of the dosage, but the patient's response to the particular drug itself. It may work the way antibiotics do: if you take the wrong antibiotic for your infection, it won't help, and the wrong antibiotic for your infection may be the right one for mine. Individual bodies respond differently even to the same substance. The answer probably varies. There are some people who won't respond to chemotherapy at any dose; there are some who will respond equally well to normal or huge doses, and there are some who will respond to huge doses but not to normal ones. Unfortunately, at this stage we don't know which are which.

But the big question is, does BMT really cure patients with metastatic disease? David Eddy, from the Center for Health Policy Research and Education, at Duke University, did a review study in April 1992[3] of all the existing data on autologous (from your own body) bone marrow transplant in metastatic disease. He found that although at that point there had been a number of studies, none were randomized control studies that put people into separate groups, one getting standard chemotherapy and the other bone marrow transplant.

Keep in mind that up to 27 percent of women with metastatic breast cancer will have a significant remission with hormones or standard chemotherapy. In the limited studies we have, the *complete* response rate to BMT is higher than it is in standard chemotherapy—it's 36 percent versus 8 percent. Remember, you can have a remission without having a complete response. And the overall (both complete and partial) response rate is good—70 percent. But the duration of the response is the same—eight months. And the median survival is about 16 months—compared to a median survival of over two years following conventional therapy in a large percentage of trials. There's 43 percent overall survival in two years, versus 39 percent two-year survival with standard chemotherapy, essentially no difference.[4] A direct, randomized controlled study of bone marrow transplant has never been done. All that has been done is to compare the data from the bone marrow studies against that in other studies of chemotherapy. The problem is, we can't be sure if the comparisons are accurate, since there's no control for age, general health, and other factors. A variety of women are included: those who respond well to chemo and those who don't; those who, apart from the cancer, are physically strong and those who are weakened by age or by other illnesses. A difference in the sample could seriously skew any study. In general, the people who have bone marrow transplants are younger, because they have to be able to withstand the incredible assault on their bodies. A 65-year-old with a bad heart isn't a candidate for BMT. Transplant patients are those who usually have metastatic disease identified in only one spot rather than all over their bodies and therefore are considered more "curable." To be sure of the efficacy of bone marrow transplant, we'd have to study women who have had the procedure in contrast to the same *type* of women treated with standard chemotherapy.

To ensure that they are transplanting only women who are likely to benefit, oncologists now give patients three or four cycles of chemotherapy first, and, if the patient demonstrates a response to that, they then give her the bone marrow transplant. This makes sense: if you don't respond to chemotherapy at all, you're unlikely to respond to it in megadoses. However, it makes comparisons with the overall population of women treated with standard chemo (responders and nonresponders) even trickier. We really need to have randomized control studies. Some of those are now taking place, but we don't have the data from them yet.

David Eddy, when he reviewed the data, found that, even looking at the most impressive results, there was a projected disease-free survival rate of 14 percent in six years. But he emphasizes that it's only a projection. In fact, at the time of his study only one woman had been observed—for six years. Another had been observed for slightly over four years and a third for slightly over three. While that's encouraging, it's not a lot of data to go on.

Further, with conventional chemotherapy, 10 percent of patients are alive in 10 years. So it's not a difference between zero and 14 percent, even if it's accurate. It's between 10 and 14. And with such small numbers of women studied for long-term survival with BMT, if one dies, the percentage shrinks dramatically. Eddy concluded that although the results were promising, they didn't suggest that BMT was the great answer, at least not yet.

A very important consideration in all this is the danger of the procedure itself. Five to 10 percent of women die during the procedure. This must be factored in when we talk about increased survival.

Bone marrow transplant is still an unproven therapy. We have a lot to learn about it. It may prove very useful to women in earlier stages of breast cancer. The fact that it's been done chiefly on women with metastatic disease works against its effecting long-term cures. Many advocates point out that it will probably work better in patients whose disease has not noticeably spread—those we believe to have micrometastatic disease. Now it's being tested on women who have 10 or more positive lymph nodes (see Chapter 28).

I think that bone marrow transplant will probably prove to have a place in the treatment of metastatic disease, and that there is a subgroup of women for whom it will make a difference. But we don't quite know how to pick those women out yet. The problem is that because there are no controlled studies and we don't have the absolute data yet, there's a tendency for doctors to say to women with metastatic disease, "The chances of our curing you with conventional therapy are very low. We've got this new experimental treatment that may or may not work, but it's your only chance." And too often the patient, understandably grasping for hope, hears that as "This will work and traditional therapy won't." And she goes for it.

Then we run into the problem of cost. Bone marrow transplant is a very expensive procedure, and many insurance companies won't pay for it because they regard it as experimental. It may sound harsh, but I think they're right. We have no way yet of accurately gauging whether it will help a patient more than traditional chemotherapy, or even kill her itself. I think any woman who wants to have bone marrow transplant, for metastatic disease, should have it only as part of a controlled study, so we can get the information. It's frustrating to realize that had all bone marrow transplants performed to date been part of controlled studies, we would probably have the answers we need.

Blue Cross–Blue Shield on the East Coast did a great thing in the early 1990s. They realized that if a woman with metastatic disease believed BMT was her only chance, she might sue her insurance company for refusing to pay for it. If the case was tried by a jury of her peers, the company would look like the villain and would lose the case. So Blue Cross–Blue Shield decided to avoid that by agreeing to pay for the transplant, if it were part of a clinical trial comparing high-dose chemotherapy through bone marrow transplant versus high-dose chemotherapy alone.

This doesn't mean every woman who wants it will get the transplant. Half the group will get one treatment and half the other, and by definition the distribution is random. But half the women who apply will get the procedure, and the others will be getting the treatment we know to be the most effective available treatment to date.

Unfortunately, bone marrow transplants are good business. Hospitals love them, because hospitals like to fill beds. Here's a procedure that keeps a patient in bed for two weeks. It's a high-income, high-tech operation: it uses a lot of blood transfusions and blood tests and drugs and all the things that hospitals need to pay their bills. Thus, many small community hospitals have developed their own bone marrow transplant programs. They don't have the expertise to do it, and their mortality rates are as high as 10 percent. But it's the hot new thing. In America, we tend to believe if it hurts more and you suffer more, it must work better—particularly if somebody is trying to prevent you from getting it. So there are probably a lot more people getting bone marrow transplants than there should be. If I seem adamant, it's because I've seen firsthand the negative as well as the positive effects of the procedure. One of my patients was one of the very first breast cancer patients of Bill Peters, who is now the head of the transplant program at Duke. He was then at the Dana Farber, as was I. She had had breast cancer that had recurred locally while she was having chemotherapy. She had the transplant and got through it well. But two weeks after she got out of the hospital she had another recurrence. I had another patient more recently with a recurrence in a lymph node above her collarbone. As we discussed in Chapter 31, that kind of recurrence almost always means the disease has metastasized. She agonized about it, and decided to have the transplant. She died from the transplant. She probably would have died of breast cancer, but maybe not for another 5 or 10 years.

So when I say that 5 to 10 percent of women die from the procedure, I'm not just quoting statistics—I'm thinking about real women. If you decide on bone marrow transplant, you're gambling on a long shot versus a slight danger of immediate death. If you live five years with or without the transplant, you may well be alive within the time we find a treatment that will work for metastatic disease, and that may be a less drastic treatment than bone marrow transplant.

I'm not by any means dismissing BMT. There are women who have had transplants and have done very well. But there are also women who have had standard chemotherapy, or hormone treatments, who have done very well. It's hard to know what the right thing to do is. It's also very hard for someone who's been told she has metastatic disease not to go for the biggest, strongest thing she can find. But before you sign up for a transplant you need to get a couple of opinions. If, after thoroughly researching the advisability of getting bone marrow transplant, you decide to do it, you have more research to do. You need to find out the best place to have it done. You can't make convenience your criterion in something this dangerous. If it means traveling three states away to get the best procedure, travel three states away. Look for a hospital that has a program doing a clinical trial and that has done the procedure frequently, rather than a community hospital that's done only a few and has no relation to any of the studies being done. The mortality rate is probably less at the larger centers. You're risking years of life, and you want to minimize the risk as much as you can.

Other Treatments

I've been talking about systemic therapies so far, but sometimes local treatment is called for. There are certain kinds of metastatic disease that respond best to local treatments because they're really local problems.

Radiation, for example, works best if the cancer has spread to your eye. Spinal cord involvement, impending bone fracture (in which your bone is so weakened that it is about to break)—this kind of local problem, where one spot can be radiated, also lends itself well to radiation.

If you're being treated with radiation for metastatic cancer rather than the initial breast cancer, there are some slight differences. The treatment is the same, but it's for a different purpose—to alleviate pain or other symptoms. It usually takes a couple of weeks before the pain noticeably lessens.

The timing is somewhat different as well. There are usually 10 to 15 treatments, spread over two and a half to four weeks. A smaller dose of radiation is used. While a primary radiation treatment might use 6,000 centigrays of radiation over six and a half weeks, with 180 centigrays per treatment, the treatment for someone with, for example, bone metastasis in the hip might use 3,000 centigrays over 10 treatments of 300 centigrays each.

Surgery, as we mentioned in Chapter 31, is best if there is one spot in the lung or brain. If the cancer has recurred in several places, however, systemic treatment is best.

Pain Control

In terms of palliation—getting rid of symptoms so you feel better— treatments of the cancer itself aren't the only options. We've come an enormous way in pain control. So if, for example, you're in severe pain because of bone metastasis, we now have ways of putting a catheter in the space along the spinal cord and dripping continuous low-dose morphine in to get rid of all the pain. Administered this way, it won't affect your mind the way it would if administered systemically. This won't cure you, but in your last three or four months of life, when systemic therapy is no longer working, it can give you quality time and reduce or eliminate suffering. It's amazing that the leading medical textbooks on breast diseases and breast cancer have no chapter about pain management. Yet there's a whole specialty now on pain control—a combination of anesthesiologists, internists, and psychiatrists. There's a lot of knowledge now about chronic pain and how to deal with it. Anybody who is having chronic pain because of metastatic cancer, and isn't getting relief, should ask to be referred to a pain unit. A lot of oncologists and people who work on cancer are so focused on treating and curing the disease that they forget about these ancillary things that can make an enormous difference in the patient's life. So ask to see a pain specialist: it may mean having to travel to the local medical school, but it can make a big difference to you.

Experimental Treatments for Metastatic Breast Cancer

Throughout this book I've been encouraging women to participate in phase three clinical trials (see Chapter 33)—trials of drugs or treatments that have been tested in earlier phases and have been shown to cause no harm to the patient. There is a trickier area to consider with metastatic cancer, and that is phase one or two trials. These are much earlier trials, designed to determine first the toxicity of a possibly useful drug, and then its efficacy.

Since you now know that, unlike the case with your first diagnosis, the traditional treatments offer only a slim chance at best of saving your life, an experimental treatment may be worth considering. It's a gamble, but one in which the gain might be considerable.

When is the best time to become involved in an experimental trial? Classically people do it when nothing else has helped and they've run out of options. The problem is that when you have run out of options you're least likely to respond to the new treatment: you have no resources left. So the best time may be when you have metastatic disease but are asymptomatic. A chest X ray or bone scan shows a lesion but actually you have no other signs. At this stage, there's no rush to use chemotherapy or hormonal therapy, since, as we said earlier, there's no evidence that treating with chemo earlier will give you better survival odds than waiting until you have symptoms. This, however, is a good time to try something experimental. You have an opportunity to see if it works, and then if it doesn't, you can get chemotherapy when your symptoms surface.

These kinds of treatments will not be routinely offered by your doctor, unless she or he is a doctor who is working on the experiments. The best way to find out about them is to go to your local medical school and see what they're involved in. You can also call the Physician Data Query (PDQ) at the National Cancer Institute (1-800-4-CANCER), which is a computerized searching system, and they will print out for you a list of every clinical trial that you're eligible for, in your geographic area, or in the whole United States if you're willing and able to travel (see Appendix B).

I think this is really worthwhile. It's a gamble, but sometimes the gamble pays off. For example, the women who first participated in the tests for Taxol, the drug that comes from the bark of the yew tree, had a remarkable response lasting 18 months to two years.

There are two exciting new experiments being worked on for metastatic disease. One, initiated at UCLA and now being done at several centers around the country, is a combination of chemotherapy with what's called a "biological response modifier." They've developed an antibody to the Her 2 neu oncogene, which we discussed in Chapter 14. As we noted, 30 percent of women are overexpressors of the Her 2 neu oncogene. We're seeing remarkable responses in people who haven't responded to other drugs. The theory behind the treatment is that the chemotherapy drug cisplatinum causes DNA damage. Normally when your body has DNA damage it simply repairs it, but we are hoping that we will do more damage to the DNA in the cancer cells than the body can handle. The antibody to the Her 2 neu oncogene will block DNA repair in those cancer cells which have overexpression of the oncogene. Now you've got drugs both causing the damage, and blocking its repair, and you've got a much stronger effect.

This concept is on the forefront of what we're going to see in the future—combinations of biological response modifiers, growth hormones, antibodies, and chemotherapy to make all of them work better.

A similar idea is an anti-angiogenesis drug. Angiogenesis is the cancer's attempt to develop new blood vessels to support its growth. With drugs that will block this function the cancer theoretically will not be able to get enough nourishment from its inadequate blood vessels and will die. Clinical trials are going on now with this category of drugs.

The best quality of life is being in remission—not having symptoms from cancer. But only you can decide what price in toxicity you are willing to pay. Some women want to try everything new and others do not. Don't let yourself be pushed by your doctor or family. Decide in your own heart what the best approach is for you.

33

Clinical Trials

As a woman and a physician, I've always been frustrated by the lack of information about women's health. Virtually all of the medical research in the past was done on men. Even the rat research was done on male rats. In the course of reading this book you've probably noticed how often I have said, "We don't know whether . . . " or "More research is needed before we know . . . ". You're probably tired of reading it. I know I'm tired of writing it. But the answers aren't there.

So what can we do about it? There are a couple of things. We can get involved in the political work that has sprung up around breast cancer and women's health (see Chapter 34) and demand more research. And we can participate in the research when we get the funding for it. As women, we can't complain that there are no data on diseases relevant to us, and then remain aloof from studies when they exist. Our demands for research are slowly getting met, and there is some very important research going on now that offers women the opportunity to participate. The silicone implant studies we discussed in Chapter 5, for example, will finally tell us whether the implants are safe or not. The tamoxifen prevention study will help us to learn whether tamoxifen can help women at high risk for breast cancer (see Chapter 17). The Women's Health Initiative is studying all of the health issues faced by postmenopausal women, including the safety of taking estrogen and progesterone, and the efficacy of calcium and vitamin D supplements. I think women should seek out these studies—and especially women who have been under-represented in research in the past: lesbians, older women, women of various racial and ethnic minorities. I realize that this may be hard for some people, since I'm asking women who have already suffered from the insensitivity of the health establishment to involve themselves deeply with that establishment. But the only way to learn about women's health is to have women in studies, and the way to be in studies is to sign up for them.

The silicone implant controversy, which we discussed at length in Chapter 5, has dramatically demonstrated the problem that can arise when, as so often happens, a new medical procedure or substance is used before it's been sufficiently tested. The only way we find out it's problematical is when problems erupt months or years later. We need to move into a new mode in which we test every new treatment or procedure in the beginning, and continually for years thereafter, to see whether or not it's safe or even effective. If we'd done that with silicone, we'd know whether or not it causes the autoimmune diseases many women are now suffering. If we'd done it with DES, we would have saved a lot of women's lives.

All these studies are what we call research protocols (sometimes also known as clinical trials). Although the term "protocol" sounds like we're talking about who goes into the operating room first, a medical protocol is actually a research program designed to answer some specific questions about the effectiveness of a particular approach. The questions can be about methods of diagnosis, types of treatment, dosage of drugs, timing of administration of drugs, or type of drugs used. So a protocol for breast cancer treatment, for example, might study node-negative breast cancers in premenopausal women to see whether or not they would benefit from chemotherapy. A large enough group of patients who fit the criteria is recruited, and they're randomized (picked at random either to receive the treatment or not). Those selected to receive the drugs will be given them on a very strict regimen: for instance, they will be given x amount, on day 1 and 3, and a particular blood test will be given on day 5. This precision is important for the question to be answered—no variation is permitted, or our understanding of how well the treatment works will be impaired. The other women, or control group, will not receive the new drugs but will be followed just as rigorously, and will be given the standard treatment. What makes it a protocol is the fact that it is asking a question: will the women receiving the chemotherapy do better than the women who are not? Other protocols might compare two different treatments to see which is the best. By participating in these studies these women will get reasonable treatments and at the same time help us to figure out the answers.

New treatments used in protocols are tried out in three phases. Phase-one treatments are aimed at determining the safety of a technique or the toxicity and most effective dose of a treatment. For example, one protocol I am involved in is testing the usefulness of a breast duct endoscope, a tiny scope that I am trying to put into breast ducts to see if we can explore them noninvasively. This study doesn't compare one group to another but is done under controlled conditions to determine both the safety and efficacy of this tool. We are first trying it on women who are about to have a mastectomy and who have given us permission to do the experiment. For 15 minutes after the patient has been put under the anesthetic, we try to find the milk ducts and insert the endoscope into the breast that is to be removed. After the breast has been taken off, we examine it to determine if we have caused any damage. If this phase of the study shows that we don't damage the breast, we can go onto the next phase.

In the case of chemotherapy drugs, phase-one studies usually involve people who have advanced disease and are informed and willing to try unproven therapies, on the long shot that this may be the miracle that saves them. In addition, the researchers are trying to give patients the drugs in the doses that will be effective if the drugs do work. These are usually new drugs, and there is always the chance that one of them will be effective. If phase one shows the drug to be tolerated by patients, the study moves on to phase two, with the best and safest dose found in phase one. Here we are testing to see if the drug has any effect on the disease. (In the case of my ductoscopy, the phase-two study will try to determine whether this technique has the ability to diagnose precancer at an earlier stage.) A phase-two drug study looking at breast cancer is often done on women whose cancer has spread but who are not in an immediate life-threatening situation—women who have metastatic disease but are still asymptomatic, and are willing to gamble on the long shot that some experimental new treatment will be the breakthrough that they've been hoping for. Taxol, a new chemotherapy drug, is a good example of that—it did turn out to be a very effective drug for metastatic disease and is being studied now as an adjuvant treatment.

Once we've determined the effectiveness and safety of the technique or drugs (and, with drugs, the best dosages), we're at phase three. An example of a phase-three study for my ductoscope might be comparing it to mammography for certain high-risk women. With drugs, phase-three studies might take a new drug that seems to show some effectiveness without undue toxicity, and compare it to the standard treatment. Phase-three cancer studies use patients with all degrees of cancer.

People often have an inaccurate perception of phase-three trials. They think it's all or nothing: the experimental group gets the new treatment and the control group gets nothing. But that's never the case. The trials compare new treatment against the standard treatment. So, for example, if you're part of a study comparing very high dose chemotherapy with the standard dose, and you end up in the control group, you'll still get adequate doses of chemotherapy, based on the therapy you would have gotten if you weren't in the study. The experimental group would get the higher doses to see if more is better. This way you know you're getting the best treatment that we currently know of, since we don't know if the new treatment will be better or less effective. It's a good gamble: you either get the best we have or something that may be better. Phase three can be thought of as a comparison between what we hope will be the next step and the best we currently have.

This is an ethical way to experiment with drugs and new techniques, but it does create some limitations. Since in phase one we use only patients who have not responded well to standard therapy, we can't be sure that, if our new treatment fails also, it would not have worked with a patient whose disease was less widespread. In fact, there are now efforts to try some new drugs earlier, at the first sign of recurrence, which may indeed be a fairer way to test them. Even with the current limitation, however, we've made amazing advances in treatments and techniques in the past decade.

A phase-three protocol is never an early stage of experimentation. By the time we have a large-scale protocol, we're using drugs or treatment approaches that are already in use. What we're changing is dosages, timing, combinations of drugs or their indications. Often what's being studied is the dosage of a particular drug we know to be effective, or timing of treatments. In these studies patients are randomly divided into two groups, one given the standard dosage and one the "new twist." If one group does better than the other, we'll know which dose is best; if both do the same, we know the approach with the least side effects is all that's needed. Although it may seem a little scary to participate in research, it is important to remember that no doctor should put you on a protocol or clinical trial without being convinced that the treatment being investigated will be at least as helpful to you as the standard treatment. By definition, any trial sponsored by the National Cancer Institute and other peer-reviewed groups has safeguards built in. Your treatment will be chosen by an unbiased computer. You could be part of the group that gets the new combination of treatments, or of the control group that gets standard treatment. In addition, there is a Human Experimentation Committee in every hospital that reviews each protocol to make sure it is safe and well-designed. They oversee all clinical trials and are responsible for making sure that the informed consent is readable and that the potential benefits of the study outweigh its risks for the subjects being studied. Of course, you'll always be given the choice. It's both unethical and illegal for a doctor to put you on a protocol treatment or clinical trial without your full and informed consent, and you have every right to refuse. If you're on an experiment and become convinced that it's harming you, you can leave it, though this should be done only as a last resort, since losing a subject affects the study results. You and your doctor both have the right to take you off the study at any time.

There are very good reasons for participating in a protocol. Aside from its usefulness to women in the future, studies assure the patient herself that she will get the best possible care. For these reasons, many women are eager to be part of studies. Susan McKenney, a nurse practitioner and oncology nurse who works extensively with breast cancer patients, has talked with many patients at the Dana Farber Institute and finds that, once they understand they're not just guinea pigs and that the treatments can be helpful both to them and to other women, they are often anxious to participate. "Breast cancer treatment has changed over the last 20 years because women have participated in protocols," she says.

Patients I've spoken with back this up. One woman who was diagnosed in 1990 with a stage 3 cancer became involved in a study using far higher doses of chemotherapy than the standard—the dose was adjusted upward as far as the patient's tolerance allowed. Aside from the treatments in the hospital, which occurred every three weeks, she gave herself nightly injections of a material that stimulated the growth of the bone marrow that had been destroyed by the chemotherapy.

She had a difficult time with the treatment, throwing up so often that she slept on the bathroom floor for weeks. "They called me the nausea queen," she recalls ruefully. But her experiment paid off. Although in this study the patients went straight into chemotherapy, without having surgery or radiation beforehand, they had been warned that they would probably require both when the chemotherapy course was over. But her tumor shrunk so dramatically and so completely that she did not need either. "I feel that the only reason I'm alive is because I did that trial," she says today. One of the other women in the trial, with whom she became close friends, survived in spite of the fact that she had a very aggressive inflammatory cancer. Not all women are so lucky, of course, but all have the satisfaction of contributing to medical knowledge.

There are many ways for patients to participate in protocols. One of my recent patients was part of the duct endoscopy study—and managed to participate in two others in the same operation. She was scheduled to have a mastectomy with immediate reconstruction with a free flap (see Chapter 26). First she participated in a phase-three study comparing one anesthetic gas to another. Then she was part of my phase-one breast duct endoscopy study, after she had been put to sleep and prior to her mastectomy. Finally, she was part of a study exploring two different ways of estimating the size of the flap that the plastic surgeon creates following the mastectomy on a patient who is having immediate reconstruction. None of these studies affected her treatment in any way other than adding about 15 minutes to the time she spent under anesthesia, and yet she was able to contribute important information in many areas.

If you're considering being part of a study, you have a right to know everything about it. Ask the researchers what exactly they're giving you; find out the possible side effects; find out what they know and don't know. You have to sign an informed consent form, which is often many pages long. (The form for the study of high-dosage chemotherapy was 27 pages long.) Read it, thoroughly: it's worth the effort. Write your questions down. Sit down with the doctor, go over any questions about anything that's unclear. Also ask to speak to another breast cancer survivor who has gone through the same program ahead of you.

Some studies are actually begun by patients themselves. You can get a group in the community together and initiate a study on your own terms. For example, if you want to research lesbians and breast cancer, you can go to the local medical school or a researcher and say, "This is a study we want to see done. We'll supply the participants— do you have anyone who can work with us?" A number of recent studies have begun that way. For example, a group of women on Long Island were very disturbed at the high level of breast cancer in their community. They lobbied the National Cancer Institute, and got a study that will be investigating possible environmental pollutants on Long Island and their relation to breast cancer. Other women in Cape Cod have set up a similar study for Massachusetts.

The political action of breast cancer activists has resulted in increased funds for breast cancer research, and now that the door is beginning to open we're getting more and more studies on women and disease. As a National Breast Cancer Coalition says in its Research Agenda statement, "We encourage innovative ideas and would like to see an increase in investigator-initiated research rather than . . . proposals where researchers are solicited to submit grant applications aimed toward research in a particular area the NCI has determined has merit, which in essence controls the breadth of approaches." The scientists are glad for the money, but they sometimes need to be reminded that if they want women to participate in their studies, they have to involve them in designing the studies, so that the studies themselves make sense.

This kind of active effort to create and participate in studies has been very effective in the AIDS community. AIDS patients were angry and frustrated because new drugs weren't being released fast enough, and they were able to set up a whole system of community clinical trials, which allowed the new drugs to be used and studied at the same time. Then they very eagerly participated in the studies, so some answers came in. Unfortunately the answers have not yet included a cure. Scientific discoveries don't always yield quick results, even with interest, more money, and active participation. But they never yield results without them. I think we need to follow the example of the AIDS activists.

So far, we haven't done so to a large enough extent. Only about 3 percent of breast cancer patients in the U.S. participate in protocols. This is much lower than in Europe, and not something for us to be proud of. But we can't wholly blame the patients for this. Many hospitals or doctors here simply don't offer protocols. If you're being treated at a research hospital or major cancer center you'll usually be offered protocols if you qualify, and large numbers of patients there do participate. Women who choose such hospitals for treatment tend to be those who seek out the most advanced, sophisticated treatments; that's why they go to a big research hospital. They feel safer in an environment whose major purpose is studying and fighting cancer. But the ability to offer protocols isn't limited to these hospitals. There is now a mechanism allowing community hospitals to offer participation in protocols. A program called CCOP (Cancer Center Outreach Program) links community hospitals with large medical centers, allowing you to participate locally. And that participation assures that your doctor is keeping up to date, and that you're getting the best medicine has to offer.

Protocols are more available than a lot of doctors admit—or even know about. There are four or five national cooperative groups around the country that do studies in many centers. At UCLA we're a member of the Southwestern Oncology Group (SWOG), and there are many protocols that we, along with a lot of other centers, participate in. You can be sure, if you're on a SWOG protocol, that you're getting quality care—and you may or may not be getting that same quality care with your own doctor. Other national groups are ECOG (Eastern Cooperative Oncology Group), CALGB (Cancer and Leukemia Group B), and NSABP (National Surgical Adjuvant Breast and Bowel Project).

All hospitals and all doctors could offer patients some form of participation in protocols, if they choose to do so. Many don't. There are several reasons for this. Some aren't convinced that protocols—or a particular protocol—offer as good a treatment as the standard treatment. Others don't want to bother. They have to fill out a lot of forms, and do blood tests on very specific days—a protocol is more work for the doctor. Still, many others are willing enough to offer protocols, but haven't the interest or the ability to explain them well. If a doctor simply says, "You can have the standard treatment or be part of an experiment," you're probably going to take the former. If you're not offered a protocol, it is important for you to ask your doctor why he or she is suggesting a particular treatment. Sometimes it's because there is scientific evidence that supports it, but more often than not, it is because they feel, based on their experience, that it is the right treatment. Both of these may be valid reasons, but you deserve to know which is being used or whether both apply. And you need to know why they are not recommending a study. You need to ask your doctor what protocols you are eligible for.

If you ask your doctor about trials and are told they don't know of any and don't want to bother finding out, you can call 1-800 4 CANCER, at the National Cancer Institute. They'll hook you into their Physician Data Query (PDQ) computer program and give you a list of every clinical trial you're eligible for. They'll also tell you what area the trials are in so you'll know whether or not a given study is being conducted near you. Then you can go with that information to your doctor and work with it from there.

It's not as easy in terms of noncancer studies, but you can call the Office on Women's Health and get some information on major trials. The Women's Health Initiative has a number you can call to find out the nearest center (see Appendix B).

In a clinical trial, the study doesn't end when the treatment ends. You're followed for the rest of your life, since the point of the trial is to see how a new treatment affects patients in the long run. So when you sign on to a clinical trial, you're accepting a long-term commitment— and getting one, since it can only benefit you to be followed so closely that any problem will be caught as early as possible.

Often doctors will tell you they are using the same "protocol" as the one used at a cancer center, when what they mean is that they are using the same drugs in the same dosages. But unless it's part of a study designed to answer a fundamental question, it isn't really a protocol.

We should also mention the financial aspects of studies, since they vary greatly depending on the nature of the study. For a study that offers no benefit and some inconvenience to the subject, payment may be offered as an incentive—those are the studies college kids often get on to earn a couple of hundred dollars. In fact, I participated in a study of DES as a contraceptive when I was in medical school to help pay my tuition. Some studies that might benefit the subject, or that cause the subject no inconvenience (like my endoscope study), involve no financial exchange at all. Occasionally a study of a treatment that can benefit the patient will be offered to the patient at a reduced fee, like an asthma and visualization study my co-author participated in.. Finally, as is the case with the chemotherapy studies I've discussed here, the patient (or the insurance company) pays the full price for the procedure, being rewarded by the hoped-for benefits of the treatment and by the quality control that follows it. (New drugs are usually free.)

Unfortunately, even when they're offered protocols, only a small percentage of women accept the offer. Here too there are a number of reasons. Some women are afraid of being randomized. They want to get the best treatment and they find it hard to believe that the medical profession doesn't know what that is. Or they have strong feelings about getting a particular treatment and they don't want to experiment with anything else.

Often women don't want to be in studies because they're not allowed to decide which group they'll be in. "I'll be in a study comparing chemotherapy and tamoxifen," a woman will tell me, "if I can choose which one I'll get." That can't be done, since the treatments need to be chosen randomly for the study to be valid.

Another reason some women don't participate in clinical trials is that they think we already have the answers. For example, they assume that the standard treatments will save their lives, and they don't want to rock the boat with something new. But it's precisely because the standard treatments *don't* always work that we do experiments. The courageous women who participated in the phase-one and -two trials of Adriamycin and Taxol have benefited not only themselves but the many women who have followed.

Some women fail to understand the whole idea of a study. They want to choose their own treatment, rather than participate in a protocol. After the treatment is finished, they want that treatment and its effects on them to be studied. But of course, that isn't the way it works. For a study of a treatment to give us any clear information, it must be done under controlled circumstances, defined by the researchers and strictly followed. After-the-fact statistics have had their use, but that's not the same as following a particular subject on a particular treatment, and we can never get the same level of information with this kind of observational study that we can with randomized control studies. You can't have your cake and eat it too. If you want the information that comes with being part of a controlled study, you have to be on that study from the beginning.

Ironically, some women swing to the other extreme, and I find that equally frustrating. Once in a while, a highly publicized experimental procedure comes along that people think is the miracle we've been searching for. Then the attitude toward being in a study turns around. You don't fear being part of an experiment; you demand what you think will be your share of the miracle.

This had been the case with so-called bone marrow transplant, high-dose chemotherapy with bone marrow rescue (see Chapter 32). This has gotten so much good press that people often fail to understand that its impact on cure rates is still unknown—we don't as yet know if it will work. Yet many women with aggressive breast cancer are jumping into it. This isn't wholly the media's fault. Many oncologists are pushing it. An oncologist will say to a patient, "You have a terrible prognosis. Standard chemotherapy isn't going to work all that well; you'd better have a bone marrow transplant, it's your only chance." The patient assumes the doctor knows it will work. But in truth, the doctor can't be certain about whether it will work or not, and is suggesting a gamble. So we have the frightening phenomenon of women accepting experimental treatment without the safety net of being part of a carefully monitored study. From the beginning, we should have entered all women who wanted to undergo bone marrow transplant in a clinical trial. Then we'd know today whether it works. Having failed to do that back then, we should do it now. Until we do, we're working on no knowledge and a lot of wishful thinking. No one should be getting bone marrow transplants unless she's doing it as part of a study. But as I said earlier, the problem usually isn't that women are jumping into new treatments; it's that they aren't participating enough in studies of new treatments or in comparison studies.

One reason may be recent adverse publicity regarding one cooperative group, the National Surgical Adjuvant Breast and Bowel Project. It got a lot of press in the spring of 1994. The media coverage was so confusing that it bears discussing here. In large organizations like the NSABP, cooperative groups are formed by many different centers that want to participate in clinical research. This is wonderful, because it gives us the ability to do really large-scale studies. But it can cause some confusion. One NSABP study showed that a combination of lumpectomy and radiation is as effective in treating primary breast cancer as mastectomy. Among the centers was one in Montreal. One of the researchers in that center was found to have falsified some data used in the study. Because of this the media called the conclusion of the study into question, without checking whether the conclusions had been corroborated by other studies. In reality, regrettable though it was, the level of falsification was minor. For example, the study had strict guidelines about how many days after surgery a subject could begin to participate. The Montreal center researcher had altered its reports so that one woman's surgery appeared to have taken place two days before it actually did, thus enabling her to be used in the study. There were a few equally minor alterations. I do not excuse any of them, and the media were right to criticize them. But having done so, they had an ethical responsibility to go further and explore the implications of the alterations on the accuracy of the study's findings. Had they done so, they would have discovered that the falsifications did not change the study's findings in any substantial way: after it had discovered the fraud, the NSABP did a reanalysis of their data, excluding the altered data, and found that the results remained the same. They would also have learned that there are many other studies validating the NSABP's conclusions about breast conservation. They did not investigate, and so gave the public a partial and inaccurate presentation of the facts.

This case shows how important the large cooperative groups are. If that study had been done in just one center and the center was cheating on the data, the whole study would have been thrown out. But since the Montreal center was only one of many centers and represented only a fraction of the total study, it did not affect the outcome at all. The other lesson from this episode is that it is important to have women with breast cancer involved in the design and monitoring of the studies. The real problem was that the administration of the NSABP knew about the falsified data and did not disclose it to the other investigators or to the public. If women with breast cancer had been involved as representatives of the women in the study, we would hope to have greater public accountability and to have known much sooner. As the NSABP wrote in a statement about the falsification: "In response to the public's outcry that information had been kept from it, a top official of NCI was quoted as saying that if a year or two ago he had 'intuited' women's concerns to the NCI/NSABP behavior, NCI would have acted differently. There is a fundamental deficiency in a system where a public servant believes he must intuit how the public may react to decisions made by his agency. Had a consumer advocate—a woman with breast cancer—been part of the process, the public's peace of mind and women's lives would not have been left to the uncertainty of an individual's intuitive abilities." The paper goes on to criticize the "club-like atmosphere among researchers" that is created in the absence of consumer advocate participation.

It's also important to note that the problem in the NSABP study was with the collection and monitoring of data, not with the safety of the study. There are strong safeguards in research regarding the design and safety of the protocol. As we said earlier, each experiment must be evaluated by an institutional review board, which includes laypeople. The board members read the protocol, evaluate the scientific basis, and make sure that nothing done during the study will harm the participants.

The cooperative groups noted earlier run many protocols, working with doctors all over the country. The National Cancer Institute (see Appendix B) also has many protocols and will pay the expenses of any woman who participates. The drawback for women in other parts of the country is that you must be treated at the Institute, which is in Washington, DC.

There is also the Community Cancer Outreach Program, which includes 52 community programs in 31 states and so is accessible to many more women. These have been selected by the National Cancer Institute to participate in the introduction of the newest clinical protocols and to bring patients to clinical trials. Finally, all doctors have access to a computer program from the National Cancer Institute that lists all the available protocols for breast cancer, and the latest treatments.

Of course, after learning what protocols there are you may decide that none of them offers the treatment you want. But you owe it to yourself, and to other women, to find out what the protocols that you are eligible for are and what they involve, before you decide. My patient who took part in the high-dose chemotherapy experiment says that if she had a friend newly diagnosed with breast cancer, she would strongly urge her to look into protocols. "I'd tell her not to jump into anything," she says, "but to explore everything. Find out what's there; weigh it in your mind. 'Latest' isn't always best, and it may be that what you find isn't right for you. But there's a very good chance that you'll find that what's best for you is in a clinical trial."

Whether or not you decide to become part of a clinical trial in terms of your treatment, there's another way you can contribute to the research on breast cancer—and do yourself a favor as well. If you have any surgical procedure—whether a biopsy, a wide excision, a mastectomy, or even breast reduction—make sure that any tissue removed from your breast is kept in a tissue bank (see Chapter 12). This is becoming more and more possible because one of the things we're pushing for politically is regional and national tissue banks. You can have this done in any hospital you're in.

If the tissue is cancerous, it's especially useful to you. If it's just a biopsy and the tumor is benign, we have that tissue to study. When they remove the cancer they take what they need to make a diagnosis, look at margins, and determine the prognosis. If it's big enough they can still have some left over, and they can take a little chunk and freeze it. Then if five years from now we have a better prognostic indicator, you can go back and have the old tissue tested.

As we get new indicators, and we want to test them to see how effective they are, we have the tissue available; we don't have to go out and find it. So I think this is important for any high-risk women who undergo any surgery in which tissue is removed. Even women at no known risk for breast cancer have a contribution to make: we also need a pool of benign tissue for research. You should routinely ask the surgeon or pathologist to save some tissue for potential use in a tissue bank. If they say they don't have a tissue bank at the hospital, tell them to save it in a minus 80-degree celsius freezer and when you're over your surgery, you'll find out where they can send it. It's important that they freeze it right away. Then you can call the NCI 800 number (see Appendix B) and get the information you need. They can also save it as a paraffin block, but tissue that's been frozen allows us to do many more types of research.

This is the most painless, risk-free method of participating in trials. The kind of experiments I was discussing earlier—experiments with various kinds of treatments—are more of a gamble. I'm not trying to sound like a pollyanna, or give you false promises. There's no guarantee that being part of a trial will save or even prolong your life. My high-dose chemotherapy patient who is convinced that the experiment saved her life was part of a group of eight women who had their treatments together. Of the eight, six have since died. Probably they would have died on standard treatment as well. It's a gamble. But it's a gamble either way, with standard treatment or with experimental treatment. We have no guaranteed cures—if we did, there'd be no need for trials. But with trials, the guarantee we do have is that we are learning whatever we can to help women in the future. Already, we can see some of the results of trials. Not too long ago, any woman with breast cancer had no choice but to lose her breast. But a number of women participated in the first breast conservation studies, and were randomized to get either mastectomy or lumpectomy or radiation. They were very courageous women, going against the standard thinking to see if there wasn't an alternative. Thanks to them, thousands of women today have been able to save their breasts. As you make the complex, difficult decisions about your own treatment, keep those women in mind—the brave experimenters, and all of us who have benefited from their courage.

34

≡

The Politics
of Breast Cancer

If "everything is political," as they say, the politics of cancer have their roots in the 1950s. In 1952 the American Cancer Society started the Reach to Recovery program. This was a group of women helping women: survivors of breast cancer helping newly diagnosed women. Members of Reach to Recovery, all of whom had had mastectomies, would visit the patient in the hospital and reassure her that there was life after mastectomy. They were, and continue to be, a wonderful resource for women with breast cancer.

From there, support groups for women with breast cancer evolved. Women sat together and talked about their experiences and their feelings. It was tremendously helpful for these people to learn they were not alone in their feelings about a disease that was shrouded in so much mystery and fear.

All this underlined the fact that there was no psychosocial support from the medical profession—you had to get it from somewhere else. And since the disease remained one hidden from public view, there was still an aura of something shameful and disreputable about it.

The politics of breast cancer accelerated in the 1970s, when Shirley Temple Black, Betty Ford, and Happy Rockefeller told the world they had breast cancer. Their openness began to create an environment in which breast cancer could be looked at as a dangerous disease that

needed to be addressed by public institutions, rather than a private and shameful secret. There was a dramatic increase in the number of women in America who got mammograms, and in the number of breast cancer cases diagnosed.

Those were the days of the one-step procedure. You'd go in for the biopsy; it would be done under general anesthetic and, if the lump was positive, your breast would be immediately removed. You'd go under the anesthetic not knowing whether you'd have a breast when you woke up. There was no psychosocial support: your doctor wouldn't talk with you beyond telling you it was cancer (if they even told you that) and they removed your breast.

In 1977 Rose Kushner, a writer with breast cancer, wrote a terribly important book, *Why Me?* It ushered in the two-step procedure. Kushner saw no reason for a woman to have to decide whether to have a mastectomy before she even knew if she had breast cancer. She argued passionately that it was important for the woman to have her biopsy, learn if she had cancer, and then, if she did, decide what route to pursue. Doctors were still working on the erroneous assumption that time was everything: if they didn't get the cancer out the instant they found it, it would spread and kill the patient. Kushner had done enough research to realize that wasn't the case—that a few weeks between diagnosis and treatment wouldn't do any medical harm, and would do a great deal of emotional good. She pushed for the two-step procedure, and her book influenced large numbers of women to demand it for themselves. She became a national figure, representing women with breast cancer on the boards designing national studies, moving closer into the realm of politics. She died of breast cancer many years later, in January 1990.

Another force on the horizon at that time was Nancy Brinker. Brinker's sister, Susan G. Komen, was diagnosed with breast cancer in 1977 and died in 1980. In 1983 Brinker founded the Susan G. Komen Breast Cancer Foundation, which is based in Dallas, Texas. Ironically, she herself got breast cancer soon afterward. Since the mid-1980s, they've been working to raise money for research. They also try to encourage funding for women to get mammography. They organize the yearly Race for the Cure, which takes place in a number of cities. Brinker's husband is a wealthy businessman, active in Republican politics, and through him she became acquainted with the Bushes, the Reagans, the Quayles, and other important Republicans whose support she was able to enlist in some of her breast-cancer work.

For a long time, that was pretty much all that was going on around breast cancer. Then in the late 1980s, almost spontaneously, in different parts of the country a number of political women's cancer groups sprang up. One was in the Boston area, started by a patient of mine, Susan Shapiro, who had breast cancer. When she was diagnosed, she began to search for anyone working on the political issues around women and cancer, and she couldn't find anything. Yet she was passionately convinced that there were political implications to cancer, and particularly to women's cancers. She wrote an article in the feminist newspaper *Sojourner*, called "Cancer as a Feminist Issue," and at the end of it she announced a meeting at the Cambridge Women's Center. A lot of women showed up, women who had been as frustrated as she by the lack of political response to their disease. They formed the Women's Community Cancer Project. Their scope was fairly broad, including all cancers that women got and the role of women as caretakers for children, spouses, and parents with cancer. Inevitably, much of the focus was on breast cancer. Shapiro died in January 1990, but the project continues to flourish.

At about the same time the Women's Community Cancer Project was beginning, another group in Oakland, California, The Women's Cancer Resource Center, started, founded by a lesbian named Jackie Winnow. It too was a political group. There was a second group in the Bay Area, Breast Cancer Action, founded by Eleanor Pred, an older woman with breast cancer who modeled her work on some AIDS activism.

In Washington, D.C., the Mary-Helen Mautner Project for Lesbians with Cancer was formed by Susan Hester after Mautner, her partner, died of breast cancer. Its purpose was to provide support for lesbians with cancer, based on the model of the AIDS buddy programs.

These four groups emerged at around the same time. There were obvious differences: in two cases, the focus was lesbians, and in two the focus was all cancers. But all were based on the premise that there were political, not just personal, aspects of cancer that affected women.

All of these groups were aware of the work the AIDS movement had been doing. For the first time we were seeing people with a killer disease aggressively demanding more money for research, changes in insurance bias, and job protection. Women with breast cancer took note of that—particularly those women who had been part of the feminist movement, and were geared, as the gay activists with AIDS were, to the idea of identifying oppression and confronting it politically.

At the time these groups were emerging, I was finishing work on the first edition of this book. As I went on my book tour, talking with women, I began to realize how deep women's anger was, and how ready they were to do something. The key moment for me was in Salt Lake City in June 1990, when I gave a talk for 600 women. It was the middle of the afternoon, during the week, and the audience was mostly older women. It was a pretty long talk, and at the end, I said, "We don't know the answers, and I don't know what we have to do to make President Bush wake up and do something about breast cancer. Maybe we should march topless on the White House." I was making a wisecrack, hoping to end a somber talk with a little lightness.

I got a great response, and afterward women came up to me asking when the march was, how they could sign up for it, and what they could do to help organize it. I realized that, throughout the country, this issue touched all kinds of women, and that they were all fed up with the fact that this virtual epidemic was being ignored. I saw that it wasn't just in the big centers like San Francisco and Boston and Washington, D.C., where I'd expect to see political movements springing up. It was everywhere—everywhere women were ready to fight for attention to breast cancer.

I felt we needed to have some sort of national organization to give these women the hook they needed to begin organizing. I went to Washington to give a talk to the Mautner Project. Before the talk, I went out to dinner with Susan Hester, the founder of the project and two of her friends. I was talking about the thoughts I'd had after the Salt Lake City speech. My idea was that maybe we should have a big march, and end it with the formation of a new national organization. Hester thought we needed to go about it the other way around: if we formed the organization, we could get its members to come to a big march.

When I left, I called Amy Langer, the president of NABCO, the National Association of Breast Cancer Organizations, a group dedicated to giving individuals and groups breast cancer information. I asked what she thought of the idea, and she liked it. I also contacted Nancy Brinker of the Komen Foundation.

The four of us met for breakfast in Washington on December 11, 1990, during a breast cancer event—Susan, Amy, Nancy, and I—and we discussed it further. We all were enthusiastic and the result was a planning meeting. We invited Sharon Greene, the executive director of Y-Me, a very large support group organization in Chicago. Then we got Ann McGuire from the Women's Community Cancer Project, and we invited Eleanor Pred from Breast Cancer Action and Kim Calder from Cancer Care and Canact from New York.

We discussed whether or not any one of the existing groups wanted to take on the political piece, and although everyone was very enthusiastic no one felt they could handle this aspect, so we decided to go for a coalition of groups. The Komen Foundation dropped out and the other groups became the planning committee for the new coalition. We set up several task forces to figure out how we'd go about it and what our goals would be. Amy Langer used NABCO's list and others threw in their lists for an invitation to an organizing meeting in May 1991. Then we called an open meeting, to be held in Washington, and wrote to every women's group we knew of.

We had no idea who'd show up. On the day of the meeting the room was packed. There were representatives from all kinds of groups: the American Cancer Society and the American Jewish Congress were there. So was the Human Rights Campaign Fund, a big gay and lesbian group. There were members of breast cancer support groups from all around the country— such as Arm in Arm from Baltimore, the Linda Creed group from Philadelphia, and Share from New York. Overall there were about 100 or so individuals representing 75 organizations. We were overwhelmed, and we started the National Breast Cancer Coalition on the spot. Out of that meeting came the first Board of the Coalition.

NABCO agreed to be the administrator of the planning committee. Its expenses would be reimbursed from the other groups. As a result Amy chaired the meetings until bylaws and officers could be chosen. A year later Fran Visco, a lawyer from Philadelphia who had had breast cancer in her late 30s, became the first elected president. She has since taken a leave of absence from her law office and remains the president today.

From this first group of eager participants we formed a volunteer working board. Our first action, in the fall of 1991, was a project we called "Do the Write Thing." We wanted to collect and deliver to

Washington 175,000 letters, representing the 175,000 women who would be diagnosed with breast cancer that year. The letters would go both to the president and to various members of Congress.

This was spring, and we were planning this for October, Breast Cancer Awareness Month. Not only did we want 175,000 letters altogether, we wanted the number from each state to match the number in that state who would get breast cancer. We managed to identify groups in each state who could work with us. In October, we ended up with 600,000 letters—it was an enormous response. We delivered them to the White House. The guards just stood there; nobody would help us lift the boxes. All these women who'd had mastectomies were lifting heavy boxes of letters onto the conveyer belt.

We were all certain that the letters would just be dumped into the shredder. To make things worse, we hardly got any media coverage, because the Clarence Thomas–Anita Hill hearings were going on. So we were afraid that our first action had been a flop. But in reality, we had succeeded in a number of ways.

For one thing, we had organized in such a way that we had a group in every state. That meant a large and potentially powerful organization. For another, even if the White House ignored us, the congresspeople didn't. When we started lobbying for increased research money the members of Congress granted us $43 million more, raising the 1993 appropriation to $132 million. That was a small triumph.

One of the things we realized, however, was that we had to do more research ourselves. When we lobbied, the congresspeople who were interested in what we had to say kept asking, "Well, how much money do you need?" And we didn't know.

We realized we had to find out, and quickly. Mary Jo Kahn from the Virginia Breast Cancer Group suggested that we ask the scientists themselves, and Amy Langer suggested we hold research hearings, which we did in February 1992. We invited scientists from around the country who studied breast cancer to come to the hearings. Since we had no money, they had to pay for their own trips. We got $10,000 from a donor in Philadelphia to fund the hearings, and there were other donations as well. We rented a hotel hall, and 15 major research scientists came. They testified about what research wasn't getting done because of lack of funding, and how much money they thought they really needed.

Those hearings went on for a day, and it was one of the first times that scientists and activists interested in breast cancer had met together. The next morning we had a congressional breakfast; many of the scientists came with us and spoke to several of the congressional representatives.

We created an interesting coalition. If the scientists alone lobby for more research money, it looks like they're doing it out of self-interest. But our involvement made it clear that this wasn't about ivory-tower research, but about work that really could save human lives.

We met again after the hearings and came up with a figure: we needed $433 million for breast cancer research. The total 1992 budget was $93 million. So we started lobbying for $300 million more, armed with our report based on the scientists' testimony.

At first the reaction was overwhelmingly negative. Everybody in Congress kept saying there was no money and it would be impossible to come up with anything like another $300 million. People kept insisting that we should reduce it; we were defeating ourselves by demanding so much. But we insisted. What we were being "greedy" for was women's lives, and we weren't willing to compromise.

The National Cancer Institute didn't initially support our efforts. For one thing, it would have embarrassed them. The Institute is bound by law to give a budget to the president every year, called the bypass budget, which is their best estimate of how much money they need. (A leftover from the Nixon administration's War on Cancer, it's called the bypass budget because it bypasses Congress and goes straight to the president.) The bypass budget had only asked for something like $197 million, so they didn't feel like they could support a new demand for $433 million more.

But we kept at it, and when the politicians told us there wasn't any more money, we said, "Well, you found money for the Savings and Loan bailout. You found money for the Gulf War. We think you can find this money too, if you really decide it's important that women are dying." We testified at the Senate, and at the House. We lobbied, we sent faxes, and we called. Eventually we got somewhere—in the fall of 1992 Senator Tom Harkin, who was very sympathetic to us because his two sisters had died of breast cancer, was the chair of the Senate Appropriations Committee in charge of NIH funding. He made sure that the budgeted amount for breast cancer spending at the NIH was $220 million. But that wasn't enough. In order to get the rest of our $433 million total he tried to put forth a transfer amendment that would move money from the Defense Department to the domestic budget. It didn't work.

But we had another advantage at this point—this was the year of the woman. Because of Anita Hill, a lot of congressmen were looking bad when it came to women's issues. They needed to spiff up their images—especially since it was an election year. They realized that breast cancer was a safe thing. There was no racial issue, no question about whether someone was telling the truth or not, no important male judge's reputation at stake—just the stark fact that women were dying. Add to this the demographics of breast cancer—it's most prevalent among white and middle- to upper-class women. These men were being asked to support their own wives, mothers, and sisters, as well as the women who are most likely to vote. So we got a lot of support from men not usually known as feminists or progressives— Arlen Specter was running radio ads in Philadelphia about how important it was to fight breast cancer. Alphonse D'Amato in New York came up with an amendment saying Congress should take 3 percent of the Defense Department's budget to give us our $300 million.

We also, of course, had the more predictable allies—Ted Kennedy held hearings in my office at the Faulkner in Boston on breast cancer research. And, of course, we had strong support from a number of congresswomen, who had their own understanding of the importance of fighting breast cancer.

Then Senator Harkin noticed that, amazingly, in the past there actually had been some money for breast cancer in the Defense Department—$25 million spent on mammogram machines for the army. At our urging he decided to try and increase that to $210 million.

The Defense Department people decided that with all these attacks on their budget, they didn't want to risk their budget being wiped out. If the money officially left their budget, they'd never get it back when they applied for the following year's budget. But if the money stayed in their budget, they could fund breast cancer research this year; and then next year, with the budget still the same or higher, they could spend that money on bombers or whatever else they decided was important. So they agreed to a bill using $210 million of defense money for breast cancer research and it passed.

About 20 senators who had voted against it left while the roll call went on. When it became clear that it was going to pass, these senators literally ran back to the room and down to the podium to change their votes. Presumably they preferred to be on the winning side. Coalition vice-president Jane Reese Colbourne and others watched on C-SPAN as the senators did their undignified but useful turnaround. We ended up with a final vote of 89 to 4, with seven abstentions.

After all that, our victory was almost destroyed. President Bush challenged the decision because medical research funding was domestic spending and Department of Defense funding was military spending. As Jane Reese Colbourne describes it, "We ended up doing a vigil in front of the Senate while they had a meeting to determine whether we could really use that money. Senator Harkin fought for it. We were ready to call in people from Richmond and Baltimore to relieve us and keep the vigil going. Then Senator Inouye came out and told us we had the money."

So there was $210 million in the Department of Defense budget and the extra $220 million in the NCI budget. That's $430 million total. Against all odds, we had succeeded. Part of it was being in the right place at the right time. But most of it was the enormous amount of work all the women in the coalition and around the country had put in. Overnight, we had an enormous amount of clout and were well recognized for a group that had just begun.

We were ready to move on to our next step. It was one thing to raise money, but we wanted to have a say in how it was spent. We wanted women from our groups, women with breast cancer, to be involved in the decision-making panels on review boards for grants, on the National Cancer Advisory Board, and in all the decision making. We started lobbying for that, and our next major project was to deliver 2.6 million signatures to the White House in October 1993 to represent the 2.6 million women living with breast cancer at the time—1.6 million who knew they had breast cancer, and 1 million who were yet to be diagnosed. We mobilized around the country collecting signatures, and we delivered our 2.6 million signatures to President Clinton on October 18. As a measure of how far we'd gone from October 1991 when the boxes went on the conveyor belt into the shredder, this time we were welcomed in the East Room, where Fran Visco and I shared the stage with both Hillary and Bill Clinton, along with Secretary of Health and Human Services Donna Shalala. The room was filled with 200 of our people. It was an awesome moment.

And President Clinton followed up. In December we had a meeting to set national strategy—a meeting of activists, politicians, scientists, doctors, laypeople, businesspeople. We came up with a National Action Plan. In each one of the subgroups working on this plan, there was one of our activist members. We were at the table and we were changing the policy of business as usual around breast cancer.

Being with the scientists, talking and working with them, the activists were able to learn that the answers aren't always easy, that scientists have to work months and years to come up with one useful discovery. The scientists saw that the activists weren't shrill, uninformed troublemakers, but intelligent, concerned people fighting to save their own and others' lives.

Meanwhile, as in any successful movement, there's been a backlash. It's come from two places. One is from the people who have been working with breast cancer for a long time. They see the National Breast Cancer Coalition as the brash new upstart trying to shake up the status quo. And indeed we are. Nothing had changed for years, and it is time that we had some action around this issue.

There's also been a backlash from some of the scientists. They're glad for the funding, but they don't like the idea of having medical research funds earmarked for specific diseases. They point out that some of the discoveries about breast cancer have come from studying other things—which is true. One gene found in studying a rare eye cancer turned out to be present also in breast cancer. But there are an awful lot of things they've studied that haven't told us anything about breast cancer. They have this romantic notion about how only the curiosity of a scientist can bring about a medical miracle—you throw seeds into the fields and among the weeds the wildflowers will come up. And we're saying, yes, but we'll get more of the particular flowers we need if we do a little cultivation.

What it's really about is power—who gets to decide how the money is spent. Should it be decided by the taxpayer, whose money, after all, it is? Or should it be decided by the scientists in terms of their curiosity? They say, "We can't just give the money to whoever yells the loudest, and we can't politicize research and science." But research and science have always been political—it just depends on whose research and whose politics it is. Is it Nixon's war on cancer, or Jerry Lewis's Muscular Dystrophy, or the Heart Association clammering for more money and more research? What's different is that now there is a new group in the melee. And that's really what the backlash is about.

In fact, the National Breast Cancer Coalition has had a strict policy from the beginning to try not to rob one disease for another. We have always been clear that we want a bigger pie, not a bigger piece of a pie that's never been large enough in the first place. That's one of the reasons it's so important the increased funding we got this year came from the Department of Defense—not from AIDS research or asthma research or any other essential medical area.

The scientists then argue that eventually the money won't come from the military or some other budget, that it will come from some other disease research. But that "eventually" is a long way off—there's a lot of useless government spending that we can go after first.

The other argument is that the amount of money per case of cancer should be equal across all cancers. X amount of money per case of breast cancer, X amount for lung cancer. But that's too simplistic a way to measure it. The important measure is what we know about the disease. We know what causes lung cancer. But we don't know what to do about breast cancer yet. This doesn't mean the other diseases don't need money. We need to fight the tobacco industry and do better anti-smoking campaigns. But we need much more money for diseases like breast cancer, for which we don't yet have the information to get out to people.

The exciting thing is that one of the goals we had was to get researchers into the field. Generally speaking, there are only about eight centers that are specializing in breast cancer in the country.

One of the reasons we wanted the money from the Department of Defense was to attract new people, to get researchers working on new aspects of breast cancer. And it worked. With the $210 million made available by the Department of Defense, they got 2,400 grant applications. Many of these were people who had never done breast cancer research before.

And we now have representation at many of the levels at which decisions are made. Fran Visco sits as one of three members of the President's Cancer Panel. Kay Dickersin, from Arm in Arm in Maryland, was just appointed to the National Cancer Advisory Board. We were on the oversight committee for the Department of Defense money and involved in the study sections. We are forging the National Action Plan with the Department of Health and Human Services.

Our goals remain the same. We want access for all women to high-quality screening and treatment for breast cancer. The Mammography Quality Standards Act (see Chapter 10) is a first step. Health care reform will be another. We want influence for women with breast cancer. We are currently training activists to be effective advocates and contribute when they get a seat at the table. And we want research into the cause of breast cancer, how to prevent it and how to cure it. The increase in environmental research as well as basic research is in part in response to our efforts. We want more basic research, rather than focus our energies on how to treat existing disease. We need both, of course, but ultimately, the goal is to stop the cancer before a woman gets it in the first place.

I've learned through this that you really can affect how the government acts. A small group of committed people can do a lot. So few people let their feelings be known that the people who do it, and do it vociferously, get an undue amount of power. We didn't have any money—not like the gun lobby or the tobacco industry. But we organized. And now some of the groups with money started to help us—Revlon has been supporting women's lives as well as their looks. They paid for the petition campaign.

Many of the women in the coalition have never been involved in political action before, and they're finding themselves working side by side with baby boomers who marched in the '60s and learned the value of political protest—and now are confronting breast cancer, and realizing that like civil rights and war resistance and the early women's movement issues, breast cancer research needs to be fought for.

At the same time, breast cancer affects women of all ages, and all political stripes. Eighty-year-old women get breast cancer; thirty-year-old women get breast cancer. Democrats and Republicans and radicals and conservatives get breast cancer. Heterosexual and bisexual and lesbian women get breast cancer. Caucasian, African American, Hispanic, and Asian women get breast cancer.

This is an issue we can all agree on and one we have to all fight for. We can't afford to be good girls any longer. We can't let this disease pass on to another generation. Our lives and the lives of our daughters depend on it.

Last year in Los Angeles at the "War Mammorial," created by artist Melanie Winter, white plaster casts of women's torsos, 1,300 of them, were set on a hill. From a distance they looked like graves but up close they showed the variety of women's bodies: large breasts, small breasts, some with mastectomies and some with implants. Katie, my five-year-old daughter, was walking around trying to figure out which breasts she wanted when she grew up. Then she turned serious.

"Are these the graves of women with breast cancer?" she asked.

"No, these women are all alive," I told her. "But some women do die from breast cancer."

"Well, you're trying to stop that aren't you, Mommy?"

"Yes, Katie, I would like to stop breast cancer before you grow up."

She thought about that a minute. "What if you die first?" she asked.

"I'd like to stop breast cancer before I die," I replied. She thought again, then turned to me and said, "If there is breast cancer left after you die it is a big problem. Because I'm not going to be a breast surgeon. I'm going to be a ballerina."

Well, Katie doesn't have to worry—she can go ahead and be a ballerina. And she won't be haunted, as so many women are now, by the fear of getting breast cancer. As long as we keep fighting, the discoveries we're making, buttressed by the political activism that lets the scientists and the government know that we won't let up until we've ended breast cancer, will bring about her wish. That's what keeps me going. Twenty years from now, a comfortable retiree with no more breast cancer to worry about, I can sit in the audience waiting for the curtain to rise and my beautiful, healthy daughter to pirouette across the stage.

APPENDICES

A

Drugs Used for Systemic Treatment of Breast Cancer

This chart lists drugs, their method(s) of administration, and some common and less common side effects and toxicities. It is not meant to be exhaustive. Check with your oncologist about your specific drugs. Unusual signs and symptoms should be reported to your doctor immediately.

I. Chemotherapy

cyclophosphamide (Cytoxan)	oral, IV	**common:** nausea, vomiting, loss of appetite, menstrual irregularities, low blood counts, hair loss
		rare: liver problems, infertility
methotrexate	IV	**common:** nausea, vomiting, mouth sores, low blood counts, conjunctivitis, ulcers, rash
		rare: hair loss, headache, liver problems, blurred vision, lung injury
5 fluorouracil (5 Fu)	IV	**common:** mouth sores, nausea, vomiting, diarrhea, low blood counts, loss of appetite, hair loss, sore throat
		rare: rash, nail changes, skin darkening

doxorubicin (Adriamycin)	IV	**common:** hair loss, mouth sores, nausea, vomiting, low blood counts
		rare: heart problems, nail and skin darkening, liver problems
chlorambucil (Leukeran)	oral	**common:** low blood counts, tiredness
		rare: hair loss, nausea, vomiting, menstrual irregularities
melphalan (L-Pam)	oral	**common:** low blood counts, nausea, vomiting
		rare: rash, loss of appetite, mouth sores, lung problems
Taxol	IV	**common**: low blood counts, nausea, vomiting
		rare: numbness in hands and feet
thiotepa	IV	**common:** low blood count, nausea, vomiting, pain at IV site
		rare: stomach pain, rash, loss of appetite, menstrual irregularities, hair loss, headache, dizziness
vincristine	IV	**common:** hair loss, tingling and numbness in fingers and toes, pain at IV site, constipation, headache
		rare: muscle and jaw pain, loss of reflexes, depression, insomnia
vinblastine (Velban)	IV	**common:** nausea, vomiting, low blood count, hair loss
		rare: numbness and tingling and weakness in hands and feet, jaw pain, constipation
mitomycin	IV	**common:** low blood count, nausea, vomiting
		rare: blood in urine, loss of appetite, mouth sores, hair loss, rash, lung or kidney damage
mitoxanthrone	IV	**common:** low blood count, mild nausea, vomiting, bluish discoloration along vein, blue-green urine
		rare: hair loss

II. Hormonal Therapy

tamoxifen (Novaldex)	oral	**common:** hot flashes, temporary nausea, menstrual bleeding or itching
		rare: headache, flare of bone pain, depression
progestins (Megace)	oral	**common:** weight gain, edema, breast tenderness
		rare: carpal tunnel syndrome, hair loss
aminoglutethimide	oral	**common:** sleepiness, fatigue, rash
		rare: low thyroid, headache, liver toxicity, may need cortisone replacement
diethylstilbestrol (DES)	oral	**common:** weight gain due to fluid retention, nausea, increase in blood pressure, breast swelling and tenderness
		rare: blood clots, increased body hair
halotestin	oral	**common:** fluid retention, lowering of voice, skin changes, increased libido, changes in period
		rare: nausea, vomiting, liver damage
prednisone	oral	**common:** mood changes, increased appetite, fluid retention
		rare: after prolonged use: acne, muscle weakness, diabetes, high blood pressure

Common combinations of chemotherapy used in breast cancer:

CMF	Cytoxan, methotrexate, 5 fluorouracil
CAF	Cytoxan, Adriamycin, 5 fluorouracil
CMFVP	Cytoxan, methotrexate, 5 fluorouracil, vincristine, prednisone
CFP	Cytoxan, 5 fluorouracil, prednisone
FAC	5 fluorouracil, Adriamycin, Cytoxan

B

Resources, References, and Additional Reading

This Appendix has been culled from my own experience as well as from many other sources and is by no means exhaustive. Individuals are listed only if I think they provide a unique service. Although I believe each listing is helpful, I am not personally familiar with every one, and welcome any feedback, comments, and additions that readers may have. These can be sent to the Revlon/UCLA Breast Center, 200 UCLA Medical Plaza, Suite 510, Los Angeles, CA 90024-7028. Much of the Appendix is reprinted with permission from, and thanks to, the annual resource guide published by the National Alliance of Breast Cancer Organizations.

Many of the cancer-related pamphlets are from one of three major organizations:

American Cancer Society (ACS). For materials listed, contact your local ACS unit or state-chartered division. If the material is not available locally, contact the ACS National Office, 1599 Clifton Road NE, Atlanta, GA 30829-4251. (800) ACS-2345.

National Cancer Institute (NCI). Order all materials from Office of Cancer Communications, NCI, Building 31, Room 10 A 18, Bethesda, MD 20205. (800) 4-CANCER or (301) 496-5583.

National Alliance of Breast Cancer Organizations (NABCO). Order all NABCO fact sheets and *NABCO News* articles from NABCO, 9 East 37th Street, 10th Floor, New York, NY 10016. (212) 719-0154, fax (212) 689-1213.

The Healthy Breast

NORMAL FEMALE ANATOMY AND DEVELOPMENT

National Women's Health Network, 1325 G Street NW, Washington, DC 20005. *Written packets and booklets on many aspects of women's health, including menopause and benign and malignant breast diseases.*

Daphna Ayalah and Issac J. Weinstock, *Breasts: Women Speak about Their Breasts and Their Lives* (New York: Summit Books, 1979). *Wonderful book of photographs and interviews about women and their breasts.*

Sheila Kitzinger, *Woman's Experience of Sex* (New York: Putnam, 1983).

The Boston Women's Health Book Collective, *The New Our Bodies Ourselves* (New York: Simon & Schuster, 1984). *Still the feminist bible for women's health issues.*

Penny Wise Budoff, M.D., *No More Menstrual Cramps and Other Good News* (New York: Penguin Books, 1980).

Paula Brown Doress, Diana Laskin Siegel, and The Midlife and Older Women Book Project, *Ourselves, Growing Older* (New York: Simon & Schuster, 1987). *Good overview of midlife and beyond, written in cooperation with the Boston Women's Health Book Collective.*

Sadja Greenwood, M.D., *Menopause Naturally: Preparing for the Second Half of Life* (San Francisco: Volcano Press, 1984; revised 1989). *Good discussion of menopause without hormone replacement therapy and discussion of dangers of hormonal replacement.*

Rosetta Reitz, *Menopause: A Positive Approach* (New York: Penguin Books, 1977).

Susan Flamholtz Trien, *Change of Life* (New York: Fawcett Columbine, 1986).

Sandra Coney, *The Menopause Industry: How the Medical Establishment Exploits Women* (Alameida, CA: Hunter House, 1994). *May be ordered by calling (800) 266-5592. This book contains the most accurate view of menopause I have seen. It will wake you up.*

Dee Ito, *Without Estrogen: Natural Remedies for Menopause and Beyond* (New York: Carol Southern Books, 1994).

Women's Health Initiative. (800) 54-WOMEN. *This is the first controlled, national study to look at postmenopausal women and their health, including hormone replacement therapy, diet, calcium, and exercise. If we do not participate, we will never know the answers. Call to find the center closest to you.*

BREAST FEEDING

La Leche League International, P.O. Box 1209, Franklin Park, IL 60131-8209. *Best source of support and information about breast feeding. Send a stamped, self-addressed envelope to LLLI and request a copy of the LLLI directory (No. 504). This publication lists two key representatives of every area of the U.S. and 43 other countries. Contact the particular representatives for names and addresses of groups near you. The League is very zealous about the virtues of breast feeding; if you're at all ambivalent, they may not be the best resource for you. In addition, the La Leche League has over 200 information sheets, reprints, and booklets covering many aspects of breast feeding including such topics as sore nipples, prevention of plugged ducts and breast infections, nursing twins, nursing an adopted child, nursing and working. A catalogue (No. 501) will be sent if you send a stamped, self-addressed business-sized envelope. For information in languages other than English ask for the Translation List (No. 508).*

La Leche League International, *The Womanly Art of Breastfeeding*, 3rd ed. (New York: New American Library, 1981). *A very supportive book.*

Marsha Walker and Jeanne Watson Driscoll, "Expressing, Storing and Transporting Breastmilk." Pamphlet available from Lactation Associates, Educators and Consultants to Health Care Professionals, 254 Conant Road, Weston, MA 02193. (617) 893-3553.

Margot Edwards, "A Working Mother Can Breastfeed When . . ." Pennypress, Inc., 1100 23rd Avenue East, Seattle, WA 98112.

Ruth Lawrence, *Breastfeeding: A Guide for the Medical Profession*, 2nd ed. (St. Louis, MO: Mosby, 1989). *Written by a professor of pediatrics, this is a good source of scientific information as well as practical advice about breast feeding.*

VARIATIONS AND PLASTIC SURGERY

Nancy Bruning, *Breast Implants: Everything You Need to Know* (Alameda, CA: Hunter House, 1992). Paperback. *Valuable resource for any woman considering breast implants or for those who already have implants. New edition in 1995.*

Command Trust Network, *The Breast Implant Information Network*. For information call (800) 887-6828; for attorney settlement information call (513) 651-9770. *A network established to provide assistance and information to women with or considering implants.*

Amy J. Goldrich, *Command Trust Network's Introduction to the Legal System* (1992). Available for $18 from Command Trust Network, 256 South Linden Drive, Beverly Hills, CA 90212. (310) 556-1738. *Reference booklet for women with implants who are pursuing lawsuits against implant manufacturers.*

American Society of Plastic and Reconstructive Surgeons, 444 East Algonquin Road, Arlington Heights, Il 60005. (312) 228-9900, (800) 635-0635 (referral message tape). *Will provide written information and mail a list of certified reconstructive surgeons by geographical area after caller provides details on above (800) message tape.*

Robert Goldwyn, *The Patient and the Plastic Surgeon* (Boston: Little, Brown, 1981). *An easy-to-read book written for doctors but very informative for patients about the various procedures and their pitfalls.*

Common Problems of the Breast

Kerry A. McGuinn, *The Informed Woman's Guide to Breast Health* (Palo Alto, CA: Bull Publishing, 1992). Paperback. *A thorough review of breast lumps and benign conditions.*

Questions and Answers about Breast Calcifications (91-3198, 1990). 3 pages. NCI (800) 4-CANCER.

Understanding Breast Changes: A Health Guide for All Women (94-3636, revised April 1994). 56-page booklet from NCI. (800) 4-CANCER. *This book explains how to evaluate breast lumps and other normal breast changes that often occur and are confused with breast cancer. It is for all asymptomatic women.*

"Stereotactic core needle biopsy of the breast" (Fisher Imaging Corporation, 1993). *Video describes the procedure. 28 minutes. Single copies free from marketing department, (800) 825-8257.*

"When you can't feel it—needle localization and breast biopsy" (Beth Israel Medical Center, NY, 1991). *Video describes the procedure, 16 minutes, $15.00. To order call (212) 420-2069.*

American College of Surgeons, 55 East Erie Street, Chicago IL 60611. (312) 664-4050. *Will provide names of certified surgeons specializing in breast surgery by geographical area.*

Cushman Haagensen, ed., *Diseases of the Breast*, 3rd ed. (Philadelphia: W.B. Saunders, 1986). *This textbook is the ultimate reference for benign breast tumors. However, his approach to breast cancer is dated.*

Risks, Prevention and Detection of Breast Cancer

RISKS AND PREVENTION

M. Margaret Kemeny and Paula Dranov, *Breast Cancer and Ovarian Cancer: Beating the Odds* (Reading, MA: Addison-Wesley, 1992). *Reviews risk factors.*

Renee Royak-Schaler and Beryl Lieff Benderly, *Challenging the Breast Cancer Legacy* (New York: HarperCollins, 1993). Paperback. *For concerns about family history.*

"DES Exposure: Questions and Answers for Mothers, Daughters and Sons" (1990). $2. DES Action, 1615 Broadway, Suite 510, Oakland, CA 94612. *Authoritative booklet. 20 pages.*

"Questions and Answers About the Breast Cancer Prevention Trial (1994). Fact sheet from NCI. (800) 4-CANCER. *Describes the BCPT tamoxifen trials for preventing breast cancer in women at risk.*

"What Are Chemoprevention Clinical Trials?"(93-3459) NCI. *Explains the background and purpose of chemoprevention research in a community setting.*

Patricia T. Kelly, *Understanding Breast Cancer Risk* (Philadelphia: Temple University Press, 1992). *Includes the role women should take in designing their own breast health programs.*

"The Epidemiology of Breast Cancer" (3494, 1991). Booklet from American Cancer Society. (800) ACS-2345.

"Lesbians and Cancer." Free pamphlet available in English and Spanish from Mautner Project, P.O. Box 90437, Washington, DC 20090. (202) 332-5536.

Nancy C. Baker, *Relative Risk: Living with a Family History of Breast Cancer* (New York: Viking, 1991). *Discusses risk factors as well as women's reactions to being at "increased risk."*

Mary Dan Eades, *Breast Cancer–If It Runs in Your Family* (New York: Bantam Books, 1991).

I. Craig Henderson, "What Can a Women Do About Her Risk of Dying of Breast Cancer?" *Current Problems in Cancer*, vol. 24, no. 4. (St. Louis, MO: Mosby Year Book, 1990). *Excellent summary of the literature on risk factors and prevention. Unfortunately it has no magic answers. It will probably have to be obtained in a hospital or medical library.*

Basil Stoll, ed. *Reducing Breast Cancer Risk in Women* (Norwell, MA: Kluwer Academic Publishers, 1995). *Review of what is currently known about prevention, limited as it is.*

"Diet, Nutrition and Cancer Prevention: A Guide to Food Choices" (87-2878). National Cancer Institute. *This booklet describes what is known about diet, nutrition, and cancer prevention.*

Alice Holyoke Bakemeier, "The Potential Role of Vitamins A, C, and E and Selenium in Cancer Prevention," *Oncology Nursing Forum*, vol. 15, no. 6 (1988): 785–791. *You will probably have to get this from a hospital or medical library. A good review of the field in a readable format.*

R. Bohannon, T. P. Wuerthner, and K. K. Weinstock, *Food for Life: The Cancer Prevention Cookbook* (Chicago: Contemporary Books, 1987).

Ruth Spear, *Low Fat and Loving It* (New York: Warner Books, 1990). *Over 200 recipes.*

National Women's Health Network, *The Diet Your Doctor Won't Give You* (1987). NWHN, 1325 G Street NW, Washington, DC 20005. $1. (202) 347-1140.

National Women's Health Network, *Hearts, Bones, Hot Flashes, and Hormones* (1994). NWHN, 1325 G Street NW, Washington, DC 20005. *An excellent review of the current state of knowledge about postmenopausal hormone therapy.*

Charles B. Simone, *Cancer and Nutrition* (Garden City Park, NY: Avery, 1992).

Earl Mindell, *Earl Mindell's Vitamin Bible* (New York: Warner, 1994).

Committee on the Relationship between Oral Contraceptives and Breast Cancer, Institute of Medicine, *Oral Contraceptives and Breast Cancer* (Washington, DC: National Academy Press, 1991).

Carol Rinzler, *Estrogen and Breast Cancer: A Warning to Women.* Order from BCA Bookstore, 1280 Columbus Avenue, Suite 204, San Francisco, CA 94133.

Risk Counseling and Research Centers

— Revlon/UCLA Breast Center has a multidisciplinary high risk program including psychosocial evaluation, nutrition counseling, and excercise as well as risk assessment. (800) 825-2144.

— Alta Bates-Herrick, Comprehensive Cancer Center. Breast cancer risk counseling offered by Dr. Patricia Kelly, a geneticist, in Oakland, CA. (510) 204-4286. Other affiliated facilities include: Mt. Sinai Comprehensive Cancer Center, Miami Beach, FL, (305) 535-3350; The Comprehensive Cancer Center at JFK Medical Center, Atlantis, FL, (407) 642-3970; Komen Alliance Clinical Breast Center, Dallas, TX, (214) 820-2626.

— Strang Cancer Prevention Center is a free, national resource for breast cancer risk counseling and research into breast cancer risk. Strang operates a National High Risk Registry for purposes of research and education and publishes a newsletter. 428 East 72nd Street, New York, NY 10021. (800) 521-9356, or (212) 794-4900.

— Women at Risk is a research, diagnosis and treatment group for women at high risk of developing breast cancer. Columbia-Presbyterian Medical Center, Breast Service, New York, NY 10032. (212) 305-9926.

DETECTION

"The Older You Get, The More You Need a Mammogram" (5020, 1993). Booklet from American Cancer Society. (800) ACS-2345.

"Questions and Answers about Choosing a Mammography Facility" (94-3228, 1994). This four-page brochure should accompany "Are You Age 50 or Over? A Mammogram Could Save Your Life," from NCI. (800) 4-CANCER.

Agency for Health Care Policy and Research, *Quality Determinants of Mammography.* Guidelines for consumers and health care professionals on what is necessary for the best possible test. To order a copy of the consumer or professional guidelines, call (800) 358-9295.

National Consortium of Breast Centers, c/o Barbara Rabinowitz, RN, MSW, ACSW, Comprehensive Breast Center, Robert Wood Johnson Medical School, One Robert Wood Johnson Place, CN19, New Brunswick, NJ 08903-0019. *They will send you a list of breast centers throughout the country registered with them. Many are diagnostic only and others are involved in both diagnosis and treatment.*

Practical Advice: How to Find a Qualified Mammography Provider.

— As of October 1994, the Mammography Quality Standards Act required all facilities in the United States, except those of the Dept. of Veterans Affairs, to be FDA-certified as meeting quality standards. The American College of Radiology (ACR) is the largest FDA-approved accreditation body. To locate an ACR-accredited facility in your area, call the National Cancer Institute at (800) 4-CANCER or the American Cancer Society at (800) ACS-2345.

Making the Diagnosis of Breast Cancer

BREAST CANCER IN GENERAL

Cancer Information Service, National Cancer Institute. This information service can be reached toll-free at (800) 4-CANCER. *They give information and direction through their national and regional network on all aspects of cancer. Spanish-speaking staff members are available on request.*

Cancer Information Service (Canada). Ontario region only, (800) 263-6750. *In other provinces contact the local branch of the Canadian Cancer Society.*

National Alliance of Breast Cancer Organizations (NABCO), 1180 Avenue of the Americas, second floor, New York, NY 10036. (212) 719-0154. *Central source of information about breast cancer. Provides up-to-date information packets and resource list on written request.*

AMC Cancer Research Center's Cancer Information Line 1-800-525-3777. *Professional cancer counselors provide answers to questions about cancer, support, and advice and will mail instructive free publications upon request. Equipped for deaf and hearing-impaired callers.*

American Cancer Society. (800) ACS-2345. *National toll-free hotline provides information on all forms of cancer, and referrals for the ACS-sponsored "Reach to Recovery" program.*

Y-ME National Breast Cancer Organization. *Provides support and counseling through their national toll-free hotline (800) 221-2141 (9 am to 5 pm CST or 24 hours at (312) 986-8228). Trained volunteers are matched by background and experience to callers; Y-ME also has a hotline for partners. Y-ME offers information on establishing local support programs, and has chapters in 12 states. Call or write 212 W. Van Buren Street, Chicago, IL 60607. (312) 986-8228.*

Komen Alliance. *A comprehensive program for the research, education, diagnosis, and treatment of breast disease. Information on screening, BSE, treatment and support, including the booklet "Caring for Your Breasts," is available by calling (800) I'M AWARE or contacting the Susan G. Komen Foundation, Occidental Tower, 5005 LBJ Freeway, Suite 370, Dallas, TX 75244. (214) 450-1777.*

Kathy LaTour, *The Breast Cancer Companion* (New York: William Morrow, 1994). *Guidebook offers useful tips, insights of 75 survivors, and background information about advocacy and politics of breast cancer.*

Linda Brown Harris, *Breast Cancer Handbook: A Basic Guide for Gathering Information, Understanding the Diagnosis, and Choosing the Treatment* (1992). *A great booklet on breast cancer with many questions you should pose to your doctors.* Melpomene Institute for Women's Health Research, 1010 University Avenue, St. Paul, MN 55104. (612) 642-1951.

Joan Swirsky and Barbara Balaban, *The Breast Cancer Handbook: Taking Control after You've Found a Lump* (New York: HarperCollins, 1994). *Easy-to-read guide takes you step by step through diagnosis and treatment.*

"Breast Cancer: Risk, Protection, Detection, and Treatment." 1990. *Booklet on factors that may influence chances of having the disease, how to detect early signs, and treatment options.* Available in French. $2.50. Order from DES Action, 1615 Broadway, Oakland, CA 94612.

Roberta Altman and Michael J. Sarg, *The Cancer Dictionary* (New York: Facts on File, 1992). *Includes acronyms for chemotherapy protocols and simple anatomical illustrations. Order from Facts on File, (800) 322-8755.*

Rose Kushner, Breast Cancer Advisory Center, "If You've Thought About Breast Cancer" (1994). *Updated general pamphlet on breast cancer detection and treatment.* Order from The Rose Kushner Breast Cancer Advisory Center, P.O. Box 224, Kensington, MD 20895. (301) 949-2531.

National Women's Health Resource Center, "Making Sense of the News about Breast Cancer," in September/October 1992 issue of *National Women's Health Report* on breast cancer diagnosis and treatment. Available for $2 by calling (202) 293-6045.

J. R. Harris, S. Hellman, I. C. Henderson, and D. W. Kinne, *Breast Diseases* (Philadelphia: J.B. Lippincott, 1991). *Medical textbook with a very comprehensive overview of treatment of breast cancer.* New edition in press.

PSYCHOLOGICAL ASPECTS

Ronnie Kaye, *Spinning Straw into Gold: Your Emotional Recovery from Breast Cancer* (New York: Simon & Schuster, 1991). *Excellent guide to the emotional aspects of this disease from a psychologist who is also a survivor.*

Wellness Community facilities providing free psychosocial care to cancer patients and their families. Started in California with many centers across the country. Call 310-314-2555.

Cancer Care, Inc., and the National Cancer Care Foundation, 1180 Avenue of the Americas, New York, NY 10036. (212) 211-3300. *A social service agency which helps patients and their families cope with the impact of cancer. Direct services are limited to the Greater New York area, but callers will be referred to similar assistance available in their areas.*

Mimi Greenberg, Ph.D., *Invisible Scars: A Guide to Coping with the Emotional Impact of Breast Cancer* (New York: Walker, 1988). 204 pages. *A useful guide which will help you be in charge of your treatment.*

Judi Johnson and Linda Klein, *I Can Cope* (Minnetonka, MN: DCI Publishing, 1988). *A co-founder of ACS's 8-week "I Can Cope" program has published a guide to staying healthy with cancer using the experiences of several cancer patients.*

Danette G. Kauffman, *Surviving Cancer* (Washington, DC: Acropolis Books, 1989). *A practical guide to experiencing cancer and its treatment, with an emphasis on lists of resources for managing the medical, emotional, and financial aspects of this disease.*

"Taking Time: Support for the People with Cancer and the People Who Care about Them" (92-2059, June 1990). 31 pages. National Cancer Institute. *Addresses the feelings of other people in similar situations and how they coped.*

We Can Weekends, c/o Judi Johnson, RN, PhD, North Cancer Center, 3300 Oakdale North, Robbinsdale, MN 55422. (612) 520-5155. *Weekend retreats for families dealing with cancer. Provides an opportunity to focus on the problems and concerns that are encountered in living with cancer. Designed for families with children. Scholarships and babysitters available.* Contact North Cancer Center to learn if there is a local group.

Pat Brack and Ben Brack, *Moms Don't Get Sick* (Aberdeen, SD: Melius Publishing, 1990). *One woman's story as told through her eyes and those of her ten-year-old son. Excellent for women with children.*

Carolyn Stearns Parkinson, *My Mommy Has Cancer* (Rochester, NY: Solace Publishing, 1992).

"Helping Children Cope When a Parent Has Cancer." 12 pages. American Cancer Society. *A booklet to help you help your children.*

Judylaine Fine, *Afraid to Ask, A Book for Families to Share About Cancer* (New York City: Lothrop, Lee and Shepard Books, 1986).

Roz Perry, *Rose Penski* (Tallahassee, FL: Naiad Press, 1989). *A novel about a lesbian and her lover going through diagnosis and initial treatment of breast cancer.*

Larry Althouse and Valerie Althouse, *You Can Save Your Breast: One Woman's Experience with Radiation Therapy* (New York: W.W. Norton, 1982).

Barbara Bergholz and Eva Shaw, *Diana's Gift* (La Jolla, CA: Gentle Winds Press, 1992).

R. C. Cantor, *And a Time to Live: Toward Emotional Well-Being During the Crisis of Cancer* (New York: Harper & Row, 1978).

Helene Davis, *Chemo-poet and Other Poems* (Cambridge, MA: Alice James Books, 1989).

Judy Hart, *Love, Judy: Letters of Hope and Healing for Women with Breast Cancer* (Berkeley, CA: Conari Press, 1993).

L. LeShan, *You Can Fight for Your Life: Emotional Factors in the Treatment of Cancer* (New York: M. Evans, 1980).

L. LeShan, *Cancer as a Turning Point: A Handbook for People with Cancer, Their Families and Health Professionals* (New York: E.P. Dutton, 1989).

Leatrice Lifshitz, *Her Soul Beneath the Bone: Women's Poetry on Breast Cancer* (Urbana, IL: University of Illinois, 1988).

Personal Stories

"Victories: Three Women Triumph over Breast Disease" MBM Communications, San Francisco, CA, 1989. *Videotape of three personal stories (mastectomy/*

reconstruction, benign disease, lumpectomy/chemo/RT, recurrence). Includes group discussions, husband/wife counseling and mammography. To order call (415) 642-0460. 23 minutes, $195.00/$45.00 rental.

"Not Alone—Women Coping with Breast Cancer" Adelphi Oncology Support Program, Garden City, NY, Fall 1988). *Filmed during actual sessions, a group of breast cancer patients accompanied by a social worker discuss their concerns and offer mutual support.* 22-minute video, $150.00. Order from Adelphi, (516) 877-4444.

Judy Brady, *One in Three: Women with Cancer Confront an Epidemic* (Pittsburgh, PA: Clei's Press, 1991). *Collection of essays by women involved in grassroots cancer activism.*

Nancy Brinker, with Catherine McEvily Harris, *The Race Is Run One Step at a Time: My Personal Struggle and Everywoman's Guide to Taking Charge of Breast Cancer* (New York: Simon & Schuster, 1990). *Also available on audio cassette, account of the battle against breast cancer by the author and her sister, Susan Komen.*

Sandra Butler and Barbara Rosenblum, *Cancer in Two Voices* (Minneapolis, MN: Spinsters Book Co., 1991). *A particularly moving and honest account of the authors' last year together based on diary excerpts. One of the few descriptions of the breast cancer experience from a lesbian perspective.*

Donna Cederberg, Daria Davidson, Joy Edwards, Carol Hebestreit, Betsy Lambert, Amy Langer, Cathy Masamitsu, Sally Snodgrass, Carol Stack, and Carol Washington, *Breast Cancer? Let Me Check My Schedule* (Vancouver, WA: Innovative Medical Education Consortium, 1994). $12.95. *Ten professional women share their wisdom and experience about living with breast cancer.* Order from IMEC, 500 W. 8th Street, Suite 100A, Vancouver, WA 98660.

Linda Dackman, *Up Front: Sex and the Post-Mastectomy Woman* (New York: Viking, 1990). *A personal account, with frank details about the intimate challenges faced by a single woman in her 30's.*

Gayle Feldman, *You Don't Have to Be Your Mother* (New York: W. W. Norton, 1994). *Courageous account of a 40-year-old pregnant woman's struggle to deal with breast cancer and to come to terms with the death of her mother, who died of breast cancer.*

Amy Gross and Dee Ito, *Women Talk about Breast Surgery, from Diagnosis to Recovery* (New York: Clarkson Potter, 1990). *Women's stories describing the range of situations and treatments. Better for its support aspects than the accuracy of the medical information.*

Lois Hjelmstad, *Fine Black Lines: Reflections on Facing Cancer, Fear and Loneliness.* Order from BCA Bookstore, 1280 Columbus Avenue, Suite 204, San Francisco, CA 94133. $14.95 plus $2 postage.

Deborah Kahane, *No Less a Woman, Ten Women Shatter the Myths about Breast Cancer* (New York: Prentice-Hall Press, 1990). *A cross-section of women with breast cancer tell their own stories.*

Audre Lorde, *The Cancer Journals* (San Francisco: Aunt Lute Books, 1980). *Reflections on her breast cancer by an extraordinary black, lesbian poet.* Available from Aunt Lute Books, (415) 558-8116.

Dorothea Lynch and Eugene Richards, *Exploding into Life* (New York: Aperture, 1986). *A true-to-life-and-death account of Ms. Lynch's battle with breast cancer illustrated with photographs by her husband.* Aperture, 20 East 23 Street, NY 10010. (212) 505-5555.

Jacque Miller, *The Lopsided Gal—The Humor, Blessings and Trials of Breast Cancer* (Parker, CO: Parker Printing, 1987).

Musa Mayer, *Examining Myself: One Woman's Story of Breast Cancer Treatment and Recovery* (Winchester, MA: Faber and Faber, 1993). *Exploration of the emotional aspects of disease and recovery. Faber and Faber is donating a portion of the book's proceeds to the National Breast Cancer Coalition.*

Madeleine Meldin, *The Tender Bud: A Physician's Journal Through Breast Cancer* (Hillsdale, NJ: Analytic Press, 1993). *Written from the point of view of a psychiatrist attempting to keep her professional life intact during breast cancer treatment.*

Deena Metzger, *Tree* (Oakland, CA: Wingbow Press, 1983). *Written by the woman pictured in the well-known poster of an exultant woman with a mastectomy and a tattoo of a tree on her scar.* The poster can be obtained from Tree, P.O. Box 186, Topanga, CA 90290.

Fitzhugh Mullan, *Vital Signs: A Young Doctor's Struggle with Cancer* (New York: Farrar, Straus & Giroux, 1983).

Andy Murcia and Bob Stewart, *Man to Man: When the Woman You Love Has Breast Cancer* (New York: St. Martin's Press, 1990).

Phyllis Newman, *Just in Time* (New York: Simon & Schuster, 1988).

Betty Rollin, *First, You Cry* (New York: Harper, 1976). *Autobiographical account by NBC News correspondent.*

Allie Fair Sawyer and Norma Suzette Jones, *Journey: A Breast Cancer Survival Guide* (Alexander, NC: WorldComm Press, 1992).

Joyce Wadler, *My Breast: One Woman's Cancer Story* (Reading, MA: Addison-Wesley, 1992). *Memoir by former New York correspondent of the Washington Post.*

Carolyn Walter and Julienne Oklay, *Breast Cancer in the Life Course: Women's Experiences* (New York: Springer, 1991).

Ken Wilber, *Grace and Grit: Spirituality and Healing in the Life and Death of Treya Killam Wilber* (Boston: Shambala, 1993).

Susan Winn, *Chemo and Lunch: One Woman's Triumph over Hereditary Breast Cancer* (Santa Barbara, CA: Fithian Press, 1990).

Juliet Wittman, *Breast Cancer Journal: A Century of Petals* (Golden, CO: Fulcrum, 1993). *Well-written, honest, personal story by a journalist.*

NOTE: Several other notable personal stories are out of print but can be found in libraries, including: *Getting Better: Conversations with Myself and Other Friends,* by Anne Hargrave; *Life Wish,* by Jill Ireland; and *Of Tears and Triumphs: The Family Victory That Has Inspired Thousands of Cancer Patients,* by Georgia and Bud Photopulos.

Treating Breast Cancer

TREATMENT OPTIONS

Cancerfax. *This service allows access to NCI's Physician's Data Query (PDQ) system (see entry below) via fax machine, 24 hours/day, 7 days/week, at no charge. Two versions of the treatment are available: one for health care professionals and the other for laypeople. Information is also available in Spanish.* For information and list of necessary codes call (301) 402-5874 or (800) 4-CANCER.

PDQ (Physician Data Query). *The cancer information database of the NCI, providing prognostic, stage, and treatment information and more than 1,500 clinical trials that are open to patient accrual. Access by computer equipped with a modem, and by fax (see above).* For more information call the NCI at (800) 4-CANCER.

CANHELP. *Will research patient's treatment options (including alternative therapies) based on your medical records. A personalized 10–15 page packet will be mailed within seven working days for $400.00.* Contact CANHELP, 3111 Paradise Bay Road, Port Ludlow, WA 98365-9771. (206) 437-2291.

NIH Consensus Conference Statement: Treatment of Early Stage Breast Cancer (June 1990, vol. 8, no. 6). *Still the current standard, the treatment recommendations of the expert panel convened by the National Institutes of Health.* Copies available at no charge from NABCO. (212) 719-0154.

Wendy Schlessel Harpham, *Diagnosis Cancer: Your Guide Through the First Few Months* (New York: W. W. Norton, 1992). *Guide for newly diagnosed cancer patients, written by an internist who is also a cancer survivor.*

"Cathy Saved Her Life" (1989). *Videotape of televised story of Cathy Masamitsu, an ABC "Home Show" staff member who had breast cancer.* 90 minutes. $7.50. Order from Woody Fraser Productions, P.O. Box 7548, Burbank, CA 91510-7548.

"Power to Choose: Breakthroughs in Breast Cancer" (1990). Published by Zeneca Pharmaceuticals, *Videotape about three breast cancer patients whose diagnoses span the last 15 years.* 30 minutes. $5.00. Order from National Breast Cancer Awareness Month, P.O. Box 57424, Washington, DC 20036. (202) 785-0710.

SURGERY

Reach to Recovery, American Cancer Society. *A national program sponsored by the American Cancer Society in which women who have had breast surgery visit and directly counsel women after surgery, providing practical information and support. Includes women who have mastectomies with and without reconstruction as well as women who have had lumpectomies.* Contact your local branch.

"Mastectomy: A Treatment for Breast Cancer" (87-658, August 1987). 24 pages. National Cancer Institute. *Information about different types of breast surgery.*

"Standards for Breast-Conservation Treatment" (3405, 1992). ACS booklet, call (800) ACS-2345.

"The Surgical Management of Primary Breast Cancer" (3493, 1991). ACS booklet, call (800) ACS-2345.

Rosalind Dolores Benedet, *Healing: A Woman's Recovery Guide to Recovery After Mastectomy* (San Francisco: R. Benedet, 1993). *Guide to postoperative care after a mastectomy.* To order send $10 plus $1 shipping to R. Benedet Publishing, 220 Montgomery Street, Penthouse #2, San Francisco, CA 94104.

Practical Advice: How to Find a Breast Specialist

— Ask your family doctor or gynecologist for a referral. Your doctor can also contact the American Society of Clinical Oncology (ASCO) for names of local surgical oncologists who are ASCO members. The American Board of Medical Specialists at (800) 776-2378 can verify a physician's board certification by specialty and year, and will refer callers to local board-certified doctors.

— Call the National Cancer Institute's Cancer Information Service at (800) 4-CANCER for the names of NCI-affiliated Clinical or Comprehensive Cancer Centers in your state, or members of the NCI's COOP program. If none of these centers is conveniently located, call the Department of Surgery at the nearest one and ask for a local referral.

— Ask-A-Nurse is a free service providing 24-hour health care information and referrals from registered nurses in select locations around the country. Call (800) 535-1111 to find out if there is an office in your area.

— For referrals to a plastic surgeon for corrective or reconstructive procedures, call the American Society of Plastic and Reconstructive Surgeons message tape at (800) 635-0635 and a list of surgeons will be mailed to you.

RADIATION

"Radiation Therapy: A Treatment for Early Stage Breast Cancer" (87-659, September 1987). 20 pages. National Cancer Institute, (800) 4-CANCER. *This booklet discusses the treatment and side effects of primary radiation therapy.*

"Radiation Therapy and You: A Guide to Self-Help During Treatment" (94-2227, 1993). 52 pages. National Cancer Institute, (800) 4-CANCER. *Written for the patient receiving radiation.*

"The Role of Radiation Therapy in the Management of Primary Breast Cancer" (3492, 1991). ACS booklet, (800) ACS-2345.

SYSTEMIC THERAPY

"Chemotherapy and You: A Guide to Self-Help during Treatment" (94-1136, 1993). *A question-and-answer booklet, including glossary and guide to side effects.* 56 pages. NCI, (800) 4-CANCER.

"Chemotherapy: *Your* Weapon Against Cancer" (1991 edition). *Explanation of the benefits and side effects of chemo.* One copy free from the Chemotherapy Foundation, 183 Madison Avenue, Suite 403, New York, NY 10016. (212) 213-9292.

"Chemotherapy: What It Is, How it Helps (4512, 1990). *Brief introduction to chemotherapy.* (800) ACS-2345.

Community Clinical Oncology Program ("CCOP") (April 1993, updated periodically). List of the 70 medical centers in 32 states and Puerto Rico selected by NCI to participate in newest clinical protocols and to accrue patients to clinical trials. (800) 4-CANCER.

"Coping with the Side Effects of Chemotherapy" (1992). 19-page booklet. Order from Wyeth-Ayerst, (800) 395-9938.

"Questions and Answers About Tamoxifen" (1994). *Fact sheet on tamoxifen (Nolvadex) and its side effects.* 4 pages. NCI, (800) 4-CANCER.

Nancy Bruning, *Coping with Chemotherapy* (New York: Ballantine Books, 1993). *Overview of medical and emotional effects of chemotherapy.*

Joyce Slayton-Mitchell, *Winning the Chemo Battle* (New York: W. W. Norton, 1991). *Personal account of chemotherapy treatment from a woman who has "been there."*

1994 Directory of Prescription Drug Indigent Programs. *A listing of pharmaceutical companies that offer certain drugs at low or no cost. Includes specific drugs, patient eligibility and instructions for making the request. Free to health professionals. Request copies on letterhead.* Pharmaceutical Manufacturers Assn., 1100 15th Street NW, Washington, DC 20005. (800) PMA-INFO.

"The Role of Chemotherapy in the Management of Primary Breast Cancer" (3356, 1991). Booklet from ACS. (800) ACS-2345.

BMT Newsletter. A bimonthly newsletter covering various topics related to bone marrow transplant. Subscriptions are free; voluntary donations appreciated. 1985 Spruce Avenue, Highland Park, IL 60035. (708) 831-1913.

Susan K. Stewart, *Bone Marrow Transplants: A Book of Basics for Patients* (BMT Newsletter, Highland Park, IL, 1992). *Compilation of articles from back issues of the newsletter. Valuable chapter on insurance issues.* Order from BMT Newsletter, 1985 Spruce Avenue, Highland Park, IL 60035. (708) 831-1913.

National Bone Marrow Transplant Link. *Information clearinghouse on bone marrow transplants which also links patients or family with former patients or family.* 29209 Northwestern Highway, #624, Southfield, MI 48034. (313) 932-8483.

"Autologous Bone Marrow Transplantation: Facing the Challenge" (NABCO, NY, 1992). *Video reviewing information on ABMT/high-dose chemo, intended to be viewed by patients and their families in consultation with their medical teams.* 30 minutes. One copy free to health professionals. Order from NABCO. (212) 719-0154.

"Both Sides Now" (AMGEN, makers of Neupogen, 1994). *Four health professionals, who all have undergone chemotherapy, share their stories.* 20 minutes. Call Amgen, (800) 926-4369, to be referred to a sales representative in your area for a free copy.

American Society of Clinical Oncology (ASCO), 435 North Michigan Avenue, Suite 1717, Chicago, IL 60611. (312) 644-0828. *Will mail to medical professionals a list of member oncologists by geographical area.*

COMPLEMENTARY THERAPIES

Harold H. Benjamin, *The Wellness Community Guide to Fighting for Recovery—From Victim to Victor* (New York: Dell, 1987).

Herbert Benson, *The Relaxation Response* (New York: Avon Books, 1985).

Joan Borysenko, *Minding the Body, Mending the Mind* (Menlo Park, CA: Addison-Wesley, 1987).

Norman Cousins, *The Healing Heart* (New York: Avon Books, 1983).

Norman Cousins, *Anatomy of an Illness* (New York: Bantam Books, 1986).

Linda Dackman, *Affirmations, Meditations, and Encouragements for Women Living with Breast Cancer* (San Francisco: Harper, 1992). *Uses quotes and anecdotes to provide insight into the process.*

Larry Dossey, M.D., *Healing Words: The Power of Prayer and the Practice of Medicine* (San Francisco: HarperCollins, 1993).

Neil Fiore, *The Road Back to Health* (New York: Bantam Books, 1984). *Good explanation on how to make your own visualization tapes, by a psychologist and former cancer patient. Book is out of print but may be found in some libraries.*

Anne Fogelsanger, "See Yourself Well: For People with Cancer" (Brooklyn, NY: Equinox, 1994). *Audiocassette provides series of mental exercises to encourage relaxation.*

Humor Project. *A resource for humorous materials; free catalogue available. Quarterly magazine,* Laughing Matters, *available for $16/year. Conferences are held on using humor to cope with illness.* 110 Spring Street, Saratoga Springs, NY 12866-3397. (518) 587-8770.

Jon Kabat-Zinn, *Full Catastrophe Living: Using the Wisdom of Your Body and Mind to Face Stress, Pain and Illness* (New York: Delta Books, 1990).

Michael Lerner, *Choices in Healing: Integrating the Best of Conventional and Complementary Approaches to Cancer* (Cambridge, MA: MIT Press, 1994). *Useful book.*

Prevention magazine, (eds., Emmaus, PA: Rodale Press, 1984) *Fighting Disease: The Complete Guide to Natural Immune Power.*

Bill Moyers, *Healing and the Mind* (New York: Doubleday, 1993).

P. C. Roud, *Making Miracles: An Exploration into the Dynamics of Self-Healing* (New York: Warner Books, 1990).

Bernie Siegel, M.D., *Love, Medicine and Miracles* (New York: Perennial Library, 1987). *Promotes visualization, meditation, discussion and positive thinking.*

David Spiegel, *Living Beyond Limits: New Hope and Help for Facing Life-Threatening Illness* (New York: Times Books, 1993).

"Talking with Your Doctor" (4638-PS, 1987). *Suggestions for effective doctor/ patient communication.* 6 pages. American Cancer Society, (800) ACS-2345.

"Teamwork: The Cancer Patients' Guide to Talking with Your Doctor." National Coalition for Cancer Survivorship. 32 pages. Order from NCCS, 1010 Wayne Avenue, 5th floor, Silver Spring, MD 20910.

Institute for the Advancement of Health, 16 East 53rd Street, New York, NY 10022. (212) 832-8282. *A national organization devoted to promoting awareness of mind-body health interactions. Supplies information on behavioral techniques to promote comfort and health.*

Planetree Health Resource Center. *A nonprofit, consumer-oriented resource for health information, including materials on relaxation and visualization techniques.* Write or call for a catalogue and price list: 2040 Webster Street, San Francisco, CA 95115. (415) 923-3680.

ALTERNATIVE THERAPIES

"Unproven Methods of Cancer Management"(3028, 1988). American Cancer Society. *The local division offices have statements providing details on each of 27 treatment methods listed in this brochure.*

National Council Against Health Fraud. Call the Council's Resource Center, (800) 821-6671, or write to Dr. John Renner, Consumer Health Information Research Institute, 3521 Broadway, Kansas City, MO 64111.

Ralph Moss, *Cancer Therapy: The Independent Consumer's Guide to Non-Toxic Treatment and Prevention* (New York: Equinox Press, 1992). *Discusses nearly 100 nontoxic modes of cancer prevention and treatment.*

FINANCIAL AID

Adria Patient Assistance Plan, Adria Laboratories, P.O. Box 16529, Columbus, OH 43216-6529. (614) 764-8100. *Provides chemotherapy drugs (Adriamycin, vincristine, vinblastine) free-of-charge to patients with financial need. Request must be made by the patient's doctor to Adria Laboratories or local Adria representative.*

Bristol-Myers Indigent Patient Assistance Program, Bristol-Myers Oncology Division, 2404 West Pennsylvania Street, Evansville, IN 47721. (812) 429-5000. *Provides chemotherapy (Cytoxan) free-of-charge to patients with financial need. Request must be made by patient's physician.*

ICI Pharmaceutical Novaldex (tamoxifen) Patient Assistance Program, Manager Professional Services, ICI Pharmaceuticals, Division of ICI Americas, Inc., Wilmington, DE 19897. (800) 456-5678. *Provides tamoxifen to patients with financial need. Write for application.*

American Association of Retired People (AARP) Pharmacy Service. Catalog Dept., Box 19229, Alexandria, VA 22320. *Members can use their nonprofit service to save on prescriptions delivered by mail. Good for tamoxifen (Novaldex). Write for free catalog.*

Corporate Angel Network, Inc. (CAN), Westchester County Airport, Building 1, White Plains, NY 10604. (914) 328-1313. *A nationwide program designed to give patients with cancer the use of available seats on corporate aircraft to get to and from recognized treatment centers. There is no cost or any financial need requirement.*

Mission Air Transportation Network (Canada), 77 Bloor Street West, Suite 1711, Toronto, Ont. M5S 3A1. (416) 924-9333. *Same as above.*

National Cancer Institute, Bethesda, MD 20892-4200. (800) 638-6694. *Patients who are treated here as part of a clinical study receive their treatment free and may be housed free-of-charge at the hospital facilities of the NCI.*

Living with Breast Cancer

National Coalition for Cancer Survivorship, 323 Eighth Street SW, Albuquerque, NM 87102. (505) 764-9956. *A national network of independent groups and individuals concerned with survivorship and sources of support for cancer patients and their families.*

Marion Morra and Eva Potts, *Triumph, Getting Back to Normal When You Have Cancer* (New York: Avon Books, 1990).

"Look Good . . . Feel Better" (LGFB). A public service program from the Cosmetic, Toilet and Fragrance Association Foundation in partnership with the American Cancer Society and the National Cosmetology Association. *Designed to help women recovering from cancer deal with changes in their appearance resulting from cancer treatment. The program's print and videotape materials are designed for both patients and health professionals.* Call (800) 395-LOOK or your local ACS office.

"Look Good . . . Feel Better: Caring for Yourself Inside and Out." (CTFA Foundation, 1988). *The LGFB program's video for cancer patients undergoing chemotherapy and radiation therapy. Women discuss their experiences, and beauty professionals review ways to look and feel better during treatment, including makeup, nail care, and wigs.* 16 minutes. Order from CTFA. (800) 395-LOOK.

American Hair Loss Council. *Source of information on hair loss.* (800) 274-8717.

"Best Look Forward" (1991). *Videotape in which a makeup artist and hairdresser give advice and demonstrations, including on eyebrows and lashes.* 30 minutes. $45.00. Order from the Graduate Hospital Cancer Program, 1840 South Street, Philadelphia, PA 19146; or call Eileen Murphy, (215) 893-7298.

Buyer's Guide to Wigs and Hairpieces. Two-page summary from Ruth L. Weintraub, 420 Madison Avenue, Suite 406, NY 10017. (212) 838-1333.

Charming with Dignity. *Supplies fashion-designed turbans and the "Softee Comfort Form" prosthesis for use immediately following breast surgery.* Call for catalog. 112 West 34th Street, Suite 1617, NY 10120. (800) 477-8188.

Edith Imre Foundation for Loss of Hair. *Provides counseling and support as well as wig selection.* 30 West 57th Street, NY 10019. (212) 757-8160 or Wig Hotline (212) 765-8397.

External Reconstruction Technology. *The "Third Alternative" is a nonsurgical procedure that sculpts a breast from a cast of your body and then colors it to match your skin tone.* 4535 Benner Street, Philadelphia, PA 19135. (215) 333-8424.

Ladies' First Choice. *Post–breast surgery boutique.* Newsletter. Medicare, mail orders accepted. 6465 Sunnyside Road SE, Salem, OR 97306. (503) 363-3940.

Lady Grace Stores. *Chain of post–breast surgery stores with locations in Mass., N.H., Fla., and Me.* Newsletter. Medicare, mail orders accepted. (800) 922-0504.

My Secret. *Post-surgery boutique. Support groups and counseling available.* Medicare/Medicaid accepted. Phone orders. 41 West 86th Street, NY 10024. (212) 877-8860.

New Beginnings. *Post-mastectomy fashion service.* Phone orders. 1556 Third Avenue, Room 603, NY 10128. (212) 369-6630.

Schwartz' Intimate Apparel. *Post-surgery boutique.* Medicare/Medicaid accepted. 108 Skokie Boulevard, Wilmette, IL 60091. (708) 251-1118.

Soft Options. *Soft, washable, stretchy cap that is a comfortable alternative to wigs.* 6345 Galletta Drive, Newark, CA 94560. (510) 797-8188.

Underneath It All. *Post–breast surgery boutique which provides massage, cosmetic makeovers, and seminars.* Phone orders. 444 East 75th Street, NY 10021. (212) 717-1976.

Y-ME Prosthesis and Wig Bank. *Prosthesis and wig bank for women with financial need.* If the appropriate size is available, Y-ME will mail anywhere in the country for a nominal handling fee. (800) 221-2141.

"Maintaining a Positive Image with Breast Cancer Surgery." *Videotape covering prosthetic, lingerie, and swimsuit choices following breast cancer surgery.* $19.95 plus $2 postage. Johanna's On-Call to Mend Esteem, 199 New Scotland Avenue, Albany, NY 12208. (518) 482-4178.

"Maintaining a Positive Image with Hair Loss and Cancer Therapy." *Videotape providing useful tips for maintaining self-esteem during treatment.* $19.95 plus $2 postage. Johanna's On-Call to Mend Esteem, 199 New Scotland Avenue, Albany, NY 12208. (518) 482-4178.

"In Touch for Life" (Zeneca Pharmaceuticals, 1991). *A wellness program, with a two-videotape kit for mastectomy and lumpectomy.* Call Zeneca/Novaldex at (800) 842-9920 to be referred to a sales representative in your area for a free copy.

Practical Advice: How to Find Post-Mastectomy Products

— Prostheses. The lingerie areas in some department stores employ professionals who will fit you with a prosthesis and a bra to wear with it. Smaller lingerie boutiques in major cities often perform this function as well. Check your local yellow pages under "Lingerie" or "Brassieres," or, in larger cities, under "Breast Prosthesis." Prostheses may also be ordered from select surgical supply stores, often listed under "Surgical

Appliances and Supplies." Temporary prostheses can be ordered by mail. Women who cannot afford a prosthesis may wish to contact the Y-ME Prosthesis Bank (see listing above).

— Bathing suits and lingerie. Contact the sources mentioned above. In addition, a number of specialty boutiques have opened that sell clothing with post-mastectomy needs in mind, although there is not yet a national chain. Consult your yellow pages under "lingerie."

If you have difficulty locating a local retailer, contact the Reach to Recovery volunteer at your American Cancer Society office, call a local breast cancer support group, or contact the social work department of your hospital.

RECONSTRUCTION

"Breast Reconstruction Following Mastectomy." American Society of Plastic and Reconstructive Surgeons, 444 East Algonquin Road, Arlington Heights, IL 60005. (312) 228-9900. For referrals call the society's message tape at (800) 635-0635.

"Breast Reconstruction After Mastectomy." (4630, 1991). American Cancer Society. *Describes types of surgery with photographs and drawings and answers commonly asked questions.* 20 pages. (800) ACS-2345.

Marilyn Snyder, *An Informed Decision: Understanding Breast Reconstruction* (New York: M. Evans/Little, Brown, 1989). Paperback, $12.95. *An informative mixture of one woman's account and clearly presented illustrated information about breast reconstruction after mastectomy.*

"A Sense of Balance: Breast Reconstruction." *Interactive videotape developed by the staff at the Breast Evaluation Center, Dana Farber Cancer Institute, to inform about the pros and cons of various types of reconstruction.* $29.95. To order call (617) 732-3379.

LYMPHEDEMA

National Lymphedema Network and Network Hotline. *Nonprofit organization provides patients and professionals with information about prevention and treatment of this complication of lymph node surgery.* 2211 Post Street, Suite 404, San Francisco, CA 94115. Call hotline for referrals for medical treatment, physical therapy, general information, and support in your area. Information packet available. (800) 541-3259.

Breast Cancer Physical Therapy Center. *Provides booklet on exercises to help manage lymphedema.* 1905 Spruce Street, Philadelphia, PA 19103. $8.95.

EXERCISE

YWCA Encore Program, 624 9th Street NW Washington, DC 20001-5394. *Provides supportive discussion and rehabilitative exercise for women who have been treated for breast cancer.* To find the location of the program nearest you call (202) 628-3636.

"Get Up and Go: After Breast Surgery." (ACS/University of Michigan, Oak Park, MI 21989). Order from *Health Tapes Inc.* (313) 662-5100. *Total body exercises demonstrated by five women who have had a mastectomy, lumpectomy, or reconstructive surgery. Increasingly challenging levels.* 60 minutes, $39.95.

"Get Up and Go After Breast Surgery" (Varied Directions, 69 Elm Street, Camden, ME 04843). *Exercise tape.* 60 minutes, $29.95 plus $5 shipping. (800) 888-5236.

"Beginning Ballet for the Post-Mastectomy Woman" (First Position Productions, 1990). *Videotape of a class of women who have had mastectomies.* 50 minutes, $39.95. First Position Productions, Star Route Box 472, Sausalito, CA 94965. (415) 381-9034.

Stretch Exercise Program (1988). *An eight-week exercise/support program for women who have had surgery for breast cancer. Manual, video materials and sessions offered free through volunteer services.* Call the Alabama Division of the ACS, (205) 879-2242.

EMOTIONAL EXERCISE

Wellness Community. *Extensive support and education programs encourage emotional recovery and a feeling of wellness.* 1235 Fifth Street, Santa Monica, CA 90401. (310) 393-1415.

National Self-Help Clearinghouse. *Refers written inquiries to regional self-help services.* c/o Graduate School and University Center of City University of New York, 33 West 42nd Street, Room 620N, New York, NY 10036.

Cancer Wellness Center/Barbara Kassel Brotman House. *Offers free emotional support on its 24-hour hotline and through support groups, relaxation groups, educational workshops, and library.* 215 Revere Drive, Northbrook, IL 50062. (708) 509-9595.

Coping. Bimonthly magazine for cancer patients and survivors. Media America, 2019 North Carothers, Franklin, TN 37064. Subscription $18/year. (615) 790-2400.

"For Single Women with Breast Cancer" (1994). *Y-ME booklet offers practical guidance and emotional support for women without partners or those who live alone. Single copies available free.* (800) 221-2141.

Reach to Recovery, American Cancer Society. *Trained volunteers visit newly diagnosed patients.* (800) ACS-2345.

"Taking Time: Support for People with Cancer and the People Who Care About Them" (93-2059, 1993). National Cancer Institute. *Booklet for persons with cancer and their families.* 69 pages. (800) 4-CANCER.

Lonnie Barbach, *For Each Other: Sharing Sexual Intimacy* (New York: Signet, 1984).

M. Colgrove, H. H. Bloomfield, and P. McWilliams, *How to Survive the Loss of a Love* (New York: Bantam Books, 1977).

Betty J. Eadie, *Embraced by the Light* (Placerville, CA: Gold Leaf Press, 1992).

Anne Fogelsanger, *See Yourself Well: For People with Cancer* (Brooklyn, NY: Equinox). Audiocassette. Helpful while under treatment.

Carlton Fredericks, *Winning the Fight Against Breast Cancer* (New York: Grosset & Dunlap, 1977).

Amy Harwell and K. Tomasik, *When Your Friend Gets Cancer* (Wheaton, IL: Harold Shaw Publishers, 1987).

Judy Johnson, *Intimacy: Living as a Woman After Cancer* (Toronto: NC Press, 1987).

"Sexuality and Cancer" (1988). American Cancer Society. *Booklet about cancer and sexuality in areas that might concern the patient and her partner.* 40 pages.

D. G. Kauffman, *Surviving Cancer: A Practical Guide for Those Fighting to Win* (Washington, DC: Acropolis Books, 1989).

Raymond A. Moody, M.D., *The Light Beyond: New Explorations by the Author of Life After Life* (New York: Bantam, 1988).

Fitzhugh Mullan, Barbara Hoffman, and the National Coalition for Cancer Survivorship, *Charting the Journal: An Almanac of Practical Resources for Cancer Survivors* (Mt. Vernon, NY: Consumer Reports Books, 1990). *Collection of resources, suggestions, strategies, and feelings, with a detailed appendix directory.*

Susan Nessim and Judith Ellis, *Cancervive: The Challenge of Life After Cancer* (Boston: Houghton Mifflin, 1992). *Addresses practical and emotional issues faced by cancer survivors such as insurance, relationships, infertility, and long-term side effects of treatment.* $8.95.

Midge Stocker, ed., *Confronting Cancer, Constructing Change: New Perspectives on Women and Cancer. Essays confronting cancer myths.* (Chicago, IL: Third Side Press, 1993).

J. Tatelbaum, *The Courage to Grieve: Creative Living, Recovery and Growth Through Grief* (New York: Harper & Row, 1980).

J. Tatelbaum, *You Don't Have to Suffer: A Handbook for Moving Beyond Life's Crises* (New York: Harper & Row, 1989).

"Facing Forward: A Guide for Cancer Survivors" (93-2424, 1992). National Cancer Institute. *Addresses the special needs of cancer survivors and their families.* 43 pages. (800) 4-CANCER.

Practical Advice: How to Find a Breast Cancer Support Group

— Inquire at a local major hospital's Breast Center or Department of Social Work or Psychiatry.

— Call the National Cancer Institute's Cancer Information Service at (800) 4-CANCER for the names of the American College of Radiology (ACR) accredited mammography providers in your area, and ask these providers for support-group suggestions.

— Contact the American Cancer Society at (800) ACS-2345 for local groups that they or others sponsor.

— Call a group on the *List* in Appendix C and ask if they know of any groups located nearer to you.

— To start your own support group, contact your local ACS office or Y-ME at (800) 221-2141.

Please note that some people benefit more from individual counseling than from group support.

INSURANCE AND EMPLOYMENT

Information and Counseling about Cancer and the Workplace. Phyllis Stein, Radcliffe Career Services, Radcliffe College, 10 Garden Street, Cambridge, MA 02138. (617) 495-8631; and Barbara Lazarus, Associate Provost for Academic Programs, Carnegie-Mellon University, Pittsburgh, PA 15213. (412) 268-6994.

"What You Should Know About Health Insurance" (731, July 1987). "What You Should Know About Disability Insurance" (733, October 1987). Health Insurance Association of America, 1025 Connecticut Avenue, NW, Washington, DC 20004-3998. (202) 334-7780.

Karen M. Hassey, "Pregnancy and Parenthood After Treatment for Breast Cancer," *Oncology Nursing Forum,* vol. 15(4):439–444, 1988. *You will probably have to get this from a hospital or medical library. A very good review of all that has been published on the subject.*

"The Americans with Disabilities Act: Protection for Cancer Patients Against Employment Discrimination" (4585, 1993). American Cancer Society. *Brochure defines the ADA law by describing employment rights of the cancer patient.* (800) ACS-2345.

"Cancer. Your Job, Insurance and the Law" (4585-PS, 1987). American Cancer Society. *Summarizes cancer patients' legal rights; gives complaint procedure instructions.* 6 pages. (800) ACS-2345.

"What Cancer Survivors Need to Know About Health Insurance" (1993). National Coalition for Cancer Survivorship. *Provides clear understanding of health insurance and how to receive maximum reimbursement on claims.* 37 pages. Single copies available free. (301) 650-8868.

Charles B. Inlander and Eugene I. Pavalon, *Your Medical Rights.* (Allentown, PA: People's Medical Society, 1994).

RECURRENCE AND METASTASIS

"After Breast Cancer: A Guide to Follow-Up Care" (87–2400). National Cancer Institute. *Considers the importance of follow-up, signs of recurrence, and the physical and emotional effects of having had breast cancer.* 11 pages.

"When Cancer Recurs: Meeting the Challenge Again (9302709, 1992). National Cancer Institute. *Details types of recurrence, types of treatment, and coping with cancer's return.*

Lucy Shapero and Anthony Goodman, *Never Say Die* (East Norwalk, CT: Appleton and Lange, 1980). *A woman and her doctor discuss her care through metastatic breast cancer. Book is out of print but may still be found in libraries.*

"Advanced Cancer: Living Each Day" (85–856). National Cancer Institute. *Booklet written to make living with advanced cancer easier.* 30 pages.

"Questions and Answers About Pain Control: A Guide for People with Cancer and Their Families" (4518-PS, 1992). American Cancer Society. *Discusses pain control using both medical and nonmedical methods.* 76 pages. (800) ACS-2345 or (800) 4-CANCER (National Cancer Institute).

"Caring for the Patient with Cancer at Home: A Guide for Patients and Families" (4656-PS, 1988). *Guidebook provides detailed helpful information on how to care for the patient at home.* 40 pages.

National Hospice Organization. *Provides a directory of hospice programs by state.* 1901 North Moore Street, Suite 901, Arlington, VA 22209. (703) 243-5900.

Royal Victoria Hospital Palliative Care Service. *Independent national organization of groups providing palliative care and hospice in Canada.* 687 Pine Avenue West, Montreal, Que. H3A 1A1. (514) 843-1542.

Choice In Dying. *Nonprofit educational organization distributes the living will, a document that records a patient's wishes during treatment and in regard to terminal care.* 200 Varick Street, New York, NY 10014. (212) 366-5540.

CLINICAL TRIALS

"What Are Clinical Trials All About?" (85–2706, 1985). National Cancer Institute. *Booklet helps explain what clinical trials (protocols) are all about and helps you decide if you want to participate.* 23 pages.

Community Clinical Oncology Program (CCOP). (April 1993, updated periodically). National Cancer Institute. *Lists the 70 community programs in 32 states and Puerto Rico selected by the National Cancer Institute to participate in the introduction of the newest clinical protocols and to accrue patients to clinical trials.* (800) 4-CANCER.

National Surgical Adjuvant Breast and Bowel Project (NSABP). *For information on physicians participating in trials in your area.* 3550 Terrace Street, Room 914, Pittsburgh, PA 15261. (412) 648-9720.

Physician Data Query (PDQ). Cancer information database of the National Cancer Institute. *Provides information on prognostic, stage, and treatment and over 1,500 clinical trials open to patient accrual. Updated monthly. Access by computer equipped with a modem, and by fax.* Information is available by phone (800) 4-CANCER or fax (301) 402-5874 in English or Spanish, in formats designed for both patients and professionals. (Also see the NCI's booklet, "What Are Clinical Trials All About?")

"Pharmaceutical Frontiers: Research on Breast Cancer" (1993). *Brochure providing overview of the latest research options. Lists approved medications used in treating breast cancer and the drugs in clinical trials.* One copy free from Editor, Pharmaceutical Frontiers, Pharmaceutical Manufacturer's Association, 1100 15th Street NW, Washington, DC 20005.

"What Are Clinical Trials All About?" (92–2706, 1992). National Cancer Institute. *Booklet designed for patients considering participating in cancer treatment trials.* 22 pages. (800) 4-CANCER.

POLITICS

Virginia M. Soffa, *The Journey beyond Breast Cancer: From the Personal to the Political* (Rochester, VT: Inner Traditions, 1994).

Practical Advice: How to Get Involved with Breast Cancer Organizations

— *Advocacy.* Although individuals can become active by contacting their elected officials, the most effective way to change policy is by taking part in a national movement. The National Breast Cancer Coalition (NBCC) was formed in 1991 as a public policy effort to involve women with breast cancer and those who care about them in changing public policy. The NBCC's goals include increasing breast cancer research funding and improving access to screening, increasing the influence breast cancer survivors have over research, clinical trials, national policy, and care for all women. The NBCC welcomes individuals as members of its National Action Network and organizations that wish to join its more than 300 current member organizations and thousands of individuals. Write or call the National Breast Cancer Coalition at P.O. Box 66373, Washington, DC 20035, (202) 296-7477.

— *Volunteering.* Many breast cancer education and support organizations have limited staff budgets, so your help is often eagerly accepted. Before you make arrangements, consider the tasks you are willing to perform, including clerical work and patient contact, and if you can commit to a regular schedule or would prefer to be called for special projects. To find a local breast cancer organization where your volunteer help is needed, consult Appendix C or your local major medical center, hospital, or American Cancer Society office.

— *Financial Support.* Many organizations formed in recent years accept charitable contributions to fund breast cancer research or education. To investigate, check to be sure they are registered with your state's Office of the Attorney General or Office of Charities Registration. Your local major medical center or hospital may also accept support directed to breast cancer.

C

Regional Support
Organizations
for Cancer and
Breast Cancer Patients

Alabama

Gadsden	Woman to Woman	(205) 543-8896
Tuscaloosa	UPFRONT Support Group	(205) 759-7000

Alaska

Anchorage	The Anchorage Women's Breast Cancer Support Group	(907) 261-3151

Arizona

Phoenix	Maryvale Samaritan Hospital/ New Beginnings	(602) 848-5588
Scottsdale	Y-ME Breast Cancer Network of Arizona	(602) 952-9793
Tucson	Cerelle Center for Women's Health Breast Cancer Resource Center	(602) 325-3000
	Arizona Cancer Center	(602) 626-6044

Arkansas

Fort Smith	Phillips Cancer Support House	(501) 782-6302
Little Rock	CARTI CancerAnswers	(501) 664-8573

Reprinted with the kind permission of the National Alliance of Breast Cancer Organizations

California

Anaheim	Breast Care for Life Program Anaheim Memorial Hospital	(714) 999-3800/ beeper #35283
Berkeley	Women's Cancer Resource Center	(510) 548-9272
Chico	Enloe Hospital Breast Screening Center	(916) 891-7445
Culver City	Breast Cancer Recovery Plus	(310) 391-0068
Escondido	The Health Concern–Pallmar Pomerado Health System	(619) 737-3960
Fresno	St. Agnes Medical Center/Breast Cancer Support Group	(209) 449-5222
	Family Service Center	(209) 227-3576
La Habra	Bloomers–Y-ME of Orange County	(714) 447-6975
La Jolla	Stevens Cancer Center–Scripps Memorial Hospital	(619) 457-6756
Lancaster	Ladies of Courage/Y-ME	(805) 266-4811
Long Beach	Y-ME South Bay/Long Beach	(310) 984-8456
	Long Beach Memorial Breast Center	(310) 933-7821
Los Angeles	Rhonda Fleming Mann Resource Center for Women with Cancer	(310) 794-6644
Monterey	Breast Self-Help Group	(408) 649-1772
Napa	Bosom Buddies	(707) 257-4047
Orange	The Breast Care Center	(714) 541-0101
	Breast Cancer Support Group–UC Irvine Medical Center	(714) 456-6968
Palm Springs	Desert Hospital	(619) 323-6676
Palo Alto	Discovery Breast Cancer Support Group (also offers an exercise class for women who have had breast cancer)	(415) 494-0972
Pasadena	Breast Cancer Networking Group	(818) 796-1083
Sacramento	Save Ourselves/Y-ME of Sacramento	(916) 921-9747
San Clemente	Orange County Chapter Susan G. Komen Foundation	(714) 496-5624
San Diego	Women's Cancer Task Force/Y-ME San Diego Chapter	(619) 239-9283
	Breast Cancer Peer Support Group–UC San Diego Cancer Center	(619) 543-7397
San Francisco	The Cancer Support Community	(415) 648-9400
	Bay Area Lymphedema Support Group	(415) 921-2911

	Breast Cancer Action	(415) 922-8279
	The Breast Health Resource Center	(415) 502-1439
San Jose	Bay Area Breast Cancer Network	(408) 261-1425
Santa Monica	Wellness Community	(310) 314-2555
Sausalito	Center for Attitudinal Healing	(415) 435-5022
Van Nuys	The Breast Center	(818) 787-9911
Walnut Creek	John Muir Breast Care Resource Center	(510) 947-3322
West Covina	Queen of the Valley Breast Cancer Support Group	(818) 814-2401

Colorado

Colorado City	Daryleen Emmons Breast Cancer Support Group/Penrose Cancer Center	(719) 630-5273
Denver	AMC Cancer Research Center	(303) 239-3393 / (800) 321-9526
	Rose Breast Center	(303) 320-7142
	Rose Breast Center–Men's Discussion Group (for male partners of women with breast cancer)	(303) 320-7142

Connecticut

Branford	Y-ME of New England	(203) 483-8200 / (800) 933-4963
Danbury	I Can	(203) 830-4621
Hartford	St. Francis Hospital and Medical Center	(203) 548-4366
Norwalk	Cancer Care, Inc.	(203) 854-9911
Ridgefield	Ridgefield Breast Cancer Support Group–The Revivers	(203) 438-5555

Delaware

Wilmington	Looking Ahead Support Group	(302) 421-4161

District of Columbia

	Lombardi Breast Cancer Support Group Georgetown University	(202) 784-4000
	The Mary-Helen Mautner Project for Lesbians with Cancer	(202) 332-5536
	George Washington University	(202) 994-4589
	Betty Ford Comprehensive Breast Center	(202) 293-6654

Florida

Coral Springs	Y-ME of Florida	(305) 752-2101
Daytona Beach	Halifax Medical Center Women's Services	(904) 254-4211

Jacksonville	Bosom Buddies	(904) 633-8246
Miami	South Florida Comprehensive Cancer Center	(305) 227-5582
Orlando	Center for Women's Medicine– Florida Hospital	(407) 897-1617
	Women's Center/East Orlando Breast Cancer Support Group– Bosom Buddies	(407) 281-8663
Pensacola	Ann L. Baroco Center for Women's Health	(904) 474-7878
Sarasota	Sarasota Memorial Hospital Woman to Woman	(813) 953-1375
Tallahassee	Woman to Woman–Women's Resource Center Tallahassee Memorial Regional Medical Center	(904) 681-2255
Tampa	FACTORS/H. Lee Moffit Cancer Center	(813) 972-8407

Georgia

Atlanta	Northside Hospital	(404) 851-8954/ 6100
Tucker	Bosom Buddies of GA, Inc. (also offers a bone marrow transplant support group)	(404) 493-7517
	Bosom Buddies of GA–Men's Bereavement Support Group	(404) 493-7517

Hawaii

Honolulu	Queens Medical Center	(808) 537-7555

Idaho

Boise	Mountain States Tumor Institute	(208) 386-2764
Coeur d'Alene	North Idaho Cancer Center	(208) 666-3800
Ketchum	The Wellness Group Hospice of the Wood River Valley	(208) 726-8464

Illinois

Alton	CARE–Alton Memorial Hospital	(618) 463-7150
Barrington	A Time to Heal Wellspring Women's Health Center	(708) 381-9600 ext. 5330
Belleville	St. Elizabeth Hospital Mastectomy Club	(618) 234-1293
Elmhurst	Breast Cancer Support Group– Elmhurst Memorial Hospital	(708) 833-0143 pager
Joliet	Positive People–Sister Theresa Cancer Care Center/St. Joseph Medical Center	(815) 741-7560

Macomb	McDonough District Hospital Women's Health Resource Center	(309) 833-4101 ext. 3198
Moline	Quad City Mastectomy Support Group	(309) 764-2888
Pekin	Pekin Hospital–Mastectomy Support Group	(309) 353-0807
Peoria	Susan G. Komen Breast Center	(309) 689-6622
Rockford	Breast Cancer Support Group for Younger Women	(815) 961-6215
Springfield	Sangamon Breast Cancer Support Group	(217) 787-7187

Indiana

Bluffton	Women's Cancer Support Group	(219) 824-6493
Gary	Yes, We Can Methodist Hospital, Northlake Campus	(219) 886-4328/ (800) 952-7337
Indianapolis	Uplifter's Breast Cancer Support Group	(317) 355-1411
	Y-ME of Central Indiana	(317) 823-7292
Terre Haute	Y-ME of Wabash Valley	(812) 877-3025/ 877-9259
Warsaw	Women Winning Against Cancer	(219) 269-9911

Iowa

Cedar Rapids	"ESPECIALLY FOR YOU" After Breast Cancer	(800) 642-6329/ (319) 365-HOPE
Marshalltown	Marshalltown Cancer Support Group	(515) 752-8775
Sioux City	ABC–After Breast Cancer Support Group	(712) 279-2989

Kansas

| Wichita | Breast Cancer Care Group Victory in the Valley | (316) 262-7559 |

Kentucky

Ashland	Breast Cancer Support Group	(606) 327-4535
Edgewood	St. Elizabeth Women's Center	(606) 344-3939
Lexington	The Thursday Group	(606) 269-4836/ 233-3601
Louisville	LAMA (Louisville Area Mastectomy Association)	(502) 634-0087
Prestonsburg	Breast Cancer Support Group	(606) 886-8511 ext. 160

Louisiana

| Marrero | Bosom Buddies–West Jefferson Medical Center | (504) 349-1640 |

Metairie	Center for Living with Cancer	(504) 454-5071
New Orleans	Breast Cancer Support Group	(504) 897-5860
	Lakeland Medical Center	(504) 245-4855
	Patricia Trost Friedler Cancer Counseling	(504) 587-2120
Slidell	Bosom Buddies–NorthShore Regional Medical Center	(504) 646-5014

Maryland

Hagerstown	Y-ME of the Cumberland Valley	(301) 791-5843
Timonium	Arm in Arm	(410) 561-1650

Massachusetts

Amherst	Margaret Gozlin Counseling Center	(413) 256-4600
Boston	Cross Roads Dana Farber Cancer Institute	(617) 632-3459
	Evening Exchange New England Medical Center	(617) 956-5757
	Life After Breast Cancer New England Medical Center	(617) 956-5261
	Living with Recurrent Breast Cancer New England Medical Center	(617) 956-5261
Burlington	Lahey Clinic Breast Cancer Treatment Center	(617) 273-8989
Cambridge	Harvard University	(617) 495-2936
Framingham	Metro West Medical Center Cancer Care Center	(508) 383-1240
Jamaica Plain	Faulkner Breast Centre Support Group	(617) 983-7777
Lee	Y-ME of the Berkshires	(413) 243-4822/ (800) 439-4821
Marion	Strength for Tomorrow	(508) 748-1611
Worcester	UMass Breast Cancer Education Awareness Group	(508) 752-2210

Michigan

Ann Arbor	Breast Cancer Support Group	(313) 936-6000
Capac	Breast Cancer Support Group	(313) 395-7626
Detroit	Comprehensive Breast Center– Harper Hospital	(313) 745-2754
	Breast Cancer Support Group	(313) 343-3684
	Michigan Cancer Foundation– Breast Cancer Detection Center	(313) 833-7700
Farmington	Berry Health Center	(313) 493-6507

Flint	McLaren Mastectomy Support Group	(313) 762-2375
Grand Rapids	Woman to Woman–St. Mary's Breast Center	(616) 774-6756
	"EXPRESSIONS" for Women	(616) 957-3223
Lansing	WINS Support Group–Sparrow Hospital	(517) 483-2689
Marquette	Marquette General Hospital	(906) 225-3500
Midland	Midland Community Cancer Services	(517) 835-4841/ (800) 999-3199
Petoskey	Just for Us	(616) 347-8443
Rockwood	"Unique" Breast Cancer Support Group	(313) 833-0710 ext. 770

Minnesota

Duluth	Duluth Clinic–Breast Diagnostic Center	(218) 725-3195
Fridley	Mercy Hospital Oncology Program	(612) 422-4524
St. Louis Park	Cancer Center, Methodist Hospital	(612) 932-6086

Mississippi

Biloxi	Biloxi Regional Medical Center	(601) 436-1694

Missouri

Chesterfield	FOCUS St. Luke's Hospital	(314) 851-6090
Kansas City	Menorah Medical Center TOUCH Breast Cancer Program	(816) 276-8848
	Cancer Hotline	(816) 932-8453
	The Cancer Institute of Health Midwest	(816) 751-2629
Springfield	Reach Together	(417) 886-LADY
	Mid America Cancer Center–Breast Cancer Network (St. John's)	(800) 432-CARE (800) 364-6120
St. Charles	St. Joseph Health Center–Hospital West	(314) 947-5614/ (800) 835-1212
St. Louis	"We Can" Missouri Baptist Medical Center	(314) 569-5263
	St. John's Mercy Cancer Center	(314) 569-6400
	SHARE Breast Cancer Education and Support Program	(314) 991-4424
	Reflections and Can Survive–Barnes Jewish Hospital Breast Cancer Support Groups	(314) 362-5574
	Young Mothers with Breast Cancer–Jewish Hospital CIRCLE	(314) 454-7474

Montana

Sidney	Bosom Buddies	(406) 482-2423

Nebraska

Lincoln	St. Elizabeth Community Health Center	(402) 486-7567

Nevada

Reno	On With Life–St. Mary's Women's Center	(702) 789-3282

New Hampshire

Concord	Concord Hospital	(603) 225-2711 ext. 3872
	Mastectomy Survivors	(603) 224-2051
Lebanon	North Cotton Cancer Center	(603) 650-5789
Manchester	Catholic Medical Center	(603) 626-2049
	Elliot Hospital	(603) 628-2338

New Jersey

Bricktown	Breast Disease and Surgery Center	(908) 458-4600
Camden	Comprehensive Breast Care Center Cooper Hospital University Medical Center	(609) 342-2474
Dover	Dover General Hospital and Medical Center	(201) 989-3106
Fair Haven	Mid Monmouth County Recurrence Support Group	(908) 229-9535
Hackensack	Hackensack Medical Center	(201) 996-5800
Livingston	St. Barnabas Medical Center	(201) 533-5633
Long Branch	Cancer Center at Monmouth Medical	(908) 870-5429
Medford	Elm Lifelines Center for Cancer Counseling and Support	(609) 654-4044
Millburn	Cancer Care, Inc.	(201) 379-7500
Neptune	Woman to Woman–Jersey Shore Medical Center	(908) 776-4240
New Brunswick	Cancer Institute of New Jersey	(908) 235-6790
Ocean County	Breast Cancer Support Group	(908) 367-7934
Point Pleasant	Brick Hospital	(908) 295-6427
Pomona	Atlantic City Medical Center RNS Regional Cancer Center	(609) 652-3500
	B.E.S.T Care–Ruth Newman Shapiro Medical Center	(609) 652-3500
Princeton	Breast Cancer Resource Center Princeton YWCA (for men and women)	(609) 497-2126/ 252-2003
	Beyond Cancer	(609) 683-0692

Randolf	Women at Risk (for women considering prophylactic mastectomies)	(800) 82-BREAST
Red Bank	Riverview Regional Cancer Center	(908) 530-2382/ (800) 564-3551
Ridgewood	Cancer Care, Inc.	(201) 444-6630
	Talking It Over–Valley Hospital	(201) 447-8656
Somerville	After Breast Cancer Support Group at Somerset Medical Center	(908) 685-2953
South River	WISE–Women's International Support Environment	(908) 257-6611/ (800) 870-6616
Three Bridges	Breast Cancer Support Group	(908) 782-8708
Toms River	Community Medical Center	(908) 240-8076
Washington	After Breast Cancer Surgery	(201) 666-6610
Westfield	CHEMOcare	(800) 55-CHEMO (908) 233-1103

New Mexico

| Albuquerque | People Living Through Cancer | (505) 242-3263 |

New York

Binghamton	Breast Cancer Support Group	(607) 693-1759
Brooklyn	Othmer Cancer Center at Long Island College Hospital	(718) 780-1135
	Cancer Institute of Brooklyn	(718) 972-5816
Buffalo	Breast Cancer Network of Western New York	(716) 845-8086
Elmhurst	St. John's Queens Hospital	(718) 457-1300 ext. 2250
Elmsford	Side by Side	(914) 347-2649
Flushing	Flushing Hospital Medical Center	(718) 670-5640
Garden City	Adelphi Support Group for Women Under 40	(516) 877-4314
	Adelphi Breast Cancer HOTLINE and Support Program	(516) 877-4444
Glens Falls	After Breast Cancer–Glens Falls Hospital	(518) 251-3126
Huntington	Huntington Hospital	(516) 351-2568
Ithaca	Tompkins Community Hospital	(607) 274-4101
Johnson City	Women's Health Connection– United Health Services	(607) 763-6546
Manhasset	Oncology Support Program for Cancer Patients and Their Families	(516) 926-HELP
New Hyde Park	Long Island Jewish Medical Center Post-Lumpectomy Support Group	(718) 470-7188

New York City	SHARE: Support Services for Women with Breast or Ovarian Cancer	(212) 719-0364
	Post-Treatment Resource Program Memorial Sloan-Kettering Cancer Center	(212) 639-3292
	Cancer Care, Inc.	(212) 302-2400
	New Beginnings Beth Israel Medical Center North Division	(212) 870-9502
	Breast Friends–Mount Sinai Medical Center	(212) 241-7748
	Breast Examination Center of Harlem	(212) 864-0600
Port Jefferson	John T. Mather Memorial Hospital Live, Love and Laugh Again	(516) 476-2707
Putnam Valley	Breast Cancer Support Group	(914) 528-8213
Rochester	Cancer Action, Inc.	(716) 423-9700
	University of Rochester Cancer Center	(716) 275-5908
Rye Brook	Cancer Support Team, Inc.	(914) 253-5334
Valley Stream	Franklin General Hospital Mastectomy Discussion Group	(516) 825-8800 ext. 2205
Woodbury	Cancer Care, Inc.	(516) 364-8130
North Carolina		
Asheville	Life After Cancer/Pathways, Inc.	(704) 252-4106
Chapel Hill	Chapel Hill Support	(919) 929-7022
Charlotte	Charlotte Organization for Breast Cancer Education	(704) 846-2190
	Presbyterian Hospital	(704) 384-4750
	Women Living with Cancer	(704) 355-3789
Durham	Duke Cancer Patient Support Program–Duke Comprehensive Cancer Center	(919) 684-4497
Greensboro	Living with Cancer	(910) 379-3900
Mebane	Breast Cancer Coalition of North Carolina	(800) 419-5481
Raleigh	Triangle Breast Cancer Support Group	(919) 881-9754/ (919) 781-7070
Rocky Mount	Rocky Mount Area Breast Cancer Alliance	(919) 443-1018
	Boice Willis Clinic	(919) 937-0202
Wilson	Kathy Farris Memorial Mastectomy Group	(919) 237-0439

Winston-Salem	Pink Broomstick–Cancer Services, Inc.	(910) 725-7421/ (800) 228-7421
North Dakota		
Bismarck	Great Plains Rehabilitation Services–Mastectomy Support Group	(701) 224-7988
Ohio		
Cincinnati	Cancer Family Care	(513) 731-3346
	Bethesda Oak Hospital Breast Center	(513) 569-5152
	University of Cincinnati Hospital	(513) 558-3465
Columbus	Arthur G. James Cancer Hospital Support Groups for Women	(614) 293-3237
	Elizabeth Blackwell Center Post–Mastectomy Support Group	(614) 566-5153
	Riverside Regional Cancer Institute	(614) 566-4321/ (800) 752-9119
Dayton	St. Elizabeth Breast Center	(513) 229-7474
	Y-ME of the Greater Dayton Area	(513) 274-9151
Hamilton	Fort Hamilton Hughes Hospital Women's Health Choice	(513) 867-2700
Kettering	SOAR/Strength, Optimism & Recovery	(513) 296-7231
Marietta	Evening Exchange–Marietta Memorial Hospital	(614) 374-1450
Springfield	HERS–Breast Cancer Support Network Mercy Medical Center	(513) 390-5030
Youngstown	Southside Medical Center	(216) 740-4176/ (216) 788-5048
Oklahoma		
Oklahoma City	Central Oklahoma Cancer Center SW Medical Center	(405) 636-7104
	Oklahoma Breast Care Center	(405) 755-2273/ (800) 422-4626
Oregon		
Portland	St. Vincent Hospital and Medical Center	(503) 291-4673
Springfield	McKenzie-Willamette Hospital	(503) 726-4452
Tualatin	Meridian Park Hospital	(503) 692-2113
Pennsylvania		
Allentown	John and Dorothy Morgan Cancer Center	(215) 402-0500
Bryn Mawr	Bryn Mawr Hospital	(215) 526-3073

Camp Hill	WomanCare Resource Center Harrisburg Hospital	(717) 731-4035/ 558-2125
Coatesville	Brandywine ABC Support Group	(215) 383-8549
Dresher	"A New Beginning" Self-Help Group Abington Memorial Hospital	(215) 646-4954
Ft. Washington	Advanced Care Associates	(800) 289-8001
Hershey	Penn State University Milton S. Hershey Medical Center	(717) 531-5867
Kingston	Wyoming Valley Health Care System	(717) 283-7851
Lancaster	Lancaster Breast Cancer Network	(717) 393-7477
Norristown	Montgomery Breast Cancer Support Program	(610) 270-2703
Philadelphia	Fox Chase Cancer Center	(215) 728-2668
	Linda Creed Breast Cancer Foundation	(215) 955-4354
	Thomas Jefferson University Hospital Bodine Center for Cancer Treatment	(215) 955-8227
Pittsburgh	Cancer Support Network	(412) 361-8600
	Magee-Women's Hospital	(412) 641-1178
	Cancer Guidance Hotline	(412) 261-2211
	Magee-Women's Hospital Peer Counseling Program	(412) 641-4253
Ridley Park	Taylor Hospital Caring and Sharing	(610) 595-6000
York	York Hospital Outpatient Cancer Center	(717) 741-8100
Rhode Island		
Coventry	Focus on Us	(401) 822-0095
Providence	Roger Williams Medical Center	(401) 456-2284
	Hope Center for Life Enhancement	(401) 454-0404
	Breast Health	(401) 751-6890
Warwick	Breast Cancer Coalition	(800) 216-1040
South Carolina		
Columbia	Breast Cancer Support Group	(803) 434-3378
	Bosom Buddies and Man to Man	(803) 771-5244
Florence	McLeod Resource Center Caring Friends Support Group	(803) 667-2888
Lexington	Supporting Sisters	(803) 796-6009

South Dakota

Sioux Falls	Friends Against Breast Cancer/ Y-ME of South Dakota	(605) 339-HELP

Tennessee

Chattanooga	Y-ME of Chattanooga	(615) 886-4171
Knoxville	Knoxville Breast Center	(615) 584-0291
	Breast Cancer Networker	(615) 546-4661
Nashville	The Breast Concerns Mastectomy Support Group	(615) 665-0628

Texas

Arlington	Together We Will	(817) 277-7434
Dallas	Virginia R. Cetko Patient Education/Baylor-Charles A. Sammons Cancer Center	(214) 820-2608
	Komen Kares/The Susan G. Komen Foundation	(214) 692-8893
	Between US	(214) 521-5225
	Patient to Patient	(214) 821-2962
	Woman to Woman–Presbyterian Hospital of Dallas	(214) 345-2600
El Paso	Not Alone–Y-ME of El Paso	(915) 584-6063
Ft. Worth	Breast Reconstruction Educational Support Group	(817) 332-4311
	Doris Kupferle Breast Center	(817) 882-3650
Houston	The Rose Garden (Pasadena)	(713) 484-4708
	The Rosebuds (Southwest)	(713) 665-2729
McKinney	Women's Information Network Medical City Hospital, Dallas	(214) 562-7717
Plano	North Texas Cancer Center	(214) 824-4639
Richardson	Bosom Buddies/Women's Center	(214) 238-9516
San Antonio	The Jewels	(210) 599-0908

Utah

Salt Lake City	Holy Cross Hospital Breast Care Services	(801) 350-4973
Vernal	Ashley Valley Medical Center	(801) 789-3342

Vermont

Burlington	Breast Care Center	(802) 656-2262
Rutland	Woman to Woman–Rutland Regional Medical Center	(802) 747-3713

Virginia

Alexandria	My Image After Breast Cancer	(703) 461-9616 / (800) 970-4411
Charlottesville	Cardwell Cancer Center–Martha Jefferson Hospital	(804) 982-8407

Falls Church	Fairfax Hospital	(703) 698-3731
Harrisonburg	Women's Health Focus–Rockingham Memorial Hospital	(703) 433-4641
Norfolk	Santara Leigh Hospital	(804) 466-6837
Richmond	Massey Cancer Center	(804) 786-0450
	M.C.V. Hospital	(804) 225-4164
Salem	Lewis-Gale Regional Cancer Center	(800) 543-5660

Washington

Bellevue	Overlake Hospital	(206) 688-5385
Bremerton	Breast Cancer Support Group of Kitsap County	(206) 373-1057
Edmonds	Puget Sound Tumor Institute	(206) 640-4300
Everett	Providence Hospital	(206) 258-7255
Kirkland	Evergreen Hospital	(206) 899-2264
Olympia	A Touch of Strength St. Peter Hospital Regional Cancer Center	(206) 493-7510
Port Angeles	Operation Uplift	(206) 457-5141
Seattle	Seattle Breast Center/Northwest Hospital	(206) 368-1457
	Providence/Breast Cancer Support Group	(206) 320-2100
	Highline Community Hospital Cancer Care Program	(206) 439-5577
	Cancer Lifeline	(206) 461-4542
	Swedish Hospital Tumor Institute	(206) 386-2323

West Virginia

Charleston	CAMC Family Resource Center Women & Children's Hospital	(304) 348-2545

Wisconsin

Madison	Meriter Hospital Women's Center–After Breast Surgery	(608) 258-3750
Sheboygan	Lifestream Women's Health Center–Sheboygan Memorial Medical Center	(414) 459-5536

Wyoming

Cheyenne	United Medical Center	(307) 633-7895

Canada

Burlington, Ont.	Burlington Breast Cancer Support Services	(905) 634-2333
St. Catharine's, Ont.	Breast Cancer Research and Education Fund	(905) 687-3333

D

Comprehensive
Cancer Centers*

Alabama

Albert F. LoBuglio, M.D.**
Director, Comprehensive Cancer
Center
University of Alabama, University
Station
1824 Sixth Avenue South
Birmingham, AL 35294-3300
Tel: 205/934-5077
Fax: 205/975-7428

Arizona

Sydney E. Salmon, M.D.**
Director, Arizona Cancer Center
University of Arizona
College of Medicine
1501 North Campbell Avenue
Tucson, AZ 85724
Tel: 602/626-7925
Fax: 602/626-2284

California

Peter A. Jones, Ph.D.**
Director
Kenneth Norris, Jr. Comprehensive
Cancer Center
University of Southern California
P.O. Box 33800
Los Angeles, CA 90033-0800
Tel: 213/224-6465
Fax: 213/224-6417

Rodney H. Withers, M.D.**
Interim Director
Jonsson Comprehensive Cancer
Center
University of California
Louis Factor Building, Room 10-234
10833 LeConte Avenue
Los Angeles, CA 90024-1781
Tel: 310/825-5268
Fax: 310/206-5553

****   Laboratory/Basic   12
***   Clinical   13
**   Comprehensive   27
*   Consortium   1

*Reprinted with the kind permission of the National Cancer Institute

Erkki Ruoslahti, M.D.****
President and Scientific Director
La Jolla Cancer Research Foundation
10901 North Torrey Pines Road
La Jolla, CA 92037
  Tel: 619/455-6480
  Fax: 619/455-0181

William M. Hryniuk, M.D.***
Director, UCSD Cancer Center
University of California San Diego
225 Dickinson Street
San Diego, CA 92103-8421
  Tel: 619/543-3325
  Fax: 619/543-2639

John Kovach, M.D.***
Director, Cancer Research Center
Beckman Research Institute
City of Hope
1450 East Duarte Road
Duarte, CA 91010
  Tel: 818/359-8111 x2454
  Fax: 818/301-8111

Walter Eckhart, Ph.D.****
Professor and Director
Armand Hammer Center for Cancer
  Biology
Salk Institute
P.O. Box 85800
San Diego, CA 92186-5800
  Tel: 619/453-4100 x386
  Fax: 619/457-4765

Colorado

Paul A. Bunn, Jr., M.D.***
Director, Cancer Center
University of Colorado Health
  Sciences Center
4200 East 9th Avenue, Box B-188
Denver, CO 80262
  Tel: 303/270-3007
  Fax: 303/270-3304

Connecticut

Vincent T. DeVita, Jr., M.D.**
Director, Comprehensive Cancer
  Center
School of Medicine
Yale University
333 Cedar Street, Room 205-WWW
New Haven, CT 06520-8028
  Tel: 203/785-4095
  Fax: 203/785-4116

District of Columbia

Marc E. Lippman, M.D.**
Director
Lombardi Cancer Research Center
Georgetown University Medical
  Center
3800 Reservoir Road, N.W.
Washington, DC 20007
  Tel: 202/687-2110
  Fax: 202/687-6402

Florida

Azorides R. Morales, M.D.**
Director, Sylvester Comprehensive
  Cancer Center
University of Miami Medical School
P.O. Box 016960 (D72)
Miami, FL 33101
  Tel: 305/548-4918 or 4919
  Fax: 305/548-4684

Illinois

Richard L. Schilsky, M.D.***
Director, Cancer Research Center
University of Chicago Cancer
  Reearch Center
5841 South Maryland Avenue,
  MC1140
Chicago, IL 60637-1470
  Tel: 312/702-6180
  Fax: 312/702-9311

Steven Rosen, M.D.***
Director, Lurie Cancer Center
Northwestern University
303 East Chicago Avenue
Olson 8250
Chicago, IL 60611
　Tel: 312/908-5250
　Fax: 312/908-1372

Indiana

William M. Baird, Ph.D.****
Director, Cancer Center
Purdue University
Hansen Life Sciences Research
　Building
South University Street
West Lafayette, IN 47907-1524
　Tel: 317/494-9129 or 6275
　Fax: 317/494-9193

Maine

Kenneth Paigen, Ph.D.****
Director
The Jackson Laboratory
600 Main Street
Bar Harbor, ME 04609-0800
　Tel: 207/288-3371 x1206
　Fax: 207/288-5094

Maryland

Martin D. Abeloff, M.D.**
Center Director
Johns Hopkins Oncology Center
600 North Wolfe Street, Room 157
Baltimore, MD 21287-8943
　Tel: 410/955-8822
　Fax: 410/955-6787

Massachusetts

Christopher T. Walsh, Ph.D.**
Director, Cancer Center
Dana Farber Cancer Institute
44 Binney Street
Boston, MA 02115
　Tel: 617/632-2155
　Fax: 617/632-2161

Richard O. Hynes, Ph.D.****
Director and Professor of Biology
Center for Cancer Research
Massachusetts Institute of
　Technology
77 Massachusetts Avenue, Room
　E17-110
Cambridge, MA 02139-4307
　Tel: 617/253-6422
　Fax: 617/253-8357

Michigan

Richard Santen, M.D.**
Interim Director
Meyer L. Prentis Comprehensive
　Cancer Center
Wayne State University
3990 John R. Street, 1 Brush South
Detroit, MI 48201
　Tel: 313/745-8870
　Fax: 313/993-0304

Max S. Wicha, M.D.**
Director, Comprehensive Cancer
　Center
University of Michigan
101 Simpson Drive
Ann Arbor, MI 48109-0752
　Tel: 313/936-2516
　Fax: 313/936-9582

Minnesota

Director (Vacant)**
Comprehensive Cancer Center
Mayo Clinic, East 12
200 First Street, S.W.
Rochester, MN 55905
  Tel: 507/284-4718
  Fax: 507/284-1803

Nebraska

Raymond Ruddon, Jr., M.D.,
  Ph.D.****
Director
Eppley Institute
University of Nebraska Medical
  Center
600 South 42nd Street
Omaha, NE 68198-6805
  Tel: 402/559-4238
  Fax: 402/559-4651

New Hampshire

E. Robert Greenberg, M.D.**
Director
Norris Cotton Cancer Center
Dartmouth-Hitchcock Medical
  Center
One Medical Center Drive
Lebanon, NH 03756
  Tel: 603/650-4141
  Fax: 603/650-4150

New York

Bruce W. Stillman, Ph.D.****
Director
Cold Spring Harbor Laboratory
P.O. Box 100
Cold Spring Harbor, NY 11724
  Tel: 516/367-8383
  Fax: 516/367-8879

Paul A. Marks, M.D.**
President
Memorial Sloan-Kettering Cancer
  Center
1275 York Avenue
New York, NY 10021
  Tel: 212/639-6561
  Fax: 212/717-3299

Thomas B. Tomasi, M.D., Ph.D.**
Director
Roswell Park Cancer Institute
Elm and Carlton Streets
Buffalo, NY 14263-0001
  Tel: 716/845-5770
  Fax: 716/845-8261

Matthew D. Scharff, M.D.***
Director, Cancer Research Center
Albert Einstein College of Medicine
Chanin Building, Room 330
1300 Morris Park Avenue
Bronx, NY 10461
  Tel: 718/430-2302
  Fax: 718/822-6538

I. Bernard Weinstein, M.D.***
Director, Columbia-Presbyterian
  Cancer Center
College of Physicians and Surgeons
Columbia University
701 West 168th Street, Room 1509
New York, NY 10032
  Tel: 212/305-6921
  Fax: 212/305-6889

Vittorio Defendi, M.D.**
Director
Kaplan Comprehensive Cancer
  Center
New York University Medical
  Center
550 First Avenue
New York, NY 10016
  Tel: 212/263-5349
  Fax: 212/263-8211

Richard F. Borch, M.D., Ph.D.***
Deans Professor and Interim
  Director
Cancer Center
University of Rochester Medical
  Center
601 Elmwood Avenue, Box 704
Rochester, NY 14642
  Tel: 716/275-4865
  Fax: 716/273-1042

Ernst L. Wynder, M.D.****
President and Medical Director
American Health Foundation
320 East 43rd Street
New York, NY 10017
  Tel: 212/953-1900 x212
  Fax: 212/687-2339

North Carolina

Robert Bell, Ph.D.**
Interim Director
Comprehensive Cancer Center
Duke University Medical Center
Box 3843
Durham, NC 27710
  Tel: 919/684-3377
  Fax: 919/684-5653

Joseph S. Pagano, M.D.**
Professor of Cancer Research and
  Director, Lineberger
  Comprehensive Cancer Center
University of North Carolina
School of Medicine, Chapel Hill,
  CB-7295
Chapel Hill, NC 27599-7295
  Tel: 919/966-3036
  Fax: 919/966-3015

Frank M. Torti, M.D.**
Director, Comprehensive Cancer
  Center
Wake Forest University
Bowman Gray School of Medicine
Medical Center Boulevard
Winston-Salem, NC 27157-1082
  Tel: 910/716-4464
  Fax: 910/716-5687

Ohio

David E. Schuller, M.D.**
Director, Comprehensive Cancer
  Center
Arthur G. James Cancer Hospital
Ohio State University
300 West 10th Avenue, Room 521
Columbus, OH 43210-1240
  Tel: 614/293-4878
  Fax: 614/293-3132

Nathan A. Berger, M.D.***
Director, Cancer Research Center
Case Western Reserve University
2074 Abington Road, Wearn 152
Cleveland, OH 44106
  Tel: 216/844-8453
  Fax: 216/844-3000

Pennsylvania

Robert C. Young, M.D.**
President
Fox Chase Cancer Center
7701 Burholme Avenue
Philadelphia, PA 19111
  Tel: 215/728-2781
  Fax: 215/728-2571

John H. Glick, M.D.**
Director, Cancer Center
University of Pennsylvania
6th Floor Penn Tower
3400 Spruce Street
Philadelphia, PA 19104-4283
Tel: 215/662-6334
Fax: 215/349-5326

Giovanni Rovera, M.D.****
Director
Wistar Institute Cancer Center
36th Street at Spruce
Philadelphia, PA 19104-4268
Tel: 215/898-3926
Fax: 215/573-2097

E. Premkumar Reddy, Ph.D.****
Director
Fels Institute
Temple University School of
  Medicine
3420 North Broad Street
Philadelphia, PA 19140-5199
Tel: 215/707-4307
Fax: 215/707-1454

Ronald B. Herberman, M.D.**
Director, Pittsburgh Cancer Institute
University of Pittsburgh
200 Meyran Avenue
Pittsburgh, PA 15213-3305
Tel: 412/647-2072
Fax: 412/621-9354

Tennessee

Arthur W. Nienhuis, M.D.***
Director
St. Jude Children's Research
  Hospital
332 North Lauderdale
P.O. Box 318
Memphis, TN 38101-0318
Tel: 901/522-0301
Fax: 901/525-2720

Louis J. Bernard, M.D.*
Director
Drew-Meharry-Morehouse
  Consortium Cancer Center
1005 D.B. Todd Boulevard
Nashville, TN 37208
Tel: 615/327-6315
Tel: (Calif.) 213/754-2961
Fax: 615/327-6296

Texas

Charles A. LeMaistre, M.D.,
  President**
Frederick F. Becker, M.D., P.I., Vice
  President for Research
University of Texas
M.D. Anderson Cancer Center
1515 Holcombe Boulevard, Box 91
Houston, TX 77030
Tel: 713/792-7500
Fax: 713/790-9492

Charles A. Coltman, Jr., M.D.***
Director
San Antonio Cancer Institute
8122 Datapoint Drive, Suite 600
San Antonio, TX 78229
Tel: 210/677-3850
Fax: 210/677-0058

Utah

Dwight T. Janerich, DDS, MPH***
Professor and Interim Director
Utah Regional Cancer Center
University of Utah Health Sciences
  Center
50 North Medical Drive, Room
  2C110
Salt Lake City, UT 84132
Tel: 801/581-4048
Fax: 801/585-5763

Vermont

Richard J. Albertini, M.D., Ph.D.**
Director, Vermont Regional Cancer
  Center
University of Vermont
1 South Prospect Street
Burlington, VT 05401-3498
  Tel: 802/656-4414
  Fax: 802/656-8788

Virginia

I. David Goldman, M.D.***
Director
Massey Cancer Center
Medical College of Virginia/VCU
Box 230
Richmond, VA 23298-0230
  Tel: 804/786-9722
  Fax: 804/371-8079

Charles E. Myers, Jr., M.D.****
Director, Cancer Center
University of Virginia, School of
  Medicine
Health Sciences Center, Box 334
Charlottesville, VA 22908
  Tel: 804/924-1948
  Fax: 804/982-1071

Washington

Robert W. Day, M.D., Ph.D.**
President and Director
Fred Hutchinson Cancer Research
  Center
1124 Columbia Street, LY301
Seattle, WA 98104
  Tel: 206/667-4302
  Fax: 206/667-5268

Wisconsin

Paul P. Carbone, M.D.**
Director, Comprehensive Cancer
  Center
University of Wisconsin
600 Highland Avenue
Madison, WI 53792-0001
  Tel: 608/263-8610
  Fax: 608/263-8613

Norman R. Drinkwater, Ph.D.****
Director
McArdle Laboratory for Cancer
  Research
University of Wisconsin Medical
  School
1400 University Avenue, Room 1009
Madison, WI 53706
  Tel: 608/262-2177 or 7992
  Fax: 608/262-2824

For information in Canada, call or write:

Canadian Breast Cancer
  Foundation—Ontario Chapter
790 Bay Street
Suite 1000
Toronto, Ontario M5G 1N8
Canada
  Tel: 416/596-6773
  Fax: 416/596-7857

Canadian Breast Cancer
  Foundation—British Columbia
  Chapter
F5 British Columbia's Womens
  Hospital and Health Centre
4500 Oak Street
Vancouver, British Columbia
  V6H 3N1
Canada
  Tel: 604/875-2020
  Fax: 604/875-2646

E

$$\equiv$$

Chartered Divisions of the American Cancer Society*

Alabama Division, Inc.
504 Brookwood Boulevard
Homewood, Alabama 35209
(205) 879-2242

Alaska Division, Inc.
406 West Fireweed Lane
Anchorage, Alaska 99503
(907) 277-8696

Arizona Division, Inc.
2929 East Thomas Road
Phoenix, Arizona 85016
(602) 224-0524

Arkansas Division, Inc.
901 North University
Little Rock, Arkansas 72203
(501) 664-3480

California Division, Inc.
1710 Webster Street
Oakland, California 94612
(510) 893-7900

Colorado Division, Inc.
2255 South Oneida
Denver, Colorado 80224
(303) 758-2030

Connecticut Division, Inc.
Barnes Park South
14 Village Lane
Wallingford, Connecticut 06492
(203) 265-7161

Delaware Division, Inc.
92 Read's Way
New Castle, Delaware 19720
(302) 324-4227

District of Columbia Division, Inc.
1875 Connecticut Avenue, N.W.
Washington, DC 20009
(202) 483-2600

Florida Division, Inc.
3709 West Jetton Avenue
Tampa, Florida 33629-5146
(813) 253-0541

*National Headquarters: American Cancer Society, Inc., 1599 Clifton Road N.E., Atlanta, GA 30329-4251. Phone: (404) 320-3333.

Georgia Division, Inc.
2200 Lake Blvd.
Atlanta, Georgia 30319
(404) 816-7800

Hawaii Pacific Division, Inc.
Community Services Center Bldg.
200 North Vineyard Boulevard
Honolulu, Hawaii 96817
(808) 531-1662

Idaho Division, Inc.
2676 Vista Avenue
Boise, Idaho 83705-0836
(208) 643-4609

Illinois Division, Inc.
77 East Monroe
Chicago, Illinois 60603-5795
(312) 647-6150

Indiana Division, Inc.
8730 Commerce Park Place
Indianapolis, Indiana 46268
(317) 872-4432

Iowa Division, Inc.
8364 Hickman Road
Des Moines, Iowa 50325
(515) 253-0147

Kansas Division, Inc.
1315 SW Arrowhead Road
Topeka, Kansas 66604
(913) 273-4114

Kentucky Division, Inc.
701 West Muhammad Ali Blvd.
Louisville, Kentucky 40203-1909
(502) 584-6782

Louisiana Division, Inc.
2200 Veteran's Memorial Blvd.
Suite 214
Kenner, Louisiana 70062
(504) 469-0021

Maine Division, Inc.
52 Federal Street
Brunswick, Maine 04011
(207) 729-3339

Maryland Division, Inc.
8219 Town Center Drive
Baltimore, Maryland 21236-0026
(410) 931-6868

Massachusetts Division, Inc.
247 Commonwealth Avenue
Boston, Massachusetts 02116
(617) 267-2650

Michigan Division, Inc.
1205 East Saginaw Street
Lansing, Michigan 48906
(517) 371-2920

Minnesota Division, Inc.
3316 West 66th Street
Minneapolis, Minnesota 55435
(612) 925-2772

Mississippi Division, Inc.
1380 Livingston Lane
Lakeover Office Park
Jackson, Mississippi 39213
(601) 362-8874

Missouri Division, Inc.
3322 American Avenue
Jefferson City, Missouri 65102
(314) 893-4800

Montana Division, Inc.
17 North 26th
Billings, Montana 59101
(406) 252-7111

Nebraska Division, Inc.
8502 West Center Road
Omaha, Nebraska 68124-5255
(402) 393-5800

Nevada Division, Inc.
1325 East Harmon
Las Vegas, Nevada 89119
(702) 798-6857

New Hampshire Division, Inc.
360 Route 101, Unit 503
Bedford, New Hampshire 03110
(603) 472-8899

New Jersey Division, Inc.
2600 US Highway 1
North Brunswick, New Jersey 08902
(908) 297-8000

New Mexico Division, Inc.
5800 Lomas Blvd., NE
Albuquerque, New Mexico 87110
(505) 260-2105

New York State Division, Inc.
6725 Lyons Street
East Syracuse, New York 13057
(315) 437-7025

- Long Island Division, Inc.
75 Davids Drive
Hauppauge, New York 11788
(516) 436-7070

- New York City Division, Inc.
19 West 56th Street
New York, New York 10019
(212) 586-8700

- Queens Division, Inc.
112-25 Queens Boulevard
Forest Hills, New York 11375
(718) 263-2224

- Westchester Division, Inc.
30 Glenn Street
White Plains, New York 10603
(914) 949-4800

North Carolina Division, Inc.
11 South Boylan Avenue
Raleigh, North Carolina 27603
(919) 834-8463

North Dakota Division, Inc.
123 Roberts Street
Fargo, North Dakota 58102
(701) 232-1385

Ohio Division, Inc.
5555 Frantz Road
Dublin, Ohio 43017
(614) 889-9565

Oklahoma Division, Inc.
4323 63rd, Suite 110
Oklahoma City, Oklahoma 73116
(405) 843-9888

Oregon Division, Inc.
0330 SW Curry
Portland, Oregon 97201
(503) 295-6422

Pennsylvania Division, Inc.
Route 422 & Sipe Avenue
Hershey, Pennsylvania 17033-0897
(717) 533-6144

- Philadelphia Division, Inc.
1422 Chestnut Street
Philadelphia, Pennsylvania 19102
(215) 665-2900

Puerto Rico Division, Inc.
Calle Alverio #577
Esquina Sargento Medina
Hato Rey, Puerto Rico 00918
(809) 764-2295

Rhode Island Division, Inc.
400 Main Street
Pawtucket, Rhode Island 02860
(401) 722-8480

South Carolina Division, Inc.
128 Stonemark Lane
Columbia, South Carolina 29210
(803) 750-1693

South Dakota Division, Inc.
4101 Carnegie Place
Sioux Falls, South Dakota 57106
(605) 361-8277

Tennessee Division, Inc.
1315 Eighth Avenue, South
Nashville, Tennessee 37203
(615) 255-1227

Texas Division, Inc.
2433 Ridgepoint Drive
Austin, Texas 78754
(512) 928-2262

Utah Division, Inc.
941 East 3300 S.
Salt Lake City, Utah 84106
(801) 483-1500

Vermont Division, Inc.
13 Loomis Street
Montpelier, Vermont 05602
(802) 223-2348

Virginia Division, Inc.
P.O. Box 6359
Glen Allen, Virginia 23058-6359
(804) 527-3700

Washington Division, Inc.
2120 First Avenue North
Seattle, Washington 98109-1140
(206) 283-1152

West Virginia Division, Inc.
2428 Kanawha Boulevard East
Charleston, West Virginia 25311
(304) 344-3611

Wisconsin Division, Inc.
P.O. Box 902
Pewaukee, Wisconsin 53072-0902
(414) 523-5500

Wyoming Division, Inc.
2222 House Avenue
Cheyenne, Wyoming 82001
(307) 638-3331

F

The Wellness Community
Physician/Patient Statement*

In 1990, six prominent Los Angeles oncologists met with the staff of The Wellness Community, over a period of six months, to answer the question, "What can cancer patients expect from their oncologists?" The question was considered important since they believed that the relationship between the patient and the physician can affect the course of the illness. After many meetings they arrived at *The Wellness Community Patient/Oncologist Statement*. They then tested the *Statement* with their patients and found that a great majority of their patients had confidence in their physician and considered their relationship "excellent": However, there was agreement among patients that the issues considered in the *Statement* were important to a continuation of such "excellent" relationship. The *Statement* below was then published in the *UCLA, Jonsson Comprehensive Cancer Center Bulletin* and is given by physicians to their patients.

The effective treatment of serious illness requires a considerable effort by both the patient and the physician. A clear understanding by both of us as to what each of us can realistically and reasonably expect of the other will do much to enhance the outlook. I am giving this "statement" to you as one step in making our relationship as effective and productive as possible. It might be helpful if you would read this statement and, if you think it appropriate, discuss it with me. As your physician I will make every effort to:

1. Provide you with the care most likely to be beneficial to you.
2. Inform and educate you about your situation, and the various treatment alternatives. How detailed an explanation is given will be dependent upon your specific desires.

*Reprinted with the kind permission of The Wellness Community

3. Encourage you to ask questions about your illness and its treatment and to answer your questions as clearly as possible. I will also attempt to answer the questions asked by your family; however, my primary responsibility is to you, and I will discuss your medical situation only with those people authorized by you.
4. Remain aware that all major decisions about the course of your care shall be made by you. However, I will accept the responsibility for making certain decisions if you want me to.
5. Assist you to obtain other professional opinions if you desire, or if I believe it to be in your best interests.
6. Relate to you as one competent adult to another, always attempting to consider your emotional, social and psychological needs as well as your physical needs.
7. Spend a reasonable amount of time with you on each return visit unless required by something urgent to do otherwise, and give you my undivided attention during that time.
8. Honor all appointment times unless required by something urgent to do otherwise.
9. Return phone calls as promptly as possible, especially those you indicate are urgent.
10. Make available test results promptly if you desire such reports and I will indicate to you, at the time the test is given, when you can expect the results and who you should call to get them.
11. Provide you with any information you request concerning my professional training, experience, philosophy and fees.
12. Respect your desire to try treatment that might not be conventionally accepted. However, I will give you my honest opinion about such unconventional treatments.
13. Maintain my active support and attention throughout the course of the illness.

I hope that you as the patient will make every effort to:

1. Comply with our agreed-upon treatment plan.
2. Be as candid as possible with me about what you need and expect from me.
3. Inform me if you desire another professional opinion.
4. Inform me of all forms of therapy you are involved with.
5. Honor all appointment times unless required by something urgent to do otherwise.
6. Be as considerate as possible of my need to adhere to a schedule to see other patients.
7. Attempt to make all phone calls to me during the working hours. Call on nights and weekends only when absolutely necessary.
8. Attempt to coordinate the requests of your family and confidantes, so that I do not have to answer the same questions about you to several different persons.

Notes

INTRODUCTION

1. Turnbull N. Women go topless. *Sojourner* 1985; August:13.
2. Welch CE, Cancer of the breast. *Journal of Clinical Surgery* 1982; 1:425.

CHAPTER 1. THE BREAST AND ITS DEVELOPMENT

1. Ayalah D, Weinstock IJ. *Breasts*. New York: Summit Books, 1979.
2. Robinson JE, Short RV. Changes in breast sensitivity at puberty, during the menstrual cycle, and at parturition. *British Medical Journal* 1977; 1:1188.
3. Stanway A, Stanway P. *The Breast*. London: Granada Publishing, 1982:23.
4. Ibid.

CHAPTER 2. GETTING ACQUAINTED
WITH YOUR BREASTS

1. Kash K, Holland J, Halper M, et al. Psychological distress and surveillance behaviors of women with a family history of breast cancer. *Journal of the National Cancer Institute* 1992; 84:24.

CHAPTER 3. BREAST FEEDING

1. Guinee VF, Olsson H, Moller T, et al. Effect of pregnancy on prognosis for young women with breast cancer. *Lancet* 1994; 343:1587.
2. Petrek J. Breast cancer during pregnancy. *Cancer Supplement* 1994; 74(1).
3. London S, Colditz G, Stampfer M, et al. Lactation and risk of breast cancer in a cohort of U.S. women. *American Journal of Epidemiology* 1990; 132(7):17.
4. Yuan J, Yu MC. Risk factors for breast cancer in Chinese women in Shanghai. *Cancer Research* 1988; 48:1949.
5. Newcomb PA, Storer BE, Longnecker MP, et al. Lactation and a reduced risk of premenopausal breast cancer. *New England Journal of Medicine* 1994; 330(2):81.
6. Little RE, Anderson KW, Irvin CH, et al. Maternal alcohol use during breast feeding and infant mental and motor development at one year. *New England Journal of Medicine* 1989; 321:425.

CHAPTER 4. VARIATIONS IN DEVELOPMENT

1. Stanway A, Stanway P. *The Breast*. London: Granada Publishing, 1982:23.

CHAPTER 5. PLASTIC SURGERY

1. Letterman G, Schurter M.A. A History of Mammoplasty with Emphasis on Correction of Ptosis and Macromastia, in R. Goldwyn, ed., *Plastic and Reconstructive Surgery of the Breast* (Boston: Little, Brown, 1976), p. 361.
2. Hatcher C, Brooks L, Love C. Breast cancer and silicone implants: Psychological consequences for women. *Journal of the National Cancer Institute* 1993; 85(17):1361.
3. Szycher M, Siciliano AA. An assessment of 2,4 TDA formation of a polyurethan foam under simulated physiologic conditions. *Journal of Biomaterial Applications* 1991; 5:323.
4. Szycher M, Siciliano AA. Polyurethan-covered mammary prosthesis: A nine-year postimplant assessment. *Journal of Biomaterial Applications* 1991; 5:282.
5. Merkatz RB, Bagley GP, McCarthy EJ. A qualitative analysis of self-reported experiences among women encountering difficulties with silicone breast implants. *Journal of Women's Health* 1993; 2(2):105.
6. Winer EP, Fee-Fulkerson K, Fulkerson CC, et al. Silicone controversy: A survey of women with breast cancer and silicone implants. *Journal of the National Cancer Institute* 1993; 85(17):1407.
7. Fiala TGS, Lee WPA, May JW. Augmentation mammoplasty: Results of a patient survey. *Annals of Plastic Surgery* 1993; 30(6):503.
8. Silverstein MJ, Gierson ED, Gamagami P, Handel N, Waisman JR. Breast cancer diagnosis and prognosis in women augmented with silicone gel-filled implants. *Cancer* 1990; 66(July 1):97.
9. Gabriel SE, O'Fallon M, Kurland LT, Beard CM, Woods JE, Melton LJ III. Risk of connective-tissue diseases and other disorders after breast implantation. *New England Journal of Medicine* 1994; 330(24):1697.
10. Berkel H, Birdsell D, Jenkins H. Breast augmentation: A risk factor for breast cancer? *New England Journal of Medicine* 1992; 326(25):1649.
11. Levine J, Ilowite N. Sclerodermalike esophageal disease in children breast-fed by mothers with silicone breast implants (comments). *Journal of the American Medical Association* 1994; 271(3):213.

12. Heuston, JT. Unilateral Ageness and Hypoplasia: Difficulties and Suggestions In: A. Goldwyn, ed., *Plastic and Reconstructive Surgery of the Breast*. Boston: Little, Brown, 1976, p. 361.

13. Gifford, S. Emotional Attitudes toward Cosmetic Breast Surgery: Loss and Restitution of the Ideal Self. In: R. Goldwyn, ed., *Plastic and Reconstructive Surgery of the Breast*. Boston: Little, Brown, 1976, p. 117.

CHAPTER 6. THE MYTH OF FIBROCYSTIC DISEASE

1. Love SM, Gelman RS, Silen WS. Fibrocystic "disease" of the breast: A nondisease. *New England Journal of Medicine* 1982; 307:1010.

2. Page DL, Vanderzwagg R, Rogers LW, et al. Relationship between the component parts of fibrocystic disease complex and breast cancer. *Journal of the National Cancer Institute* 1978; 61:1055.

3. Dupont WD, Page DL. Risk factors for breast cancer in women with proliferative breast disease. *New England Journal of Medicine* 1985; 312:146.

4. Cancer Committee of the American College of Pathologists. Is "fibrocystic" disease of the breast precancerous? *Archives of Pathology and Laboratory Medicine* 1986; 110:173.

5. Minton JP, Foecking MK, Webster DJT, et al. Response of fibrocystic disease to caffeine withdrawal and correlation of cyclic nucleotides with breast disease. *American Journal of Obstetrics and Gynecology* 1980; 135:157.

6. Ernster VL, Mason L, Goodson WH, et al. Effects of caffeine-free diet on benign breast disease: A randomized trial. *Surgery* 1985; 91:263.

7. Allen SS, Froberg DC. The effect of decreased caffeine consumption on benign proliferative breast disease: A randomized clinical trial. *Surgery* 1986; 101:720.

8. Petrek JA, Sandberg WA, Cole MN, et al. The inhibitory effect of caffeine on hormone-induced rat breast cancer. *Cancer* 1977; 56:1977.

9. Lubin F, Ron E, Wax Y, et al. A case control study of caffeine and methylzanthine in benign breast disease. *Journal of the American Medical Association* 1985; 253:2388.

10. Lubin F, Ron E, Wax Y, et al. Coffee and methylxanthines and breast cancer: A case-control study. *Journal of the National Cancer Institute* 1985; 74:569.

11. Abrams A. Use of vitamin E in chronic cystic mastitis. *New England Journal of Medicine* 1965; 272:2388.

12. London RS, Solomon ED, et al. Mammary dysplasia: Clinical response and urinary excretion of 11-deoxy-17-detosteroids and prenanediol following alpha tocopherol therapy. *Breast* 1978; 4:19.

13. London RS, Sundaram GS, Murphy L, et al. The effect of vitamin E on mammary dysplasia: A double-blind study. *Obstetrics and Gynecology* 1985; 65:104.

CHAPTER 7. BREAST PAIN

1. Preece PE, Mansel RE, Hughes LE. Mastalgia: Psychoneurosis or organic disease? *British Medical Journal* 1979; 1:29.

2. Birkett J. *The Diseases of the Breast*. London: Longman & Co., 1850.

3. Patey DH. Two common non-malignant conditions of the breast. *British Medical Journal* 1949; 1:96.

4. Goodson WH, Mailman R, Jacobson M, et al. What do breast symptoms mean? *American Journal of Surgery* 1985; 150:271.

5. Kuttenin F, Fournier S, Sitruk-Ware R, et al. Progesterone insufficiency in benign breast disease. In: Angeli A, Bradlow HL, Dogliotti R, ed. *Endocrinology of Cystic Breast Disease.* New York: Raven Press, 1983.

6. Ayres J, Gidwani G. The "luteal breast": Hormonal and sonographic investigations of benign breast disease in patients with cyclic mastalgia. *Fertility and Sterility* 1983; 40:779.

7. Preece PE, Hughes LE, Mansel RE, et al. Clinical syndromes of mastalgia. *Lancet* 1976; 2:670.

8. Sitruk-Ware R, Sterkers N, Mauvais-Jarvis P. Benign breast disease: I. Hormonal investigation. *Obstetrics and Gynecology* 1979; 53:457.

9. Watt-Boolsen S, Eskildsen PC, Blaehr H. Release of prolactin, thyrotropin, and growth hormone in women with cyclical mastalgia and fibrocystic disease of the breast. *Cancer* 1985; 56:500.

10. Kumar S, Mansel RE, Hughes LE, et al. Prolactin response to thyrotropin-releasing hormone stimulation and dopaminergic inhibition in benign breast disease. *Cancer* 1984; 53:1311.

11. Page JK, Mansel RE, Hughes LE. Clinical experience of drug treatments for mastalgia. *Lancet* 1985; 2:373.

12. Miller DR, Rosenberg L, Kaufman DW, et al. Breast cancer before age 45 and oral contraceptive use: New findings. *American Journal of Epidemiology* 1989; 129:269.

13. Blichert-Toft M, Anderson AN, Henriksen OB, et al. Treatment of mastalgia with bromocriptine: A double-blind crossover study. *British Medical Journal* 1979; 1:237.

14. Greenblatt RB, Dmowsky WP, Mahesh VB, et al. Clinical studies with an anti-gonadotropin-Manazol. *Fertility and Sterility* 1971; 22:102.

15. Estes NC. Mastodynia due to fibrocystic disease of the breast controlled with thyroid hormone. *American Journal of Surgery* 1981; 142:102.

16. Fentiman IS, Caleffi M, Brame K, et al. Double-blind controlled trial of tamoxifen therapy for mastalgia. *Lancet* 1986; 1:287.

17. Boyd N, McGuire V, Shannon P, et al. Effect of low-fat, high carbohydrate diet on symptoms of cyclical mastopathy. *Lancet* 1988; 2(8603):128.

18. LeBan MM, Meerscharet JR, Taylor RS. Breast pain: A symptom of cervical radiculopathy. *Archives of Physical Medicine and Rehabilitation* 1979; 60:315.

19. Page, JR, 1985.

20. Preece, PE, 1976.

CHAPTER 8. BREAST INFECTIONS AND NIPPLE PROBLEMS

1. Thomsen AC, Espersen MD, Maigaard S. Course and treatment of milk stasis, noninfectious inflammation of the breast and infectious mastitis in nursing women. *American Journal of Obstetrics and Gynecology* 1984; 149:492.

2. Maier WP, Berger A, Derrick BM. Periareolar abscess in the nonlactating breast. *American Journal of Obstetrics and Gynecology* 1982; 149:492.

3. Sartorius O. Personal communication.

4. Watt-Boolsen S, Ryegaard R, Blichert-Toft M. Primary periareolar abscess in the nonlactating breast: Risk of recurrence. *American Journal of Surgery* 1987; 153:571.

5. Love SM, Schnitt SJ, Connolly JL, Shirley RL. Benign breast diseases. In: Harris JR, Hellman S, Henderson IC, Kinne DW, ed. *Breast Diseases.* Philadelphia: J.B. Lippincott, 1987:22.

CHAPTER 9. LUMPS AND LUMPINESS

1. Tabar L, Pentek Z, Dean PB. The diagnostic and therapeutic value of breast cyst puncture and pneumocystography. *Radiology* 1981; 14:1659.
2. Herrman JB. Mammary cancer subsequent to aspiration of cysts in the breast. *Annals of Surgery* 1971; 173:40.
3. Haagensen CD. The relationship of gross cystic disease of the breast and carcinoma. *Annals of Surgery* 1977; 185:375.
4. Dupont WD, Page DL. Risk factors for breast cancer in women with proliferative breast disease. *New England Journal of Medicine* 1985; 312:146.
5. Dupont WD, Page DL, Parl FF, et al. Long-term risk of breast cancer in women with fibroadenoma. *New England Journal of Medicine* 1994; 331(1):10.

CHAPTER 10. DIAGNOSTIC MAMMOGRAPHY

1. Bailar JC. Mammography: A contrary view. *Annals of Internal Medicine* 1976; 84:77.
2. Sadowski N. Personal communication. 1988.
3. Kornguth P, Rimer B, Conaway M, et al. Impact of patient-controlled compression on the mammography experience. *Radiology* 1993; 186(1):99.
4. Homer MJ. Nonpalpable breast microcalcifications: Frequency, management, and results of incisional biopsy. *Radiology* 1992; 185:411.
5. Berend ME, Sullivan DC, Kornguth PJ, et al. The natural history of mammographic calcifications subjected to interval follow-up. *Archives of Surgery* 1992; 127(November):1309.
6. Stomper P, Kopans D, Sadowski N, et al. Is mammograph painful? A multicenter patient survey. *Archives of Internal Medicine* 1988; 148(3):521.

CHAPTER 11. OTHER IMAGING TECHNIQUES

1. Parker SH, Lovin JD, Jobe WE, et al. Stereotactic breast biopsy with a biopsy gun. *Radiology* 1990; 176(September):741.
2. Petro J, Klein S, Niazi Z, Salzberg C, Byrne D. Evaluation of ultrasound as a tool in the follow-up of patients with breast implants: A preliminary, prospective study. *Annals of Plastic Surgery* 1994; 32(6):580.
3. Cross M, Harms S, Cheek J, Peteres G, Jones R. New horizons in the diagnosis and treatment of breast cancer using magnetic resonance imaging. *American Journal of Surgery* 1983; 166(6):749.
4. Harms S. Breast MRI. The potentials and dangers: Are you informed? *Adm Radiology* 1992; 11(11):111.
5. Merchant TE, Obertop H, de Graaf PW. Advantages of magnetic resonance imaging in breast surgery treatment planning. *Breast Cancer Research and Treatment* 1993; 25:257.
6. Ahn C, Shaw W, Marayanan K, et al. Definitive diagnosis of breast implant rupture using magnetic resonance imaging. *Plastic Reconstructive Surgery* 1993; 92(4):681
7. Tse N, Hoh C, Hawkins R, et al. The application of positron emission tomographic imaging with fluorodeoxyglucose to the evaluation of breast disease. *Annals of Surgery* 1992; 216(1):27.

8. Waxman AD, Ramanna L, Memsic LD, Foster CE, et al. Thallium scintigraphy in the evaluation of mass abnormalities of the breast. *Journal of Nuclear Medicine* 1993; 34:18.

CHAPTER 12. BIOPSY

1. Layfield LJ, Parkinson B, Wong J, Guiliano AE, Bassett LW. Mammographically guided fine-needle aspiration biopsy of nonpalpable breast lesions. *Cancer* 1991; 68:2007.
2. Martelli G, Pilotti S, de Yoldi GC, et al. Diagnostic efficacy of physical examination, mammography, fine-needle aspiration, cytology (triple-test) in solid breast lumps: An analysis of 1708 cases. *Tumori* 1990; 76:476.
3. Parker SH, Lovin JD, Jobe WE, et al. Stereotactic breast biopsy with a biopsy gun. *Radiology* 1990; 176(September):741.
4. Martelli et al., 1990.

CHAPTER 13. GENES AND ENVIRONMENT

1. Cavanee W, Dryja T, Phillips R, et al. Expression of recessive alleles by chromosomal mechanisms in retinoblastoma. *Nature* 1983; 305:779.
2. Frebourg T, Friend S. Cancer risks from germline p53 mutations. *Journal of Clinical Investigations* 1992; 90(5):1637.
3. Swift M, Reitnauer P, Morrell D, Chase C. Breast and other cancers in families with ataxia telangiectasia. *New England Journal of Medicine* 1987; 316(21):1289.
4. Slamon D, Godolphin W, Jones L, et al. Studies of the Her-2/neu proto-oncogene in human breast and ovarian cancer. *Science* 1989; 244(4905):707.
5. Miki Y, Swenson J, Shattuck-Eidens PA, et al. Isolation of a strong candidate for the 17q linked breast and ovarian cancer susceptibility gene BRCA1. *Science* 1994; 266:66.

CHAPTER 14. RISK FACTORS: GENETIC AND HORMONAL

1. Newell GR, Vogel VG. Personal risk factors: What do they mean? *Cancer* 1988; 62:1695.
2. Cuzick J. Women at high risk of breast cancer. *Reviews on Endocrine-Related Cancer* 1987; 25:5.
3. Miller AB. Epidemiology and prevention. In: Harris JR, Hellman S, Henderson IC, Kinne DW, ed. *Breast Diseases*. Philadelphia: J.B. Lippincott, 1987:
4. Seidman H, Stellman SD, Mushinski MH. A different perspective on breast cancer risk factors: Some implications of the nonattributable risk. *CA: A Cancer Journal for Clinicians* 1982; 32:301.
5. Eley JW, Hill HA, Chen VW, et al. Racial differences in survival from breast cancer. Results of the National Cancer Institute Black/White Cancer Survival Study. *Journal of the American Medical Association* 1994; 272(12):947.
6. Kelsey JL, Berkowitz GS. Breast cancer epidemiology. *Cancer Research* 1988; 48:5615.
7. Haynes S, Prevention and early detection of breast cancer in lesbians. Presentation at National Lesbian and Gay Health Conference. July 9-10, 1992.

8. Lynch HT, Albano WA, Heieck JJ, et al. Genetics, biomarkers, and control of breast cancer: A review. *Cancer, Genetics, and Cytogenetics* 1984; 13:43.

9. King M-C, Rowell S, Love SM. Inherited breast and ovarian cancer. *Journal of the American Medical Association* 1993; 269(15):1975.

10. Anderson DE. Some characteristics of familial breast cancer. *Cancer* 1971; 28:1500.

11. Adami HO, Hansen J, Jung B, et al. Characteristics of familial breast cancer in Sweden: Absence of relation of age and unilateral versus bilateral disease. *Cancer* 1981; 48:1688.

12. Ibid.

13. Sellers TA, Potter JD, Rich SS, et al. Familial clustering of breast and prostate cancers and risk of postmenopausal breast cancer. *Journal of the National Cancer Institute* 1994; 86(24):1860.

14. MacMahon B, Cole P, Brown J. Etiology of human breast cancer: A review. *Journal of the National Cancer Institute* 1973; 50:21.

15. Rosenberg L, Palmer JR, Kaufman DW, Strom BL, Schottenfeld D, Shapiro S. Breast cancer in relation to the occurrence and time of induced and spontaneous abortion. *American Journal of Epidemiology* 1988; 127:981.

16. Dahling JR, Malone KE, Voigt LF, White E, Weiss NS. Risk of breast cancer among young women: Relationship to induced abortion. *Journal of the National Cancer Institute* 1994; 86(21):1584.

17. Henderson BE, Ross RK, Judd HL, Krailo MD, Pike MC. Do regular ovulatory cycles increase breast cancer risk? *Cancer* 1985; 56:1206.

18. Olsson H, Ranstam J, Olsson ML. The number of menstrual cycles prior to the first full-term pregnancy an important risk factor of breast cancer? *Acta Oncologica* 1987; 26:387.

19. Bernstein L, Yuan J-M, Ross RK, et al. Serum hormone levels in pre-menopausal Chinese women in Shanghai and white women in Los Angeles: Results from two breast cancer case-control studies. *Cancer Causes and Control* 1990; 1:51.

20. Ibid.

21. Yuan J, Yu MC. Risk factors for breast cancer in Chinese women in Shanghai. *Cancer Research* 1988; 48:1949.

22. Anonymous. Breast feeding and the risk of breast cancer in young women. United Kingdom National Case-Control Study Group. *British Medical Journal* 1993; 307(6895):17.

CHAPTER 15. RISK FACTORS: EXTERNAL

1. Miller AB. Epidemiology and prevention. In: Harris JR, Hellman S, Henderson IC, Kinne DW, ed. *Breast Diseases*. Philadelphia: J.B. Lippincott, 1987.

2. Wydner EL. Reflections on diet, nutrition and cancer. *Cancer Research* 1983; 43:3024.

3. Armstrong B, Doll R. Environmental factors and cancer incidence and mortality with special reference to dietary practices. *International Journal of Cancer* 1975;15:617.

4. MacMahon B. Incidence trends in North America, Japan and Hawaii. In: Magnus K, ed. *Trends in Cancer Incidence*. New York: McGraw-Hill, 1982.

5. Bjarnson O, Day M, Snaedal G, et al. The effect of year of birth on the breast cancer age incidence curve in Iceland. *Journal of Cancer* 1974; 13:689.

6. Buell P. Changing incidence of breast cancer in Japanese-American women. *Journal of the National Cancer Institute* 1973; 51:1479.

7. Phillips RL, Garfinkel L, Kuzma JW, et al. Mortality among California Seventh Day Adventists for selected cancer sites. *Journal of the National Cancer Institute* 1980; 65:1097.

8. Kinlen LJ. Meat and fat consumption and cancer mortality: A study of religious orders in Britain. *Lancet* 1982; 946-949.

9. Chen J, Campbell TC, Junyao L, Peto R. The dietary, lifestyles and mortality characteristics of 65 rural populations in the People's Republic of China. Division of Nutritional Sciences, Cornell University, Ithaca, New York, 1987.

10. Willet WC, Stampfer MJ, Colditz GA, Rosner BA, Hennekens CH, Speizer FE. Dietary fat and the risk of breast cancer. *New England Journal of Medicine* 1987; 316:22.

11. Trichopoulou A, Katsouyanni K, Stuver S, et al. Consumption of olive oil and specific food groups in relation to breast cancer risk in Greece. *Journal of the National Cancer Institute* 1995; 87:110.

12. Martin-Moreno J, Willet W, Gorgojo L, et al. Dietary fat olive oil intake and breast cancer risk. *International Journal of Cancer* 1994; 58:774.

13. de Waard F, Baanders-van Haliwijn EA. A prospective study in general practice on breast cancer risk in postmenopausal women. *International Journal of Cancer* 1974; 1714:153.

14. Peterson G, Barnes S. Genistein inhibition of the growth of human breast cancer cells: Independence from estrogen receptors and the multi-drug resistance gene. *Biochemistry Biophysics Research Community* 1991; 179(1):661.

15. Rohan TE, Howe GR, Friedenreich CM, Jain M, Miller AB. Dietary fiber, vitamins A, C, and E, and risk of breast cancer: A cohort study. *Cancer Causes and Control* 1993; 4:29.

16. London SJ, Sacks FM, Caesar J, Stampfer MJ, Siguel E, Willet WC. Fatty acid composition of subcutaneous adipose tissue and diet in postmenopausal US women. *American Journal of Clinical Nutrition* 1991; 54(2):340.

17. Goldin BR, Adelercreutz H, Gorbach SL, et al. Estrogen excretion patterns and plasma levels in vegetarian and omnivorous women. *New England Journal of Medicine* 1982; 307:1542.

18. Willet WC, Stampfer MJ, Colditz GA, Rosner BA, Hennekens CJ, Speizer FE. Moderate alcohol consumption and the risk of breast cancer. *New England Journal of Medicine* 1980; 316:1174.

19. Schatzkin A, Jones DY, Hoover RN, et al. Alcohol consumption and breast cancer in the epidemiologic follow-up study of the first national health and nutrition examination study. *New England Journal of Medicine* 1987; 316:1169.

20. Harvey EB, Schairer C, Bringon LA, Hoover RN, Fraumeni JR Jr. Alcohol consumption and breast cancer. *Journal of the National Cancer Institute* 1987; 78:657.

21. Tokunaga M, Land CE, Yamamoto T, et al. Breast cancer among atomic bomb survivors. In: Boice JD Jr., Fraumeni JF Jr., eds. *Radiation Carcinogenesis Epidemiology and Biological Significance*. New York: Raven Press, 1984:45.

22. Miller AB, Howe GR, Sherman GJ, et al. Mortality from breast cancer after irradiation during fluoroscopic examinations in patients being treated for tuberculosis. *New England Journal of Medicine,* 1989; 321:1285.

23. Mettler FA, Hempelmann LH, Dutton AM, Pifer JW, Toyooka ET, Ames WR. Breast neoplasma in women treated with X rays for acute postpartum mastitis. A pilot study. *Journal of the National Cancer Institute* 1969; 43:803.

24. Hoffman DA, Lonstein JE, Morin MM, et al. Breast cancer in women with scoliosis exposed to multiple diagnostic X rays. *Journal of the National Cancer Institute* 1989; 81:1307.

25. Simon N. Breast cancer induced by radiation. Relation to mammography and treatment of acne. *Journal of the American Medical Association* 1977; 237(8): 789.

26. Hildreth NG, Shore RE, Dvoretsky PM. The risk of breast cancer after irradiation of the thymus in infancy. *New England Journal of Medicine* 1989; 321:1281.

27. Boice JD, Day NE, Anderson A, et al. Second cancer following radiation treatment for cervical cancer. An international collaboration among cancer registries. *Journal of the National Cancer Institute* 1985; 74:955.

28. Tucker MA, Coleman CN, Cox RS, et al. Risk of second cancers after treatment for Hodgkin's disease. *New England Journal of Medicine* 1988; 318:76.

29. Li FP, Corkery J, Vawter G, et al. Breast carcinoma after cancer therapy in childhood. *Cancer* 1983; 51:521.

30. Rosenberg L, Miller DR, Kaufman DW, et al. Breast cancer and oral contraceptive use. *American Journal of Epidemiology* 1984; 119:167.

31. Kelsey JL, Fischer DB, Holford TR, et al. Exogenous estrogens and other factors in the epidemiology of breast cancer. *Journal of the National Cancer Institute* 1981; 55:327.

32. Bernstein L, Ross R, Henderson B. Relationship of hormone use to cancer risk. *Monograph of the National Cancer Institute* 1992; 12:137.

33. Colletta AA, Wakefield LM, Howell FV, Danielpour D, Baum M, Sporn MB. The growth inhibition of human breast cancer cells by a novel synthetic progestin involves the induction of transforming growth factor beta. *Journal of Clinical Investigations* 1991; 87:277.

34. Greenberg ER, Barnes AB, Resseguie L, et al. Breast cancer in mothers given diethylstilbestrol in pregnancy. *New England Journal of Medicine* 1984; 311:1393.

35. Kelsey JL, Berkowitz GS. Breast cancer epidemiology. *Cancer Research* 1988; 48:5615.

36. Ibid.

37. Gambrell RD. Role of progestins in the prevention of breast cancer. *Mauritas* 1986; 8:169.

38. Barrett-Connor E. The risks and benefits of long-term estrogen replacement therapy. *Public Health Reports Supplement* 1989; (September/October):62.

39. The Writing Group for the PEPI Trial. Effects of estrogen or estrogen/progestin regimens on heart disease risk factors in postmenopausal women: The postmenopausal estrogen/progestin interventions (PEPI) trial. *Journal of the American Medical Association* 1995; 273(3):199.

40. Bergkvist L, Adami AO, Persson I, et al. The risk of breast cancer after estrogen and estrogen-progestin replacement. *New England Journal of Medicine* 1989; 321:293.

41. Coney S. *The Menopause Industry: How the Medical Establishment Exploits Women.* Alameda, CA: Hunter House, 1994.

42. Lindsay R. Estrogen therapy in the prevention and management of osteoporosis. *American Journal of Obstetrics and Gynecology* 1987; 5(May):1347.

43. Grady D, Rubin SM, Petitti DB, et al. Hormone therapy to prevent disease and prolong life in postmenopausal women. *Annals of Internal Medicine* 1992; 117(12):1016.

44. Ibid.

45. Goldin BR. Nonsteroidal estrogens and estrogen antagonists: Mechanism of action and health implications. *Journal of the National Cancer Institute* 1994; 86(23):1741.

46. Whittemore AS. The risk of ovarian cancer after treatment for infertility. *New England Journal of Medicine* 1994; 331(12):805.

47. Wolff MS, Toniolo PG, Lee EW, Rivera M, Dubin N. Blood levels of organochlorine residues and risk of breast cancer. *Journal of the National Cancer Institute* 1993; 85:648.

48. Krieger NK, Wolff MS, Hiatt RA, et al. Breast cancer and serum organochlorines: A prospective study among white, black and Asian women. *Journal of the National Cancer Institute* 1994; 86:589.

49. Loomis DP, Savitz DA, Ananth CV. Breast cancer mortality among female electrical workers in the United States. *Journal of the National Cancer Institute* 1994; 86(12):921.

50. Demers PA, Thomas DB, Rosenblatt KA, et al. Occupational exposure to electromagnetic fields and breast cancer in men. *American Journal of Epidemiology* 1991; 134(4):340.

51. Wilson ST, Blask DE, Lemus-Wilson AM. Melantonin augments the sensitivity of MCF-7 human breast cancer cells to tamoxifen in vitro. *Journal of Clinical Endocrinology and Metabolism* 1992; 275:669.

CHAPTER 16. PRECANCEROUS CONDITIONS

1. Davis HH, Simons M, Davis JB. Cystic disease of the breast: Relationship to cancer. *Cancer* 1974; 17:957.

2. Dupont WD, Page DL. Risk factors for breast cancer in women with proliferative breast disease. *New England Journal of Medicine* 1985; 312:146.

3. Haagensen CD, Lane N, Lattes R, et al. Lobular neoplasia (so-called lobular carcinoma *in situ*) of the breast. *Cancer* 1978; 42:737.

4. Wheeler JEW, Enterline HT, Rosenman JM, et al. Lobular carcinoma in situ of the breast: Long-term follow-up. *Cancer* 1974; 34:554.

5. Anderson JA. Lobular carcinoma in situ: A long-term follow-up in 52 cases. *Acta Pathology and Microbiology of Scandinavia (A)* 1974; 82:519.

6. Rosen PP, Lieberman PH, Braun DW. Lobular carcinoma of the breast. *American Journal of Surgical Pathology* 1987; 2:225.

7. Rosen PP, Braun DW, Kinne DE. The clinical significance of preinvasive breast carcinoma. *Cancer* 1980; 46:919.

8. Alpers CE, Wellings SR. The prevalence of carcinoma *in situ* in normal and cancer-associated breasts. *Human Pathology* 1985; 16:796.

9. Nielsen M, Jensen J, Andersen J. Precancerous and cancerous breast lesions during lifetime and at autopsy. *Cancer* 1984; 54:612.

10. Betsill WL, Rosen PP, Lieberman PH, et al. Intraductal carcinoma: Long-term follow-up after treatment by biopsy alone. *Journal of the American Medical Association* 1978; 239:1863.

11. Page DL, Dupont WD. Intraductal carcinoma of the breast. *Cancer* 1982; 49:751.

12. Poller D, Silverstein M, Galea M, et al. Ideas in pathology. Ductal carcinoma in situ of the breast: A proposal for a new simplified histological classification association between cellular proliferation and c-erbB-2 protein expression. *Modern Pathology* 1994; 7(2):257.

13. Lagios M. Duct carcinoma in situ: Pathology and treatment. *Surgical Clinics of North America* 1990; 70:853.

14. Silverstein M, Waisman J, Giersons E, Colburn W, Gamagami P, Lewinsky B. Radiation therapy for intraductal carcinoma: Is it an equal alternative? *Archives of Surgery* 1991; 126(4):424.

15. Anastassiades O, Iakovou E, Stavridou N, et al. Multicentricity in breast cancer: A study of 366 cases. *American Journal of Clinical Pathology* 1993; 99:238.

16. Rosen P, Fracchia A, Urban J, et al. "Residual" mammary carcinoma following simulated partial mastectomy. *Cancer* 1975; 35:739.

17. Holland R, Hendriks J, Verberek A, et al. Extent, distribution and mammographic/histological correlations of breast ductal carcinoma in situ. *Lancet* 1990; 335:519.

18. Lagios MD, Westdahl PR, Margolin FR, et al. Duct carcinoma in situ. *Cancer* 1982; 50:1309.

19. Lagios M. Management of non-invasive carcinoma of the breast. Fifteenth Annual Symposium on Diagnostic Imaging, Brown University, Providence, Rhode Island, August 6–8, 1994.

20. Recht A, Danoff BS, Solin LJ, et al. Intraductal carcinoma of the breast: Results of treatment with excisional biopsy and irradiation. *Journal of Clinical Oncology* 1983; 6:281.

21. Findlay P, Goodman R. Radiation therapy for treatment of intraductal carcinoma of the breast. *American Journal of Clinical Oncology* 1983; 6:281.

22. Montague ED. Conservative surgery and radiation therapy in the treatment of operable breast cancer. *Cancer* 1984; 53:700.

23. Fisher ER, Sass R, Fisher B, et al. Pathological findings from the National Surgical Adjuvant Breast and Bowel Project (Protocol 6) 1. Intraductal carcinoma (DCIS). *Cancer* 1986; 57:197.

24. Fisher B, Costantino J, Redmond C, et al. Lumpectomy compared with lumpectomy and radiation therapy for the treatment of intraductal breast cancer. *New England Journal of Medicine* 1993; 328(22):1581.

25. Finkelstein SD, Sayegh R, Thompson WR. Late recurrence of ductal carcinoma in situ at the cutaneous end of surgical drainage following total mastectomy. *American Surgeon* 1993; 59(July):410.

26. Fisher DE, Schnitt SJ, Christian R, Harris JR, Henderson IC. Chest wall recurrence of ductal carcinoma *in situ* of the breast after mastectomy. *Cancer* 1993; 71(10):3025.

27. Silverstein M, Waisman J, Gamagami P, et al. Intraductal carcinoma of the breast (208 cases). Clinical factors influencing treatment choice. *Cancer* 1990; 66(1):102.

CHAPTER 17. PREVENTION

1. Miller AB. Approaches to the control of breast cancer. In: Rich MA, Hager JC, Furmanski P, ed. *Understanding Cancer. Clinical and Laboratory Concepts.* New York: Marcel Dekker, 1983:3.

2. Fabian C, Zalles C, Kamel S, et al. Correlation of breast tissue biomarkers with hyperplasia and dysplasia in fine-needle aspirates (FNAs) of women at high and low risk for breast cancer. *Proceedings of Annual Meeting of American Association of Cancer Researchers* 1994; 35(A1703).

3. Lee M, Petrakis N, Wrensch M, King E, Miike R, Sickles E. Association of abnormal nipple aspirate cytology and mammographic pattern and density. *Cancer Epidemiology Biomarkers Prevention* 1994; 3(1):33.

4. Bernstein L, Henderson BE, Hanisch R, Sullivan-Halley J, Ross RK. Physical exercise activity and reduced risk of breast cancer in young women. *Journal of the National Cancer Institute* 1994; 86:1403.

5. Bernstein L, Ross RK, Lobo RA, Hanisch R, Krailo MD, Henderson BE. The effects of moderate physical activity on menstrual cycle patterns in adolescence: Implications for breast cancer prevention. *British Journal of Cancer* 1987; 55:681.

6. Frisch RE, Wyshak G, Albright N, et al. Lower lifetime occurrence of breast cancer and cancer of the reproductive system among former college athletes. *American Journal of Clinical Nutrition* 1987; 45:328.

7. Fisher ER, Fisher B, Wickerham DL, Costantino JP, Redmond C. Response: Endometrial cancer in tamoxifen-treated breast cancer patients: Findings from the National Surgical Adjuvant Breast and Bowel Project (NSABP) B-14. *Journal of the National Cancer Institute* 1994; 86(16):1253.

8. Veronesi U, DePalo G, Costa A. Chemoprevention of breast cancer with retinoids. *NCI Monographs* 1992; 12:93.

9. Spicer DV, Pike MC, Pike A, Rude R, Shoupe D, Richardson J. Pilot trial of a gonadotropin hormone agonist with replacement hormones as a prototype contraceptive to prevent breast cancer. *Contraception* 1993; 47:427.

10. Spicer D, Ursin G, Parisky YR, et al. Changes in mammographic densities induced by a hormonal contraceptive designed to reduce breast cancer risk. *Journal of the National Cancer Institute* 1994; 86(6):431.

11. Temple W, Lindsay R, Magi E, Urbanski S. Technical considerations for prophylactic mastectomy in patients at high risk for breast cancer. *American Journal of Surgery* 1991; 161(4):413.

12. Jackson CF, Palmquist M, Swanson J, et al. The effectiveness of prophylactic subcutaneous mastectomy in Sprague-Dawley rats induced with 7,12 dimethylbenzanthracene. *Plastic and Reconstructive Surgery* 1984; 73:249.

13. Nelson H, Miller S, Buck D, Demuth R, Fletcher W, Buehler P. Effectiveness of prophylactic mastectomy in the prevention of breast tumors in C3H mice. *Plastic and Reconstructive Surgery* 1989; 83(4):662.

14. Goldman LD, Goldwyn RM. Some anatomical considerations of subcutaneous mastectomy. *Plastic and Reconstructive Surgery* 1973; 51:501.

15. Pennesi V, Capozzi A. Subcutaneous mastectomy data: A final statistical analysis of 1500 patients. *Aesthetic Plastic Surgery* 1989; 13(1):15.

16. King M-C, Rowell S, Love SM. Inherited breast and ovarian cancer. *Journal of the American Medical Association* 1993; 269(15):1975.

CHAPTER 18. SCREENING

1. Wolfe JN. Breast cancer screening. *Breast Cancer Research and Treatment* 1991; 18:S89.

2. Ibid.

3. Senie R, Rosen P, Lesser M, Kinne D. Breast self-examination and medical examination related to breast cancer stage. *American Journal of Public Health* 1981; 71:583.

4. Anonymous U.K. trial of early detection of breast cancer group: First results on mortality reduction in the U.K. trial of early detection of breast cancer. *Lancet* 1988; ii:411.

5. Shapiro S, Venet W, Strax P, et al. Ten- to fourteen-year effects of screening on breast cancer mortality. *Journal of the National Cancer Institute* 1982; 69:349.

6. Ibid.

7. Chu KC, Smart CR, Tarone RE. Analysis of breast cancer mortality and stage distribution by age for the health insurance plan clinical trial. *Journal of the National Cancer Institute* 1988; 80:1195.

8. Miller A, Baines C, To T, Wall C. Canadian National Breast Screening Study: 2. Breast cancer detection and death rates among women aged 50–59 years. *Canadian Medical Association Journal* 1992; 147(10):1477.

9. Fletcher SW, Black W, Harris R, Rimer BK., Shapiro S. Report of the international workshop for screening for breast cancer. *Journal of the National Cancer Institute* 1993; 85(20):1644.

10. Kopans DB. NBSS Revisited–Again (response). *Journal of the National Cancer Institute* 1993; 85(21):1774.

11. Eddy DM, Hasselblad B, McGivney W, Hendee W. The value of mammography screening in women under age 50 years. *Journal of the American Medical Association* 1988; 259:1512.

CHAPTER 19. UNDERSTANDING BREAST CANCER

1. Robbins G, ed. *Silvergirl's Surgery: The Breast*. Austin, TX: Silvergirl, 1984:

2. Fisher B. Laboratory and clinical research in breast cancer—a personal adventure. The David Karnofsky Memorial Lecture. *Cancer Research* 1980; 40:3863.

3. Gershon-Cohen J, Berger SM, Klickstein HS. Roentgenography of breast cancer moderating concept of "biological predeterminism." *Cancer* 1963; 16:961.

4. Fisher B, Redmond CB, Fisher E, et al. Ten-year results of randomized clinical trial comparing radical mastectomy and total mastectomy with or without radiation. *New England Journal of Medicine* 1985; 312:674.

5. Harris JR, Osteen RT. Patients with early breast cancer benefit from effective axillary treatment. *Breast Cancer Research and Treatment* 1985; 5:17.

6. Tabar L, Fagerberg CJG, Grad A, et al. Reduction in mortality from breast cancer after mass screening with mammography randomized trial from the Breast Cancer Screening Working Group of the Swedish National Board of Health and Wellness. *Lancet* 1985; 1:829.

CHAPTER 20. DIAGNOSIS AND TYPES OF BREAST CANCER

1. Fisher ER, Sass R, Fisher B. Biological considerations regarding the one- and two-step procedures in the management of patients with invasive carcinoma of the breast. *Surgery, Gynecology, and Obstetrics* 1985; 161:245.

2. Dixon JM, Anderson TJ, Page DL, et al. Infiltrating lobular carcinoma of the breast: An evaluation of the incidence and consequence of bilateral disease. *British Journal of Surgery* 1983; 70:513.

3. Gotteland M, May E, May-Levin F, Contesso G, Delarue J-C, Mouriesse H. Estrogen receptors (ER) in human breast cancer. *Cancer* 1994; 74(3):864.

4. Ewers S-V, Attewell R, Baldetorp B, et al. Prognostic significance of flow cytometric DNA analysis and estrogen receptor content in breast carcinomas—a 10-year survival study. *Breast Cancer Research and Treatment* 1992; 24:115.

5. Slamon D, Godolphin W, Jones L, et al. Studies of the Her-2/*neu* proto-oncogene in human breast and ovarian cancer. *Science* 1989; 244(4905):707.

6. Tetu B, Brisson J. Prognostic significance of Her-2/*neu* oncoprotein expression in node-positive breast cancer. *Cancer* 1994; 73(9):2359.

7. Muss H, Thor A, Kute T, et al. c-erbB-2 expression and response to adjuvant therapy in women with node-positive early breast cancer. *New England Journal of Medicine* 1994; 330(18):1260.

8. Wong WW, Vijayakumar S, Weichselbaum RR. Prognostic indicators in node-negative early stage breast cancer. *American Journal of Medicine* 1992; 92:539.

CHAPTER 21. STAGING: HOW WE GUESS IF YOUR CANCER HAS SPREAD

1. Ciatto S, Pacini P, Azzini V, et al. Preoperative staging of primary breast cancer. A multicentric study. *Cancer* 1988; 61(5):1038.

2. Haagensen C. *Diseases of the Breast*. (2nd ed.) Philadelphia: W.B. Saunders, 1971.

3. Wong WW, Vijayakumar S, Weichselbaum RR. Prognostic indicators in node-negative early stage breast cancer. *American Journal of Medicine* 1992; 92:539.

4. Lorde A. *A Burst of Light*. New York: Firebrand Books, 1988:550.

CHAPTER 22. FEARS AND FEELINGS

1. Rollin B. *First, You Cry*. New York: New American Library, 1976:111.

2. Kushner R. *Alternatives*. Cambridge, MA: Kensington Press, 1984:192.

3. Peters-Golden H. Breast cancer: Varied perceptions of social support in the illness experience. *Social Science Medicine* 1982; 16:483.

4. Telephone interview with Anne Kaspar.

5. Taylor SE, Lichtman RR, Wood JV. Attributions, beliefs about control and adjustment to breast cancer. *Journal of Perspectives on Sociology and Psychology* 1984; 46:489.

6. Taylor et al., 1984.

7. Wellisch DK, Gritz ER, Schain W, Wang HJ, Siau J. Psychological functioning of daughters of breast cancer patients. Part II: Characterizing the distressed daughter of the breast cancer patient. *Psychosomatics* 1992; 33(2):171.

8. Lichtman RR, Taylor SE, et al. Relations with children after breast cancer: The mother-daughter relationship at risk. *Journal of Psychosociology and Oncology* 1984; 2:1.

CHAPTER 23. TREATMENT OPTIONS: OVERVIEW

1. Veronesi U. Randomized trials comparing conservative techniques with conventional surgery: An overview. In: Tobias JS, Peckham MJ, eds. *Primary Management of Breast Cancer: Alternatives to Mastectomy Management of Malignant Disease Series*. London: E. Arnold, 1985.

2. Fisher B, Redmond C, Poisson R, et al. Eight-year results of a randomized clinical trial comparing total mastectomy and segmental mastectomy with or without radiation in the treatment of breast cancer. *New England Journal of Medicine* 1989; 320:822.

3. Rech A, Connolly JL, Schnitt SJ, et al. Conservative surgery and primary radiation therapy for early breast cancer: Results, controversies and unresolved problems. *Seminars in Oncology* 1986; 13:434.

4. Harris JR, Connolly JL, Schnitt SJ, et al. The use of pathological features in selecting the extent of surgical resection necessary for breast cancer patients treated by primary radiation therapy. *Annals of Surgery* 1985; 201:164.

5. Calle R, Viloq JR, Zafrani B, et al. Local control and survival of breast cancer treated by limited surgery followed by irradiation. *International Journal of Radiology, Oncology and Biophysics* 1986; 12:873.

6. Lindley R, Bulman A, Parsons P, et al. Histological features predictive of an increased risk of early local recurrence after treatment of breast cancer by local tumor excision and radical radiotherapy. *Surgery* 1989; 105:13.

7. Brenner M, Schnitt SJ, Connolly JL, et al. The use of reexcision in primary radiation therapy for stage I and II breast carcinoma. *International Journal of Radiology, Oncology and Biophysics* 1985; 11(Supplement 1):186.

8. Schnitt SJ, Abner A, Gelman R, et al. The relationship between microscopic margins of resection and the risk of local recurrence in patients with breast cancer treated with breast conserving surgery and radiotherapy. *Cancer* 1994; 74:1746.

9. Rosen PP, Kinne DW, Lesser M, et al. Are prognostic factors for local control of breast cancer treated by primary radiotherapy significant for patients treated by mastectomy? *Cancer* 1986; 57:1415.

10. Schnitt et al., 1994.

11. Fisher et al., 1989.

12. Schnitt SJ, Pierce S, Gelman R, et al. A prospective study of conservative surgery alone in the treatment of selected patients with Stage I breast cancer. *In preparation*.

13. Silverstein MJ, Gierson ED, Waisman JR, Senofsky GM, Colburn WJ, Gamagami P. Axillary lymph node dissection for T1a breast carcinoma: Is it indicated? *Cancer* 1994; 73(3):664.

14. Osteen RT, Steele GD Jr., Menck HR, Winchester DP. Regional differences in surgical management of breast cancer. *CA: A Cancer Journal for Clinicians* 1992; 42(1):39.

15. Kushner R. *Why Me?* Cambridge, MA: Kensington Press, 1982:372.

16. Group EBCTC. Effects of adjuvant tamoxifen and of cytotoxic therapy on mortality in early breast cancer: An overview of 61 randomized trials among 28,896 women. *New England Journal of Medicine* 1988; 319:1681.

17. Butta A, MacLennan K, Flanders KC, et al. Induction of transforming growth factor beta 1 in human breast cancer in vivo following tamoxifen treatment. *Cancer Research* 1992; 52(15):4261.

18. Group EBCTC, 1988.

19. Jordan VC, Fritz NF, Langan-Fahey S, Thompson M, Tormey DC. Alteration of endocrine parameters in premenopausal women with breast cancer during long-term adjuvant therapy with tamoxifen as the single agent. *Journal of the National Cancer Institute* 1991; 83(20):1488.

20. Group EBCTC, 1988.

21. Ibid.

22. Bonadonna G, Valagussa VE, Rossi A, et al. Ten-year experience with CMF-based adjuvant chemotherapy in resectable breast cancer. *Breast Cancer Research and Treatment* 1985; 5:95.

23. Wolmark N, Fisher B. Adjuvant chemotherapy in Stage II breast cancer: An overview of the NSABP clinical trials. *Breast Cancer Research and Treatment* 1983; 3(Supplement):S19.

24. Group EBCTC, 1988.

25. Ibid.

26. Wickerham D, Fisher B, Brown A, et al. Two months of Adriamycin-cyclophosphomide with and without interval reinduction therapy vs. six months of conventional CMF in positive node breast cancer. *Annual Meeting of the American Society of Clinical Oncologists* 1990; 9(A73).

27. Kitten L, Osbourne K. Antiestrogens antagonize melphalan but not cyclophosphomide cytotoxity in human breast cancer cells by estrogen receptor independent mechanisms. *Proceedings of the Annual Meeting of the American Society of Clinical Oncologists* 1988; 7:A31.

28. Peters WP, Ross M, Vrendenburgh JJ, et al. High dose chemotherapy and autologous bone marrow support as consolidation after standard dose adjuvant therapy for high risk primary breast cancer. *Journal of Clinical Oncology* 1993; 11(6):1132.

29. Bonadonna G, Veronesi U, Brambilla C, et al. Primary chemotherapy to avoid mastectomy in tumors with diameters of three centimeters or more. *Journal of the National Cancer Institute* 1990; 82(19):1539.

CHAPTER 24. SPECIAL CASES

1. Hortobagyi GN, Blumenschein GR, Spanos W, et al. Multimodal treatment of locally advanced breast cancer. *Cancer* 1983; 51:763.

2. Perez CA, Graham ML, Taylor ME, et al. Management of locally advanced carcinoma of the breast: I. Noninflammatory. *Cancer Supplement* 1994; 74(1):453.

3. Haagensen C. *Diseases of the Breast*. (2nd ed.) Philadelphia: W.B. Saunders, 1971.

4. Perez CA, Fields JN, Fracasso PM, et al. Management of locally advanced carcinoma of the breast: II. Inflammatory carcinoma. *Cancer* 1994; 74:466.

5. Ashikari R, Rosen PP, Urban JA, et al. Breast cancer presenting as an axillary mass. *Annals of Surgery* 1976; 183:415.

6. Viloq JR, Ferme F, et al. Conservative treatment of axillary adenopathy due to probable subclinical breast cancer. *Archives of Surgery* 1982; 117:1136.

7. Montague ED. Axillary metastases from unknown primary sites. In: Fletcher G, ed. *Textbook of Radiotherapy*. Philadelphia: Lea and Febiger, 1980.

8. Feigenberg Z, Zer M, Dintsman M. Axillary metastases from an unknown primary source: A diagnostic and therapeutic approach. *Israeli Journal of Medical Science* 1976; 12:1153.

9. van Ooijen B, Bontenbal M, Henzen-Logmans SC, Koper PC. Axillary nodal metastases from an occult primary consistent with breast carcinoma. *British Journal of Surgery* 1993; 80(10):1299.

10. Lagios MD, Westdahl PR, Rose MR, et al. Paget's disease of the nipple. *Cancer* 1984; 54:545.

11. Kister SJ, Haagensen CD. Paget's disease of the breast. *American Journal of Surgery* 1970; 119:606.

12. Malak G, Tapolcsanyi L. Characteristics of Paget's carcinoma of the nipple and problems of its negligence. *Oncology* 1974; 30:278.

13. Lagios MD, 1984.

14. Haagensen C. *Diseases of the Breast*. (2nd ed.) Philadelphia: W.B. Saunders, 1975:227.

15. Guinee VF, Olsson H, Moller T, et al. Effect of pregnancy on prognosis for young women with breast cancer. *Lancet* 1994; 343:1587.

16. Lambe M, Hsieh C-C, Trichopoulos D, Ekbom A, Pavia M, Adami H-O. Transient increase in the risk of breast cancer after giving birth. *New England Journal of Medicine* 1994; 331(1):5.

17. Thompson WD. Genetic epidemiology of breast cancer. *Cancer* 1994; 74:279.

18. McCormick B. Selection criteria for breast conservation: The impact of young and old age and collagen vascular disease. *Cancer* 1994; 74:430.

19. Lee CG, McCormick B, Mazumdar M, Vetto J, Borgen PI. Infiltrating breast carcinoma in patients age 30 years and younger: Long-term outcome for life, relapse, and second primary tumors. *International Journal of Radiation, Oncology, Biology, and Physics* 1992; 23:969.

20. Silliman RA, Balducci L, Goodwin JS, Holmes FF, Leventhal EA. Breast cancer care in old age: What we know, don't know, and do. *Journal of the National Cancer Institute* 1993; 85(3):190.

21. Horobin JM, Preece PE, Dewar JA, Wood RAB, Cuschieri A. Long-term follow-up of elderly patients with locoregional breast cancer treated with tamoxifen alone. *British Journal of Surgery* 1991; 78(January):213.

22. Bates T, Riley DL, Houghton J, Fallowfield L, Baum M. Breast cancer in elderly women: A Cancer Research Campaign trial comparing treatment with tamoxifen and optimal surgery with tamoxifen alone. *British Journal of Surgery* 1991; 78(May):591.

23. Guinee et al., 1994.

24. Lambe et al., 1994.

25. Deapen MD, Pike MC, Casagrande JT, et al. The relationship between breast cancer and augmentation mammoplasty: An epidemiologic study. *Plastic and Reconstructive Surgery* 1986; 77:361.

26. Jacobson GM, Sause WT, Thomson JW, Plenk HP. Breast irradiation following silicone gel implants. *International Journal of Radiation, Oncology, Biology, and Physics* 1986; 12(5):835.

27. Schwartz RM, Newell RB, Hauch JF, et al. A study of familial male breast carcinoma and a second report. *Cancer* 1980; 46:2629.

28. Jackson AW, et al. Carcinoma of the male breast in association with the Klinefelter syndrome. *British Medical Journal* 1965; 1:223.

29. Campbell JH, Cummins SD. Metastases simulating mammary cancer in prostatic carcinoma under estrogenic therapy. *Cancer* 1951; 4:303.

CHAPTER 25. SURGERY

1. Hrushesky WJM, Bluming AZ, Gruber SA, Sothern RB. Menstrual influence on surgical cure of breast cancer. *Lancet* 1989; 2:949.

2. Veronesi U, Luini A, Mariani L, et al. Effect of menstrual phase on surgical treatment of breast cancer. *Lancet* 1994; 343(June 18):1545.

3. Lanzafame RJ, McCormick CJ, Rogers DW, et al. Mechanisms of the reduction of tumor recurrence with the carbon dioxide laser in experimental mammary tumors. *Surgery, Gynecology and Obstetrics* 1988; 67:493.

4. Silen W, Matory WE, Love SM. *Evolving Techniques in Breast Surgery: An Atlas.* Philadelphia: J.B. Lippincott. In press.

5. Troyan S. Personal communication.

6. Rosen PP, Lesser MT, Kinne DW, et al. Discontinuous or "skip" metastases in breast carcinoma; Analysis of 1228 axillary dissections. *Annals of Surgery* 1983; 197:276.

7. Siegel BM, Mayzel KA, Love SM. Level I and II axillary dissection in the treatment of early stage breast cancer; an analysis of 259 consecutive patients. *Archives of Surgery* 1990; 125:1144.

8. Lorde A. *The Cancer Journals.* New York: Spinsters, 1980:16.

9. Lerner R. Complete Decongestive Physiotherapy (CDP). The ideal treatment for lymphedema. *Massage Therapy Journal* 1992; (Winter):37.

10. Casley-Smith JR, Morgan RG, Piller NB. Treatment of lymphedema of the arms and legs with 5,6-Benso(alpha)-pyrone. *New England Journal of Medicine* 1993; 329:1158.

CHAPTER 26. PROSTHESIS AND RECONSTRUCTION

1. Lorde A. *The Cancer Journals.* New York: Spinsters, 1980:16.

2. Metzger D. *Tree and The Woman Who Slept with Men to Take the War Out of Them.* Oakland, CA: Wingbow Press, 1983.

3. Rollin B. *First, You Cry.* New York: New American Library, 1976:111.

4. Kushner R. *Why Me?* Cambridge, MA: Kensington Press, 1982:372.

5. Johnson CH, van Heerden JA, Donohue JH, et al. Oncological aspects of immediate breast reconstruction following mastectomy for malignancy. *Archives of Surgery* 1989; 124:819.

CHAPTER 27. RADIATION THERAPY

1. Cuzick J, Stewart H, Peto R, et al. Overview of randomized trials of postoperative adjuvant radiotherapy in breast cancer. *Cancer Treatment Report* 1987; 71:15.

2. Kurtz JM, Amalric R, Brandone H, et al. Contralateral breast cancer and other second malignancies in patients treated by breast-conserving therapy with radiation. *International Journal of Radiation, Oncology, Biology, and Physics* 1987; 15:277.

CHAPTER 28. SYSTEMIC TREATMENTS

1. Bonadonna G, Valagussa VE, Rossi A, et al. Ten-year experience with CMF-based adjuvant chemotherapy in resectable breast cancer. *Breast Cancer Research and Treatment* 1985; 5:95.

2. ASCO. American Society of Clinical Oncology recommendations for the use of hematopoetic colony stimulating factors: Evidence-based clinical practice guidelines. *Journal of Clinical Oncology* 1994; 12:247.

3. Denmark-Wahnefried W, Winer EP, Rimer BK. Why women gain weight with adjuvant chemotherapy for breast cancer. *Journal of Clinical Oncology* 1993; 11(7):1418.

4. Fisher B, Rockette H, Fisher ER, et al. Leukemia in breast cancer patients following adjuvant chemotherapy or postoperative radiation: The NSABP experience. *Journal of Clinical Oncology* 1985; 3:1640.

5. Klewer SE, Goldberg SJ, Donnerstein RL, Berg RA, Hutter JJ Jr. Dobutamine stress echocardiography: A sensitive indicator of diminished myocardial function in asymptomatic doxorubicin-treated long-term survivors of childhood cancer. *Journal of the American College of Cardiologists* 1992; 19(2):394.

6. Siegel BS. *Love, Medicine and Miracles*. New York: Harper & Row, 1986:133.

7. Saphner T, Tormey DC, Gray R. Venous and arterial thrombosis in patients who received adjuvant therapy for breast cancer. *Journal of Clinical Oncology* 1991; 9(2):286.

8. Fisher B, Costantino JP, Redmond CK, et al. Endometrial cancer in tamoxifen-treated breast cancer patients: Findings from the National Surgical Adjuvant Breast and Bowel Project (NSABP) B-14. *Journal of the National Cancer Institute* 1994; 86(7):527.

9. Caleffi M, Fentiman IS, Clark GM, et al. Effect of tamoxifen on oestrogen binding, lipid and lipoprotein concentrations and blood clotting parameters in premenopausal women with breast pain. *Journal of Endocrinology* 1988; 119(2):335.

10. Kristensen B, Ejlertsen B, Dalgaard P, et al. Tamoxifen and bone metabolism in postmenopausal low-risk breast cancer patients: A randomized study. *Journal of Clinical Oncology* 1994; 12(5):992.

11. Jordan VC, Fritz NF, Langan-Fahey S, Thompson M, Tormey DC. Alteration of endocrine parameters in premenopausal women with breast cancer during long-term adjuvant therapy with tamoxifen as the single agent. *Journal of the National Cancer Institute* 1991; 83(20):1488.

CHAPTER 29. COMPLEMENTARY AND ALTERNATIVE TREATMENTS

1. Cousins N. *Anatomy of an Illness*. New York: Bantam Books, 1979:45.

2. Spiegel D, Bloom JR, Kraemer HC, Gottheil E. Effect of psychosocial treatment on survival of patients with metastatic breast cancer. *Lancet* 1989; 2(8668):888.

3. Fawzy FI, Fawzy NW, Hyun CS, et al. Malignant melanoma. Effects of an early structured psychiatric intervention, coping, and affective state on recurrence and survival six years later. *Archives of General Psychiatry* 1993; 50(9):681.

4. Duckro, P, Magaletta, PR, "The Effect of Prayer on Physical Health: Experimental Evidence" in *Journal of Health and Religion*.

5. Dossey L. *Healing Words: The Healing Power of Prayer*. San Francisco: Harper, 1993.

6. Fiore N. *The Road Back to Health*. New York: Bantam Books, 1984:149.

7. Cousins, 1979.

8. Ibid.

9. Benson H. *Beyond the Relaxation Response*. New York: Berkley Books, 1985.

10. Mella DL. *The Legendary and Practical Use of Gems and Stones*. Albuquerque, NM: Domel, 1979.

11. Boyar AP, Rose DP, Loughride JR, et al. Response to a diet low in total fat in women with postmenopausal breast cancer: A pilot study. *Nutrition and Cancer* 1988; 11:93.

12. Frederick C. *Winning the Fight against Breast Cancer: The Nutritional Approach*. New York: Grosset & Dunlap, 1977.

13. Kushi M. *The Cancer Prevention Diet*. New York: St. Martin's Press, 1983:157.

14. Kennedy D. Food and Drug Administration's warning on laetrile.

15. Lorde A. *A Burst of Light*. New York: Firebrand Books, 1988:550.

CHAPTER 30. LIFE AFTER BREAST CANCER

1. Robbins GF, Berg JW. Bilateral primary breast cancers: A prospective clinical pathological study. *Cancer* 1964; 17:1501.

2. Haagensen CD, Lane N, Bodian C. Coexisting lobular neoplasia and carcinoma of the breast. *Cancer* 1983; 51:1468.

3. Anonymous. Impact of follow-up testing on survival and health-related quality of life in breast cancer patients. A multicenter randomized controlled trial. The GIVO Investigators. *Journal of the American Medical Association* 1994; 271(20):1587.

4. Stierer M, Rosen HR. Influence of early diagnosis on prognosis of recurrent breast cancer. *Cancer* 1989; 64:1128.

5. Cobleigh MA, Berris RF, Bush T, et al. Estrogen replacement therapy in breast cancer survivors: A time for change. *Journal of the American Medical Association* 1994; 272(7):540.

6. Ibid.

7. Kitzinger S. *Woman's Experience of Sex*. New York: G.P. Putnam's Sons, 1983:308.

8. Mignot L, et al. Breast cancer and subsequent pregnancy. *American Society of Clinical Oncology Proceedings* 1986; 5:57.

9. Peters M. The effect of pregnancy in breast cancer. *Prognostic Factors in Breast Cancer* 1968; 65.

CHAPTER 31. WHEN CANCER COMES BACK

1. Fisher B, Anderson S, Fisher ER, et al. Significance of ipsilateral breast tumour recurrence after lumpectomy. *Lancet* 1991; 338(August 10):327.

2. Ibid.

3. Toonkel LM, Fix I, Jacobson LH, Wallach CB. The significance of local recurrence of carcinoma of the breast. *International Journal of Radiation, Oncology, Biology, and Physics* 1983; 9(1):33.

4. Borner M, Bacchi A, Goldhirsch A, et al. First isolated locoregional recurrence followng mastectomy for breast cancer: Results of a phase III multicenter study comparing systemic treatment with observation after excision and radiation. *Journal of Clinical Oncology* 1994; 12:2071.

5. Slavin SA, Love SM, Goldwyn RM. Recurrent breast cancer following immediate reconstruction with myocutaneous flaps. *Plastic and Reconstructive Surgery* 1994; 93(May):1191.

6. Marks LB, Halperin EC, Prosnitz LR, et al. Post-mastectomy radiotherapy following adjuvant chemotherapy and autologous bone marrow transplantation for breast cancer patients with ≥ 10 positive axillary lymph nodes. *International Journal of Radiation, Oncology, Biology, and Physics* 1992; 23(5):1021.

7. Recht A, Pierce S, Abner A, et al. Regional nodal failure after conservative surgery and radiotherapy for early-stage breast carcinoma. *Journal of Clinical Oncology* 1991; 9:988.

8. Clark GM, Sledge WJ Jr., Osbourne CK, et al. Survivial from first recurrence: Relative importance of prognostic factors in 1,015 breast cancer patients. *Journal of Clinical Oncology* 1987; 5:55.

9. Ibid.

10. Robinson RG, Preston DF, Baxter KG, Dusing RW, Spicer JA. Clinical experience with strontium-89 in prostatic and breast cancer patients. *Seminars in Oncology* 1993; 20(3 Supplement 2):44.

11. Spiegel D, Bloom JR, Kraemer HC, Gottheil E. Effect of psychosocial treatment on survival of patients with metastatic breast cancer. *Lancet* 1989; 2(8668):888.

12. Spiegel, D, *Living Beyond Limits: New Hope and Help for Facing Life-Threatening Illness.* New York: Times Book, 1993.

CHAPTER 32. METASTATIC DISEASE: TREATMENTS

1. Powles TJ, Smith IE, Ford HT, et al. Failure of chemotherapy to prolong survival in a group of patients with metastatic breast cancer. *Lancet* 1980; 1:580.

2. Ross MB, Buzdar AU, Smith TL, et al. Improved survival of patients with metastatic breast cancer receiving combination chemotherapy. *Cancer* 1985; 55(2):341.

3. Eddy DM. High-dose chemotherapy with autologous bone marrow transplantation for the treatment of metastatic breast cancer. *Journal of Clinical Oncology* 1992; 10(4):657.

4. Ibid.

CHAPTER 34. THE POLITICS OF BREAST CANCER

1. "War Mammorial" copyright 1993. Melanie Winter created to bring attention to the problem during National Breast Cancer Awareness Month, as well as to publicize the newly formed Los Angeles Breast Cancer Alliance.

Glossary

abscess: Infection which has formed a pocket of pus.

adenocarcinoma: Cancer arising in gland forming tissue. Breast cancer is a type of adenocarcinoma.

adjuvant chemotherapy: Anticancer drugs used in combination with surgery and/or radiation as an initial treatment before there is detectable spread, to prevent or delay recurrence.

adrenal gland: Small gland found above each kidney which secretes cortisone, adrenalin, aldosterone, and many other important hormones.

alopecia: Hair loss, a common side effect of chemotherapy.

amenorrhea: Absence or stoppage of menstrual period.

androgen: Hormone which produces male characteristics.

aneuploid: Abnormal amount of DNA in a cell, can correlate with a worse cancer.

anorexia: Loss of appetite.

areola: Area of pigment around the nipple.

aspiration: Putting a hypodermic needle into a tissue and drawing back on the syringe to obtain fluid or cells.

asymmetrical: Not matching.

ataxia telangiectasia: Disease of the nervous system; carriers of the gene are more sensitive to radiation and have a higher risk of cancer.

603

atypical cell: Mild to moderately abnormal cell.

atypical hyperplasia: Cells that are not only abnormal but increased in number.

augmented: Added to, such as an augmented breast; one that has had a silicone implant added to it.

autologous: From the same person. An autologous blood transfusion is blood removed and then transfused back to the same person at a later date.

axilla: Armpit.

axillary lymph node dissection: Surgical removal of lymph nodes found in the armpit region.

axillary lymph nodes: Lymph nodes found in the armpit area.

benign: Not cancerous.

bilateral: Involving both sides, such as both breasts.

biological response modifier: Usually natural substances, such as colony stimulating factor which stimulates the bone marrow to make blood cells, that alter the body's natural response.

biopsy: Removal of tissue. This term does not indicate how *much* tissue will be removed.

bone marrow: The soft inner part of large bones that produces blood cells.

bone scan: Test to determine if there is any sign of cancer in the bones.

brachial plexus: A bundle of nerves in the armpit which go on to supply your arm.

breast reconstruction: Creation of artificial breast after mastectomy by a plastic surgeon.

bromocriptine: Drug used to block the hormone prolactin.

calcifications: Small calcium deposits in the breast tissue that can be seen by mammography.

Cathepsin D: Enzyme which helps in process of invasion. A high level is thought to correlate with worse prognosis.

carcinoembryonic antigen (CEA): Nonspecific (not specific to cancer) blood test used to follow women with metastatic breast cancer to help determine if the treatment is working.

carcinogen: Substance that can cause cancer.

carcinoma: Cancer arising in the epithelial tissue (skin, glands, and lining of internal organs). Most cancers are carcinomas.

cellulitis: Infection of the soft tissues.

centigray: Measurement of radiation-absorbed dose; same as a rad.

chemotherapy: Treatment of disease with certain chemicals. The term usually refers to *cytotoxic* drugs given for cancer treatment.

colostrum: Liquid produced by the breast before the milk comes in: pre milk.

comedo: Type of DCIS where the cells filling the duct are more aggressive looking.

comedon: Whitehead pimple.

contracture: Formation of a thick scar tissue; in the breast a contracture can form around an implant.

core biopsy: Type of needle biopsy where a small core of tissue is removed from a lump without surgery.

corpus luteum: Ovarian follicle after ovulation.

cortisol: Hormone produced by the adrenal gland.

costochondritis: Inflammation of the connection between ribs and breastbone; a type of arthritis.

cribiform: Type of DCIS where the cells filling the duct have punched out areas.

cyclical: According to a cycle such as the menstrual cycle.

cyst: Fluid-filled sac.

cystosarcoma phylloides: Unusual type of breast tumor.

cytologist: One who specializes in studying cells.

cytology: Study of cells.

cytotoxic: Causing the death of cells. The term usually refers to drugs used in chemotherapy.

danazol: Drug used to block hormones from the pituitary gland, used in endometriosis and (rarely) breast pain.

diethylstilbesterol (DES): Synthetic estrogen once used to prevent miscarriages, now shown to cause vaginal cancer in the daughters of the women who took it. DES is sometimes used to treat metastatic breast cancer.

differentiated: Clearly defined. Differentiated tumor cells are similar in appearance to normal cells.

diploid: Normal amount of DNA in a cell, can correlate with a better prognosis.

doubling time: Time it takes the cell population to double in number.

ductal carcinoma in situ: Ductal cancer cells that have not grown outside of their site of origin, sometimes referred to as precancer.

edema: Swelling caused by a collection of fluid in the soft tissues.

electrocautery: Instrument used in surgery to cut, coagulate, or destroy tissue by heating it with an electric current.

embolus: Plug or clot of tumor cells within a blood vessel.

engorgement: Swelling with fluid as in a breast engorged with milk.

esophagus (esophageal): Organ carrying food from the mouth and the stomach.

estrogen: Female sex hormones produced by the ovaries, adrenal glands, placenta, and fat.

estrogen receptor: Protein found on some cells to which estrogen molecules will attach. If a tumor is positive for estrogen receptors it is sensitive to hormones.

excema: Skin irritation characterized by redness and open weeping.

excisional biopsy: Taking the whole lump out.

fat necrosis: Area of dead fat usually following some form of trauma or surgery; a cause of lumps.

fibroadenoma: Benign fibrous tumor of the breast most common in young women.

fibrocystic disease: Much misused term for any benign condition of the breast.

fibroid: Benign fibrous tumor of the uterus (not in the breast).

flow cytometry: Test that measures DNA content in tumors.

fluoroscopy: Use of an X ray machine to examine parts of the body directly rather than taking a picture and developing it, as in conventional X rays. Fluoroscopy uses more radiation than a single X ray.

follicle stimulating hormone (FSH): Hormone from the pituitary gland which stimulates the ovary.

follicles: In the ovaries eggs encased in their developmental sacs.

frozen section: Freezing and slicing tissue to make a slide immediately for diagnosis.

frozen shoulder: Stiffness of the shoulder which is painful and makes it hard to lift the arm over the head.

galactocele: Milk cyst sometimes found in a nursing mother's breast.

genetic: Relating to genes or inherited characteristics.

ghostectomy: Removal of breast tissue in the area where there was a previous lump.

gynecomastia: Swollen breast tissue in a man or boy.

hemangioma: A birth mark consisting of overgrowth of blood vessels.

hematoma: Collection of blood in the tissues. Hematomas may occur in the breast after surgery.

hemorrhage: Bleeding.

heterogeneous: Composed of many different elements. In relation to breast cancer, heterogeneous refers to the fact that there are many different types of breast cancer cells within one tumor.

homeopathy: System of therapy using very small doses of drugs which can produce in healthy people symptoms similar to those of the disease being treated. These are believed to stimulate the immune system.

hormone: Chemical substance produced by glands in the body which enters the bloodstream and causes effects in other tissues.

hot flashes: Sudden sensations of heat and swelling associated with menopause.

human choriogonadotropin (HCG): Hormone produced by the *corpus luteum*.

hyperplasia: Excessive growth of cells.

hypothalamus: Area at the base of the brain that controls various functions including hormone production in the pituitary.

hysterectomy: Removal of the uterus. Hysterectomy does not necessarily mean the removal of ovaries *(oophorectomy)*.

immune system: Complex system by which the body is able to protect itself from foreign invaders.

immunocytochemistry: Study of the chemistry of cells using techniques that employ immune mechanisms.

incisional biopsy: Taking a piece of the lump out.

infiltrating cancer: Cancer that can grow beyond its site of origin into neighboring tissue. Infiltrating does not imply that the cancer has already spread outside the breast. Infiltrating has the same meaning as invasive.

informed consent: Process in which the patient is fully informed of all risks and complications of a planned procedure and agrees to proceed.

in situ: In the site of. In regard to cancer, in situ refers to tumors that haven't grown beyond their site of origin and invaded neighboring tissue.

intraductal: Within the duct. Intraductal can describe a benign or malignant process.

intraductal papilloma: Benign tumor which projects like a finger from the lining of the duct.

invasive cancer: Cancers that are capable of growing beyond their site of origin and invading neighboring tissue. Invasive does not imply that the cancer is aggressive or has already spread.

lactation: Production of milk from the breast.

latissimus flap: Flap of skin and muscle taken from the back and used for reconstruction after mastectomy or partial mastectomy.

lidocaine: Drug most commonly used for local anesthesia.

lobular: Having to do with the lobules of the breast.

lobular carcinoma in situ: Abnormal cells within the lobule which don't form lumps. They can serve as a marker of future cancer risk.

lobules: Parts of the breast capable of making milk.

local treatment of cancer: Treatment of the tumor only .

luteinizing hormone: Hormone produced by the pituitary which helps control the menstrual cycle.

lumpectomy: Surgery to remove lump with small rim of normal tissue around it.

lymphatic vessels: Vessels that carry lymph (tissue fluid) to and from lymph nodes.

lymphedema: Milk arm. This swelling of the arm can follow surgery to the lymph nodes under the arm. It can be temporary or permanent and occur immediately or any time later.

lymph nodes: Glands found throughout the body which help defend against foreign invaders such as bacteria. Lymph nodes can be a location of cancer spread.

malignant: Cancerous.

mastalgia: Pain in the breast.

mastitis: Infection of the breast. Mastitis is sometimes used loosely to refer to any benign process in the breast.

mastodynia: Pain in the breast.

mastopexy: Uplift of the breast through plastic surgery.

melatonin: Hormone produced by the pineal gland.

menarche: First menstrual period.

metastasis: Spread of cancer to another organ, usually through the bloodstream.

metastasizing: Spreading to a distant site.

methylxanthine: Chemical group to which caffeine belongs.

microcalcification: Tiny calcifications in the breast tissue usually seen only on a mammogram. When clustered can be a sign of ductal carcinoma in situ.

micrometastasis: Microscopic and as yet undetectable but presumed spread of tumor cells to other organs.

micropapillary: Type of DCIS where the cells filling the duct take the form of "finger" projections into the center.

myocutaneous flap: Flap of skin and muscle and fat taken from one part of the body to fill in an empty space.

necrosis: Dead tissue.

nodular: Forming little nodules.

nuclear magnetic resonance (NMR or MRI): Imaging technique using a magnet and electrical coil to transmit radio waves through the body.

oncogene: Tumor genes present in the body. These can be activated by carcinogens and cause cells to grow uncontrollably.

oncology: Study of cancer.

oophorectomy: Removal of the ovaries.

osteoporosis: Softening of the bones that occurs with age in some people.

oxytocin: Hormone produced by the pituitary gland, involved in lactation.

palliation: Act of relieving a symptom without curing the cause.

palpable: Can be felt.

pathologist: Doctor who specializes in examining tissue and diagnosing disease.

pectoralis major: Muscle which lies under the breast.

phlebitis: Irritation of a vein.

pituitary gland: A gland located in the brain which secretes many hormones to regulate other glands in the body: the master gland.

Poland's syndrome: A congenital condition where there is no breast development on one side of the chest.

polygenic: Relating to more than one gene.

polymastia: Literally many breasts. Existence of an extra breast or breasts.

postmenopausal: After the menopause has occurred.

Premarin: Estrogen which is sometimes given to women after menopause.

progesterone: Hormone produced by the ovary involved in the normal menstrual cycle.

prognosis: Expected or probable outcome.

prolactin: Hormone produced by the pituitary that stimulates progesterone production by the ovaries and lactation.

prophylactic subcutaneous mastectomies: Removal of all breast tissue beneath the skin and nipple, to prevent future breast cancer risk.

prosthesis: Artificial substitute for an absent part of the body, as in breast prosthesis.

protocol: Research designed to answer a hypothesis. Protocols often involve testing a specific new treatment under controlled conditions.

proto-oncogene: Normal gene controlling cell growth or turnover.

Provera: Progesterone which is sometimes given to women in combination with Premarin after menopause.

pseudolump: Breast tissue that feels like a lump but when removed proves to be normal.

ptosis: Drooping, as in breasts that hang down.

punch biopsy: A biopsy of skin that punches a small hole out of the skin.

quadrantectomy: Removal of a quarter of the breast.

rad: Radiation-absorbed dose; same as centigray. One chest X ray equals 1/10 of a rad.

randomized: Chosen at random. In regard to a research study it means choosing the subjects to be given a particular treatment by means of a computer programmed to choose names at random.

recurrence: Return of cancer after its apparent complete disappearance.

remission: Disappearance of detectable disease.

sarcoma: Cancer arising in the connective tissue.

scleroderma: An autoimmune disease which involves thickening of the skin and difficulty swallowing among other symptoms.

scoliosis: Deformity of the backbone which causes a person to bend to one side or the other.

sebaceous: Oily, cheesy material secreted by glands in the skin.

selenium: Metallic element found in food.

seroma: Collection of tissue fluid.

side effect: Unintentional or undesirable secondary effect of treatment.

silicone: Synthetic material used in breast implants because of its flexibility, resilience, and durability.

S-phase fraction: Measure of number of cells dividing at any one time.

subareolar abscess: Infection of the glands under the nipple.

subcutaneous tissue: The tissue under the skin.

systemic treatment: Treatment involving the whole body, usually using drugs.

tamoxifen: Estrogen blocker used in treating breast cancer.

thoracic: Concerning the chest (thorax).

thoracic nerves: Nerves in the chest area.

thoracoepigastric vein: Vein that starts under the arm and passes along the side of the breast and then down into the abdomen.

titration: Systems of balancing. In chemotherapy titration means using the largest amount of a drug possible while keeping the side effects from becoming intolerable.

trauma: Wound or injury.

triglyceride: Form in which fat is stored in the body, consisting of glycerol and three fatty acids.

tru-cut biopsy: Type of core needle biopsy where a small core of tissue is removed from a lump without surgery.

tumor: Abnormal mass of tissue. Strictly speaking, a tumor can be benign or malignant.

virginal hypertrophy: Inappropriately large breasts in a young woman.

xeroradiography: Type of mammogram taken on a Xerox plate rather than X ray film.

Index

Note: Page numbers in italics refer to illustrations in the text.

About the Authors

SUSAN M. LOVE M.D., a practicing breast surgeon, is Director of the Revlon/ UCLA Breast Center in Los Angeles, California. She is Associate Professor of Clinical Surgery at UCLA and the Revlon Chair in Women's Health. Dr. Love has been a proponent of innovative approaches to treatment, authoring many articles, chapters and co-authoring the *Atlas of Breast Surgery*. She works tirelessly to politicize the epidemic of breast cancer, having co-founded the National Breast Cancer Coalition in 1990 and serving on the President's National Action Plan for Breast Cancer as well as other scientific and government committees. Appearing regularly on "Oprah," "Dateline," "Nightline," "Good Morning America," and many other television and radio shows, she believes every woman deserves to have accurate information in order to make choices. She shares her home in Southern California with her life partner, Helen Cooksey M.D., their daughter Katie, Brownie the dog, and Sugar the cat.

KAREN LINDSEY is author of *Divorced, Beheaded, Survived: A Feminist Reinterpretation of the Wives of Henry VIII* (Addison-Wesley), *Friends as Family* (Beacon Press), and *Falling Off the Roof* (Alice James Books). Her articles have appeared in *Ms, The Women's Review of Books, Sojourner, International Figure Skating*, and many other publications and anthologies. She teaches women's studies at the University of Massachusetts/Boston, and writing at Emerson College.